Water Pollution and Hazardous Wastes

ENVIRONMENTAL LAW

VOLUME ONE
Environmental Decisionmaking and NEPA

VOLUME TWO
Water Pollution and Hazardous Wastes

VOLUME THREE
Air Pollution

Water Pollution and Hazardous Wastes

JACKSON B. BATTLE
Professor of Law
University of Wyoming

ENVIRONMENTAL LAW VOLUME TWO
Anderson Publishing Co. / Cincinnati, Ohio

ENVIRONMENTAL LAW VOLUME TWO: Water Pollution and Hazardous Wastes

Library of Congress Cataloging in Publication Data

Battle, Jackson B.
  Environmental law.

  Contents: v. 1. Environmental decisionmaking and
NEPA — v. 2. Water pollution and hazardous wastes.
  1. Environmental law—United States—Cases. I. Title.
KF3775.A7B37   1985   344.73'046   84-9341
ISBN 0-87084-084-3 (v. 1)   347.30446

Anderson Publishing Co. / Cincinnati, Ohio

Jean C. Martin, Executive Editor   William A. Burden, Managing Editor

Contents

Preface

This casebook is one of a three-volume series on environmental law intended for classroom use, either as a complete package or by selection of only one or two volumes for incorporation into a course designed by the professor to cover other subjects not treated in this series. I have written and compiled this volume and Volume One. The author of Volume Three is Mark Squillace.

My impression from discussions with my colleagues who are teaching in the field is that few want to cover exactly the same subjects under the broad heading of an environmental law course. In the usual three-hour law school course, most will begin with the material included in Volume One: first, the basic legal framework of standing, administrative, and constitutional law which forms the background for environmental regulation and, second, the National Environmental Policy Act. After this, most law professors prefer to move into areas most pertinent to their own region of the country and/or to their own interests and expertise. If the course fits my personal concept of environmental law—that is, it does not include land-use planning, natural resources development, or public lands—then the professor will want to cover at least one of the subjects to which the other two volumes in this series are devoted: water pollution and hazardous wastes (Volume Two) or air pollution (Volume Three). For example, the professor may prefer to rely on Volume Two to illustrate the intricacies of a complex federal regulatory scheme in the context of the Clean Water Act, and then spend the rest of the course covering his or her own preferred subject—*e.g.*, wildlife conservation, coastal zone management, or surface mining—through use of supplementary materials. The basic idea behind this "modular" concept is to allow professors to design their own courses around their own notions of "environmental law," without insisting that students purchase large hardbound casebooks containing hundreds of pages of materials that will not be covered in their courses.

Also, I anticipate that the individual volumes will be utilized in special courses and seminars which are concerned only with the particular subject of the volume: *e.g.*, air pollution. And I am aware that some law schools combine environmental law with other law in a given field: for example, including water pollution control with water rights in a "water law" course. Finally, I have noticed that other academic departments—such as biology, agriculture, engineering, and political science—are increasingly including environmental law relevant to their disciplines in their courses; and I hope that one or more of these books might fit their needs.

So much for the reason for the modular approach. Now a description of the format and pedagogical theory which I have followed in the first two volumes, and which are continued by Professor Squillace in Volume Three.

First and foremost, they are *casebooks*. They use the traditional case-study method to comprehensively develop the overall structure and application of major pieces of environmental legislation. The decision to adhere to the traditional format of primary emphasis on cases (rather than on textual explanations and excerpted articles) was basically due to my preference as a teacher for casebooks which allow *me* to do the teaching. Particularly in a field so inviting of strong and divergent opinions as environmental law, it seems especially intrusive of an author to comment too freely on the issues. Even if all bias could be eliminated, however, I still prefer a text which allows the professor and students room for their own views.

I suspect that this is the feeling of most law professors, but until recently it was difficult to cover the major issues in any area of environmental law without producing more of a treatise than a casebook. Although a few statutory provisions still require some explanation without the benefit of cases on point, at least the most important areas of environmental law have by now "matured" sufficiently—that is, enough issues have been litigated and decided by the courts—that this sort of casebook is possible.

Even with three volumes, their scope is rather restricted. Other than the introductory and background materials in the first part of Volume One, coverage is limited to NEPA, the Clean Water Act, the Resource Conservation and Recovery Act, the "Superfund" Act, and the Clean Air Act. Why this selection? First, as anyone involved in environmental law is well aware, the field is hardly narrow. Any attempt to cover only federal environmental law would involve treatment of at least a dozen major pieces of legislation, many approaching the Internal Revenue Code in complexity. To try to cover the whole spectrum would be like seeing Europe in eight days. Such a broadbrush survey would leave a student with little more than a nodding acquaintance with any particular act.

Much more can be accomplished by devoting one's efforts to an in-depth study of a few of the most significant pieces of federal legislation. We have chosen NEPA, RCRA, Superfund, and the Clean Water and Air Acts because they are the most comprehensive, the most complex, the most ambitious, the most difficult and expensive to comply with, and, consequently, far and away the most heavily litigated—over two-thirds of each volume of *Environment Reporter* being devoted to cases involving these acts. Therefore, a student somewhat versed in this legislation should be prepared for the majority of disputes he or she will encounter in a general environmental law practice. More importantly, and more relevant to law school instruction, the student will be well prepared in the sense that he or she will have been involved in intensive analysis of a "typical" environmental statute. The analytical processes and legal method studied in dissecting this legislation should better serve a student when confronted with a statute not studied in the course than would superficial treatment of black letter law soon forgotten. This assumption, that the best law school can offer is transferable legal skills, is incurably traditional.

State and local environmental laws are also of great importance; but, of course, it would be impossible to treat them directly in texts intended for nationwide use. Little can be gained from using a particular state's law for illustration: there are often few, if any, state court interpretive decisions, and the law varies greatly from state to state—except where its structure is essentially dictated by federal law. In this latter sense, the emphasis in Volumes Two and Three on the Clean Water and Air Acts includes coverage of the largest and most uniform portions of state environmental law. In general, the principal features of one state's plan implementing the federal Clean Air or Water Act do not differ significantly from those of another state with a qualifying plan. In studying NEPA, also, much of what is learned will be applicable in states which have impact statement requirements. Thus, in most instances, the student with strong local interests should not feel slighted. Again, skills learned in the course should be readily transferable to state law problems.

Each of the volumes contains between three hundred and four hundred pages of text. Thus, if a professor chooses to use all three volumes in a three semester-hour course, he or she will need to prune the material for coverage, or else handle twenty-five-page assignments (something which neither my students nor I have ever found possible). On the other hand, a single volume could be supplemented to fill a specialized two-hour course. When, as in Volume Two, limited space has not been used for inclusion of the relevant statutes, my recommendation is that the legislation covered be reproduced and distributed separately or that students purchase one of the commercially-bound compilations of these statutes.

My intention is to supplement these volumes annually, either with reproducible mailings of recent developments or with a single paperbound volume covering all areas.

Jack Battle
April, 1986

Acknowledgments

The author gratefully acknowledges the permissions granted to reproduce the following copyrighted material:

Schnapf, *State Hazardous Waste Programs Under the Federal Resource Conservation and Recovery Act,* 12 ENVTL. L. 679 (1982). Reprinted with permission of the editors of Environmental Law and the author.

Garrett, *Hazardous Waste Management Under RCRA: An Overview of the Statute and the EPA's Current Program,* 13 NAT. RESOURCES L. NEWSLETTER 1 (1981). Reprinted with permission of the American Bar Association Press.

Bromm, *EPA's New Land Disposal Standards,* 12 ELR 15027 (1982). Reprinted with permission of the Environmental Law Institute, Washington, D.C.

Rosbe & Gulley, *The Hazardous and Solid Waste Amendments of 1984: A Dramatic Overhaul of the Way America Manages Its Hazardous Wastes,* 14 ELR 10458 (1984). Reprinted with permission of the Environmental Law Institute, Washington, D.C.

Comment, *Superfund at Square One: Promising Statutory Framework Requires Forceful EPA Implementation,* 11 ELR 10101 (1981). Reprinted with permission of the Environmental Law Institute, Washington, D.C.

Table of Cases

The principal cases are in italic type. Cases cited or discussed are in Roman type. References are to page numbers.

I
THE CLEAN WATER ACT

1 INTRODUCTION

Nature of and Trends in Water Pollutants

Environmental Protection Agency, The Economics of
Clean Water—1973, pp. 9-12.

INTRODUCTION TO POLLUTION PROBLEMS

No one has described completely the quality of a body of water. To do so would entail chemical analyses of a near-infinite number of solid, liquid, and gaseous compounds, as well as a complete identification of all biota present in the water from viruses to vertebrates. Thus, any practical description of water quality can only be concerned with a very limited subset of all conceivable physical, chemical, and biological aspects of actual waterbodies. Typical water quality measurements are, in fact, oriented toward a small group of commonly observed pollution problems.

Harmful Substances

A stream of seemingly clean and pure water may be highly polluted due to the presence of toxic substances in very low concentrations. For example, certain chemicals in concentrations of only several parts per billion may be deadly to the mayfly, an important link in the aquatic food chain. Certain harmful substances may be natural, such as acids from bogs. Most, however, are manmade such as industrial and agricultural chemicals. A few of these are well known—heavy metals, pesticides, herbicides, and polychlorinated biphenyls (PCB's), for example.

Toxicity effects can be dramatic, as in the case of large fishkills, or they can be subtle, as in the case of minute concentrations causing decreasing fertility or changing reproductive or predation habits over a long period of time. Detecting any chemical and tracing it back to its sources can be difficult, particularly in the case of widely used and highly persistent substances such as mercury, dieldrin, or PCB's. Sources can be diverse, ranging from industrial or municipal sewage discharges to urban stormwater, agricultural runoff, or atmospheric particle "fallout." It is therefore not safe to assume that the only major sources of harmful substances are industrial discharges.

Analysis of these harmful substances is complicated because they do not usually remain dissolved or suspended in water but are taken up by sediments, plants, and animals. In the case of DDT, concentrations in fish will be at least one order of magnitude greater than in sediments, which in turn have concentrations at least one order of magnitude greater than the overlying waters. Since most other important pesticides are insoluble (and many toxic metals form insoluble salts), water concentrations by themselves do not form reliable indicators. For the same reasons, water concentrations will tend to be very low—on the order of parts per billion—making results extremely sensitive to the specific chemical analysis methods used. For instance, older gas chromatographic methods for DDT were unable to distinguish DDT clearly from PCB's. Since PCB's are often found in substantially higher concentrations than DDT, these older results are quite unreliable.

Physical Modification

Aquatic habitats are sensitive to fluctuations of many physical characteristics of water including temperature and transparency. Temperature fluctuations occurring naturally can be amplified by human activities through large discharges of industrial cooling water, such as from power plants or steel mills, from release of warm surface water held in reservoirs, or from de-struction of shade trees along stream banks. Warm discharges do not automatically cause ecological damage—some increase desirable biological activity. Large thermal discharges into small or relatively stagnant bodies of water, however, can cause large temperature increases. If such increases occur in critical "zones of passage" or spawning grounds, they can disrupt important biological communities.

Natural waters lose transparency due to sediment loads. Aside from natural sources of sediment there are human sources including construction activities, strip mining and farming practices. Transparency can also be lost by excess microorganism growth stimulated by nutrient-rich agricultural runoff, urban stormwater or sewer overflows, and sewage treatment plant discharges. Reduced transparency has a serious effect other than aesthetic degradation: It reduces the amount of light available to underwater plants and thus decreases a primary food source for certain fish and birds.

Another significant alteration of key aquatic habitats results from physical modification of shores, banks, and channels. Artificial draining of marshland to create waterfront property destroys the highly productive environment necessary for spawning of certain fish species and feeding of migratory birds. Construction of breakwaters can reduce "flushing" of bays to the point where the effect of pollutant discharges to these bays is greatly magnified by stagnant water conditions. Channel and watershed "improvement" destroys biological communities on stream banks and, in some cases, can accelerate erosion and sediment.

Finally, dams and their impoundments can produce profound changes in the physical and biological characteristics of a stream. These changes include beneficial as well as negative effects.

Not all aspects of physical modifications of streams and estuaries are quantifiable. In fact, only a few simple measures of the extent of

harmful physical modifications (including suspended solids, turbidity, color, and temperature) are known. Some other physical measures that would be useful are often not routinely made; among these are sediment cores to analyze the nature of bottom deposit buildup, and settleable solids to measure the materials deposited on the bottom.

Eutrophication

An adequate crop of algae is the beginning of the food chain for most aquatic communities. However, relatively stagnant waters (such as lakes and slow-moving estuaries) rich in nutrients can grow such heavy crops of algal and other aquatic plants that the decay of dead cell matter may seriously deplete the bottom waters of oxygen. This prevents the survival of oxygen-sensitive food species and fish. In extreme cases floating algal mats, thick bottom slimes, and odors result.

There are many waters in the nation that are or were naturally eutrophic. On the other hand, artificial addition of any one of the 100 or so nutrients necessary to plant growth may stimulate algal blooms (heavy growths) in stagnant waters where that nutrient is normally undersupplied. In addition to the well-known nutrients, phosphorus and nitrogen, there are others equally essential to plants, including carbon dioxide, potassium, magnesium, and vitamin B-12. Man adds nutrients to water by many means. Perhaps one of the most important sources is runoff of agricultural fertilizers, which yield large loads of phosphorus, nitrogen,and potassium; other sources include treated municipal sewage, industrial discharges, and sewer overflows.

The only direct measure of eutrophication is a complete biological study of the waters in question. Indirect measures of eutrophication are biomass, standing algal crops, chlorophyll, nutrient uptake and benthic (that is, stream or lake bottom) oxygen demand. Unfortunately, most of these are almost never monitored routinely. Nutrient levels can be useful, although not necessarily conclusive, measures of the potential for eutrophication. Of the 100 or so nutrients essential for plant growth, only compounds of nitrogen and phosphorus are routinely measured, making it difficult to use normal monitoring evidence to specify either nitrogen or phosphorus as the direct cause of a bloom.

Salinity, Acidity, and Alkalinity

Major changes in the salt content of water can seriously disrupt aquatic communities and decrease the value of water for irrigation and water supply purposes. Where the fresh water inflow of estuaries is reduced through upstream consumption or diversion of freshwater, the saline front advances upstream. This advance decreases the low salinity area of the estuary necessary for spawning or growth of important species such as striped bass. Many inland streams are naturally saline, due to the salt content of solids and minerals in their drainage basins. In certain areas, this natural salinity has been substantially increased by man's activities. Irrigation in saline soil areas increases stream salinity, because of increased evaporation (both on land and in reservoirs) and leaching of salt from the soil into the irrigation return flow. In certain basins, mine and quarry drainage can also add substantial salt loads to rivers.

Acidity changes can be equally damaging to aquatic life. The most important acid sources are drainage from mines and acid rain downwind from major sulfur-polluted air regions. The importance of sulfur air pollution has only recently been recognized; several small lakes have suffered such serious increases in acidity within only one decade as to almost eliminate many desirable fish species. Highly acidic industrial and municipal discharges that are large relative to the receiving stream can also cause damage.

Alkalinity presents problems in many areas, particularly west of the Mississippi River. The problems range from reduced agricultural production to the fouling of water pipes. Most alkaline pollutants are from natural sources such as sodium carbonate deposits. However, certain industries such as the gypsum board industry may also contribute to an alkaline condition.

Quantitative analysis of salinity normally uses total dissolved solids as an indicator of total salts; common individual salts such as sulfates and chlorides are also sometimes measured. To some extent, specific ecological damage due to salinity depends on the composition of the salts present. Acidity/alkalinity measures are considerably more complex. pH, the measure of free hydrogen ions present, measures the stream's capacity to neutralize or "inactivate" bases. Alkalinity measures the stream's capacity to buffer acids. Thus, if a given stream shows little pH trend over the last 10 years, but alkalinity has decreased markedly, one can predict that the stream will be considerably more vulnerable to relatively small acid discharges.

Oxygen Depletion

Oxygen dissolved in water is one of many substances essential to sustaining aquatic animal life. The dissolved oxygen (DO) level is widely considered to be the single most important indicator of pollution; actually, there is no reason to consider it more or less important than indicators such as toxicity, salinity, and algal population.

Dissolved oxygen is consumed whenever any substance is oxidized in water. This oxidation can be a direct chemical process, or it can be a biological process. All aquatic animals, from bacteria to fish, consume dissolved oxygen in metabolizing food substances. Such food substances range from sugars and starches, which are consumed by microorganisms in days, to paper pulp or oils, which are consumed by microorganisms only after months. Rapidly consumable substances create oxygen deficits within a few days of stream travel from their sources, while slowly consumable substances create deficits weeks or months of stream travel away from their source.

Thus, slowly consumable substances may not cause significant oxygen loss in the stream at all; instead, they may be consumed in a downstream lake, reservoir, estuary, or ocean where they may or may not pose a problem. Naturally, the rate of consumption for a specific food substance or waste is highly sensitive to temperature; higher water temperatures greatly accelerate the growth and metabolism of the microorganisms that feed on the waste. On the other hand, many toxic substances slow this growth and can give a misleading picture of oxygen sufficiency.

Oxygen-consuming or oxygen-demanding substances can be attributed to many sources. There are large natural sources, including leaves, soil organic matter, and wildlife droppings washed into rivers by storm runoff. Agricultural areas contribute additional runoff-carried oxygen demand from livestock manure and topsoil erosion. There are also the classical "point" sources: municipal sewage treatment plant discharges and a wide variety of industrial waste discharges.[1] However, some urbanized areas contribute oxygen-demanding loads by other routes, including storm sewers, sewer overflows, intentional treatment plant bypasses, sewer leaks, and unsewered runoff.

The direct quantitative measures of oxygen content of water are the absolute concentration of DO present, and the percent of saturation for DO corrected for temperature and pressure (since warm or low pressure water can dissolve less oxygen than cold or high pressure water). The latter measure is based on theoretical tables of saturation values for dissolved oxygen in distilled water, but many substances found in impure water can either raise or lower saturation levels of DO. Supersaturated values of up to 140 percent are seen, particularly in waters where algae contribute substantial oxygen.

In describing the oxygen-depleting characteristics of wastes, 5-day biochemical oxygen demand (BOD_5) and chemical oxygen demand (COD) are the most common measures. In BOD_5, the waste or stream sample is incubated in a bottle (sometimes inoculated with stream microorganisms) at 20°C. for 5 days, and the weight of oxygen metabolically consumed by the microorganisms is measured. Among the many deficiencies of the BOD_5 measurement are: It has very poor repeatability; bottle conditions are far from stream conditions; trace toxicants can seriously inhibit microorganism growth and reduce apparent oxygen demand; and the 5-day reading gives no indication of depletion rate over shorter or longer periods. In measurement of COD, a sample of water is chemically oxidized to give an approximate upper bound on the amount of biologically oxidizable material present; COD cannot be measured in salty water, however, and it also fails to capture volatile oxidizable substances such as organic acids, alcohols, and ammonia.

Health Hazards and Aesthetic Degradation

An assessment of health hazards from polluted water involves considerable uncertainty. There is little doubt that human feces carry infectious pathogens for a number of intestinal diseases, typhoid fever, hepatitis, brucellosis, encephalitis, poliomyelitis, psittacosis, and tuberculosis. However, there are grave uncertainties about the die-off rates of pathogens in natural waters as well as their infectiousness for swimmers or other recreational water users. Note that the issue of drinking water is not at stake, since its safety depends on disinfection treatment by the water supply system. The evidence that water polluted with fecal matter can transmit diseases to swimmers is sparse and uncertain, particularly since it has been discovered that swimmers in unpolluted water also have higher incidences of common ear, eye, and nose infections. There is some evidence that hepatitis can be transmitted via shellfish from polluted waters; unfortunately, the usual antibacterial measure—chlorination of sewage effluents—may not abate this problem for viral forms of hepatitis.

The evidence for waterborne toxicity hazards via fish, shellfish, and perhaps drinking water is somewhat stronger, at least in the case of relatively high concentrations of mercury and cadmium. On the other hand, considerably less effort has been expended on the chronic health hazards of low-level, long-term toxicants in

[1]The term "point source" means any discernible, confined and discrete conveyance, including but not limited to any pipe, ditch, channel, tunnel, conduit, well, discrete fissure, container, rolling stock, concentrated animal feeding operation, or vessel or other floating craft, from which pollutants are or may be discharged. [§502, 33 U.S.C. §1362(14) (1972).]

A non-point source is any non-confined area from which pollutants are discharged into a body of water, i.e., agricultural run-off, urban run-off, and sedimentation from construction sites. The term would also apply to drainage and seepage from mining, and salt water intrusion into rivers, lakes, and estuaries resulting from the reduction of fresh water flow. [208 (b)(2)(F)-(I), 33 U.S.C.A. §1288(b)(2)(F)-(I).]

drinking water (and fish) than on the infectious disease problem. Consequently, little can be said in this area, since even monitoring data are sparse.

Despite the paucity of evidence regarding waterborne transmission of diseases to recreational users, public health agencies since the turn of the century have assumed that the problem exists. Because of the expense of direct identification of specific pathogens in water, these agencies traditionally have used several indirect and nonspecific measures of bacterial populations in water: total coliforms, fecal coliforms, and fecal streptococci. These bacteria are not pathogenic, nor do they simulate the die-off rates of pathogens. Fecal bacterial counts are good indicators of the presence of undisinfected municipal sewage, when runoff sources are either low or insignificant. Unfortunately, fecal coliforms are also found in runoff from agricultural and wilderness lands and from urban areas. In fact, it is possible that fecal coliforms can multiply significantly in streams under certain conditions.

Water bodies can be degraded aesthetically by increases in murkiness, color, algal scums, floating solids and oils, and odors. Murkiness is approximately measured by turbidity, which has been discussed, together with color, under Physical Modifications. Algal growth has been discussed under Eutrophication. Floating solids and oils, in areas with properly functioning treatment plants and oil separators, generally come from combined sewer overflows, storm sewer discharges, and unsewered runoff, as evidenced by the major increases in these measures directly after rainstorms. Unaesthetic odors can stem from many sources, including decaying organic matter in water or on the bottom and a myriad of industrial chemicals. Among chemicals, phenols are traditionally singled out for special attention by pollution control agencies.

In the broad area of health hazards and aesthetic degradation, only a few measures are routinely monitored. The ones available for analysis are total coliform, fecal coliform, fecal streptococci, phenols, and odors.

The Clean Water Act: An Introductory Overview

History of Water Pollution Control

The first statutory involvement of the federal government in the control of discharges into the nation's waters began with enactment of the Rivers and Harbors Act of 1889. Section 13, generally called the "Refuse Act," prohibited discharge of refuse matter of any kind into any navigable waters of the United States, with enforcement authority granted to the Secretary of the Army. For seventy years, however, his authority rarely was exercised to control liquid pollution discharges, but rather was used to control disposal of trash and floating debris.

Congress attempted to broaden protection of the nation's waters in 1948 by enactment of the original Federal Water Pollution Control Act (FWPCA). This act gave the states primary enforcement authority for control of water pollution, an approach which proved to be ineffective.

Although the FWPCA was amended five times between 1948 and 1972, basic flaws made enforcement difficult; and there were few improvements in water quality throughout the nation. Nearly all of the federal and state water pollution laws focused upon maintaining the ambient quality of water, which varied with the uses to which different water bodies were put. Receiving waters that were used primarily for industrial purposes were allowed to be heavily polluted. Low ambient standards provided no incentive for cleanup of rivers and lakes used for industrial waste and municipal sewage disposal.

Reliance upon receiving water, or ambient, standards was also flawed by difficulty of enforcement in areas where several discharges were contributing to water quality problems. Without a means of identifying and regulating discharges by individual polluters, state enforcement authorities were unable to force cleanup of water bodies.

In the post-Earth-Day atmosphere of public concern about protection of the environment, Congress enacted a comprehensive system for water pollution control in the 1972 Amendments to the Federal Water Pollution Control Act. The Senate committee reporting the 1972 Amendments found that there had been an almost total lack of enforcement of the FWPCA and that new measures were required to curtail the use of rivers, lakes, and streams as waste treatment systems.

With the enactment of these Amendments, Congress fixed a firm course to clean up the nation's waters. The primary innovation in the Amendments was to focus upon the chemical and biological nature of pollution discharges, with a secondary emphasis upon the quality of receiving waters. It was determined that the most effective approach to cleaning up the nation's waters would be to impose discharge limitations upon individual polluters and to base those limitations upon the capabilities of modern control technologies.

The Act was again amended in 1977, when the name was officially changed to the "Clean Water Act."

Organization of the Clean Water Act

The 1972 version of the Act contained three basic elements aimed at achieving the goal of eliminating the discharge of pollutants into the waters of the United States. First, the Environmental Protection Agency was directed to conduct a research program and develop methods for waste treatment. Second, the Act authorized a massive construction program for municipal waste treatment works, with federal financial assistance. Third, the Act established a comprehensive system of standards, permits, and enforcement methods for control of the complete spectrum of polluting materials.

With the 1972 Amendments, Congress established several new goals and national policies:
(a) That discharge of pollutants into the navigable waters be eliminated by 1985;
(b) That the interim goal of nationwide water quality providing for protection of fish and wildlife and for water recreation uses be achieved by 1983;
(c) That discharge of toxic pollutants in toxic amounts be prohibited;
(d) That federal financial assistance be provided to construct publicly owned treatment works;
(e) That areawide waste treatment planning programs be implemented in each state; and
(f) That the states have the primary responsibility to control water pollution.

Effluent Limitations and Standards for Point Sources

Title III of the Clean Water Act establishes a comprehensive system of procedures for regulation of a variety of pollution problems caused by point source discharges. Separate but sometimes overlapping provisions govern control of "conventional" pollutants (primarily those which deplete water-dissolved oxygen); "toxic" pollutants (those which cause death, disease, or malformation of organisms); thermal pollution; and other non-toxic, non-conventional pollutants. (This Title also contains a separate regulatory framework for spills of harmful amounts of oil and hazardous substances, discussion of which will be deferred until that section is reached. Other titles govern disposal of dredged and fill material and "nonpoint source" pollution.)

A conspicuous feature of Title III is that different standards of performance are imposed upon existing industrial point sources, new sources, and publicly owned treatment works (or "POTWs"). Sections 301 and 304 provide for development of effluent limitations for existing point sources (including POTWs), Section 306 provides the same for new sources, and Sections 302 and 303 give supplemental authority for development of more stringent standards for protection of the quality of individual water bodies. Sections 308, 309, 505, and 508 supply the means to enforce all these standards.

1. Effluent Limitations for Existing Sources

The Clean Water Act distinguishes pollution discharged from pipes, ditches and other discrete conveyances, collectively termed "point sources,"[1] from runoff from agricultural operations, industrial sites, and other "nonpoint sources." Point sources are to be regulated by "effluent limitations,"[2] restrictions upon the contents and nature of discharged substances. These limitations are to be applied on a class-specific, industry-wide basis for each regulated pollutant.

Point source regulation is Congress' answer to the difficulties of working backwards from desired receiving water quality standards. As "end-of-pipe" standards, effluent limitations are applied at the source of discharge, usually in terms of specified quantities of pollutants per unit of total discharge volume.

The amounts of pollutants that may be discharged from a point source are based upon applicable target-date statutory technology requirements. In 1972, Congress, recognizing that compliance with new technology-based standards would be expensive and time consuming, established two categories of performance standards for existing point sources. The first category, or stage, for compliance was that "best practicable control technology currently available" (BPT) be achieved by all direct dischargers, other than publicly owned treatment works, by July 1, 1977. The second stage was achievement of "best available technology economically achievable" (BAT), originally mandated by July 1, 1983, for all direct dischargers other than treatment works. Publicly owned treatment works were to meet "secondary treatment" requirements by July 1, 1977, and apply "best practicable waste treatment technology" (BPWTT) by July 1, 1983.

In making the 1977 Amendments, Congress found that some existing point sources were unable to achieve PBT limitations by the July 1977 deadline. Accordingly, the Act was amended to give EPA authority to grant case-by-case extensions of the 1977 deadline to industrial dischargers who were found to have made a good faith attempt to comply and who were committed to making "reasonable further progress" toward compliance. Under such extensions, full compliance with BPT limitations was required by April 1, 1979.

The 1977 Amendments also made changes in the 1983 BAT requirement. Three categories of pollutants were created—with the standard, the compliance deadline, and the availability of waivers dependent on the particular category.

  a. Discharges of "conventional pollutants," including suspended solids, coliform bacteria, pH, and oxygen-demanding pollutants, were to be controlled by the "best conventional pollutant control technology" (BCT) by July 1, 1984. No waivers of this requirement nor extensions of the 1984 compliance deadline were statutorily provided.
  b. Discharges of "toxic pollutants" were to be controlled by application of BAT by July 1, 1984. For these pollutants no waivers were expressly made available, but extensions to allow utilization of more effective "innovative technology" could postpone the compliance deadline up to July, 1987.

---

[1]"The term 'point source' means any discernible, confined and discrete conveyance, including but not limited to any pipe, ditch, channel, tunnel, conduit, well, discrete fissure, container, rolling stock, concentrated animal feeding operation, or vessel or other floating craft, from which pollutants are or may be discharged. This term does not include return flows from irrigated agriculture." Section 502 (14).

[2]"The term 'effluent limitation' means any restriction established by a State or the Administrator on quantities, rates, and concentrations of chemical, physical, biological, and other constituents which are discharged from point sources into navigable waters, the waters of the contiguous zone, or the ocean, including schedules of compliance." Section 502 (11).

c. Discharges of all other pollutants (termed "nonconventionals") not in the above two categories were to be controlled by application of BAT not later than three years after new limitations were established, or not later than July 1, 1984, whichever is later, but in no case later
than July 1, 1987. The BAT limitations for these nonconventional pollutants might be modified on a case-by-case basis upon a showing of either economic infeasibility or absence of any
interference with water quality standards. Innovative technology extensions were also
made available.

For publicly owned treatment works unable to meet the July 1977 "secondary treatment"
deadline because of delays in federal funding or construction difficulties, the 1977 Amendments
authorized extensions of up to six years. When even the extended 1983 deadlines for secondary
treatment loomed too close, and adequate federal funds still were not available, Congress in 1981
provided for extensions up to July, 1988, and at the same time relaxed the definition of secondary
treatment. Also in the 1981 Amendments Congress repealed entirely the second-stage standard of
"best practicable waste treatment technology" and its attainment date.

EPA was given responsibility under the Act for study and development of effluent limitations
following consultation with other agencies and affected persons. The first step was to be issuance
of "guidelines" under Section 304, which contain descriptions of the abilities of available technology to reduce pollution from classes and categories of point sources, and which specify economic
and engineering factors to be considered for individual point sources. The statutory provisions
for these guidelines place more emphasis on economic factors for "best practicable" technologies
than for "best available" technologies. The second step was to be issuance of "limitations" pursuant to Section 301. EPA in fact combined these two steps as a matter of convenience and issued
"effluent limitations guidelines" for each regulated industry.

EPA has generally defined BPT by the selection of the average of the best control technologies in current use in each industry, rejecting industry arguments that BPT should reflect only
the average technology currently in use. BPT limitations do not require the use of a specified technology, but EPA must set a limitation which is achievable by at least one available method or
process. EPA has interpreted Congress' intent to require a uniform nationwide application of BPT
limitations; consequently, BPT standards require a uniform degree of effluent reduction for each
industry regulated.

Promulgation of best available technology limitations (BAT) requires less emphasis upon
cost/benefit analysis than BPT. Costs are to be considered by EPA as a factor affecting selection
of BAT limitations, but only to the extent that costs of achieving such limitations might be
unreasonable.

2. Point Source Regulation

Section 301 (a) makes unlawful the discharge of any pollutant except in compliance with
provisions of the Clean Water Act. The mechanism by which effluent limitations are applied to
individual point sources is provided in Section 402 of the Act, setting up a permit system called
the National Pollutant Discharge Elimination System (NPDES). No person may discharge from
a point source without such a permit. Processing of permit applications must include public notice
and opportunities for interested persons to object to permit issuance.

Section 402 authorizes states with approved enforcement programs to regulate point sources,
subject to EPA's continuing oversight. State agencies obtain EPA approval by showing that state
law provides adequate authority to enforce standards set by EPA under Title III of the Act. A
majority of the states have received EPA approval of their enforcement programs.

3. New Source Standards

Effluent limitations described above (BPT, BCT, and BAT) are to be applied to existing point
sources. A separate provision, Section 306 (which parallels the Sections 301-304 effluent limitations procedure) governs regulation of point source discharges from new sources.

New sources are defined in Section 306 to include, at a minimum, a lengthy list of industrial manufacturing and processing facilities which are required to meet stringent standards of performance upon commencement of commercial operations. EPA is directed to promulgate such standards for each category of new sources, allowing for differences among classes, types, and sizes within the categories.

These new source standards of performance are to reflect the greatest degree of effluent reduction achievable with the "best available demonstrated control technology." The Act does not indicate how such standards rank in comparison to the BAT standards for existing sources under Section 301; but the statutory language as well as policy considerations seem to require that they be no less stringent than BAT. The relative ease with which advanced technology can be designed into new facilities is a factor which may encourage even higher performance standards, but the deterrence of modernization that could result militates against such an interpretation.

There is no variance procedure for new sources; but, once a new source is constructed in compliance with current performance standards, no more stringent standard may be imposed upon that source for ten years.

4. Toxic Substances

Protection of living organisms, especially humans, from disease, cancer, birth defects, and poisoning caused by waterborne pollutants is governed by Section 307, titled "Toxic and Pretreatment Effluent Standards." EPA is directed to develop toxic pollutant effluent standards that provide an ample margin of safety for humans and other potentially affected organisms. These standards are to be developed on a pollutant-by-pollutant basis, in contrast to Sections 301 and 306 effluent limitations developed on an industry-by-industry basis.

The 1972 Amendments directed EPA to list and set standards for particularly toxic compounds within a short statutory time frame, but the agency failed to implement standards for any toxic pollutants by the deadline, primarily because of lack of sufficient data regarding toxicity and persistence in the environment. Several suits were brought by environmental organizations to force EPA to promulgate regulations. Settlement of these suits in 1976 generated a toxics strategy emphasizing BAT effluent limitations guidelines, new source performance standards, and pretreatment standards on an industry-by-industry basis, and with only secondary reliance on the Section's pollutant-specific approach. Twenty-one industrial categories were selected for priority regulation, with attention given to 65 toxic substances, including heavy metals, chlorinated hydrocarbon pesticides, dioxin, acrylonitrile, vinyl chloride, and PCBs, among others.

The 1977 Amendments essentially codified the 1976 consent decree, with a one-year extension granted for compliance with BAT limitations to July 1, 1984. EPA also retained its original discretion to develop effluent limitations more stringent than BAT, based not on technology but instead upon the effects that toxics have on human and animal health (health-based limitations).

Section 307 (b) empowers EPA to establish pretreatment standards controlling discharges into publicly owned waste treatment works for all pollutants which are not treatable by such public works or which would interfere with effective operation of such works. Special attention is given to pretreatment of toxic pollutants by both existing and new sources.

5. Water Quality Standards

Prior to 1972 most states had adopted ambient water quality standards to limit the effects of discharges upon receiving waters. In amending the Act, Congress decided to preserve the right of states to enforce such standards, so long as they provided as much or more protection than the new federal source-specific effluent limitations. Section 303 authorizes states to enforce pre-existing standards and to develop new ones consistent with the Act. In addition, it requires EPA to promulgate water quality standards for states that fail to do so.

Water-quality-based effluent standards are established by determination of the levels of effluent discharges that can be assimilated by receiving water bodies without deterioration of designated uses. Availability of control technology is not a relevant factor. States are directed to identify those waters within their boundaries for which federal effluent limitations are inadequate, develop priorities for protection or cleanup of such waters, and proceed to determine the "total maximum daily load" of pollutants that the receiving waters can handle without destruction of their designated water qualities. Any effluent limitations and compliance schedules necessary to achieve water quality standards must then be developed, with EPA assistance and approval. These steps are to be part of the continuing planning processes required by Sections 303 and 208. Whether or not a state fulfills its duty to set effluent limitations to protect its water quality standards, under Section 301(b)(1)(C) neither the state nor EPA can lawfully issue a permit without whatever limitations are necessary to achieve the designated quality standard.

Section 302 authorizes EPA to establish stricter effluent limitations for particular point sources whenever BAT limitations prove insufficient to maintain high ambient water quality. Economic analysis comparing the costs of implementing such stricter limitations to the benefits to be realized must accompany development of the limitations. If the benefits of high quality water are found to justify whatever economic and social costs will result, EPA is required to set the effluent limitations accordingly.

6. Thermal Pollution

The definition of "pollutant" includes thermal discharges, which are thus subject to regulation under Sections 301 (existing point sources) and 306 (new sources). Point source operators, however, may obtain modification of thermal effluent limitations upon demonstration that discharge of warmer water will not interfere with propagation of fish, shellfish, and wildlife, pursuant to Section 316 of the Act.

Disposal of Dredged and Fill Material

Section 404 of the Act gives the U.S. Army Corps of Engineers authority to regulate discharges of dredged and fill material[3] into the navigable waters of the United States, except that limited authority may be delegated to states with approved programs to regulate discharges into small streams and lakes and associated wetlands. EPA may object to issuance of "404 permits" by either the Corps or a state at sites where discharge would have an unacceptable adverse impact upon the environment.

Administration of Section 404 under the 1972 Act engendered widespread controversy for three principal reasons: First, the jurisdiction of the Corps had been extended far beyond the limits of traditionally navigable waters of the United States; second, discharge of silt from farming and logging operations was arguably subject to 404 regulation; and third, administrative backlogs were delaying processing of permits for routine construction activities that threatened only minor discharges of soil and silt. In 1977 Congress amended the section (1) to exempt normal farming, ranching, and timbering activities; (2) to give the states permitting authority over "non-navigable" waters; and (3) to authorize the Corps to issue five-year general permits on state, regional, or national bases for categories of activities that would have only minimal cumulative adverse effects on the environment.

---

[3]Dredged material is defined as material that is excavated or dredged from the waters of the United States, while fill material means any material used to replace aquatic areas with dry land or to change the bottom elevation of a water body. 33 CFR § 323.2 (k) (m), 42 Fed. Register §7145 (July 19, 1977).

Congress also exempted all federal projects which are specifically authorized by Congress, following consideration of environmental impact statements, from regulation by both federal and state dredge and fill permit programs.

Areawide Waste Treatment Management

Section 208 directs states to develop comprehensive plans for control of "nonpoint" source pollution and coordination of areawide waste treatment. Nonpoint sources are those activities (such as mining, farming, construction, and timbering) that generate pollutants which find their way to water bodies other than through discrete or confined outlets. Runoff of precipitation, irrigation, and drainage water from such sources commonly deposits significant amounts of silt, salts, and chemical pollutants (such as pesticides) into streams and lakes. In some areas these sources of pollution degrade ambient water quality more severely than point source discharges, but they are much more difficult to regulate.

"Areawide waste treatment management plans" are to be developed by local planning agencies established by state governors in each area determined to have substantial water quality problems. The states themselves are to prepare the plans for the areas in which the needs are not so critical. The required ingredients of such plans, which are specified in Section 208(b)(2), fall into three broad categories: assurance of adequate POTWs; regulation of industrial, commercial, and residential development so as to minimize water quality impacts; and control of nonpoint sources of pollution.

Regulation of nonpoint sources, including, *inter alia,* irrigation runoff and solid waste disposal, is to be accomplished by imposition of "best management practices" (BMPs)[4] under approved state programs. Best management practices under Section 208 are site-specific, considering the quality of the receiving water body and local variation in soil type, slope, and vegetation. (Under the 1977 Amendments, Section 304 (e), BMPs may also be developed by EPA on an industry-wide basis to control toxic or hazardous runoff from facility sites which also contain point sources.) Where substantial water quality problems do not exist, nonpoint source regulation by BMPs may be unnecessary; however, where water quality falls below governing standards, stringent land use and other controls may be required under the 208 regulatory framework.

Section 208 areawide planning bears so close a relationship to state duties to develop waste management plans under Section 303 that EPA has combined the obligations under both sections, terming the results "water quality management plans." These combined plans include identification of waters which are not adequately protected by effluent limitations (Section 303 (d)) and of waters which require protection by regulation of nonpoint sources (Section 208 (b)), and then development of the appropriate strategies to achieve the applicable water quality standards (Section 303 (e)). Development and implementation of Section 208 plans are the sole responsibility of the states acting through local planning agencies; EPA's role is limited to providing technical and financial support.

Enforcement and Citizen Suits

Enforcement procedures governing violations of effluent limitations, new source standards, toxic standards, and terms of NPDES and dredge and fill permits are provided in Section 309. Recogniz-

---

[4]BMPs are generally defined as "practices or combinations of practices that are determined by a designated planning agency after problem assessment, examination of alternative practices, and appropriate public participation to be the most effective practicable means of preventing or reducing the amount of pollution generated by nonpoint sources to a level compatible with water quality goals." 40 CFR 130.2 (q) 1977.

ing that states with approved enforcement programs are primarily responsible for enforcement, EPA's authority is supposed to be generally supervisory and supplemental. If EPA finds that a person is in violation of an applicable condition or limitation, it may issue an order requiring the person to comply or bring a civil action in federal court for money penalties and/or injunctive relief or it may notify the person and the responsible state of the finding of violation. If the latter course of action is taken, and if the state fails to act within 30 days of notification, EPA may act to require compliance.

Whenever it appears to EPA that violations are so widespread within a state as to indicate lax state enforcement, the state is to be notified and EPA is to assume primary enforcement duties until the state shows that it will perform adequate enforcement.

Any person who violates applicable conditions and limitations is subject to imposition of civil penalties not to exceed $10,000 per day of violation. Any person found to be willfully or negligently violating is subject to criminal punishment: fines range from $2,500 to $25,000 per day of violation for first offenders, plus imprisonment of up to one year. Punishment for subsequent criminal convictions may reach $50,000 per day of violation, or imprisonment for not more than two years, or both.

Section 308 authorizes EPA to require operators of point sources to maintain records and monitoring equipment and to sample effluent discharges as appropriate. Enforcement personnel are authorized to enter upon premises to inspect records and observe operation of point sources. Copies of monitoring records and other information maintained by point source operators are to be made available to the public, except that trade secrets may be protected from disclosure. States seeking approval of their enforcement programs must develop procedures for inspection, monitoring, and entry that conform with this section. Additional record-keeping requirements are imposed by Sections 310 (d) and 312 (g) upon specified categories of point sources.

Section 508 authorizes EPA to list persons, including corporations, convicted of willful or negligent violations under Section 309 (c) as ineligible to receive federal grants, contracts, and loans. A listing excludes only the violating facility from such programs and does not affect other facilities owned by the convicted person. The listing procedure includes opportunity for hearing objections and subsequent petition for "de-listing." The procedure has rarely been implemented, but provides a useful tool for settlement of enforcement actions.

The Clean Water Act contains a provision similar to the Clean Air Act's authorization for any citizen to bring a civil action to enforce standards, limitations, permit conditions, and compliance orders. Such actions may be brought directly against any person, including governmental entities, alleged to be in violation, or against EPA to compel performance of non-discretionary regulatory duties. No citizen suit may be commenced before sixty days' notice has been given to the alleged violator, EPA, and the appropriate state agency. Citizens suits may be brought by any person or corporation alleging an interest which is or may be affected, and attorneys' fees may be awarded at the discretion of the court.

Citizens suits have been more frequently used to compel EPA to develop regulations and standards under Sections 301, 304, and 307 than to redress violations by individual point sources.

There you have it — a "brief overview." As you no doubt suspect, much more detail awaits.

Environmental Protection Agency
v.
California ex rel. State Water Resources Control Board
426 U.S. 200 (1976)

MR. JUSTICE WHITE delivered the opinion of the Court.

The issue in this case which arises under the Federal Water Pollution Control Act Amendments of 1972 (Amendments) is whether federal installations discharging water pollutants in a State with a federally approved permit program are to secure their permits from the State, or from the Environmental Protection Agency (EPA). As with the related Clean Air Act issue decided this day in *Hancock v. Train*, 96 S.Ct. 2006, decision of the specific statutory question — whether obtaining a state permit is among those "requirements respecting control and abatement of pollution" with which federal facilities must comply under § 313 of the Amendments — is informed by constitutional principles governing submission of federal installations to state regulatory authority.

Before it was amended in 1972, the Federal Water Pollution Control Act employed ambient water quality standards specifying the acceptable levels of pollution in a State's interstate navigable waters as the primary mechanism in its program for the control of water pollution. This program based on water quality standards, which were to serve both to guide performance by polluters and to trigger legal action to abate pollution, proved ineffective. The problems stemmed from the character of the standards themselves, which focused on the tolerable effects rather than the preventable causes of water pollution, from the awkwardly shared federal and state responsibility for promulgating such standards,[4] and from the cumbrous enforcement procedures. These combined to make it very difficult to develop and enforce standards to govern the conduct of individual polluters.

Some States developed water quality standards and plans to implement and enforce them, and some relied on discharge permit systems for enforcement. Others did not, and to strengthen the abatement system federal officials revised the Refuse Act of 1899, 33 U.S.C.A. § 407, which prohibits the discharge of any matter into the Nation's navigable waters except with a federal permit. Although this direct approach to water pollution abatement proved helpful, it also was deficient in several respects: the goal of the discharge permit conditions was to achieve water quality standards rather than to require individual polluters to minimize effluent discharge, the permit program was applied only to industrial polluters, some dischargers were required to obtain both federal and state permits, and federal permit authority was shared by two federal agencies.

In 1972, prompted by the conclusion of the Senate Committee on Public Works that "the Federal water pollution control program *** has been inadequate in every vital aspect," Congress enacted the Amendments, declaring "the national goal that the discharge of pollutants into the navigable waters be *eliminated* by 1985." For present purposes the Amendments introduced two major changes in the methods to set and enforce standards to abate and control water pollution. First, the Amendments are aimed at achieving maximum "effluent limitations" on "point sources," as well as achieving acceptable water quality standards. A point source is "any discernible, confined and discrete conveyance *** from which pollutants are or may be discharged." An "effluent limitation" in turn is "any restriction established by a State or the Administrator on quantities, rates, and concentrations of chemical, physical, biological or other consti-

---

[4]The States were to promulgate water quality standards and an implementation plan meeting certain criteria. If a State did not establish such standards and a plan, the Administrator was charged to promulgate water quality standards—but not a plan—in cooperation with state officials.

tuents which are discharged from point sources, *** including schedules of compliance." Such direct restrictions on discharges facilitate enforcement by making it unnecessary to work backward from an overpolluted body of water to determine which point sources are responsible and which must be abated. In addition, a discharger's performance is now measured against strict technology-based[11] effluent limitations — specified levels of treatment — to which it must conform, rather than against limitations derived from water quality standards to which it and other polluters must collectively conform.[12]

Second, the Amendments establish the National Pollutant Discharge Elimination System (NPDES) as a means of achieving and enforcing the effluent limitations. Under NPDES, it is unlawful for any person to discharge a pollutant without obtaining a permit and complying with its terms.[14] An NPDES permit serves to transform generally applicable effluent limitations and other standards — including those based on water quality — into the obligations (including a timetable for compliance) of the individual discharger, and the Amendments provide for direct administrative and judicial enforcement of permits. §§ 309 and 505. With few exceptions, for enforcement purposes a discharger in compliance with the terms and conditions of an NPDES permit is deemed to be in compliance with those sections of the Amendments on which the permit conditions are based. § 402(k). In short, the permit defines, and facilitates compliance with and enforcement of,

a preponderance of a discharger's obligations under the Amendments.

NPDES permits are secured, in the first instance, from EPA, which issues permits under the authority of § 402(a)(1). Section 402(a)(3) requires the EPA permit program and permits to conform to the "terms, conditions, and requirements" of § 402(b). Consonant with its policy "to recognize, preserve, and protect the primary responsibilities and rights of the States to prevent, reduce, and eliminate pollution," Congress also provided that a State may issue NPDES permits "for discharges into navigable waters within its jurisdiction," but only upon EPA approval of the State's proposal to administer its own program. EPA may require modification or revision of a submitted program but when a plan is in compliance with EPA's guidelines under § 304(h)(2) and is supported by adequate authority to achieve the ends of § 402(b)(1) — (9) and to administer the described program, EPA shall approve the program and "suspend the issuance of permits under [§ 402(a)] as to those navigable waters subject to such program."

The EPA retains authority to review operation of a State's permit program. Unless the EPA waives review for particular classes of point sources or for a particular permit application, § 402(d)(3), (e), a State is to forward a copy of each permit application to EPA for review, and no permit may issue if EPA objects that issuance of the permit would be "outside the guidelines and requirements" of the Amendments. § 402(d)(1), (2). In addition to this review authority, after notice and opportunity to take action, EPA may withdraw approval of a state permit program which is not being administered in compliance with § 402. § 402(c)(3).

The Amendments also sought to enlist "every Federal agency . . . to provide national leadership in the control of water pollution in [its] operations." To do so, 33 U.S.C.A § 1171(a), which required federal agencies, "consistent with the paramount interest of the United States as determined by the President [to] insure compliance with applicable water quality standards," was amended by adding § 313, providing that federal installations must "comply with Federal, State,

[11]Point sources other than publicly owned treatment works must achieve effluent limitations requiring application of the "best practicable control technology currently availiable" by June 1, 1977, and application of the "best available technology economically achievable" by June 1, 1983. §§301(b)(1)(A), (2)(A).

[12]Water quality standards are retained as a supplementary basis for effluent limitations, however, so that numerous point sources, despite individual compliance with effluent limitations, may be further regulated to prevent water quality from falling below acceptable levels. See §§ 301(c), 302, 303.

[14]Section 301(a) makes unlawful "the discharge of any pollutant by any person" except in compliance with numerous provisions of the Amendments, including § 402 which establishes NPDES.
In effect, NPDES terminates operation of the Refuse Act permit program. §§ 402(a)(4), (5), 402(k).

interstate, and local requirements respecting control and abatement of pollution to the same extent that any person is subject to such requirements."

*   *   *

Our decision in this case is governed by the same fundamental principles applied today in *Hancock v. Train:* federal installations are subject to state regulation only when and to the extent that congressional authorization is clear and unambiguous. As in *Hancock v. Train,* we must determine whether Congress has subjected federal installations to the degree of state control urged by the States. The only section of the Amendments expressly obliging federal installations to comply with general measures to abate water pollution is § 313, which provides in part:

"Each department, agency, or instrumentality of the executive, legislative, and judicial branches of the Federal Government (1) having jurisdiction over any property or facility, or (2) engaged in any activity resulting, or which may result, in the discharge or runoff of pollutants shall comply with Federal, State, interstate, and local requirements respecting control and abatement of pollution to the same extent that any person is subject to such requirements, including the payment of reasonable service charges."

Except for the reference to service charges, § 313 is virtually identical to § 118 of the Clean Air Act. Taken alone, § 313, like § 118 of the Clean Air Act, states only to what extent — the same as any person — federal installations must comply with applicable state requirements. Section 313 does not expressly provide that federal dischargers must obtain state NPDES permits. Nor does § 313 or any other section of the Amendments expressly state that obtaining a state NPDES permit is a "requirement respecting control or abatement of pollution."

The EPA's position is that the Amendments make clear "only that facilities of the executive, legislative and judicial branches operating within the states must comply with the applicable effluent limitations and compliance schedules promulgated by the particular state pursuant to its EPA-approved implementation plan," as incorporated in EPA-issued permits, not that they comply with "state regulations demanding that sources of discharges — including federal facilities — obtain discharge permits." The States claim that this distinction "between permits and effluent 'limitations' . . . ignores the fact that the mechanism by which such 'limitations' are formulated and applied to individual dischargers is by the permit system established in section 402." From this the States, recognizing that § 313 itself does not subject federal dischargers to their permit programs, derive their principal argument that a State's authority to subject federal installations to its EPA-approved permit program must be implied from the practical needs of administering an NPDES permit program, and that this implication is sufficiently clear to satisfy the governing constitutional standard.
***
Congress used virtually the same language in § 313 as in § 118 of the Clean Air Act; and our conclusion in *Hancock v. Train* that the Clean Air Act is without clear indication that Congress intended federal installations emitting air pollutants to be subject to the permit program of a State's implementation plan makes it difficult for the States to establish that for similar purposes the same language becomes sufficiently clear in § 313 of the Amendments. There are, of course, significant differences between the Clean Air Act and the Amendments. Only the Amendments expressly provide for a permit program to aid in abating pollution. In comparison with the Clean Air Act, the Amendments give the EPA a more prominent role in relation to the States; a State is not required to develop an NPDES permit program, and until a State does develop a permit program *all* discharges in the State are subject to a permit program developed and carried out by the EPA. In addition, under the Amendments the EPA's role in developing the effluent limitations that serve as the basis for a State's NPDES permit conditions is more prominent than in developing the ambient air quality standards which are the foundation of the emission standards in a State's Clean Air Act implementation plan. ***

*   *   *

The Court of Appeals also found textual support for its conclusion in § 510 of the Amendments. This section, which is patterned after § 116 of the Clean Air Act, provides that the States may set more restrictive standards, limitations, and requirements than those imposed under the Amendments. Section 510 quite plainly was intended to strengthen state authority. It may also have been intended to permit the States to impose stricter standards and effluent limitations on federal installations than would have been imposed under an EPA permit in the absence of an approved state NPDES program. But this hardly answers the question before us, which is whether these higher standards are to be enforced through a State rather than an EPA permit system. ***

Another contention drawing upon § 510 is that a State's authority to impose stricter substantive standards on federal installations is meaningless if a State cannot subject federal dischargers to its permit system. This is simply an adjunct to the States' primary argument that no state NPDES permit system can function effectively unless federal dischargers are required to obtain state permits and that federal installations are therefore impliedly, but clearly subject to state permit programs. We cannot agree.

Before a State has its NPDES program approved, it is the EPA which issues permits for all dischargers, federal and nonfederal. Since the Amendments do not require the States to develop NPDES programs, we must assume that the Congress was satisfied that EPA could administer the program, not only by promulgating the nationwide effluent limitations and other standards required by the Amendments, but also by translating those limitations into the conditions of individual permits for individual federal and nonfederal dischargers. We must also assume that the Congress contemplated that there may be some States which would elect not to develop an NPDES program but would nonetheless determine — as § 510 permits — to adopt water quality standards or other limitations stricter than those EPA itself had promulgated and would otherwise apply. This being the case, Congress must have contemplated that EPA was capable of issuing permits in that State —

to both federal and nonfederal dischargers — and of enforcing those stricter standards. Some of those standards — in fact-all but those pegged to the quality of the receiving waters — could be translated into permit conditions for each discharger without coordinating the conditions in other permits, because the effluent limitations in the Amendments are technology-based and the timetable by which compliance is to be achieved is not made to depend on the performance of other dischargers. Other standards, primarily those involving water quality standards, would require coordination among the permit conditions of numerous polluters — federal and nonfederal, and it is evident that Congress contemplated that EPA was capable of carrying out this function as well.

*   *   *

The States, like the Court of Appeals, also find support for their position in § 505 of the Amendments; which provides that a citizen may commence civil actions in district court "against any person (including *** the United States ***) who is alleged to be in violation of *** an effluent standard or limitation under this Act ***." § 505(a)(1). *** Thus, while §§ 505(f)(2)-(4) permit suits for violation of effluent standards or limitations promulgated under §§ 301, 302, 306, and 307, a suit against a permit holder will necessarily be brought under the definition in § 505(f)(6); unless the plaintiff can show violation of the permit condition, violation of the Amendments cannot be established. This is true both for conditions imposed in accordance with EPA-promulgated effluent limitations and standards and for those imposed in accordance with more stringent standards and limitations established by a State pursuant to § 510. ***

*   *   *

IV

Our conclusion is that the Federal Water Pollution Control Act Amendments of 1972 do not subject federal facilities to state NPDES permit requirements with the requisite degree of clarity. Should it be the intent of Congress to have EPA approve a state NPDES program regulating federal as well as nonfederal point sources and suspend issuance of NPDES permits as to all point sources discharging into the navigable waters subject to the State's program, it may legislate to make that intention manifest.

The judgment of the Court of Appeals is Reversed.

NOTES

1. *EPA v. California* was the Supreme Court's first encounter with the Water Act and is included in these materials primarily for its good description of the NPDES permitting scheme.

2. As to the merits, do you agree that obtaining a state permit was not among the "requirements" with which federal facilities were to comply under Section 313 of the 1972 Amendments?

3. In any event, Congress responded in 1977 by amending Section 313 in line with the Court's invitation. See the amended version in your statutory supplement. Has Congress now made its wishes "clear and unambiguous"?

4. For an unusual case illustrating the extremes to which Section 313 can lead, *see Weinberger v. Romero-Barcelo,* 456 U.S. 305 (1982), included in this text *infra*. There the First Circuit had held that the Navy's discharge of ordnance into the coastal waters of Puerto Rico was unlawful without first obtaining an NPDES permit. Would this seem to be the sort of case likely to prompt a Presidential exemption?

2 EFFLUENT LIMITATIONS

E.I. du Pont de Nemours & Co. v. Train
430 U.S. 112 (1977)

MR. JUSTICE STEVENS delivered the opinion of the Court.

Inorganic chemical manufacturing plants operated by the eight petitioners discharge various pollutants into the Nation's waters and therefore are "point sources" within the meaning of the Federal Water Pollution Control Act Amendments of 1972 ("The Act"). The Environmental Protection Agency has promulgated industry-wide regulations imposing three sets of precise limitations on petitioners' discharges. The first two impose progressively higher levels of pollutant control on existing point sources after July 1, 1977, and after July 1, 1983, respectively. The third set imposes limits on "new sources" that may be constructed in the future.

These cases present three important questions of statutory construction: (1) whether EPA has the authority under § 301 of the Act to issue industry-wide regulations limiting discharges by existing plants; (2) whether the Court of Appeals, which admittedly is authorized to review the standards for new sources, also has jurisdiction under § 509 to review the regulations concerning existing plants; and (3) whether the new source standards issued under § 306 must allow variances for individual plants.

As a preface to our discussion of these three questions, we summarize relevant portions of the statute and then describe the procedure which EPA followed in promulgating the challenged regulations.

The Statute

The statute, enacted on October 18, 1972, authorized a series of steps to be taken to achieve the goal of eliminating all discharges of pollutants into the Nation's waters by 1985. § 101(a)(1).

The first steps required by the Act are described in § 304, which directs the Administrator to develop and publish various kinds of technical data to provide guidance in discharging responsibilities imposed by other sections of the Act.*** Within 270 days, he was to develop the information to be used in formulating standards for new plants pursuant to § 306. § 304(c). And within one year he was to publish regulations providing guidance for effluent limitations on existing point sources. Section 304(b) goes into great detail concerning the contents of these regulations. They must identify the degree of effluent reduction attainable through use of the best practicable or best available technology for a class of plants. The guidelines must also "specify factors to be taken into account" in determining the control measures applicable to point sources within these classes. A list of factors to be considered then follows. The Administrator was also directed to develop and publish, within one year, elaborate criteria for water quality accurately reflecting the most current scientific knowledge, and also technical information on factors necessary to restore and maintain water quality. § 304(a). The title of § 304 describes it as the "information and guidelines" portion of the statute.

Section 301 is captioned "effluent limitations." Section 301(a) makes the discharge of any pollutant unlawful unless the discharge is in compliance with certain enumerated sections of the Act. The enumerated sections which are relevant to this case are § 301 itself, § 306, and § 402.

A brief word about each of these sections is necessary.

Section 402 authorizes the Administrator to issue permits for individual point sources, and also authorizes him to review and approve the plan of any State desiring to administer its own permit program. These permits serve "to transform generally applicable effluent limitations . . . into the obligations (including a timetable for compliance) of the individual discharger[s.] . . ." *EPA v. State Water Resources Control Board.* 426 U.S. 200, 205. Petitioner chemical companies' position in this litigation is that § 402 provides the only statutory authority for the issuance of enforceable limitations on the discharge of pollutants by existing plants. It is noteworthy, however, that although this section authorizes the imposition of limitations in individual permits, the section itself does not mandate either the Administrator or the States to use permits as the method of prescribing effluent limitations.

Section 306 directs the Administrator to publish within 90 days a list of categories of sources discharging pollutants and, within one year thereafter, to publish regulations establishing national standards of performance for new sources within each category. Section 306 contains no provision for exceptions from the standards for individual plants; on the contrary, subsection (c) expressly makes it unlawful to operate a new source in violation of the applicable standard of performance after its effective date. The statute provides that the new source standards shall reflect the greatest degree of effluent reduction achievable through application of the best available demonstrated control technology.

Section 301(b) defines the effluent limitations that shall be achieved by existing point sources in two stages. By July 1, 1977, the effluent limitations shall require the application of the best *practicable* control technology currently available; by July 1, 1983, the limitations shall require application of the best *available* technology economically achievable. The statute expressly provides that the limitations which are to become effective in 1983 are applicable to "categories and classes of point sources"; this

phrase is omitted from the description of the 1977 limitations. While § 301 states that these limitations "shall be achieved," it fails to state who will establish the limitations.

Section 301(c) authorizes the Administrator to grant variances from the 1983 limitations. Section 301(e) states that effluent limitations established pursuant to § 301 shall be applied to all point sources.

To summarize, § 301(b) requires the achievement of effluent limitations requiring use of the "best practicable" or "best available" technology. It refers to § 304 for a definition of these terms. Section 304 requires the publication of "regulations, providing guidelines for effluent limitations." Finally, permits issued under § 402 must require compliance with § 301 effluent limitations. Nowhere are we told who sets the § 301 effluent limitations, or precisely how they relate to § 304 guidelines and § 402 permits.

The Regulations

The various deadlines imposed on the Administrator were too ambitious for him to meet. For that reason, the procedure which he followed in adopting the regulations applicable to the inorganic chemical industry and to other classes of point sources, is somewhat different from that apparently contemplated by the statute. Specifically, as will appear, he did not adopt guidelines pursuant to § 304 before defining the effluent limitations for existing sources described in § 301(b) or the national standards for new sources described in § 306. This case illustrates the approach the Administrator followed in implementing the Act.

EPA began by engaging a private contractor to prepare a Development Document. This document provided detailed technical study of pollution control in the industry. The study first divided the industry into categories. For each category, present levels of pollution were measured and plants with exemplary pollution control were investigated. Based on this information, other technical data, and economic studies, a determination was made of the degree of pollution control which could be achieved by the various levels of technology mandated by the statute. The study was made available to the public and circulated to interested persons. It formed the basis of "effluent limitation guideline" regulations issued by EPA after receiving public comment on proposed regulations. These regulations divide the industry into 22 subcategories. Within each subcategory, precise numerical limits are set for various pollutants.[9] The regulations for each subcategory contain a variance clause applicable only to the 1977 limitations.[10]

Eight chemical companies filed petitions in the United States Court of Appeals for the Fourth Circuit for review of these regulations. The Court of Appeals rejected their challenge to EPA's authority to issue precise, single-number limitations for discharges of pollutants from existing sources. It held, however, that these limitations and the new plant standards were only "presumptively applicable" to individual plants. We granted the chemical companies' petitions for certiorari in order to consider the scope of EPA's authority to issue existing-source regulations. We also granted the Government's cross-petition for review of the ruling that new source standards are only presumptively applicable. For convenience, we will refer to the chemical companies as the "petitioners."

The Issues

The broad outlines of the parties' respective theories may be stated briefly. EPA contends that 301(b) authorizes it to issue regulations establishing effluent limitations for classes of plants. The permits granted under § 402, in EPA's view, simply incorporate these across-the-board limitations, except for the limited variances allowed by the regulations themselves and

by § 301(c). The § 304(b) guidelines, according to EPA, were intended to guide it in later establishing § 301 effluent limitation regulations. Because the process proved more time consuming than Congress assumed when it established this two-stage process, EPA condensed the two stages into a single regulation.

In contrast, petitioners contend that § 301 is not an independent source of authority for setting effluent limitations by regulation. Instead, § 301 is seen as merely a description of the effluent limitations which are set for each plant on an individual basis during the permit-issuance process. Under the industry view, the § 304 guidelines serve the function of guiding the permit issuer in setting the effluent limitations.

*   *   *

I

We think § 301 itself is the key to the problem. The statutory language concerning the 1983 limitation, in particular, leaves no doubt that these limitations are to be set by regulation. Subsection (b)(2)(A) of § 301 states that by 1983 "effluent limitations *for categories and classes* of point sources" are to be achieved which will require "application of the best available technology economically achievable *for such category or class.*" (Emphasis added.) These effluent limitations are to require elimination of all discharges if "such elimination is technologically and economically achievable for a *category or class* of point sources." (Emphasis added.) This is "language difficult to reconcile with the view that individual effluent limitations are to be set when each permit is issued." The statute thus focuses expressly on the characteristics of the "category or class" rather than the characteristics of individual point sources. Normally, such class-wide determinations would be made by regulation, not in the course of issuing a permit to one member of the class.

Thus, we find that § 301 unambiguously provides for the use of regulations to establish the 1983 effluent limitations. Different language is used in § 301 with respect to the 1977 limitations. Here, the statute speaks of "effluent limitations for point sources," rather than "effluent limitations for categories and classes of point

---

[9]Some subcategories are required to eliminate all discharges by 1977. Other subcategories are subject to less stringent restrictions. For instance, by 1977 plants producing titanium dioxide by the chloride process must reduce average daily discharges of dissolved iron to 0.72 pounds per thousand pounds of product. This limit is cut in half for existing plants in 1983 and for all new plants.

[10]These limitations may be made "either more or less stringent" to the extent that "factors relating to the equipment or facilities involved, the process applied, or other such factors related to such discharges are fundamentally different from the factors considered" in establishing the limitations. ***

sources." Nothing elsewhere in the Act, however, suggests any radical difference in the mechanism used to impose limitations for the 1977 and 1983 deadlines. For instance, there is no indication in either § 301 or § 304 that the § 304 guidelines play a different role in setting 1977 limitations.*** We conclude that the statute authorizes the 1977 limitations as well as the 1983 limitations to be set by regulation, so long as some allowance is made for variations in individual plants, as EPA has done by including a variance clause in its 1977 limitations.[19]

The question of the form of § 301 limitations is tied to the question whether the Act requires the Administrator or the permit issuer to establish the limitations. Section 301 does not itself answer this question, for it speaks only in the passive voice of the achievement and establishment of the limitations. But other parts of the statute leave little doubt on this score. Section 304(b) states that "[f]or the purpose of adopting or revising effluent limitations . . . the Administrator shall" issue guideline regulations; while the judicial review section (§ 509(b)(1)) speaks of "the Administrator's action . . . in approving or promulgating any effluent limitation or other limitation under section 301 . . . ." And § 101(d) requires us to resolve any ambiguity on this score in favor of the Administrator. It provides that "[e]xcept as otherwise *expressly* provided in this Act, the Administrator of the Environmental Protection Agency . . . shall administer this Act." (Emphasis added.) In sum, the language of the statute supports the view that § 301 limitations are to be adopted by the Administrator, that they are to be based primarily on classes and categories, and that they are to take the form of regulations.

The legislative history supports this reading of § 301.*** The Conference Report on § 301 states that "the determination of the economic impact of an effluent limitation [will be made] on the basis of classes and categories of point sources, as distinguished from a plant by plant determination." Leg. Hist., at 304. In presenting the Conference Report to the Senate, Senator

Muskie, perhaps the Act's primary author, emphasized the importance of uniformity in setting § 301 limitations. He explained that this goal of uniformity required that EPA focus on classes or categories of sources in formulating effluent limitations. Regarding the requirement contained in § 301 that plants use the "best practicable control technology" by 1977, he stated:

"The modification of subsection 304(b)(1) is intended to clarify what is meant by the term 'practicable.' The balancing test between total cost and effluent reduction benefits is intended to limit the application of technology only where the additional degree of effluent reduction is wholly out of proportion to the costs of achieving such marginal level of reduction for *any class or category* of sources.

"The Conferees agreed upon this limited cost-benefit analysis in order to maintain *uniformity within a class and category* of point sources subject to effluent limitations, and to avoid imposing on the Administrator any requirement to consider the location of sources within a category or to ascertain water quality impact of effluent controls or to determine the economic impact of controls on any individual plant in a single community." Leg. Hist., at 170 (emphasis added).

*   *   *

This legislative history supports our reading of § 301 and makes it clear that the § 304 guidelines are not merely aimed at guiding the discretion of permit issuers in setting limitations for individual plants.

What, then, is the function of the § 304(b) guidelines? As we noted earlier, § 304(b) requires EPA to identify the amount of effluent reduction attainable through use of the best practicable or available technology and to "specify factors to be taken into account" in determining the pollution control methods "to be applicable to point sources . . . within such categories or classes." These guidelines are to be issued "[f]or the purpose of adopting or revising

---

[19]We agree with the Court of Appeals, 541 F.2d, at 1028, that consideration of whether EPA's variance provision has the proper scope would be premature.

effluent limitations under this Act." As we read it, § 301 requires that the guidelines survey the practicable or available pollution control technology for an industry and assess its effectiveness. The guidelines are then to describe the methodology EPA intends to use in the § 301 regulations to determine the effluent limitations for particular plants. If the technical complexity of the task had not prevented EPA from issuing the guidelines within the statutory deadline, they could have provided valuable guidance to permit issuers, industry and the public, prior to the issuance of the § 301 regulations.

Our construction of the Act is supported by § 501(a), which gives EPA the power to make "such regulations as are necessary to carry out" its functions and by § 101(d), which charges the agency with the duty of administering the Act. *** The petitioners' view of the Act would place an impossible burden on EPA. It would require EPA to give individual consideration to the circumstances of each of the more than 42,000 dischargers who have applied for permits and to issue or approve all these permits well in advance of the 1977 deadline in order to give industry time to install the necessary pollution control equipment. We do not believe that Congress would have failed so conspicuously to provide EPA with the authority needed to achieve the statutory goals.

*   *   *

Language we recently employed in another case involving the validity of EPA regulations applies equally to this case:

> "We therefore conclude that the Agency's interpretation . . . was 'correct,' to the extent that it can be said with complete assurance that any particular interpretation of a complex statute such as this is the 'correct' one. Given this conclusion, as well as the facts that the Agency is charged with administration of the Act, and that there has undoubtedly been reliance upon its interpretation by the States and other parties affected by the Act, we have no doubt whatever that its construction was sufficiently reasonable to preclude

> the Court of Appeals from substituting its judgment for that of the Agency." *Train v. Natural Resources Defense Council,* 421 U.S. 60, 87.

When as in this case, the Agency's interpretation is also supported by thorough, scholarly opinions written by some of our finest judges, and has received the overwhelming support of the courts of appeals, we would be reluctant indeed to upset the Agency's judgment. In this case, on the contrary, our independent examination confirms the correctness of the Agency's construction of the statute.

Consequently, we hold that EPA has the authority to issue regulations setting forth uniform effluent limitations for categories of plants.

II

Our holding that § 301 does authorize the Administrator to promulgate effluent limitations for classes and categories of existing point sources necessarily resolves the jurisdictional issue as well. For, as we have already pointed out, § 509(b)(1) provides that "[r]eview of the Administrator's action . . . in approving or promulgating any effluent limitation or other limitation under section 301, 302, or 306, . . . may be had by any interested person in the Circuit Court of Appeals of the United States for the Federal judicial district in which such person resides or transacts such business . . . ."

*   *   *

III

The remaining issue in this case concerns new plants. Under § 306, EPA is to promulgate "regulations establishing Federal standards of performance for new sources . . . ." § 306(b)(1)(B). A "standard of performance" is a "standard for the control of the discharge of pollutants which reflects the greatest degree of effluent reduction which the Administrator determines to be achievable through application of the best available demonstrated control technology, . . . including, where practicable, a standard permitting no discharge of pollutants." § 306(a)(1). In setting the standard, "[t]he Administrator may distinguish among classes, types, and sizes within categories of new sources . . . and shall consider the type of process employed (including whether batch or continuous)." § 306(b)(2). ***

The Court of Appeals held that:

"Neither the Act nor the regulations contain any variance provision for new sources. The rule of presumptive applicability applies to new sources as well as existing sources. On remand EPA should come forward with some limited escape mechanism for new sources." 541 F.2d at 1028.

The Court's rationale was that "[p]rovisions for variances, modifications, and exceptions are appropriate to the regulatory process." *Ibid.*

The question, however, is not what a court thinks is generally appropriate to the regulatory process; it is what Congress intended for *these* regulations. It is clear that Congress intended these regulations to be absolute prohibitions. The use of the word "standards" implies as much. So does the description of the preferred standard as one "permitting *no* discharge of pollutants." (Emphasis added.) It is "unlawful for *any* owner or operator of *any* new source to operate such source in violation of any standard of performance applicable to such source." § 306(e) (emphasis added). In striking contrast to § 301(c), there is no statutory provision for variances, and a variance provision would be inappropriate in a standard that was intended to insure national uniformity and "maximum feasible control of new sources."

That portion of the judgment of the Court of Appeals requiring EPA to provide a variance procedure for new sources is reversed. In all other aspects, the judgment of the Court of Appeals is affirmed.

*   *   *

NOTES

1. Was du Pont's position unreasonable? Was it an unreasonable construction of the Act?

2. Is a uniform national standard workable and realistic? Given the substantial amount of variation in production processes in most industries, is a uniform national standard fair and equitable?

3. How are the variations in facilities to be taken into account? In the permitting process? In subcategorizing within a category of point sources? In granting "variances"?

4. Are variances from BPT limitations permissible? On what statutory authority? Why should new source standards be any more rigidly applied?

5. With a system largely based on uniform national standards, what role is left for the states? Is there as much incentive for a state to adopt an NPDES permitting plan as there is for it to adopt a state implementation plan under the Clean Air Act? Note that, as guaranteed by § 510, a state might maintain its own more stringent effluent limitations, and as provided in § 401, EPA could not issue a permit to a discharger without state certification that the state standards were met. (In fact, states were significantly slower to seek Water Act permitting authority. By 1983, for example, the State of Texas had yet to adopt an NPDES plan.)

6. For an example of the difficulty in challenging national effluent limitations set by EPA, see the largely unsuccessful efforts by the pesticide industry to convince the First Circuit to overturn BPT standards applicable to them. *BASF Wyandotte Corp. v. Castle*, 598 F.2d 637 (1st Cir. 1979).

Association of Pacific Fisheries
v.
Environmental Protection Agency

615 F. 2d 794 (9th Cir. 1980)

Before TRASK, SNEED, and KENNEDY, Circuit Judges.

KENNEDY, Circuit Judge:

In 1972 Congress, intending "to restore and maintain the chemical, physical, and biological integrity of the Nation's waters," amended the Federal Water Pollution Control Act (Act), 33 U.S.C. § 1251 *et seq.* Congress established national pollution goals to be achieved by specific dates. By July 1, 1977, industries discharging pollutants into the nation's waters were to have achieved "the best practicable control technology currently available (BPT)." Section 301(b)(1)(A). By 1983, industry is to achieve "the best available technology economically achievable (BEA)." Section 301(b)(2)(A). The Environmental Protection Agency (EPA or Agency) was entrusted with the responsibility of defining and policing the efficient and prompt achievement of these goals.

This case involves a challenge to regulations promulgated by the Agency establishing effluent guidelines for the Canned and Preserved Seafood Processing Point Source Category. 40 C.F.R. §§ 408.10 *et seq.* ***

*** These *** regulations covered nineteen separate subcategories. *** At issue are the regulations which apply to Alaskan hand-butchered salmon (Subpart P), Alaskan mechanized salmon (Subpart Q), west coast hand-butchered salmon (Subpart R), west coast mechanized salmon (Subpart S), Alaskan bottomfish (Subpart T), west coast bottomfish (Subparts U and V), Alaskan scallops (Subpart AC), and herring fillets (Subparts AE and AF).

The effluent which is the subject of the regulations consists of unused fish residuals. This discharge includes heads, tails, and internal residuals of the processed fish. Substantial quantities of water are used at various stages of the plant operations. This water comes into contact with the fish residuals and contains pollutants when discharged. The regulations prescribe limitations on discharge, and utilize three measures of pollution: five-day biochemical oxygen demand (BOD_5); total suspended solids (TSS); and oil and grease (O & G). The regulations establish daily maximum levels and monthly average levels for each subcategory, and are measured in terms of the amount of pollutant per thousand pounds of fish processed.

The prescribed 1977 BPT for processors not located in Alaska, and Alaska processors located in "population or processing centers," is the installation of screens to trap the larger fish particles before the effluent is discharged from the plant.[3] Residuals trapped by the screens may be disposed of in ways discussed below. Alaska processors in "remote" locations are subject only to limitations on the size of particles in the effluent, a requirement that can be met by grinding the solids before discharge.

By 1983 the fisheries must comply with more rigorous technology requirements and effluent limitations. For nonremote facilities, the Agency directed that a dissolved air flotation unit be installed at each location and that the end-of-pipe effluent be channeled through this system before it is discharged into the receiving water. These regulations apply to all nonremote subcategories except Subpart V, Conventional Bottomfish. There, the Administrator has prescribed aerated lagoons as the BEA. Remote Alaska fish processors will be required by the 1983 regulations to screen the effluent before discharging it into the receiving waters.

---

[3]Although the Agency prescribed screening as the BPT, "processors may select alternative methods . . . to meet the published effluent limitations."

*   *   *

1977 REGULATIONS

*   *   *

B. *Cost-Benefit Comparisons and the Question of Screening*

The parties dispute whether or not the requirement of screening plus barging or land-based disposal was reached after a proper evaluation of costs and benefits. The disagreement extends both to questions of interpreting the statute and to whether the Agency followed the Act even assuming its own interpretation is correct.

Section 304(b)(1)(B) of the Act provides in part:

> Factors relating to the assessment of best practicable control technology currently available to comply with subsection (b)(1) of section 301 of this Act shall include consideration of the total cost of application of technology in relation to the effluent reduction benefits to be achieved from such application.

We think it plain that, as a general rule, the EPA is required to consider the costs and benefits of a proposed technology in its inquiry to determine the BPT. The Agency has broad discretion in weighing these competing factors, however. When considering different levels of technology, it must be shown that increased costs are wholly disproportionate to potential effluent reduction before the Agency is permitted to rely on a cost-benefit comparison to select a lower level of technology as the BPT. ***

It is relevant in this case, moreover, to consider the definition of the benefits the Agency is directed to weigh. We agree with the Agency's contention that Congress intended BPT standards to be based primarily on employment of available technology for reducing effluent discharge, and not primarily on demonstrated changes in water quality. Congress was aware that prior enforcement efforts based on water quality standards had not been successful. It determined, accordingly, that the Agency should

have the authority to require effluent reduction benefits as defined by the amount or degree of reduction achieved by a level of technology applied to discharge, without the necessity of demonstrating the incremental effect of that technology on the quality of the receiving water. As the D.C. Circuit explained in *Weyerhaeuser Co. v. Costle*, 590 F.2d at 1041-44, the "effluent reduction benefits" referred to in the Act are not primarily water quality benefits; rather, "[e]ffluent reduction occurs whenever less effluent is discharged, *i.e.*, whenever a plant treats its wastes before discharge." *Id.*, 590 F.2d at 1044 n. 49.

In light of these principles, we evaluate the petitioners' claim that the Agency overestimated the benefits of screening and improperly ignored or underestimated the benefits of grinding. Petitioners assert that grinding should have been considered expressly by the Agency as an alternate technology. It was used by a significant number of plants before the regulations became effective, and the Agency expressly permitted grinding for plants in remote areas. Petitioners assert that the Agency's failure to consider grinding makes its analysis deficient and invalidates the cost-benefit determination that justifies prescribing screening for nonremote processors. According to petitioners, the record demonstrates that "every 'adverse environmental impact' identified by respondent is either eliminated by grinding and dispersion or not alleviated by screening at all."

We do not understand petitioners to dispute seriously that removing solids by screening is superior to grinding in terms of reducing both the total amount of fish solids and pollutants as defined by the measures used by the EPA. Their point, rather, is that the EPA's determination of BPT must be evaluated by taking into account the methods of disposing of the collected fish products that are permitted by the regulations in question. Petitioners contend that the ultimate reduction in pollution achieved by screening is the same as grinding, since the EPA permits screened solids to be barged and dumped at specified ocean sites located only ½ to 2½ miles from the processing plants. We think petitioners' reasoning is flawed in various respects.

Barging of solids for dumping at ocean sites is only one of various waste disposal alternatives permitted. Transportation to landfills or pet food processing plants, where the by-products can be sold to the food processors, are also possible methods of handling collected solids. It was reasonable for the Agency to find that given a choice between barging and transporting to a land-based reduction center, some plants would choose the latter. To the extent that screened solids are not returned to the receiving waters, fewer pollutants are discharged, and presumably TSS, BOD and O & G are also reduced.***

The Agency says further that the receiving waters into which it approved discharge of barged solids "are not the same waters" as those used by processors to discharge their ground effluent, because the approved sites are farther offshore. While the petitioners argue that this is irrelevant, there is support for the Agency's distinction in the legislative history of the Act. The Agency has not explained to this court as clearly as it might have how the asserted water quality benefits of discharging a given amount of effluent farther offshore should be considered within the statutory framework of technology-based, not water quality-based, pollution limitations. But even assuming, contrary to our conclusion in the previous paragraph, that application of the BPT would result in no decrease in the amount of pollutants discharged into receiving waters (both nearshore and offshore), we think that the Act permits the EPA to consider an improvement in nearshore water quality to be an "effluent reduction benefit."*** No doubt Congress sought in the Act to do more than simply have the EPA relocate the same amount of effluent discharge, but we doubt that it prohibited the EPA from requiring relocation of that discharge where environmental benefits of such a relocation have been demonstrated.[9]

The record contains evidence that because of inadequate tidal dispersion in various locations

affected by the regulation, discharges by processors caused aesthetic and environmental harm by forming sludgebeds at or near beaches and shoreline. The Agency cites studies showing such effects at Kodiak, Cordova, Petersburg, and Anchorage. The Agency also considered a study by the Canadian Environmental Protection Service which indicated that effluent from fish processing facilities can have harmful environmental effects up to one mile from the discharging facility, altering the environmental balance of the receiving waters and creating toxic waste products. The dumping sites approved by the Agency are located in deeper waters and in areas of high tidal activity. These factors facilitate dispersion and decomposition of discharged fish solids.

*   *   *

The costs of screening were also considered by the Agency. For example, the Agency projected that for mechanized Alaskan salmon canning plants, "Grinding costs ranged from $30,000 for a 20 ton per-day plant to $54,000 for a 150 ton per-day plant respectively. Screening and barging costs varied from $72,000 to $146,000 for the same plants." The figures for Alaskan Bottom Fish indicate that grinding costs ranged from $20,000 capital outlay and $50/day operation and maintenance (O & M) for a 13.6 ton per-day plant to $38,000 capital and $60/day O & M for a 105.6 ton per-day plant. Screening and barging costs varied from $55,000 capital outlay and $150/day O & M for the smaller plant to $98,000 capital outlay and $190/day O & M for the larger plant.

After estimating the costs for affected subcategories, the Agency concluded the total internal costs of the 1977 effluent limitations would be $6.2 million for investment and $1.3 million of annual expenditures. External costs included a minor effect on prices and the expected closure of some processing plants because of inability to comply economically with the regulations. The effect of these closures on the domestic industry capacity was anticipated to be small.

[9]We decline at this time to discuss the extent to which, if the EPA relies on water quality evidence in measuring the benefits of requiring a particular technology for a category or subcategory of point sources, it must also consider water quality evidence at particular sites in passing on applications for variances.

Petitioners argue that the number of plants estimated to close as a result of the regulations demonstrates that the costs of implementing the technology are wholly out of proportion to the effluent reduction benefits, and thus that the regulations do not prescribe a practicable technology. We do not find the Agency's action can be set aside on this issue.

Precisely how many plants in nonremote locations the EPA estimated would close as a result of the 1977 BPT is not completely clear from the record. In the Preamble to the Regulations, the Agency states only that "a number of small plants are projected to be adversely affected by the effluent limitations." The record shows that in affected subcategories 28 out of 172 plants were projected to close as a result of the 1977 BPT. In its brief, the Agency argues that for several reasons, stated in the record, its original estimate of the number of plant closings was too high. It does not, however, point to any revised estimate. Thus, the most concrete estimate available is that contained in EPA's Economic Analysis. These data also disclose that in Alaska nonremote subcategories—the Alaska subcategories where screening is the BPT—seven out of sixteen plants were predicted to close as a result of inability to meet BPT.

Petitioners agree Congress contemplated that implementing BPT might result in plant closures in some industries. The proportion of plants estimated to close in the nonremote Alaska subcategories (57% for nonremote Alaskan fresh and frozen salmon and 33% for nonremote Alaskan salmon canning) is substantially higher than that approved in some other cases.*** The Agency determined, however, that the effect on prices of implementing the BPT would be small: "price increases generally in the range of 0.3 to 0.5 percent are projected," 40 Fed.Reg. at 55777. It also found that "domestic industry capacity is not expected to be affected by the potential closure of these particular small plants." Id. The percentage of estimated plant closures in the seafood processing category generally is low. Given these findings, the estimated number of plant closings in the nonremote Alaska subcategories, standing by itself, does not invalidate its cost/benefit analysis or require us to set aside the Agency's determination that the required technology was practicable.

The Agency need not balance the costs of compliance against effluent reduction benefits with pinpoint precision, in part because many of the benefits resulting from the effluent reduction are incapable of precise quantification. See also Appalachian Power Co. v. Train, 545 F.2d 1351, 1361 (4th Cir. 1976) ("[W]e [reject] Industry's contention that benefits derived from a particular level of effluent reduction must be quantified in monetary terms . . . This reflects the simple fact that such benefits often cannot be reduced to dollars and cents.").

The Agency, upon consideration of the effluent reduction benefits thought to be achieved by screening, both the water quality benefits and the amount of pollutants discharged into the receiving waters, determined that the costs of screening were justified. We conclude the Agency complied with the Act's mandate to consider the costs of technology in relation to effluent reduction benefits.

C. *Accuracy of the Agency's Data and Methodology*

*   *   *

In determining the effluent guidelines for the subcategories, the Agency employed a model plant analysis. Because the Agency determined that treatment practices in the industry were inadequate, it constructed a model plant utilizing processing data gathered from operating processors during the 1973 season, and financial data from 1968 through 1972. The Agency used peak flow in gallons per minute as the major determinant of the size and cost of treatment equipment which would be required.

As we understand petitioners' challenge, it is that the Agency's model plant for nonremote Alaskan canned salmon facilities (and presumably other subcategories as well) underestimated the amount of fish processed per hour at actual processors, since the data gathered by the EPA were collected during the 1973 season, an unproductive season not representative of most years. As a result, petitioners say, the model plant analysis underestimated the costs of installing and operating required screening technology. The increased costs would result from the necessity of installing larger screens to handle the greater flow, and possibly also from requirements for more trucks or barges to handle the screened solids.

***To make petitioners' claim more concrete, if a large processor had a water flow rate of 2.2 gallons per minute (the EPA figure) and processed 40 tons of raw material per hour instead of the model plant figure of approximately 8, the cost of compliance with the regulations, while perhaps not being exactly five times as expensive as predicted by the EPA, would nevertheless be substantially higher than the predicted figure.

The Agency defends the model plant as being designed on the basis of figures obtained from actual processors. The Agency also supports its analysis with at least two further arguments. It first notes that the relation, if any, between tons of fish processed per hour and the cost of installing appropriate screening technology is not linear. One cost comparison made by the Agency indicated that a facility which processes ten times as much fish per hour would probably spend only 1.4 times as much as the small facility for the screening technology. Thus, any underestimation regarding plant production would not affect the Agency's cost estimations to such a degree that its analysis must be set aside.

The Agency's other argument is that several of the facilities sampled had or could have had a water use rate of substantially less than 2.2 gallons per pound of raw material, the figure assumed for the model plant. Therefore, even if the tons of raw material processed per hour at a plant were greater than the EPA estimated, its cost figures were not unreasonable estimates, because the plant could process more than 8.3 tons of material per hour using the same flow rate as the model plant, and the cost of installing screens to handle the flow rate would thus be similar to that of the model plant.

The Agency may or may not have constructed the model plant with complete accuracy, but that is not the question for this court. After consulting with members of the processing industry and other knowledgeable sources, the

EPA engaged in sampling procedures designed to collect representative data given the constraints imposed by time and difficulties of data collection.

***The Agency had relevant information before it and considered this information in formulating its production and cost estimates. We decline to second guess the Agency's expert determinations as to the model plant, since there is adequate support for those conclusions in the record.

*   *   *

1983 REGULATIONS

The regulations promulgated by the Administrator for 1983 are to reflect the "best available technology economically achievable." Section 301(b)(2)(A). For the regulations to be affirmed, the Agency must demonstrate that the technology required is "available" and the effluent limitations are "economically achievable."

A. *Dissolved Air Flotation Unit.*

A dissolved air flotation unit is the prescribed technology for the following subcategories: west coast hand-butchered salmon (Subpart R), west coast mechanized salmon (Subpart S), non-Alaskan mechanized bottomfish (Subpart V), and non-Alaskan herring fillet (Subpart AF).

The system operates as follows: Effluent passes into a holding tank. Air enters the effluent under pressure and attaches to solid particles. Buoyed by the air, the particles rise to the surface and are skimmed off. The particles can be used as animal feed or fertilizer. The clarified water is withdrawn from the bottom of the tank. Before entering the receiving waters, this effluent remainder must be within certain maximum limitations. The regulations set forth limitations for BOD_5, TSS, O & G, and acidity for each category.

The numerical limitations were based on the assumption that a DAF unit will reduce BOD_5 by 75%, TSS by 90%, and O & G by 90%. Petitioners claim these figures were the result of a single study conducted by the British Columbia seafood industry in conjunction with the Canadian Fisheries Research Board. The study measured the amount of reduced pollutants in the effluent from a salmon processing plant. The DAF unit reduced the BOD_5 by 80%, the TSS by 90%, and the oil and grease by 95%. Petitioners argue that the Agency was arbitrary and capricious in basing its 1983 technology regulations on a single study.

The legislative history of the 1983 regulations indicates that regulations establishing BEA can be based on statistics from a single plant. The House Report states:

> It will be sufficient for the purposes of setting the level of control under available technology, that there be one operating facility which demonstrates that the level can be achieved or that there is sufficient information and data from a relevant pilot plant or semi-works plant to provide the needed economic and technical justification for such new source.

Although only one salmon study was in the record, the Administrator also considered numerous other DAF studies involving herring, groundfish, stickwater, sardines, shrimp, tuna, mackerel, scabbard, yellow croaker, and menhaden bailwater. Each of these studies revealed a substantial reduction in pollution levels. Although the pollution reduction in some studies was not as dramatic as others, the EPA is not charged with burden of showing that all DAF units could meet the limitations, but rather that the best existing DAF units can meet the limitations. Further, to the extent that some of these studies are best viewed as implicating "transfer technology," the Agency did not misuse its discretion in finding the technology to be transferable to the subcategories at issue. The EPA's data base was sufficient to show that the technology required to meet the 1983 limitations is "available."

*   *   *

The next question is whether the Agency properly evaluated the costs of meeting the 1983 guidelines. In describing the role of costs in promulgating BEA, the Conference Report stated:

> While cost should be a factor in the Administrator's judgment, no balancing test will be required. The Administrator will be bound by a test of reasonableness. In this case, the reasonableness of what is 'economically achievable' should reflect an evaluation of what needs to be done to move toward the elimination of the discharge of pollutants and what is achievable through the application of available technology—without regard to cost.

L.H. at 170. Although the wording of the statute clearly states that the 1983 limitations must be "economically achievable," there is some disagreement among the circuits as to whether the costs of compliance should be considered in a review of the 1983 limitations. We hold, in agreement with the court in *Weyerhaeuser, supra*, 590 F.2d at 1044-45, that the EPA must consider the economic consequences of the 1983 regulations, along with the other factors mentioned in section 304(b)(2)(B).

Petitioners maintain that the Agency must balance the ecological benefits against the associated costs in determining whether the technology is economically achievable. They cite in support of this proposition *Appalachian Power Co. v. Train*, 545 F.2d 1351 (4th Cir. 1976). In remanding the 1983 regulations affecting electrical power companies, the court there stated:

> [I]n choosing among alternative strategies, EPA must not only set forth the cost of achieving a particular level of heat reduction but must also state the expected environmental benefits, that is to say the effect on the environment, which will take place as a result of reduction, for it is only after EPA has fully explicated its course of conduct in this manner that a reviewing court can determine whether the agency has, in light of the goal to be achieved, acted arbitrarily or capriciously in adopting a particular effluent reduction level.

Id. at 1364-65 (footnote omitted). According to petitioners, the Agency did not consider the incremental benefit to the environment to be achieved by the dissolved air flotation units, and the regulations must be set aside. We cannot agree. As noted by the court in *Weyerhaeuser, supra,* 590 F.2d at 1045-46, the language of the statute indicates that the EPA's consideration of cost in determining BPT and BEA was to be different. In prescribing the appropriate 1977 technology, the Agency was to "include consideration of the total cost of application of technology *in relation to the effluent reduction benefits to be achieved from such application.*" Section 304(b)(1)(B) (emphasis added). In determining the 1983 control technology, however, the EPA must "take into account . . . the cost of achieving such effluent reduction," along with various other factors. Section 304(b)(2)(B). The conspicuous absence of the comparative language contained in section 304(b)(1)(B) leads us to the conclusion that Congress did not intend the Agency or this court to engage in marginal cost-benefit comparisons.

The intent of Congress is stated in 33 U.S.C. § 1251(a)(1): "[I]t is the national goal that the discharge of pollutants into the navigable waters be eliminated by 1985 . . . ." The regulations that will be applied in 1983 are intended to result "in reasonable further progress toward the national goal of eliminating the discharge of all pollutants . . . ." 33 U.S.C. § 1311(b)(2)(A). These express declarations of congressional intent cannot be ignored in determining the reasonableness of the 1983 regulations. So long as the required technology reduces the discharge of pollutants, our inquiry will be limited to whether the Agency considered the cost of technology, along with the other statutory factors, and whether its conclusion is reasonable. Of course, at some point extremely costly more refined treatment will have a de minimis effect on the receiving waters. But that point has not been reached in these BEA regulations.

The record discloses that the Agency studied the cost of complying with the 1983 regulations. It set forth the cost of compliance for plants that produced various amounts of effluent per minute, both in terms of capital costs and operation and maintenance costs. The projections include estimates of the costs of construction, labor, power, chemicals and fuel. Although land acquisition costs were not considered, the amount of land necessary for the air flotation unit is minimal. In contrast to our conclusion regarding aerated lagoons, the Agency was not arbitrary in concluding that the DAF unit could be installed on existing plant locations without necessitating additional land acquisitions.

Finally, it does not appear that the cost of complying with the 1983 regulations is unreasonable. The cost of compliance for the Northwest Canned Salmon subcategory, for example, is estimated to be $157,000 for initial investment and $32,000 of annual expenditures for the average size plants. According to the EPA's economic analysis, the total annual costs of pollution abatement averaged between one and two percent of the total sales figures of each subcategory. Depreciation is available for the capital outlays and tax deductions are available for business expenses. The Agency concluded that the benefits justified the costs, and petitioners have not shown that conclusion to be arbitrary or capricious.

Although the number of plants estimated to close as a result of the 1983 regulations was not stated clearly to us, it appears to be a lesser proportion of affected plants than that which we approved for the 1977 regulations. Since Congress contemplated the closure of some marginal plants, we do not consider the regulations to be arbitrary and capricious.

For these reasons, we conclude that the 1983 regulations requiring dissolved air flotation units for West Coast fish processors should be upheld.

B. *Aerated Lagoons*

The aerated lagoon is the required technology for the non-Alaskan conventional bottomfish subcategory. Aerated lagoons are still ponds in which waste water is treated biologically. They are usually three to four feet deep. With oxidation taking place in the upper eighteen inches, the water will remain in the lagoon from three to fifty days. Mechanically aerated lagoons are between six and twenty feet deep and receive oxygen from a floating aerator. Because of the length of detention time, the lagoons must be large in relation to the square footage of a processing plant to handle peak wasteload production.

*   *   *

The final question presented is whether the Agency gave adequate consideration to costs in the determination that aerated lagoons are achievable technology. The major disadvantage of aerated lagoons is that they require large amounts of readily-accessible land. The Agency did not consider the cost of acquiring land in determining the economic impact of the regulations. The reason given for this omission is that the costs of acquiring land are "site-specific" and vary depending upon the location and surrounding area. Although this may be true, it does not follow that the cost of acquiring land should be completely ignored in determining whether the technology is achievable. Where a significant amount of land proximate to a plant is an inherent requirement of a control technology, the Agency must attempt to determine the economic impact of acquiring the land. The Agency may set forth the amount of land necessary for various size plants, the average cost of land in the vicinity of identified processing plants, and, finally, whether it is reasonable to conclude that land will be available for the aerated lagoons.

We recognize this holding may be at odds with *American Iron and Steel Inst. v. EPA*, 526 F.2d 1027, 1053 (3d Cir. 1976). The court there determined that the cost of land acquisition should not be considered because it is "inherently site-specific" and that petitioners have the burden of showing "the magnitude of these excluded costs factors." *Id.* at 1053. We respectfully disagree on both counts.

The Agency has successfully projected other average costs that might be termed "site-specific" such as the cost of in-plant process changes, the cost of barging and screening and the cost of other control technology. Each of these costs is subject to variability, depending on plant design and location. Similarly, when a significant amount of land is required for implementation of the regulation, we think the Agency must take land availability or land cost into account in some manner before it can make a reasoned determination that the regulations are economically achievable, especially when actual plant sites can be studied for this purpose. Failure to do so results in an incomplete consideration of the economic impact of the regulations. This is especially true where, as here, it appears many plant sites are located on waterfront areas where proximate land is not available or is in all probability expensive. That the cost or practicality of acquiring land is difficult to discern does not excuse the Agency from making some estimate of those factors. The amount of land necessary for this control technology is quite significant, and we think it is essential that the Agency give express consideration to that aspect of the 1983 regulations.

*   *   *

We therefore remand the regulation requiring aerated lagoons to the Agency in order that it may promulgate new 1983 regulations for the non-Alaskan conventional bottomfish subcategory. The remaining regulations are sustained upon the reasoning set forth above.

AFFIRMED in part and REMANDED in part.

NOTES

1. As illustrated by the effluent limitations for the seafood processing industry at issue in this case, the control technology prescribed for meeting the limitations is not always very complex. In fact, in the case of BPT limitations, the modifications and equipment necessary to meet the standards are often quite rudimentary: screens, settling ponds, skimmers and other such uncomplicated devices. This is not to say that they are necessarily inexpensive or that their costs can be painlessly borne by the industry. Consider the capital and operating costs recited in this case, page 29, which EPA forecast would be imposed by BPT on Alaskan salmon and bottomfish processing plants. Also, notice that the agency estimated that imposition of this first round of standards on the nonremote Alaskan fresh and frozen salmon industry would put 57 percent of the plants in that subcategory out of business. Does this indicate that the survival of some businesses depends on their ability to continue uncontrolled pollution? If so, should it be deemed "practicable" to force them under?

2. The most significant of the factors specified in Section 304 (b)(1)(B) for the Administrator's consideration in setting BPT limitations is "the total cost of application of technology in relation to the effluent reduction benefits to be achieved from such application."

Does this require—like Executive Order 12291—that the total benefits of the limitation established outweigh its total costs? Thus far, in construing this phrase, most reviewing courts have recited the statement in the Conference Committee report on the bill which became the Amendments of 1972:

> The balancing test between total cost and effluent reduction benefits is intended to limit the application of technology only where the additional degree of effluent reduction is wholly out of proportion to the costs of achieving such marginal level of reduction for any class or category of sources.

Deferring to the agency's exercise of broad discretion in striking the proper balance, courts have not insisted that EPA demonstrate that its promulgated standard is cost beneficial. Could EPA, however, strictly apply the Executive Order to its setting of BPT limitations?

3. In challenging BPT standards, affected industries have often complained of EPA's refusal to consider the costs and benefits of levels of pollution abatement other than those corresponding to the limited number of control technologies selected for evaluation. Such a restricted analysis, it has been argued, prevents determination of the most "cost effective" pollution control technology. Where this argument has been raised, it has been rejected in favor of EPA's "broad discretion" to select those control technologies which are available and the costs and benefits of which it will evaluate. Is this an "intellectual fraud"? See American Iron & Steel Institute v. EPA, 568 F. 2d 284 (3d Cir. 1977).

On the other hand, would it bog the agency down in research of marginal relevance to require it to undertake measurement of the costs and benefits of each additional increment of waste treatment control, from bare minimum to zero discharge? This was the opinion of the D.C. Circuit in Weyerhaeuser Co. v. Costle, 590 F. 2d 1011, 1047-48 (D.C. Cir. 1978).

4. EPA's preferred method of determining the best practicable control technology currently available (BPT) has been to find existing facilities within the particular category at issue which employ exemplary pollution treatment technology. The effluent reduction achieved, and costs incurred, by these plants are then studied, and these results are used to arrive at the average costs and benefits experienced by these exemplary facilities. This method of determining BPT from the "average of the best existing performance" has been attacked by industry, which has argued that EPA should instead base its BPT regulations on the average performance of all plants in the industrial category. Not surprisingly, EPA's approach has been sustained. See Kennecott Copper Corp. v. EPA, 612 F. 2d 1232 (10th Cir. 1979); American Frozen Food Institute v. Train, 539 F. 2d 107 (D.C. Cir. 1976). When EPA can point to economically viable commercial scale plants achieving a certain level of pollution reduction—including no pollutant discharge at all—it is quite difficult for industry to mount a successful attack. See Kennecott Copper Corp., 612 F. 2d 1232 (challenge to "zero discharge" BPT standard for gold and silver cyanidation mills failed when five active mills were already in compliance).

5. If EPA determines that the level of effluent reduction achieved in a particular category is uniformly inadequate and that, therefore, no existing facilities are "exemplary," it may resort to other means of setting BPT. One method is to look to control technology used by plants in other industries which is transferable to the industry with which it is concerned. Of course, such reliance on "transfer technology" is permissible only if the technology can practicably be applied to facilities within that industry. *See Tanners' Council, Inc. v. Train,* 540 F.2d 1188, 1991 (4th Cir. 1976).

Another method, the one employed by EPA in *Pacific Fisheries,* is the utilization of "model plant analysis." Here it took a simple control device, the installation of screens (but one which was apparently not used in existing Alaskan salmon canning plants), and "modelled" its effectiveness, and the costs which it would impose, based on data obtained from actual processors. Obviously, the weakness of such a hypothetical construct is that its results may not be borne out in actual practice. In *Pacific Fisheries,* however, despite demonstrated weaknesses in EPA's data collection and analysis, the court was willing to accept its conclusions, "given the limitations the agency faced when it adopted industry standards for the first time." 615 F.2d at 809 (quotation not included in edited text).

6. Probably the most difficult issue in the *Pacific Fisheries* case was raised by petitioners' charge that, in requiring screening of wastes, which could then be barged and dumped in deep water, rather than allowing grinding, EPA had impermissibly considered the nature of the receiving waters. It was somewhat anomalous for an industry's challenge to be cast in this form; more typically an industry group has argued for consideration of differences in water quality benefits in setting effluent limitations.

In *Weyerhaeuser Co. v. Costle,* 590 F.2d 1011 (D.C. Cir. 1978), for example, paper mills which discharged their wastes into the Pacific Ocean argued that the capacity of ocean salts to buffer acid discharges and the infinitesimal effect of wastes with high BOD upon all the dissolved oxygen in the ocean should have been considered by EPA in setting BOD and pH levels for BPT for the pulp and paper industry. (Their most forceful argument was that EPA should have created a separate subcategory for ocean-discharging plants.) The D.C. Circuit stood solidly behind the position which EPA there took: that receiving water capacity to dilute or naturally treat effluents could not be considered in setting 301 limitations.

> . . .[B]ased on long experience, and aware of the limits of technological knowledge and administrative flexibility, Congress made the deliberate decision to rule out arguments based on receiving water capacity.
>
> Moreover, by eliminating the issue of the capacity of particular bodies of receiving water, Congress made nationwide uniformity in effluent regulation possible. . . . In addition, national uniformity made pollution clean-up possible without engaging in the divisive task of favoring some regions of the country over others.
>
> . . . In only one limited instance, thermal pollution, is receiving water capacity to be considered in relaxing standards, and the section allowing such consideration was drafted as a clear exception. Section 316 (a) of the Act. Otherwise, receiving water quality was to be considered only in setting "more stringent" standards than effluent limitations otherwise would prescribe. Section 301 (b) (1) (C) of the Act.

590 F.2d at 1042.

Given such precedent, EPA might have felt hard-pressed to take a position in *Pacific Fisheries* that it could consider the difference between a discharge into nearshore waters (via an outfall pipe) and a discharge into offshore waters (via a barge). Didn't the court, however, essentially validate such a position when it held that EPA could consider an improvement in nearshore water quality to be an "effluent reduction benefit," even though it was achieved simply by a relocation of the discharge?

7. What do you think the result would have been if, instead, EPA had required *grinding* and the processing plants had challenged EPA's promulgation of such a requirement without considering the advantages of screening and barging to a deepwater site?

What if EPA set a TSS percentage removal requirement for an industry based upon an assumption that shore-based settling ponds would be used and a discharger argued that he was entitled to meet such terms in his permit by screening out the suspended solids and dumping them in other waters?

8. Certainly the language of Section 304 (b)(1)(B), requiring BPT limitations to be based on considerations of costs "in relation to effluent reduction benefits," supports some general consideration of water quality effects. But what about in the setting of BAT standards? Notice that in *Pacific Fisheries* EPA had set screening requirements under BAT for remote Alaskan salmon canning plants by July, 1983.

9. Consider the different statutory verbage used in Section 301 (b)(2)(A) to describe the 1983 effluent limitations (usually referred to as BAT, not "BEA" as denominated by this court). Also compare the factors specified in Section 304 (b)(2)(B) to be taken into account in setting BAT with those contained in 304 (b)(1)(B) for BPT. What is the significance of the different language concerning cost considerations? Should any different meanings be given to the term "available" as used in the two standards?

10. As discussed in the *Pacific Fisheries* opinion, at least for purposes of assessing BAT, courts allow EPA to base a finding of "availability" on at least three different sorts of evidence: (1) performance by a single operating facility, (2) data from a pilot plant, or (3) results obtained from other types of facilities that use technology "transferable" to the category at issue.

11. This court's rejection of the argument that cost-benefit balancing was required of EPA in setting BAT standards is consistent with the vast majority of holdings on the issue. Its requirement only that EPA be shown to have "considered" the cost imposed by the technology in question and that the extent of its attention to those costs be "reasonable," given the evidence as to the other factors assessed, is quite typical of the approach in other Circuits.

Compare, however, the quotation on page 32 of the Fourth Circuit's view in *Appalachian Power Co. v. Train.* Is there a significant difference?

American Petroleum Institute
v.
Environmental Protection Agency

661 F.2d 340 (5th Cir. 1981)

Before Brown, Thornberry and Williams, Circuit Judges.

John R. Brown, Circuit Judge:

In this Battle of Acronyms, the American Petroleum Institute (API) takes the field against the Environmental Protection Agency (EPA) to protest its actions with regard to National Pollutant Discharge Elimination System (NPDES) permits for oil and gas installations employing best practicable control technology currently available (BPT). At one end of the battleground stands the arm of the federal government charged with the protection of our environment, surrounded by a phalanx of regulations. Arrayed against it stands API, a trade organization that represents the Nation's petroleum industry, joined with its allies, some fifteen oil companies. Both parties court our assistance, hoping with our intervention to rout the enemy and emerge victorious. Declining the invitation, we judge the clash to be a draw.

API requests us to reverse or remand certain EPA Guidelines that limit the discharge of wastes generated by oil and gas production facilities. In the period since it filed these petitions, API has negotiated with EPA on many of the issues involved. Having resolved all the major problems, the couple has started down the aisle but pauses for a last question or two. Their differences boil down to four narrow points: upset, bypass, recategorization of certain wells, and "stripper" wells. As to those final questions, we affirm EPA's actions with regard to upset and bypass, but remand to the Agency for further consideration of the remaining two issues.

*　　　*　　　*

Oil Wells That End Well

Americans have drilled for oil since 1859. Initially, oilmen conducted their operations exclusively on land. Offshore oil development began at the close of the century with the drilling of wells from wooden docks extending short distances from the coastline. As man's uses and need for oil and its by-products have increased, so have the industry's efforts to obtain it. Today, the oil industry operates in three different spheres. *Exploration* involves mapping, subsurface surveys, and exploratory drilling to ascertain the existence of oil and gas deposits. Through *drilling,* which necessitates the boring of wells deep into the earth's crust, oil producers exploit reservoirs of oil, gas and water lying hundreds or thousands of feet inside the earth. *Production* involves bringing these elements to the surface and then processing them into the finished products for which our society has found so many uses.

Today, in addition to a landscape of oil rigs throughout many parts of our Nation, offshore activities take place in the seas off both the Atlantic and Pacific coasts, in the Gulf of Mex-

ico, and in the frigid waters around Alaska. Offshore drilling produces approximately 1.3 million barrels of oil per day, about 16% of the Nation's total.

Just as one finds a variety of architectural styles in the average suburb, so one finds different types of oil rigs in the offshore neighborhood. Mobile rigs drill from floating barges or hulls. Especially in coastal areas, oil companies drill wells from barges, with production facilities established adjacent to the well on platforms or artificial islands. Yet others are floated into place and then raised on telescoping legs. Stationary rigs, by contrast, sit astride steel platforms resting on the seabed which do justice to Rube Goldberg.

The oil companies operate in excess of one thousand offshore facilities, the majority of which are in the Gulf of Mexico. They drill in water ranging from less than 100 feet to over 1000 feet deep. Some wells are within swimming distance while others are located as far as 100 miles from shore. Despite these differences, all oil and gas production facilities share one common trait: EPA regulation of waste discharges. And it is primarily upon that issue that API finds fault with EPA's final regulations.

All oil wells generate wastes. To produce the oil that our energy-hungry nation demands, one must take the bitter with the sweet, the waste water with the black gold. Oil wells produce three basic types of effluent. The first two, deck drainage and sanitary wastes from kitchens and toilets, are not in question here.

The third, and inevitable by-product of oil drilling, is "produced water". The underground reservoirs that contain oil also contain fossil seawater—water that has been in the ground during the time of oil formation. This unsavory mineral water rises to the surface in large quantities with the oil during production. The mixture of oil and water is then processed and separated. The oil goes into a pipeline for further processing, but the water remains, an unwanted commodity. Onshore facilities customarily reinject this produced water underground. Offshore facilities cannot do so. The problem then arises, what to do with the produced water? In most cases, it is treated on the rig. Existing technology furnishes several methods for treating produced water.[10] The goal of all methods is to cause oil that is dissolved in the water to rise to the surface, where it is skimmed off. Following treatment, the water is pumped over-board into the sea from which it came eons ago.

In certain areas of Louisiana and Texas, adjacent to bodies of saline water, wells located on terra firma have for many years, with the approval of the relevant state authorities, emptied this produced water into bays, inlets, estuaries, and marshes rather than reinject it.

*   *   *

EPA by the Horns

*   *   *

EPA's efforts to comply with the congressional mandate actually began in 1974 with a study of oil and gas platforms operating in the estuarine, coastal and outer Continental Shelf areas. The study led to a preliminary report entitled "Best Practicable Control Technology and Effluent Limitations for Offshore Oil and Gas Operations." The preliminary report identified the major sources of pollution from the platforms and analyzed the pollution control technology that offshore operators used. It took note of the distinction between treatment in offshore areas and on land-based platforms. In onshore areas, the discharge of produced water is forbidden because it is salt water while the receiving waters are fresh. Thus, operators must reinject the produced water underground. While the salt/fresh water dichotomy creates no problem for the offshore operators, the discharge of produced water there is equally impermissible. Yet reinjection of produced water on offshore platforms is virtually impossible because space restrictions limit the feasibility of installing the necessary equipment.

---

[10]"The simplest form involves holding the water in "ponds" for a sufficient time to allow the oil to float to the top. Other methods include: gas flotation, where bubbles of gas are injected and, as they rise, attach themselves to oil droplets; parallel plate coalescers, a pack of tilted parallel plates which guide rising oil droplets to the surface; and media and fibrous media coalescers. EPA Development Document at 74-80.

Relying upon the conclusions of the preliminary report, EPA in late 1974 published a "Draft Development Document for Effluent Limitations Guidelines and New Source Performance Standards for the Oil and Gas Extraction Point Source Category" (Draft Development Document). The Document selected the treatment systems that constituted BPT and then proposed appropriate effluent limitations. For onshore areas, BPT allowed for no discharge of produced water. Offshore, a platform could discharge produced water providing it installed treatment systems to remove oil and grease from the water before dumping it overboard.

EPA OKs API BPT

EPA circulated this Draft Development Document to interested parties and, after reviewing their comments, published interim final regulations for the offshore segment. Onshore regulations followed in October 1976. Once again, EPA solicited and received comments. Representatives of the oil and gas industry expressed their concerns and made suggestions for improvements. The industry also filed these petitions for review of EPA's actions in this and the Ninth Circuit.

In the interim, the record grew as the parties composed their differences by parcel post. In an encouraging spirit of cooperation, industry representatives wrote to EPA offering criticisms, suggestions and commentary, and EPA responded in kind. Out of this exchange of information, much good has come. EPA took some changes to heart and entered into Stipulations of Final Settlement in the Ninth Circuit regarding the offshore regulations and in this Circuit for the onshore regulations.

EPA promulgated the final Guidelines on April 13, 1979. *Effluent Guidelines and Standards, Oil and Gas Extraction Point Source Category,* 44 Fed. Reg. 22069. They apply to the offshore, onshore, coastal, and wildlife use subcategories in the oil and gas extraction industry[20]

---

[20]The agricultural and wildlife subcategories are not relevant to this action; they apply to those parts of the Nation where produced water from oil and gas drilling, lacking substantial salt content, may safely be used for the irrigation of crops or watering of livestock.

and incorporate the Stipulations of Partial Settlement with the changes agreed upon by the
parties. Combining both segments in one Guideline, this new set superseded the earlier, interim
final Guidelines.

The Guidelines combined the far offshore
and near offshore subcategories into a single, offshore subcategory. They revised the description
of the coastal subcategory, as a result of which
the Texas and Louisiana wells located on land but
which traditionally had discharged produced
water into coastal waters could no longer do so.
The Guidelines made some changes in the "stripper" subcategory definition, but once again
deferred setting effluent limitations due to a lack
of information. Perhaps most important, despite
strenuous objection by petitioners API and the
oil and gas producers, EPA declined to incorporate upset and bypass provisions in the Guidelines themselves. EPA explained that such
provisions "should be included in NPDES permits," adding that the upset and bypass issue
"should be dealt with in the context of permit
issuance."

***The parties' commendable willingness to
negotiate their differences should not, and does
not, go unnoticed by this Court. Nor do we hesitate to say that, as a result of these stipulations,
the issues before us today are four in number,
but narrow in scope.

Issues and Answers

Upset and Bypass. This issue lies at the heart
of the parties' continuing disagreement. "Upset"
refers to the problem where, for reasons beyond
the operator's control, waste treatment equipment fails to operate at the level required by EPA
regulations. Examples of upsets include equipment malfunctions, changes in the nature and
rate of flow of water through the treatment system, chemical changes or reactions, and routine
platform operations that affect the treatment
system. As both parties acknowledge, upsets are
an inherent part of current technology. API and
EPA diverge, however, on the question of the
appropriate treatment of upsets within the
Guidelines' format.

"Bypass" refers to the necessity, from time
to time, to route wastes around all or portions

of treatment systems so that operators can perform maintenance. Even in our era of technological derring-do, equipment from time to time
requires cleaning, overhauling or routine repair.
Given the cost of treatment equipment and space
limitations on platforms, operators cannot carry
spares; when such maintenance becomes necessary, some pollutants must inevitably be discharged.[21] On this issue, too, API and EPA have
failed to reach an agreement.

API insists that upset and bypass provisions
be included within the Guidelines themselves.
EPA, it points out, based BPT limitations upon
surveys that expressly excluded upset and bypass
discharge figures from the data base. As a result,
BPT figures are skewed—they reflect ideal operating conditions rather than reality. Moreover,
BPT is based upon standards that the model
wells could meet only 99% of the time. In other
words, not even the technologically superior
wells upon which EPA based BPT limitations can
meet the requirements of those limitations all
the time. If EPA does not include upset and
bypass provisions within the Guidelines, then,
API asserts, all wells will of necessity be in violation of EPA's standards—through no fault of
their own—at least 1% of the time.

Recategorization of Coastal Discharge. API
also attacks EPA's recategorization from the
coastal subcategory to the onshore subcategory
of those onshore wells that historically have discharged produced water into coastal waterways.
The coastal subcategory, as initially defined,
described a fixed geographical area in Louisiana
and Texas, where state law permitted the dis-

---

[21]Although the parties argue as though bypasses
were a daily event of critical proportions, the amount
and frequency of such discharges, in fact, are low. An
API survey concluded that bypasses occur during
eight-tenths of one percent (0.8%) of overall operating time and discharge on average 22.2 gallons of oil
and grease out of 73,836 gallons of produced water.
As petitioners noted, "the objective of offshore activity
is to produce and sell oil—not to dump it into the
ocean." Ninth Circuit brief at 17. The equipment which
separates oil and gas from produced water, functioning alone, removes all but trace elements of oil and
grease from the water before it enters the treatment
facilities. Even when the treatment facilities shut
down—which rarely happens, as the operators can
usually bypass portions of the equipment rather than
the entire system—the discharge is not great.

charge of produced water into brackish or saline surface waters.[25] EPA has now concluded that coastal means coastal and onshore means onshore, and the twain, presumably, shall not meet. Accordingly, it requires those wells previously denominated coastal but which sit on dry land to adhere to the "no discharge of produced water" standard applicable to onshore wells that have always reinjected the water underground. API asserts that this change will prove "devastating", forcing well operators to the Hobson's choice of incurring tremendous costs of reinjecting the produced water or ceasing operation altogether.

Stripper Wells. Stripper wells[26] are those wells that produce less than ten barrels per day of crude oil although operating at the maximum feasible rate of production. The EPA guidelines for strippers merely describe the subcategory, reserving the limitations for a later date.[27] They apply only to stripper oil wells and nowhere mention marginal wells producing natural gas. API asserts that the criteria upon which EPA relied to describe the stripper subcategory for oil wells apply equally to marginal gas wells, and that the Agency's exclusion of the gas wells from the subcategory was arbitrary and capricious.

Thicket in Overton Park

Before proceeding, we must specify the standard of review that we follow. That is no mean task. As the EPA's promulgation of regulations governing effluent limitations amounts to "rulemaking" for the purposes of the Administrative Procedure Act, we first turn for guidance to the appropriate section of that Act, 5 U.S.C § 706***

*   *   *

Less than fully illumined by the statutory language, we turn to the Supreme Court's authoritative pronouncement in *Citizens to Preserve Overton Park v. Volpe*, 401 U.S. 402 (1971). *Overton Park* requires a reviewing court "to engage in a substantial inquiry." An agency decision "is entitled to a presumption of regularity. But that presumption is not to shield [the agency's] action from a thorough, probing, in-depth review." 401 U.S. at 415. In assessing the decision, a court must consider "whether the decision was based on a consideration of the relevant factors and whether there has been a clear error of judgment." Although the review of the facts "is to be searching and careful, the ultimate standard of review is a narrow one. The court is not empowered to substitute its judgment for that of the agency." 401 U.S. at 416.

*   *   *

In summary, we must accord the agency considerable, but not too much deference; it is entitled to exercise its discretion, but only so far and no further; and its decision need not be ideal or even, perhaps, correct so long as not "arbitrary" or "capricious" and so long as the agency gave at least minimal consideration to the relevant facts as contained in the record.

Our first feat is to plunge into the record, which in this case hardly deserves that appellation. Bereft of testimony or factual findings,[28] it consists of 23,243 pages of charts, graphs, tables, computer printouts, and scientific studies helpful only in that many contradict one another. Moreover, since APA labored under a judicial order to produce regulations before it was prepared to do so, it in effect developed the record after it issued the regulations. We must, therefore, work backwards from EPA's final Guidelines to the mass of material in the record. Notwithstanding the possibility of judicial omniscience, we of necessity heed Judge Griffin Bell's admonition. "While the *Overton Park* mandate does require that we base our review on the entire record before the agency, we do not interpret it to require that we plunge into

---

[25]When EPA amended the definitions, it moved these wells to the onshore category but redefined coastal to include any body of water landward of the inner boundary of the territorial seas as well as wetlands adjacent to such water. 40 C.F.R. § 435.41(e),(f).

[26]Nowhere in the briefs do the petitioners or respondent explain the origins of this term; perhaps such things are better left unsaid.

[27]EPA explains that it "does not yet have sufficient technical data to promulgate effluent limitations for this subcategory." 44 Fed. Reg. at 22069.

[28]Since this case came to us on direct review of the Agency's actions, there were not proceedings below to generate a testimonial record or otherwise to tidy up the mass of data accumulated by the parties.

the record unaided by the parties. . . . Lest we make of this case a career, we must generally restrict our consideration to the parties' specific citations." *Texas v. EPA*, 499 F. 2d 289, 297 (5th Cir. 1974) (Bell, J.), *cert. denied sub nom. Exxon Corp. v. EPA*, 427 U.S. 905 (1976). And so in this case.

How do you spell relief?

That EPA's Final Effluent Regulations must adequately provide for upsets and bypasses, no one denies. The record proves that upsets and bypasses are as much a part of BPT as modern equipment and technological data. Despite best efforts at compliance, even a facility employing the best available equipment will occasionally exceed discharge limitations. Relying on the language of the Clean Water Act, 33 U.S.C. § 1314 (b)(1)(A), API argues persuasively that current BPT *includes* occasional upsets and bypasses. The statutory language specifically requires consideration of such factors as "the age of equipment and facilities involved", "engineering aspects" and "process changes". EPA cannot regulate by whim; it must take into account both the technological potential *and* existing limitations when it sets BPT standards. Without some absolution for the oil and gas producers from the harsh penalties that the Act imposes on "exceedances", EPA's final regulations would indeed suffer from serious infirmities.

We do not understand EPA to dispute this contention. Their answer, quite simply, is that the [permitting] Regulations, not the Guidelines, take care of this problem. The final Regulations contain upset and bypass provisions which largely satisfy API's concerns. Not yet content, API desires they be expressly included in the Guidelines. It contends that to leave the matter in the hands of the permit issuer amounts to a grant of discretion, with no guarantee that a facility will receive upset and bypass relief when it needs it. API refers us to two cases to buttress its argument. *Marathon Oil Company v. EPA*, 564 F.2d 1253 (9th Cir. 1977), a case remarkably similar to the present action, involved a challenge to EPA effluent limitations. The oil company insisted that the use of "confidence intervals" and BPT necessitated upset and

bypass provisions. EPA refused, promising to exercise prosecutorial discretion. API argued that discretion did not satisfy the statute. The Court agreed. To confirm that we understand its decision, we must look carefully at what the Court did and did not say.

*   *   *

***The Federal Water Pollution Control Act requires point sources of pollution to utilize the "best practicable control technology currently available" prior to 1983. The EPA cannot impose a higher standard without violating the Control Act. And yet the permits as currently written do exactly that. The permits on their face require petitioners to meet the standards 100 percent of the time. But platforms using BPCTCA can only be expected to achieve the effluent standards 97.5 percent of the time in the case of deck drainage and 99 percent of the time in the case of produced water. We, therefore, remand to the EPA with instructions to insert upset provisions into the permits.

It is not an adequate response that the EPA will informally take BPCTCA into account in deciding whether or not to prosecute "violators." First, there is no guarantee that the EPA will choose to exercise this discretion. And once a prosecution is brought, the courts have no authority to dismiss the complaint on the grounds that the permit holder could not have avoided the violation.

The Ninth Circuit's holding is of no avail to API. The Court required EPA to furnish a more reliable and certain means of upset and bypass relief than its promise to be nice. It did not obligate EPA to insert the provisions in the applicable Guidelines. *Marathon* supports the proposition that EPA must afford the oil companies *some* means of upset and bypass forgiveness, but it does not require the Agency to insert those provisions in the Guidelines under review.

FMC Corp. v. Train, 539 F.2d 973 (4th Cir. 1976), is to the same effect.***

API further points out that the logical repository of provisions tailored to the needs and characteristics of the oil industry is in the oil and gas Guidelines rather than in generic regulations applicable to an assortment of unrelated industries.***

EPA retorts that API has lost sight of the forest and the trees as well. It avers that upset and bypass provisions properly belong in the generic NPDES regulations and that such inclusion more than suffices to dispel the industry's fears.

The upset and bypass provisions are contained in 40 C.F.R. § 122.60, entitled "Additional Conditions Applicable to All Permits", which expressly states:

> The following conditions, in addition to those set forth in § 122.7, apply to *all* NPDES permits:***
>
> (g) bypass . . .
>
> (h) upset . . .

(emphasis added). These provisions *"are required* to be included in *all* proposed permits issued by EPA." All NPDES permits, whether issued by EPA or by a state, *must* incorporate these provisions. If, as EPA assures us, these provisions do apply to *all* gas and oil NPDES permits, whether issued by the EPA or the states, then our conclusion furnishes the assurance that in defense of enforcement proceedings, these provisions are as much included as though spelled out in the formal Guidelines.

*   *   *

While we confess to some puzzlement over EPA's obstinate refusal to include the upset and bypass provisions in the Guidelines in order to conserve a few paragraphs in the Federal Register, an alteration that counsel in oral argument conceded would make little or no difference to the Agency, we hesitate to declare the Agency's action arbitrary or capricious.

*   *   *

The Coastal Subcategory Reclassification

As we have noted, API challenges EPA's action in reclassifying certain wells from coastal to onshore as a violation of the Administrative Procedure Act and of the Clean Water Act, § 304(b)(1)(B). We will deal with those issues in order.

Uttering its battle cry "arbitrary and capricious", API attacks EPA's decision to reclassify as onshore those oil and gas wells that discharge into coastal (i. e., saline) waters. For support, API clings to the interim final Guidelines which had placed those wells in the coastal category. The primary reason for the coastal/onshore distinction was that onshore wells would discharge into fresh water if not required to reinject their produced water. The wells in question, however, discharge into salt water. Therefore, API triumphantly concludes, the reclassification, placing those wells in the category that EPA had created to prevent discharge into fresh water, is illogical, and thus arbitrary and capricious.

While on first blush API's complaint seems well-taken, a moment's reflection reveals the flaw. Granted that EPA originally placed the wells in question in the coastal category, the simple fact is, the Agency changed its mind. Nothing in the Administrative Procedure Act prohibits an agency from changing its mind, if that change aids it in its appointed task. Here, EPA concluded that water quality and the environment would benefit from a prohibition of produced water discharge. Such a decision falls squarely within EPA's discretion as well as the statutory purpose, and we are loathe to disturb it on appeal.

Having found that the EPA did not violate the Administrative Procedure Act, we now turn to API's challenge under the Clean Water Act. API contends that the Agency failed to take into account the cost of compliance when it made the recategorization. § 304(b)(1)(B) of the Act requires the Agency to consider "the total cost of application of technology in relation to the effluent reduction benefits to be achieved from such application." Courts have viewed this requirement in different ways. "[W]hile it is clear that the Administrator must consider cost," the Third Circuit reasoned, "some amount of economic disruption was contemplated as a necessary price to pay in the effort to clean up the Nation's waters, and the Administrator was given considerable discretion in weighing costs." *American Iron & Steel Institute v. EPA, supra* at 1052. *** The question, explains the Tenth Circuit, is whether "EPA made a serious, careful, and comprehensive study of the costs which compliance will impose on the industry." *American Petroleum Institute v. EPA, supra* at 1038.

The legislative history of the Clean Water Act casts but pale light on our problem. A singularly unhelpful source of information, legislative history always contains self-serving statements that support either side of an argument and most points between. So it is here. Senator Muskie, one of the bill's chief sponsors, at one point called it a "limited cost-benefit analysis"; yet comparison of BPT regulations with BAT regulations indicates that Congress did intend a more substantial review of costs in the former case.

To calculate the economic impact of the EPA's revised regulations, EPA hired Arthur D. Little, Inc., a management consulting firm (ADL). The ADL study concluded that "the reinjection requirement is not expected to close any on-land, non-stripper wells in Louisiana and Texas . . . ." It estimated the investment required to install reinjection equipment at $80 million and the amount of oil foregone as a result at 3 million barrels, approximately 1.8% of "the projected remaining lifetime production of the impacted *[sic]* wells." The average increase in production costs as a result of the reinjection requirement would total $.34 per barrel.

The ADL figures mask an important methodological flaw. At the time of the study, the wells in question were in the coastal subcategory. EPA based its conclusion that reinjection would have no dramatic effect on cost or energy production on the fact that most onshore wells already were reinjecting produced water. Yet EPA forgot to add the wells whose status it sought to revise to the onshore subcategory before making that determination. In other words, the ADL study ignored the very wells in question. Before estimating the number of affected wells and the cost figures, ADL should have grouped the coastal wells in question in the onshore category. The sizeable amount the wells would have to spend to comply, EPA, in effect, overlooked.

Believing that EPA had "grossly underestimated the economic impact" of the change, API employed H. J. Gruy & Associates, Inc., an engineering consultant firm (Gruy), to analyze the ADL study. Its results differed, to say the least. Gruy actually performed two surveys. In the first, it found 21 wells in Louisiana and 430 in Texas for which "neither (i) the injection facility capital costs and/or the additional injection operating cost nor (ii) the expense of hauling produced water for off-site disposal could be economically justified." Gruy estimated the volume of production foregone at 9,771,000 barrels. While ADL had ignored gas wells, the Gruy study determined that 39,152 million cubic feet of natural gas would be lost. Moreover, the new reinjection equipment would consume approximately six million barrels of fuel annually. Gruy set the total cost of compliance at $357.5 million.

At EPA's request, API commissioned Gruy to prepare an addendum to the study, excluding stripper wells from the data. Gruy concluded that, even with stripper wells excepted, 7.6 million barrels of oil and 32 billion cubic feet of gas would be lost, at a total cost of compliance of $307.3 million.

On a second front, API questions the Agency's finding that "deregulation of domestic oil and gas will *drastically* affect [the Gruy] predictions," that "it is unlikely that any significant loss of oil will actually occur." EPA offers no explanation and no support for these conclusions. It ignores the fact that only "high-cost natural gas", as the Natural Gas Policy Act, 15 U.S.C. § 3301 *et seq.* defines the term, is deregulated. The price of all other natural gas remains subject to regulation at least until January 1, 1985.

*   *   *

We have no way of knowing whose study is more correct, nor do we regard that as an appropriate matter for judicial inquiry. What is clear is that the parties' figures differ radically. Although EPA has made an effort to calculate the total cost, as required by the Act, the discrepancy between the ADL and Gruy studies, a discrepancy unexplained by EPA, leads us to conclude that EPA has not satisfactorily fulfilled its obligation of cost analysis. Its failure necessitates a remand for the purpose of comparing and explaining the differences.

Stripper Wells

API aims the last bow in its quiver at EPA's failure to include stripper gas wells within the regulations applicable to stripper oil wells. Although it seems ironic that API would contest EPA's *failure* to regulate, in fact that failure has serious repercussions. The deregulation of the price of natural gas, as EPA has pointed out, created substantial incentives for the producers to crank up their wells. Yet without EPA guidelines, operators of stripper gas wells presumably are subject to the full panoply of Clean Water Act restrictions and penalties—a harsh load indeed, one that might well deter gas production.

Relying on the Gruy studies, EPA explains that "marginal wells were not a large problem" and that "there was not sufficient data to justify including marginal gas wells in the stripper subcategory."*** API now regards the problem as worthy of our consideration. It cites Federal Energy Regulatory Commission data that lists 12,429 stripper gas wells with an estimated annual production of about 103 billion cubic feet. Such figures belie EPA's contention that there exists nothing to regulate. The number of wells to which API has drawn our attention indicates that EPA should examine once again the problem of stripper gas wells and consider adding them to the final Guidelines for stripper oil wells. While we of course express no opinion as to whether or not EPA must include stripper gas wells in the stripper subcategory regulations, we agree with API that EPA should at least consider the problem again in the light of this new information. Should the Agency conclude as before that stripper gas wells do not belong in the Guidelines, then API and EPA may climb into the ring yet again.

Accordingly, we remand this issue to the EPA for further proceedings.

Recapitulation and Grand Finale

Aware that the length of this opinion may have caused the drowsy reader to lose track of our conclusions, we repeat them here. The EPA upset and bypass provisions are affirmed. As to the recategorization of coastal wells and the failure to regulate stripper gas wells, we reverse and remand to EPA for further consideration.

NOTES

1. Only Judge John R. Brown can make a complex environmental case so readable. Fortunately, there are reasons beyond the entertainment value of the decision for its inclusion.

2. In addressing the challenge to EPA's reclassification of wells from the "coastal" subcategory to the "onshore" subcategory, notice that Judge Brown first found the subcategorization decision not to have been "arbitrary and capricious," but then went on to find it not to have been in compliance with the Clean Water Act. Obviously, this implies that categorization is not purely discretionary with EPA. But what are the standards which EPA must follow in making such classifications of industry, and where in the Act are they to be found? EPA's response, uniformly accepted by the courts, is that it is to look to the same factors specified in Section 304 (b) (1) (B) (for BPT) for consideration in setting the numerical effluent limitations for each category and subcategory: costs, age of equipment and facilities, process employed, non-water quality impacts, etc. Certainly this is quite logical. *See American Iron & Steel Inst. v. EPA,* 568 F.2d 284, 297-300 (3d Cir. 1977).

Judge Brown's holding that EPA failed to properly assess the cost of compliance when it made the coastal-to-onshore recategorization illustrates the application of the statutory cost-benefit factor to such decisions.

Only rarely does a court vacate an effluent limitation set by EPA because of flawed supporting economic analysis. Usually it takes a blatant methodological defect before a reviewing court will overturn agency conclusions based on technical studies. Can EPA's reliance on A.D. Little's study of the economic impact of requiring onshore wells to reinject their wastes be aptly so characterized?

3. Should EPA's failure to include gas wells within the subcategory applicable to "stripper" oil wells have also been treated as unsupported by the record?

Was it so unusual for API to insist that marginal gas wells be included in the stripper subcategory, given that EPA imposed no limitations on discharges from wells within that subcategory? See footnote 27 to the opinion. Should EPA be allowed to carve out a subcategory within an industry for which it imposes no effluent limitations because of insufficient existing data? Could it create a subcategory within which there were no effluent limitations because the cost of any pollution controls were too great for plants within the subcategory to bear?

In the *American Iron & Steel Inst.* case, the Third Circuit held that EPA could not exempt the small, economically-marginal plants in the Mahoning River Valley of Ohio from the BPT limitations otherwise applicable to the iron and steel industry. In holding that, under Section 301 (e), an *exemption* was not a permissible means of accommodating diversity, the court emphasized that it was not deciding whether the Act allowed EPA to "afford special treatment on the basis of location." 568 F.2d at 306-08. Do you think that EPA could create a "Mahoning Valley" subcategory within the iron and steel industry? Should it be able to base such a decision on the inability of Mahoning Valley plants to bear the same costs as others within the industry? Reconsider this question after you have read the Supreme Court's decision in *EPA v. National Crushed Stone Ass'n, infra* p.67.

4. Did Judge Brown rule correctly in sustaining EPA's refusal to include provisions for "upset" and "bypass" within the BPT limitations for offshore oil and gas production facilities? Wasn't the argument quite persuasive that such allowances were required if even a facility employing the best practicable control technology currently available would meet the limitations only 99 percent of the time?

As the court held, some means of upset and bypass relief was necessary. The only real issue was whether such relief had to be made part of the BPT limitations themselves? Why do you suppose that the oil producers were less than happy with the following requirement for special upset and bypass terms in discharge permits that is contained in EPA's general regulations governing permitting?

(g) Bypass—(1) Definitions. (i) "Bypass" means the intentional diversion of waste streams from any portion of a treatment facility.

(ii) "Severe property damage" means substantial physical damage to property, damage to the treatment facilities which causes them to become inoperable, or substantial and permanent loss of natural resources which can reasonably be expected to occur in the absence of a bypass. Severe property damage does not mean economic loss caused by delays in production.

*   *   *

(4) Prohibition of bypass. (i) Bypass is prohibited, and the Director may take enforcement action against a permittee for bypass, unless:

(A) Bypass was unavoidable to prevent loss of life, personal injury, or severe property damage;

(B) There were no feasible alternatives to the bypass, such as the use of auxiliary treatment facilities, retention of untreated wastes, or maintenance during normal periods of equipment downtime. This condition is not satisfied if the permittee could have installed adequate backup equipment.

(h) Upset.— (1) Definition. "Upset" means an exceptional incident in which there is unintentional and temporary noncompliance with technology-based permit effluent limitations because of factors beyond the reasonable control of the permittee. An upset does not include noncompliance to the extent caused by operational error, improperly designed treatment facilities, inadequate treatment facilities, lack of preventive maintenance, or careless or improper operation.

(2) Effect of an upset. An upset constitutes an affirmative defense to an action brought for noncompliance with such technology-based permit effluent limitations if the requirements of paragraph (g)(3) of this section are met. [Notice within 24 hours of an upset, etc.]***

(4) Burden of proof. In any enforcement proceeding the permittee seeking to establish the occurrence of an upset has the burden of proof.

40 C.F.R. § 122-60 (g), (h).

In *CPC International, Inc. v. Train,* 540 F.2d 1329, 1336-38 (8th Cir. 1976), on the other hand, the court seemed to hold that no relief from the new source limitations for the corn wet milling industry for such "excursions" was required, other than that available under EPA's "prosecutorial discretion," because the record indicated that excursions should not occur in properly-designed new plants.

Washington v. Environmental Protection Agency
573 F.2d 583 (9th Cir. 1978)

Before KOELSCH, DUNIWAY and GOODWIN, Circuit Judges.

KOELSCH, Circuit Judge:

These three matters arise under the Federal Water Pollution Control Act Amendments of 1972.

They commonly concern objections of the Regional Administrator of the United States Environmental Protection Agency (EPA) to a National Pollutant Discharge Elimination System (NPDES) permit issued by the State of Washington through its Department of Ecology (DOE) to Scott Paper Company (Scott) for the discharge of sulphite wastes from the latter's wood pulp and paper mill near Anacortes, Washington, into the waters of Puget Sound (The Anacortes permit).

Prior to issuing the permit, DOE transmitted a copy to the Administrator, who registered his formal objection to the permit as proposed by DOE. Notwithstanding the Administrator's purported veto under § 402(d) of the Act, DOE issued the permit to Scott; the Administrator then proceeded to impose sanctions on Scott.[6] This precipitated these several proceedings.

*   *   *

Although we hold that the district court has jurisdiction to entertain Scott's challenge to the Administrator's objection to the Anacortes permit, we need not, in light of the record before us, remand the case for additional proceedings. That course is made unnecessary by the presence of a dispositive legal issue which we resolve in the interests of judicial economy. ***

Scott contends that in the absence of effluent limitation guidelines promulgated by EPA in the form of regulations and applicable to point sources of the Anacortes type, the Administrator lacks authority under § 402(d) of

---

[6]The sanctions took the form of an enforcement order issued by the Administrator pursuant to § 309(a)(3) of the Act requiring Scott to submit a compliance schedule meeting EPA's best estimate of BPT at the Anacortes plant.

the Act to object to state-issued NPDES permits. We are compelled to agree, based upon an examination of the statutory scheme and a consideration of the procedural consequences of a contrary holding.

As indicated, although commanded by Congress to "publish within one year of enactment of this title [i.e., by October 18, 1973], regulations, providing guidelines for effluent limitations" (§304 (b)), "[t]he various deadlines imposed on the Administrator were too ambitious for him to meet." *E.I. du Pont de Nemours & Co. v. Train*, 430 U.S. 112, 122 (1977). Specifically, as of the date the Administrator purported to object to the Anacortes permit under § 402 (d), he had not yet published effluent limitation guidelines applicable to the pulp and paper industry in the form of regulations as called for by § 304 (b) of the Act.[8] In the absence of such guideline regulations the Administrator perforce relied on other grounds in purporting to find that the Anacortes permit did not reflect best practicable control technology (or "BPT") and was therefore "outside the guidelines and requirements of [the] Act" within the meaning of § 402 (d) (2) (B). The technical basis upon which the Administrator relied in objecting to the Anacortes permit consisted of certain "interim guidance documents" which, according to the Administrator, provided technical data approximating BPT values for facilities of the Anacortes type which would have been applicable had effluent limitation guidelines for pulp and paper point sources been timely issued in the form of regulations as contemplated by § 304 (b).

We conclude, however, that as a matter of statutory interpretation the Administrator's exercise of the veto power conferred by § 402 (d) is contingent upon the antecedent formulation of guideline regulations under § 304 (b) in conformity with the rule making provisions of the Administrative Procedure Act. 5 U.S.C. § 553.

As noted, the Administrator's exercise of the veto power under § 402 (d) is expressly conditioned upon and confined to a finding that the state-issued NPDES permit in question is "outside the guidelines and requirements of [the] Act." § 402 (d) (2) (B). It is conceded that the Administrator objected to the Anacortes permit as proposed by DOE on the specific ground that the permit failed to require the achievement of BPT at the Anacortes plant within the meaning of § 301 (b)(1)(A).

We first dispose of the Administrator's contention that the term "guidelines" as used in § 402 (d)(2)(B) refers only to the guidelines establishing uniform procedures for state-administered NPDES permit programs which the Administrator is required to issue by § 304 (h). The language of the statute itself plainly suggests that Congress intended the effluent limitation guidelines to take the form of regulations. Subsection 304 (b) provides that "[f]or the purpose of adopting . . . effluent limitations under this Act the Administrator shall . . . publish . . . *regulations*, providing guidelines for effluent limitations . . . ." (Emphasis added.) Moreover, in discharging his guideline development function under § 304 (b), Congress directed the Administrator to consult "with appropriate Federal and State agencies and *other interested persons. . . .*" *Id.* Recourse to the legislative history of the Act indicates that in enacting the clause emphasized above, Congress intended the Administrator to promulgate §304 (b) guidelines in accordance with the rule making provisions of the APA.***In light of the language of § 304 (b) and the relevant legislative history, we are clear that Congress intended the Administrator to formulate effluent limitation guidelines expressing BPT for classes and categories of point sources only after giving "interested persons an opportunity to participate in the [effluent limitation guideline] rule making through submission of written data, views, or arguments with or without opportunity for oral presentation." 5 U.S.C. § 553. That he did not do here. As we will endeavor to show later in this opinion, that failure is fatal to his position.

Had the Administrator issued § 304 (b) guidelines for pulp and paper point sources in conformity with the procedure prescribed by 5 U.S.C. § 553 prior to the time he purported to object to the Anacortes permit, Scott could not now complain that it had not had its day before

---

[8]Proposed effluent guidelines and standards (*see E.I. du Pont de Nemours & Co. v. Train, supra.* 430 U.S. at 124 and n.13) applicable to the pulp, paper and paperboard point source category were subsequently published in the Federal Register, 41 Fed. Reg. 7661 (February 19, 1976).

the Administrator in the formulation of generally applicable effluent limitation standards. The Administrator could have measured the effluent limitations imposed upon Scott's Anacortes plant as proposed by DOE against the general standards applicable to classes and categories of pulp and paper point sources developed in the course of the § 301 (b) rule making process and, on a finding that the BPT requirements proposed by DOE were "outside the guidelines and requirements of [the] Act," vetoed the permit under § 402 (d) (2) (B). Scott (or any other aggrieved party) could then have secured judicial review of the Administrator's objection under the provisions of § 10 of the APA and relevant case law.***

We necessarily adopt the subjunctive tense in outlining the procedural course that matters might have taken had the Administrator timely published effluent limitation guideline regulations under § 304 (b) prior to objecting to the Anacortes permit. As matters stand, however, the Administrator has purported to nullify a state-issued NPDES permit and to threaten the permit applicant with civil penalties on the basis of criteria that have not been subjected to the safeguards of public rule making poceedings. We are clear, upon a review of the statutory scheme, that Congress did not intend to deprive permit applicants of the significant procedural opportunity to contribute to the formulation of administrative guidelines through participation in public rule making proceedings by permitting the Administrator to object to a proposed state-issued NPDES permit in the absence of duly published guideline regulations and on the basis of what is in effect an *ad hoc* determination of what constitutes BPT for an individual point source.

We must determine, however, whether the achievement of effluent reductions through the application of BPT is a ". . . requirement of [the] Act" within the meaning of § 402 (d) in the absence of § 304 (b) guideline regulations. Reluctantly, we conclude that it is not. The express language of § 301 (b) of the Act does not in terms require the reduction of effluents through the application of BPT no matter how expressed or determined. Rather, it calls for the achievement of "effluent limitations . . . which shall require

the application of [BPT] *as defined by the Administrator pursuant to Section 304 (b) of the Act. . . .* " § 301 (b)(1)(A); emphasis added. Section 304 (b), in turn, provides that

"(b) for the purpose of adopting or revising effluent limitations under this Act the Administrator shall . . . publish within one year of enactment of this title, regulations, providing guidelines for effluent limitations . . . ."

Thus, "[t]o summarize, § 301(b) requires the achievement of effluent limitations requiring use of the 'best practicable' . . . technology. It refers to § 304 for a definition of these terms. Section 304 requires the publication of 'regulations, providing guidelines for effluent limitations.' " *E.I. du Pont de Nemours & Co. v. Train, supra,* 430 U.S. at 121.

The term "guidelines" appears again in the operative clause of § 402 (d) (2) (B)—circumscribing the Administrator's use of the veto power — without explication. We are clear that the term "guidelines" as used in defining the veto power of § 402 (d) includes the effluent limitation guidelines which the Administrator is required by § 304 (b) to develop and issue in the form of regulations. The "guidelines and requirements" clause of § 402 (d)(2)(B) thus points back to the guideline regulations of § 304 (b), the existence of which, as indicated, is an explicit precondition for the statutory *requirement* of § 301 (b) that effluent reductions be achieved through the application of BPT.

Our conclusion that the Administrator's power of objection under § 402 (d) is conditioned upon the existence of § 304 (b) guideline regulations prescribing BPT for classes and categories of point sources is not only commanded by a fair reading of the statutory language but is also operationally consistent with the permit issuing sequence contemplated by the Act. As we construe the mechanics of the statutory scheme, Congress envisioned that the Administrator would not have occasion to exercise the veto power conferred by § 402 (d) in the absence of effluent limitation guideline regulations promulgated under § 304 (b).

As contemplated by the Act, issuance of effluent limitation guideline regulations under

§ 304 (b) would precede the transfer of the NPDES permitting function from EPA to the several states. The § 304 (b) guidelines would thus perform their intended function of guiding state NPDES permit authorities in determining BPT for individual point sources by expressing effluent limitation values achievable through application of the technical requirements and methodology prescribed by § 304 (b). "The Act's text and its legislative history make clear that as a general matter the Section 304 (b) (1) guidelines and the section 301 (b) (1) limitations were to be developed prior to the issuance of permits." *Natural Resources Defense Council, Inc. v. Train,* 510 F.2d 692, 707 (D.C. Cir. 1975). The subsequent issuance of individual NPDES permits by state authorities would then serve "to transform generally applicable effluent limitations . . . into the obligations . . . of the individual discharger . . . ." *EPA v. State Water Resources Control Board,* 426 U.S. 200, 205 (1976).

We accordingly agree with the Court of Appeals for the Sixth Circuit that "[t]he presence within the Act of successive deadlines for promulgation of standards, issuance of permits, and conformance with effluent limitations bespeaks a rational implementation strategy anticipating a discrete sequence of events[.]" *Republic Steel Corp. v. Train,* 557 F.2d 91, 95 (6th Cir. 1977). Although Congress intended that dischargers of pollutants be required to achieve effluent reductions applying the best practicable control technology currently available (as indicated by § 301 (b) (1) (A)), it elected to require that such a result be achieved through a complex administrative mechanism which contemplates the formulation by the Administrator of regulations developed under 304 (b) (1) (A) expressing such effluent limitations as general standards applicable to classes and categories of point sources prior to the transfer of the permitting authority to the states and thus necessarily prior to the Administrator's exercise of the veto power conferred by 402 (d).

*   *   *

In the absence of a valid objection under § 402 (d), the compliance order issued by the Administrator requiring Scott to submit a plan designed to achieve effluent reductions based on the Administrator's unilateral determination of BPT at Anacortes is without statutory warrant.

*   *   *

NOTES

1. Was this decision correct? As a matter of law? As a matter of policy?

2. Since EPA does not in fact issue "guidelines" under Section 304 apart from "limitations" under Section 301, does this decision mean that, until EPA has issued a final nationwide 301 limitation for a point source category, it cannot veto any permit for a point source within such a category which is issued by a state with NPDES permitting authority? Can the state be as lenient as it wants? Can it disregard its own state limitations? Can it allow violation of water quality standards?

3. What if a state has not been delegated NPDES permitting authority and EPA retains responsibility for issuance of permits? *See* Section 402 (a) (1). This section has been utilized by EPA and interpreted by the courts to allow EPA to make individualized BPT determinations prior to promulgation of uniform national standards. Is such potential discrepancy between standards in states with NPDES authority and those without desirable?

4. Was the court correct that an EPA veto in the absence of 304 guidelines would deprive the applicant of any opportunity for input on the relevant technical and legal issues? See Section 402 (d) (4).

3 THE COMPLIANCE DEADLINE

Republic Steel Corp. v. Train
557 F.2d 91 (6th Cir. 1977)

Before: CELEBREZZE and LIVELY, Circuit Judges, and RUBIN, District Judge.

CELEBREZZE, Circuit Judge:

This case of first impression arises under the 1972 amendments to the Federal Water Pollution Control Act, P.L. 92-500. The question presented is whether failure of the Administrator of the United States Environmental Protection Agency (EPA) to define interim effluent limitations reflecting a given level of pollution control technology, as required by the Act, frees an authorized state agency to issue a discharge permit which sanctions noncompliance with the statutory deadline for achieving that degree of effluent abatement.

***Key to this litigation is the subsection 301(b)(1)(A)(i) requirement of conformity by July 1, 1977 with "effluent limitations for point sources *** which shall require the application of the best practicable control technology currently available [BPT]as defined by the Administrator pursuant to section [304(b)] of [the Act] *** ." Section 304(b)(1), in turn, obligates the Administrator to publish by October 18, 1973, regulations establishing effluent guidelines reflecting BPT for categories of dischargers including iron and steel manufacturing.

*   *   *

In July, 1972, Republic Steel Corporation (Republic) applied for a federal permit to continue discharging effluents from its Canton, Ohio steel mill into Nimishillen Creek. The Canton mill is an integrated steel manufacturing operation engaged primarily in the processing of alloy and stainless steel. In March, 1974, Ohio received approval from EPA under section 402(b) to begin

issuing NPDES permits, and Republic immediately commenced to negotiate with the Ohio Environmental Protection Agency (Ohio EPA).

In June, 1974, Ohio EPA issued a draft permit for the Canton mill which incorporated *state defined* effluent limitations under state estimates of BPT. *** At that time EPA had failed to promulgate any section 304(b) effluent limitation guidelines for iron and steel manufacturing. As of the present date no final regulations exist covering alloy and stainless steel operation.

Understandably, in the absence of controlling federal regulations, Republic sought to exploit available state administrative procedures to secure the most favorable permit terms and conditions. *** On August 1, 1975, eight months after the last date envisioned by Congress for routine issuance of NPDES permits, final agreement was reached and the implementation period commenced to run. However, Republic continued to assert that full compliance within 24 months was physically impossible. This prompted further adjudication hearings at which Republic presented unchallenged engineering and procurement data which convinced Ohio EPA to modify the permit to allow 42 months for development and installation of antipollution devices. Ohio EPA was aware that this change extended compliance beyond the July 1, 1977, date imposed by section 301(b)(1)(A)(i).***

In January, 1976, Ohio EPA transmitted the final NPDES permit to EPA's Region V office as required by section 402 (d)(1). Within 90 days the Director of the Enforcement Division of Region V objected to its issuance, exercising his authority under section 402(d)(2)(B). He did not expressly question the reasonableness of the state's BPT effluent standards or the 42 month implementation schedule. Rather, he concluded that the permit violated section 301 because full compliance would not be achieved until after July 1, 1977. Republic filed a timely petition for judicial review, pursuant to section 509(b)(1)(F), challenging this determination.

We do not question EPA's good faith in attempting to discharge the ambitious and often ambiguous duties imposed upon it by a "poorly drafted and astonishingly imprecise statute." *E.I. du Pont de Nemours & Company v. Train*, 541 F.2d 1018, 1026 (4th Cir. 1976). Many factors, some admittedly beyond EPA's control, have conspired to frustrate its legitimate compliance efforts. In particular, virtually every exercise of the agency's discretion has precipitated protracted litigation challenging the legitimacy of its authority or the substance of its "final" regulations.

*** The inability of EPA to meet its statutory obligations has distorted the regulatory scheme and imposed additional burdens which must be equitably distributed. This task is a difficult one because of the nature of the available options. Either the affected discharger must be compelled to risk potential enforcement proceedings in spite of an abbreviated compliance schedule, or society must tolerate slippage of an interim pollution abatement deadline.

Republic contends that the language of section 301(b)(1) (A)(i) expressly conditions adherence to the July 1, 1977, deadline upon definition *by the Administrator* of BPT effluent limitation and guidelines *pursuant to section 304(b) of the Act*. Therefore, the Administrator's failure to satisfy this condition precedent by publishing final regulations for alloy and stainless steel manufacturing excuses Republic's noncompliance with the July 1 date. We reluctantly agree. The import of the section is unequivocal: federal regulations must exist before dischargers can be compelled to honor dates for implementing them. The presence within the Act of successive deadlines for promulgation of standards, issuance of permits, and conformance with effluent limitations bespeaks a rational implementation strategy anticipating a discrete sequence of events:

*** Under the final version of the Act, effluent limitations and permits would be required by December 31, 1974, in order to provide polluters 30 months to comply with the July 1, 1977, deadline. *Natural Resources Defense Council, Inc. v. Train*, 510 F.2d 692, 707-708 (D.C. Cir. 1975) (footnotes omitted).

*   *   *

EPA correctly points out that the Act is devoid of language countenancing exceptions to the July 1, 1977, deadline under any condition. *** Nevertheless, nothing cited to us by EPA suggests that Congress anticipated the "Catch 22" situation inherent in the facts of this case. The language of the Act and its legislative history make clear that Congress expected EPA to define the rules before subjecting dischargers to potential civil and criminal penalties.

EPA attempts to bolster its position by emphasizing its authority under section 402 (a)(1), in advance of formally promulgated regulations, to issue and enforce NPDES permits imposing "such conditions as the Administrator determines are necessary to carry out the provisions of the Act. *Id.* From this, it would have us conclude that the duty of the discharger to achieve BPT by July 1, 1977 must be independent of EPA's obligation to promulgate the necessary guidelines by October 18, 1973. EPA cites *Bethlehem Steel Corporation v. Train*, 544 F.2d 657 (3rd Cir. 1976), and *United States v. Cutter Laboratories, Inc.*, 413 F. Supp. 1295 (E.D. Tenn. 1976), in support of this position.

A careful reading of both opinions confirms that EPA's reliance upon them is misplaced.*** In the *Bethlehem Steel* case EPA granted the permit on December 31, 1974, the last day mandated by Congress for routine issuance of NPDES permits. Therefore, Bethlehem Steel enjoyed a 30 month compliance schedule, the minimum period possible under the statutory scheme assuming no administrative slippage. In contrast, Republic's permit was issued by a state agency eight months after expiration of the permit granting deadline, affording Republic only 24 months for compliance.***

We read the *Bethlehem Steel* and *Cutter*

Laboratory decisions as standing for the limited proposition that a July 1, 1977, deadline, written into an NPDES permit *issued by EPA on or before December 31, 1974,* is enforceable despite the absence of BPT federal guidelines. Although we may share this view, we find no persuasive authority for extending its application to permits issued by EPA after 1974. In addition, we are convinced that the Act expressly forecloses this result when the permit issuing authority is a state agency. Section 402 (1)(A) empowers states to issue NPDES permits which "apply, and

insure compliance with, any applicable requirements of section 301, *** of [the Act]."*Id.* Our holding that section 301(b)(1)(A)(i) is made unenforceable by the Administrator's failure to promulgate necessary regulations is tantamount to a finding that the July 1, 1977, deadline is no longer an "applicable requirement" of the Act. Therefore, in this case, Ohio EPA was not bound to apply it and EPA was without authority to object to the proposed permit on this ground.

*   *   *

State Water Control Board v. Train
559 F.2d 921 (4th Cir. 1977)

Before RUSSELL, Circuit Judge, FIELD, Senior Circuit Judge, and WIDENER, Circuit Judge.

RUSSELL, Circuit Judge:

The State Water Control Board of the Commonwealth of Virginia brought this action against the Administrator of the United States Environmental Protection Agency (EPA) on behalf of the Commonwealth of Virginia and certain of her political subdivisions, seeking a declaration that the effluent limitations of Section 301 (b)(1) of the Federal Water Pollution Control Act Amendments of 1972 (FWPCA) do not apply to publicly owned sewage treatment plants which have not received federal grants under Title II of the FWPCA.[3] The district court denied the relief sought and the Board appeals. For the reasons stated below, we affirm.

---

[3]The complaint requested the district court to declare *inter alia,* that
for each publicly-owned sewage treatment plant that cannot be put into compliance with the July 1, 1977, deadline under § 301(b)(1) of the Act, such plant shall not be required to comply with applicable limitations under [that section] until such time as federal grant funds are available in an amount sufficient to underwrite 75 percent of the eligible costs of construction thereof and a reasonable time has been allowed to complete the necessary construction.

I.

The FWPCA seeks to eliminate the discharge of pollutants into the navigable waters by 1985 in order to "restore and maintain the chemical, physical, and biological integrity of the Nation's waters." As an initial step toward that goal, Section 301 (b)(1)(B) requires publicly owned treatment works to achieve, by July 1, 1977, the degree of effluent reduction attainable through application of secondary treatment.[8] In addition, such plants must satisfy any limitations which are necessary to implement any applicable water quality standard.

These criteria are applied to individual treatment plants primarily through the national permit system established by Section 402. Under that system, no person may discharge pollutants without a permit issued by EPA or an EPA-approved state permit program. Section 402 requires that such permits be conditioned on compliance with the requirements of, *inter alia,* Section 301. Discharge of pollutants without a permit or in violation of a permit condition may result in civil and criminal penalties as well as injunctive sanctions.

---

[8]The degree of effluent reduction attainable through the application of secondary treatment is determined by reference to information published by EPA pursuant to FWPCA § 304(d)(1). 33 U.S.C. § 1314(3)(1).

To assist in financing the facilities necessary to accomplish the effluent reductions mandated by Section 301, Title II of the Act establishes a program of federal grants to states, municipalities and intergovernmental agencies for the construction of publicly owned treatment plants. Section 202 (a) provides that the amount of any grant made under this program shall be 75% of approved construction costs; and Section 207 authorizes the appropriation of $18 billion for fiscal years 1973 through 1975 for such grants.

Unfortunately, however, the grant program's effectiveness in facilitating compliance with the 1977 effluent limitations has been limited. Grants have not been available for many construction projects because the money authorized by Section 207 is insufficient to finance 75% of the cost of every needed sewage treatment plant in the country. Moreover, disbursement of the authorized funds has been substantially delayed by Presidential impoundment[18] and by the time consumed by administrative processing of grant applications.[19] These problems, together with the fiscal difficulties now confronting most State and local governments, have made it economically impossible for many localities to accomplish the required effluent reductions by the 1977 deadline.

Motivated by this circumstance, appellant contends that, under a proper construction of the Act, receipt of Title II grant money is a condition precedent to the duty to comply with the 1977 effluent standards. We cannot agree.

II.

Our analysis begins with the undisputed fact that appellant's position is not supported by the text of the statute. Section 301(b)(1)'s effluent limitations are, on their face, unconditional; and no other provision indicates any link between their enforceability and the timely receipt of federal assistance.

Appellant, relying on the Act's legislative history, asks us to hold that such a link is, nevertheless, implicit in the statutory scheme. However, as the following discussion demonstrates, that history actually tends to reinforce the "plain meaning" of the text.

As the Third Circuit has noted, "all discussion of this date [the July 1, 1977 deadline] in the legislative history indicates that Congress viewed it as an inflexible target." *Bethlehem Steel Corp. v. Train* (3rd Cir. 1976) 544 F.2d 657, 661.***

*   *   *

More importantly, Congress actually declined to write the statute as appellant would now have us construe it. During hearings on the House bill, William Ruckelshaus, then head of EPA, and appellee Train, then Chairman of the Council on Environmental Quality, urged that the Act permit extension of the 1977 deadline in cases where, despite good faith efforts, compliance is impossible. Significantly, Mr. Ruckelshaus also recommended that "the secondary treatment requirement [of Section 301(b)(1)(B)] should only apply to projects for which new Federal grants are provided." The bill which the House subsequently passed empowered EPA to extend the 1977 deadline for up to two years in cases where compliance is physically or legally impossible; but, despite the recommendation of Mr. Ruckelshaus, it did not limit the applicability of Section 301 (b) (1) (B) to those facilities receiving federal assistance. Moreover, even the provision authorizing case-by-case extension of the deadline was later deleted without comment by the Conference Committee. This clearly provides strong support for the conclusion that Congress meant for the July 1, 1977 deadline to be rigid and that it did not intend that sewage treatment plants not receiving timely federal grants should be exempt from that deadline.***

Appellant argues, however, that Congress would have so intended if it had foreseen the

---

[18]After the Act was passed over his veto, President Nixon, by letter dated November 22, 1972, directed the Administrator to allot among the States "[n]o more than $2 billion of the [$5 billion] authorized for the fiscal year 1973, and no more than $3 billion of the [$6 billion] authorized for the fiscal year 1974 . . . ." For fiscal year 1975, the Administrator allotted only $4 billion of the $7 billion authorized for that year. However, *Train v. City of New York*, 420 U.S. 35 (1975), held that the Administrator lacks authority to allot less than the amounts specified by Section 207 and the impounded funds were finally allotted in fiscal year 1976.

[19]The district court found that approval of a grant request requires approximately six months to one year.

funding delays and shortfalls which have plagued the grant program. Like the court below, we are not convinced that Congress was, in fact, unaware that some necessary projects might not receive timely grants. Nor, accepting that premise, is there any reason to believe that Congress would have expressly provided the blanket exemption now advocated by appellant if it had been accurately forewarned about the deficiencies which have surfaced in the grant program — it seems more likely that Congress' response, if any, to such forewarning would have been to retain the provision of the House bill empowering EPA to extend the deadline on a case-by-case basis where compliance is impossible. But in any event, we do not think that, on the record before us, it is within our judicial function to speculate as to how Congress might have written the statute had it been more prescient. Where, as here, Congress has chosen not to incorporate a suggested provision into legislation, we must abide by that decision even though it appears in retrospect to have been based on a false premise. *Cf. Youngstown Co. v. Sawyer, supra.* In such cases, reconsideration of the matter is a task for Congress, not the courts.

III.

Our holding in this case does not mean that, absent Congressional action, severe sanctions will inevitably be imposed on municipalities who, despite good faith efforts, are economically or physically unable to comply with the 1977 deadline. We fully expect that, in the exercise of its prosecutorial discretion, EPA will decline to bring enforcement proceedings against such municipalities. Furthermore, in cases where enforcement proceedings are brought, whether by EPA or by private citizens, the courts retain equitable discretion to determine whether and to what extent fines and injunctive sanctions should be imposed for violations brought about by good faith inability to comply with the deadline. In exercising such discretion, EPA and the district courts should, of course, consider the extent to which a community's inability to comply results from municipal profligacy.

CONCLUSION

For the reasons stated, we conclude the appellant is not entitled to the relief requested. Accordingly, the judgment of the district court is

AFFIRMED.

NOTES

1. Only the Sixth Circuit provided any relief whatsoever from the July 1, 1977, deadline for either secondary treatment by treatment works or BPT for industrial dischargers.

2. Obviously, some severe problems arose for industries and treatment works which were unable to meet the deadline. The Act authorized the Administrator to bring civil actions for injunctive relief, seek civil penalties up to $10,000 per day of violation or criminal fines up to $25,000 per day of violation ($50,000 for second offenders), and proceed in court against treatment works to prohibit new ties-ins.

States had similar enforcement authority to penalize noncompliance with the 1977 deadline, and some were not afraid to use it. For example, shortly after the deadline passed, Michigan pursued seven firms to settlements totaling over $3.6 million. Ford Motor Company alone was penalized $1.6 million for failing to meet the deadline at three plants and agreed to spend $36 million on new treatment projects in the state. See ENV'T. REP. CURRENT DEV. 549 (1977).

3. Section 309 of the Act, containing the primary enforcement provisions, also gave the Administrator the authority to issue a compliance order in lieu of bringing a civil action; but, under the Act prior to the 1977 Amendments, the time specified for compliance could not exceed thirty days. (With the 1977 Amendments the Administrator could specify a time for compliance which he determined to be "reasonable.")

Could a court grant any relief from such a compliance order?

Could the Administrator refuse to initiate either administrative or judicial sanctions? Consider the "citizen suit" provisions in Section 505.

If EPA or a citizen asked a court to enjoin a violation of BPT past the deadline, would the court have discretion to refuse injunctive relief or structure it to allow more time for compliance? Reconsider *TVA v. Hill*?

4 THE 1977 AMENDMENTS AND CONGRESSIONAL RELIEF

In the 1977 amendments, Congress provided some measure of relief.

EPA was given the authority to grant case-by-case extensions of the July 1, 1977, BPT requirements for industrial dischargers who had made good faith attempts to comply. However, such extensions could not extend past April 1, 1979.

The agency was allowed to extend the 1977 deadline for installation of secondary sewage treatment for up to six years where the failure to comply was due to lack of federal construction grant funds or to delays in completion of treatment facility construction. (When even such extended 1983 deadlines for secondary treatment loomed too close, and adequate federal funds still were not available, Congress in 1981 provided for extensions up to July, 1988, and at the same time relaxed the definition of secondary treatment. In 1981 Congress also repealed entirely the second stage standard of "best practicable waste treatment technology" and its attainment date.)

Also, the amendments made several changes in the original requirement for attainment of BAT by industries by 1983. The standard was changed and the deadline was moved up one year, to July 1, 1984, for discharges of "conventional pollutants," such as biological oxygen demand and suspended solids. Congress also provided an additional year for installation of BAT for controlling discharges of 65 "toxic" pollutants. For all other pollutants, those not in the conventional or toxic category, a deadline of no later than July 1, 1987, was set; but EPA was empowered to modify the BAT standards for these "nonconventional" pollutants on a case-by-case basis.

Republic Steel Corp. v. Costle

581 F.2d 1228 (6th Cir. 1978)

Before: CELEBREZZE, LIVELY and KEITH, Circuit Judges.

CELEBREZZE, Circuit Judge:

This case is before the Court on remand from the Supreme Court for further consideration in light of the Clean Water Act of 1977, P.L. 95-217. In our previous decision we held that the Administrator of the United States Environmental Protection Agency (EPA) had improperly vetoed issuance of a water pollution permit to petitioner Republic Steel Corporation (Republic) for its Canton, Ohio, mill. *Republic Steel Corp. v. Train,* 557 F.2d 91 (6th Cir. 1977) (hereinafter referred to as *Republic Steel I*).

       *   *   *[4]

[4]As of oral argument in this case (June 1978) EPA had still not promulgated final BPT guidelines for iron and steel manufacturing. In the absence of general standards, BPT has been determined on a case-by-case basis, either by the Administrator or by the responsible state agency.

We reluctantly concluded that EPA's failure to timely define BPT precluded the Administrator from imposing a July 1, 1977, compliance deadline, since Congress had apparently established promulgation of regulations under § 304(b) as a necessary precondition for imposition of the deadline in § 301(b)(1)(A)(i). Our decision was designed "to relieve the discharger of the unfair consequences" of being forced to comply with the deadline in the absence of applicable standards for guidance.

This Court stayed its mandate in *Republic Steel I* pending the EPA's petition for a writ of certiorari from the Supreme Court. Shortly after EPA filed its petition for certiorari, Congress enacted the Clean Water Act of 1977, which substantially revised the FWPCA. In the wake of that enactment, the Supreme Court granted EPA's petition, vacated our judgment in *Republic Steel I,* and remanded the case to this Court for further consideration in light of the new law, *Costle v. Republic Steel Corp.*, 434 U.S. 1030, 46 U.S.L.W. 3452 (1978).

We have reviewed the 1977 Act and conclude that its provisions have effectively overruled our previous decision. Although neither § 301(b)(1)(A)(i), requiring industrial dischargers to achieve BPT no later than July 1, 1977, nor § 304(b) requiring EPA to define BPT by October 18, 1973, were amended by the 1977 Act. Congress did add a new § 309(a)(5)(B) providing as follows:

> (B) The Administrator may, if he determines (i) that any person who is a violator of, or any person who is otherwise not in compliance with, the time requirements under this Act or in any permit issued under this Act, has acted in good faith and has made a commitment (in the form of contracts or other securities) of necessary resources to achieve compliance by the earliest possible date after July 1, 1977, but not later than April 1, 1979; (ii) that any extension under this provision will not result in the imposition of any additional controls on any other point or nonpoint source; (iii) that an application for a permit under section 402 of this Act was filed for such person prior to December 31, 1974; and (iv) that the facilities necessary for compliance with such requirements are under construction, grant an extension of the date referred to in section 301(b)(1)(A) to a date which will achieve compliance at the earliest time possible but not later than April 1, 1979.

The legislative history of this provision makes it abundantly clear that Congress intended the procedure outlined therein to be the exclusive avenue of relief from the dictates of a mandatory and unconditional July 1, 1977, deadline. The Senate Report expressly rejected the rationale of *Republic Steel I*.

> Under existing law there are no circumstances that justify a time for compliance extending beyond July 1, 1977. The Administrator can only issue an

enforcement order requiring compliance within 30 days or initiate civil or criminal action. Thus, the decision of the U.S. Court of Appeals for the Sixth Circuit in *Republic Steel Corporation v. Train* et al and *Williams*, ___ F.2d___ (6th Cir. 1977) was an incorrect interpretation of existing law. This amendment responds to the legitimate concern of dischargers who, despite good faith efforts, will not comply with the 1977 requirements. To accommodate this objective, the committee amended section 309(a) of the act to authorize the Administrator in his discretion, to pursue one of two new options with regard to a discharger out of compliance.

*   *   *

The import of the statute is now plain: the July 1, 1977 deadline cannot be waived by the courts. To the extent that noncompliance occurs despite good faith efforts as defined in § 309(a)(5)(B), relief is available only via discretionary extension of the deadline by the Administrator.

*   *   *

***Moreover, the 1977 Act effectively responds to the concern we expressed in *Republic Steel I* that a discharger might suffer "unfair consequences" from EPA's failure to timely promulgate relevant BPT regulations. Under prior law, the Administrator had no clear statutory authority to extend the July 1, 1977, deadline and a discharger could be subjected to liability without any consideration for the reasons for his noncompliance.[8] The new § 309(a)(5)(B) clearly permits the Administrator to extend the deadline where noncompliance was caused solely by the lack of BPT guidelines.

We conclude, then, that the Administrator can properly object under § 402(d)(2)(B) of the Act to a proposed permit for a point source governed by § 301(b)(1)(A)(i) if that permit does

---

[8]Prior to the 1977 Act, EPA did provide relief from the 1977 deadline on an informal basis. Under the "Enforcement Compliance Schedule Letter" (ECSL) program, the Administrator would agree to refrain from enforcement of the statutory deadline against certain dischargers who made good faith attempts at compliance.

not require attainment of BPT by July 1,1977, unless the Adminstrator has determined that a time extension is warranted pursuant to § 309(a)(5)(B).

This does not, however, end our inquiry. We must decide whether the 1977 Act may be applied in the context of this case, which was pending before the Supreme Court at the time the new law took effect.

The general rule is that "a court is to apply the law in effect at the time of its decision, unless doing so would result in manifest injustice or there is statutory direction of legislative history to the contrary." This principle applies with full force to an appellate court in reconsidering a decision that has been vacated and remanded by the Supreme Court in light of an intervening change in the law.

The Clean Water Act of 1977 contains no "statutory direction or legislative history" militating against application of § 309(a)(5)(B) to pending cases.***

Nor do we think that application of current law would result in manifest injustice. If Republic has made good faith efforts at compliance with the law that have been delayed only by EPA's failure to timely promulgate BPT standards, then the company will be eligible for an extension under § 309(a)(5)(B). There is nothing fundamentally unfair in predicating relief from the deadline on a showing to the responsible agency that the polluter has made a "reasonable attempt to comply with the mandates of the law."***[13]

The situation might be different if Republic could claim that its noncompliance was induced by administrative or judicial construction of § 301(b)(1)(A)(i) to the effect that the July 1, 1977, deadline was waived by EPA's failure to promulgate BPT guidelines. But in the years following enactment of FWPCA, EPA consistently took the official position that the statutory compliance date was absolute and that it was not waived by the absence of BPT guidelines. The first draft permit for the Canton mill issued by OEPA in June 1974 required compliance by September 1976. EPA's position as to the Act's time requirement was not challenged by a court of appeals until our decision in *Republic Steel I* on June 23, 1977—only days before the July 1, 1977, deadline. Republic can hardly claim that its noncompliance was induced by that decision, since by even the most conservative estimates the necessary equipment would take many months to construct. Nor can the company maintain that it ever had a vested right in the result ordered in *Republic Steel I,* since our mandate there never took effect, and since the Supreme Court later vacated the judgment altogether.

In any event, Republic does not seriously claim that its noncompliance with the July 1, 1977, deadline is the result of an honest belief that the deadline was invalid. Rather the company maintains that it was unable to meet the deadline, despite good faith efforts, because of the absence of BPT guidelines from EPA. If this is true, then the new § 309(a)(5)(B) procedure can provide any justified relief.[17]

The petition for review is dismissed.

---

[13]According to the Senate Report, ninety percent of the nation's major industrial dischargers were expected to meet the 1977 deadline.

[17]We do not mean to suggest that Republic may in any sense be *entitled* to an extension as a matter of law. The decision on whether or not to grant an extension is committed to the Administrator's discretion, based on his assessment of the factors listed in § 309(a)(5)(B).***

NOTES

1. What if now, after April 1, 1979, an industrial point source *still* is not in compliance with BPT?
Could EPA create a compliance schedule giving it another year or two?
Could a court cast injunctive relief in such a form?

2. What if EPA refused to grant an extension under Section 309 (a)(5)(B)? Could a court compel such an extension? If so, under what circumstances?

3. What if the state disagreed with such an extension? What, if anything, could it do to block it?

American Paper Institute
v.
Environmental Protection Agency
660 F.2d 954 (4th Cir. 1981)

Before WIDENER, PHILLIPS and ERVIN, Circuit Judges.

ERVIN, Circuit Judge:

The petitioners in these consolidated cases seek judicial review of the actions of the Administrator of the Environmental Protection Agency (EPA) in issuing regulations pursuant to section 304(b)(4)(B) of the Clean Water Act ("the Act") promulgating effluent water limitations controlling conventional pollutants[2] from private industrial sources in accordance with section 301(b)(2)(E) of the Act.[3]***

Although the petitioners challenge the best conventional technology (BCT) regulations issued pursuant to section 304(b)(4)(B), their primary objection is to the methodology used by the Administrator in promulgating the regulations. In particular, the petitioners contend that Congress in section 304(b)(4)(B) mandated that EPA incorporate two main factors in its methodology for determining BCT: an industry cost-effectiveness test and a test that compares the cost for private industry to reduce its effluent levels with that incurred by publicly owned treatment works (POTWs) for a similar purpose. The petitioners assert that EPA considered only the latter factor and that EPA's benchmark for this latter factor was arbitrary and capricious.***

We hold that all the regulations promulgated pursuant to section 301(b)(2)(E) must be invalidated on the ground that EPA did not consider all the factors mandated by section 304(b)(4)(B).***

I. BACKGROUND

In 1972, Congress amended the Federal Water Pollution Control Act to establish a timetable for achieving certain water pollution control objectives. Congress declared as its policy that the discharge of pollutants in our nation's navigable waters "be eliminated by 1985." 33 U.S.C. § 1251(a)(1). With respect to private

---

[2]Conventional pollutants are defined in the Act to include but not to be limited to, those "classified as biological oxygen demanding, suspended solids, fecal coliform, and pH." 33 U.S.C. § 1314(a)(4). ***

[3]33 U.S.C. § 1311(b)(2)(E). This provision of the Act provides in relevant part:
in order to carry out the objectives of this chapter there shall be achieved . . . not later than July 1, 1984, effluent limitations for categories and classes of point sources, other than publicly owned treatment works, which in the case of pollutants identified pursuant to section 1314(a)(4) of this title shall require application of the best conventional pollutant control technology as determined in accordance with regulations issued by the Administrator pursuant to section 1314(b)(4) of this title.

industrial sources, such as these petitioners, this achievement was to be accomplished in two stages: an interim level of control effective in 1977, and a final level effective in 1983. The 1977 standard was designated "best practicable technology" (BPT) and the more stringent 1983 standard was "best available technology" (BAT).

Five years later Congress undertook to re-examine these standards. Ultimately, the Federal Water Pollution Control Act was amended again, and the Act as amended became known as the Clean Water Act. Under the Clean Water Act, the 1977 requirements (BPT) were left intact, but changes were made in the 1983 requirements (BAT). As part of these changes, Congress established various standards and schedules for three classifications of pollutants: (1) conventional pollutants; (2) toxic substances; and (3) non-conventional non-toxic pollutants not otherwise classified. 33 U.S.C. § 1311. The strict BAT standards were retained for toxic pollutants known to be dangerous and for non-conventional non-toxic pollutants the effects of which are uncertain, but the effective date for both categories was delayed.

While the parties disagree over precisely what Congress intended to do when it enacted the 1977 amendments to the Act and draw markedly different conclusions from the language of the amendments and the legislative history, it is clear that Congress felt that the results produced by the BPT had provided a high degree of water quality improvement, and that in some instances, BAT for conventional pollutants about which much was known might require treatment not deemed necessary to meet the 1983 water quality goals of the Act. Concern was expressed about requiring "treatment for treatment's sake," and there was much discussion about comparing the cost of treatment with the benefits obtained from the reductions achieved.

Out of this came the development of a new standard, best conventional pollutant control technology (BCT). The new requirement was described by one Senate-House conferee as "the equivalent of best practical technology or something a little bit better, even as far as best available technology in some circumstances."

In directing EPA to promulgate regulations concerning BCT standards, Congress passed section 304(b)(4)(B) of the Act, which provides in part:

> Factors relating to the assessment of best conventional pollutant control technology (including measures and practices) shall include consideration of the reasonableness of the relationship between the costs of attaining a reduction in effluents and the effluent reduction benefits derived, and the comparison of the cost and level of reduction of such pollutant from the discharge from publicly owned treatment works to the cost and level of reduction of such pollutants from a class or category of industrial sources, and shall take into account the age of equipment and facilities involved, the process employed, the engineering aspects of the application of various types of control techniques, process changes, non-water quality environment impact (including energy requirements), and such other factors as the Administrator deems appropriate. 33 U.S.C. § 1314(b)(4)(B).

In addition, in section 73 of the 1977 amendments, Congress directed EPA to "review every effluent guideline promulgated prior to the enactment of this Act which is final or interim final."[12] This required review of all outstanding BAT limitations for conventional pollutants for all secondary industrial sources within 90 days after the effective date of the amendments.

Pursuant to this Congressional Directive, EPA proceeded to carry out its duties. On

---

[12] 91 Stat. 1609.

At the time this action was filed, EPA had evaluated all the BAT regulations for the thirteen secondary industry categories having final or interim final BAT effluent guidelines.***

Secondary industries were defined by the Administrator to include those industries not covered in the settlement agreement reached in *National Resources Defense Council, Inc. v. Train*, 8 E.R.C. 2120 (D.D.C. 1976). EPA made it clear in its final rules in which it used the contested methodology that it intended to use the same methodology when it reviewed conventional pollutant requirements for the primary industries, i.e., those included in the above mentioned 1976 Consent Agreement. 44 Fed. Reg. 50,732 (1979).

*　　　*　　　*

August 23, 1978, proposed rules were published relating to 13 secondary industry categories. These rules also contained a methodology for determining the reasonableness of any proposed effluent limitation under the BCT criteria. Critical comments were received, and on April 2, 1979, a notice was published indicating that the use of two additional documents was being considered for the data contained therein and that such data might be used in the future for computing the costs and levels of pollutants from POTW's. EPA published its final BCT determinations on August 29, 1979, and the petitioners filed these petitions on May 9, 1980, thus presenting these final regulations for our review.

II. ANALYSIS

A. *COST EFFECTIVENESS TEST*

EPA's position is that Congress did not require it to utilize an industry cost-effectiveness test, but instead only mandated a POTW cost comparison standard in arriving at BCT regulations for industry. In interpreting section 304(b)(4)(B), EPA concludes that the proposed effluent guidelines are not required to pass two reasonableness tests. In support of its position, EPA reads the seemingly dual requirements of section 304(b)(4)(B) as one, commanding only a consideration of reasonableness. It contends that the second clause in the relevant portion of section 304(b)(4)(B) sets forth the benchmark of reasonableness—a comparison of the proposed BCT cost and level of effluent reduction for industry to the cost and level of reduction from the discharge of POTWs.

We are unable to accept this suggested statutory interpretation. When faced with such a question, our starting point for discerning congressional intent is the words of the statute itself. The law which empowers EPA to act directs that EPA's effluent regulations "shall . . . specify factors to be taken into account in determining the best conventional pollutant control technology measures and practices to comply with section 1311(b)(2)(E) of this title to be applicable to any point source (other than publicly owned treatment works) within such categories or classes." 33 U.S.C. § 1314(b)(4)(B).

Congress did not leave EPA free to select these factors. The statute continues:

> Factors relating to the assessment of best conventional pollutant control technology . . . *shall* include consideration of the reasonableness of the relationship between the costs of attaining a reduction in effluents and the effluent reduction benefits derived, *and* the comparison of the cost and level of reduction of such pollutants from the discharge from publicly owned treatment works to the cost and level of reduction of such pollutants from a class or category of industrial sources. *Id.* (emphasis added).

We find the language of this statute to be clear and straight-forward. We thus find no reason to resort to additional rules of statutory construction or to rely on the legislative history, which has minimum probative value because of the numerous conflicts contained therein.

EPA's construction of section 304(b)(4)(B) is contrary to the plain meaning of the words contained therein. EPA ignores the mandatory language of the law ("shall"), disregards the conjunctive ("and"), and completely eliminates the first factor. By its own admission, the agency made no effort to determine what it would cost an affected industry to remove a pound of pollutant past the BPT level nor did it compare the cost of such removal with the benefits derived from the removal, as specifically required by statute.

***Where, as here, the language of the Act is unambiguous and EPA has failed to comply with its directives, we must grant the petitions to set aside the regulations involved and remand the regulations to EPA for reconsideration. On remand EPA is to develop an industry cost-effectiveness test in accordance with the provisions of section 304(b)(4)(B), employ that test in a manner consistent with the statute, and reexamine all existing BCT regulations to ensure that they are not inconsistent with the proper employment of this industry cost-effectiveness test.

B. *POTW COMPARISON TEST*

The petitioners also challenge the action of EPA in the formation and application of the POTW comparison test. They argue that EPA erred in using an incremental approach, i.e., one going beyond the cost of normal secondary treatment for POTWs, in arriving at a POTW benchmark. They also contend that even if EPA were permitted to use an incremental POTW comparison, it acted arbitrarily and capriciously because the increment was too large to comply with congressional intent. The petitioners also object to the POTW cost data as being inadequate and statistically unreliable. We reject each of these challenges, except the one directed to the errors in the cost data.

For rule making procedures conducted pursuant to Section 4 of the Administrative Procedure Act, 5 U.S.C. § 553, as these were, we must strike "agency action, findings, and conclusions" that we find to be "arbitrary, capricious, an abuse of discretion, or otherwise not in accordance with law." 5 U.S.C. § 706(2)(A). In discussing the scope of judicial review under similar circumstances, this court has emphasized that "[t]he ultimate standard of review is narrow. This court is not empowered to substitute its judgment for that of the agency."***

1.

The petitioners specifically argue that EPA erred in concluding that it was appropriate to consider the cost of upgrading POTWs beyond secondary treatment.[16] The petitioners object to the POTW benchmark for several reasons because: (1) secondary treatment is the only specifically defined treatment level that POTWs are required by law to meet; (2) advanced secondary treatment (AST),[18] the

increment which EPA chose, was not in existence when Congress enacted section 304 of the Act; and (3) the legislative history indicates that the POTW benchmark should be based on the average cost of normal secondary treatment.

We reject the petitioners' contentions. Section 304(b)(4)(B) explicitly authorizes EPA in establishing BCT limitations to compare "the cost and level of reduction of such pollutants from the discharge from publicly owned treatment works to the cost and level of reduction of such pollutants from a class or category of industrial sources." This controlling statute unequivocally directs EPA to employ a POTW comparison test. Contrary to the suggestions, we find nothing on the face of the statute or in the legislative history to suggest that Congress intended for EPA to use a specific POTW benchmark. Although Congress specifically directed the use of this comparison test, it did not issue any instructions as to how EPA was to structure or administer the test.

EPA considered a number of ways in which a POTW test could be formulated. One of the suggestions was that the POTW benchmark be based on the average pollutant removal costs for secondary treatment at POTWs, i.e., the increment from no treatment to secondary treatment. In addition to looking at average POTW costs for secondary treatment, EPA considered various incremental approaches below secondary treatment. EPA rejected these proposals primarily because it felt that a proper POTW benchmark should be one roughly paralleling that with which it is to be compared—the industrial increment from BPT to BAT. Whereas industry was required to be at a BPT level in 1977, POTWs were required to have met effluent limitations based upon secondary treatment by 1977. EPA believed that a relevant basis of comparison for

---

[16]Secondary treatment is the level of treatment that POTWs were required to have achieved by July 1, 1977 unless granted an extension. 33 U.S.C. § 1311(b)(1)(B). Secondary treatment has been broken down by the Administrator into three categories: biochemical oxygen demand (BOD), suspended solids (TSS), and pH. The parameters within each category are set forth in the Administrator's regulations. 40 C.F.R. § 133.102.

[18]AST is not a technology-based limitation that is currently applicable to POTWs. Instead, AST was a term developed by EPA for a construction grant program for POTWs. AST is used to refer to a treatment facility that "can produce effluent of a higher quality than secondary, still using primarily secondary treatment technology." 44 Fed. Reg. 29,534 (1979).***

POTWs would be at an incremental level beyond secondary treatment since BCT would be at a level at least equal to BPT and in many cases beyond BPT. EPA considered several such increments. After a careful consideration of various alternatives, EPA adopted a test employing a comparison of the cost of upgrading POTWs from secondary treatment levels. The selection of this upgrade comparison does not do violence to the language of the statute, and we do not find it to be arbitrary or capricious.

2.

Not only do the petitioners object to an incremental POTW benchmark, but they also object specifically to the use of the increment from secondary to AST as being too costly. In essence, the petitioners contend that even if EPA were permitted to use an incremental POTW benchmark, it should have used a narrower increment, one that more closely straddles the marginal cost of secondary treatment.

We reject this contention. We cannot substitute our judgment for that of EPA and condemn EPA for not choosing what we may consider to be the best increment.***

*   *   *

As indicated by the above comments of the Corn Refiners and the CWPS, there may be any number of increments based on slightly different technology or slightly different sizes of a given technology that EPA could have used. It is clear from the record that EPA was not oblivi-ous to these comments. Instead of using POTW cost reasonableness figures based on specific separate and distinct technologies employed by small and large POTWs, as it had proposed initially, in its final rules, EPA used a single POTW cost reasonableness figure based on the average of all cost-effective technologies used by POTWs operating beyond secondary treatment, but employing basic secondary treatment technology.

We cannot conclude that EPA acted arbitrarily and capriciously in choosing AST as the increment beyond secondary treatment for the POTW benchmark. While EPA sought to use an increment that narrowly straddled secondary treatment, i.e., one that closely approximated marginal costs, and although it admitted its failure to find the narrowest increment that would have more closely approximated marginal cost, there is no statutory mandate requiring EPA to use an increment that equals marginal cost.

*   *   *

III. CONCLUSION

We find no merit to the petitioners' other challenges. Accordingly, we vacate the regulations promulgated pursuant to section 304 of the Act. We remand this action to the agency with instructions to devise a cost-effectiveness test in accordance with the guidelines of this opinion and to correct its data errors.

AFFIRMED IN PART, REVERSED IN PART AND REMANDED.

NOTES

1. Did EPA have a prayer in defending its "single requirement" reading of Section 304 (b)(4)(B) so as not to mandate an industry cost-effectiveness test?

Judge Phillips dissented from the majority opinion on this issue:

Attempting, as does the court, to divine the provision's plain meaning by parsing the convoluted key sentence only reveals, I suggest, that it will not effectively parse. It is true that the two critical clauses from which the two-pronged test requirement is found by the court are phrased in the conjunctive, implying that they express parallel thoughts. But a look at their content reveals that they can only be made parallel in thought by importing into the first clause a phrase, "by means of an industry cost-effectiveness test," that is not literally or plainly there. Without that imported language—actually a construct out of whole cloth by the petitioners that has the happy effect of resolving the issue in their favor—the first clause simply lays down reasonableness of the cost/benefit relationship as a general standard for formulating the BCT regulations rather than positing, as the second clause surely does, a specific test by which reasonableness is to be gauged.***

660 F.2d at 965.

2. Compare the cost and benefit consideration language used in Section 304 (b)(4)(B) for identification of BCT with that used in Section 304 (b)(1)(B) for identification of BPT. Is there any significant difference in this "plain language"?

Given that the federal courts had heretofore interpreted Section 304 (b)(1)(B) not to require EPA to apply a strict cost-effectiveness test in setting BPT, was it correct for the court to find a more specific requirement in Section 304 (b)(4)(B)?

If on its face Section 304 requires no more serious cost-benefit balancing for BCT than for BPT, then wasn't EPA correct in its position that the only thing new required by subsection (b)(4)(B) was a POTW cost-comparison test?

3. If EPA must actually apply sound cost-benefit analysis in setting BCT limitations for each category of point source dischargers, how is it to assess the benefits? Can it seriously attempt to do so without considering the nature, location and quality of the receiving waters for each discharger (potential as well as present?) within each point source category? Realistically, can this be done? Even if it could be, would it be consistent with the basic principle that 301 limitations are not to be based on water quality considerations?

4. After the 1977 Amendments, did EPA have to review its BAT standard for seafood processing plants (which set limits for BOD, oil and grease, and TSS). Recall *Association of Pacific Fisheries v. EPA*, page 27 *supra*. Does this mean, for example, that non-remote salmon canners *might* not have to use screens? That they *would* not?

5. For a good description of how the BPT, BAT, BAD, and BCT standards have been interpreted by EPA and by the courts, see Baum, *Legislating Cost-Benefit Analysis: The Federal Water Pollution Control Act Experience,* 9 COLUM. J. ENVTL. L. 75 (1983). Mr. Baum concludes that the verbose and ambiguous statutory language requiring some sort of unspecified cost-benefit balancing allows the agency to set virtually any level of effluent limitations it desires.

5 VARIANCES

Environmental Protection Agency
v.
National Crushed Stone Association
449 U.S. 64 (1980)

JUSTICE WHITE delivered the opinion of the Court.

In April and July 1977, the Environmental Protection Agency (EPA), acting under the Federal Water Pollution Control Act Amendments of 1972 (Act), promulgated pollution discharge limitations for the coal mining industry and for that portion of the mineral mining and processing industry comprising the crushed stone, construction sand, and gravel categories. Although the Act does not expressly authorize or require variances from the 1977 limitation, each set of regulations contained a variance provision.[2]

Respondents sought review of the regulations in various courts of appeals, challenging both the substantive standards and the variance clause. All of the petitions for review were transferred to the Court of Appeals for the Fourth Circuit. In *National Crushed Stone Association v. EPA,* 601 F. 2d 111 (CA4 1979), and in *Consolidation Coal Company v. Costle,* 604 F. 2d 239 (CA4 1979), the Court of Appeals set aside the variance provision as "unduly restrictive" and remanded the provision to EPA for reconsideration.

To obtain a variance from the 1977 uniform discharge limitations a discharger must demonstrate that the "factors relating to the equipment or facilities involved, the process applied, or other such factors relating to such discharger are fundamentally different from the factors considered in the establishment of the guidelines." Although a greater than normal cost of implementation will be considered in acting on a request for a variance, economic ability to meet the costs will not be considered.[5] A variance,

---

[2]The variance provision reads as follows:
"In establishing the limitations set forth in this section, EPA took into account all information it was able to collect, develop and solicit with respect to factors (such as age and size of plant, raw materials, manufacturing processes, products produced, treatment technology available, energy requirements and costs) which can affect the industry subcategorization and effluent levels established. It is, however, possible that data which would affect these limitations have not been available and, as a result, these limitations should be adjusted for certain plants in this industry. An individual discharger or other interested person may submit evidence to the Regional Administrator (or to the State, if the State has the authority to issue NPDES permits) that factors relating to the equipment or facilities involved, the process applied, or other such factors related to such discharger are fundamentally different from the factors considered in the establishment of the guidelines. On the basis of such evidence or other available information, the Regional Administrator (or the State) will make a written finding that such factors are or are not fundamentally different for that facility compared to those specified in the Development Document. If such fundamentally different factors are found to exist, the Regional Administrator or the State shall establish for

the discharger effluent limitations in the NPDES permit either more or less stringent than the limitations established herein, to the extent dictated by such fundamentally different factors. Such limitation must be approved by the Administrator of the Environmental Protection Agency. The Administrator may approve or disapprove such limitations, specify other limitations, or initiate proceedings to revise these regulations."

[5]EPA has explained its position as follows:
"Thus a plant may be able to secure a BPT variance by showing that the plant's own compliance costs with the national guideline limitation would be x times greater than the compliance costs of the plants EPA

therefore, will not be granted on the basis of the applicant's economic inability to meet the costs of implementing the uniform standard.

The Court of Appeals for the Fourth Circuit rejected this position. It required EPA to "take into consideration, among other things, the statutory factors set out in § 301 (c)," which authorizes variances from the more restrictive pollution limitations to become effective in 1987 and which specifies economic capability as a major factor to be taken into account.[6] The court held that

> " 'if [a plant] is doing all that the maximum use of technology within its economic capability will permit and if such use will result in reasonable further progress toward the elimination of the discharge of pollutants . . . no reason appears why [it] should not be able to secure such a variance should it comply with any other requirements of the variance.' " 601 F. 2d, at 124, quoting from *Appalachian Power Co. v. Train*, 545 F. 2d 1351, 1378 (CA4 1976).

*   *   *

I

We shall first briefly outline the basic structure of the Act, which translates Congress' broad goal of eliminating "the discharge of pollutants into the navigable waters" into specific requirements that must be met by individual point sources.

Section 301 (b) of the Act, 33 U.S.C. § 1311 (b), authorizes the Administrator to set effluent limitations for categories of point sources. With respect to existing point sources, the section provides for implementation of increasingly strin-

gent effluent limitations in two steps. The first step, to be accomplished by July 1, 1977, requires all point sources to meet standards based on "the application of the best practicable control technology currently available [BPT] as defined by the Administrator . . . ." § 301 (b)(1)(A). The second step***requires all point sources to meet standards based on application of the "best available technology economically achievable [BAT] for such category or class . . . ."[9] § 301 (b)(2)(A). Both sets of limitations are to be based upon regulatory guidelines established under § 304 (b).

Section 304 (b) of the Act is again divided into two sections corresponding to the two levels of technology, BPT and BAT. Under § 304 (b)(1) the Administrator is to quantify "the degree of effluent reduction attainable through the application of the best practicable control technology currently available [BPT] for classes and categories of point sources . . . ." In assessing the BPT the Administrator is to consider:

> "The total cost of application of technology in relation to the effluent reduction benefits to be achieved from such application, . . . the age of equipment and facilities involved, the process employed, the engineering aspects of the application of various types of control techniques, process changes, non-water quality environmental impact (including energy requirements), and such other factors as the Administrator deems appropriate."

Similar directions are given the Administrator for determining effluent reductions attainable from the BAT except that in assessing BAT total cost is no longer to be considered in comparison to effluent reduction benefits.

Section 402 authorizes the establishment of the National Pollutant Discharge Elimination System (NPDES), under which every discharger of pollutants is required to obtain a permit. The

---

considered in setting the national BPT limitation. A plant may not, however, secure a BPT variance by alleging that the plant's own financial status is such that it cannot afford to comply with the national BPT limitation." 43 Fed. Reg. 50042.

[6]Section 301 (c), 33 U. S. C. § 1311 (c) allows the Administrator to grant a variance "upon a showing by the owner or operator . . . that such modified requirements (1) will represent the maximum use of technology within the economic capability of the owner or operator; and (2) will result in reasonable further progress toward the elimination of the discharge of pollutants."

[9]The 1972 Amendments required that the second stage standards be met by 1983. This deadline was extended in the Clean Water Act Amendments of 1977. Depending on the nature of the pollutant, the deadline for the more stringent limitations now falls between July 1, 1984 and July 1, 1987.***

permit requires the discharger to meet all the applicable requirements specified in the regulations issued under § 301. Permits are issued by either the Administrator or state agencies that have been approved by the Administrator.[11]***

Section 301 (c) of the Act explicitly provides for modifying the 1987 (BAT) effluent limitations with respect to individual point sources. A variance under § 301 (c) may be obtained upon a showing "that such modified requirements (1) will represent the maximum use of technology within the economic capability of the owner or operator; and (2) will result in reasonable further progress toward elimination of the discharge of pollutants." Thus, the economic ability of the individual operator to meet the costs of effluent reductions may in some circumstances justify granting a variance from the 1987 limitations.

No such explicit variance provision exists with respect to BPT standards, but in *E.I. du Pont de Nemours v. Train*, 430 U.S. 112 (1977), we indicated that a variance provision was a necessary aspect of BPT limitations applicable by regulations to classes and categories of point sources. The issue in this case is whether the BPT variance provision must allow consideration of the economic capability of an individual discharger to afford the costs of the BPT limitation. For the reasons that follow, our answer is in the negative.

II

The plain language of the statute does not support the position taken by the Court of Appeals. Section 301 (c) is limited on its face to modifications of the 1987 BAT limitations. It says nothing about relief from the 1977 BPT requirements.***

The two factors listed in § 301 (c)— "maximum use of technology within the economic capability of the owner or operator" and "reasonable further progress toward the elimination of the discharge of pollutants"—parallel the general definition of BAT standards as limitations that "require application of the best available technology economically achievable for such category or class, which will result in reasona-

ble further progress toward . . . eliminating the discharge of all pollutants. . . . " § 301 (b) (2). A § 301 (c) variance, thus, creates for a particular point source a BAT standard that represents for it the same sort of economic and technological commitment as the general BAT standard creates for the class. As with the general BAT standard, the variance assumes that the 1977 BPT has been met by the point source and that the modification represents a commitment of the maximum resources economically possible to the ultimate goal of eliminating all polluting discharges. No one who can afford the best available technology can secure a variance.

There is no similar connection between § 301 (c) and the considerations underlying the establishment of the 1977 BPT limitations. First, § 301 (c)'s requirement of "reasonable further progress" must have reference to some prior standard. BPT serves as the prior standard with respect to BAT. There is, however, no comparable, prior standard with respect to BPT limitations. Second, BPT limitations do not require an industrial category to commit the maximum economic resources possible to pollution control, even if affordable. Those point sources already using a satisfactory pollution control technology need take no additional steps at all. The § 301 (c) variance factor, the "maximum use of technology within the economic capability of the owner or operator," would therefore be inapposite in the BPT context. It would not have the same effect there that it has with respect to BAT's, *i.e.*, it would not apply the general requirements to an individual point source.

More importantly, to allow a variance based on the maximum technology affordable by the point source, even if that technology fails to meet BPT effluent limitations, would undercut the purpose and function of BPT limitations. Rather than the 1987 requirement of the best measures economically and technologically feasible, the statutory provisions for 1977 contemplate regulations prohibiting discharges from any point source in excess of the effluent produced by the best practicable technology currently available in the industry. The Administrator was referred to the industry and to existing practices to determine BPT. He was to categorize point sources,

---

[11]***At present, over 30 States and covered territories operate their own NPDES programs.

examine control practices in exemplary plants in each category, and after weighing benefits and costs and considering other factors specified by § 304, determine and define the best practicable technology at a level that would affect the obvious statutory goal for 1977 of substantially reducing the total pollution produced by each category of the industry.[15] Necessarily, if pollution is to be diminished, limitations based on BPT must forbid the level of effluent produced by the most pollution-prone segment of the industry, that segment not measuring up to "the average of the best existing performance." So understood, the statute contemplated regulations that would require a substantial number of point sources with the poorest performances either to conform to BPT standards or to cease production. To allow a variance based on economic capability and not to require adherence to the prescribed minimum technology would permit the employment of the very practices that the Administrator had rejected in establishing the best practicable technology currently in use in the industry.

To put the matter another way, under § 304, the Administrator is directed to consider the benefits of effluent reductions as compared to the costs of pollution control in determining BPT limitations. Thus, every BPT limitation represents a conclusion by the Administrator that the costs imposed on the industry are worth the benefits in pollution reduction that will be gained by meeting those limits. To grant a variance because a particular owner or operator cannot meet the normal costs of the technological requirements imposed on him, and not because there has been a recalculation of the benefits compared to the costs, would be inconsistent with this legislative scheme and would allow a level of pollution inconsistent with the judgment of the Administrator.

In terms of the scheme implemented by BPT limitations, the factors that the Administrator

considers in granting variances do not suggest that economic capability must also be a determinant. The regulations permit a variance where "factors relating to the equipment or facilities involved, the process applied or such other factors relating to such discharger are fundamentally different from the factors considered in the establishment of the guidelines." If a point source can show that its situation, including its costs of compliance, is not within the range of circumstances considered by the Administrator, then it may receive a variance, whether or not the source could afford to comply with the minimum standard. In such situations, the variance is an acknowledgement that the uniform BPT limitation was set without reference to the full range of current practices, to which the Administrator was to refer. Insofar as a BPT limitation was determined without consideration of a current practice fundamentally different from those that were considered by the Administrator, that limitation is incomplete. A variance based on economic capability, however, would not have this character; it would allow a variance simply because the point source could not afford a compliance cost that is not fundamentally different from those the Administrator has already considered in determining BPT. ***

Because the 1977 limitations were intended to reduce the total pollution produced by an industry, requiring compliance with BPT standards necessarily imposed additional costs on the segment of the industry with the least effective technology. If the statutory goal is to be achieved, these costs must be borne or the point source eliminated. In our view, requiring variances from otherwise valid regulations where dischargers cannot afford normal costs of compliance would undermine the purpose and the intended operative effect of the 1977 regulations.

III

The Administrator's present interpretation of the language of the statute is amply supported by the legislative history, which persuades us that Congress understood that the economic capability provision of § 301 (c) was limited to BAT variances; that Congress foresaw and accepted the economic hardship,

---

[15]EPA defines BPT as "the average of the best existing performance by plants of various sizes, ages and unit processes within each industrial category or subcategory. This average is not based upon a broad range of plants within an industrial category or subcategory, but is based upon performance levels achieved by exemplary plants."***

including the closing of some plants, that effluent limitations would cause; and that Congress took certain steps to alleviate this hardship, steps which did not include allowing a BPT variance based on economic capability.

*   *   *

Nor did Congress restrict the reach of § 301 (c) without understanding the economic hardships that uniform standards would impose. Prior to passage of the Act, Congress had before it a report jointly prepared by EPA, the Commerce Dept., and the Council on Environmental Quality on the impact of the pollution control measures on industry. That report estimated that there would be 200 to 300 plant closings caused by the first set of pollution limitations.***

Congress did not respond to this foreseen economic impact by making room for variances based on economic impact.*** Instead of economic variances, Congress specifically added two other provisions to address the problem of economic hardship.

First, provision was made for low-cost loans to small businesses to help them meet the cost of technological improvements.***

Second, an employee protection provision was added, giving EPA authority to investigate any plant's claim that it must cut back production or close down because of pollution control regulations. § 507 (e). This provision had two purposes: to allow EPA constantly to monitor the economic effect on industry of pollution control rules and to undercut economic threats by industry that would create pressure to relax effluent limitation rules.***

The only protection offered by the provision, however, is the assurance that there will be a public inquiry into the facts behind such an economic threat.***

As we see it, Congress anticipated that the 1977 regulations would cause economic hardship and plant closings: "[T]he question . . . is not what a court thinks is generally appropriate to the regulatory process; it is what Congress intended for *these* regulations." *Du Pont, supra,* at 138.

IV

It is by now a commonplace that "when faced with a problem of statutory construction, this Court shows great deference to the interpretation given the statute by the officers or agency charged with its administration." The statute itself does not provide for BPT variances in connection with permits for individual point sources, and we had no occasion in *du Pont* to address the adequacy of the Administrator's 1977 variance provision. In the face of § 301 (c)'s explicit limitation and in the absence of any other specific direction to provide for variances in connection with permits for individual point sources, we believe that the Administrator has adopted a reasonable construction of the statutory mandate.

*   *   *

We conclude, therefore, that the Court of Appeals erred in not accepting EPA's interpretation of the Act. EPA is not required by the Act to consider economic capability in granting variances from its uniform BPT regulations.

The judgment of the Court of Appeals is Reversed.

NOTES

1. Did this decision turn on a reading of the controlling statutory language? If so, *what* statutory language?

In either the 1972 or the 1977 Amendments was there any statutory provision for a variance from BPT limitations?

Was not the availability of a BPT variance simply created out of whole cloth by EPA, and acknowledged in passing as necessary by the Court in *du Pont*? Was its creation necessary to the establishment of uniform national standards, or in opposition to that principle?

Was the issue before the Court one which only a lawyer could appreciate: Did EPA act within its statutory authority in setting the criteria for obtaining variance when no statutory authority had been found?

2. Putting aside such academic objections, what are grounds for obtaining a BPT variance?

Must an applicant show a "fundamental difference" in one of the factors specified in Section 304 (b)(1)(B) for setting BPT limitations and for establishing point source categories?

Or must the applicant demonstrate a "fundamentally different factor" affecting its facility, in the sense of a type of influence or effect not even considered by EPA in setting the 301 limitation?

3. Do you understand the distinction drawn by EPA, and approved by the Court, between fundamentally different costs and economic inability to meet costs not fundamentally different from those considered by EPA in setting the BPT standard?

Does this mean that BPT limitations could put some plants out of business? Should BPT for a point source category be set at a level which will cause severe economic dislocations, or only a small amount? Recall the fifty-seven percent closures forecast in *Pacific Fisheries* for non-remote Alaskan fresh and frozen salmon plants.

4. On what grounds can a variance from BAT be granted? Does Section 301 (c) specify the exclusive ground? Has EPA acted outside its statutory authority in applying the "fundamentally different factors" variance concept to BAT? (This was the issue that subsequently came before the Court in *Chemical Manufacturers Ass'n v. Natural Resources Defense Council, Inc., infra* p. 79.)

Does Section 301(c) apply to BCT — the second-stage limitations for conventional pollutants? If not, may any variance from BCT be granted? May the "fundamentally different factors" standard be used?

5. Focusing more closely on BPT variances, precisely what sort of factors may EPA properly consider in passing on an application?

What if an applicant showed that the only convenient location for disposal of the large amount of sludge captured by BPT was a wildlife habitat threatened by such sludge disposal?

If a combined pulp/alcohol/byproducts plant produces less *raw waste per ton of product* than the exemplary pulp mills used by EPA in setting the BPT limitations which were expressed in terms of *BOD per ton of raw waste,* may the combined facility obtain a variance which will allow it to discharge waste with higher BOD per ton of waste? For an opinion sustaining EPA's negative answer, see *Georgia-Pacific Corp. v. EPA,* 671 F.2d 1235 (9th cir. 1982).

6. Can a state with NPDES permitting authority grant a BPT variance? If so, does it act with complete autonomy? Does EPA have the power to veto a state-issued variance? If so, on what grounds? See footnote 2 to the *Crushed Stone* decision.

7. Could the present EPA reverse its position and provide for BPT variances based upon economic incapability?

Crown Simpson Pulp Company v. Costle

642 F. 2d 323 (9th Cir. 1981)

Before DUNIWAY, CHOY and SNEED, Circuit Judges.

DUNIWAY, Circuit Judge:

Crown Simpson Pulp Company and Louisiana-Pacific Corporation petition for review of the decision of the Environmental Protection Agency (EPA) to veto two pollutant discharge permits that the California State Water Resources Control Board proposed to issue to the Companies. The proposed permits would grant the Companies variances from two EPA effluent limitations. ***

1. The Facts.

*   *   *

The Companies operate two bleached kraft pulp mills located on the Samoa Peninsula, on the west side of Humboldt Bay in California. Each mill discharges effluent into the Pacific Ocean through a separate deepwater outfall diffuser system designed in consultation with the State. In February, 1976, acting under Section 301(b) of the Act, the EPA issued effluent limitations for different types of bleached kraft pulp, paper and paperboard mills discharging into navigable waters. As required by this section of the Act, these regulations impose discharge limits, for the period July 1, 1977 to July 1, 1983, based on "the application of the best practicable control technology currently available as defined by the Administrator." The regulations also include a provision for a variance from the discharge limits where the discharger demonstrates that "factors relating to the equipment or facilities involved, the processes applied, or other such factors related to such discharger are *fundamentally different* from the factors considered in the establishment of the guidelines."

In March, 1977, the California State Water Resources Control Board — an agency approved by the EPA under § 402(b) of the Act to grant discharge permits — proposed to issue discharge permits to the Companies that included variances from two of the effluent limitations set by the EPA guidelines for bleached kraft pulp mills.

Under § 402 of the Act, all dischargers must obtain such discharge permits to continue discharging and permits are granted only to dischargers who either conform to EPA's effluent limits or merit a variance.

Subject to the approval of the Administrator of EPA, the State Board granted variances to the Companies from EPA guidelines for biochemical oxygen demand of effluent (BOD) — "The BOD of a waste exerts an adverse effect upon the dissolved oxygen resources of a body of water by reducing the oxygen available to fish, plant life, and other aquatic species" — and for the pH, e.g., acidity or alkalinity, of effluent. The State Board concluded after several days of hearings that the non-water quality environmental effects of adhering to these guidelines — adherence to the EPA guidelines for BOD and pH would require construction and operation of a treatment facility — outweighed the water quality benefits. It said: ". . . the existing discharges result in no water quality problems . . . there is no expected or predictable water quality improvement to be achieved as the result of imposition of the EPA Guidelines. In light of . . . the magnitude of the chemical and energy requirements, and the potential air and land management problems associated with sludge disposal . . . we can only conclude the evidence justified the variance requested." Accordingly the State Board proposed to grant permits to the Companies, authorizing limits of BOD and pH far above those set in EPA's guidelines.

In a lengthy decision issued September 15, 1977, the Administrator vetoed the permits and denied the variance requests. The Administrator emphasized that the State Board had not found — as the variance provision required — that the non-water quality environmental effects of adherence to the limitations in this case were "fundamentally different" from those considered by EPA in publishing effluent limitations for the industry as a whole: "It is clear that the Board did not find a 'fundamental difference' in terms of non-water quality impact itself but instead found non-water quality impact to be significant *because of lack of improvement of local receiving water quality.* In effect, the State granted an exemption from minimum national technology-based standards because of local water quality considerations. This was contrary to the letter and intent of the [Act] and I have no choice but to disapprove the state action." (emphasis in original). The Companies petition for review of EPA's decision.

II. The Merits

To begin with, we note that the issue in this case is not whether a variance may be granted because of such factors as the non-water environmental effects of adherence to the general effluent limitations. The agency has now explicitly stated, both in its opinion in this case as well as in more recent regulations, that the factors which the agency must consider under § 304(b)(1) in determining the standard of best practicable technology will also be considered by the agency in deciding whether a plant is fundamentally different and thus whether a variance is appropriate. These factors include non-water quality environmental impact, energy requirements, and cost in relation to effluent reduction benefit as well as several other factors

Nor is the issue whether the agency may insist that a particular discharger show a "fundamental difference" in his plant as to one or more of the factors considered by EPA in setting the guidelines for the industry category before granting a variance. The Companies do not challenge the fundamental difference requirement and it has been upheld explicitly in *Weyerhaeuser Co. v. Costle, supra,* 590F.2d at 1040, a case to which Crown Simpson was a party, as well as implicitly in the recent opinion in *EPA v. National Crushed Stone Association.*

Rather, the issue is whether, in insisting that a particular discharger show a "fundamental difference" in his plant before granting a variance, the agency must consider receiving water quality as a factor that may make a fundamental difference—either in itself or because other factors may be considered fundamentally differ-

ent when assessed in the light of receiving water quality. Thus, the Companies contend that a variance must be granted where the non-water environmental costs of adherence to the guidelines are high—although not "fundamentally different"—*and* the benefits of adherence to the receiving water are apparently negligible. We disagree.

In granting a variance on the basis of non-water quality environmental effects viewed in the light of receiving water quality, the State Board nowhere found that the non-water environmental effects of adherence to EPA's guidelines would be "fundamentally different" for these two companies' plants as opposed to others in the industry. This was not simply a failure by the State Board to make itself clear. The State Board fully understood the requirement: It rejected the Companies' claim that their costs of adherence justified a variance by finding that these costs were not "substantially different from the costs EPA found would be sustained on an industry-wide basis." Moreover, one of the Companies' own witnesses gave testimony to the State Board specifically denying any fundamental difference as to non-water quality environmental impact***.

Thus, we reject the Companies' suggestion that the State Board found a fundamental difference as to non-water quality environmental impact in substance and merely failed to enunciate the exact words or that receiving water quality played only a subsidiary part in the Board's decision to grant variances. To the contrary, it is clear from the State Board's opinion that it would not have granted the variances except for its consideration of receiving water quality. And it was because of this heavy reliance on receiving water quality that the Administrator felt compelled, in view of his interpretation of the Act, to disapprove the variances. It is thus upon this interpretation of the Act that the dispute hinges.

When faced with a problem of statutory construction, "[we show] great deference to the interpretation given the statute by the officers or agency charged with its administration." The opinion of the Administrator persuasively argues that to base effluent limitations or variances from these limitations on local water quality considerations would be inconsistent with the Act and its legislative history. 10 E.R.C. at 1846-50. Judge McGowan's enlightening opinion in *Weyerhaeuser Co. v. Costle, supra*, reached the same conclusion, finding "that based on long experience, and aware of the limits of technological and administrative flexibility, Congress made the deliberate decision to rule out arguments based on receiving water quality." 590F.2d at 1042.***

We need not repeat here the exhaustive discussions of the legislative history of the Act provided by the Administrator's decision and by the court in *Weyerhaeuser Co. v. Costle, supra*. These discussions demonstrate that a fundamental purpose of the Act was to shift pollution control from a focus on receiving water quality to a focus on the technological control of effluent. Above all the Act seeks to "avoid imposing on the Administrator any requirement to consider the location of sources within a category or to ascertain water quality impact of effluent controls." *Weyerhaeuser Co. v. Costle, supra*, 590 F.2d at 1045 n.52 (quoting Senator Muskie). We therefore affirm the agency's decision that the State Board erred in proposing a variance for reasons relating to receiving water quality. Without finding a fundamental difference as to any factor or combination of factors considered by EPA in setting effluent limitations for the industry category, the State Board could not, consistently with the Act, grant variances on the basis of receiving water quality.

Our holding does not deprive the Act or industry of a meaningful variance provision or the states of a significant role in administering the Act. Under EPA regulations variances have been granted, and are appropriately granted, by the state or EPA when a discharger's plant is substantially or fundamentally different as to those factors considered by the EPA in drawing up the guidelines. Indeed, in his opinion in this case the Administrator took care not to foreclose the possibility of a future variance for the two Companies here, and emphasized the continuing importance of the State Board in the variance and permit process ***. To rule out variances granted in large measure because of receiving

water quality merely requires that the states or EPA grant variances in accordance with the basic purpose of the Act; it does not put an end to variances or to the state's role in granting them.

Our holding in this case is consistent with our decision in *Association of Pacific Fisheries v. EPA, supra*, 615F.2d at 794. In *Pacific Fisheries* we upheld EPA's issuance of permits to certain Alaskan fish processors. The best practicable control technology for these processors was determined to be the installation of screens to strain out larger fish particles from the plants' discharge. The permits issued to certain of these processors allowed, among several methods of disposal, the barging and dumping of screened-out solids at certain offshore ocean sites. EPA had not considered water quality in categorizing the industry or in setting effluent limitations for each category. It considered water quality only in issuing certain permits. Plaintiff did not challenge EPA's consideration of water quality in issuing permits but argued that if barging and dumping were permissible so too should grinding and dispersion of effluent be permissible.

Although noting that "[t]he Agency has not explained to this court as clearly as it might have how the asserted water quality benefits of discharging a given amount of effluent farther offshore should be considered within the statutory framework of technology-based, not water quality-based, pollution limitations," we held that "[i]t was not an abuse of discretion for the Agency to consider an improvement in nearshore water quality as one factor in support of the effluent limitation." 615F.2d at 807. We found specific support in the legislative history for a limited consideration of water quality in framing effluent standards for the Alaskan fish processing industry.

We certainly did not hold in *Pacific Fisheries*, as the Companies appear to contend, that the agency *must* consider water quality in framing effluent guidelines. Indeed, we explicitly affirmed the D.C. Circuit's position that the Act seeks to reduce pollution by technology based standards and not by standards based on receiving water quality. Thus, we only permitted a limited consideration of receiving water quality in an unusual factual setting.

Moreover, we explicitly declined to decide "the extent to which, if the EPA relies on water quality evidence in measuring the benefits of requiring a particular technology for a category or subcategory of point sources, it must also consider water quality evidence at particular sites in passing on applications for variances." 615 F.2d at 807 n.9. Here, EPA did not rely on water quality evidence and thus the question posed but not answered in *Pacific Fisheries* need not be answered here. We also note, as we did there, that a fundamental purpose of the Act was to free EPA from the incubus "of proving in every case the application of an effluent limitation at a specific site will improve water quality at that site." 615 F.2d at 807 n.8. Thus, even if EPA could base industry guidelines to a limited degree on local water quality considerations, if we were to permit companies to seek variances from these guidelines on the basis of water quality at particular sites, we would be returning water pollution control to its ineffective pre-1972 status in defiance of Congress's desire "to restore and maintain the chemical, physical, and biological integrity of the Nation's waters."

In short, our decision in *Pacific Fisheries* has not suddenly rehabilitated the discredited approach of water quality based pollution control. The Administrator's holding that the Act does not permit either industry-wide guidelines or variances to be based solely or in large part on local water quality considerations is not inconsistent with our *Pacific Fisheries* opinion.

*   *   *

The decision of the Administrator is affirmed.

NOTES

1. Was this case correctly decided? If so, does it mean that the technology-based standards of Section 301 can sometimes require "treatment for treatment's sake"? Might they sometimes even require environmentally harmful action to be taken? In this case, the Redwood Chapter of the Sierra Club supported the variances because of fears that treatment facilities required by the national standards would harm a nearby dune-wetland area and create other sludge disposal problems.

2. The court's reasoning was that only those factors designated in Section 304(b)(1) for consideration in setting the national BPT effluent limitations may be grounds for a variance from such limitations. Notice, however, that the primary factor for EPA to consider in setting BPT standards is "the total cost of application of technology *in relation to the effluent reduction benefits to be achieved* from such application." § 304(b)(1)(B) (emphasis added). Can't the nature of the receiving waters be such that a "fundamental difference" in the cost-benefit balance will result? In other words, *Crushed Stone* recognized that fundamentally higher costs would justify a variance; shouldn't fundamentally lower benefits be treated the same?

Regardless of whether Section 304(b)(1)(B) could be read to support variances based on receiving water quality, does the overall statutory scheme do so?

3. Was the *Pacific Fisheries* case artfully distinguished? What if (as in *Pacific Fisheries*) the BPT standard had in fact been based in part on water quality considerations? For example, what if a nonremote Alaskan salmon canner asked for a variance from the screening requirement because the strong tides and deep water in the particular nearshore site at which it discharged achieved the same sort of pollutant dispersal as would occur at offshore barge dump sites?

4. Could EPA create a separate subcategory, with much lower BOD and pH limitations, for "deep ocean dischargers" within the pulp and paper mill category? The industry's attempt to

force the agency to do so failed in *Weyerhaeuser Co. v. Costle,* 590F.2d 1011, 1041-44 (D.C. Cir.1978), quoted supra, p. 75.

5. At the time *Crown Simpson* was decided, in only two instances did the act allow the assimilative capacity of receiving water to be considered in relaxing standards: for thermal pollution and for ocean discharges from publicly-owned treatment works. *See* Section 316 and 301(h) of the Act. These clearly were written to be exceptions to the general rule. Are they distinguishable? Are they justified? The wholesale granting of Section 316 variances from thermal pollution limitations has been the subject of much criticism: "That limited exemption has been turned into a gaping loophole." S. REP. No. 370, 95th Cong., 1st Sess. 8.

6. Before the Crown Simpson and Louisiana-Pacific pulp mills were required to comply with BPT effluent limitations, Congress amended Section 301 of the Clean Water Act to include the following special variance provision:

(m)(l) The Administrator, with the concurrence of the State, may issue a permit under section 402 which modifies the requirements of subsections (b)(1)(A) and(b)(2)(E) of this section, and of section 403, with respect to effluent limitations to the extent such limitations relate to biochemical oxygen demand and pH from discharges by an industrial discharger in such State into deep waters of the territorial seas, if the applicant demonstrates and the Administrator finds that—

(A) the facility for which modification is sought is covered at the time of the enactment of this subsection by National Pollutant Discharge Elimination System permit number CA0005894 or CA0005282;

(B) the energy and environmental costs of meeting such requirements of subsections (b)(1)(A) and (b)(2)(E) and section 403 exceed by an unreasonable amount the benefits to be obtained, including the objectives of this Act;

(C) the applicant has established a system for monitoring the impact of such discharges on a representative sample of aquatic biota;

(D) such modified requirements will not result in any additional requirements on any other point or nonpoint source;

(E) there will be no new or substantially increased discharges from the point source of the pollutant to which the modification applies above that volume of discharge specified in the permit;

(F) the discharge is into waters where there is strong tidal movement and other hydrological and geological characteristics which are necessary to allow compliance with this subsection and section 101(a)(2) of this Act;

(G) the applicant accepts as a condition to the permit a contractual obligation to use funds in the amount required (but not less than $250,000 per year for ten years) for research and development of water pollution control technology, including but not limited to closed cycle technology;

(H) the facts and circumstances present a unique situation which, if relief is granted, will not establish a precedent or the relaxation of the requirements of this Act applicable to similarly situated discharges; and

(I) no owner or operator of a facility comparable to that of the applicant situated in the United States has demonstrated that it would be put at a competitive disadvantage to the applicant (or the parent company or any subsidiary thereof) as a result of the issuance of a permit under this subsection.

(2) The effluent limitations established under a permit issued under paragraph (1) shall be sufficient to implement the applicable State water quality standards, to assure the protection of public water supplies and protection and propagation of a balanced, indigenous

population of shellfish, fish, fauna, wildlife, and other aquatic organisms, and to allow recreational activities in and on the water. In setting such limitations, the Administrator shall take into account any seasonal variations and the need for an adequate margin of safety, considering the lack of essential knowledge concerning the relationship between effluent limitations and water quality and the lack of essential knowledge of the effects of discharges on beneficial uses of the receiving waters.

(3) A permit under this subsection may be issued for a period not to exceed five years, and such a permit may be renewed for one additional period not to exceed five years upon a demonstration by the applicant and a finding by the Administrator at the time of application for any such renewal that the provisions of this subsection are met.

(4) The Administrator may terminate a permit issued under this subsection if the Administrator determines that there has been a decline in ambient water quality of the receiving waters during the period of the permit even if a direct cause and effect relationship cannot be shown; *Provided,* that if the effluent from a source with a permit issued under this subsection is contributing to a decline in ambient water quality of the receiving waters, the Administrator shall terminate such permit.

Of course, Crown Simpson and Louisiana-Pacific hold permits numbered CA0005894 and CA0005282. And, of course, this legislation was introduced by the congressman whose district included the two pulp mills.

7. Assuming that the two mills meet the rigid requirements for the variance, is this special treatment justified? Should the same relief be available to any discharger who can meet these requirements?

Would making such a variance available to any discharger who could meet its terms threaten the fabric of Section 301 and its technology-based standards? Would it threaten the environment? Your attention is called to the finding required by subparagraph (m)(1)(B).

8. In general, Section 403 requires EPA to establish "ocean discharge criteria" which, unless satisfied by the requirements of Section 301, must be met by additional permit terms. Notice that the new subsection (m) to Section 301 authorizes a variance from Section 403 as well as Section 301(b)(1)(A) and (b)(2)(E).

Chemical Manufacturers Association
v.
Natural Resources Defense Council, Inc.

105 S. Ct. 1102 (1985)

JUSTICE WHITE delivered the opinion of the Court.

*　　*　　*

I

As part of a consolidated lawsuit, respondent National Resources Defense Counsel (NRDC) sought a declaration that § 301(l) of the Clean Water Act prohibited EPA from issuing "fundamentally different factor" (FDF) variances for pollutants listed as toxic under the Act. Petitioners EPA and Chemical Manufacturers Association (CMA) argued otherwise. To understand the nature of this controversy, some background with respect to the statute and the case law is necessary.

*　　*　　*

Indirect dischargers—those whose waste water passes through publicly owned treatment plants—are *** required to comply with pretreatment standards promulgated by EPA under § 307 of the Act for pollutants not susceptible to treatment by sewage systems or which would interfere with the operation of those systems. Relying upon legislative history suggesting that pretreatment standards are to be comparable to limitations for direct dischargers, and pursuant to a consent decree,[4] EPA

has set effluent limitations for indirect dischargers under the same two-phase approach applied to those discharging waste directly into navigable waters.

Thus, for both direct and indirect dischargers, EPA considers specific statutory factors and promulgates regulations creating categories and classes of sources and setting uniform discharge limitations for those classes and categories. Since application of the statutory factors varies on the basis of the industrial process used and a variety of other factors, EPA has faced substantial burdens in collecting information adequate to create categories and classes suitable for uniform effluent limits, a burden complicated by the time deadlines it has been under to accomplish the task. Some plants may find themselves classified within a category of sources from which they are, or claim to be, fundamentally different in terms of the statutory factors. As a result, EPA has developed its FDF variance as a mechanism for ensuring that its necessarily rough-hewn categories do not unfairly burden atypical plants. Any interested party may seek an FDF variance to make effluent limitations either more or less stringent if the standards applied to a given source, because of factors fundamentally different from those considered by EPA in setting the limitation, are either too lenient or too strict.[8]

The 1977 amendments to the Clean Water Act reflected Congress' increased concern with the dangers of toxic pollutants. The Act, as then amended, allows specific statutory

---

[4]Lawsuits by NRDC resulted in a consent decree placing EPA under deadlines for promulgating categorical pretreatment standards based on BPT and BAT criteria. *NRDC* v. *Train,* 8 ERC 2120 (DC 1976), modified *sub nom., NRDC* v. *Costle,* 12 ERC 1833 (DC 1979), modified *sub nom., NRDC* v. *Gorsuch,* No. 72 2153 (DC Oct. 26, 1982), modified *sub nom., NRDC* v. *Ruckelshaus.* No. 73-2153 (DC Aug. 2, 1983 and Jan. 6, 1984). In the 1977 amendments to the Act, Congress sanctioned this approach to establishing pretreatment standards for indirect dischargers. *Environmental Defense Fund, Inc.* v. *Costle,* 205 U. S. App. D. C. 101, 115-116, 636 F. 2d 1229, 1243-1244 (1980).

[8]Sources subject to new source performance standards (NSPS) under the Act are those who begin construction after the publication of proposed new source standards, 33 U. S. C. § 1316, and they are ineligible for FDF variances. See 40 CFR § 403.13(b).

modifications of effluent limitations for economic and water quality reasons in § 301(c) and (g).[9] Section 301(*l*), however, added by the 1977 amendments, provides:

> "The Administrator may not modify any requirement of this section as it applies to any specific pollutant which is on the toxic pollutant list under section 1317(a)(1) of this title." 91 Stat. 1590.

In the aftermath of the 1977 amendments, EPA continued its practice of occasionally granting FDF variances for BPT requirements. The Agency also promulgated regulations explicitly allowing FDF variances for pretreatment standards and BAT requirements. Under these regulations, EPA granted FDF variances, but infrequently.[12]

---

[9]33 U. S. C. § § 1311(c) and (g). Those provisions explain in relevant part:
"(c) The Administrator may modify the requirements of [§ 301's effluent limitations] with respect to any point source for which a permit application is filed after July 1, 1977, upon a showing by the owner or operator of such point source satisfactory to the Administrator that such modified requirements (1) will represent the maximum use of technology within the economic capability of the owner or operator; and (2) will result in reasonable further progress toward the elimination of the discharge of pollutants."

*   *   *

"(g)(1) The Administrator, with the concurrence of the State, shall modify the requirements of [§ 301's effluent limitations] with respect to the discharge of any pollutant (other than pollutants identified pursuant to section 1314(a)(4) of this title, toxic pollutants subject to section 1317(a) of this title, and the thermal component of discharges) from any point source upon a showing by the owner or operator of such a point source satisfactory to the Administrator that—

*   *   *

"(C) such modification will not interfere with the attainment or maintenance of that water quality which shall assure protection of public water supplies, and the protection and propagation of a balanced population of shellfish, fish, and wildlife, and allow recreational activities, in and on the water and such modification will not result in the discharge of pollutants in quantities which may reasonably be anticipated to pose an unacceptable risk to human health or the environment . . ."
EPA and NRDC appear to be at odds as to whether § 301(c) and § 301(g) modifications are available to indirect dischargers as well as direct dischargers. Resolution of the seeming disagreement is not necessary to adjudicate this case.
[12]NRDC acknowledges the limited availability of FDF variances. *** By 1984, a total of four FDF vari-

As part of its consolidated lawsuit, respondent NRDC here challenged pretreatment standards for indirect dischargers and sought a declaration that § 301(*l*) barred any FDF variance with respect to toxic pollutants. *** ***[T]he Third Circuit here ruled in favor of NRDC, and against petitioners EPA and CMA***. ***We reverse.

II

Section 301(*l*) states that EPA may not "modify" any requirement of § 301 insofar as toxic materials are concerned. EPA insists that § 301(*l*) prohibits only those modifications expressly permitted by other provisions of § 301, namely, those that § 301(c) and § 301(g) would allow on economic or water-quality grounds. Section 301(*l*), it is urged, does not address the very different issue of FDF variances. This view of the agency charged with administering the statute is entitled to considerable deference; and to sustain it, we need not find that it is the only permissible construction that EPA might have adopted but only that EPA's understanding of this very "complex statute" is a sufficiently rational one to preclude a court from substituting its judgment for that of EPA. *Train* v. *NRDC*, 421 U.S. 60, 75, 87 (1975); see also *Chevron, U.S.A. Inc.* v. *NRDC*, 467 U.S. __ (1984). Of course, if Congress has clearly expressed an intent contrary to that of the Agency, our duty is to enforce the will of Congress.

A

NRDC insists that the language of § 301(*l*) is itself enough to require affirmance of the Court of Appeals, since on its face it forbids any modifications of the effluent limitations that EPA must promulgate for toxic pollutants. If the word "modify" in § 301(*l*) is read in its broadest sense, that is, to encompass any change or alteration in the standards, NRDC is correct. But it makes little sense to construe the section to forbid EPA to amend its own standards, even to correct an error or to impose stricter requirements. *** As NRDC does and must concede, § 301(*l*) cannot be read to forbid every change in the toxic waste standards. The

---

ances had been granted to direct dischargers and none had been granted to an indirect discharger.***

word "modify" thus has no plain meaning as used in § 301(*l*), and is the proper subject of construction by EPA and the courts. *** We should defer to [EPA's] view unless the legislative history or the purpose and structure of the statute clearly reveal a contrary intent on the part of Congress. NRDC submits that the legislative materials evinces such a contrary intent. We disagree.

B

The legislative history of § 301(*l*) is best understood in light of its evolution. The 1972 amendments to the Act added § 301(c), which allowed EPA to waive BAT and pretreatment requirements on a case-by-case basis when economic circumstances justified such a waiver. In 1977, the Senate proposed amending § 301(c) by prohibiting such waivers for toxic pollutants. At the same time, the Senate bill added what became § 301(g), which allowed waivers from BAT and pretreatment standards where such waivers would not impair water quality, but which like § 301(c), prohibited waivers for toxic pollutants. The bill did not contain § 301(*l*). That section was proposed by the Conference Committee, which also deleted the toxic pollutant prohibition in § 301(c) and redrafted § 301(g) to prohibit water quality waivers for conventional pollutants and thermal discharges as well as for toxic pollutants. While the Conference Committee Report did not explain the reason for proposing § 301(*l*), Representative Roberts, the House floor manager, stated:

> "Due to the nature of toxic pollutants, those identified for regulation will not be subject to waivers from or modification of the requirements prescribed under this section, *specifically, neither section 301(c) waivers based on the economic capability of the discharger nor 301(g) waivers based on water quality considerations shall be available."* Leg. Hist. 328-329 (emphasis added).

Another indication that Congress did not intend to forbid FDF waivers as well as § 301(c) and (g) modifications is its silence on the issue. Under NRDC's theory, the Conference Committee did not merely tinker with the wording of the Senate bill, but boldly moved to eliminate FDF variances. But if that was the Committee's intention, it is odd that the Committee did not communicate it to either House, for only a few months before we had construed the Act to permit the very FDF variance NRDC insists the Conference Committee was silently proposing to abolish. In *E.I. du Pont de Nemours & Co. v. Train,* 430 U. S. 112 (1977), we upheld EPA's class and category effluent limitations, relying on the availability of FDF waivers. Congress was undoubtedly aware of *du Pont,* and absent an expression of legislative will, we are reluctant to infer an intent to amend the Act so as to ignore the thrust of an important decision.

NRDC argues that Congress's discussion of the Act's provisions supports its position. Several legislators' comments seemed to equate "modifications" with "waivers" or "variances". Many of these statements, however, came in the specific context of discussing the "waiver" provisions of § 301(c) and (g), not the prohibition in § 301(*l*). ***

After examining the wording and legislative history of the statute, we agree with EPA and CMA that the legislative history itself does not evince an unambiguous congressional intention to forbid all FDF waivers with respect to toxic materials.

C

Neither are we convinced that FDF variances threaten to frustrate the goals and operation of the statutory scheme set up by Congress. The nature of FDF variances has been spelled out both by this Court and by the Agency itself. The regulation explains that its purpose is to remedy categories which were not accurately drawn because information was either not available to or not considered by the Administrator in setting the original categories and limitations. An FDF variance does not excuse compliance with a correct requirement, but instead represents an acknowledgement that not all relevant factors were taken sufficiently into account in framing that requirement originally, and that those relevant factors, properly considered, would have justified—indeed, required—the creation of a subcategory for the discharger in question. As we have recognized, the FDF variance is a laudable corrective mechanism, "an acknowledgment that the uniform . . . limitation was set without reference to the full range of current practices, to which the Administrator was to refer." *EPA* v. *National Crushed Stone Assn.*, 449 U. S. 64, 77-78 (1980). It is, essentially, not an exception to the standard-setting process, but rather a more fine-tuned application of it.

We are not persuaded by NRDC's argument that granting FDF variances is inconsistent with the goal of uniform effluent limitations under the Act. ***

NRDC concedes that EPA could promulgate rules under § 307 of the Act creating a subcategory for each source which is fundamentally different from the rest of the class under the factors the EPA must consider in drawing categories. The same result is produced by the issuance of an FDF variance for the same failure properly to subdivide a broad category. Since the dispute is therefore reduced to an argument over the means used by EPA to define subcategories of indirect dischargers in order to achieve the goals of the Act, this is a particularly persuasive case for deference to the Agency's interpretation.

NRDC argues, echoing the concern of the Court of Appeals below, that allowing FDF variances will render meaningless the § 301(*l*) prohibition against modifications on the basis of economic and water quality factors. That argument ignores the clear difference between the purpose of FDF waivers and that of § 301(c) and (g) modifications, a difference we explained in *National Crushed Stone*. A discharger that satisfies the requirements of § 301(c) qualifies for a variance "simply because [it] could not afford a compliance cost that is not fundamentally different from those the Administrator has already considered" in creating a category and setting an effluent limitation. 449 U.S., at 78. A § 301(c) modification forces "a displacement of calculations already performed, not because those calculations were incomplete or had unexpected effects, but only because the costs happened to fall on one particular operator, rather than on another who might be economically better off." *Ibid.* FDF

variances are specifically unavailable for the grounds that would justify the statutory modifications. Both a source's inability to pay the foreseen costs, grounds for a § 301(c) modification, and the lack of a significant impact on water quality, grounds for a § 301(g) modification, are irrelevant under FDF variance procedures.

EPA and CMA point out that the availability of FDF variances makes bearable the enormous burden faced by EPA in promulgating categories of sources and setting effluent limitations. Acting under stringent timetables, EPA must collect and analyze large amounts of technical information concerning complex industrial categories. Understandably, EPA may not be apprised of and will fail to consider unique factors applicable to atypical plants during the categorical rulemaking process, and it is thus important that EPA's nationally binding categorical pretreatment standards for indirect dischargers be tempered with the flexibility that the FDF variance mechanism offers, a mechanism repugnant to neither the goals nor the operation of the Act.

III

Viewed in its entirety, neither the language nor the legislative history of the Act demonstrates a clear Congressional intent to forbid EPA's sensible variance mechanism for tailoring the categories it promulgates. In the absence of Congressional directive to the contrary, we accept EPA's conclusion that § 301(*l*) does not prohibit FDF variances.***

*   *   *

The judgement of the Court of Appeals is reversed.

It is so ordered.

JUSTICE MARSHALL, with whom JUSTICE BLACKMUM and JUSTICE STEVENS join, and with whom JUSTICE O'CONNOR joins as to Parts I, II, and III, dissenting.

In this case, the Environmental Protection Agency (EPA) maintains that it may issue, on a case-by-case basis, individualized variances from the national standards that limit the discharge of toxic water pollutants. EPA asserts this power in the face of a provision of the Clean

Water Act that expressly withdraws from the agency the authority to "modify" the national standards for such pollutants. The Court today defers to EPA's interpretation of the Clean Water Act even though that interpretation is inconsistent with the clear intent of Congress, as evidenced by the statutory language, history, structure, and purpose. I had not read our cases to permit judicial deference to an agency's construction of a statute when the construction is inconsistent with the clear intent of Congress.

I

*   *   *

This case is not about whether exceptions are useful adjuncts to regulatory schemes of general applicability. That is a policy choice on which courts should defer to Congress in the first instance, and to the administrative agency in the absence of a clear congressional mandate. Here, Congress has made the policy choice. It has weighed competing goals and determined that, whatever the general merits of exceptions schemes, they are simply inappropriate in the context of the control of toxic water pollution. As a result, an exceptions scheme such as the one challenged here simply cannot stand.

II

I first consider EPA's argument that § 301(l) proscribes only those modifications otherwise authorized by § 301(c) and (g). *** This limited view of § 301(l)'s scope is clearly inconsistent with congressional intent; the plain meaning of the statute and its legislative history show a clear congressional intent to ban all "modifications."

*   *   *

B

*** [T]he legislative history demonstrates that Congress meant what it said, and it evidences a clear congressional intent to ban all "modifications." First, the legislative history firmly establishes that § 301(l) was enacted as part of a program to deal effectively and comprehensively with the problem of toxic pollutants, and that its prohibition was an integral

part of this program. Under any canon of statutory construction, the congressional purposes in enacting a provision would be deemed relevant to the question of the scope of that provision, but the Court simply fails to discuss this issue.

*   *   *

The primary purpose of the 1977 amendments was to strengthen the regulation "of the increasingly evident toxic hazard." The § 301(l) ban on "modifications" was an integral part of this effort to make the environment safe from toxics, and through it, Congress sought to prevent *any* weakening of the categorical standards for the control of toxic pollutants. It is clear that Congress knew full well what effects the rule might have on industry, and that it went forward nonetheless. ***

It is readily apparent that a complete ban on modifications would most directly and completely accomplish the congressional goal. EPA offers no evidence in the legislative history to explain why this goal would be promoted by banning the statutory modifications of § 301(c) and (g), but would not more effectively be advanced by banning other modifications as well. It points to no evidence that Congress singled out the § 301(c) and (g) modifications as more pernicious from the standpoint of an effective toxic control program than modifications based on other factors. In fact, the statutory scheme suggests that the converse is true, as Congress specifically provided for statutory exemptions in these areas but not in other areas.

In the case of § 301(c), Congress was aware that certain firms would be driven to bankruptcy if they were required to comply strictly with the categorical standards. Congress determined that avoiding bankruptcies was an important social goal, and one that was not automatically outweighed by the goal of protecting the environment. Section 301(c) reflects the tension between these two goals: As long as a firm can make reasonable pollution control progress, it will not be driven to bankruptcy by its inability to meet higher pollution control standards.

Similarly, in the case of § 301(g) water quality modifications, Congress decided not to force dischargers to meet standards higher than those that could be justified by legitimate environmental considerations. Thus, as long as a discharge did not interfere with the attainment of adequate water quality, a discharger would not be forced to expend additional resources in pollution control merely because a higher standard was "economically achievable." Cf. 1977 Leg. Hist. 326, 123 Cong. Rec. 38960 (1977) (Rep. Roberts).

If these two modifications are the only ones now prohibited, the result is wholly counterintuitive. EPA is in effect contending that economic and water quality factors present the most compelling case for modification of the standard in the nontoxic context—as they are explicitly authorized by statue—but the least compelling case for modification in the toxic context—as they are the only modifications prohibited by § 301(l). As might be expected, EPA does not present any theory, much less a logical argument, or evidence in the legislative history, to support this extremely inconsistent result.

Moreover, if Congress had not intended to prohibit all modifications, it would almost certainly either have defined explicitly the scope of permissible modifications, or given the agency some guidance on how to go about doing so. Only in this way would Congress have had any assurance that modifications would be allowed only when they promoted interests of sufficient importance to outweigh Congress's foremost goal of protecting the environment against toxic pollution.

*   *   *

D

The Court and EPA both attach great importance to the Congressional silence regarding FDF variances. EPA argues that *E.I. Du Pont de Nemours v. Train*, 430 U. S. 112 (1977), held that FDF variances are "appropriate." According to EPA, if Congress had intended to reverse this result it would have made its intention clear. This contention, which the Court finds persuasive, is based on a misunderstanding of what was at stake in *Du Pont*. That case did not authorize the issuance of variances in any context that is relevant here.

Du Pont involved a challenge to EPA's authority to issue, to direct dischargers, categorical effluent limitations for BPT and BAT. The Court had little difficulty in upholding such categorical limitations in the BAT context, as the statute provided that the limitations be set for "categories and classes" of dischargers, § 301(b)(1)(B). *See Du Pont, supra* at 127. In contrast, the statute provided that BPT limitations be set for "point sources." § 301(b)(1)(A). Several chemical manufacturers argued that, given this language, individualized BPT limitations were necessary, and that regulation by categories and classes of dischargers was inappropriate. This Court rejected the industry's challenge, holding that BPT limitations could be set by industry-wide regulation, so long as some allowance—such as FDF variances—was made for variations in individual plants. 430 U. S., at 128.

In support of its position that the Court broadly endorsed the issuance of FDF variances and that the Congressional silence is noteworthy, EPA cites as dispositive one sentence in the opinion, which reads:

> "We conclude that the statute authorizes the 1977 limitations [BPT] as well as the 1983 limitations [BAT] to be set by regulation, so long as some allowance is made for variations in individual plants, as EPA has done by including a variance clause in its 1977 limitations." *Id.*, at 128.

Only by taking this sentence out of context can one find support for the proposition that *Du Pont* requires FDF variances from BAT limitations, just as it does in the case of BPT limitations. When read in context, the sentence cited by EPA clearly means that BPT standards, like BAT standards, can be set by regulation, but if EPA does so in the BPT context, it must allow for variances. ***

Furthermore, the Court upheld the regulations challenged in *Du Pont* even though they did not contain an FDF variance clause for BAT limitations. If the sentence in question has the meaning that EPA now ascribes to it, the Court would presumably have had to reverse on that point.

*   *   *

*** We should scarcely attribute any significance to the legislative failure to discuss *Du Pont* because *Du Pont* considered a fundamentally different scheme of regulation. It may be that one day the Clean Water Act will be read to permit, for nontoxic pollutants, FDF variances from BAT and pretreatment standards; however, there is no reason why Congress should have said anything in 1977, when it enacted § 301(*l*), about a legal development that has not yet taken place, eight years later.

*   *   *

F

The determination that Congress clearly intended that § 301(*l*) do more than just ban modifications otherwise permitted by § 301(c) and (g) compels the conclusion that EPA's construction to the contrary cannot stand. As this Court has repeatedly stated,

> "The interpretation put on the statute by the agency charged with administering it is entitled to deference, but the courts are the final authorities on issues of statutory construction. They must reject administrative constructions of the statute, whether reached by adjudication or by rulemaking, that are inconsistent with the statutory mandate or that frustrate the policy that Congress sought to implement." *FEC v. Democratic Senatorial Campaign Committee*, 454 U. S. 27, 31-32 (1981) (citations omitted).

*   *   *

III

EPA's second construction of the statutory scheme is, on the surface, a more plausible one. EPA argues that FDF variances do not excuse compliance with the correct standards, but instead provide a means for setting more appropriate standards. It is clear that, pursuant to § 307(b)(2), EPA can "revise" the pretreatment standards, as long as it does so "following the procedure established. . .for the promulgation of such standards." The statute contemplates that the standards will be set and revised through notice-and-comment rulemaking and will be applicable to categories of sources. EPA argues that such a "revision," which is clearly not proscribed by § 301(*l*), would be substantively indistinguishable from an FDF variance. ***

To support its argument, EPA points out that the factors that may justify an FDF variance are the same factors that may be taken into account in setting and revising the national pretreatment standards. *** EPA acknowledges that the statute requires that the national pretreatment standards be established—and therefore revised—for "categories" of dischargers and not on a case-by-case basis. It argues, however, that nothing in the Clean Water Act precludes EPA from defining a subcategory that has only one discharger.

The logic of EPA's position is superficially powerful. If EPA can, through rulemaking, define a subcategory that includes only one discharger, why should it not be able to do so through a variance procedure? In fact, if rulemaking and the variance procedure were alternate means to the same end, I might have no quarrel with EPA's position, which the Court has accepted. ***

However, the agency's position does not withstand more than superficial analysis. An examination of the legislative history of the 1972 amendments to the Clean Water Act—the relevance of which both the Court and EPA ignore—reveals that Congress attached great *substantive* significance to the method used for establishing pollution control requirements.

The Conference Committee Report directed EPA to "make the determination of the economic impact of an effluent limitation on the basis of classes and categories of point sources, *as distinguished from a plant by plant determination.*" 1972 Leg. Hist. 304 (emphasis added). ***

*   *   *

The legislative history also makes clear why Congress found it so important that the standards be set for "categories" of dischargers, and not for individual dischargers. Congress intended to use the standard as a means to "force" the introduction of more effective pollution control technology. *** By requiring that the standards be set by reference to either the "average of the best" or very "best" technology, the Act seeks to foster technological innovation. ***

Unlike the statutory revision mechanism of § 307(b), FDF variances are set not by reference to a category of dischargers, but instead by reference to a single discharger. In evaluating an application for a variance, EPA does not look at the group of dischargers in the same position as the applicant, but instead focuses solely on the characteristics of the applicant itself. Under the FDF program, there is no mechanism for EPA to ascertain whether there are any other dischargers in that position. Moreover, there is no mechanism for EPA to group together similarly situated dischargers. Quite to the contrary, a scheme in which the initial screening may be done by the individual States, at times determined by when the variance application is filed, is unlikely to lead to the identification of new subcategories.

*   *   *

In the aggregate, if EPA defines a new pretreatment subcategory through rulemaking, the BAT-level pollution control requirement of each discharger would be determined by reference to the capability of the "best" performer. In contrast, if EPA provides individual variances to each plant in this group, only one discharger would have a requirement based on the capability of the best performer—the best performer itself. The others would necessarily be subject to less stringent standards.

*   *   *

It is true, of course, that even the statutory revision procedure might identify a subcategory with only one discharger. That procedure, however, will have established that this discharger is indeed uniquely situated. In contrast, an FDF variance sets an individual requirement even where there may be similarly situated dischargers.

In summary, whatever else FDF variances might do, they do not further the same congressional goals as the notice-and-comment rulemaking required for § 307(b) revisions. *Vermont Yankee* is simply inapposite; Congress intended, for substantive reasons, that the pretreatment standards be set and revised through rulemaking for categories of dischargers. The Court's conclusion to the contrary stems exclusively from its failure to consider why Congress chose to require categorical standards.

*   *   *

NOTES

1. Do you agree with this decision? Which opinion do you think is better reasoned — the majority by Justice White or the dissent by Justice Marshall?

2. Is it sensible to conclude that in enacting Section 301(*l*) Congress barred for toxics the only variances mentioned in the legislation, but not the implied FDF variance?

What, if anything, can be inferred from congressional silence as to the applicability of Section 301(*l*) to FDF variances when Congress had remained silent *on FDF variances themselves*?

Is it significant that EPA had not even provided for FDF variances from BAT limitations at the time the 1977 amendments were passed? (This extension beyond BPT was not made until 1978.) If it is significant, which way does it cut?

3. Is the majority persuasive that an FDF variance is substantively indistinguishable from a revision and subcategorization, particularly to create a subcategory of *one*?

4. Probably EPA's best argument was the "practical necessity" of providing for FDF variances. Wasn't this argument somewhat undercut, however, by the fact that only four FDF variances (even from BPT limitations) had been granted by 1984?

Perhaps the application of BAT limitations in 1984 will intensify the pressure for FDF variances; and, after EPA reinstates their availability in response to the Court's approval, perhaps we will see a greater number of applications granted. Remember that states, too, may grant FDF variances, subject to EPA approval.

5. How much does the majority decision turn on deference to EPA's construction of its statutory authority? Could EPA tire of the administrative headaches of passing on so many variance applications and adopt NRDC's position?

6. Are FDF variances available to direct as well as indirect dischargers?

7. Are FDF variances available to new sources? Indeed, is any sort of variance available from new source performance standards? When new source standards are set at the same levels as BAT and BCT, the only difference between the treatment of new and existing sources now may be the availability of variances.

8. Precisely what sorts of variances are available, for what sorts of pollutants, and to whom? Perhaps the statutory complexity yields much less than first meets the eye.

FDF variances would seem to be available to both direct and indirect dischargers, and from the full range of standards (BPT, BCT, and BAT) applicable to all types of pollutants (conventionals, toxics, and non-conventionals).

Water-quality-based variances under Section 301(g), on the other hand, are much less widely available. On the face of the statute, they are not applicable to toxic or conventional pollutants or to thermal discharge standards. This leaves only the relatively small range of pollutants that do not fall into these categories — what have come to be called "non-conventionals" (primarily ammonia, color, iron, chloride and nitrate).

Feasibility-based variances under Section 301(c) are similarly restricted. Looking only at the language of subsection (c), they would seem to be available for toxics as well as non-conventional pollutants (since both are referenced in subsection (b)(2)(A)). However, EPA has read Section 301(*l*) to bar 301(c) variances for toxics, this construction was approved by the Court in *Chemical Manufacturers*, and it would seem to be necessary in order to give Section 301(*l*) any substance. This variance provision, therefore, is also restricted to non-conventionals.

9. Are the variances provided by Sections 301(c) and 301(g) from BAT limitations for non-conventionals available to indirect dischargers as well as direct dischargers? A negative answer was given in *Koppers Co. v. EPA*, 23 ERC 1013 (3d Cir. 1985), in which the court adopted the reasoning employed by EPA Administrator Ruckelshaus in denying a request for a 301(g) variance by an indirect discharger (seemingly contrary to the impression indicated by the Supreme Court in footnote 9 to the *Chemical Manufacturers* decision).

Administrator Ruckelshaus's reasoning was that, by its terms, Section 301(g) authorized modifications only "with respect to the discharge of any [non-conventional] pollutant," and that "discharge of a pollutant" was defined in Section 502(12) only to include *direct* discharges by point sources into navigable waters. This limitation of Section 301(g) to direct dischargers Ruckelshaus found supported by his reading of Section 301(c). Noting that a modification under subsection (c) was available when a "permit application" was filed, the Administrator reasoned that, since Congress was aware that only direct dischargers were required to obtain permits, feasibility-based variances under Section 301(c) were likewise unavailable to indirect dischargers. This and other statutory construction, as well as legislative history and practical considerations, convinced Administrator Ruckelshaus, and apparently the Third Circuit, that Sections 301(c) and 301(g) were meant to be "companion" provisions, neither of which was available to indirect dischargers.

10. FDF variances, therefore, are now the only variances available to anyone — other than the very limited 301(c) and (g) variances for direct dischargers from BAT limitations for nonconventionals.

Isn't it amazing that just about the only meaningful variances remaining are those nowhere mentioned in the Clean Water Act?

6 NEW SOURCE STANDARDS OF PERFORMANCE

Senate Report (Public Works Committee) No. 92-414
Oct. 28, 1971 [To accompany S. 2770]

* * *

* * *

SECTION 306—NATIONAL STANDARDS OF PERFORMANCE

New sources of pollution in at least twenty-eight specified industries must be constructed to meet a standard that reflects the greatest degree of effluent reduction that can be achieved by use of the latest available control technology. If it is practicable, this could be a standard that permits no discharge of pollution. EPA must promulgate the best available technology standard for each industry.***

* * *

It should be noted that the Committee considered use of the phrase 'latest available control technology', but rejected it in favor of 'best available control technology.'

The Committee agreed that, although used in the Clean Air Act, the term 'latest' may not (as intended) be interpreted as the best. The Committee has substituted the word 'best' in this bill to make clear its intention.

As used in this section, the term 'available control technology' is intended to direct the Administrator to examine the degree of effluent reduction that has been or can be achieved through the application of technology which is available or normally can be made available. This does not mean that the technology must be in actual, routine use somewhere. Rather, it means that the technology must be available at a cost and at a time which the Administrator determines to be reasonable.

The implicit consideration of economic factors in determining whether technology is 'available' should not affect the usefulness of this section. The overriding purpose of this section would be to prevent new water pollution problems, and toward that end, maximum feasible control of new sources, at the time of their construction, is considered by the Committee to be the most effective and, in the long run, the least expensive approach to pollution control.

This section requires that the Administrator, within 90 days following enactment of this Act, publish a list of categories of industrial groups for which he will establish standards of performance.

EPA was further directed in Section 306 to propose national standards of performance for all new sources, within each category listed, within one year of enactment. Section 306(b)(1)(B). Final regulations were to be promulgated within 120 days following proposal of standards; such final regulations were to be effective immediately upon promulgation.

Factors to be considered in establishing new source standards generally parallel the considerations for Section 301 effluent limitations—the costs of installing control systems and the capabilities of available technologies.

At this point you should read Section 306. (It's short.)

American Iron and Steel Institute
v.
Environmental Protection Agency

526 F.2d 1027 (3d Cir. 1975)

Before ADAMS, HUNTER and GARTH, Circuit Judges.

JAMES HUNTER, III, Circuit Judge:

This is a petition brought by the American Iron and Steel Institute and several individual steel companies to review regulations promulgated by the Administrator of the Environmental Protection Agency on June 28, 1974. In these regulations, entitled "Effluent Guidelines and Standards, Iron and Steel Manufacturing Point Source Category," the Administrator established nationwide single number effluent limitations for point sources in the iron and steel industry engaged in "primary" (or basic manufacturing) operations.***

*   *   *

Thus far, we have been addressing petitioners' various contentions pertaining to the Administrator's promulgation of regulations for existing point sources under sections 301 and 304 of the Act. In this section we shall consider petitioners' challenge to the Administrator's interpretation of his power to promulgate effluent limitations for new point sources under section 306.***

The Act refers to three distinct levels of technology which must be attained. For existing sources, the standard to be applicable in 1977 is the "best practicable control technology currently available," or "BPCTCA." The 1983 standard for existing sources is the "best available technology economically achievable," or "BATEA." The standard applicable to new sources is the "best available demonstrated control technology," or "BADCT." It is unquestioned that the 1977 "BPCTCA" is the least stringent of the three. The dispute focuses on the relative degree of stringency between the 1983 "BATEA" standards and the new source "BADCT" standards. The Administrator took the view that these two standards were essentially similar. In his establishment of

"BADCT" standards, he merely incorporated by reference the relevant "BATEA" standards. The only independent analysis he conducted in defining "BADCT" levels was to determine as required by section 306, whether a "zero discharge" level was "practicable." Since he determined in each case that a "zero discharge" level for new sources was not practicable, he merely adopted the "BATEA" standards. Petitioners, however, contend that the new source standards should be less stringent than the 1983 "BATEA" standards, since the Act requires that the new source standards be "demonstrated" and that they be achievable now rather than by 1983.

We reject petitioners' contention that it was necessarily error for the Administrator to equate the two standards. While it is true that the new source standards, unlike the 1983 standards for existing sources, must be based on technology whose present availability is "demonstrated," it is clear that Congress did not intend by that phrase to limit the technology to that which is widely in use. As the House Report stated:

"It will be sufficient, for the purpose of setting the level of control under available technology, that there be one operating facility which demonstrates that the level can be achieved or that there is sufficient information and data from a relevant pilot plant or semi-work plant to provide the needed economic and technical justification for such new source."

Furthermore, Congress was clearly appreciative of the fact that the most effective and least expensive approach to water pollution would be to prevent new water pollution problems by requiring "maximum feasible control of new sources, at the time of their construction." Thus, Congress recognized that new sources could attain discharge levels more easily and at less cost than existing sources which must be retrofitted.***This awareness of the lower costs that would be incurred by new sources led Congress to require that less weight be given to costs under section 306 than under section 304.***

In sum, given Congress' clearly expressed belief that it would be easier for new sources to attain a particular level of effluent control than it would be for existing sources, and given the fact that the Administrator was permitted to rely on pilot projects (or "transfer technology") to determine whether a particular standard was "demonstrated," we do not believe that it was arbitrary or an abuse of discretion for the Administrator to equate the "BADCT" levels for new sources with the "BATEA" levels for existing sources. The fact that Congress anticipated that new sources could achieve particular effluent limitations more easily than existing sources points in the direction of *greater* stringency for new source standards and counterbalances somewhat the requirement that technology for new sources be "demonstrated"–a requirement which, as we have seen, can be met through reliance on pilot projects. We thus conclude that it was not necessary for the Administrator to conduct a separate study of technology for new sources and that he acted within the permissible scope of his discretion in relying on the portions of the Final Development Document which discuss the "BATEA" standards. Rather than invalidate the section 306 limitations totally, we believe it is more appropriate to examine each one being challenged to determine whether the record supports the Administrator's conclusion that the standard has been "demonstrated."

Petitioners also contend that the Administrator failed to consider factors which section 306 required him to consider in establishing new source standards.***Petitioners contend that the Administrator failed "to make the requisite cost/benefit analysis." However, no cost/benefit analysis is required under section 306. Rather, the Administrator is required only to take costs "into consideration." This language is virtually identical to that appearing in section (b)(2)(B), which requires the Administrator to take costs "into account" in assessing "BATEA" levels and which is distinct from the limited cost/benefit analysis required in section 304(b)(1)(B). Furthermore***cost was to be given even less weight under section 306 than for existing sources.

*   *   *

1. *Flow Rates.*—Petitioners first challenge the 100 gallon per ton flow rate for new by-product coke plants. As noted previously, we are satisfied that the Administrator did not act arbitrarily and capriciously in using a 175 gallon per ton flow rate for 1977 "BPCTCA" limitations in the by-product coke subcategory. However, we agree with petitioners that a 100 gallon per ton flow rate has not been "demonstrated." None of the sampled plants achieved such a flow rate, and the Administrator has not pointed to any transfer technology indicating that such a flow rate is achievable for by-product coke. The Administrator instead relies on the Koppers Report, claiming that the Report's recommendation supports a 100 gallon per ton rate. The Koppers Report, however, merely makes a recommendation, and even that is for a 300 gallon per ton rate. Even if the Administrator is correct in saying that a 1:1 dilution is not necessary and that certain effluents were improperly included in the Koppers Report, we do not believe that the "recommendation" there can satisfy the requirement in section 306 that the technology be "demonstrated." We see no evidence in the record that an actual plant—pilot project or otherwise—has achieved a 100 gallon per ton flow rate. Thus, the new source standards for by-product coke should be reconsidered in light of a new and "demonstrated" flow rate.

*   *   *

NOTES

1. Compare the consideration required to be given to costs and the "demonstration" of the "availability" of the control technology necessary to satisify the terms of section 306 with the manner in which costs and availability are treated in setting BPT and BAT limitations under sections 301 and 304. *See Association of Pacific Fisheries v. EPA*, and notes following, pages 27-37 of this text *supra*.

2. Do you see any significant difference in the acceptable ways for EPA to demonstrate "availability" in promulgating new source standards and the means of showing the availability required in setting BPT and BAT limitations? Do actual existing plants with the desired pollution control equipment in place have to be located in setting any of the three standards? Are "pilot projects" and "transfer technology" enough for EPA to rely upon in promulgating all three?

3. If EPA does demonstrate availability through a pilot project, what if commercial-scale plants which install the technology specified are unable to meet the effluent limitations in the standard? Is this a defense to an enforcement action? Would it entitle a plant to a variance?

4. By now it seems well established that no cost/benefit analysis need be made in setting BAT or new source standards. *See CPC International, Inc. v. Train*, 540 F.2d 1329 (8th Cir. 1976). But how much discretion does EPA have in considering costs? Might it employ cost/benefit analysis if it so desires, and set the standards at the point at which benefits clearly exceed costs?

May EPA set new source standards more stringent than BAT — to the extent of imposing so much greater costs on new plants than existing ones that modernization of an industry is discouraged? May it set more stringent BAT standards? If it were to do so, would this not produce some anomalous results after July, 1984?

5. Such considerations have caused EPA usually to set new source and BAT standards at the same levels. Industry petitioners, however, have occasionally objected to this practice, arguing that plants built before 1984 should not have to install systems that achieve BAT performance levels. Consider the scheme that was set up by Congress:

(1) A plant built before the effective date of applicable new source standards must have met BPT limitations by 1977, unless excused until 1979.

(2) A new source built, for example, in 1977 must have met any Section 306 performance standards that were proposed before construction commenced — that is, best available demonstrated technology. Once compliance with those standards is achieved, no more stringent standard may be imposed on the plant for a ten-year grace period (extending in the example to 1987), excepting pollutants not regulated by new source standards but later regulated under Section 301 (BAT).

(3) The existing plant described in (1) above, which presumably achieved BPT compliance by 1979, must upgrade its control to comply with best available technology by 1984.

(4) Meanwhile, the clock is running on the ten-year grace period for the new source described in paragraph (2), which must achieve compliance with BAT, including timely-revised BAT limitations, by the end of the grace period (in the example, 1987).

The best technology *available* for 1984 applications (Section 301) may be more advanced and, therefore, more stringent and perhaps more costly, than the best technology *demonstrated* earlier when 306 standards were promulgated. Did Congress intend to allow new sources to install less effective controls before 1984 than existing sources must install by 1984?

How could a practice allowing new sources to install less effective controls be reconciled with Congress' observations that new plants could install more effective controls at lower costs?

National Renderers Association
v.
Environmental Protection Agency

541 F.2d 1281 (8th Cir. 1976)

Before GIBSON, Chief Judge, and HEANEY and WEBSTER, Circuit Judges.

HEANEY, Circuit Judge.

*   *   *

THE RELATIONSHIP BETWEEN NEW SOURCE AND 1983 STANDARDS

There is an additional important problem with respect to the new source standards. Unlike some other standards promulgated by the EPA, *see, e. g.,* wet corn milling standards discussed in *CPC I,* the new source standards permit higher levels of effluent than do the 1983 existing guidelines, notwithstanding the fact that the best available effluent control technology would appear to permit achievement of the 1983 standards in new plants. There is no explanation for this anomaly in the briefs, and counsel for the EPA was unable to give a rational reason for it at oral argument. The standards would thus appear on their face to be inconsistent with Congressional intent that new sources employ the most advanced current technology:

> The standards of performance for new sources of water pollution would require the achievement of the greatest degree of pollution reduction that can be achieved through the application of best available effluent control technology.***Such a maximum use of available means to prevent and control water pollution is essential to the prevention of new pollution problems and the eventual attainment of the goal of no discharge.

*   *   *

The *overriding* purpose of this section would be to prevent new water pollution problems, and towards that end, maximum feasible control of new sources, at the time of their construction, is considered by the Committee to be the most effective and, in the long run, the least expensive approach to pollution control.

A Legislative History of the Water Pollution Control Act Amendments of 1972, 93rd Cong., 1st Sess. (Comm. Print 1973) at 1475—1476 [Emphasis added.]

The House Public Works Committee was similarly emphatic:

> In section 306, the Committee recognizes two of the most significant factors in the attainment of clean water. These factors are (1) the need to preclude the construction of new sources or the modification of existing sources which use less than the best available control technology for the reduction or elimination of the discharge of pollutants and (2) the recognition of the significantly lower expense of attaining a given level of effluent control in a new facility as compared to the future cost of retrofitting an existing facility to meet stringent water pollution control measures.

*   *   *

> New sources [that] discharge pollutants *** *must* be constructed to meet a standard of performance that reflects the *greatest* degree of effluent reduction that can be achieved by use of the best available demonstrated control technology, processes, or operating methods for that category of sources, and for class, types, and sizes within categories of new sources. If it is practicable, a new source performance standard could prohibit any discharge of pollutants.

Id. at 797-798 [Emphasis added.].

We could speculate from the record and from the arguments that had been advanced that the new source standards were set at lower levels because the EPA felt that the cost of including the technology necessary to meet the 1983 standard would be so high that no new plants would be built. If this is the reason, then the EPA should say so forthrightly. If this is not the reason, the real reason should be given and justification should be set forth in the record.

We do not suggest that the new source standards should be the same as the 1983 standards. We suggest only that the matter be thoroughly reviewed on remand. In this connection, the EPA may, because of the unique nature of this industry, find it necessary to develop variable standards based on geography and/or plant size. Standards based on these criteria might do more towards meeting the congressional goals than the present standards which simply exempts small plants from all federal effluent controls. We have no desire to limit the choices available to the EPA; we intend only to encourage it to make the choices which will best effectuate congressional intent and to explicate fully its reasons for so doing. ***

*   *   *

NOTES

Whether a source is "new" depends upon two events: commencement of construction of a source, and proposal of new source performance standards by EPA. If construction of a plant commences after proposal but before promulgation of final standards, the plant is a "new source" for purposes of applying those standards.

Bear in mind that EPA may propose standards for different pollutants at different times; thus a "new source" for purposes of controlling one pollutant may only have to meet BPT limitations for those pollutants for which new source standards had not been proposed as of the date of first construction.

What happens when EPA proposes a new source standard but fails to promulgate the standard as final within the statutory 120-day period? Is a source "new" if it started construction after proposal? Should the proposal be set aside or re-proposed?

Pennsylvania v. Environmental Protection Agency

618 F.2d 99L (3d Cir. 1980)

Before: GIBBONS, HIGGINBOTHAM and SLOVITER, *Circuit Judges*

*   *   *

OPINION ON REHEARING

GIBBONS, *Circuit Judge*

The petitioner and the respondent in this action seeking review of an order of the Environmental Protection Agency (EPA) have jointly petitioned for rehearing by the original panel.*** The petitioner and the respondent have called to our attention the fact that in No. 79-1466 petitioners also challenged the definition of "new source" coal mines contained in the regulations as promulgated.***

The contested regulation was promulgated on the authority of section 306 of the Act. 33 U.S.C. § 1316, which defines a new source as:

any source, the construction of which is commenced after the publication of proposed regulations prescribing a standard of performance under this section which will be applicable to such source, if such standard is thereafter promulgated in accordance with this section.

Id. § 1316(a)(2). In the promulgated standard, however, the EPA noted that promulgation of the regulations was delayed for more that one hundred twenty days after publication of proposed regulations because the agency needed additional time to address the substantial number of comments received on its proposal. It therefore made the effective date of the new source regulations the date of promulgation rather than the date of proposal.***

The Act provides that when the Administrator designates a category of sources, here coal mines, as subject to section 306, then "[a]s soon as practicable, but in no case more than one year" thereafter he "shall propose and publish regulations establishing Federal standards of performance for new sources within such category," 33 U.S.C. § 1316(b)(1)(B). "After considering . . . comments, he shall promulgate, within one hundred and twenty days after publication of such proposed regulations, such standards with such adjustments as he deems appropriate." *Id.* The quoted time limits are couched in mandatory language. The same subsection states that "[s]tandards of performance, or revisions thereof, shall become effective upon promulgation." *Id.*

Petitioners urge that the effective date provision in section 306 (b)(1)(B) must be read together with the new source definition in section 306 (a)(2) quoted above: that is, the regulations apply upon promulgation to all new sources constructed after the standards are proposed. Otherwise, they argue, the mandatory time limits in section 306 (b)(1)(B) will be easily circumvented. Thus, they urge, the EPA cannot rely on its own foot dragging as a reason for avoiding application of the promulgated standards to new sources constructed between the date of proposal and the date of promulgation. EPA, on the other hand, contends that taking into account its budgetary restraints and the technical subject matter with which it deals, we should read the deadlines and effective date provision in section 306 as directory only. Otherwise,

EPA suggests, it will merely avoid the deadlines and the effective date provision by reproposing and repromulgating standards.***

We start our analysis with the plain language of the statute. Section 306 requires that once a category of sources has been identified by the Administrator as subject to the section, regulations governing new sources within that category must be proposed within one year. In equally mandatory terms, the section requires promulgation of the regulations within one hundred and twenty days after proposal and defines a "new source" as one the construction of which was commenced after proposal of regulations, "if such [regulations are] thereafter promulgated in accordance with this section." 33 U.S.C. § 1316(a)(2). Seizing upon this quoted provision, EPA argues that its failure to promulgate within one hundred and twenty days is a failure to promulgate in accordance with the section which renders the statutory new source definition inapplicable. The legislative history of the Act reveals that the original Senate bill defined new sources solely with reference to the date of proposal of the regulations.***

                    *   *   *

Although the legislative history is inconclusive, the time limit appears to serve a dual purpose. It advances the public interest in a prompt abatement of polluting discharges. It also serves to limit the period during which businesses contemplating construction, put on notice by a proposal for a standard, are left in a state of uncertainty with respect to final agency action. Congress said, in effect, that it is not unreasonable, once a business has been put on notice of a proposed standard affecting it, for that business to pattern its conduct for four months to the likely application of the standard. We reject the government's suggestion that it can postpone indefinitely the period of uncertainty by the expedient of periodic reproposal.

Assuming such a congressional purpose for the one hundred and twenty day provision in section 306, the next question is the consequence of EPA failure to meet that deadline. There are several alternative possibilities. That espoused by EPA here is the recognition of its power to disregard entirely the provision in section 306 defining new sources as those constructed after proposal of standards, and to apply the standards only to post-promulgation construction. The effect of such recognition, however, is to place possibly competing businesses, equally on notice of a proposed standard, in different positions because one took a chance on starting construction in the meantime while the other did not. Such a policy would conflict with***the Supreme Court's indication that escape from the standards of section 306 should be minimized. *See E.I. du Pont de Nemours & Co. v. Train.* 430 U.S. 112, 137-39 (1977) (holding that Congress intended that no new source may be granted a variance from § 306 standards). A second possibility is to hold that the one hundred and twenty day provision in section 306(b)(1)(B) shall be read into the new source definition in section 306(a)(2). This would mean that if promulgation were delayed for more than one hundred and twenty days the standard would apply only to new construction commenced in the last one hundred twenty days before promulgation. While that construction would give some effect to the congressional intention to make standards applicable to those businesses which go forward in the face of notice of the proposed regulation, it would, like the EPA construction of section 306, draw an arbitrary line between businesses, equally on notice, on the basis of when they took the chance of starting construction. Neither of these constructions seems consistent with the public interest in maximizing elimination of sources of pollution. Neither, moreover, is consistent with the policy we recognized in *AISI I* and *AISI II* of preventing the exemption from coverage of the Act of a group of businesses, that should have been included, to the disadvantage of their competitors. The third construction, that espoused by petitioners, is that section 306 means what it says; that the proposal of new source standards puts the world on notice, and that the regulations, whenever promulgated,

apply to all who have been put on notice.

We conclude that this last construction is the only one consistent with the basic policies of the Act. It is not at all unfair, because businesses contemplating new construction which may be covered by the proposed standards are put on notice.[1] EPA acknowledges, it is true, that its record of compliance with the one hundred and twenty day limitation is less than perfect. Thus some businesses may, because of agency inaction, be left in a state of uncertainty for a time longer than Congress contemplated. But those businesses are not without remedy. They can resort to the district court under the citizens' suit provisions of section 505 of the Act to compel agency compliance with the spirit if not with the letter of the section 306 time limits.***Given the availability of that remedy we see no reason for construing section 306 in a manner which distorts its plain meaning. That plain meaning is that promulgated new source standards apply to construction commenced after publication of proposed regulations. If the agency fails to meet the one hundred and twenty day time limit, the remedy is a section 505 suit in the district court to compel prompt agency action.

The petition for review in No. 79-1466, insofar as it challenges that provision in the new source standards for coal mines making them effective only as to construction commenced after the date of promulgation rather than after the date of proposal will be granted, and the case remanded to EPA for modification of the promulgated regulations in accordance with this opinion. In all other respects the petition for review will be denied for the reasons set forth in our prior opinion.

---

[1] We reserve judgment on the issue, not presented in the instant case, of the proper interpretation of the Act in circumstances involving the combination of a substantial time deviation and a substantial change in the substance of the regulations between the dates of proposal and of promulgation.

7 TOXIC POLLUTANTS

Environmental Defense Fund, Inc. v. Environmental Protection Agency

598 F.2d 62 (D.C. Cir. 1978)

Before TAMM and ROBINSON, Circuit Judges, and CHARLES R. RICHEY, District Judge.

TAMM, Circuit Judge:

We are called upon in these consolidated cases to review challenges to the Environmental Protection Agency's (EPA) first regulations prohibiting discharge into the nation's waterways of a toxic substance polychlorinated biphenyls (PCBs), under the Federal Water Pollution Control Act Amendments.[1] For the reasons that follow, we uphold the EPA's regulations.

I. FACTS AND PRIOR PROCEEDINGS

A. *Factual Background on PCBs*

PCBs are a group of related chlorinated hydrocarbon chemicals useful in several industrial processes and toxic to a wide variety of organisms, including man. The chemistry of PCBs figures prominently in this case and will be discussed below. At this point, we need note only that PCBs fall into two chemical categories: PCBs with a low chlorine content (less chlorinated PCBs) and PCBs with a high chlorine content (more chlorinated PCBs). More chlorinated PCBs have been manufactured and used since 1929. For decades, they served in a variety of industrial uses such as ink solvents, plasticizers, adhesives, and textile coatings, but their principal use was and is in electrical equipment. PCBs are nonflammable liquids that are highly resistant to electrical current. Therefore, they have been widely used to fill electrical devices such as capacitors and transformers, aiding in the storage of electrical charge without creating the fire hazard that would occur if a flammable filler were used.

---

[1]Section 307(a) of the Federal Water Pollution Control Act Amendments of 1972, 33 U.S.C. §1317(a) (1976), provides as follows:

(1) The Administrator shall, within ninety days after October 18, 1972, publish (and from time to time thereafter revise) a list which includes any toxic pollutant or combination of such pollutants for which an effluent standard (which may include a prohibition of the discharge of such pollutants or combination of such pollutants) will be established under this section. The Administrator in publishing such list shall take into account the toxicity of the pollutant, its persistence, degradability, the usual or potential presence of the affected organisms in any waters, the importance of the affected organisms and the nature and extent of the effect of the toxic pollutant on such organisms.

(2) Within one hundred and eighty days after the date of publication of any list, or revision thereof, containing toxic pollutants or combination of pollutants under paragraph (1) of the subsection, the Administrator, in accordance with section 553 of Title 5, shall publish a proposed effluent standard (or a prohibition) for such pollutant or combination of pollutants, which shall take into account the toxicity of the pollutant, its persistence, degradability, the use or potential presence of the affected organisms in any waters, the importance of the affected organisms and the nature and extent of the effect of the toxic pollutant on such organisms, and he shall publish a notice for a public hearing on such proposed standard to be held within thirty days. As soon as possible after such hearing, but not later than six months after publication of the proposed effluent standard (or prohibition), unless the Administrator finds, on the record, that a modification of such proposed standard (or prohibition) is justi-

fied based upon a preponderance of evidence adduced at such hearings, such standard (or prohibition) shall be promulgated.

    *   *   *

(4) Any effluent standard promulgated under this section shall be at that level which the Administrator determines provides an ample margin of safety.

(5) When proposing or promulgating any effluent standard (or prohibition) under this section, the Administrator shall designate the category or categories of sources to which the effluent standard (or prohibition) shall apply.***

    *   *   *

This section was amended by section 53 of the Clean Water Act of 1977, 33 U.S.C.A. § 1317(a) (1977).

Awareness of the danger from PCBs to the environment and to man was slow to develop. Although large quantities of PCBs were manufactured and leaked into the environment, the PCBs detected in the environment were long mistaken for pesticide residues, which they resemble chemically. It was not until the mid-1960's that the presence of PCBs in the environment and the harm they inflict were recognized and distinguished from the pesticide problem. As we shall discuss below, it became apparent from scientific studies that more chlorinated PCBs built up to dangerous levels in the sediments of waterways, in the water, in fish, and ultimately in humans, creating a serious risk of death for aquatic organisms and disease (particularly cancer) for man.

In 1971-72, in response to public and government pressure, PCBs manufacturers and users took initial steps to reduce the PCBs danger. Manufacture was shifted from the more chlorinated PCBs to the less chlorinated PCBs because it was hoped that less chlorinated PCBs were less dangerous. PCBs use was limited to closed electrical equipment, where the need was greatest and the leakage was least. Some effort was made to control discharge of PCBs into waterways.

*   *   *

Developments in the early and mid-1970's heightened the public concern about PCBs and resulted in new regulatory efforts in late 1975 and early 1976. Monitoring of residues in fish revealed that in industrial discharges of PCBs were rendering fish in many waterways unhealthy for human consumption.[7] This monitoring culminated in a state proceeding. General Electric Co., 6 Envir. I., Rep. (Envir. Law Inst.) 30007 (1976), in which New York's Department of Environmental Conservation found that discharges of PCBs by General Electric, a major manufacturer of electrical equipment containing PCBs, had rendered most upper Hudson River fish dangerous to eat. Similar situations threatened the fishing industry in the Great Lakes and elsewhere.

*   *   *

Following the 1975 renewal of EPA's regulatory effort, further information accumulated with respect to the health hazards posed by PCB. Morever, substitutes for PCBs were developed in this country and in Japan that would serve adequately in electrical equipment without creating a fire hazard. Congress became impatient and wrote a special provision devoted solely to PCBs into the Toxic Substances Control Act of 1976, 15 U.S.C. §§ 2601-2629 (1976). See section 6(e), 15 U.S.C. § 2605(e) (1976). Considering that there are few statutes aimed so particularly at control of an individual chemical, we construe this provision as a significant comment on the failure of existing regulatory mechanisms. Failure of existing regulatory mechanisms to control PCBs contributed materially both to passage of the preventive sections of the Toxic Substances Control Act and to strengthening, in 1977, of the toxics provision of Federal Water Pollution Control Act Amendments of 1972. See 33 U.S.C.A. § 1317 (a) (1977).

Further, the failures in initial efforts at controlling PCBs were a major factor in new administrative initiatives.***

B. *PCBs Proceedings.*

***In sum, the history of EPA's PCBs proceedings is a history of frustration of a congressional mandate for action. Regulatory steps that Congress expected to take little more than one year took four years.

---

[7]PCBs discharged into the waterways by manufacturers of PCBs and electrical equipment constitute only a small part of the total discharge and emission of PCBs into the environment. It is estimated that about ten million pounds of PCBs enter the environment yearly, mainly through vaporization, leaks, and spills. See Comment, supra note 3, 6 ENVIR. I., REP. (ENVIR. LAW INST.) at 10057. It is estimated that about ten thousand pounds of PCBs are discharged yearly into the nation's waterways by manufacturers of PCBs and electrical equipment, with direct discharges accounting for less than one-third of this amount. 41 Fed. Reg. 30469 (1976): App. I 28. However, such discharges have greater significance than their small part of the total would suggest, because these discharges occur at fixed geographic points in concentrated form supplementing previous discharges, whereas other types of PCBs leakage into the environment occur from nonpoint sources in diffuse form. For example, the facility involved in the General Electric case created a health hazard by discharging little more than two pounds of PCBs per day at the time of suit, *General Electric Co.*, 6 ENVIR. L, REP (ENVIR. LAW INST.) 30007, 30010 (1976).

On October 18, 1972, Congress enacted the Federal Water Pollution Control Act Amendments of 1972. The 1972 Act prescribed a rigid schedule for promulgation of effluent standards for toxic substances. Section 307 (a), 33 U.S.C. § 1317(a) (1976), directed EPA to publish a list of toxic substances within ninety days, propose effluent standards for the listed substances within 180 days after listing, and promulgate final effluent standards within six months after the proposed standards. Thus, EPA was to promulgate toxic effluent regulations by early 1974.

In May 1973, after EPA failed to meet its first deadline, the Natural Resources Defense Council, Inc. (NRDC) sued EPA to hasten EPA action and bring about publication of a toxic substances list. This suit ended in a consent decree in June 1973, fixing a timetable for EPA. Pursuant to this timetable EPA issued, in July 1973, a proposed list of nine toxic substances, including PCBs, and, in September 1973, a final list of the same nine substances. In December 1973, EPA proposed standards for the nine substances. In April and May 1974, EPA held an evidentiary hearing on the proposed standards in which numerous objecting parties participated.

However, after the hearing, EPA failed to promulgate final standards for any of the nine substances. There were several causes for this failure. EPA contended that it lacked sufficient data to set regulations that would survive judicial review. Congressmen later expressed their belief that the procedures employed by EPA substantially impeded effective regulation due to their excessive complexity and formality.***

EPA's failure to promulgate any toxic standards triggered a wave of suits by environmental groups seeking to compel EPA to promulgate regulations for PCBs and other toxic substances. Before those suits could be resolved, EPA developed a new approach to toxics regulation, and negotiated a consent degree with the environmental groups that was accepted, with modifications, in June 1976, by the United States District Court for the District of Columbia. *NRDC v. Train*, 8 ERC (BNA) 2120, 2122 (1976) ("Flannery decree"), *rev'd in part on other*

grounds sub nom. NRDC v. Costle, 561 F.2d 904 (D.C. Cir. 1977). EPA's new approach had two elements. First, EPA committed itself to controlling toxic substances under provisions of the 1972 Act other than section 307(a), chiefly sections 301 and 304, which allowed EPA to regulate on an industry-by-industry basis using informal rulemaking proceedings and feasibility criteria. Second, EPA committed itself to make at least limited use of section 307(a): it would regulate some substances, including PCBs, under the provision; and it would use the provision to limit or prohibit discharges of hazardous substances for some or all industrial categories as a supplement to its industry-by-industry approach.

Following the failure in 1974 of its initial regulatory efforts, and consistent with the regulatory program and consent decree eventually adopted, EPA set out in 1975 to investigate PCBs more thoroughly.***

Based on these preparations, EPA proposed effluent standards for PCBs discharges on July 14, 1976. The proposed standards allowed on the average no more than one part per billion of PCBs in certain discharges by manufacturers of electrical equipment, and prohibited any PCBs in other discharges by manufacturers of electrical equipment and in all discharges by manufacturers of PCBs. The proposed regulations made no distinction between more chlorinated PCBs and less chlorinated PCBs. *See* 41 Fed. Reg. 30476-77 (1976).

On August 20, EPA commenced a formal rulemaking hearing before an administrative law judge on the proposed PCBs standards, which was concluded on November 30 after twenty-one days of testimony.*** At the close of the hearing, the record was furnished to the EPA Administrator (Administrator) for his consideration.

In January 1977, the Administrator filed his final decision on PCBs standards with the EPA hearing clerk, and, on February 2, 1977, published the standards. The final standards were more stringent than the proposed standards in that they prohibited any PCBs in discharges of manufacturers of electrical equipment.

*   *   *

II. STATUTORY FRAMEWORK

*   *   *

The Supreme Court and this court have previously reviewed industrial source effluent regulations. However, no court has previously reviewed toxic pollutant effluent regulations adopted pursuant to section 307(a). The toxics standards provision of the 1972 Act, section 307 (a), poses a number of difficult interpretive problems. Fortunately, we have some aids in interpreting this section, including both a prior and a subsequent legislative enactment. Prior to the 1972 Act, Congress passed the Clean Air Act Amendments of 1970, containing a hazardous air pollutant provision that bears a marked resemblance to the toxics provision. Subsequent to the 1972 Act, Congress amended the toxics provision in the Clean Water Act of 1977.***

Prior to 1972, there was no special provision in the federal water pollution laws to cope with toxic pollutants. As the number and amount of chemicals discharged into the nation's waterways increased in recent decades, it became apparent that some groups of chemicals posed a special danger to public health and the environment. There were two leading examples of such groups: chlorinated hydrocarbons, a group that included both pesticides (such as DDT, endrin, and toxaphene) and industrial chemicals (such as PCBs); and heavy metals, a group that included cadmium, mercury, and others.

Toxic substances, such as these, create a special danger in several ways. As demonstrated by a number of disasters involving widespread human poisoning or massive kills or contamination of fish, shellfish, birds, and other wildlife, many chemicals discharged into waters are lethal or injurious even in minute doses.[31] Toxic chemicals have been identified repeatedly as a cause of cancer, through studies both of persons exposed to such chemicals on the job and elsewhere, and of animals in the laboratory and the field. Moreover, toxic substances often have characteristics besides toxicity that magnify

their danger. These characteristics include (1) physical and chemical factors such as resistance to detoxification by sunlight and water, and mobility in the air and water; and (2) biological factors, such as tendencies not to be safely degraded by organisms, but rather to accumulate in organisms or to degrade into other toxic substances. Finally, a most troubling characteristic of toxic substances is how little they are understood by scientists. New discoveries about their nature and effects are made constantly, but existing knowledge seems inadequate to measure their full danger.

Congress's response to the toxics problem was section 307 of the 1972 Act. Other interlocking sections gave prominence to section 307. Section 101 (a)(3) of the Act, 33 U.S.C. § 1251 (a)(3) (1976), stated that "it is the national policy that the discharge of toxic pollutants in toxic amounts be prohibited." Section 502 (13), 33 U.S.C. § 1362(13) (1976), gave a broad definition[34] to "toxic pollutant," drawing on the wide array of direct and indirect effects of such substances.*** The 1977 amendments to the Act continued this highlighting tendency, by declaring that toxic pollutant standards are not subject to individual waiver or modification as are other standards.

Section 307(a) sets forth the substantive considerations and procedures for EPA to use in formulating toxics standards. In the substantive provisions, section 307(a) (2) requires EPA to "take into account" six factors that were intended to cover comprehensively the effects of toxic substances in the environment. Section

---

[31]Perhaps the most famous and horrifying disaster was the poisoning of hundreds of people in Japan by PCBs in 1968, which figured prominently in debate over the adequacy of environmental legislation and regulation. *See* Star, note 11 *supra*, I HARV. E.L. REV. at 561-62.

---

[34]Section 502(13), 33 U.S.C. § 1362(13) (1976) provides:

The term "toxic pollutant" means those pollutants, or combinations of pollutants, including disease-causing agents, which after discharge and upon exposure, ingestion, inhalation or assimilation into any organism, either directly from the environment or indirectly by ingestion through food chains, will, on the basis of information available to the Administrator, cause death, disease, behavorial abnormalities, cancer, genetic mutations, physiological malfunctions (including malfunctions in reproduction) or physical deformations, in such organisms or their offspring.

*   *   *

307(a)(5) allows EPA to set different standards for industrial categories using different processes. Section 307 (a)(4) directs EPA to set the standards at a level that provides "an ample margin of safety," a phrase that is the section's polestar — its guiding principle in protecting against incompletely understood dangers.

More complex than the section's substantive provisions are its procedural provisions, which mingle formal with informal rulemaking.***

In the Clean Water Act of 1977, Congress amended the toxics provision in major part to solve the problems revealed in the course of the 1973-76 proceedings. Congress adopted its own list of sixty-five families of toxic substances in place of EPA's older, shorter lists, and created two procedures for EPA to use, separately or in tandem. Under the first procedure, amended section 307 (a)(2) directed EPA to set industry-by-industry regulations based on technological feasibility criteria. Under the second procedure, which was based on the 1972 provision, amended section 307(a)(2) directed EPA to set health-based effluent standards on a pollutant-by-pollutant basis using the original factors of toxicity, persistence, degradability etc., and the familiar "ample margin of safety" standard. The original cumbersome procedures were relaxed: formal procedures were replaced by informal ones, and the timeable for rulemaking was enlarged.

*   *   *

IV. INTERACTION WITH TOXIC SUBSTANCES CONTROL ACT.

Congress enacted the Toxic Substances Control Act (TSCA), 15 U.S.C. §§ 2601-2629 (1976), during the pendency of EPA's proceedings on the proposed PCBs effluent standards. TSCA requires notice of intent to manufacture, and pre-manufacture testing of, chemical substances, and confers authority on EPA to regulate the manufacture, processing, distribution in commerce, use, or disposal of such substances. In addition to the provisions applicable to chemical substances in general, TSCA includes a specific provision concerned solely with poly-chlorinated biphenyls, section 6(e), 15 U.S.C.

§ 2605(e) (1976). Section 6(e) provides for a gradual phasing out of PCBs use over a two and one-half year period with limited provision for exemptions.[54]

Industry petitioners contend that this section of TSCA was intended to "preempt" EPA's authority under the 1972 Act. They assert that EPA's ban on discharges of PCBs into waterways makes manufacture and processing of PCBs impossible and that TSCA's phase-out timetable and exemption authority show that Congress did not intend PCBs to be completely and immediately phased out. Therefore, the argument goes, EPA should not achieve this result by the use of its authority under another regulatory provision, the toxics section of the 1972 Act. EPA responds that Congress did not intend section 6(e) to deprive it of its authority under the 1972 Act.

We agree with EPA. Strictly speaking the claim made by industry petitioners is one of "repeal by implication," the overriding of one statute by a later enactment *sub silentio*, rather than a claim of "preemption." "It is, of course, a cardinal principle of statutory construction that repeals by implication are not favored."***

*   *   *

Section 9(b) leaves EPA the choice of regulating toxic substances under TSCA, other statutes (such as the 1972 Act), or both.***

*   *   *

V. EVIDENTIARY BASIS FOR REGULATIONS OF LESS CHLORINATED PCBs

A. *Arguments of the Parties*

The principal claim of industry petitioners is that EPA's regulations lack an adequate basis

---

[54]One year after the effective date (January 1, 1977), PCBs manufacture, processing, distribution in commerce or use is forbidden "other than in a totally enclosed manner." One year thereafter, "no person may manufacture any polychlorinated biphenyl"; six months beyond that, "no person may process or distribute in commerce any polychlorinated biphenyl." This phase-out is limited by the EPA Administrator's discretionary authority to grant temporary conditional exemptions for petitioners who qualify to his satisfaction under two tests.***

in the record to the extent that they cover less chlorinated PCBs because the record consists, in large part, of studies of related, but different substances (more chlorinated PCBs). In order to rule on this claim, we have no alternative except to venture into a difficult realm of chemistry and toxicology, for, however deferential may be our review, we cannot rule on an issue without a firm grasp of it.

PCBs are a group of related chemicals that have two aspects in common. First, they share a basic chemical structure known as the "biphenyl" structure, consisting of two rings of carbon atoms with hydrogen atoms attached. Second, instead of a simple biphenyl structure PCBs have one or more chlorine atoms substituting for one or more hydrogen atoms. From these two aspects comes the name "polychlorinated biphenyls." PCBs vary with respect to how much chlorine is substituted for hydrogen, ranging from one to ten chlorine atoms per molecule of PCBs.

Commercially, PCBs are manufactured and sold in the form of mixtures. Some mixtures contain predominantly PCBs with few chlorine atoms per molecule; these are termed "less chlorinated PCBs." Other PCBs mixtures contain predominantly PCBs with more chlorine atoms per molecule; these are termed "more chlorinated PCBs."

As we have discussed, more chlorinated PCBs were the main PCBs in use from 1929 until the early 1970's. In the early 1970's under public and government pressure, PCBs manufacturers and users shifted from more chlorinated to less chlorinated PCBs. The chemical and electrical industries were able to shift relatively rapidly from use of one PCBs mixture to another. However, this shift created the "knowledge gap" that underlies the principal issue in this proceeding. As a practical matter, scientific knowledge about the effects of chemicals cannot keep up with the ability of industrial laboratories to create new ones. Most of the available scientific studies on PCBs concern more chlorinated PCBs, either because the studies were conducted over the decades when more chlorinated PCBs were the main PCBs in use, or because, even after

the early 1970's, scientists continued to study the more chlorinated PCBs.

Accordingly, EPA faced a familiar choice in this proceeding. On one hand, it could regulate a substance whose properties were incompletely understood (less chlorinated PCBs) by relying, in major part, upon its knowledge about more familiar substances (more chlorinated PCBs), despite the uncertainties of extrapolation from one substance to another. On the other hand, it could delay regulation until science could more fully explore the risks of the new substance.

Industry petitioners contend that EPA lacked an adequate basis for regulation because of this incompleteness in the scientific knowledge about less chlorinated PCBs mixtures. They argue that EPA "could not have reasonably hoped to regulate Aroclors 1016 and 1242 [less chlorinated PCBs] without commissioning extensive studies on comparative mammalian toxicity.*** They insist that EPA must trace a line of direct causation from each substance it regulates to the danger requiring regulation.

In response, EPA disputes that it must produce such direct proof concerning the danger posed by every regulated substance. EPA notes that the statutory standard calls for setting discharge levels at the level that will provide "an ample margin of safety," and cites prior authority, particularly *Ethyl Corp. v. EPA*, 541 F.2d 1 (D.C. Cir.) (en banc), *cert. denied*, 426 U.S. 941 (1976), to support its position. In EPA's view, action need not be delayed while a risky situation persists — that is, until the extent of the danger is fully ascertained. EPA contends that ample evidence showing the danger of more chlorinated PCBs together with scientific reasoning and evidence that less chlorinated PCBs share some dangerous qualities of more chlorinated PCBs, constitutes an adequate basis for regulation.

B. *Applicable Legal Standards*

Section 307 (a)(2) sets forth the relevant factors for setting toxic effluent standards. It requires EPA to "take into account" six factors in proposing such standards: "the toxicity of the pollutant, its persistence, degradability, the usual or potential presence of the affected organisms in any waters, the importance of the affected organisms and the nature and extent of the effect of the toxic pollutant on such organisms."

***Toxicity concerns the adverse biological effects of toxic substances on life in the environment. Persistence concerns the physical and chemical effects of the nonliving environment (such as sunlight and water) on toxic substances. Degradability concerns the effects of the living environment on toxic substances. Taken together, the three factors were intended to cover comprehensively the fate of toxic substances in the environment and their effects on living organisms.

The last three factors concern "affected organisms": their presence (usual or potential) "in any waters," their importance, and the effect on them of the toxic substance. Inclusion of these factors requires EPA to focus on specific effects on specific important organisms as well as on the general toxicity, persistence, and degradability of the substance. On the list of "affected organisms" is, of course, man, although other organisms may certainly trigger the last three factors.

Based on these factors, section 307 (a)(4) directs EPA to set discharge standards at a level providing an "ample margin of safety."***

＊　　＊　　＊

[T]he term "margin of safety" was intended to provide protection "against hazards which research has not yet identified." If administrative responsibility to protect against unknown dangers presents a difficult task, indeed, a veritable paradox — calling as it does for knowledge of that which is unknown — then, the term "margin of safety" is Congress's directive that means be found to carry out the task and to reconcile the paradox. Addition of a generous measure — "ample"— is Congress's recognition that the EPA would need great latitude in meeting its responsibility.

C. *Scope of Review*

EPA's decision is reviewed under the "substantial evidence" test.*** In *Consolidated Edison Co. v. NLRB*, 305 U.S. 197, 229 (1938), Chief Justice Hughes described "substantial

evidence" as "more than a mere scintilla. It means such relevant evidence as a reasonable mind might accept as adequate to support a conclusion."***

Recent lower court decisions have elucidated a significant aspect of the "substantial evidence" test in review of scientific rulemaking. Recently, in *Industrial Union Department, AFL-CIO v. Hodgson*, 499 F.2d 467 (D.C. Cir. 1974), this court construed a section of the Occupational Safety and Health Act of 1970 that provides for judicial review of rulemaking under the "substantial evidence" test. The court distinguished between those administrative determinations that were "factual," and those that were "legislative" *i.e.,* involved policy judgements.*** The central conclusion of *Industrial Union* — when an agency must resolve issues "on the frontiers of scientific knowledge," the reviewing court will uphold agency conclusions based on policy judgements in lieu of factual determinations — has gained acceptance in many statutory contexts.***

D. *Adequacy of the Basis for EPA Regulations*

1. EPA's policy judgements concerning extrapolation.

Industry petitioners contend that EPA lacked an adequate basis for the incomplete scientific knowledge about less chlorinated PCBs. In effect, they assert that EPA must demonstrate the toxicity of each chemical it seeks to regulate through studies demonstrating a clear line of causation between a particular chemical and harm to public health or the environment. We do not agree.

The principal basis for rejecting petitioners' views is the wording of the statute. As we stated, the "ample margin of safety" provision directs EPA to guard against incompletely known dangers. EPA, in its expert policy judgement, relied on its knowledge about a known substance to assess the danger of one about which less is known. Petitioners suggest no alternative approach for the agency short of waiting for conclusive proof about the danger posed by a less understood substance. However, by requiring EPA to set standards providing an "ample margin of safety," Congress authorized and, indeed, required EPA to protect against dangers before their extent is conclusively ascertained.***

Proper deference in judicial review to the scientific expertise of the Administrator also militates against precluding EPA from regulating less chlorinated PCBs on the basis of what is known about related substances. The risks posed by toxic substances, and the extent to which one substance has effects similar to those of related substances, are matters on the frontiers of scientific knowledge. EPA, not the court, has the technical expertise to decide what inferences may be drawn from the characteristics of related substances and to formulate policy with respect to what risks are acceptable.

*   *   *

Finally, in reviewing EPA's policy of regulating less chlorinated PCBs in part on the basis of what is known about more chlorinated PCBs, we must recognize considerations of administrative feasibility. The number of toxic substances subject to regulation seems very large.[81] Regulation of so many substances could well be extremely difficult if EPA were precluded from drawing inferences from available data on well-known, related substances.***

2. EPA's factual determination of the particular risks here.

We now review the evidence presented by EPA, industry petitioners, and others. EPA did not rely on a single approach or study, but acted on the basis of a variety of studies and types of evidence.*** The evidence on scientific matters need not consist of one dispositive study, but may be varied and cumulative.

We have structured our review under the "substantial evidence" test according to the primary factors of section 307 (a)(2): toxicity (including carcinogenicity), persistence, and degradability as they relate to affected organisms.

a. Toxicity

The evidence presented concerning toxicity

may be divided into (i) evidence bearing on aquatic organisms, (ii) evidence bearing on man, and (iii) evidence concerning the special quality of carcinogenicity.

*   *   *

iii. Carcinogenicity

In the EPA proceedings, as in the public debate over PCBs, an issue of considerable importance was whether PCBs cause cancer. EPA introduced studies showing that exposure to more chlorinated PCBs produces cancer and cancer-like growths in rats. EPA also introduced studies showing that more chlorinated PCBs are mutagenic, which, according to commentators, suggests that they may be carcinogenic. Finally, EPA introduced studies that PCBs including less chlorinated PCBs, are enzyme inducers, indicating that they may be co-carcinogenic — that is, that they may produce cancer when they act in combination with other substances. EDF introduced evidence showing that on-the-job exposure to more chlorinated PCBs decades ago resulted eventually in a high incidence of cancer.

Industry petitioners respond that the evidence that less chlorinated PCBs are carcinogenic is far from conclusive. Again, they earnestly contend that evidence concerning more chlorinated PCBs fails to support regulation of less chlorinated PCBs. In response to the studies showing that less chlorinated PCBs are enzyme inducers, they introduced expert testimony disputing that enzyme inducers are necessarily carcinogenic or co-carcinogenic.***

After review of the authorities on the difficult issue of carcinogenic effect, we conclude that EPA's evidence furnishes adequate support for its prohibition. An administrator has a "heavy burden" to "explain the basis for his decision to permit the continued use of a chemical known to produce cancer in experimental animals." *EDF v. Ruckelshaus* [DDT], 439 F.2d 584, 596 n.41 (D.C. Cir. 1971)***. When firm evidence establishes that a chemical is a carcinogen, statutes generally leave an administrator no alternative but to step in to protect the public.

On the other hand, when the evidence is less than firm, but merely suggests that a chemical may be a carcinogen, the same "heavy burden" may not attend administrative inaction. The deci-

---

[81]The Clean Water Act of 1977 listed 65 families, containing at least 129, and possibly thousands of individual substances. *See* 8 ENVIR. REP. (BNA) 1131 (1977). Moreover, this listing was intended only as a beginning; the number of potentially toxic substances must be reckoned in the thousands.***

sion to act in such a case has been held to fall within the discretion of the Administrator. For example, in *Reserve Mining Co. v. EPA*, 514 F.2d 492 (8th Cir. 1975) (en banc), EPA sought to abate discharge of mining refuse into Lake Superior "under an acceptable but unproved medical theory," that the discharges were carcinogenic. The court concluded that the discharges should be abated, even though there would be a heavy cost, including possible loss of many jobs, to the local economy. Similarly, in *Certified Color Manufacturers Association v. Mathews*, 543 F.2d 284 (D.C. Cir. 1976), the Food and Drug Administration (FDA) terminated its provisional approval of a color additive used to dye food on the basis of a vigorously debated study of the additive's carcinogenic effects. This court concluded that the FDA action should be upheld, based upon FDA's scientific judgment that the study was not conclusive, but was merely suggestive of carcinogenicity. "Courts have traditionally recognized a special judicial interest in protecting the public health, particularly where 'the matter involved is as sensitive and fright-laden as cancer.' Where the harm envisaged is cancer, courts have recognized the need for action based upon lower standards of proof than otherwise applicable." *Id.* at 297-98.***

These cases demonstrate the inevitable tension attending regulation of carcinogens. Frequently, such regulations have severe economic impact. Indeed, sometimes, as alleged by industry petitioners in this case, such regulations may jeopardize plants or whole industries, and the jobs depending on them. In such circumstances, the temptation to demand that the agency furnish conclusive proof of carcinogenicity as support for the regulations is great. However, the decision to delegate authority to an agency to control suspected carcinogens is a legislative judgment that is not open to question in this court. Congress's direction to EPA to protect against incompletely understood dangers could not be carried out if we were to adopt the proof requirements advocated by industry petitioners.

What scientists know about the causes of cancer is how limited is their knowledge. The record in this case demonstrates that it may take decades for human exposure to carcinogens to result in cancer; in the meantime, the case for inferring a cancer danger with respect to an incompletely understood substance is vigorously disputed. If regulation were withheld until the danger was demonstrated conclusively, untold injury to public health could result. Accordingly, we find that Congress has allowed EPA to support a prohibition on the basis of strongly contested and merely suggestive proof. We conclude that the evidence in this case is at least suggestive of carcinogenicity and thus supports EPA's decision.

b. Persistence

EPA summarized studies showing that PCBs tend to accumulate in the environment over many years, are mobile, and adhere to sediments. This court has noted before that such characteristics intensify the dangers posed by toxic substances, because they increase the exposure of persons and vulnerable organisms of all kinds to those substances. Accordingly, these studies provide support for EPA's prohibition.

c. Degradability

EPA summarized a number of studies concerning the degradation of both less and more chlorinated PCBs by living organisms. PCBs were shown to resist degradation, to bioaccumulate (build up) to high levels in simple organisms, and then to bioaccumulate further as those simple organisms are consumed by higher organisms.[104] When degradation does occur, it may result in creation of other harmful substances, either as intermediates, or as end products of degradation. Industry petitioners disputed EPA's evidence, and produced their own evidence that less chlorinated PCBs are more easily metabolized and eliminated, and less likely to bioaccumulate than more chlorinated PCBs. They also contended that these substances degrade by safe routes into non-dangerous substances.

---

[104]For example, microorganisms collect in their bodies the PCBs in the water, and PCBs are further concentrated as, successively, the microorganisms are consumed by invertebrates, the invertebrates by small fish, the small fish by larger fish, and the large fish by man.

However, the conclusions advanced by industry petitioners do not necessarily weaken the support for EPA's prohibition. It was not necessary for EPA to prove that less chlorinated PCBs were as dangerous as more chlorinated PCBs in order to justify a prohibition. The central issue is not whether less chlorinated PCBs are less degradable than more chlorinated PCBs, but whether less chlorinated PCBs are insufficiently degradable. Our task in reviewing the record is not to choose between these conflicting studies, but rather to determine whether EPA's decision had substantial evidence on the whole record. Viewed as a whole, the record provided substantial support for EPA's conclusions.

3. Conclusion.

Under the substantial evidence standard of review, EPA is not required to "prove" its case in the reviewing court "in some sense of weight of the evidence." Its policy decisions are subject to deferential review, and its factual conclusions are upheld although they many not be supported by all the evidence, or even by most of it. It suffices that EPA's conclusions are supported by "such relevant evidence as a reasonable mind might accept as adequate to support [the] conclusion[s]." *Consolidated Edison Co. v. NL, RB,* 305 U.S. at 229. On this record, it is clear that EPA's prohibition on discharges of PCBs must be upheld.

*   *   *

NOTES

1. Besides telling you more than you probably wanted to know about PCBs, this lengthy (and greatly edited) case should provide some feel for the extent of the problems arising in regulation of toxic water pollutants: both the difficulty of EPA's job in assessing the dangers from toxic discharges and the jeopardy in which industry can be placed when a mere possibility of a carcinogenic effect can mandate a "zero discharge" standard and, conceivably, a shutdown.

The decision also contains a good summary of Section 307 and recount of the history of its implementation. Another quick review of the basic regulatory scheme, past and present, might be helpful.

2. Prior to the 1977 Amendments, Section 307 specified a single approach to the regulation of discharges of toxic pollutants. EPA was directed to set health-based, nationally-uniform, toxic effluent standards on a pollutant-by-pollutant basis. Since the technological or economic feasibility of compliance was not a consideration, the spectre of plant closures hung heavily over each step in the regulatory process — the most burdensome of which were the full-blown adversary hearings required to precede the promulgation of any such standard. Couple with this the scarcity and inconclusiveness of relevant scientific data concerning toxic substances and the seeming logical incongruity in a statutory mandate to set uniform national standards based on health effects (which typically depend upon the nature of the receiving waters), and it is not hard to see why EPA lagged for so long in setting toxic effluent standards. None had been promulgated by 1976.

The lawsuit by several environmental organizations to compel EPA to move more quickly and take its obligations more seriously resulted in a consent decree — the "Flannery decree" — which changed the course of regulation of toxic water pollutants. *Natural Resources Defense Council, Inc. v. Train,* 8 ERC 2120 (D.D.C. 1976). Under the Flannery decree, EPA agreed to control the discharges of 65 listed toxic substances produced by 21 categories of industries by utilization of the more workable vehicles of Sections 301, 303, and 306 of the Act — primarily the BAT limitations. The health-based approach of Section 307 would be resorted to only as a backup — when effective health protection could not be achieved under the other sections of the Act.

This shift from the pitfalls of the health-based approach to the proven course of technology-based regulation of toxic pollutants was statutorily adopted in the 1977 Clean Water Act. Essentially, the Flannery decree was incorporated into the amended Sections 307 and 301. The 1977 Amendments specified the same list of 65 toxic pollutants, but also gave EPA the authority to make additions or deletions to the list based upon its assessment of the dangers posed by particular substances, applying the criteria of Section 307 (a) (toxicity, persistence, degradability, etc.). Consistent with the consent decree, the amendments required BAT (as well as new source and "pretreatment" standards) to be promulgated for each of the listed substances and industrial categories by July, 1980, with compliance achieved by July, 1984. Needless to say, EPA did not adhere to this timetable; as of July, 1984, it had not even promulgated BAT limitations for some of the listed point-source categories, and many dischargers were far from compliance with the standards which had been promulgated. EPA's delay, and pleas of administrative and budgetary infeasibility, resulted in modification of the Flannery decree and its timetables, *NRDC, Inc. v. Costle*, 12 ERC 1833 (D.D.C. 1979), although on appeal of the modified decree the D.C. Circuit reaffirmed the settlement against the argument that it had been superseded by the 1977 Amendments. *See EDF, Inc. v. Costle*, 636 F.2d 1229 (D.C. Cir. 1980).

3. Section 307 (a) of the Act contains the standards and procedures under which EPA is to undertake the two-pronged approach to regulation of toxic pollutants. It is understandable and should be read carefully.

4. Even though EPA's setting of health-based standards now appears discretionary, it has promulgated such uniform national standards for six substances (all chlorinated hydrocarbons): aldrin/dieldrin, DDT, endrin, toxaphene, benzidine, and PCBs. *See* 40 CFR Part 129 (1984). The agency's reluctance to promulgate more health-based toxic standards is, presumedly, due to its primary reliance on BAT technology-based limitations.

5. The case which you have read concerned challenges to the first of these health-based toxic standards: those set for PCBs.

Does the decision justify EPA's previous lack of confidence that it had sufficient scientific evidence upon which to base such standards?

How could EPA pass the "substantial evidence" test for a "zero discharge" standard for *less* chlorinated PCBs when almost all of its evidence on toxicity pertained to *more* chlorinated PCBs?

Review the court's construction of the "ample margin of safety" concept, its expressed deference to agency expertise on "policy" issues "on the frontiers of scientific knowledge," and its refusal to require EPA to demonstrate a "clear line of causation." Would not an approach to judicial review combining these ingredients allow EPA to set a zero discharge standard for any suspected carcinogen? Despite severe economic impacts?

6. Given the court's deference to EPA, could the agency properly have reached a decision *not* to regulate less chlorinated PCBs based on the same evidence? Could the present EPA rescind these standards? Could it do so for economic reasons?

7. For another example of the D.C. Circuit's deference to EPA's judgement in setting toxic pollutant standards, see *Hercules, Inc. v. EPA*, 598 F.2d 91 (D.C. Cir. 1978), in which the health-based standards for the pesticides toxaphene and endrin were sustained. The minimal scrutiny applied by the court in that case allowed EPA, among other things, to base its toxic effluent standards on studies of toxicity to organisms that were highly susceptible to these pesticides — even though those organisms were not present in the receiving waters of the only existing plants discharging such substances.

8   PRETREATMENT STANDARDS

Cerro Copper Products Company
v.
Ruckelshaus
766 F.2d 1060 (7th Cir. 1985)

Before ESCHBACH and COFFEY, Circuit Judges, and DOYLE, Senior District Judge.

COFFEY, Circuit Judge.

The petitioners, Cerro Copper Products Co. and the Village of Sauget, Illinois, seek review of certain regulations promulgated by the Environmental Protection Agency concerning the pretreatment of wastewater discharge from industrial copper-forming facilities. We deny the petition for review.

I

In 1972 and 1977, Congress amended the Clean Water Act ("Act") in an effort to control water pollution and "to restore and maintain the chemical, physical, and biological integrity of the Nation's waters." The Act presently provides that direct dischargers—those who expel wastewater directly into navigable waters—must comply with the "best practicable control technology currently available" by July 1, 1977, to limit pollutants within their wastewater discharge, commonly referred to as effluent. The Act further provides that by July 1, 1984, the direct dischargers must comply with the more stringent standard of "best available technology economically achievable" in regulating effluent pollutants. In addition, the act provides that indirect dischargers—those whose wastewater passes through a publicly owned treatment works plant ("POTW")—pretreat their wastewater discharge before passing it along to the POTW for further treatment. Congress directed the Environmental Protection Agency ("EPA") to administer, implement, and enforce the provisions of the Act, and in this capacity, the EPA is to establish "pretreatment standards for introduction of pollutants into treatment works ... which are publicly owned for those pollutants which are determined not to be susceptible to treatment by such treatment works or which would interfere with the operation of such treatment works." 33 U.S.C. § 1317(b)(1). Congress instructed the EPA to "establish national pretreatment standards for toxic pollutants based on the best available technology economically achievable, or any more stringent effluent standards...." H.R.Conf.Rep. No. 830, 95th Cong., 1st Sess. 87.

The requirement that indirect dischargers remove pollutants from their effluent through pretreatment procedures, before introducing such wastewater into the POTW, creates the potential for unnecessary, duplicative wastewater treatment procedures if the POTW is capable of efficiently removing those same pollutants. Thus, in an effort "to avoid treatment for treatment's sake," the Act provides that:

"[i]f, in the case of any toxic pollutant under subsection (a) of this section introduced by a source into a publicly owned treatment works, the treatment by such works removes all of any part of such toxic pollutant and the discharge from such works does not violate that effluent limitation or standard which would be applicable to such toxic pollutant if it were discharged by such source other than through a publicly owned treatment works, and does not prevent sludge use or disposal by such works in accordance with section 1345 of this title, then the pretreatment requirements for the sources actually discharging such toxic pollutant into such publicly owned treatment works may be revised by the owner or operator of such works to reflect the removal of such toxic pollutant by such works.''

33 U.S.C. § 1317(b)(1). This statutory removal credit program allows indirect dischargers to modify the pollutant levels within their wastewater discharge based upon the degree of pollution reduction achieved by the POTW. In effect, the indirect dischargers, when pretreating their wastewater, are not required to remove those pollutants that can be efficiently treated and removed by the POTW. The statutory removal credit program ensures that the combination of pretreatment by the indirect discharger and further treatment by the POTW achieves ''at least that level of treatment which would be required if the industrial source were making a direct discharge.'' H.R.Conf.Rep. No. 830, 95th Cong., 1st Sess. 87.

In June 1978, the EPA promulgated regulations implementing the general wastewater pretreatment standards for indirect dischargers and setting forth the guidelines to be followed by indirect dischargers and POTWs in qualifying for removal credits.*** The regulations require that pollutants introduced into POTWs by indirect dischargers ''shall not Pass Through the POTW or Interfere with the operation or performance of the works.'' 40 C.F.R. § 403.5(a). The regulations direct POTWs ''with a total design flow greater than 5 million gallons per day (mgd) and receiving from Industrial Users pollutants which Pass Through or Interfere with the operation of the POTW ... to establish a POTW Pretreatment Program....'' 40 C.F.R. § 403.8(a). The EPA defines pretreatment as ''the reduction of the amount of pollutants, the elimination of pollutants, or the alteration of the nature of pollutant properties in wastewater prior to or in lieu of discharging or otherwise introducing such pollutants into a POTW.'' 40 C.F.R. § 403.3(q). Thus, the POTW must formulate a pretreat-

ment program to ensure that the pollutant levels within the wastewater discharge of those industrial facilities who use the POTW are in compliance with the EPA standards.

The regulations further provide that the POTW may revise the pretreatment program for an industrial user in order to reflect the POTW's removal of pollutants. To qualify for these ''removal credits,'' the POTW must have an EPA-approved pretreatment program and must submit periodic data to the EPA concerning the quantity and quality of the POTW's normal influent and effluent flow. The EPA will approve the revised pretreatment program and grant removal credits only where ''the POTW demonstrates Consistent Removal of each pollutant for which the discharge limit in a categorical Pretreatment Standard is to be revised....'' 40 C.F.R. § 403.7(b). Indeed, the removal credit will be granted only for the actual removal of the pollutant mass by the POTW, not for a reduction in the concentration of the pollution through dilution of the wastewater. If the POTW's pretreatment standards meet with EPA approval and the POTW establishes that it is capable of removing pollutant mass from the wastewater of an indirect discharger, the POTW is authorized to issue revised effluent pollutant limitations for the indirect discharger. This revised discharge limit is calculated through a mathematical formula; dividing the EPA's pretreatment standard for a given pollutant by the sum of one minus the POTW's consistent removal rate of that pollutant. For example, if the EPA's pretreatment standard is one pound of pollutant discharge for every thousand pounds of mass used in the manufacturing process, and the POTW can remove 75% of that pollutant, then the revised discharge limit for the indirect discharger would be four pounds of pollutant discharge for every thousand pounds of mass used in the manufacturing process. The POTW would remove 75%, or three of the four pounds of the pollutant, thus bringing the wastewater into compliance with the EPA's pretreatment standard of one pound of pollutant for every thousand pounds of discharged mass.

The EPA regulations also provide that

each industrial discharger of water pollutants within the United States will be classified within an industrial category. The EPA is to promulgate individual pretreatment standards for each industrial category, specifying the quantity and concentration of pollutants that indirect dischargers may release to their respective POTWs. Realizing that "it may be necessary on a case-by-case basis to adjust the limits in categorical Pretreatment Standards, making them either more or less stringent, as they apply to a certain Industrial User," the EPA included "a fundamentally different factors" ("FDF") variance for each industrial category.***

On August 15, 1983, the EPA issued the pretreatment standards and effluent limitations for the direct and indirect dischargers within the copper-forming industry. According to the EPA, "[t]he Agency considered a number of factors to determine whether subcategorization is needed in the copper forming category. After consideration of these factors, the Agency has determined that the copper forming category is most appropriately regulated as a single subcategory." 48 Fed. Reg. 36,944 (1983). The EPA based this conclusion upon the fact that the 176 copper-forming facilities within the United States perform five basic operations—hot rolling, cold rolling, extrusion, drawing, and forging—that utilize water, oil-water emulsions, or soluble oil-water mixtures as lubricants that are included within the wastewater discharge. The EPA's thorough and exhaustive study of the copper-forming industry revealed that:

"[p]ollutants found in significant amounts in copper forming waste streams include: chromium, copper, lead, nickel and zinc; toxic organics; and suspended solids, pH, and oil and grease. In addition, the sludges generated by treatment of these wastewaters usually contain large quantities of toxic metals.

*   *   *

Id. at 36,945. The EPA found that in the copper-forming industry, the POTWs were ineffective in treating the toxic pollutants — including chromium, copper, lead, nickel, zinc, and toxic organics — present in the wastewater of copper-forming facilities. According to the EPA:

"[i]n the copper forming category, the Agency has concluded that the toxic metals regulated under these standards (chromium, copper, lead, nickel, and zinc) pass through the POTW. The nationwide average percentage of these same toxic metals removed by a well-operated POTW meeting secondary treatment requirements is about 50 percent (ranging from 20 to 70 percent), whereas the percentage that can be removed by a copper forming direct discharger applying the best available technology economically achievable is about 90 percent. Accordingly, these pollutants pass through a POTW."

Id. at 36,947. Thus, the EPA issued pretreatment regulations requiring, inter alia, flow reduction techniques and "end-of-pipe" pre-discharge treatment in the form of "[c]hemical reduction of chromium; chemical precipitation of metal ions using hydroxides or carbonates; removal of precipitated metals by settling; pH control; oil skimming; chemical emulsion breaking; and filtration." Id. at 36,945. In effect, the EPA regulations placed numerical limitations upon the toxic pollutant mass that could be discharged from copper-forming facilities. The EPA concluded that these pretreatment regulations "will not result in any closures [or] job losses" for the forty-five indirect dischargers within the copper-forming industry. Id. at 36,949. The EPA added, of course, that these pretreatment standards for the copper-forming industry were "subject to the 'fundamentally different factors' variance and credits for pollutants removed by POTW." Id. at 36,955. In compliance with section 307(b)(1) of the Clean Water Act, the EPA required indirect dischargers in the copper-forming industry to comply with the pretreatment standards within three years of their promulgation. Thus, the forty-five indirect dischargers in the copper-forming industry must have wastewater pretreatment programs that comply with the "best available technology economically achievable" in operation by August 15, 1986.

*   *   *

Turning to the facts in the present case, the record reveals that the petitioner, Cerro Copper Products Co., ("Cerro") is a copper-forming facility located in Sauget, Illinois, that manufactures seamless copper tubing for plumbing, industrial, and refrigeration uses. The EPA classifies Cerro as an indirect discharger of toxic organic pollutants as well as the toxic metal pollutants of chromium, copper, lead, nickel, and zinc. The co-petitioner, Village of Sauget, Illinois, owns and operates the Sauget POTW, which treats the wastewater discharge of Cerro and various other industries within Sauget and the surrounding area. The Sauget POTW was built in the early 1970's after a study by the local industries revealed that the most cost-effective treatment of industrial wastewater would be through the construction and operation of a centrally located POTW. The record reveals that the local industries within the Sauget area contributed $7,870,000 to the $8,670,000 construction cost of the POTW, while the Village of Sauget and the Federal Government funded the remainder of the costs. According to the EPA, the Sauget POTW is not presently in compliance with the EPA's regulations concerning effluent pollutant limitations for "secondary treatment" POTWs. Moreover, the EPA claims that the Sauget POTW's removal of toxic pollutants discharged by Cerro is not at the level of "best available control technology economically achievable" as required by the EPA regulations.

The petitioners respond that construction of a regional wastewater treatment plant to serve southwestern Illinois is in progress and upon completion in 1986, the regional plant will treat Cerro's wastewater discharge to the degree necessary to comply with the EPA standards. The costs for this regional POTW are being funded in large measure (85%) through Federal Government monies, with the remaining funds being secured through the issuance of revenue bonds guaranteed by the local industries of Sauget, including Cerro. This regional POTW, when completed, will treat sewage from cities and municipalities in southwestern Illinois as well as industrial wastewater that has already passed through the Sauget POTW.*** According to the petitioners, the Sauget POTW is a reasonable alternative to installing pretreatment equipment at Cerro's manufacturing plant because the Sauget POTW will pretreat the wastewater discharge before passing it along to the soon to be completed regional POTW. The petitioners, in effect, argue that Cerro's pretreatment of its wastewater discharge will be unnecessary and wasteful once the regional treatment facility is completed and in full operation in the immediate future. The petitioners claim that the EPA failed to take these unique circumstances into account when it formulated uniform, national pretreatment standards for the copper-forming industry. The petitioners further contend that the EPA regulations implementing the removal credits program are invalid because they do not address the unique situation presented in this case where the Sauget POTW, and the soon to be completed regional POTW, will successfully remove the toxic pollutants discharged by Cerro.

II

This court has jurisdiction to review the regulations promulgated by the EPA for the pretreatment of wastewater discharge from industrial copper-forming facilities pursuant to 33 U.S.C. § 1369(b)(1)***.***

The petitioners claim that following completion of the regional POTW, the wastewater discharged from that facility will satisfy the "best available control technology economically achievable," as required by the EPA. According to the petitioners, once the regional POTW is completed, the Sauget POTW will become a pretreatment facility and the regional POTW will become the POTW, within the meaning of the Clean Water Act. The petitioners contend that in view of the present stage of development and the contemplated completion date of the regional treatment plant, there is no need for Cerro to install additional pretreatment equipment at its manufacturing plant. The petitioners claim that the EPA failed to consider this alleged unique situation when it promulgated uniform, national wastewater pretreatment standards for the copper-forming industry.

We summarily dispose of the petitioners' attack upon the EPA's uniform, national pretreatment standards for the copper-forming industry as the legislative history of the Clean Water Act clearly reveals that Congress intended the EPA to promulgate wastewater pretreatment standards on a nationwide basis.*** Thus, Congress expressly intended that the EPA, when establishing national wastewater pretreatment standards for the various industrial categories, not take into account the individual characteristics of each industrial facility and POTW. Congress realized that due to the many variables existing throughout the wide range of industries, it would be impossible for the uniform, national pretreatment standards to accommodate each and every facility within an industrial category. According to the Senate Report:

"[a]nother reason for minimizing the consideration of removals in the development of national pretreatment standards is that the performance of treatment works on industrial waste, except in those few cases where the system is specifically designed to treat a certain type of industrial waste, is extremely variable. Data that have [sic] been presented to this committee indicate that secondary treatment removal efficiency for metals varies from between 10 and 70 percent. Variability of such magnitude makes the assumption of specific level of removal, when setting national standards, almost impossible."

S.Rep. No. 370, 95th Cong., 1st Sess. 58, *reprinted in* 1977 U.S.Code Cong. & Ad. News 4326, 4383. In view of the variety of industrial facilities and POTWs subject to the uniform, national pretreatment standards, Congress enacted the removal credit program to allow indirect dischargers to modify the pollutant levels within their wastewater discharge based

upon the degree of pollution reduction achieved by the POTW.*** Accordingly, the legislative history of the Clean Water Act reveals that Congress intended the EPA to promulgate uniform, national wastewater pretreatment standards and then permit modification of these standards through the removal credits program.

In the present case, the EPA conducted a thorough and exhaustive study of the copper-forming industry. The EPA solicited information from all 176 facilities within the industry concerning the copper-forming processes used; the mass pollutant content of the wastewater discharge; the size, age, and land availability of the facility; and the existing pollution treatment devices in use. Based upon this industry-wide study, the EPA found that the wastewater discharge of all facilities within the copper-forming industry contained toxic organic pollutants as well as toxic metal pollutants, including chromium, copper, lead, nickel, and zinc. The EPA found that the average POTW was unable to remove these toxic pollutants from the wastewater at the required level of "best available control technology economically achievable." Thus, the EPA promulgated uniform, national pretreatment standards, requiring copper-forming facilities to use pretreatment procedures to remove toxic pollutants from their wastewater before passing such water along to the POTW. In view of Congress' mandate to promulgate uniform, national pretreatment standards and the EPA's exhaustive review of the copper-forming industry, we uphold the EPA's wastewater pretreatment regulations for the copper-forming industry as a fair, reasonable, and proper embodiment of clear Congressional intent.

The petitioners further claim that the EPA's removal credit program is invalid because its application requires Cerro to pretreat its wastewater discharge before passing it along to the Sauget POTW. The petitioners argue that Cerro's pretreatment amounts to nothing more than "treatment for treatment's sake" because the Sauget POTW and the soon to be completed regional POTW are capable of removing pollutants to satisfy the EPA's pollutant discharge limitations. The Clean Water

Act provides that the Federal Court of Appeals may review the EPA regulations implementing the removal credit program only if the petitioner filed a petition "within ninety days from the date of such determination, approval, promulgation, issuance or denial, or after such date only if such application is based solely on grounds which arose after such ninetieth day." 33 U.S.C. § 1369(b)(1). In the present case, the EPA regulations for the removal credit program were promulgated and available to the public in January 1981, but the petitioners failed to challenge the regulations until November 1983, when they filed a petition for review before this court.*** The petitioners failed to challenge the removal credit formula within the ninety day statutory period, and we believe that it contravenes the principles of fairness and equity to permit the petitioners to circumvent this limitation, some three years later, by attempting a collateral challenge upon the very same removal credit formula.***

We do note that the EPA's removal credit program is an integral component of the Clean Water Act and is vital to the EPA's implementation of the Act.*** Thus, in reviewing the uniform, national pretreatment standards promulgated by the EPA for the copper-forming industry, we must also examine the removal credits program which permits qualifying POTWs and indirect dischargers to revise the EPA pretreatment standards. The EPA's removal credit regulation consists of a formula that permits indirect dischargers to receive credit for the POTW's removal of pollutants. *See* 40 C.F.R. § 403.7(d)(4). The POTW must actually remove the pollutant mass from

the wastewater and removal credits are not to be granted for simple dilution, i.e., increasing the volume of water and thereby decreasing the number of pollutants per unit of water.*** According to the House Report, "[i]n promulgating national pretreatment standards the Administrator shall include a provision recognizing the option of [a POTW] to modify the requirements to reflect the degree of *reduction* achieved by the treatment works." H.R.Conf. Rep. No. 830, 95th Cong., 1st Sess. 88, *reprinted in* 1977 U.S.Code Cong. & Ad.News 4424, 4463 (emphasis added). The removal credit program promulgated by the EPA allows indirect dischargers to modify the pollutant levels of their wastewater discharge if the POTW properly removes toxic pollutants from the wastewater within the guidelines specified by the EPA. The EPA's removal credit program effectuates Congressional intent to remove pollutants from our Nation's waters and thus we hold that the program is a proper implementation of the Clean Water Act.

As a result of the Supreme Court's reversal of the Third Circuit's opinion in *Metal Finishers*, the EPA may grant FDF variances for toxic pollutants. It is thus obvious that at the time the EPA reinstates the FDF variance provision for toxic pollutants, the petitioners will have an opportunity to present their claim of alleged unique circumstances to the EPA in an attempt to satisfy the requirements of 40 C.F.R. § 403.13 and obtain a FDF variance. In the meantime, the petitioners must comply with the EPA's pretreatment standards for the copper-forming industry by August 15, 1986.

NOTES

1. Pretreatment requirements for industrial sources which discharge into POTWs are, of course, necessary for effective control of water pollution. With direct dischargers and POTWs subject to end-of-the-pipe effluent limitations, it would be anomalous for indirect dischargers to escape regulation, pass the burden completely on to the public owners of the treatment works (or befoul the works), and gain a competitive advantage over direct dischargers. With an estimated number of over 50,000 such indirect dischargers, it is not surprising that, from the 1972 amendments forward, Congress has required EPA to promulgate pretreatment standards to prevent the discharge of pollutants into POTWs which would interfere with, pass through, or otherwise, be incompatible with such treatment works.

The General Pretreatment Regulations first promulgated by EPA in 1978 reflect its commitment to require pretreatment of indirect discharges of toxic pollutants to the same extent as required of direct discharges. The major features of the relevant statutory provisions, regulations, and agency strategy is well described in the Seventh Circuit's decision; but a reading of Section 307(b), (c) and (d) of the Act would provide a good quick perspective on the court's analysis of the issues before it.

2. Is it clear from a reading of Section 307(b) and (c) what factors the Administrator was to consider in setting categorical pretreatment standards? Is it even clear that for *existing* sources the Administrator was to set standards based upon categories of *industrial sources*, rather than upon categories of *pollutants*?

EPA's regulatory approach of setting pretreatment standards by industrial category was embodied in the "Flannery consent decree," *NRDC v. Train*, 8 ERC 2120 (D.D.C.1976), as was the decision to require indirect dischargers to apply levels of control technology similar to those which the Act mandated for direct dischargers. In this consent decree, the Administrator agreed to promulgate pretreatment standards analogous to BPT for eight specified industrial categories by May 15, 1977. Categorical pretreatment standards based on BAT for existing sources would then be promulgated for all 21 listed industrial categories by the end of 1979. Although these deadlines were subsequently relaxed somewhat, the legislative history behind the 1977 amendments has been judicially interpreted to support congressional sanction of this approach to regulation of indirect dischargers. *See Environmental Defense Fund, Inc. v. Costle*, 636 F.2d 1229, 1243-44 (1980).

In addition to these industry-specific pretreatment standards, the General Pretreatment Regulations elaborate upon the basic requirement in 307(b) and (c) that no pollutant be discharged which would pass through or interfere with a POTW. These general regulations also establish the mechanisms and procedures governing the separately promulgated categorical standards: providing, *inter-alia*, for "FDF" variances, removal credits, and adjustment of discharge limits according to a "combined wastestream formula." *See* 40 C.F.R. § 403 (1985) and *National Association of Metal Finishers v. EPA*, 719 F.2d 624 (3d Cir. 1983), in which the regulations were judicially reviewed.

3. The Act does not expressly require indirect dischargers to obtain NPDES permits; instead, both the categorical pretreatment standards and the general requirements apply to them simply as rules of law. The standards, however, are incorporated into contracts with, or permits issued by, the receiving POTWs. Also, many states require permits for indirect and direct dischargers alike.

4. Do you understand how the removal credits program operates? To be eligible to grant revisions to reflect the toxic pollutants it removes, a POTW must have its treatment program and ability to reliably revise discharge limits for specific pollutants approved by EPA or the administering state agency. To obtain authorization for each proposed removal credit, the POTW must demonstrate "consistent removal" of each pollutant sufficient to justify the revision.

5. Given this legislative and administrative scheme, do you think that Cerro had much hope of obtaining an exception for its "unique situation"—either in the form of a special subcategory for copper-forming facilities with pretreatment by a "first-stage" POTW, or in the form of modification of the removal credits provisions?

Did Cerro actually just seem to be asking for relief from the uniform national pretreatment standards without present eligibility for removal credits (because of the non-compliance of the Sauget POTW)? If the new regional POTW is in fact able to reduce the pollutants discharged to a level that complies with BAT, shouldn't Cerro *then* be eligible for removal credits for the amounts of pollutants removed by the two POTWs in tandem? But should Cerro be entitled to any relief until it is known whether in fact the two POTWs will accomplish consistent removal? What should Cerro do in the interim?

6. Should Cerro, on such a showing as this, be entitled to an FDF variance?

Recall from the discussion in the Notes following *Chemical Manufacturers Ass'n* that FDF variances are the only variances that seem to be available to indirect dischargers, regardless of the nature of the pollutants involved. At the time of the Third Circuit's decision in *Koppers Co. v. EPA*, 23 ERC 1013 (3d Cir. 1985), EPA's position, convincing to the court and supported by statutory language, was that the variances allowed for non-conventional pollutants by 301(c) and 301(g) were not available to indirect dischargers.

9 WATER QUALITY STANDARDS

Before its amendment in 1972, the Federal Water Pollution Control Act relied upon state-established water quality standards as the primary mechanism for control of water pollution. States were supposed to develop water quality standards for interstate waters within their boundaries and create implementation schedules and enforcement programs in order to assure attainment of those standards.

This approach, however, proved unsuccessful: partly because it focused only on the tolerable effects of water pollution instead of directly on the causes, partly because of the difficulties of proving responsibility under such a system, and partly because there was no provision for effective federal back-up authority — either in implementing or enforcing the standards.

Of course, the major change made by the 1972 Amendments was in providing for federally-set technology-based effluent limitations applicable directly to dischargers regardless of the nature of the receiving waters. But the 1972 Amendments also reinvigorated the water quality approach in ways which made it an important and effective second line of defense against pollution of the nation's waters.

At this point you should read Section 303, and then Section 302. After you have done so, consider the author's following summary of their operative provisions.

Pre-existing water quality standards for interstate waters were grandfathered into the new scheme, unless EPA determined that they failed to comply with the Act's requirements prior to the 1972 Amendments.

States were now required to adopt and submit to EPA water quality standards for their intrastate waters as well. These standards were also subject to EPA's judgment as to whether they complied with the requirements of the pre-1972 Act. If they did, they were to be approved and effective.

If, however, EPA judged either the interstate or the intrastate standards not to be in compliance with the pre-existing Act, it was to promulgate other standards for the state (if, after notice and opportunity, the state failed to make the necessary changes). Of course, EPA was also required to promulgate standards for any state which failed to submit them for its approval.

After the passage of the 1972 Amendments, at least once every three years, the states are required to review their water quality standards to assure continuing compliance with the Act. Any new or modified standards adopted by a state as a result of this review process must be submitted to EPA. Such revised or new water quality standards specifically must consist of (1) the designated uses of the waters involved and (2) the water quality "criteria" necessary for attainment and for maintenance of each designated use. For example, the criteria for a stream designated as a cold water fishery would comprehend all factors necessary for maintaining the stream for that use — including dissolved oxygen, temperature, sediment load, salinity, absence of toxic pollutants, etc.[1] Thus, the states at least are now provided with a clear description of what their new water quality standards should look like. In fact, this is what their original standards should have been comprised of, but often were not.

According to Section 303 (c)(2), these new and revised state water quality standards are to be:

[1]For a full description of water quality criteria, see Section 304 (a).

***such as to protect the public health or welfare, enhance the quality of water and serve the purposes of this Act. Such standards shall be established taking into consideration their use and value for public water supplies, propagation of fish and wildlife, recreational purposes, and agricultural, industrial, and other purposes, and also taking into consideration their use and value for navigation.

Obviously, these considerations are quite broad and may give the states considerable leeway. Remember, however, that declared "purposes of this Act" include no discharge by 1985, fishable/swimmable water by July, 1983, and prohibition of the discharge of toxic amounts of toxic pollutants. See Section 101 (a). Query: Don't these goals limit the states' authority to continue low quality use designations into the 1980s?

These new and revised standards are to be submitted to EPA for its approval. If it determines that the requirements of the Act — particularly those quoted above — have not been met, and if a state fails to make whatever changes are necessary for compliance, EPA is to promulgate the standards.

At this point, it might seem that EPA's power to promulgate substitute standards is triggered only when a state initiates a change or revision. However, a focus on Section 303 (c) (4) (B) reveals that EPA has the power to itself initiate a new or revised standard whenever it determines that "the requirements of the Act" necessitate it.

Once the water quality standards are established, the Act next provides a specific route for insuring that they are attained. According to Section 303 (d), each state is required to identify those of its waters for which the "1977" BPT and secondary treatment effluent limitations would not be enough to achieve the designated water quality standards. It is then supposed to establish a "priority ranking" for those waters where this is the case. The same sort of identification is to be made of any waters for which thermal discharge limitations set under Section 301 are inadequate to protect waterlife.

For each of the waters so identified as not being adequately protected by 301 limitations, the states are to determine the "total maximum daily load" of pollutants which the water can assimilate and still meet the designated water quality standard. A similar calculation is to be made of the "total maximum daily thermal load" required to protect waterlife.

In order to assist the states in this task, under Section 304 (a)(2), EPA was supposed to identify those pollutants suitable for calculation of total maximum daily loads and correlate various water qualities with such load levels. Within 180 days after EPA published this list of pollutants amenable to maximum daily load measurement, states were required to submit to EPA for its approval their total maximum daily load figures for any waters where they were required. If EPA disapproves of either a state's identification of waters in need of additional protection or its calculation of daily load, it is required to substitute its own identification and load figures.

Whether such identifications and load calculations are made by the state and approved by EPA, or promulgated by EPA, they are required by Section 303 (e) to be incorporated into a "continuing planning process," which in turn must be part of any state NPDES program in order for the state to be delegated permitting authority. The required ingredients of an approvable continuing planning process are enumerated in Section 303 (e)(3). For present purposes, the most important of these requirements are "(F)," which requires the means of assuring compliance with water quality standards, and "(A)," which requires any effluent limitations necessary to comply with Section 301 (b)(1). And, very significantly, Section 301 (b)(1)(C) requires any effluent limitations which are necessary to meet water quality standards. Thus, through this complex process, wherever necessary, states are supposed to translate their water quality standards into source-specific effluent limitations. In this manner, water-quality-based effluent limitations will be produced which are more stringent than BPT, secondary treatment, or even BAT standards.

So, what happens if a state doesn't co-operate with this scheme? Remember, EPA has the duty to promulgate water quality standards in lieu of noncomplying states. It also has the authority to establish total maximum daily loads for states whose "TMDLs" are submitted and disapproved. Section 303 (e) dealing with the "continuing planning process," however, applies only to the states. On the other hand, under Section 402 (a)(1), EPA can issue a permit only if Section 301 is complied with. And, as discussed, Section 301 (b)(1)(C) requires any more stringent limitation necessary to assure that water quality standards will be met. Thus, there is no longer supposed to be any way for a discharger legally to cause or contribute to a water quality violation.

Now back to Section 302. On its face, subsection (a) of this section appears to require all waters in the nation to meet the stringent "fishable/swimmable" standard — if not through application of BAT, then through establishment of whatever stringent effluent limitations are necessary. Even though the language might be construed so as to not make this section effective until after the BAT deadlines (1984 or later), by then at least state choices as to lower water qualities would seem to be pre-empted.

However, subsection (b) seems to take some of the sting out of the preceding subsection. It requires EPA to hold a hearing, where affected persons are to be given the opportunity to demonstrate that a limitation required for fishable/swimmable water would result in "no reasonable relationship between the economic and social costs and the benefits to be obtained." If such a demonstration is made, EPA is to relax the limitation accordingly.

There you have an exhaustive, and perhaps exhausting, description of water quality standards. Now for a few cases to illustrate how they operate.

Scott v. City of Hammond

530 F. Supp. 288 (N.D. Ill. 1981)

SHADUR, District Judge.

Illinois citizen William J. Scott ("Scott") sues the City of Hammond, Indiana ("Hammond"), the Hammond-Munster Sanitary District ("District") and the United States Environmental Protection Agency and its Administrator (collectively "EPA") because of District's alleged discharge of raw human fecal material into Lake Michigan. Scott seeks relief against Hammond and District under theories of Illinois and federal common law of nuisance, alleging that the discharges caused 1980 closings of several Chicago beaches. Scott also claims EPA has failed to perform certain allegedly nondiscretionary duties imposed by section 303 of the Federal Water Pollution Control Act (the "Act") and seeks an injunction requiring EPA to comply with those Section 303 requirements.

EPA has moved to dismiss the Complaint as it pertains to EPA. For the reasons stated in this memorandum opinion and order, EPA's motion is granted.

Claims Against EPA

1. *Statutory Framework and Nature of the Claims*

Section 303 is one component of the Act's comprehensive scheme to regulate water pollution. It requires states to establish water quality standards ("standards") applicable to the discharge of pollutants into interstate and intrastate waters. In conjunction with that requirement Act § 304 requires EPA to promulgate non-binding water quality criteria ("criteria") that designate the maximum concentration of various pollutants for a waterway that would still "protect" its designated uses.

States may and usually do use the criteria in formulating their standards. Completed standards are submitted to EPA and if approved become "the water quality standard for the applicable waters of that State." If EPA instead determines the submitted standard fails to meet the requirements of the Act it is authorized to promulgate a different standard for the state.

Section 303(d) also requires states to develop total maximum daily loads ("TMDLs") for all dischargers into waterways for which certain requirements of Act §§ 301 (b)(1)(A) and (B) are not satisfied. Lake Michigan is such a waterway. TMDLs are in turn allocated among the various dischargers to set specific limits on the amount of pollutants each entity may discharge. Unlike the formulation of standards, for which EPA provides advisory criteria under Section 304, initial promulgation of TMDLs is entirely the responsibility of the states. However, proposed TMDLs are subject to EPA approval, and if tendered TMDLs are deficient EPA is required to establish TMDLs within 30 days.

Scott alleges that Hammond and District have illegally discharged raw human fecal material into Lake Michigan. In 1977 both Indiana and Illinois submitted and obtained EPA approval of proposed standards for the discharge of fecal coliform into Lake Michigan. However, neither state has submitted any TMDLs for approval even though Section 303(d)(2) required such submissions by December 28, 1978.

Scott claims that under the Act EPA is required to adopt:

(1) criteria applicable to fecal tract virus and pathogen bacteria discharges into Lake Michigan, and
(2) TMDLs for all such discharges.

Claiming jurisdiction is proper under 28 U.S.C. §§ 1331, 1332 and 1361, and 33 U.S.C. § 1365 (citizen suits under the Act), he urges the Act imposes a non-discretionary duty on EPA to promulgate the requested criteria and TMDLs because (1) Section 303(c)(2) mandates that state standards "shall be such as to protect the public health" and (2) present standards violate that mandate because they inadequately regulate the discharge of bacteria and viruses.

2. Promulgation of Bacteria and Virus Criteria

Scott's responsive memorandum levels a barrage of charges as to EPA's non-promulgation of such criteria. Those charges, however, essentially reduce to one: Standards adopted in 1977 by Indiana and Illinois applicable to fecal material discharges into Lake Michigan are inadequate because they do not specifically regulate two alleged components of fecal pollution.

Our Court of Appeals' decision in *United States Steel Corp v. Train*, 556 F.2d 822 (7th Cir. 1977), defines the avenues for relief open to Scott. If his Complaint is read as contesting the substance of the standards he may bring only an action (1) *against the State[s]* in state court or (2) "a federal action against the state officers responsible for their [the standards'] enforcement alleging deprivation of a federal constitutional right." 556 F.2d at 836-37. Obviously, Scott has selected neither of those courses of action here. Under *United States Steel* his only other available course would have been to seek Administrative Procedure Act review of EPA's approval of the standards. 556 F.2d at 837. But as was the case in *United States Steel*, Scott's Complaint does not seek that relief and cannot be sustained on that ground either.

*   *   *

Scott's efforts to characterize his request for promulgation of virus and bacteria criteria in various ways (other than as a challenge to the sufficiency of the 1977 standards) is unpersuasive. He does not attempt to refute EPA's claim that the 1977 standards were designed to regulate fecal pollution discharges and thus could have embodied the specific criteria Scott seeks. Thus EPA and the states have acted under Section 303 to establish standards pertaining to a type of pollutant discharge (fecal). Different labels do not change the essence of Scott's attack on the substance of those standards. *United States Steel* and the EPA procedure for review of agency actions would effectively be eviscerated if a party were allowed to launch such attacks via a federal action against EPA. Scott has therefore failed to state a cause of action against EPA for its non-promulgation of fecal bacteria and virus criteria.

3. Promulgation of TMDLs

Section 303(d)(1)(C) requires each state to develop TMDLs for those waters within its boundaries where water quality standards will not be achieved by application of technology-based limitations. Under Section 303(d)(2) EPA's duty is to either approve or disapprove such [proposed TMDLs] . . . not later than thirty days after the date of submission . . . [and if disapproved] establish [TMDLs] as . . . [it] determines necessary to implement the [applicable] water quality standards.

. . .

Scott's Complaint seeks to have EPA "adopt a . . . [TMDL] for all discharges of viruses and bacteria into Lake Michigan which will ensure the attainment of the water quality criteria for viruses and bacteria." However, neither Indiana nor Illinois has submitted a proposed TMDL, and Section 303(d)(2) limits EPA's authority in this area to (1) approval of *state-submitted* TMDLs or (2) promulgation *after* disapproval of such submission. Scott has submitted no authority for the proposition that EPA may promulgate TMDLs in the absence of a state proposal, or for the proposition that EPA can in some respect enforce a state's duty to submit TMDLs.

This Court need not decide whether Scott may sue a *state* for its failure to submit TMDLs, for he has not sought to do so. Clearly the Act provides no basis for a suit against EPA for its "failure" to promulgate TMDLs in the absence of such a submission.

NOTES

1. Do you agree with the court's holding that EPA cannot be required to adopt water quality criteria for Lake Michigan that apply to fecal tract virus and pathogen bacteria?

The concentration of fecal coliform bacteria in water is far from a perfect measure of the extent of health hazards associated with the presence of untreated municipal sewage. In the first place, fecal coliforms are not pathogenic, nor do their die-off or multiplication rates simulate those of pathogens. Also, fecal coliform levels can be significantly raised by runoff from rural and urban areas, without any corresponding increase in the level of the pathogens in the water because of raw sewage discharges. See the discussion in EPA's report on "Nature of and Trends in Water Pollutants," *supra* p. 7. However, because of the difficulty and expense of direct identification of water-borne pathogens, EPA has accepted water quality criteria designed to measure the raw sewage load in a water body which are specified only in terms of fecal coliform bacteria count.

If EPA were to determine that the technology was reasonably available to measure the presence of pathogen bacteria and viruses, could it disapprove state-submitted criteria expressed only in terms of fecal coliforms and promulgate criteria for such pathogens? Could EPA, at any time such technological means became available, utilize its authority under Section 303(c)(4)(B) to replace state criteria with such "improved" criteria? Could EPA be compelled by a citizen suit brought under Section 505(a)(2) to take such action?

2. Did the court correctly construe Section 303(d)(2) to limit EPA's authority to promulgate total maximum daily loads to those instances in which states submit "TMDLs" that EPA disapproves? Is it logical to deprive EPA of the authority to act only in the case of states which make no effort to comply with the Act?

Without the authority to set TMDLs, does EPA have any means of assuring that water quality standards are met? Can this be accomplished in permitting under the authority of Section 301(b)(1)(C) without the intervening step of TMDL calculation? Could EPA disapprove a state-issued permit for failure to assure achievement of state water quality standards without reference to a TMDL study?

3. What other remedies are available to the plaintiff in this case? Shortly, in Chapter 15 of this text, we will explore the availability of common law nuisance actions in cases such as this — an issue not raised by EPA's motion to dismiss.

Do citizen suits under Section 505 of the Clean Water Act lie to compel states to regulate in compliance with the Act?

4. The basic problem is how can citizens of a downstream state, or one bordering on an interstate body of water such as a Great Lake, be protected from discharges permitted by a state where the facility is located.

Does the citizen of one state have the right to intervene and participate in permitting decisions in another state? Most importantly, does Section 301(b)(1)(C) require effluent limitations that are necessary to meet not only the water quality standards of the state where the discharger is located, but also any more stringent water quality standards established by other affected states? Or is the procedure established by Section 402(b)(5), (d)(2) and (d)(4) the only protection afforded non-permitting states?

5. Must the EPA protect the water quality preferences of a downstream state against being placed in jeopardy by lower water quality designations by upstream states? If so, does this mean that EPA must always allow a downstream state desiring high water quality to dictate to an upstream state? What statutory authority does EPA have to disapprove one state's water quality designations because of impact on another? Does Section 103(a) of the Act provide sufficient statement of purpose to be incorporated into the "purposes" requirement of Section 303(c)(2)?

Whether or not express statutory authority exists, EPA has consistently asserted the power to resolve interstate conflicts over water quality designations. In its most recent Water Quality Standards Regulations, 48 Fed. Reg. 51400 (Nov. 8, 1983), EPA has reiterated its position:

§ 131.10(B)

In designating uses of a water body and the appropriate criteria for those uses, the state shall take into consideration the water quality standards of downstream waters and shall ensure that its water quality standards provide for the attainment and maintenance of the water quality standards of downstream waters.

Would you expect such a requirement for approval by EPA to be upheld in court as a practical necessity — whether or not express authority can be found in the Act?

United States Steel Corporation v. Train

556 F.2d 822 (7th Cir. 1977)

Before CUMMINGS AND TONE Circuit Judges, and CAMPBELL, Senior District Judge.

TONE, Circuit Judge. These consolidated cases bring before us an Environmental Protection Agency (EPA) order granting a discharge permit under the Federal Water Pollution Control Act Amendments of 1972 and a related District Court judgment.***

*   *   *

The Plant

U.S. Steel's Gary Works occupies 3,700 acres on the southern shore of Lake Michigan. An integrated steel mill, Gary Works produces coke, iron, steel, and primary and finished steel shapes. The plant draws water from Lake Michigan and each day discharges up to 775 million gallons of polluted water into the lake and into the Grand Calumet River, which flows into the lake. The discharges are made through five outfalls into the lake and 14 into the river. Each day the 500 million gallons discharged into the river include an average of 180 pounds of phosphorus, 325 pounds of phenol, 3,100 pounds of cyanide, 3,400 pounds of fluorides, 5,100 pounds of ammonia, 82,000 pounds of chloride, and 180,000 pounds of sulphates. These pollutants eventually flow into lower Lake Michigan.

The EPA Permit Proceeding

*   *   *

EPA initially issued a permit for the Gary Works in October 1974, after having published notice of its proposed action. The permit contained effluent limitations, monitoring requirements, and additional conditions, together with a compliance schedule. U.S. Steel did not accept the permit but requested an administrative hearing pursuant to EPA regulations.***

After the hearing and a limited remand ordered by EPA, the Regional Administrator substantially approved the conditions contained in the permit, which had been formulated by the Regional Enforcement Division. U.S. Steel appealed, pursuant to 40 C.F.R. § 125. 36(n)(1), to the Administrator, who denied review. The permit was reissued by EPA on June 25, 1976, with a modified compliance schedule. U.S. Steel then filed its petition for review in this court.

The Permit

The permit imposes technology-based limitations governing pH, total suspended solids (TSS), and oil and grease at each individual outfall. These limitations are designed to reflect the level of pollutant discharges remaining despite installation of 1977, or best practicable, technology.***

*   *   *

Other permit limitations, imposed because they are required by Indiana regulations, govern six chemicals, *viz.*, ammonia, cyanide, phenol, chloride, sulphate, and flouride. These limitations apply to the plant's river outfalls as a group and not to individual outfalls. There are also thermal limitations based on state water quality standards.

*   *   *

Agency Refusal To Consider Validity of Indiana Water Quality Standards.

The administrative law judge held that he was without jurisdiction to consider the validity of the Indiana water quality standards upon

which certain limitations in the permit were based, a position the Administrator sustained. U.S. Steel contends that Indiana provides no judicial review of the validity of the standards and that due process therefore requested the Administrator to determine the validity of those standards.

Under § 402(a)(1) of the FWPCA, the Administrator must condition the NPDES permit upon the discharger's meeting "all applicable requirements under sections 301," *et al.* Section 301 (b)(l)(C) requires compliance by July 1, 1977 with

> "any more stringent limitation, including those necessary to meet water quality standards, treatment standards, or schedules of compliance, established pursuant to any State law or regulations (under authority preserved by section 510) . . . ."

Section 510 preserves the right of any state to impose limitations more stringent than the federal limitations under the Act. Because the Administrator is required by the Act to include in the permit any more stringent state limitations, including those necessary to meet state water quality standards, and is given no authority to set aside or modify those limitations in a permit proceeding, he correctly ruled that he had no authority to consider challenges to the validity of the state water quality standards in such a proceeding.

The Administrator's only authority to pass on state water quality standards is conferred by § 303 of the Act, which empowers him to determine whether the standard "meets" or is "consistent with the applicable requirements of this Act." In accordance with that provision he has, in a separate proceeding, considered and approved the applicable Indiana water quality standards. Authority to approve or disapprove a state's identification of polluted waters and calculation of total maximum daily loads is conferred on the Administrator by § 303(d)(2). These determinations are reviewable in an action in the district court under the judicial review provisions of the APA.

*   *   *

Permit Conditions

A. *Limitations Required by State Law or Regulation*

The limitations on the six chemicals, ammonia, cyanide, phenol, chloride, sulphate and fluoride, and the thermal limitations are, as we have seen, state limitations adopted by Indiana pursuant to its plenary power preserved by § 510. They were included in the permit because § 402(a)(1) required the Administrator to condition the discharge permit on compliance with "all applicable requirements" of, *inter alia,* § 301, and § 301(b)(1)(C) requires dischargers to achieve, in addition to the technology-based effluent limitations determined by EPA, "any more stringent limitation, including those necessary to meet water quality standards . . . established pursuant to any State law or regulation (under authority preserved by Section 510) . . . ."

(1) *Chemical Limitations*

The limitations for the six chemicals are aggregate weight limits on the total discharges that may be made from all the outfalls at which those chemicals are discharged, which are the river outfalls. The allowable discharges are not allocated among the individual outfalls.[19] Compliance, however, is determined by monitoring at each outfall.

In challenging these limitations, U.S. Steel argues that the water quality standards on which certain limitations are based are invalid. As we have held in Parts III, A(4) and III, B(1), *supra,* however, those standards are not subject to review in either of the appeals presently before us. The company also argues that the limitations on the six chemicals are impossible to achieve with present technology. Even if this is true, it does not follow that they are invalid. It is clear from §§ 301 and 510 of the Act, and

the legislative history, that the states are free to force technology. Although the Indiana Board considered technology in setting some of these limitations, it was not required to do so. Only the federal effluent limitations must be technology-based, and they represent the minimum level of pollution reduction required by the Act. If the states wish to achieve better water quality, they may, even at the cost of economic and social dislocations caused by plant closings.***

U.S. Steel also asserts in conclusory terms that the limitations on the six chemicals are not based upon substantial evidence and are arbitrary. If this is intended as an argument that the allocations are more stringent than would be necessary to achieve the water quality standards, it fails for two reasons:

First, notwithstanding EPA's overgenerous concession to the contrary, this necessity argument is not available in this proceeding, Section 301(b)(1)(C), the ultimate source of the Administrator's obligation to put the state limitations in the permit, is not limited to restrictions based on water quality standards but extends to "any more stringent limitation" the state adopts pursuant to the authority preserved by § 510. As we read the Act, the Administrator had no more authority to inquire into whether the limitations adopted by the state were necessary to achieve the water quality standards than he did to inquire into the validity of those standards.

*   *   *

We accordingly overrule the objections to the limitations on the six chemicals.

(2) *Thermal Limitations*

The permit also establishes limitations, effective July 1, 1977, on the temperature of the adjacent receiving waters of Lake Michigan and the Grand Calumet River after admixture of the discharges.[26] Monitoring requirements of the

---

[19]The permit limitations are:

	Daily Average (In lbs.)	Daily Maximum (In lbs.)
Ammonia	2,150	4,300
Cyanide	109.5	219
Phenol	25.76	51.52
Chloride	40,023	80,046
Fluride	2,778	5,556
Sulphate	95,660	191,320

These limitations are applied on a net basis.

---

[26]The limitations are different for the lake and the river, varying seasonally for each body of water. Discharges into the Grand Calumet River may not cause waters adjacent to the discharge to exceed 60°F from October through March, or 90°F during these spring and summer months. Comparably, limitations for the lake are the lower of existing temperature plus 3°F

permit enable EPA to measure U.S. Steel's compliance with the thermal limitations. The limits are taken directly from the Indiana water quality standards applicable to the two bodies of water. The permit offers U.S. Steel an alternative to compliance with these limitations as authorized by § 316(a) of the Act. Under that section, the company may attempt to

> "demonstrate to the satisfaction of the Administrator . . . that [the] effluent limitation[s] proposed for the control of the thermal component of [its] discharge . . . [are] more stringent than necessary to assure the projection [*sic*] and propagation of a balanced, indigenous population of shellfish, fish, and wildlife in and on [Lake Michigan and/or the Grand Calumet River]."

If the company's showing is successful, EPA may set less stringent thermal limitations, provided

or 45°F during January-March, 50°F in December, 55°F in April, 60°F during May and November, 65°F in October, 70°F in June, and 80°F during July-September.

they still meet the aquatic-life requirements. U.S. Steel challenges both the thermal limitations and the thermal demonstration provisions of the permit.

U.S. Steel argues that "the thermal limitations in this permit are vague, arbitrary and unreasonable." As effluent limitations based directly on state water quality standards and included in the permit pursuant to § 301(b)(1)(C), however, the thermal limitations are not open to substantive challenge in this proceeding. The company's related claim that compliance with the limits cannot be reliably determined must be rejected insofar as it is an objection to the permit's use of temperature as the measurement scale for determining compliance with thermal water quality standards. We know of no alternative measurement scale. And, although thermal monitoring is necessarily imprecise, it is possible to determine whether a discharger is in substantial compliance with thermal effluent limitations. The thermal limitations in the permit are therefore upheld.

*   *   *

NOTES

1. Probably the most striking thing about this case is the information it contains on the levels of pollutants discharged by a large steel mill such as this. Notice that, even under the permit terms here challenged, it would be allowed to discharge a daily average of 109.5 pounds of cyanide and 95,660 pounds of sulphates. But compare these figures with the 3,100 pounds of cyanide and 180,000 pounds of sulphates discharged per day prior to control.

2. Would, as the court suggests, an industry adversely affected by stringent state water quality standards be able to obtain relief from EPA upon its review of those state standards? *See* Section 303(c)(2), (3). Could EPA disapprove a state water quality standard if, in setting the standard, the state had totally ignored the value of the water for industrial uses? Could a federal reviewing court properly order either EPA or the state to take into consideration such economic factors? Reconsider the question after reading the next case.

3. If, as U.S. Steel alleged, the effluent limitations adopted by Indiana were impossible to meet and not rationally related to attainment of the state water quality standards, could it hope to prevail in a constitutional challenge? Would section 401 or section 510 of the Act shield the state from commerce clause attack? *See White v. Massachusetts Council of Construction Employees*, 103 S. Ct. 1042 (1983).

4. Do you agree with the court's statement that the thermal limitations taken directly from the Indiana water quality standards could be relaxed by the EPA Administrator if he were satisfied with a showing made pursuant to Section 316?

Note that Section 303(g) provides "Water quality standards relating to heat shall be consistent with the requirements of Section 316 of this title." But does this imply that, once such thermal water quality standards have been set by the state and approved by EPA, the Administrator could nevertheless grant variances under Section 316? Would such a variance from state water quality standards be consistent with Section 510?

5. To obtain a variance from a thermal limitation under the terms of Section 316, the applicant must not only show that indigenous populations of fish and wildlife will not be harmed by the discharge, it must also show that the cooling water intake structures reflect the "best technology available for minimizing adverse environmental impact." Section 316(b). In the licensing of the Seabrook Nuclear Power Plant on the Massachusetts coast, one issue which arose concerned the effects of its offshore intake structure upon juvenile and larval fish that might be pulled into its one-foot-per-second intake. *See Seacoast Anti-Pollution League v. Costle,* 597 F.2d 306 (1st Cir. 1979).

Homestake Mining Company
v.
Environmental Protection Agency
477 F.Supp. 1279 (D.S.D. 1979)

BOGUE, District Judge.

This case is before the Court on cross-motions for summary judgment. It concerns defendant South Dakota's adoption and defendant Environmental Protection Agency's (EPA) approval of water quality standards under the Federal Water Pollution Control Act (FWPCA). These standards were incorporated in a National Pollution Discharge Elimination System (NPDES) permit issued to Plaintiff Homestake Mining Company.

*   *   *

FACTS

Plaintiff contends that EPA's approval of South Dakota's water quality standards, which are somewhat stricter than those mandated by the FWPCA, was arbitrary, capricious and contrary to law. In 1974, South Dakota revised its water quality standards and designated Whitewood Creek for use as a cold water permanent fishery and for recreation in and on the water. This designation affected plaintiff in that plaintiff discharges waste into Gold Run Creek which

is a tributary of Whitewood Creek. On October 28, 1977, South Dakota again revised its water quality standards as required by § 303(c) of the FWPCA. These revisions did not change the designation of Whitewood Creek as a cold water permanent fishery.

Under § 402(a) of the FWPCA, EPA issued draft NPDES permits to plaintiff in 1975 and 1976. These permits contained effluent limitations based on BPT and the more stringent state water quality standards. Plaintiff was given a chance for a hearing on the terms of its permit, but eventually declined this opportunity and accepted the permit on September 17, 1976.

Plaintiff is now asking this Court to declare EPA's approval of South Dakota's more stringent water quality standards to be violative of the FWPCA. Such a declaration by this Court would free plaintiff from the requirements of its NPDES permit. In its prayer for relief plaintiff asks this Court to enjoin the application to it of both South Dakota's water quality standards and the Cheyenne River Basin Plan.

*   *   *

EPA'S APPROVAL OF SOUTH DAKOTA'S WATER QUALITY STANDARDS

In revising its water quality standards in October of 1977, South Dakota's Board of Environmental Protection was instructed by counsel that South Dakota law did not allow the Board to consider economic or social factors in establishing these standards. These standards became effective on December 15, 1977, and were conditionally approved by EPA on March 15, 1978. Plaintiff argues that South Dakota's Board of Environmental Protection was required by the FWPCA to consider economic and social factors. Because it failed to do so, plaintiff further argues that EPA's approval of the standards was arbitrary and capricious. Plaintiff's claim is based on § 303(c)(2) of the FWPCA, which reads as follows:

> Whenever the State revises or adopts a new standard, such revised or new standard shall be submitted to the Administrator. Such revised or new water quality standards shall consist of the designated uses of the navigable waters involved and the water quality criteria for such waters based upon such uses. Such standards shall be such as to protect the public health or welfare, enhance the quality of water and serve the purposes of this chapter. Such standards shall be established taking into consideration the use and value for public water supplies, propagation of fish and wildlife, recreational purposes, and agricultural, industrial, and other purposes, and also taking into consideration the use and value for navigation.

The federal regulations implementing § 303(c)(2) are also relied upon by plaintiff:

> The State shall establish water quality standards which will result in the achievement of national water quality goals specified in section 101(a)(2) of the Act, wherever obtainable. In determining whether such standards are obtainable for any particular segment, the State should take into consideration environmental, technological, social, economic,

and institutional factors. 40 C.F.R. § 130.17(c)(1).

The language of the statute and the regulations must be studied in examining plaintiff's first claim. The FWPCA states that "standards shall be established taking into consideration" the various factors listed. The applicable federal regulation states that "the State should take into consideration" the various factors. It must therefore, be determined what the phrase "taking into consideration" requires.

***Nothing in the statute seems to indicate that the states must give equal weight to all the factors listed. The *Weyerhaeuser* case indicates that the amount of weight to give each individual factor is within the State's discretion.

In support of its contention that EPA should have disapproved South Dakota's water quality standards, plaintiff cites *Kentucky v. Train,* 9 E.R.C. 1280 (E.D. Ky. 1976). In that case, EPA's disapproval of state standards was upheld because Kentucky's standards extended only to waters identified on the map entitled "Streams of Kentucky" rather than to all "waters of the United States" as required by the FWPCA. Plaintiff cites this case in support of its position that disapproval of state plans has been judicially sanctioned. However, there is an important point that distinguishes *Kentucky v. Train* from the case at bar. In *Kentucky v. Train,* EPA disapproved the state standards because they failed to meet the minimum requirements of the FWPCA. On the other hand, in the case at bar, plaintiff is asking this Court to declare invalid standards that are more stringent than those contained in the Act. Declaring state standards invalid because they are too stringent violates both the statute itself and case law interpreting the statute. Section 301(b)(1)(C) allows states to adopt more stringent standards than those established by the Act. Furthermore, §§ 303(f) and 510 of the FWPCA give the states the power to establish any effluent limitation standards which are equal to or more stringent than the Act's standards.

In *United States Steel Corporation v. Train,* 556 F.2d 822 (7th Cir. 1977), the Court dealt with the issue of more stringent state standards. The Court held that the FWPCA was not designed

to inhibit the states from adopting more stringent standards and in forcing industry to create more effective pollution control technology.
*** Furthermore, the Court held that EPA has
no authority to set aside or modify state standards which are more stringent than those mandated by the Act.***

*   *   *

South Dakota's water quality standards simply establish more stringent standards than
those required by the Act. The statute itself and
the case law make it clear that the states can
adopt more stringent standards and can force
technology. Under §§ 301 and 510 of the
FWPCA, EPA had no power to disapprove these
standards and was required to include them in
the NPDES permit. South Dakota was not
required to consider economic and social factors
and thus its failure to do so does not invalidate
its water quality standards. Even though it may
be much more difficult for plaintiff to comply
with South Dakota's standards, than it would be
to comply with the Act's standards, South
Dakota had the power to adopt the stricter standards and EPA's approval of those standards was
not arbitrary and capricious or violative of the
Act.

IMPLEMENTATION OF §§ 302 AND 303

The objective of the FWPCA is set out in
§ 101(a). This objective is generally referred to
as the goal of achieving fishable/swimmable
waters. It underlies the effluent limitations
established by both the states and EPA.

Plaintiff argues that the fishable/swimma-
ble goal is being improperly implemented. Plaintiff contends that § 302 of the FWPCA was
intended to be the primary means of implementing the fishable/swimmable goal, but instead,
EPA has improperly relied on § 303 as the
primary method of achieving this goal.***

Section 302 requires a cost-benefit hearing
prior to the establishment of new effluent limitations where the effluent limitations required
under § 301(b)(2) are not sufficient to attain the
goals of the FWPCA. Section 301(b)(2) requires
the achievement of effluent limitations applying

BAT by July 1, 1984. Therefore, as defendant
EPA points out, it appears that plaintiff's claim
is premature. Section 302 applies only when the
application of BAT will interfere with attainment
of the fishable/swimmable goal. Because many
of the standards based on BAT are not yet established, plaintiff presently is not being asked to
comply with any effluent limitation stricter than
BAT. Thus, § 302 should not be applied at this
time and plaintiff should not be allowed to complain about the lack of a hearing.

However, even if plaintiff's claim is not considered premature, the claim would still fail
because the use of § 303 by EPA has not been
improper.

*   *   *

Section 301(b)(1)(C) requires that there shall
be achieved,

> not later than July 1, 1977, any more
> stringent limitation, including those
> necessary to meet water quality stan-
> dards, treatment standards, or schedules
> of compliance, established pursuant to
> any State law or regulations (under
> authority preserved by section 1370 of
> this title) . . .

This statute clearly deals with more stringent
state limitations. Nowhere does it require that
a § 302 hearing be held before the adoption of
a standard.

*   *   *

As pointed out in the first section of this
opinion, the states clearly have the right to
establish more stringent standards than those
mandated by the FWPCA. If plaintiff's interpretation of the statute was correct, any time
state standards exceeded BAT, a cost-benefit
analysis would have to be conducted by EPA.
This would have the effect of virtually emascu-
lating the state's power, which is guaranteed
by § 510. Section 302 guarantees a hearing only
if the effluent limitations are adopted under
EPA authority, not state authority. The rights
of the states are clearly protected by the Act
and states are intended to be an integral cog in
the operation of the statute. Plaintiff's interpretation would have the effect of decreasing

the states' power. This does not appear to be intended by § 302.

Plaintiff further alleges that EPA's implementation of § 303 has been arbitrary and capricious. Plaintiff complains that through the use of a guidance document EPA illegally limited the discretion of the states in adopting their water quality standards. The guidance document indicates that the states should give prime importance to recreational uses and the preservation of aquatic biota. Plaintiff complains that EPA improperly imposed these standards on South Dakota, and in so doing, restricted South Dakota from exercising its full range of statutory authority because it prevented South Dakota from considering industrial, agricultural and other use classifications.

In support of this argument, plaintiff cites *Associated Industries of Alabama v. Train*, 9 E.R.C. 1561 (N.D. Ala. 1976). In that case, EPA disapproved Alabama's water quality standards because they did not meet EPA's "national policy" which prohibited use classification below that of "fish and wildlife." This so-called national policy was set in an EPA memorandum. EPA claimed that under § 303(a) it could declare Alabama's standards invalid because they were not consistent with the applicable requirements of the FWPCA. The plaintiff claimed EPA's actions were arbitrary and capricious.

The Court found that Alabama's water quality standards were consistent with the Act and that EPA had disapproved them because they failed to meet the "fish and wildlife" criteria. The Court found that the states were permitted by the Act to consider other use classifications, such as agricultural and industrial uses, and could not be restricted to considering fish and wildlife as the minimum use classification. The Court concluded that EPA had not properly established a national policy and therefore Alabama was not compelled to comply with the requirements in the memorandum.

Plaintiff argues that through the use of the guidance document EPA has forced the states to do exactly what the Court in *Associated Industries, supra,* said EPA could not do; that being, requiring the states to adopt 1983 fish-

able/swimmable goal in 1977. One key factor distinguishes the *Associated Industries* case from the one at bar. In *Associate Industries,* EPA attempted to force the State of Alabama to adopt water quality standards which Alabama did not want to adopt. Such is not the case here.

Assuming arguendo that the memorandum involved in *Associated Industries* and the guidance document at issue in this case are both examples of a wrongful attempt to impose water quality standards contrary to the FWPCA, the fact is that the State of South Dakota is not complaining in this case. As is shown in the first section of this opinion, the states have the right to force technology and establish stricter water quality standards. In this case, South Dakota is not complaining, as did Alabama in *Associated Industries,* that EPA is forcing it to adopt water quality standards it did not wish to adopt. South Dakota used its considerable discretion under the FWPCA and adopted the standards it felt would best serve the state. That being the case, plaintiff is in no position to complain about the standards. If South Dakota felt EPA was attempting to force it to adopt standards it did not want, it could do as Alabama did in *Associated Industries* and refuse to adopt such standards or challenge EPA in court. However, since this has not been done, it must be assumed that the water quality standards adopted for Whitewood Creek were those desired by the state and was within the State's power under the FWPCA.

APPROVAL OF THE CHEYENNE RIVER BASIN PLAN

Plaintiff next challenges EPA's approval of the § 303(e), 33 U.S.C., § 13139(e), Cheyenne River Basin Plan. A large part of western South Dakota, including Whitewood Creek, is included in the Cheyenne River Basin. The Plan establishes South Dakota's

> strategy for correcting water pollution and thereby improving and maintaining water quality in the Cheyenne River Basin. . . . It specifies the process of planning and managing pollution abate-

ment operations to achieve South Dakota's standards for pollutant discharges to, and water quality in the Basin's, lakes, rivers and tributaries.

This plan was implemented pursuant to § 303(e) of the FWPCA.

Section 303(e) provides for the establishment, by the states, of a continuing planning process. Section 303(e)(3)(C) reads as follows:

The Administrator shall approve any continuing planning process submitted to him under this section which will result in plans for all navigable waters within such State, which include, but are not limited to, the following. . . .

(C) total maximum daily load for pollutants in accordance with subsection (d) of this section.

The method of establishing the daily load is set out in § 303(d)(1). That section provides:

(A) Each State shall identify those waters within its boundaries for which the effluent limitations required by section 1311(b)(1)(A) and section 1311(b)(1)(B) of this title are not stringent enough to implement any water quality standard applicable to such waters. The State shall establish a priority ranking for such waters, taking into account the severity of the pollution and the uses to be made of such waters. . . . (C) Each State shall establish for the waters identified in paragraph (1)(A) of this subsection, and in accordance with the priority ranking, the total maximum daily load, for those pollutants which the Administrator identifies under section 1314(a)(2) of this title as suitable for such calculation. Such load shall be established at a level necessary to implement the applicable water quality standards with seasonal variations and a margin of safety which takes into account any lack of knowledge concerning the relationship between effluent limitations and water quality.

Section 304(a)(2)(D) of the FWPCA, 33 U.S.C. § 1314(a)(2)(D), requires EPA to identify pollutants which are suitable for maximum daily load calculations by October 18, 1973. Prior to the adoption of South Dakota's water quality standards defendants failed to comply with these sections of the Act in that maximum daily loads for pollutants were not established.

These procedures were meant to assist EPA and the states in implementing the requirements of the Act. Plaintiff contends that these procedures are mandatory requirements of the FWPCA. Furthermore, plaintiff argues that the failure to comply with these procedures should invalidate the entire Cheyenne River Basin Plan.

Although South Dakota did not establish total maximum daily loads as required by § 303(d), this was not required of the state until 180 days after EPA's identification of pollutants. Because EPA had not identified the pollutants at the time of the Basin Plan's adoption, South Dakota cannot be said to have failed to comply with this portion of the FWPCA. The question then becomes whether EPA's failure to identify pollutants suitable for maximum daily load calculations pursuant to § 304(a)(2)(D) is of such magnitude as to invalidate the Cheyenne River Basin Plan and in turn, to invalidate plaintiff's NPDES permit.

It appears to this Court that EPA's failure to identify pollutants does not invalidate the Basin Plan. First of all, plaintiff's attack on the entire Basin Plan is clearly an attempt to avoid having to comply with the terms of its NPDES permit. Section 509(b)(1)(F) provides that a challenge to an NPDES permit can be made within 90 days of the permit's issuance in the applicable Circuit Court of Appeals. This, plaintiff did not do.***Since plaintiff neglected its other opportunities to challenge its NPDES permit, the Court is unwilling to invalidate the entire Cheyenne River Basin Plan because of plaintiff's dissatisfaction with its permit.

Furthermore, it appears that § 402(a)(1) of the FWPCA allows the issuance of a permit prior to the taking of all implementing actions. This statute provides in part as follows:

[T]he Administrator may, after opportunity for public hearing, issue a permit for the discharge of any pollutant, . . . prior to the taking of necessary implementing actions relating to all such requirements, such conditions as the Administrator determines are necessary to carry out the provisions of this chapter.

It appears to this Court that Congress anticipated that some of the Act's requirements would not, or could not, be complied with prior to the issuance of permits. Therefore, § 402 was included in the Act to insure that the permit issuance program was not stymied because another part of the Act had not been strictly complied with.

*   *   *

The FWPCA is a complex statute. EPA clearly has more experience working with it than do most other public or private entities. In implementing and interpreting such a complex statute, EPA's interpretation must be given a great deal of weight. In approving South Dakota's Cheyenne River Basin Plan, EPA substantially complied with the Act's requirements. Furthermore, plaintiff's right to challenge the effluent limitation and its NPDES permit was preserved. Therefore, this Court sees no reason to declare the Basin Plan invalid or to find EPA's approval of it to be arbitrary and capricious.

CONCLUSION

The establishment of South Dakota's water quality standards and EPA's approval of them appear to this Court to be in compliance with the FWPCA. Therefore, the summary judgment motion of the defendants will be granted and plaintiff's motion for summary judgment will be denied.

NOTES

1. Do you agree with the court that, despite the literal terms of Section 303(c)(2), the state did not have to consider economic or social factors—*e.g.,* "agricultural" or "industrial" uses—in setting water quality standards? Was not *U.S. Steel's* application of Section 510 distinguishable?

Under this holding, could another state refuse to consider "propagation of fish and wildlife" in setting its standards?

If a state submits no water quality standards, and EPA resorts to its authority under Section 303(c)(4) to set them, what factors is it to take into consideration? Could it refuse to consider agricultural and industrial uses?

2. Do you agree with the court's construction of Section 302? Read this somewhat ambiguous section carefully.

Does it not apply until BAT limitations are imposed (now destined for July, 1984)?

Would it *ever* authorize rejection of state-set water quality standards? Does it ever apply to *water quality standards* under any circumstances—even those set by EPA? Notice that by its terms Section 302 only applies to *effluent limitations* for a particular point source necessary to achieve the "fishable/swimmable" standard required by subsection (a).

After July, 1984, would subsection (b) empower EPA to "adjust" an effluent limitation necessary to achieve a *state* fishable/swimmable standard—or only one compelled by subsection (a)?

3. Homestake's argument that EPA had improperly forced the state of South Dakota into designating Whitewood Creek as a cold water fishery was, of course, considerably undercut by the fact that South Dakota had first made that designation in 1974 and was not complaining of any federal coercion in maintaining it in 1977.

But what if South Dakota had wanted to change the creek's designation to "mine-runoff dispersion waters" and EPA had disapproved such a water quality standard and promulgated the cold water fishery standard? How could it find the state's choice "not to be consistent with the requirements" of the Act. *See* Section 303(c)(3) and (4)(A). Could EPA ever, under such circumstances, find that the state had not properly balanced the factors specified in Section 303(c)(2)? Notice that two requirements in subsection (c)(2) are that the standards be such as to "*enhance* the quality of water" and "serve the purposes of this chapter"—including the national goal in Section 101 (a)(2) of fishable/swimmable water by July, 1983. Could EPA use this as a justification to deny downgrading now that we are past 1983? Would it permit EPA to utilize Section 303(c)(4)(B) to upgrade all waters in the nation to fishable/swimmable? Notice that in 1976, in the only reported decision to squarely face EPA's power to force upgrading, the North District of Alabama denied the agency such authority. *Associated Industries v. Train*, 9 ERC 1561 (N.D. Ala. 1976).

4. The most recent expression of EPA's policies for implementing Section 303 are contained in the "Water Quality Standards Regulation" promulgated by Administrator Ruckelshaus, (after a great deal of controversy surrounding the significantly different proposal of his predecessor) on November 8, 1983. *See* 48 Fed. Reg. 51400, to be codified at 40 CFR Part 131 (1984). This regulation recites that it is designed to describe "the requirements and procedures for developing, reviewing, revising and approving water quality standards by the states," 40 CFR § 131.1; but Section 131.22(C) makes clear that, in promulgating water quality standards for states which fail to satisfy these rules, EPA is subject to the same requirements.

The "antidegradation policy" expressed in Section 131.12 provides strict protection of existing uses of all water bodies. ("Existing uses" are defined by Section 131.3(E) to be "those uses actually attained in the water body on or after November 28, 1975, whether or not they are included in the water quality standards."

§ 131.12 Antidegradation Policy.

(A) The State shall develop and adopt a statewide antidegradation policy and identify the methods for implementing such policy pursuant to this subpart. The antidegradation policy and implementation methods shall, at the minimum, be consistent with the following:

(1) Existing instream water uses and the level of water quality necessary to protect the existing uses shall be maintained and protected.

(2) Where the quality of the waters exceed levels necessary to support propagation of fish, shellfish, and wildlife and recreation in and on the water, that quality shall be maintained and protected unless the State finds, after full satisfaction of the intergovernmental coordination and public participation provisions of the State's continuing planning process, that allowing lower water quality is necessary to accommodate important economic or social development in the area in which the waters are located. In allowing such degradation or lower water quality, the State shall assure water quality adequate to protect existing uses fully. Further, the State shall assure that there shall be achieved the highest statutory and regulatory requirements for all new and existing point sources and all cost-effective and reasonable best management practices for nonpoint source control.

(3) Where high quality waters constitute an outstanding National resource, such as waters of National and State parks and wildlife refuges and waters of exceptional recreational or ecological significance, that water quality shall be maintained and protected.

(4) In those cases where potential water quality impairment associated with a thermal discharge is involved, the antidegradation policy and implementing method shall be consistent with Section 316 of the Act.

Along with this strict protection of *existing uses*, Sections 131.10(G) and (H) give the states some flexibility in changing from "designated" uses which are more stringent than those actually attained:

(G) States may remove a designated use which is not an existing use, as defined in

§ 131.3, or establish sub-categories of a use if the State can demonstrate that attaining the designated use is not feasible because

(1) Naturally occurring pollutant concentrations prevent the attainment of the use; or

(2) Natural, ephemeral, intermittent or low flow conditions or water levels prevent the attainment of the use, unless these conditions may be compensated for by the discharge of sufficient volume of effluent discharges without violating State water conservation requirements to enable uses to be met; or

(3) Human caused conditions or sources of pollution prevent the attainment of the use and cannot be remedied or would cause more environmental damage to correct than to leave in place; or

(4) Dams, diversions or other types of hydrologic modifications preclude the attainment of the use, and it is not feasible to restore the water body to its original condition or to operate such modification in a way that would result in the attainment of the use; or

(5) Physical conditions related to the natural features of the water body, such as the lack of a proper substrate, cover, flow, depth, pools, riffles, and the like, unrelated to water quality, preclude attainment of aquatic life protection uses; or

(6) Controls more stringent than those required by Sections 301(B) and 306 of the Act would result in substantial and widespread economic and social impact.

(H) States may not remove designated uses if:

(1) They are existing uses, as defined in Section 131.3, unless a use requiring more stringent criteria is added; or

(2) Such uses will be attained by implementing effluent limits required under Sections 301(B) and 306 of the Act and by implementing cost-effective and reasonable best management practices for nonpoint source control.

These subsections are followed by the mandate of § 131.10(I): "Where existing water quality standards specify designated uses less than those which are presently being attained, the state shall revise its standards to reflect the uses actually being attained."

No matter how heavily industrial the actual use of a water body, Section 131.10(A) provides: "In no case shall a state adopt waste transport or waste assimilation as a designated use for any waters of the United States."

5. Do you think that EPA has gone beyond the scope of the Act in setting some of these requirements? Do you anticipate challenges by affected industries and/or states? A facial challenge to an earlier version of EPA "antidegradation policy" which was brought by ten public utility companies was dismissed as not "ripe" outside the context of actual application in a concrete situation. *See Commonwealth Edison Co. v. Train*, 649 F.2d 481 (7th Cir. 1980). If you were now counsel to these utilities, when and how would you advise them to make their attack on the new regulations?

6. Remember that water quality standards have two required components: designated uses and water quality *criteria*. Both must be submitted by a state to EPA for its approval, and EPA may disapprove and promulgate substitutes for either or both. Section 131.11 of the new water quality regulations specifies the requirements for criteria:

§ 131.11 Criteria

(A) Inclusion of pollutants:

(1) States must adopt those water quality criteria that protect the designated use. Such criteria must be based on sound scientific rationale and must contain sufficient parameters or constituents to protect the designated use. For waters with multiple use designations, the criteria shall support the most sensitive use.

*   *   *

(B) Form of criteria: In establishing criteria, States should:
(1) Establish numerical values based on:
   (I) 304(A) Guidance; or
   (II) 304(A) Guidance modified to reflect site-specific conditions; or
   (III) other scientifically defensible methods;
(2) establish narrative criteria or criteria based upon biomonitoring methods where numerical criteria cannot be established or to supplement numerical criteria.

In its summary of responses to public comments during rule-making, EPA denied that it had any policy of "presumptive applicability" of the criteria which it had specified pursuant to Section 304(a) of the Act. Although it said that states are free to use EPA's 304(a) criteria to support state criteria, "they are equally free to use any other criteria for which they have sound scientific support." May EPA disapprove state criteria as without sound scientific support and substitute its own, when this causes state-designated uses to impose more severe limitations on dischargers than the state contemplated? Consider the following case.

Mississippi Commission on Natural Resources v. Costle
625 F.2d 1269 (5th Cir. 1980)

Before GEE, FAY and RANDALL, Circuit Judges.

FAY, Circuit Judge:

The Mississippi Commission on Natural Resources (Commission) challenges the authority of the United States Environmental Protection Agency (EPA) to promulgate a water quality standard on dissolved oxygen for Mississippi. The Commission filed a complaint seeking a declaratory judgment that EPA's rejection of the state standard and promulgation of a federal standard were arbitrary, capricious, and beyond EPA's authority.***After cross-motions for summary judgment, the court granted judgment to EPA***.

I. *Statutory Framework*

Prior to 1972, the Federal Water Pollution Control Act (FWPCA) relied primarily upon state-promulgated water quality standards as the means for reaching its goal of enhancing the quality of the nation's waters. A water quality standard has two components. The first is the use for the water in an area. Possible uses are for industry, agriculture, propagation and protection of fish and wildlife, recreation, and pub-

lic water supply. The second component is the water quality criteria necessary to meet the designated use. For most pollutants, criteria are expressed as specific numerical concentration limits. For example, a state might set the water quality standard for a certain creek by designating it as a fishing area and requiring that the chloride concentration be no greater than 250 milligrams per liter of water.

In 1965, Congress considered whether the states or a federal administrator should establish water quality standards. Concerned that federal promulgation would discourage state plans for water quality and "would place in the hands of a single Federal official the power to establish zoning measures over—to control the use of—land within watershed areas" throughout the nation. Congress gave the states primary authority to set water quality standards. The state standards and plans were submitted to the federal administrator, who determined whether they were consistent with the Act's requirements. If the state did not adopt complying standards, the administrator promulgated water quality uses and criteria.

The Act "focused on the tolerable effects

rather than the preventable causes of water pollution." Problems with translating violations of standards into limits on particular polluters, the lack of enforcement, and the "awkwardly shared federal and state responsibility" led to amendments in 1972. The major change was the establishment of the National Pollutant Discharge Elimination System (NPDES), under which it is illegal to discharge pollutants without a permit complying with the Act.***The permits are the primary means for reaching the national goal of eliminating discharge of pollutants into water by 1985 and the interim goal of reaching a level of water quality, wherever attainable, "which provides for the protection and propagation of fish, shellfish, and wildlife and provides for recreation in and on the water . . . by July 1, 1983."

As the Act was passed, states promulgate water quality standards, which are submitted to EPA for approval. EPA can promulgate standards if the state does not set standards consistent with the Act or whenever EPA determines that another "standard is necessary to meet the requirements of [the Act]." State standards are reviewed every three years. NPDES permits must contain not only any effluent limitations set by EPA and the states, but also any more stringent limits necessary to reach the water quality standards.In addition, EPA must develop and publish "criteria for water quality accurately reflecting the latest scientific knowledge."

II. *Facts*

The dispute in this case arises from EPA's refusal to approve the Mississippi water quality standard for dissolved oxygen (DO) and EPA's subsequent promulgation of a DO standard. Dissolved oxygen is necessary for the protection and propagation of fish and aquatic life, and is generally measured in milligrams per liter (mg/l).

In 1946, the Mississippi Game and Fish Commission adopted a regulation requiring a minimum average DO concentration of 3.0 mg/l and an instantaneous minimum of 2.5 mg/l. Under this standard, the DO concentration could drop as low as 2.5 so long as compensating periods at higher concentrations raised the daily average to 3.0 mg/l.

In response to state and federal legislation, the Commission adopted standards on January 17, 1967 requiring a minimum daily average DO of 4.0 mg/l. The 1972 amendments to the Act allowed preexisting water quality standards to remain in effect upon approval by EPA. These standards were approved in October, 1972.

On January 18, 1973, EPA advised the Commission that it was time for the triennial review of its standards. After public hearings, the Commission submitted to EPA a DO standard of not less than an average of 5.0 mg/l, but allowing a level of 4.0 mg/l during periods with extremely low water levels. The low flow standard applies to days with the lowest water level that occurs for seven consecutive days in ten years (7 days Q10). On May 15, 1973, EPA approved the Commission's water quality standards, stating they were in "full compliance with the 1972 Amendments to the Federal Water Pollution Control Act."

As noted above, one of EPA's duties under the amendments is to develop and publish "criteria for water quality accurately reflecting the latest scientific knowledge." These criteria were to be published one year after October 18, 1972 and from time to time thereafter. *Id.* EPA gave notice of the availability of *Quality Criteria for Water,* also called the Red Book, on October 26, 1973. It thereafter became EPA's policy to request a state to justify its standards whenever the state submitted for approval water quality criteria less stringent than those in the Red Book.

In 1976, at the time for Mississippi's triennial review, EPA conferred with the Commission about upgrading its DO standard. Although the likelihood of the 7 day Q10 rate's occurring for seven *straight* days is only once in ten years, that particular low flow rate actually occurs for significant periods virtually every year. In addition, the 4.0 mg/l 7 day Q10 standard is an average, which therefore allows the DO level to fall below 4.0 on numerous occasions each year. Higher DO concentrations reduced crowding of fish and the resulting susceptibility to disease and toxicants. Adult fish generally are more tolerant of lower DO levels than juvenile forms. Lower levels also interfere with fish spawning.

The Commission forwarded to EPA for comment a proposed standard which required 5.0 mg/l with an instantaneous minimum of 4.0 mg/l, but allowed the DO to range between 5.0 and 4.0 for short periods.***The Commission, however, abandoned the proposal and on April 22, 1977, submitted to EPA its existing 5.0 mg/l—4.0 mg/l 7 days Q10 standard.

On June 9, 1977, EPA notified the Commission that it questioned the adequacy of the DO criteria. Specifically, Mississippi's DO standard was the only one in its region below 5.0 for 7 day Q10 conditions, and it was below the 5.0 mg/l criteria established in the Red Book. In accordance with its policy, EPA requested justification for the lower standard.***On August 24, 1977, EPA notified the Commission that it found Mississippi's justification unpersuasive.***

The Commission reconsidered its standard in September, 1977, and decided the state's standard was in the public interest.

EPA found this action insufficient and on July 13, 1978, proposed a DO standard of 5.0 mg/l at all times. In September, 1978, two public hearings were held in Mississippi as part of the rulemaking process. In response to public comment, EPA revised its proposed rule and adopted the less stringent standard of 5.0 mg/l daily average with an instantaneous minimum of not less than 4.0 mg/l.***

The Commission then filed this action for an injunction and declaratory judgment.

III. *The Commission's Position*

The Commission argues that EPA exceeded its powers both in its disapproval of the state DO criteria and in its promulgation of a federal standard. As to the disapproval, the Commission emphasizes that Congress intended for the states to have primary responsibility in setting water quality standards. The Commission reasons that EPA therefore cannot substitute its judgment for the state's unless the state standard is arbitrary, capricious, or totally unreasonable. According to the Commission, since the same standard was approved in 1973, it cannot be disapproved now. Furthermore, EPA can only disapprove standards that fail to meet the requirements of the Act. The Commission argues

that EPA is enforcing its policies as though they were the Act's requirements. In addition, the Commission claims that EPA improperly failed to consider economic factors in evaluating the DO criteria and that EPA ignored and misinterpreted evidence presented at hearings.

The Commission also attacks EPA's promulgation of its own standard. Because EPA did not promulgate the standard within ninety days, it therefore, according to the Commission, lost the power to act. The Commission also claims that nothing in the record supports a 4.0 mg/l instantaneous minimum. The standards in nearby states are irrelevant. The Commission asserts that Mississippi's flat topography and subtropical summer climate result in naturally low DO concentrations. According to the Commission, Congress intended for the individual states to account for these regional variations in setting criteria and did not intend for these differences to be ignored for the sake of bureaucratic uniformity.

*   *   *

V. *Scope of Review*

The Commission does not question the application of APA section 706 to this case.***Under section 706, generally a court must consider three questions: first, whether the administrator acted in the scope of his authority; second, whether the choice made was "arbitrary, capricious, an abuse of discretion, or otherwise not in accordance with law"; and third, whether the agency followed procedural requirements.***

For EPA to promulgate a water quality standard, it must determine that the state's standard "is not consistent with the applicable requirements of [the Act]" or that "a revised or new standard is necessary to meet the requirements of [the Act]." Review is therefore centered around two issues: first, whether EPA's disapproval of Mississippi's DO standard was proper; and second, whether EPA properly promulgated the substitute standard.***

VI. *Disapproval of Mississippi's Standard*
A. *Scope of Authority*

The Commission contends that EPA exceeded its statutory authority by tipping the balance of federal and state power created by

Congress in the FWPCA. The Commission argues that EPA may substitute its judgment only if a state fails to act or acts irresponsibly. Furthermore, the Commission asserts that EPA misconstrues its authority as allowing disapprovals of standards that do not meet the requirements of EPA policy instead of those not meeting the requirements of the Act.

Congress did place primary authority for establishing water quality standards with the states. *** As noted above, the legislative history reflects congressional concern that the Act not place in the hands of a federal administrator absolute power over zoning watershed areas. The varied topographies and climates in the country call for varied water quality solutions.

Despite this primary allocation of power, the states are not given unreviewable discretion to set water quality standards. All water quality standards must be submitted to the federal Administrator. The state must review its standards at least once every three years and make the results of the review available to the Administrator. EPA is given the final voice on the standard's adequacy:

> If the Administrator determines that any such revised or new standard is not consistent with the applicable requirements of this chapter, he shall not later than the ninetieth day after the date of submission of such standard notify the State and specify the changes to meet such requirements. If such changes are not adopted by the State within ninety days after the date of notification, the Administrator shall promulgate such standard pursuant to paragraph (4) of this subsection.

***

EPA's role also is more dominant when water quality criteria are in question. Although the designation of uses and the setting of criteria are interrelating chores, the specification of a waterway as one for fishing, swimming, or public water supply is closely tied to the zoning power Congress wanted left with the states. The criteria set for a specific use are more amenable to uniformity. Congress recognized this dis-

tinction by placing with EPA the duty to develop and publish water quality criteria reflecting the latest scientific knowledge shortly after the amendment's passage and periodically thereafter. EPA correctly points out that by leaving intact the Mississippi use designations it has acted in the manner least intrusive of state prerogatives.

Nothing indicates a congressional intent to restrict EPA's review of state standards to the issue of whether the state acted arbitrarily or capriciously. The FWPCA requires EPA to determine whether the standard is "consistent with" the Act's requirements.***

The statute enumerates the following requirements for water quality standards:

> Such standards shall be such as to protect the public health or welfare, enhance the quality of water and serve the purposes of this chapter. Such standards shall be established taking into consideration their use and value for public water supplies, propagation of fish and wildlife, recreational purposes, and agricultural, industrial, and other purposes, and also taking into consideration their use and value for navigation.

One purpose of the Act is

> the national goal that wherever attainable, an interim goal of water quality which provides for the protection and propagation of fish, shellfish, and wildlife and provides for recreation in and on the water be achieved by July 1, 1983.

Id. § 1251(a)(2). The EPA administrator did not improperly construe his authority by interpreting the FWPCA as allowing him to translate these broad statutory guidelines and goals into specifics that could be used to evaluate a state's standard. One "requirement of the Act" is that EPA formulate these policies for water quality criteria. It was not unreasonable for the EPA Administrator to interpret the Act as allowing him to require states to justify standards not in conformance with the criteria policy.

*   *   *

We conclude that EPA did not exceed its statutory authority in disapproving the state water quality standard.

B. *Substantive and Procedural Aspects of the Disapproval*

We turn to a consideration of whether the disapproval was arbitrary or capricious.***

With a position that contains both procedural and substantive elements, the Commission argues that EPA's approval of the 5.0-4.0 7 days Q 10 standard in 1973 estops EPA's disapproval of it now and renders EPA's action unreasonable. This position overlooks the congressional goal of attaining fishable and swimmable waters by 1983. Triennial review of state standards is a means of evolving and upgrading water quality standards. In addition, the Act authorizes EPA to set standards whenever the Administrator determines that a *revised* standard is necessary to meet the FWPCA's requirements. If EPA were bound by its prior approvals, this power would be meaningless. We also note that the prior approval in this case was before the statutory deadline for developing criteria under § 1314 and before the Red Book was published.

The Commission asserts that EPA failed to consider all relevant factors by excluding economic considerations in setting the DO criteria. EPA determined that while economic factors are to be considered in designating uses, those factors are irrelevant to the scientific and technical factors to be considered in setting criteria to meet those uses. When criteria cannot be attained because of economic factors, EPA states that the particular water can be designated for a less restrictive use, a process called "downgrading." The Commission argues that the statute's requirement that "use and value" be considered in setting standards makes economic factors relevant to both the designation of uses and the setting of criteria. Furthermore, it claims that EPA's policies against downgrading make its suggested solution illusory.

We note at the outset that EPA states it did examine the economic impact of its criteria and "concluded that a significant impact [was] not likely to occur." Nevertheless, we are convinced that EPA's construction is correct. Congress itself separated use and criteria and stated that "the water quality criteria for such waters [shall be] based on such uses." 33 U.S.C. § 1313(c)(2) (1976). The statute requires EPA to develop criteria "reflecting the latest *scientific* knowledge." *Id.* § 1314(a)(1) (emphasis added). The interpretation that criteria were based exclusively on scientific data predates the 1972 amendments. Furthermore, when Congress wanted economics and cost to be considered, it explicitly required it.

EPA policy does permit downgrading when "substantial and widespread adverse economic social impact" would otherwise result. General downgrading is not possible in this case, however, because Mississippi has the same standard for all uses. Furthermore, the statute requires that waters be at least fishable and swimmable "wherever attainable." Mississippi's lowest use is fishable water. EPA does allow downgrading for particular stream segments, and suggested this course to the Commission in its disapproval letter.

The Commission also argues that EPA's disapproval was a clear error of judgment. EPA has determined that most fishable waters require a DO concentration of 5.0 mg/l. It determined that the fish species in Mississippi, as throughout the South, would be adversely affected by a 4.0 mg/l average during the stressful low flow periods. EPA cited laboratory and field studies supporting its position. Its disapproval of the state standards was not arbitrary or capricious.

VII. *Promulgation of the Substitute Standard*
A. *The New DO Criteria*

Because EPA's disapproval of the DO standard was proper, it was within the scope of the Administrator's authority to promulgate a substitute standard. The question is whether the EPA was arbitrary or capricious in promulgating the DO criteria.

Mississippi wants its waters to support a diversified fish population. By weight, about 85% of the Mississippi fish can be classified as coarse or rough fish, such as catfish, carp, drum, buffalo, and shad. Nevertheless, the waters also include higher oxygen demanding gamefish, such as bass, (large mouth, spotted, white, and striped), white perch, bream, crappie, flounder, redfish, speckled trout, white trout, sheephead, croaker, bluegill, and red ear sunfish. Data cited by EPA in both its disapproval and as support for its standard "point very strongly to 5[mg/l] as the lower limit of dissolved oxygen, if the complex is to maintain a desirable fish faunae under natural river conditions." Testimony and data of experts based on laboratory and field studies support EPA's position that a 5.0 mg/l concentration is needed to support a balanced and diverse fish population and that 4.0 mg/l is the lowest safe level. In addition, fish are subject to more stress as water temperatures rise, a condition usually occurring during low flow periods.

The EPA's DO criteria was not a clear error in judgment. Furthermore, EPA did not arbitrarily promulgate its 5.0 mg/l criteria without considering the Mississippi situation. After reviewing the statements from the public hearings, EPA promulgated a lower standard that allows an instantaneous minimum of 4.0 mg/l. EPA did not act in an arbitrary or capricious manner.

B. *Procedural Defects*

The Commission asserts that EPA's failure to promulgate its substitute criteria within ninety days after publishing the proposal precludes it from acting. EPA did miss the deadline.[3] The question is what are the consequences of its tardiness.

The FWPCA does not impose any sanctions for missing the deadline. The APA requires a consideration of whether prejudice has resulted.***As the district court found, no prejudice is shown on this record.

*   *   *

VIII. *Conclusion*

The district court order dissolving the injunction and granting summary judgment to the government is AFFIRMED.

---

[3]Other courts have noted that the FWPCA imposed unrealistic statutory requirements and timetables on the EPA, which is usually in good faith "attempting to discharge the ambitious and often ambiguous duties imposed upon it . . . . " *Republic Steel Corp v. Train.* 557 F.2d 91, 94 (6th Cir. 1977).*** EPA's delay cannot be condoned, but in light of its duties it is understandable.

NOTES

1. On what bases may EPA disapprove state-designated water quality criteria? Is its authority the same as in disapproving water quality uses: the reference in Section 303(c)(3) to the "applicable requirements of this chapter"? What are the requirements for criteria? Is it simply that they correspond with the designated uses? If so, must EPA defer to the judgment of a state on such technological matters? As long as there is reasonable support in the record for EPA's position, is it possible for a state to win a "battle of experts" in court?

2. Could either EPA or a state consider economic impacts in setting criteria?

3. If, in light of the new criteria, Mississippi would like to rethink some of its water quality use designations, what should it do? Would it be eligible for downgrading under Sections 131.10 and 131.12 of the 1983 regulations quoted previously?

10 PERMITTING PROCEDURES AND STATE CERTIFICATION

Costle v. Pacific Legal Foundation

445 U. S. 198 (1980)

MR. JUSTICE BLACKMUN delivered the opinion of the court.

This case, in a sense, is a tale of a great city's—and the Nation's—basic problems in disposing of human waste. "How" and "where" are the ultimate questions, and they are intertwined. The issues presently before the Court, however, center in the administrative processes by which the city and the Nation seek to resolve those basic problems.

I

Respondent city of Los Angeles owns and operates the Hyperion Wastewater Treatment Plant located in Playa Del Rey, Cal. Since 1960, the Hyperion plant has processed most of the city's sewage, and has discharged the wastes through three "outfalls" extending into the Pacific Ocean. The shortest outfall terminates about one mile from the coastline in 50 feet of water. It is operative only during emergencies caused by increased sewage flow during wet weather or by power failures at the pumping plant. The second outfall terminates about five miles out. Approximately 340 million gallons of treated wastewater are discharged every day into the ocean, at a depth of 187 feet, through that outfall. This wastewater receives at least "primary treatment,"[1] but about one-third of the

flow also receives "secondary treatment"[2] by an activated sludge process. The third outfall terminates about seven miles from the coast. It is through this third outfall that the solids that have been removed during treatment are discharged into the ocean, at a depth of 300 feet. Prior to discharge the solid materials, commonly referred to as sludge, have been digested, screened, and diluted with secondary effluent.

The Hyperion plant is operated under permits issued by the Environmental Protection Agency (EPA) and the California Regional Water Quality Control Board (CRWQCB).***[3]

***One of the requirements applicable to an NPDES permit for a publicly owned treatment works, such as the Hyperion plant, is specified

---

[1]Under applicable regulations, the Environmental Protection Agency defines "primary treatment" as "the first stage in wastewater treatment where substantially all floating or settleable solids, are removed by floatation and/or sedimentation." 40 CFR §125.58 (m) (1979).

[2]The agency by its regulations describes "secondary treatment" as that treatment which will attain "the minimum level of effluent quality . . . in terms of . . . parameters" [sic]. These so-called "parameters" [but compare any dictionary's definition of this term] are specified levels of biochemical oxygen demand, suspended solids, and pH values. 40 CFR §§ 125.58(r) and 133.102 (1979).

[3]In March 1973, the EPA and the California State Water Resources Control Board entered into an understanding that gave the State primary responsibility for administering the NPDES program in California, with the EPA retaining jurisdiction over discharges beyond the limits of the territorial sea, that is, more than three miles out from the coastline. EPA permits are thus required for the Hyperion plant's discharges through the five- and seven-mile outfalls. The CRWQCB, acting pursuant to California's Porter-Cologne Act, Cal. Water Code Ann. § 13260, et seq. (West 1977), also requires a state permit for these outfalls.

* * *

in § 301 (b)(1)(B). That provision requires such works in existence on July 1, 1977, to achieve "effluent limitations based upon secondary treatment as defined by the Administrator."

II

The EPA has promulgated regulations providing for notice and public participation in any permit proceeding under the NPDES. Those regulations, implementing the statutory requirement that any NPDES permit be issued "after opportunity for public hearing," are the focus of this case. The regulations state: "Public notice of the proposed issuance, denial or modification of every permit or denial shall be circulated in a manner designed to inform interested and potentially interested persons of the discharge and of the proposed determination to issue, deny, or modify a permit for the discharge." 40 CFR § 125.32(a) (1978). That public notice "shall include at least": (1) circulation of the notice within the affected geographical area by posting in the post office and "public places" nearest the applicant's premises, or posting "near the entrance to the applicant's premises and in nearby places," or publication in local newspapers; (2) the mailing of notice to the permit applicant and "appropriate" federal and state authorities; and (3) the mailing of notice to any person or group who has requested placement on the NPDES permit mailing list for actions affecting the geographical area.

Following the issuance of public notice the EPA Regional Administrator is directed to provide at least a 30-day period during which interested persons may submit written views concerning the proposed action or may request that a hearing be held. § 125.32(b)(1). If the Regional Administrator "finds a significant degree of public interest in a proposed permit," he is directed to hold a public hearing on the proposed action at which interested parties may submit oral or written statements and data. § 125.34. Following a determination by the Regional Administrator to take a proposed permit action, he is directed to forward a copy of that determination to any person who has submitted written comments. If the determination is substantially changed from the initial pro-

posed action, he must give public notice of that determination. In either event, his determination constitutes the final action of the EPA unless a timely request for an adjudicatory hearing is granted. § 125.35.

Any interested person, within 10 days following the date of the determination, may request an "adjudicatory hearing" or a "legal decision" with respect to the determination. § 125.36 (b). A request for an adjudicatory hearing is to be granted by the Regional Administrator if the request "[s]ets forth material issues of fact relevant to the questions of whether a permit should be issued, denied or modified." § 125.36 (c)(1)(ii). Issues of law, on the other hand, are not to be considered at an adjudicatory hearing. If a request for an adjudicatory hearing raises a legal issue, that issue is to be referred by the hearing officer to the EPA's Assistant Administrator for Enforcement and the General Counsel for resolution. If a request for an adjudicatory hearing raises only legal issues, a hearing will not be granted and the Regional Administrator will refer those issues to the aforementioned officers. § 125.36(m).

III

The EPA and the CRWQCB first issued a joint permit to the city of Los Angeles for discharges of treated sewage from the Hyperion plant in November 1974.***On August 18, 1975, the 1974 permit was rescinded by the federal and state authorities, and replaced with a permit covering all three outfalls. The 1975 permit conditioned continued discharges from the Hyperion plant on compliance by the city with a schedule designed to achieve full secondary treatment of wastewater by October 1, 1979, and the gradual elimination of the discharge of sludge into the ocean over a 30-month period following "concept approval" of a plan for alternative disposal of the sludge.

In July 1976, the EPA notified Los Angeles that its 1975 NPDES permit would expire on February 1, 1977, and that a new permit would be needed if discharges were to continue beyond that date. The city filed an application for a new permit on July 30.***On January 24, 1977, after a public hearing, the EPA and the CRWQCB did extend the expiration date of the 1975 permit from February 1, to June 30, 1977, citing inadequate time to review the city's application for a new permit. App. 93.[7]

On April 26, 1977, the EPA advised the city that it again proposed to extend the expiration date of its NPDES permit for the Hyperion plant, this time from June 30, 1977, to December 17, 1979. All other terms and conditions of the permit were to remain unchanged. Notice of the proposed action was published in the Los Angeles Times the following day.***Neither the city nor the respondent Pacific Legal Foundation (PLF), nor any other party, requested a hearing or filed comments on the proposed extension, and the EPA's Regional Administrator determined that public interest in the modification proposal was insufficient to warrant convening a public hearing. On May 23, at a public hearing, the CRWQCB officially extended the expiration date of the state permit for the Hyperion plant until December 17, 1979. On June 2, 1977, the

---

[7]In the meantime, a significant public controversy had developed concerning the EPA's approval of the city's alternative sludge disposal project. That project, to be funded by construction grants awarded under Title II of the FWCPA, 86 Stat. 833, 33 U.S.C. § 1281 *et seq.*, has been referred to as the Hyperion Treatment Plant Interim Sludge Disposal Project. (The parties, commendably, have refrained from referring to this project as the HTPISDP, and so shall we.) The project called for the implementation of a process at the plant by which the digested sludge would be dewatered, formed into cakes, and hauled by truck to a sanitary landfill in Palos Verdes. An environmental impact appraisal developed by the EPA has estimated that when the trucking project is fully operational it will require 255 round trips per week over a distance of 42 miles. The city of Los Angeles and its Chamber of Commerce opposed the project. *** Respondent Pacific Legal Foundation (PLF) also objected. ***

    *   *   *

Still another PLF lawsuit relating to the Hyperion permit and its "sludge-out" schedule is pending. In that action the PLF has sued officials of the EPA and the Department of the Interior claiming that those agencies have failed to carry out their statutory obligations under the Endangered Species Act of 1973 in approving the alternative sludge disposal project. The PLF contends that the elimination of sludge discharge into the ocean will adversely affect the food chain that supports the existence of gray whales and brown pelicans, and the trucks going to and from the landfill site will kill the El Segundo butterfly. ***

    *   *   *

Regional Administrator of the EPA transmitted to the city his final determination to extend the time of expiration of the federal permit to the same 1979 date.

When informed by telephone on June 13 that the EPA's final determination had been made on June 2, and that a request for an adjudicatory hearing could be accepted only if filed that day, *see* 40 CFR § 125.36(b)(1), respondent Kilroy, represented by PLF attorneys, filed such a request.

Respondent Kilroy's request for an adjudicatory hearing presented two issues that he wished to raise:

> "1. Whether the requirements of the permit should be modified in that the project that is the subject of the compliance schedule set forth in NPDES permit CA010991 [the Hyperion permit] is being evaluated in an EIS by the EPA pursuant to the requirements of NEPA, the compliance schedule should not be mandated in an NPDES permit until the NEPA study is completed; and
>
> "2. Whether the procedures used and the record developed were adequate [for the] issuance of an NPDES permit."

Within 10 days of receiving Kilroy's request, the Regional Administrator responded by certified mail, stating his determination that the request did not set forth material issues of fact relevant to the question whether the permit should be extended. Thus, he concluded that Kilroy's request had not met the requirements of 40 CFR § 125.36(c)(1)(ii). The Regional Administrator did construe the request, however, as one raising issues of law relating to the appropriate interpretation to be given regulations that had been promulgated under the FWPCA. He therefore certified to the EPA's General Counsel three issues of law raised by the request. Before the General Counsel's ruling on the certified issues of law was announced, respondents PLF and Kilroy, joined now by the city of Torrance, theretofore a stranger to the formal proceedings, filed a timely petition with the United States Court of Appeals for the Ninth Circuit seeking review of the Regional Administrator's action extending the expiration date of the Hyperion permit. A similar petition was filed by respondent city of Los Angeles. The petitions were consolidated for review.***

IV

The Court of Appeals remanded the matter to the Administrator for the holding of a "proper hearing."***

*   *   *

The Administrator of the EPA petitioned his Court for review of the question whether § 402(a)(1) requires the EPA to conduct an adjudicatory hearing before taking action on an NPDES permit issuance or modification where, after notice of the proposed action, no one requested a hearing before the action was taken and the only request filed subsequently raised no material issue of fact. We granted certiorari to review this important issue in a rapidly developing area of the law.

V
A

Petitioner's basic contentions are that the EPA was entitled to condition the availability of a public hearing on the extension of the Hyperion permit on the filing of a proper request, and that it similarly was entitled to condition an adjudicatory hearing following its extension decision on the identification of a disputed issue of material fact by an interested party. We agree with both contentions.

***Rather than permitting the Regional Administrator to decide, in the first instance, whether there is sufficient public interest in a proposed issuance or modification of a permit to justify a public hearing, and to limit any adjudicatory hearing to the situation where an interested party raises a material issue of fact, the Court of Appeals would require the agency to justify every failure to hold a hearing by proof that the material facts supporting its action "are not subject to dispute." This holding is contrary to this Court's approval in past decisions of agency rules, similar to those at issue here, that have required an applicant who seeks a hearing to meet a threshold burden of tendering evidence suggesting the need for a hearing.

Moreover, it is important to note that the regulations described in Part II of this opinion, *supra*, were designed to implement the statutory command that permits be issued "after *opportunity* for public hearing." § 402(a)(1) (emphasis supplied). In the past, this Court has held that a similar statutory requirement that an "opportunity" for a hearing be provided may be keyed to a *request* for a hearing. See *National Coal Operators' Assn. v. Kleppe,* 423 U.S., at 398-399. And only recently the Court re-emphasized the fundamental administrative law principle that "the formulation of procedures was basically to be left within the discretion of the agencies to which Congress had confided the responsibility for substantive judgments." *Vermont Yankee Nuclear Power Corp. v. NRDC,* 435 U.S. 519, 524 (1978).

Neither can we ignore the fact that under the standard applied by the Court of Appeals, the EPA would be required to hold hearings on most of the actions it takes with respect to NPDES permit issuances and modifications. Hearings would be required even in cases, such as this, in which the proposed action only extends a permit's expiration date without at all affecting the substantive conditions that had been considered during earlier hearings. The Administrator advises us that each year the EPA grants about 100 requests for adjudicatory hearings under the NPDES program, issues about 2,200 permits, and takes thousands of actions with respect to permits.***

Affirmance of the Court of Appeals' rationale obviously would raise serious questions about the EPA's ability to administer the NPDES program.***

We recognize the validity of respondents' contention that the legislative history of the FWPCA indicates a strong congressional desire that the public have input in decisions concerning the elimination of water pollution. The FWPCA itself recites:

"Public participation in the development, revision, and enforcement of any regulation, standard, effluent limitation, plan, or program established by the Administrator . . . under this Act shall be provided for, encouraged, and assisted by the Administrator." § 101(e).

Passages in the FWPCA's legislative history indicate that this general policy of encouraging public participation is applicable to the administration of the NPDES permit program.***

Nonetheless, we conclude that the regulations the EPA has promulgated to implement this congressional policy are fully consistent with the legislative purpose, and are valid.***

B

Having rejected the Court of Appeals' invalidation of the EPA's public participation regulations, we turn to the issues framed by respondents. First, PLF and Kilroy contend that the EPA's regulations required the Regional Administrator to hold a public hearing in this case because there was a "significant degree of public interest" in the extension of the Hyperion permit.***

Notwithstanding the orientation of these regulations toward the encouragement of public participation in the NPDES permit issuance process, our examination of the record leads us to reject respondents' contention that the EPA failed to comply with its regulations in this case. It is undisputed that the most controversial aspects of the Hyperion permit—the compliance schedule for secondary treatment, the "sludge-out" requirement, and the resultant requirement that the city develop an alternative method of sludge disposal—were all included within the 1975 permit. That permit was issued following EPA publication of advance notice of its tentative determination to revise the initial 1974 permit, and a hearing on the proposed revisions. None of the respondents objected to the issuance of the 1975 permit or requested an adjudicatory hearing. We agree with the position advanced by petitioner that respondents may not re-open consideration of substantive conditions contained within the 1975 permit through hearing requests relating to a proposed permit modification that did not even purport to affect those conditions.

The EPA's determination to modify the 1975 permit by extending its expiration date to December 17, 1979, was made following newspaper publication of the proposed action, including notice of an opportunity for submission of comments and hearing requests. Respondent Los Angeles received an individual notice of the EPA's tentative determination to extend the permit, and raised no objection. Respondents PLF and Kilroy, who argue that the EPA was aware of their interest in the Hyperion permit and their opposition to the Interim Sludge Disposal Project, could have received such individual notice if they had asked to be placed on the EPA's mailing list for notices of proposed agency actions within the pertinent geographical area. They made no such request. Under the circumstances, we think it reasonable that the Regional Administrator decided to extend the expiration date of the permit without another public hearing, on the grounds that the public had not exhibited a significant degree of interest in the action under consideration, and that information pertinent to such a decision would not have been adduced if a hearing had been held. This simply is not a case in which doubt existed concerning the need for a hearing.

*   *   *

Finally, respondents suggest that the EPA erred in not holding an adjudicatory hearing on the issues raised in respondent Kilroy's request. We agree with petitioner, however, who contends that Kilroy's request raised legal, rather than factual, issues, and who notes that respondents treated the request in that fashion in arguing the issues Kilroy presented before the EPA's General Counsel. Even in their arguments before this Court, respondents have continued to raise factual issues that are relevant only to their contention that greater adverse effects on both the marine and land environment will result from the Interim Sludge Disposal Project than from the continued discharge of sludge into the ocean. If such issues had been raised in a timely request for an adjudicatory hearing, we agree with petitioner that the EPA could have taken the position that such issues, regardless of their merits, were not pertinent to a determination to extend the Hyperion permit's expiration date. That determination had no impact on the compliance schedule for "sludge-out"that already had long been in effect.

C

In sum, we hold that the Court of Appeals erred in concluding that the EPA is required to hold a public hearing on every NPDES permit action it takes unless it can show that the material facts supporting its action "are not subject to dispute." We hold, rather, that the agency's regulations implementing the statutory requirement of "an opportunity for a public hearing" under § 402 of the FWPCA are valid. Respondents have failed to demonstrate that those regulations were not applied properly in the context of this case. The Court of Appeals' judgment remanding the case to the agency for an adjudicatory hearing on the EPA's extension of the expiration date of Los Angeles' NPDES permit for its Hyperion Wastewater Treatment Plant is reversed.

It is so ordered.

NOTES

1. States seeking approval of state enforcement programs must provide for public participation in NPDES permit procedures that are consistent with the requirements of the Clean Water Act. Prior to 1979, EPA was approving state programs on an ad hoc basis, without setting any guidelines for assessing adequacy of state public participation opportunities. An Illinois conservation group brought suit to overturn EPA's approval of that state's program, alleging that there were inadequate provisions for citizen participation. The 7th Circuit overturned EPA's approval and directed the agency to promulgate guidelines in *Citizens for a Better Environment v. EPA*, 596 F.2d 720 (7th Cir. 1979), citing §§ 304(i), 402(b) and 101(e) of the Act. The court did not, however, undertake to evaluate the adequacy of Illinois' program; review was limited to EPA's duty to develop guidelines.

What should be the standard for determining adequacy of public involvement opportunities in *state* NPDES permitting processes? Footnote 8 to the opinion in *Citizens for a Better Environment* discusses the petitioner's contentions:

> 8. Citizens contends that the federal citizen suit provision in the Act, Section 505, defines the public participation in state enforcement required by Section 101(e). This contention is based primarily on Citizens' argument that Section 402(a) (3) requires that federal and state programs be as identical as possible. The language of this Section, however, does not suggest that state programs are required to adopt the citizen participation components of the federal program; section 402(a) (3) requires only that the federal program "be subject to the same terms, conditions and requirements as apply to a state permit program." Citizens, however, also points to more general language in the statute and its legislative history indicating that Congress intended state and federal programs to be as uniform as possible. We do not decide today what provisions must be made for citizen participation in the state NPDES enforcement process in order to satisfy the requirements of the Act.

2. In *Costle v. Pacific Legal Foundation, supra*, it was held that an adjudicatory hearing is not required when no factual issues are raised; the court did not discuss what ingredients would be necessary for such a hearing when factual issues are timely raised.

Under the Federal Administrative Procedure Act, adjudicatory hearings are those required by statute to accompany decisions made "on the record;" such statutes usually apply to permit issuance proceedings. Required procedures generally include formal notice, adversarial evidentiary proceedings, a decision based solely upon evidence introduced at the hearing, initial decision by an independent administrative law judge, and review of initial decisions by the agency. (In the case of EPA, the reviewing officer would presumably be the Administrator or a Regional Administrator.) *See* Sections 554, 556, and 557 of the Federal Administrative Procedure Act. At one time, however, EPA interpreted Section 402 of the Clean Water Act as not triggering full adjudicatory hearings under the APA for NPDES permit decisions.

In *Marathon Oil Co. v. EPA*, 564 F.2d 1253 (9th Cir. 1977), the court rejected that position, holding that the requirement in Section 402(a)(1) of an "opportunity for public hearing" was enough, despite the absence of any language expressly specifying that permitting decisions were to be made "on the record." It did, however, uphold EPA's procedures, in which the appropriate Regional Administrator would issue a draft permit, which would become final unless an adjudicative hearing on the permit was requested within ten days. The adjudicative hearing was held before an Administrative Law Judge (an "ALJ") who would certify the record of the hearing back to the Regional Administrator, who would then make the final decision himself. The court held that Sections 554(d) and 557(b) of the APA, which require the ALJ to make an initial or recommended decision, were inapplicable to initial licensing such as this. It also held that nothing in this procedure, whereby the Regional Administrator, in effect, reviewed his earlier draft decision in light of the record made before the ALJ, offended the due process clause of the Constitution. (The court did, however, find that the APA was violated when the Regional Administrator "made excursions outside the record" in making his final decision.)

3. Recall from the discussion of Section 307 that in 1976 EPA adopted a complex strategy for control of toxic pollutants in settlement of lawsuits brought by environmental groups. *See Natural Resources Defense Council, Inc. v. Train*, 8 ERC 2120 (D.D.C. 1976). As part of the settlement agreement, EPA was required to include "re-opener" clauses in NPDES permits for 21 categories of industrial point sources. These clauses allow EPA to revise issued permits to require compliance with newly-promulgated toxic pollutant limitations. (EPA adopted regulations asserting even broader authority in December, 1978, requiring compliance by permit modification with any more stringent limitations issued under Sections 301(b)(2)(C) or (D), 304(b)(2), and 307(a)(2).)

EPA's authority to modify issued NPDES permits to require compliance with subsequently-adopted toxic pollutant standards was challenged in *Inland Steel Co. v. EPA*, 574 F.2d 367 (7th Cir. 1978). The following clause had been included in Inland's 1976 NPDES permit for its Indiana Harbor Works facility, pursuant to EPA regulations:

> [I]f a toxic effluent standard or prohibition (including any schedule of compliance specified in such effluent standard or prohibition) is established under Section 307(a) of the Act for a toxic pollutant which is present in the discharge and such standard or prohibition is more stringent than any limitation for such pollutant in this permit, this permit shall be revised or modified in accordance with the toxic effluent standard or prohibition and the permittee so notified.

Although there were no toxic standards applicable to Inland's plant when the permit was issued, Inland challenged the re-opener clause during EPA permit hearings and then upon petition for review to the 7th Circuit, Inland argued that Section 402(k) of the Act gave finality to issued permits for the life of each permit, somewhat analogous to the ten-year grace period given to new sources under Section 306. The first sentence of Section 402(k) states:

> Compliance with a permit issued pursuant to this section shall be deemed compliance, for purposes of sections 309 and 506, with sections 301, 302, 306, 307 and 403, except any standard imposed under section 307 for a toxic pollutant injurious to human health.

EPA responded that Section 402(k) was designed "to insure that, once a point source has obtained a permit, subsequent changes in effluent limitations will not place the permit holder in violation of the Act," and not to prevent EPA from requiring case-by-case compliance with new limitations through modification of individual NPDES permits. The court agreed with EPA, finding that "finality" related to the enforcement provisions of Sections 309 and 506, not the substantive requirements of the remaining sections cited in Section 402(k).

Inland's second argument was that EPA's authority to modify issued permits may only be exercised "for cause" under Section 402(a)(3). That section allows EPA to terminate or modify a permit for cause, including but not limited to violation of permit conditions, misrepresentation, or changed conditions. The court found that "cause" is not limited to the examples given and, further, that changed conditions could include adoption of stringent toxic pollutant standards. The court's conclusion:

> The notion that Congress intended to withhold from the Administrator the authority to include in a permit a provision authorizing modification of the permit to incorporate a subsequently adopted more stringent toxic pollutant standard is hard to square with the alternative that concededly is open to the Administrator. He could choose to issue permits of extremely short duration instead of the five-year maximum permitted by § 402(b)(1)(B), or the three years fixed for Inland's final permit, and thus assure that any new or amended toxic pollutant standard would be complied with promptly. Having given the Administrator this power, Congress would have had no reason of which we can conceive for withholding the authority he claims in this case.

> Finally, the Administrator is given a broad discretion to choose the means by which he will carry out his responsibilities. He is authorized by § 501(a) "to prescribe such regulations as are necessary to carry out his functions under this Act." He also has the responsibility under § 402(a) (1) for imposing as a condition to the issuance of a permit that the discharge meets "all applicable requirements under," *inter alia*, § 307. In addition, when a permit is issued before the promulgation of standards applicable to the subject plant's discharges, as was the permit here with respect to toxic pollutant standards, that permit is to be subject, under § 301(a)(1), to "such conditions as the Administrator determines are necessary to carry out the provisions of this Act." These expansive grants of power, considered together with the principle that the Administrator's interpretation of the Act he is responsible for administering is entitled to great deference, *see, e.g., American Meat Institute v. EPA, supra,* 526 F.2d at 449-450, would weigh heavily in favor of his interpretation even if we were not convinced, as we are, that Inland's contrary interpretation is untenable.

Inland Steel Co. v. EPA, 574 F. 2d 367, 373 (7th Cir. 1978).

American Petroleum Institute v. Costle
15 ERC 1139 (W.D.La. 1980)

The plaintiffs brought suit to enjoin the United States Environmental Protection Agency (EPA) from enforcing regulations promulgated for the administration of the National Pollutant Discharge Elimination System (NPDES) established under the Federal Water Pollution Control Act, 33 U.S.C. 1251 *et seq.****

*   *   *

The Federal Water Pollution Control Act makes unlawful the discharge of any pollutant by any person unless that discharge is authorized by a permit issued under the National Pollutant Discharge Elimination System, 33 U.S.C. §1342. Regulations promulgated under the Act initially provided for two categories of dischargers, "existing sources" and "new sources," and applied generally more stringent effluent limitation standards to the second group.

The challenged regulations create the category of "new dischargers," sources which are "new" in the sense that they began to discharge after the Act's effective date but which do not conform to the definition of "new source" used in the Act. A "new discharger" (such as the owner of a drilling barge) is required by the challenged regulations to obtain a new permit before moving to each new drilling location. It routinely requires at least six months to process the application under optimum conditions. If "any interested person" requests an evidentiary hearing, the permit will not issue until the hearings are completed. 40 CFR § 124.60(a)(1). The presiding administrative law judge may, however, authorize the source to discharge pending disposition of the application. 40 CFR § 124.60(a)(2). A new discharger is also ineligible for the extended schedules of compliance authorized for existing sources, and instead must comply with effluent limitation standards within 90 days of commencing discharge, 40 CFR § 122.66(d)(4).

Judicial review of these regulations is governed by the Administrative Procedures Act, 5 U.S.C. § 701 *et seq.* The Act authorizes a reviewing court to determine whether the challenged regulations are consistent with the mandate of the enabling legislation and were adopted pursuant to pertinent procedural requirements.

*   *   *

Moreover, in determining whether the plaintiffs are entitled to a preliminary injunction, the court must consider four factors: whether the mover's position has a substantial likelihood of success on the merits; whether the applicant will suffer irreparable harm unless the injunction issues; whether the threatened injury to applicant if relief is denied outweighs the harm to the defendant if relief is granted; and whether the grant of injunctive relief serves the public interest. ***

*   *   *

The affidavits reflect that over 150 mobile drilling rigs are operating in waters of the United States, for the most part in the Gulf of Mexico off the coasts of Texas and Louisiana. These rigs drill, on an average, three to five wells during each 12-month period. The plaintiffs contend that off-shore drilling activities cannot be precisely planned, and that although drilling programs may be planned for several years in advance, the programs are updated frequently as dictated by changes in circumstances. Among these circumstances are: success or failure of a particular drilling prospect; the activities of competitors; the availability of drilling rigs; mechanical problems with the drilling rigs; weather; unanticipated additional drilling time or deeper drilling at a particular location; correcting hole problems at a particular location; modifications to OCS lease sales scheduled by the Department of the Interior; and necessary drilling on short notice in order to maintain a lease in force. These circumstances make it impossible, the plaintiffs contend, for the industry to predict the movement of a rig sufficiently in advance to comply with the dictates of 40 CFR § 122.53(b).

A satisfactory showing has been made that the challenged regulation, 40 CFR § 122.53(b), will cause irreparable harm to the plaintiffs if its enforcement is not enjoined. The regulation requires the owner or operator of a movable rig to obtain a new permit for each new drilling location. At least six months is required to process an application for such permits. The dynamics of the offshore oil and gas industry make it extremely unlikely that the owner has any firm knowledge of the rig's location six months in the future. The rig owner's alternatives are harsh: either to be bound to a previously designated location where the services of the rig may not be in demand or to ignore the permitting process and invite civil and criminal liability for any unpermitted discharges.

A second requirement for obtaining a preliminary injunction is for the applicant to demonstrate a likelihood of prevailing on the merits. In the instant case, the plaintiffs contend that the new discharger regulations are unauthorized by the Federal Water Pollution Control Act and are arbitrary and capricious. Pretermitting the first challenge to the regulations, it is clear that the EPA acted in an arbitrary and capricious manner by requiring owners of movable drilling rigs to obtain a new permit each time they moved to a new drilling location, when six months to one and a half years is routinely required to process applications for such permits. An agency's action may be deemed arbitrary and capricious if it rejects "obviously less burdensome but equally effective controls in favor of more expensive or onerous ones."***

In the instant case, the EPA had available the alternative of issuing general permits for this category of dischargers, 40 CFR § 122.59, which, by their nature, would not require submission of a separate application each time a movable rig began operations at a new location. In fact, on August 15, 1980, the EPA proposed three general NPDES permits for movable rigs located in the Gulf of Mexico and at the same time waived the requirement that these dischargers submit permit applications 180 days prior to the commencement of discharge, 45 Fed. Reg. 54428. In light of the EPA's apparent recognition that discharges from movable rigs are regulated more efficiently through a general permit system (a system obviously less burdensome for the plaintiffs), its previous decision to require application 180 days before discharge can commence was arbitrary and capricious and should be enjoined. Therefore, the plaintiffs have successfully demonstrated a likelihood that their position will prevail at trial on the merits.

Before issuing a preliminary injunction, the court must also weigh the potential harm to the plaintiff if the injunction does not issue against the potential harm to the defendant if the relief is granted. In the instant case, the harm to the defendants is obviously minimal. The EPA has administered the NPDES for eight years without the challenged regulations and admits that it has ignored these dischargers to concentrate "on industrial dischargers considered major contributors of pollution and on discharges located near population centers."45 Fed. Reg. 54429. Moreover, the agency has clearly indicated that its preferred method of regulating dischargers of this sort is through the issuance of general permits, three of which it has already proposed in draft form. Therefore, the harm to the EPA in enjoining 40 CFR § 122.53(b) is minimal.

A final consideration in issuing a preliminary injunction is whether the public interest is thereby served. Although the public certainly has a valid interest in the protection of the nation's waters, the public interest will not be served by significant delays in exploration and extraction of needed oil and gas supplies, particularly when the delays are occasioned by a regulatory scheme which is unduly burdensome and which has been at least partially repudiated by the administrative agency. For these reasons, an injunction in the present case would be in the public interest.

*   *   *

The application for preliminary injunction seeking to enjoin enforcement of 40 CFR § 122.53 (insofar as it defines "new discharger") and 40 CFR § 122.53 is granted as those regulations relate to movable drilling rigs operating in waters within the United States and off the coast of the United States. The injunction will not apply to operations of offshore drilling rigs conducted in environmentally sensitive areas.

*   *   *

NOTES

1. If it was arbitrary and capricious for EPA to create the category of "new dischargers" for mobile drilling barges without any statutory authorization for such a category, how can the court approve of "general permits" as the "preferred method" of permitting movable drilling rigs?

Is there any mention in the Clean Water Act of "general permits"? There is — in Section 404(e), added by the 1977 Amendments — but, as you will see, this unique provision only authorizes general permits (on a state, regional, or nationwide basis) to be issued for the discharge of *dredged or fill material.*

2. Doesn't the creation of a general NPDES permit system out of whole cloth fly in the face of the basic statutory scheme? Could EPA issue a general permit to a railroad tank car hauling toxic wastes which would permit it to discharge the wastes into any body of water along the rail line? Should it be allowed to issue a general permit to a coastal drilling barge authorizing it to discharge wastewater into any part of the Laguna Madre, for 200 miles along the Texas coast? Shouldn't the characteristics of each individual discharge site be considered in a new permitting decision?

Lake Erie Alliance v. Corps of Engineers

526 F. Supp. 1063 (W.D. Pa. 1981)

WEBER, Chief Judge:

On July 19, 1979, plaintiffs filed a complaint for declaratory and injunctive relief alleging numerous violations of federal laws in connection with the issuance of construction permit No. 77-492-3 granted to United States Steel Corporation (U.S. Steel) by the United States Army Corps of Engineers for the construction of piers in Lake Erie, dredging, the installation of intake and discharge structures into its waters, and diversion of a stream leading into Lake Erie, all in connection with a proposal to construct a steelmill at this site.***

*   *   *

Violations of Sections 401 and 404 of the Clean Water Act

The next cause of action in the complaint alleges three violations of the Federal Water Pollution Control Act, commonly known as the Clean Water Act. The first violation alleged is that U.S. Steel failed to obtain a valid Section 401 certification from the State of Ohio. Section 401 of the Clean Water Act requires an applicant for a federal license to conduct any activity, including the construction or operation of facilities which may result in discharge into navigable waters, to provide the licensing agency with a certification from the state in which the discharge originates. 33 U.S.C. § 1341(a)(1). U.S. Steel obtained a 401 certification from the State

of Ohio on May 4, 1979, and a subsequent certification was reissued on June 19, 1979, to clarify the earlier one. Plaintiffs contend that this certification was invalid.

*   *   *

The OEBR [Ohio Environmental Board of Review] considered *de novo* plaintiffs' allegations that the 401 certification from Ohio was invalid and found in favor of the director of the Ohio EPA on every issue. The decision of the OEBR was affirmed by the Court of Appeals of Franklin County, Ohio. Defendants contend that the decision of the Ohio courts that the section 401 certification in question is both reasonable and lawful, is res judicata and may not be challenged in this court.

***Plaintiffs contend that res judicata does not apply here since the OEBR declined to consider whether the 401 certification satisfied the federal EPA regulations.

On the contrary, both the administrative board and the appellate courts considered the question and decided that in issuing a 401 certification, the director of the Ohio EPA is not bound by the regulations of the U.S. EPA or any other federal agency. To the extent that this particular question may raise federal issues, we agree with the finding of the Administrative Review Board and the Ohio Court of Appeals that the state certification under the Clean Water Act is set up as the exclusive prerogative of the state and is not to be reviewed by any agency of the federal government. 33 U.S.C. § 1371(c)(2). In all other respects we conclude that plaintiffs are barred from relitigating the validity of the 401 certification by the doctrine of res judicata.

Plaintiffs next argue that the Corps' issuance of permit No. 77-492-3 was unlawful because U.S. Steel did not obtain a 401 certification from the Commonwealth of Pennsylvania. It is their position that U.S. Steel is obligated to apply for and obtain a 401 certification from Pennsylvania as one of the states in which the discharge into the navigable waters of the United States will originate. This argument appears to be an afterthought since in the amended complaint plaintiffs argue only that Pennsylvania must be notified as a state whose water quality may be affected by the discharge in question and given 60 days to file objections or proposed permit conditions. The Clean Water Act requires that "any applicant for a Federal . . . permit to conduct any activity . . . which may result in discharge into the navigable waters, shall provide the licensing or permitting agency a certification from the state in which the discharge originates or will originate . . . ." 33 USC § 1341.

Plaintiffs' first contention is that certain operations of the plant located in Pennsylvania will generate water pollutants which will end up in navigable waters of Pennsylvania and that discharge pipes will be located almost on the state line. Therefore, the plant discharge will originate in Pennsylvania where one-half the facilities are located and because the plant discharges will affect Pennsylvania waters, a Pennsylvania certification is required. This position has specifically been rejected by the U.S. EPA. In an opinion issued by the General Counsel, the agency stated that when a facility is located in one state and has the end of a discharge pipe within the waters of another state, the applicant must only get a 401 certification from the state in which the facility is located and *not* from the state where the discharge pipe is located. U.S. EPA, General Counsel Opinion (No. 78-8), *emphasis added.*

***Origination of discharge is a touchstone requiring a 401 certification from a state and there is no evidence in the administrative record that any discharge will originate in Pennsylvania. Therefore, no such certification is required. Further, we note that the representatives of the Commonwealth of Pennsylvania and the Pennsylvania Department of Environmental Resources took part in the development of the final EIS and apparently agreed that there was no need for Pennsylvania to issue a 401 certification.

*   *   *

NOTES

1. If you have not yet read Section 401(a)(1) and (2), and (d), do so now. After reading these provisions in Section 401, do you agree with the court's decision? Specifically, does the requirement in Section 401(a)(1) of certification from "the State in which the discharge originates or will originate" mean that certification is required only from the state in which the *facility* is located and *not* from the state in which the *discharge pipe* is located? Does this make sense? Which state would have the greater concern with the pollution?

2. Does Section 401 (a)(2) contain adequate means for protection of water quality in states which are affected by discharges originating in other states?

Clearly Section 401(a)(2) applies when the permitting agency is the U.S. Army Corps of Engineers (for dredged or fill material). But does it apply when the permitting agency is an agency of another state?

How, if at all, does Section 401 (a)(2) mesh with Section 402 (b)(3) and (5) and with Section 402 (d)(2) and (4)? Do these provisions in Section 402 establish other procedures for protection of one state from another, which do not mandate compliance with water quality standards in affected states? Or do the two sections reinforce one another?

3. May the state in which the discharge would originate deny certification for any reason, or for no reason, and thereby block a federal permit? Consider the following case.

Roosevelt Campobello International Park Commission
v.
Environmental Protection Agency
684 F.2d 1041 (1st Cir. 1982)

COFFIN, Chief Judge. In these three consolidated appeals petitioners challenge the final decision of the EPA Administrator to issue a National Pollutant Discharge Elimination System (NPDES) permit to the Pittston Company pursuant to § 402 of the Clean Water Act, 33 U.S.C. § 1342. The permit authorizes the Pittston Co. to construct and operate a 250,000 barrel per day oil refinery and associated deep water terminal at Eastport, Maine, in accordance with specified effluent limitations, monitoring requirements, and other conditions. Petitioners contend that EPA's actions violated the National Environmental Policy Act (NEPA), the Endangered Species Act, and the Clean Water Act.

Pittston proposes to construct an oil refinery and marine terminal in Eastport, Maine, a relatively pristine area of great natural beauty near the Canadian border. The area is known for being the foggiest on the East Coast, experiencing some 750-1000 hours of fog a year; daily tides approximate twenty feet. The plan contemplates that crude oil shipments will arrive several times a week in supertankers, or Very Large Crude Carriers (VLCCs), as long as four football fields, or slightly less than a quarter of a mile. The tankers will travel through Canadian waters around the northern tip of Campobello Island, where the Roosevelt Campobello International Park is located, down Head Harbor Passage to a refinery near Eastport where they will be turned and berthed. Numerous barges and small tankers will carry the refined product from Eastport to destination markets in the Northeast.

*   *   *

Petitioners' final argument is that the ALJ erred by ruling that conditions imposed on the project by the Maine BEP under state law are not incorporated into the federal NPDES permit. They allege that the certification issued by the State of Maine pursuant to § 401(a)(1) of the Clean Water Act, though making no explicit mention of the conditions previously imposed by the Maine BEP, incorporated these terms by implication. Therefore, these requirements must also be "a condition on any Federal license or permit." § 401(d). The State of Maine, as amicus curiae, makes a somewhat different argument. It argues that the prior certification is irrelevant, because the proposal as approved by the state had been substantially modified by the ALJ. But the state contends that it has been denied its right to certify the *new* proposed discharge, and therefore the NPDES permit is invalid.***

The ALJ considered testimony and evidence to determine whether the state certification implicitly incorporated the conditions previously imposed by the Maine BEP. Contrary to respondents' contention, he found as a factual matter that "the conditions of the Maine BEP Order are conditions precedent to the effectiveness of the state's certification. He further ruled, however, as a matter of law, that § 401(d) of the Act precludes the state from including in its certification requirements of state law which do not relate to "water quality standards, effluent limitations or schedules of compliance." *See* § 301 (b)(1)(C). Finally, he concluded that "conditions of the Maine BEP relating to test runs with tankers prior to delivering oil, limiting the size of tankers . . . , requiring real time simulation studies, stating times and conditions of navigation of Head Harbor Passage, and other matters unrelated to water quality may not legally be regarded as part of the State of Maine's Sec. 401 certification, irrespective of the intention of the issuer of the certification."

Petitioners argue, with some force, that the conditions listed above *are* related to water quality, since they are designed to minimize the risk of an oil spill which would severely impair water quality. We believe that the ALJ made a more fundamental error by seeking to determine which requirements of state law were appropriately affixed to the state's certification. Section 401(a) of the Clean Water Act empowers the state to certify that a proposed discharge will comply with the Act and "with any other appropriate requirement of State law." Any such requirement "shall become a condition on any Federal license or permit." § 401(d). EPA has interpreted this provision broadly to preclude federal agency review of state certification. "Limitations contained in a State certification must be included in a NPDES permit. EPA has no authority to ignore State certification or to determine whether limitations certified by the State are more stringent than required to meet the requirements of State law," EPA, Decision of the General Counsel No. 58 (March 29, 1977); *see also* Decision of the General Counsel No. 44 (June 22, 1976). The NPDES regulations state that "[r]eview and appeals of limitations and conditions attributable to State certification shall be made through the applicable procedures of the State and may not be made" through the procedures established in the federal regulations. 40 C.F.R. § 124.55(e) (1981). The courts have consistently agreed with this interpretation, ruling that the proper forum to review the appropriateness of a state's certification is the state court, and the federal courts and agencies are without authority to review the validity of requirements imposed under state law or in a state's certification. *See United*

States Steel Corp. v. Train, 556 F.2d 822, 837-39 & n.22 (7th Cir. 1977); *Lake Erie Alliance v. U.S. Army Corps of Engineers.* 526 F.Supp. 1063, 1074 (W.D. Pa. 1981).

Our conclusion that EPA lacked authority to review the conditions imposed by the State of Maine is also supported by the statutory scheme of the Clean Water Act. Section 511(c)(2) of the Act, 33 U.S.C. § 1371(c)(2), makes clear that "[n]othing in the National Environmental Policy Act . . . shall be deemed to authorize any Federal agency . . . to review any effluent limitation or other requirement established pursuant to this Act *or the adequacy of any certification under section 401* of this Act." (emphasis added). Section 510 of the Act, 33 U.S.C. § 1370, specifically preserves the right of a state to "adopt or enforce . . . any requirement respecting control or abatement of pollution," even if it is more stringent than those adopted by the federal government. Finally, it is clear that even in the absence of state certification, EPA would be bound to include in the federal permit "any more stringent limitations . . . established pursuant to any State law or regulations (under authority preserved by Section 510)." § 301(b)(1)(C).

The regulations cited by respondents do not compel a different result. *** The new regulation, 40 C.F.R. § 124.55(d) (1981), states that "[a] condition in a draft permit may be changed during agency review in any manner consistent with" state certification without requiring recertification. This regulation clearly does not authorize EPA to amend a permit in a manner *inconsistent* with state certification by deleting conditions imposed by the state during the certification process. *** Since the state at no time waived its rights to certify the proposed discharge, and the ALJ lacked authority to exclude the previously imposed state conditions from the federal permit, these conditions must be included in any NPDES permit for the Pittston project to be issued in the future, unless the conditions are modified according to law.

*   *   *

11   NAVIGABLE WATERS

United States v. Holland

373 F. Supp. 665 (M.D. Fla. 1974)

KRENTZMAN, District Judge:

MEMORANDUM OPINION

This is an action brought by the United States to enjoin allegedly unlawful landfilling operations in an area known as Harbor Isle, adjoining Papy's Bayou, St. Petersburg, Florida. The government contends that the defendants have begun filling the waters of the bayou with sand, dirt, dredged spoil and biological materials without the permits required by 33 U.S.C.A. §§ 403, 407 and 1311(a). For relief the government requests a stoppage of further filling and a restoration of some mangrove wetland.

*   *   *

On January 9, 1974, plaintiff's motion for preliminary injunction was heard. At that proceeding the following were established to the Court's satisfaction:

1. Defendants are engaged in developing a 281 acre tract of land known as Harbor Isle.

2. For the purposes of the preliminary injunction hearing the Court accepted defendants' determination that the mean high water line is one foot above sea level.

3. Tide data, visual observation and classification of vegetation established that a substantial number of tides exceed two feet above sea level.

   (a) The United States Geological Survey tide gauge data indicated that 50-100 tides exceed two feet in the subject waters each year.

4. The parties stipulated to the accuracy of a land survey introduced by defendants. The survey and other evidence established that:

   (a) Most of the property is interlaced with artificial mosquito canals containing water.

   (b) The water in the mosquito canals is connected to Papy's Bayou.

   (c) The elevation of much of the property is less than two feet.

5. Without a permit issued under authority of Title 33, United States Code, Sections 407 and 1344, defendants have discharged sand, dirt, dredged spoil and biological materials into the man-made canals and into mangrove wetlands which are periodically inundated by tides exceeding two feet above sea level.

6. Defendants would continue to discharge sand, dirt, dredged spoil and biological materials until the fill created has effectively displaced tidal waters, thereby eliminating the normal ebb and flow of tides over the subject property.

7. Continued discharge would result in irreparable injury, loss and damage to the aquatic ecosystem of Papy's Bayou and to the commercial and sport fisheries which are dependent upon the estuaries of the Gulf of Mexico.

The Court felt these facts established acts of sufficient scope to warrant federal jurisdiction under the Federal Water Pollution Control Act, and of sufficient magnitude to justify a preliminary injunction. The motion for such an injunction was granted at the hearing. A brief order of injunction and findings was signed January 11, 1974.

Since the courts have not yet been faced with the question of whether federal jurisdiction over water pollution encompasses intertidal wetlands by virtue of the relatively new Federal Water Pollution Control Act Amendments of 1972, 33 U.S.C.A. § 1251 et seq., this opinion will offer the rationale for the grant of jurisdiction.

The Federal Water Pollution Control Act Amendments of 1972

The government charged the defendants with past and continuing violations of Section 301(a) of the Federal Water Pollution Control Act Amendments of 1972 (FWPCA). To sustain this allegation two showings had to be made. First it had to be established that the defendants' acts were such as to be prohibited if done in waters within federal jurisdiction, and second, that the waters receiving the impact of the prohibited conduct were indeed within that jurisdictional ambit.

Prohibited Activities

The FWPCA is an admirably comprehensive piece of legislation. It was designed to deal with all facets of recapturing and preserving the biological integrity of the nation's water by creating a web of complex interrelated regulatory programs. Section 301(a), the enforcement hub of the statute, however, is stated very simply. It provides that except as otherwise permitted within the Act "the discharge of a pollutant by any person shall be unlawful." The plainness of the prohibition is matched by the breadth given the definition of a "discharge of a pollutant":

> (A) Any addition of any pollutant to navigable waters from any point source,
> (B) Any addition of any pollutant to the waters of the contiguous zone or the ocean from any point source other than a vessel or other floating craft. 33 U.S.C.A. § 1362(12).

"Pollutant" is in turn defined as

> ***dredge spoil, solid waste, incinerator residue, sewage garbage, sewer sludge, munitions, chemical wastes, *biological materials*, radioactive materials, heat, wrecked or discarded equipment, rock *sand*, cellar dirt and *industrial*, municipal and agricultural waste discharged into water.***

Id. § 1362(6) (emphasis added).

And "point source" is

> ***any discernible, confined and discrete conveyance, *including* but not limited to any *pipe, ditch,* channel, tunnel, conduit, well, discrete fissure, container, *rolling stock,* concentrated animal feeding operation, or vessel or other floating craft, from which pollutants are or may be discharged. Id. § 1362(14) (emphasis added).

The evidence substantiates the defendants' admission that without a permit they have discharged and would continue to discharge from point sources, including dump trucks, drag lines, and bulldozers, materials defined as pollutants. Whether these pollutants were discharged into waters within federal jurisdiction was the key issue.

Jurisdiction under the FWPCA

Throughout the course of this litigation there has been considerable discussion about whether the mosquito ditches that connect with Papy's Bayou are "navigable" and much testimony about whether certain discharges of pollutants were above or below the "mean high water line." Argument was heard on the issue of whether federal jurisdiction under the FWPCA was limited to activities taking place in navigable waters below the mean high water line. Because the terms "navigability" and "mean high water line" have played such important parts in determining federal jurisdiction over water pollution in the past, the contention that these terms should be used in arguing jurisdiction under the FWPCA was not surprising.

For years the mainstays of the federal water pollution effort were Sections 10 and 13 of Rivers and Harbors Act of 1899. Section 10 makes it illegal to fill, excavate, alter or modify the course, condition or capacity of waters within the boundaries of a navigable waterway without authorization from the Corps of Engineers. Section 13 prohibits the deposit of refuse in, or on the bank of, a navigable waterway without a Corps of Engineers' permit. Both of these laws are by their terms limited to waters that are deemed navigable. Because of this limitation past discussion of federal jurisdiction over water pollution was largely a question of the navigability of the waterway being affected.

Why the Congress limited the Rivers and Harbors Act to navigable waters is no insoluable mystery. Although the Constitution does not mention navigable waters, it vests in Congress the power to "regulate commerce with foreign nations and among the several states." Since much of the interstate commerce of the 19th century was water borne, it was early held that the commerce power necessarily included the power to regulate navigation. Gibbons v. Ogden, 22 U.S. (9 Wheat.) 1 (1824). *** To make this control effective Congress was deemed empowered to keep navigable waters open and free and to provide sanctions for interference. *See e.g.*, Gilman v. Philadelphia, 70 U.S. (3 Wall.) 713 (1865). The Rivers and Harbors Act of 1899 was an exercise of that power.

Whether Congressional power in 1899 was limited by judicial interpretation to navigable waters is now only of historical significance. At the time of the Act's passage, "commerce" was still nearly synonymous with "transportation" and the term "interstate" was largely used in a geographical sense. The extant case law relied upon the tenth amendment as a restraint upon the federal commerce power. The effects intrastate activity might have on commerce outside the state was of little concern. ***

Although the reach of federal power under the commerce clause widened dramatically in the twentieth century, the nineteenth century legacy of "navigation" lingered to limit federal control over water pollution. Since Congress had clearly limited the Rivers and Harbors Act to navigation, any subsequent judicial broadening of jurisdiction under the statute of necessity had to be in the form of expanding the definition of "navigability."

Starting with the basic definition of waters that

> ***form in their ordinary condition by themselves, or by uniting with other waters, a continued highway over which commerce is or may be carried on with

other States or foreign countries in the customary modes in which such commerce is conducted by water. (The Daniel Ball, 77 U.S. (10 Wall.) 557 (1870).)

the test of navigability was enlarged in 1874 to embrace waters that had the capability of commercial use, not merely those in actual use. The definition was again expanded in 1921 to bring in waterbodies whose past history of commercial use made it navigable despite subsequent physical or economic changes preventing present use for commerce. In 1940 it was held that a waterway would be deemed navigable-in-fact if by "reasonable improvements" it could be made navigable. Thus the jurisdictional basis broadened until only the most insignificant body of water could escape one of the tests of navigability.

But the limitation of navigability still worked to impede efforts to forestall the degradation of the aquatic environment. Not only did small feeder streams and tributaries remain exempt from federal jurisdiction but, more importantly, the wetland areas adjoining the waterways did also.

Just as it was not surprising that Congress limited the Rivers and Harbors Act to navigable waters, it was not surprising to have limited enforcement under the statute to navigation-impeding activities taking place *in* the water. Those charged with enforcing the Act needed an easily discernible boundary for their jurisdiction power—i.e. the lateral extent of the waterbody. In tidal areas that boundary became the mean high water line.

The Mean High Water Line

Since the Rivers and Harbors Act was passed at a time when interstate commerce was thought of in a geographical sense, and since the Act was designed primarily to keep the navigable waters free of physical impediments, it was natural to draw on the property-law concept of the mean high water line to limit the scope of jurisdiction in tidal water areas. If an agency is responsible only for keeping a waterbody free of obstructions, there is little need to focus attention on activities beyond the ordinary reach of the water.

But because the mean high water line was, and is, used to demarcate authority in tidal zones does not necessarily mean that the line is an inviolate barrier to federal assumption of authority over activities landward of the line. Examining the history and use of the line underscores the point.

*   *   *

The United States Supreme Court in Borax Consolidated, Ltd. v. Los Angeles, 296 U.S. 10 (1935), *** adopted the *** "mean high water" line as the limit of a federal land grant. *Borax* became a landmark case in the law of tidal boundaries. And even though the test used by the Supreme Court was enunciated to settle a land dispute, ***the test of the mean high water mark became the inveterate standard to be applied in limiting federal authority over navigable waters. Courts were justified in relying on a rule of common law which did no harm to the purposes of the statutes in question. The need to protect the navigable capacity of a waterway above the mean high water line was obviously minimal.

If the instant case involved only the question of federal jurisdiction over non-navigable streams and wetland areas under the Rivers and Harbors Act the Court might be compelled to deny jurisdiction by the sheer weight of precedent. But such is not the case. Here the Court is presented with a dispute brought pursuant to a new federal law not limited to the traditional tests of navigability.

On October 18, 1972, the Congress exercised its power under the commerce clause by enacting the FWPCA establishing regulatory programs to combat pollution of the nation's waters. Even though it seems certain that Congress sought to broaden federal jurisdiction under the Act, it did so in a manner that appears calculated to force courts to engage in verbal acrobatics. Although using the term "navigable waters" in the prohibitory phase of the statute, the definition of "navigable waters" is stated to be "waters of the United States, including the territorial seas." 33 U.S.C.A. § 1362(7). The definition stands with no limiting language.

If indeed the Congress saw fit to define away the navigability restriction, the sole limitation on the reach of federal power remaining would be the commerce clause. Thus two questions emerge. Did Congress intend to define away the old "navigability" restriction? And does the Congress have such power?

The answer to the first question is in the affirmative. The Court is of the opinion that the clear meaning of the statutory definition may be ascertained on its face without having to rely on the well established judicial philosophy that "forbids a narrow, cramped reading" of water pollution legislation.***

The legislative history of the FWPCA supports this clear meaning.

The bill submitted to the Senate as S. 2770 defined "navigable waters" to mean "navigable waters of the United States, portions thereof, and the tributaries thereof, including the territorial seas and the Great Lakes," Legislative History of the Water Pollution Control Act Amendments of 1972, Vol. 2, p. 1698 (hereinafter cited as "Legislative History").*** The House of Representatives bill, H.R. 11896, contained a more restrictive definition: "The Navigable waters of the United States, including the territorial seas." Legislative History, Vol.1, p. 1069. Significantly, when the two bills went to the Committee of Conference, the word "navigable" was deleted from the House definition in creating the final standard. The reason for this change was stated in the Joint Explanatory Statement of the Committee of Conference:

> "The conferees fully intend that the term 'navigable waters' be given the broadest possible constitutional interpretation unencumbered by agency determinations which have been made or may be made for administrative purposes." Conference Report, Senate Report No. 92-1236, Sept. 28, 1972, page 144; Reprinted in Legislative History, Vol. 1, p. 327.

*   *   *

The foregoing compels the Court to conclude that the former test of navigability was indeed defined away in FWPCA.***

Clearly Congress has the power to eliminate the "navigability" limitation from the reach of federal control under the Commerce Clause. The "geographic" and "transportation" conception of the Commerce Clause which may have placed the navigation restriction in the Rivers and Harbors Act of 1899 has long since been abandoned in defining federal power. Now when courts are faced with a challenge to congressional power under the Commerce Clause a statute's validity is upheld by determining first if the general activity sought to be regulated is reasonably related to, or has an effect on, interstate commerce and, second, whether the specific activities in the case before the court are those intended to be reached by Congress through the statute. Perez v. United States, 402 U.S. 146 (1970); Katzenbach v. McClung, 397 U.S. 294 (1964); Heart of Atlanta Motel, Inc. v. United States, 397 U.S. 341 (1964); United States v. Darby, 312 U.S. 100 (1941).

It is beyond question that water pollution has a serious effect on interstate commerce and that the Congress has the power to regulate activities such as dredging and filling which cause such pollution. As stated by the Court in Zabel v. Tabb, 430 F.2d 199, 204 (5 Cir. 1970):

> [T]he nation knows, if the Courts do not, that the destruction of fish and wildlife in our estuarine waters does have a substantial effect on interstate commerce ***. Nor is it challenged that dredge and fill projects are activities which may tend to destroy the ecological balance and thereby affect commerce substantially."

Congress and the courts have become aware of the lethal effect pollution has on all organisms. Weakening any of the life support systems bodes disaster for the rest of the interrelated life forms. To recognize this and yet hold that pollution does not affect interstate commerce unless committed in navigable waters below the mean high water line would be contrary to reason. Congress is not limited by the "navigable waters" test in its authority to control pollution under the Commerce Clause.

Having thus ascertained that Congress had the power to go beyond the "navigability" limitation in its control over water pollution and that it intended to do so in the FWPCA, the question remains whether the Congress intended to reach the type of activities involved in the instant case—the pollution of non-navigable mosquito canals and mangrove wetland areas.

As previously noted the defendants without a permit have filled and otherwise polluted various mosquito canals which connected with the waters of Papy's Bayou. The man-made canals were found to be non-navigable for the purposes of this action.

The conclusion that Congress intended to reach water bodies such as these canals with the FWPCA is inescapable. The legislative history quoted supra manifests a clear intent to break from the limitations of the Rivers and Harbors Act to get at the sources of pollution. Polluting canals that empty into a bayou arm of Tampa Bay is clearly an activity Congress sought to regulate. The fact that these canals were man-made makes no difference. They were constructed long before the development scheme was conceived. That the defendants used them to convey the pollutants without a permit is the matter of importance.

The Court is of the opinion that the waters of the mosquito canals were within definition of "waters of the United States" and that the filling of them without a permit was a violation of the FWPCA.

Whether the FWPCA was meant to reach activities such as those committed here in mangrove wetlands above the mean high water line is slightly less apparent. An examination of Congressional intent, however, leads this Court to the conclusion that such intertidal wetlands were indeed meant to be covered.

The first glimpse of Congressional intent comes from the FWPCA itself. Section 101(a) puts forth the purpose of the Act:

> "The objective of this Act is to restore and maintain the chemical, physical, and biological integrity of the Nation's waters.***

> *   *   *

Section 404 of the Act establishes a program for permitting the discharge of dredged or fill materials into waters of the United States. Subsection (c) provides for careful consideration of whether or not such discharges will have "unacceptable adverse effect on municipal water supplies, shellfish-beds, and fishery areas (including spawning and breeding areas), wildlife, or recreational areas." 33 U.S.C.A. § 1344(c).

These *** sections do not by themselves prove conclusively that Congress sought to assume jurisdiction over activities taking place in wetlands above the mean high water line. What these sections do reveal is a sensitivity to the value of a coastal breeding ground. Composed of various interdependent ecological systems (i.e. marshes, mudflats, shallow open water, mud and sand bottoms, beach and dunes) the delicately balanced coastal environment is highly sensitive to human activities within its confines.

Congress realizes the coastal ecology is endangered by poorly planned development. It cannot be gainsaid that the discharge of pollutants into coastal, estuarine and adjacent waters have caused considerable damage to the marine environment. Estuaries, partially enclosed bodies of water within which there is a measurable dilution of sea water by fresh water run off, and other breeding zones have suffered the most damage. Salt water marshes and other wetlands constitute a major component of the estuarine system.

Estuaries are not only highly productive in organic matter, but also are valuable in replenishing oxygen for the atmosphere. Moreover, estuaries are vital to fish and shellfish. About two-thirds of all ocean animals either spend a part of their life there or feed upon a species that has lived there. The first Annual Report of the Council on Environmental Quality, 176 (1970). The FWPCA embodies the realization that pollution of these areas may be ecologically fatal.

In an attempt to combat these threats to the coastal environment, the Congress broadened its jurisdiction to encompass "all waters of the United States." In doing so Congress deemed it "essential that the discharge of pollutants be controlled *at the source.*" Legislative History Vol. 2.p.

1495. Getting at the source of pollution is going beyond the confines of a high water line. It cannot be doubted that most of the damage to marine life results from land-based and not sea-based activities.

One of the sources of pollution in the instant case was the discharge of sand, dirt and dredged spoil on land which, although above the mean high water line, was periodically inundated with the waters of Papy's Bayou. Defendants argue that such activities are beyond the reach of the FWPCA. This Court does not agree. Even the occasional lapping of the bayou waters has conveyed these pollutants into the waters of the United States. That the pollutants are not so conveyed every day is of no consequence. Pollutants have been introduced into the waters of the United States without a permit and the mean high water mark cannot be used to create a barrier behind which such activities can be excused. The environment cannot afford such safety zones.

The Court is of the opinion that the mean high water line is no limit to federal authority under the FWPCA. While the line remains a valid demarcation for other purposes, it has no rational connection to the aquatic ecosystems which the FWPCA is intended to protect.***

The defendants' filling activities on land periodically inundated by tidal waters constitute discharges entering "waters of the United States" and, since done without a permit, were thus in violation of 33 U.S.C.A. § 1311(a).

The Rivers and Harbors Act of 1899

Plaintiff has alleged violations of Sections 10 and 13 of the Rivers and Harbors Act of 1899 (33 U.S.C.A. §§ 403, 407). The evidence indicated that refuse or fill material has been deposited into navigable waters below the mean high water line. The area below the line is a small percentage of the total area for which an injunction is sought.

The government argued that any activity above mean high water which affects the quality of classical navigable-in-law waters may be properly enjoined as a violation of the 1899 Act. Plaintiff also contended that artificial mosquito canals are navigable-in-law when connected to navigable-in-fact waterbodies since the canals contain water at mean high tide.

Although these arguments are not unpersuasive, the Court's foregoing determination that the FWPCA encompasses the area included in the government's allegation under the 1899 Act makes it unnecessary to decide whether the theories based on the older statute are meritorious.

By determining that the defendants have violated the provisions of the FWPCA and by enjoining further unlawful activities, the Court has not permanently prohibited defendants from going forward with their plans. All the Court has said is that the activities cannot be continued without a federal permit.

The Court realizes that the thought of preserving huge stretches of coastline in a natural state and forbidding all commercial development in coastal areas is unrealistic. This is a societal choice which the government must observe. But the government can and should insure that the public interest in protecting all life forms is at least considered in the development plans. Any expense that might be incurred by this evaluative process will be dwarfed by the cost of neglecting the ecological interests.

Natural Resources Defense Council, Inc. v. Callaway

392 F. Supp. 685 (D.D.C. 1975)

DECLARATION AND ORDER
OF FINAL JUDGMENT

AUBREY E. ROBINSON, Jr., District Judge.

Plaintiffs have moved for an order pursuant to Rule 56 of the Federal Rules of Civil Procedure granting partial summary judgment in favor of Plaintiffs on Count I of the Complaint; and Defendants' having moved to dismiss the complaint on all counts; and the Court having heard argument of counsel, the Motion for Partial Summary Judgment on Count I of the Complaint is granted; and it is DECLARED that:

1. Congress by defining the term "navigable waters" in Section 502(7) of the Federal Water Pollution Control Act Amendments of 1972 to mean "the waters of the United States, including the territorial seas," asserted federal jurisdiction over the nation's waters to the maximum extent permissible under the Commerce Clause of the Constitution. Accordingly, as used in the Water Act, the term is not limited to the traditional tests of navigability.

2. Defendants Howard H. Callaway, Secretary of the Army, and Lt. Gen. William C. Grib- ble, Chief, Army Corps of Engineers, are without authority to amend or change the statutory definition of navigable waters and they are hereby declared to have acted unlawfully and in derogation of their responsibilities under Section 404 of the Water Act by the adoption of the definition of navigability described at 33 C.F.R. § 209.210(d)(1), 39 Federal Register 12119 (April 3, 1974) and 33 C.F.R. 209.260; and it is ordered that Defendants Callaway and Gribble:

1. Revoke and rescind so much of 39 Federal Register 12115, et seq. (April 3, 1974) as limits the permit jurisdiction of the Corps of Engineers by definition or otherwise to other than "the waters of the United States."

2. Publish within fifteen (15) days of the date of this Order proposed regulations clearly recognizing the full regulatory mandate of the Water Act.

3. Publish within thirty (30) days of the date of this Order final regulations clearly recognizing the full regulatory mandate of the Water Act;***.

*   *   *

Leslie Salt Company v. Froehlke

578 F.2d 742 (9th Cir. 1978)

SNEED, Circuit Judge:

These appeals deal with the scope of the regulatory jurisdiction of the U.S. Army Corps of Engineers ("Corps") over "navigable waters of the United States" as that term is used, first, in the Rivers and Harbors Act of 1899, 33 U.S.C. § 401 et seq., and, second, in the Federal Water Pollution Control Act of 1972, 33 U.S.C. § 1251, et seq.

Suit was initiated on March 29, 1972, by the Sierra Club against Leslie Salt Co. ("Leslie"), seeking a declaratory judgment that Leslie's diked evaporation ponds in and around Bair Island in San Francisco Bay were built in violation of the Rivers and Harbors Act of 1899 because Leslie had failed to seek or obtain permits from the Corps. The action also sought a permanent injunction ordering removal of the dikes or, in the alternative, prohibiting further construction or maintenance of dikes at Bair Island. Leslie then sued the Corps on December 20, 1973, seeking a declaration that the regulatory jurisdiction of the Corps over tidal marshlands in San Francisco Bay under both the Rivers and Harbors Act of 1899 and the Federal Water Pollution Control Act of 1972 ("FWPCA") is delimited by the line of mean high water ("MHW"). The Sierra Club was permitted to intervene in this action.

The two cases were consolidated for trial. On December 9, 1974, the district court rendered partial summary judgment in favor of the Corps and the Sierra Club in Leslie's suit against the Corps ("Leslie's suit"), holding that the Corps's jurisdiction under the FWPCA extends to the line of mean higher high water ("MHHW") on the Pacific coast. This was followed on March 11, 1976 by an opinion in both cases holding that the Corps's jurisdiction under the Rivers and Harbors Act also extends to the MHHW line on the Pacific coast. The district court further held that the Corps's jurisdiction extends to the *former* MHHW line in its unobstructed, natural state, rather than to the *present* MHHW line, which at least in part follows the bayward edge of Leslie's

dikes. *Id.* at 1102. Finally, the court held that although the Corps had timely asserted its jurisdiction over the discharge of dredged or fill material under the FWPCA of 1972, it was estopped from requiring permits under the Rivers and Harbors Act for the future maintenance of any obstruction already constructed before the Corps's assertion of jurisdiction. *Id.* at 1104. The court ruled that its estoppel holding in Leslie's suit against the Corps was also applicable to the Sierra Club's action ("Sierra Club's suit"), which later was dismissed on the court's own motion. These appeals followed.

The district court erred in holding that the Corps's jurisdiction under the Rivers and Harbors Act extends to the MHHW line on the Pacific coast, but was correct insofar as its holding subjected to the Corps's jurisdiction under the FWPCA waters which are no longer subject to tidal inundation because of Leslie's dikes, without regard to the location of historic tidal water lines in their unobstructed, natural state.***

I.

Facts

Leslie owns some 35,000 acres of property along the shores of south San Francisco Bay. Appellant Mobil Oil Estates Ltd. (Bair Island Investments) is the owner of a 3,000-acre parcel in San Mateo County known as "Bair Island." The subject lands were originally conveyed by the United States to the State of California pursuant to the Arkansas Swamp Act of 1850, and then patented by the state to Leslie's predecessors in interest. In its natural condition, the property was marshland subject to the ebb and flow of the tide. Commencing in 1860, the land was diked and reclaimed and has since that time been used primarily for salt production by means of solar evaporation of Bay waters introduced into Leslie's salt ponds. These dikes were completed, for the most part, in 1927, although some work continued through 1969. Because of these dikes, the land in question has not been subject to tidal action on a regular basis, although most of it is periodically inundated by Bay waters for salt production. The Bair Island property was removed from salt production in 1965; because of the continued maintenance of dikes on the island, it has become dry land.

In 1971 and 1972, the San Francisco District of the Corps published two Public Notices (No. 71-22 on June 11, 1971, and No. 71-22(a) on January 18, 1972), stating that the Corps had changed its policy and would henceforth require permits for all "new work" on unfilled marshland property within the line of "former mean higher high water," whether or not the property was presently diked off from the ebb and flow of the tides.

In these Public Notices the Corps purported simply to redefine the scope of its regulatory authority within the ambit of the Rivers and Harbors Act of 1899, Sections 9 and 10 of which prohibit filling or the construction of any "dam," "dike," "obstruction," or "other structures" within the "navigable water of the United States," without the prior authorization of the Corps of Engineers. 33 U.S.C. §§ 401, 403.

An understanding of the technical tide line terminology is critical to this case. Every 24.8 hours, both the Pacific and Atlantic coasts of the United States experience two complete tidal cycles, each including a high and a low tide. The Gulf coast tides, known as diurnal, have but one high and one low tide each lunar day. On the Atlantic coast, the difference between the two daily tidal cycles, known as semidiurnal tides, is relatively slight. Accordingly, there is in most instances little difference between the two high tides or between the two low tides in a given day on the east coast. The two daily Pacific coast tidal cycles (known as "mixed type" tides), however, in most locations are substantially unequal in size, with one high tide significantly higher than the other. The mean high water line is the average of both of the daily high tides over a period of 18.6 years; the mean higher high water line is the average of only the higher of the two tides for the same period of time. Thus, on the Atlantic coast the difference between the MHW and the MHHW is relatively small, while on the Pacific coast generally it is relatively large.

We shall first discuss Leslie's suit and then turn to that of the Sierra Club.

II.
Leslie's Suit
*   *   *

B. *Scope of Corps's Jurisdiction Under Rivers and Harbors Act.*

Analysis of the Rivers and Harbors Act must begin by acknowledging that it does not define the terms "navigable water of the United States" or "waters of the United States." Pertinent regulations defining these terms have recently been adopted by the Corps. On July 25, 1975, after the San Francisco District of the Corps issued the two Public Notices dealing with the use of the MHHW line as the limit of its jurisdiction, the Corps promulgated the following definition of "navigable waters of the United States":

> The term, "navigable waters of the United States," is administratively defined to mean waters that have been used in the past, are now used, or are susceptible to use as a means to transport interstate commerce landward to their ordinary high water mark and up to the head of navigation as determined by the Chief of Engineers, and also waters that are subject to the ebb and flow of the tides shoreward to their mean high water mark *(mean higher high water mark on the Pacific coast).*

33 C.F.R. § 209.120(d)(1) (emphasis added). Regulation 209.260, adopted September 9, 1972, provides in most pertinent part, as follows:

> *Shoreward limit of jurisdiction.* Regulatory jurisdiction in coastal areas extends to the line on the shore reached by the plane of the mean (average) high water. *However, on the Pacific coast, the line reached by the mean of the higher high waters is used.*

33 C.F.R. § 209.260 (k)(1)(ii) (emphasis added).
*   *   *

Leslie contends that the district court's ruling upholding the Corps's regulations is contrary to every reported decision defining the bound-

aries of tidal water bodies. Conceding that Congress may in theory have the power under the Commerce Clause to legislate with respect to land between the MHW and the MHHW line, Leslie argues that the "navigable waters of the United States" within the meaning of the Rivers and Harbors Act have consistently been judicially extended only to the MHW line. ***
Inasmuch as Leslie accurately describes the state of the authorities, the Corps and Sierra Club in effect invite us to read the Act differently than in the past to accommodate the desire of the Corps to extend its jurisdiction on the Pacific coast. We decline the invitation because we believe it is misdirected. It should be addressed to Congress rather than the Judiciary.

Turning to the authorities, the Supreme Court in 1915 held that federal regulatory jurisdiction over navigable tidal waters extends to the MHW line. *Willink v. United States,* 240 U.S. 572, 580 (1916). While *Willink* was concerned with the boundaries of the tidal waters on the Atlantic coast, the case is significant because it deals directly with the relationship between the federal navigational servitude and the Corps's regulation of "navigable waters of the United States." The servitude, which reaches to the limits of "navigable water," permits the removal of an obstruction to navigable capacity without compensation. *See* 33 U.S.C. § 403. Accordingly, an expansion of "navigable water" shoreward diminishes the protection of the Fifth Amendment. We think an interpretation of the Act which accomplishes this, first advanced seventy-two years after its enactment, should be viewed with skepticism to say the least.

*   *   *

Consistent with *Willink,* however, is the leading case defining the extent of tidal water bodies on the Pacific coast. *Borax Consolidated, Ltd. v. City of Los Angeles,* 296 U.S. 10 (1935), originated in a property dispute brought by Los Angeles to quiet title to land on an island in Los Angeles harbor. At issue was the proper boundaries between *tidelands* as to which the State possessed original title upon admittance to the Union, and *uplands,* which became public lands of the United States at the time of their acquis-

tion from Mexico. Los Angeles claimed the disputed property under a tidelands grant from the State of California, while Borax Consolidated, the upland owner, claimed under a patent issued by the United States. The specific question presented on appeal to the Supreme Court was whether this boundary line was the mean high tide line as urged by Los Angeles; or the "neap tide" line, as Borax Consolidated contended. Neap tides are those which occur monthly when the moon is in its first and third quarters, during which time the tide does not rise as high or fall as low as on the average. In contrast, "spring tides," which occur at times of new moon and full moon, are greater than average. During spring tide the high water rises higher and low water falls lower than usual.

The Supreme Court, affirming a decision of this court, held that the tideland extends to the MHW mark as technically defined by the United States Coast and Geodetic Survey; that is, "the average height of *all* the high waters" at a given place over a period of 18.6 years. (emphasis added).***

The district court below distinguishes *Borax* on the grounds that the Supreme Court was dealing with an issue of *title* and "made no reference to the federal navigational servitude under the Rivers and Harbors Act or to the distinction of MHHW and MHW." However, *Borax* cannot be brushed aside so easily. The considerations involved in the regulation of navigable waters under the commerce power are intimately connected to the question of title to tidelands. The term "navigable waters" has been judicially defined to cover: (1) nontidal waters which were navigable in the past or which could be made navigable in fact by "reasonable improvements,"***and (2) waters within the ebb and flow of the tide.*** Tideland, by definition, is the soil underlying tidal water. To fix the shoreward boundary of tideland there must be fixed the shoreward limit of tidal water which, in turn, should fix the shoreward limit of "navigable waters" in the absence of a contrary intent on the part of Congress. To fix the limit of "navigable water," for the purposes of the Rivers and Harbors Act, further shoreward than *Borax* fixed the limit of "tidal water" assumes the existence of an intent of Congress at the time of the Act's enactment of which we have no evidence.

*   *   *

This long-standing recognition that, for the purpose of fixing a shoreward limit, the terms tide water and navigable water are interchangeable strongly suggests that in *Borax* the Supreme Court, in the course of settling a title dispute, also fixed the shoreward boundary of navigable water on the Pacific coast. This is buttressed by the fact that since *Borax* and *Willink*, the MHW line has been routinely cited as the boundary of federal regulatory jurisdiction over tidal waters by every court to consider the question, with the two recent exceptions upon which the Corps and Sierra Club rely.***

Although these cases all arose on the Atlantic or Gulf coasts, each implicitly accepts *Borax*, a Pacific coast case, as enunciating a rule applicable to all coasts of the United States. Taken together, they indicate the extent to which the MHW line has been consistently accepted as the boundary of "navigable waters of the United States." To affirm the Corps's recent regulations setting the shoreward reach of federal regulatory power on the Pacific coast at the MHHW line would constitute a dramatic reversal of long-established decisional precedent.

The appellees insist that the Corps's recently promulgated regulations using the MHHW line are not an extension of jurisdiction, but merely a recognition of previously informal policy. *** Assuming *arguendo* that there was such a policy on the part of the Corps, we cannot accept an interpretation which was never stated or practiced, and which is so clearly contrary to the long-established precedent to which the Corps in its regulations prior to 1972 gave deference. Neither do we perceive how the use of MHHW on the Pacific coast and MHW elsewhere would bring any more "harmony" to the Corps's regulatory jurisdiction than has existed under the heretofore uniform application of the MHW line on all coasts.[11]

Moreover, we have already indicated that more is involved than simply an expansion of the Corps's regulatory authority. As stated by the Supreme Court in *United States v. Virginia Electric Co.*, 365 U.S. 624 (1961):

> This navigational servitude — sometimes referred to as a "dominant servitude," . . . or a "superior navigation easement," . . . — is the privilege to appropriate without compensation *which attaches to the exer-*

monthly variations between spring and neap tides, it is brought about by variations in the declination of the moon relative to the earth. Since the difference between MHHW and MHW is relatively greater on the Pacific coast, the Corps argues that its use of MHHW on the Pacific is more consistent with use of MHW elsewhere than if it simply applied MHW everywhere.

However, there are so many exceptions to the basic pattern of greater diurnal inequality on the Pacific coast than the Atlantic that the Corps' policy cannot be said to produce any "harmony." The three tide types form a continuum from semidiurnal to mixed to diurnal. As diurnal inequality increases the lower high water and higher low water tend to become equal and merge. When this occurs, there is but one high and one low water in a tidal day instead of two. Thus, this diurnal or "daily" type of tide, which is found on the Gulf coast, is actually an extreme form of the mixed type of tide found on the Pacific coast, just as the mixed tide type is a more extreme form of the semidiurnal type.

As reported in the USGS publication relied on by the Supreme Court in *Borax, supra.*, there are tremendous variations in the amounts of diurnal inequality found at various points on the different coasts. For example, there is *greater* diurnal inequality at Baltimore, Maryland, on the Atlantic coast, than at either Astoria, Oregon or Humboldt Bay, California, both on the Pacific coast. Since the difference between the once a day diurnal type of tide and the mixed tide type is strictly a matter of degree, it is not surprising that some places on the Gulf coast such as the southern end of Florida and parts of Texas actually experience Pacific-type diurnal inequality. On the other hand, the Alaskan coast (presumably part of the Pacific coast for Corps purposes) has tremendous variations all along the spectrum, from Atlantic-type semidiurnal tides at Ketchikan, Juneau, and Anchorage, to Pacific-type mixed tides at Sitka, Kodiak, and Point Barrows; to Gulf-type diurnal tides at Dutch Harbor and St. Michael.

In view of these inconsistencies in diurnal inequality, it is difficult to see the rationality of using a different standard for the Corps's jurisdiction on the Pacific coast in order to bring about an asserted uniformity. H.A. Marmer, Tidal Datum Planes, U.S. Coast and Geodetic Survey (Special Publication No. 135), at 5-7, 74-83 (1927).

---

[11]The difference between morning and afternoon tides is known as "diurnal inequality." Like the

cise of the "power of the government to control and regulate navigable waters in the interest of commerce." United States v. Commodore Park, 324 U.S. 386, 390.

United States v. Virginia Electric, 365 U.S. at 627-28 (emphasis added). The navigational servitude reaches to the shoreward limit of navigable waters. To extend the servitude on the basis of a recently formulated administrative policy is to impose an additional burden of unknown magnitude on all private property that abuts on the Pacific coast.

We wish to point out, however, that our interpretation of the Rivers and Harbors Act is not governed by a belief that the Act represents the full exertion by Congress of its authority under the Commerce Clause. To paraphrase the Court of Appeals for the Third Circuit in *Stoeco Homes, supra,* "we can put aside the question whether under the Commerce Clause, Congress could extend the regulatory jurisdiction of the Army Corps of Engineers" to the MHHW line or beyond:

> In the statute on which the government relies Congress did not do so. *It extended that jurisdiction only to the navigable waters of the United States. . . .* [The Rivers and Harbors Acts of 1890 and 1899] were enacted pursuant to the Commerce Clause, but neither reached the full extent of Congressional power over commerce. That power was exercised in 1890 to protect "waters, in respect of which the United States has jurisdiction" and in 1899 to protect "waters of the United States." Congress obviously adopted the judicial definition of those waters as of 1890. That definition was the admiralty definition.

Stoeco Homes, supra. 498 F.2d at 608-09 (emphasis added).

We hold that in tidal areas, "navigable waters of the United States," as used in the Rivers and Harbors Act, extend to all places covered by the ebb and flow of the tide to the mean high water (MHW) mark in its unobstructed, natural state. Accordingly, we reverse the district court's decision insofar as it found that the Corps's jurisdiction under the Rivers and Harbors Act includes all areas within the former line of MHHW in its unobstructed, natural state.

Our holding that the MHW line is to be fixed in accordance with its natural, unobstructed state is dictated by the principle recognized in *Willink, supra,* that one who develops areas below the MHW line does so at his peril. We recognize that under this holding issues of whether the Government's power may be surrendered or its exercise estopped, and if so, under what circumstances and to what extent, may arise. Leslie, for example, may contend that there has been a surrender by the Corps of its power under the Rivers and Harbors Act with respect to certain land below the MHW line. Such contentions, however, are not presently before us in this case. Therefore, at this time it is not necessary for us to pass on issues such as were before the court in *Stoeco, supra.*

C. *Scope of Corps's Jurisdiction Under FWPCA.*

The scope of regulatory authority under the FWPCA presents a substantially different issue. The district court's holding that the Corps's regulatory jurisdiction under the FWPCA is "coterminous" with that under the Rivers and Harbors Act, extending to "the former line of MHHW of the bay in its unobstructed, natural state," is faulty. In its opening brief in this appeal, Leslie properly concedes that:

> . . . the Corps' jurisdiction under Section 404 of the FWPCA is broader than its jurisdiction under the Rivers and Harbors Act in that it encompasses existing marshlands located above as well as below the lines of mean high water and mean higher high water which are currently subject to tidal inundation.

Brief for Appellant Leslie Salt Co. at 60. Leslie contends, however, that the use of the *former* unobstructed, natural MHHW line "extends the Corps' regulatory authority significantly further than is authorized by the FWPCA," because it results in the possibility that the Corps would be able to regulate discharges onto dry lands under an Act whose purpose is to control pollution of the nation's waters. *Id.*

This contention presents a false issue. Neither the Corps nor the Sierra Club argues for the result envisioned by Leslie. Instead, they contend that under the FWPCA, the case law interpreting it, and the Corps's own regulations, neither the MHW nor the MHHW line marks the full limit of the Corps's jurisdiction to regulate the pollution of the *waters* of the United States.***

Where the parties differ is on the question of whether the Corps's jurisdiction covers waters which are no longer subject to tidal inundation because of man-made obstructions such as Leslie's dikes. These are the waters which the district court apparently wanted to include under the aegis of the FWPCA through the use of the historic MHHW line "in its unobstructed, natural state."

*   *   *

[T]he court below actually placed undue limits on the FWPCA when it stated that "the geographical extent of the Corps' jurisdiction under the Rivers and Harbors Act is coterminous with that under FWPCA." It is clear from the legislative history of the FWPCA that for the purposes of that Act, Congress intended to expand the narrow definition of the term "navigable waters," as used in the Rivers and Harbors Act. This court has indicated that the term "navigable waters" within the meaning of the FWPCA is to be given the broadest possible constitutional interpretation under the Commerce Clause.*See United States v. Phelps Dodge Corp.*, 391 F. Supp. 1181 (D. Ariz. 1975); *United States v. Holland, supra,* 373 F. Supp. 665 (M.D. Fla. 1974). Also in *Phelps Dodge, supra,* the court interpreted the FWPCA broadly in finding that:

> ... a legal definition of "navigable waters" or "waters of the United States" within the scope of the [Federal Water Pollution Control] Act includes any waterway within the United States also including normally dry arroyos through which water may flow, where such water will ultimately end up in public waters such as a river or stream, tributary to a river or stream, lake, reservoir, bay, gulf,

sea or ocean either within or adjacent to the United States.

Phelps Dodge, supra, 391 F. Supp. at 1187. *See also, United States v. Holland, supra,* 373 F. Supp. at 670-676.

The water in Leslie's salt ponds, even though not subject to tidal action, comes from the San Francisco Bay to the extent of eight to nine billion gallons a year. We see no reason to suggest that the United States may protect these waters from pollution while they are outside of Leslie's tide gates, but may no longer do so once they have passed through these gates into Leslie's ponds. Moreover, there can be no question that activities within Leslie's salt ponds affect interstate commerce, since Leslie is a major supplier of salt for industrial, agricultural, and domestic use in the western United States. Much of the salt which Leslie harvests from the Bay's waters at the rate of about one million tons annually enters interstate and foreign commerce.

Our suggestion that the full extent of the Corps's FWPCA jurisdiction over the "waters of the United States" is in some instances not limited to the MHW or the MHHW line is reinforced by regulations published by the Corps on July 19, 1977 and found at 33 C.F.R. § 323.2.[16]

---

[16]This section sets out the definitions used in Part 323, which covers permits for discharges of dredged or fill material into waters of the United States pursuant to Section 404 of the FWPCA. In pertinent part, § 323.2 provides as follows:

> For the purpose of this regulation, the following terms are defined:
> (a) The term "waters of the United States" means:
> (1) The territorial seas with respect to the discharge of fill material. . . ;
> (2) Coastal and inland waters, lakes, rivers, and streams that are navigable waters of the United States, *including adjacent wetlands;*
> (3) Tributaries to navigable waters of the United States, *including adjacent wetlands* (manmade nontidal drainage and irrigation ditches excavated on dry land are not considered waters of the United States under this definition);
> (4) Interstate waters and their tributaries, *including adjacent wetlands;* and
> (5) *All other waters of the United States* not identified in paragraphs (1)-(4) above, *such as*

Without determining the exact limits of the scope of federal regulatory jurisdiction under

---

isolated wetlands and lakes, intermittent streams, prairie potholes, and *other waters that are not part of a tributary system to interstate waters or to navigable waters of the United States,* the degradation or destruction of which could affect interstate commerce.

*　　　*　　　*

(c) The term "wetlands" means those areas that are inundated or saturated by surface or ground water at a frequency and duration sufficient to support, and that under normal circumstances do support, a prevalence of vegetation typically adapted for life in saturated soil conditions. Wetlands generally include swamps, marshes, bogs and similar areas.

(d) The term "adjacent" means bordering, contiguous, or neighboring. *Wetlands separated from other waters of the United States by man-made dikes or barriers, natural river berms, beach dunes, and the like are "adjacent wetlands."*

*　　　*　　　*

the FWPCA, we find that the regulations at 33 C.F.R. § 323.2 are reasonable, consistent with the intent of Congress, and not contrary to the Constitution. We therefore hold that the Corps's jurisdiction under the FWPCA extends at least to waters which are no longer subject to tidal inundation because of Leslie's dikes without regard to the location of historic tidal water lines in their unobstructed, natural state. We express no opinion on the outer limits to which the Corps's jurisdiction under the FWPCA might extend.

Our holdings with respect to the Rivers and Harbors Act of 1899 and the FWPCA dispose of the declaratory judgment sought by Leslie in its case. Any claims by Leslie, which may be engendered by these holdings, and which are not also involved in Sierra Club's case, whether based on equitable considerations, estoppel, or surrender, must be made and considered in a separate and independent proceeding.

*　　　*　　　*

NOTES

1. Interpretation of the jurisdictional reach of the Clean Water Act, "navigable waters," to extend as far as the federal commerce power was a substantial departure from the more limited construction traditionally given to "navigable waters of the United States." By the time the 1972 Amendments were passed, the meaning of this latter term was well established: waters which presently, in the past, or, with reasonable improvements, in the future could be used for interstate or international commerce by water — with the shoreward boundary being the mean high water mark and the upstream demarcation being the actual limits of navigability.

Several important legal incidents have been attached to the traditional term "navigable waters of the United States": (1) it establishes federal admiralty jurisdiction, (2) it defines the line between property belonging to the state and federal governments or their respective patentees, (3) it determines the application of the federal "navigational servitude," and (4) it is the language used in prior federal legislation — most significantly to our present concerns, in Sections 10 and 13 of the Rivers and Harbors Act.

For most purposes, the older term is the more limited. *Leslie Salt,* however, illustrates one circumstance in which "navigable waters of the United States" reach further than "navigable waters" as used in the Clean Water Act: the newer term only applies to salt water presently lapped by the tide; the traditional one applies to any area below the *original* mean high tide line. Therefore, a permit from the Corps of Engineers would be required by Section 10 of the Rivers and Harbors Act for any modification of dry land which was once below the natural MHTL before the construction of a dike or seawall. The Clean Water Act applies to *more* water (in *Leslie Salt* even to man-made salt ponds above the MHTL); but at least *some* water must presently cover the area, if only intermittently.

2. The very expansive interpretation of "navigable waters" in *Holland* and *Leslie Salt* has been widely, if not uniformly, accepted. Notice that the definition in Section 502(7) expressly includes only the "territorial" part of the seas within the scope of "waters of the United States." Territorial seas extend seaward for three miles; beyond that is the "contiguous zone," which extends twelve miles from shore, and the "ocean." *See* definitions in Section 502(8), (9), and (10); Article 24 of the Convention of the Territorial Sea and the Contiguous Zone, ENVTL. L. REP. STATUTES 40326 (1985). Pollutants added to the contiguous zone or ocean are subject to 301 limitations and permitting under sections 402 or 404 only if discharged from shore or from the structures fixed on the seabed. *See* Section 502(12). The "Ocean Dumping Act," 33 U.S.C. § 1401 *et seq.*, however, restricts dumping from vessels beyond the "waters of the United States."

3. EPA's definition of "waters of the United States" for purposes of NPDES permitting under Section 402 is by now (1985) quite broad, incorporating almost every rationale employed by the courts for exercise of federal commerce power.

Waters of the United States or *Waters of the U.S. means:*

(a) All waters which are currently used, were used in the past, or may be susceptible to use in interstate or foreign commerce, including all waters which are subject to the ebb and flow of the tide;

(b) All interstate waters, including interstate "wetlands";

(c) All other waters such as intrastate lakes, rivers, streams (including intermittent streams), mudflats, sandflats, "wetlands," sloughs, prairie potholes, wet meadows, playa lakes, or natural ponds the use, degradation, or destruction of which would affect or could affect interstate or foreign commerce including any such waters:

  (1) Which are or could be used by interstate or foreign travelers for recreational or other purposes;

  (2) From which fish or shellfish are or could be taken and sold in interstate or foreign commerce; or

  (3) Which are used or could be used for industrial purposes by industries in interstate commerce;

(d) All impoundments of waters otherwise defined as waters of the United States under this definition;

(e) Tributaries of waters identified in paragraphs (a) through (d) of this definition;

(f) The territorial sea; and

(g) "Wetlands" adjacent to waters (other than waters that are themselves wetlands) identified in paragraphs (a) through (f) of this definition.

Waste treatment systems, including treatment ponds or lagoons designed to meet the requirements of the CWA (other than cooling ponds as defined in 40 CFR 423.11(m) which also meet the criteria of this definition) are not waters of the United States.

Wetlands means those areas that are inundated or saturated by surface or groundwater at a frequency and duration sufficient to support, and that under normal circumstances do support, a prevalence of vegetation typically adapted for life in saturated soil conditions. Wetlands generally include swamps, marshes, bogs, and similar areas.

40 C.F.R. § 122.2 (1985)

The definition presently used by the Corps of Engineers for issuance of permits for discharges of dredged or fill material under Section 404 is identical. *See* 33 C.F.R. § 323.2 (1985). The Corps additionally explains what is meant by "wetlands adjacent to" the waters included in the definition.

The term "adjacent" means bordering, contiguous, or neighboring. Wetlands separated from other waters of the United States by man-made dikes or barriers, natural river berms, beach dunes and the like are "adjacent wetlands."

33 C.F.R. § 323.2(d) (1985).

The basic ingredients in EPA's and the Corps' definitions reflect, and are reflected in, judicial elaborations upon the scope of the Clean Water Act; and by now little serious dispute remains over the necessity for either a 402 or a 404 permit for discharges into almost any water. The issue has long been settled as consistent with *U.S. v. Holland* as to intertidal wetlands. *See Conservation Council v. Costanzo*, 398 F.Supp. 653 (E.D.N.C.), *aff'd*, 528 F.2d 250 (4th Cir. 1975). Similarly, general agreement exists as to the Act's application to non-navigable lakes and tributaries to historically navigable freshwaters. *See Minnehaha Creek Watershed District v. Hoffman*, 597 F.2d 617 (8th Cir. 1979), included in text *infra* p. 243. Courts have also applied the Act to dry creek and lake beds and other areas only intermittently containing water. *See Avoyelles Sportsmen's League, Inc. v. Marsh*, 715 F.2d 897 (5th Cir. 1983); *United States v. Texas Pipeline Co.*, 611 F.2d 345 (10th Cir. 1979).

4. To the extent that serious disputes concerning federal regulatory jurisdiction under the Clean Water Act continued into the 1980s, they usually involved application of the dredge and fill permitting requirements of Section 404 to freshwater wetlands. The Supreme Court, however, has now had its say on the matter; and it may have largely ended the legal debate — as opposed to the regulatory policy debate.

United States
v.
Riverside Bayview Homes, Inc.
106 S.Ct. 455 (1985)

WHITE, J., delivered the opinion for a unanimous Court.

This case presents the question whether the Clean Water Act, together with certain regulations promulgated under its authority by the Army Corps of Engineers, authorizes the Corps to require landowners to obtain permits from the Corps before discharging fill material into wetlands adjacent to navigable bodies of water and their tributaries.

I

The relevant provisions of the Clean Water Act originated in the Federal Water Pollution Control Act Amendments of 1972 and have remained essentially unchanged since that time. Under §§ 301 and 502 of the Act, any discharge of dredged or fill materials into "navigable waters" — defined as the "waters of the United States" — is forbidden unless authorized by a permit issued by the Corps of Engineers pursuant to § 404.[1] After initially construing the Act to cover only waters navigable in fact, in 1975 the Corps issued interim final regulations redefining "the waters of the United States" to include not only actually navigable waters but also tributaries of such waters, interstate waters and their tributaries, and nonnavigable intrastate waters whose use or misuse could affect interstate commerce. 40

---

[1]With respect to certain waters, the Corps' authority may be transferred to States that have devised federally approved permit programs. CWA § 404(g). Absent such an approved program, the Corps retains jurisdiction under § 404 over all "waters of the United States."

Fed. Reg. 31320 (1975). More importantly for present purposes, the Corps construed the Act to cover all "freshwater wetlands" that were adjacent to other covered waters. A "freshwater wetland" was defined as an area that is "periodically inundated" and is "normally characterized by the prevalence of vegetation that requires saturated soil conditions for growth and reproduction." 33 CFR § 209.120 (d)(2)(h) (1976). In 1977, the Corps refined its definition of wetlands by eliminating the reference to periodic inundation and making other minor changes. The 1977 definition reads as follows:

"The term 'wetlands' means those areas that are inundated or saturated by surface or ground water at a frequency and duration sufficient to support, and that under normal circumstances do support, a prevalence of vegetation typically adapted for life in saturated soil conditions. Wetlands generally include swamps, marshes, bogs and similar areas." 33 CFR § 323.2(c)(1978).

In 1982, the 1977 regulations were replaced by substantively identical regulations that remain in force today. See 33 CFR § 323.2 (1985).[2]

Respondent Riverside Bayview Homes, Inc. (hereafter respondent), owns 80 acres of low-lying, marshy land near the shores of Lake St. Clair in Macomb County, Michigan. In 1976, respondent began to place fill materials on its property as part of its preparations for construction of a housing development. The Corps of Engineers, believing that the property was an "adjacent wetland" under the 1975 regulation defining "waters of the United States," filed suit in the United States District Court for the Eastern District of Michigan, seeking to enjoin respondent from filling the property without the permission of the Corps.

The District Court held that the portion of respondent's property lying below 575.5 feet above sea level was a covered wetland and enjoined respondent from filling it without a permit. Respondent appealed, and the Court of Appeals remanded for consideration of the effect of the intervening 1977 amendments to the regulation. On remand, the District Court again held the property to be a wetland subject to the Corps' permit authority.

Respondent again appealed, and the Sixth Circuit reversed. 729 F.2d 391 (1984). The court construed the Corps' regulations to exclude from the category of adjacent wetlands — and hence from that of "waters of the United States" — wetlands that were not subject to flooding by adjacent navigable waters at a frequency sufficient to support the growth of aquatic vegetation. The court adopted this construction of the regulations because, in its view, a broader definition of wetlands might result in the taking of private property without just compensation. The court also expressed its doubt that Congress, in granting the Corps jurisdiction to regulate the filling of "navigable waters," intended to allow regulation of wetlands that were not the result of flooding by navigable waters. Under the court's reading of the regulations, respondent's property was not within the Corps' jurisdiction, because its semi-aquatic characteristics were not the result of frequent flooding by the nearby navigable waters. Respondent was therefore free to fill the property without obtaining a permit.

We granted certiorari to consider the proper interpretation of the Corps' regulations defining "waters of the United States" and the scope of the Corps' jurisdiction under the Clean Water Act, both of which were called into question by the Sixth Circuit's ruling. We now reverse.

II

The question whether the Corps of Engineers may demand that respondent obtain a permit before placing fill material on its property is primarily one of regulatory and statutory interpretation: we must determine whether respondent's property is an "adjacent wetland" within the meaning of the applicable

[2]The regulations also cover certain wetlands not necessarily adjacent to other waters. See 33 CFR §§ 323.2(a)(2) and (3) (1985). These provisions are not now before us.

regulation, and, if so, whether the Corps' jurisdiction over "navigable waters" gives it statutory authority to regulate discharges of fill material into such a wetland. In this connection, we first consider the Court of Appeals' position that the Corps' regulatory authority under the statute and its implementing regulations must be narrowly construed to avoid a taking without just compensation in violation of the Fifth Amendment.

We have frequently suggested that governmental land-use regulation may under extreme circumstances amount to a "taking" of the affected property. *See*, e.g., *Williamson County Regional Planning Comm'n v. Hamilton Bank*, 473 U.S. — , 105 S.Ct. 3108 (1985); *Penn Central Transportation Co. v. New York City*, 438 U.S. 104 (1978). We have never precisely defined those circumstances; but our general approach was summed up in *Agins v. Tiburon*, 447 U.S. 255, 260 (1980), where we stated that the application of land-use regulations to a particular piece of property is a taking only "if the ordinance does not substantially advance legitimate state interests . . . or denies an owner economically viable use of his land." Moreover, we have made it quite clear that the mere assertion of regulatory jurisdiction by a governmental body does not constitute a regulatory taking. *See Hodel v. Virginia Surface Mining & Reclamation Assn.*, 452 U.S. 264, 293-297 (1981). The reasons are obvious. A requirement that a person obtain a permit before engaging in a certain use of his or her property does not itself "take" the property in any sense: after all, the very existence of a permit system implies that permission may be granted, leaving the landowner free to use the property as desired. Moreover, even if the permit is denied, there may be other viable uses available to the owner. Only when a permit is denied and the effect of the denial is to prevent "economically viable" use of the land in question can it be said that a taking has occurred.

If neither the imposition of the permit requirement itself nor the denial of a permit necessarily constitutes a taking, it follows that the Court of Appeals erred in concluding that a narrow reading of the Corps' regulatory juris-

diction over wetlands was "necessary" to avoid "a serious taking problem." We have held that in general, "[e]quitable relief is not available to enjoin an alleged taking of private property for public use, duly authorized by law, when a suit for compensation can be brought against the sovereign subsequent to a taking." *Ruckelshaus v. Monsanto Co.*, 467 U.S. __, 104 S.Ct. 2862, 2880 (1984). This maxim rests on the principle that so long as compensation is available for those whose property is in fact taken, the governmental action is not unconstitutional. For precisely the same reason, the possibility that the application of a regulatory program may in some instances result in the taking of individual pieces of property is no justification for the use of narrowing constructions to curtail the program if compensation will in any event be available in those cases where a taking has occurred. Under such circumstances, adoption of a narrowing construction does not constitute avoidance of a constitutional difficulty; it merely frustrates permissible applications of a statute or regulation.***[6]

III

Purged of its spurious constitutional overtones, the question whether the regulation at issue requires respondent to obtain a permit before filling its property is an easy one. The regulation extends the Corps' authority under § 404 to all wetlands adjacent to navigable or interstate waters and their tributaries. Wetlands, in turn, are defined as lands that are "inundated *or saturated* by surface *or ground*

---

[6]Because the Corps has now denied respondent a permit to fill its property, respondent may well have a ripe claim that a taking has occurred. On the record before us, however, we have no basis for evaluating this claim, because no evidence has been introduced that bears on the question of the extent to which denial of a permit to fill this property will prevent economically viable uses of the property or frustrate reasonable investment backed expectations. In any event, this lawsuit is not the proper forum for resolving such a dispute: if the Corps has indeed effectively taken respondent's property, respondent's proper course is not to resist the Corps' suit for enforcement by denying that the regulation covers the property, but to initiate a suit for compensation in the Claims Court.***

water at a frequency and duration sufficient to support, and that under normal circumstances do support, a prevalence of vegetation typically adapted for life in saturated soil conditions." 33 CFR § 323.2(c) (1985) (emphasis added). The plain language of the regulation refutes the Court of Appeals' conclusion that inundation or "frequent flooding" by the adjacent body of water is a *sine qua non* of a wetland under the regulation. Indeed, the regulation could hardly state more clearly that saturation by either surface or ground water is sufficient to bring an area within the category of wetlands, provided that the saturation is sufficient to and does support wetland vegetation.

The history of the regulation underscores the absence of any requirement of inundation. The interim final regulation that the current regulation replaced explicitly included a requirement of "periodi[c] inundation." In deleting the reference to "periodic inundation" from the regulation as finally promulgated, the Corps explained that it was repudiating the interpretation of that language "as requiring inundation over a record period of years." In fashioning its own requirement of "frequent flooding" the Court of Appeals improperly reintroduced into the regulation precisely what the Corps had excised.

Without the nonexistent requirement of frequent flooding, the regulatory definition of adjacent wetlands covers the property here. The District Court found that respondent's property was "characterized by the presence of vegetation that requires saturated soil conditions for growth and reproduction," and that the source of the saturated soil conditions on the property was ground water. There is no plausible suggestion that these findings are clearly erroneous, and they plainly bring the property within the category of wetlands as defined by the current regulations. In addition, the court found that the wetland located on respondent's property was adjacent to a body of navigable water, since the area characterized by saturated soil conditions and wetland vegetation extended beyond the boundary of respondent's property to Black Creek, a navigable waterway. Again, the court's finding is

not clearly erroneous. Together, these findings establish that respondent's property is a wetland adjacent to a navigable waterway. Hence, it is part of the "waters of the United States" as defined by 33 CFR § 323.2 (1985), and if the regulation itself is valid as a construction of the term "waters of the United States" as used in the Clean Water Act, a question which we now address, the property falls within the scope of the Corps' jurisdiction over "navigable waters" under § 404 of the Act.

IV
A

An agency's construction of a statute it is charged with enforcing is entitled to deference if it is reasonable and not in conflict with the expressed intent of Congress. *Chemical Manufacturers Assn. v. Natural Resources Defense Council, Inc.,* 470 U.S. __, 105 S.Ct. 1102 (1985). *Chevron, U.S.A., Inc. v. Natural Resources Defense Council, Inc.,* 467 U.S. __, 104 S.Ct. 2778 (1984). Accordingly, our review is limited to the question whether it is reasonable, in light of the language, policies, and legislative history of the Act for the Corps to exercise jurisdiction over wetlands adjacent to but not regularly flooded by rivers, streams, and other hydrographic features more conventionally identifiable as "waters."[8]

On a purely linguistic level, it may appear unreasonable to classify "lands," wet or otherwise, as "waters." Such a simplistic response, however, does justice neither to the problem faced by the Corps in defining the scope of its authority under § 404(a) nor to the realities of the problem of water pollution that the Clean Water Act was intended to combat. In determining the limits of its power to regulate discharges under the Act, the Corps must necessarily choose some point at which water ends and land begins. Our common experience tells us that this is often no easy task: the transi-

---

[8]We are not called upon to address the question of the authority of the Corps to regulate discharges of fill material into wetlands that are not adjacent to bodies of open water, see 33 CFR § 323.2(a)(2) and (3) (1985), and we do not express any opinion on that question.

tion from water to solid ground is not necessarily or even typically an abrupt one. Rather, between open waters and dry land may lie shallows, marshes, mudflats, swamps, bogs — in short, a huge array of areas that are not wholly aquatic but nevertheless fall far short of being dry land. Where on this continuum to find the limit of "waters" is far from obvious.

Faced with such a problem of defining the bounds of its regulatory authority, an agency may appropriately look to the legislative history and underlying policies of its statutory grants of authority. Neither of these sources provides unambiguous guidance for the Corps in this case, but together they do support the reasonableness of the Corps' approach of defining adjacent wetlands as "waters" within the meaning of § 404(a). Section 404 originated as part of the Federal Water Pollution Control Act Amendments of 1972, which constituted a comprehensive legislative attempt "to restore and maintain the chemical, physical, and biological integrity of the Nation's waters." CWA § 101. This objective incorporated a broad, systemic view of the goal of maintaining and improving water quality: as the House Report on the legislation put it, "the word 'integrity' . . . refers to a condition in which the natural structure and function of ecosystems is maintained." H.R. Rep. No. 92-911, p. 76 (1972). Protection of aquatic ecosystems, Congress recognized, demanded broad federal authority to control pollution, for "[w]ater moves in hydrologic cycles and it is essential that discharge of pollutants be controlled at the source." S. Rep. No. 92-414, p. 77 (1972).

In keeping with these views, Congress chose to define the waters covered by the Act broadly. Although the Act prohibits discharges into "navigable waters," the Act's definition of "navigable waters" as "the waters of the United States" makes it clear that the term "navigable" as used in the Act is of limited import. In adopting this definition of "navigable waters," Congress evidently intended to repudiate limits that had been placed on federal regulation by earlier water pollution control statutes and to exercise its powers under the Commerce Clause to regulate at least some

waters that would not be deemed "navigable" under the classical understanding of that term.

Of course, it is one thing to recognize that Congress intended to allow regulation of waters that might not satisfy traditional tests of navigability; it is another to assert that Congress intended to abandon traditional notions of "waters" and include in that term "wetlands" as well. Nonetheless, the evident breadth of congressional concern for protection of water quality and aquatic ecosystems suggests that it is reasonable for the Corps to interpret the term "waters" to encompass wetlands adjacent to waters as more conventionally defined. Following the lead of the Environmental Protection Agency, the Corps has determined that wetlands adjacent to navigable waters do as a general matter play a key role in protecting and enhancing water quality:

> "The regulation of activities that cause water pollution cannot rely on . . . artificial lines . . . but must focus on all waters that together form the entire aquatic system. Water moves in hydrologic cycles, and the pollution of this part of the aquatic system, regardless of whether it is above or below an ordinary high water mark, or mean high tide line, will affect the water quality of the other waters within that aquatic system.
>
> "For this reason, the landward limit of Federal jurisdiction under Section 404 must include any adjacent wetlands that form the border of or are in reasonable proximity to other waters of the United States, as these wetlands are part of this aquatic system." 42 Fed. Reg. 37128 (1977).

We cannot say that the Corps' conclusion that adjacent wetlands are inseparably bound up with the "waters" of the United States — based as it is on the Corps' and EPA's technical expertise — is unreasonable. In view of the breadth of federal regulatory authority contemplated by the Act itself and the inherent difficulties of defining precise bounds to regulable waters, the Corps' ecological judgment about the relationship between waters and their adjacent wetlands provides an adequate basis for a legal judgment that adjacent wetlands may be defined as waters under the Act.

This holds true even for wetlands that are not the result of flooding or permeation by water having its source in adjacent bodies of open water. The Corps has concluded that wetlands may affect the water quality of adjacent lakes, rivers, and streams even when the waters of those bodies do not actually inundate the wetlands. For example, wetlands that are not flooded by adjacent waters may still tend to drain into those waters. In such circumstances, the Corps has concluded that wetlands may serve to filter and purify water draining into adjacent bodies of water and to slow the flow of surface runoff into lakes, rivers, and streams and thus prevent flooding and erosion. In addition, adjacent wetlands may "serve significant natural biological functions, including food chain production, general habitat, and nesting, spawning, rearing and resting sites for aquatic . . . species." 33 CFR § 320.4(b)(2)(i) (1985). In short, the Corps has concluded that wetlands adjacent to lakes, rivers, streams and other bodies of water may function as integral parts of the aquatic environment even when the moisture creating the wetlands does not find its source in the adjacent bodies of water. Again, we cannot say that the Corps' judgment on these matters is unreasonable, and we therefore conclude that a definition of "waters of the United States" encompassing all wetlands adjacent to other bodies of water over which the Corps has jurisdiction is a permissible interpretation of the Act. Because respondent's property is part of a wetland that actually abuts on a navigable waterway, respondent was required to have a permit in this case.[9]

B

Following promulgation of the Corps' interim final regulations in 1975, the Corps' assertion of authority under § 404 over waters not actually navigable engendered some congressional opposition. The controversy came to a head during Congress' consideration of the Clean Water Act of 1977, a major piece of legislation aimed at achieving "interim improvements within the existing framework" of the Clean Water Act. In the end, however, as we shall explain, Congress acquiesced in the administrative construction.

Critics of the Corps' permit program attempted to insert limitations on the Corps' § 404 jurisdiction into the 1977 legislation: the House bill as reported out of committee proposed a redefinition of "navigable waters" that would have limited the Corps' authority under § 404 to waters navigable in fact and their adjacent wetlands (defined as wetlands periodically inundated by contiguous navigable waters). The bill reported by the Senate Committee on Environment and Public Works, by contrast, contained no redefinition of the scope of the "navigable waters" covered by § 404, and dealt with the perceived problem of overregulation by the Corps by exempting certain activities (primarily agricultural) from the permit requirement and by providing for assumption of some of the Corps' regulatory duties by federally approved state programs. On the floor of the Senate, however, an amendment was proposed limiting the scope of "navigable waters" along the lines set forth in the House bill.

In both chambers, debate on the proposals to narrow the definition of navigable waters centered largely on the issue of wetlands preservation. Proponents of a more limited § 404 jurisdiction contended that the Corps' asser-

---

[9]Of course, it may well be that not every adjacent wetland is of great importance to the environment of adjoining bodies of water. But the existence of such cases does not seriously undermine the Corps' decision to define all adjacent wetlands as "waters." If it is reasonable for the Corps to conclude that in the majority of cases, adjacent wetlands have significant effects on water quality and the aquatic ecosystem, its definition can stand. That the definition may

include some wetlands that are not significantly intertwined with the ecosystem of adjacent waterways is of little moment, for where it appears that a wetland covered by the Corps' definition is in fact lacking in importance to the aquatic environment — or where its importance is outweighed by other values — the Corps may always allow development of the wetland for other uses simply by issuing a permit. See 33 CFR § 320.4(b)(4) (1985).

tion of jurisdiction over wetlands and other nonnavigable "waters" had far exceeded what Congress had intended in enacting § 404. Opponents of the proposed changes argued that a narrower definition of "navigable waters" for purposes of § 404 would exclude vast stretches of crucial wetlands from the Corps' jurisdiction, with detrimental effects on wetlands ecosystems, water quality, and the aquatic environment generally. The debate, particularly in the Senate, was lengthy. In the House, the debate ended with the adoption of a narrowed definition of "waters"; but in the Senate the limiting amendment was defeated and the old definition retained. The Conference Committee adopted the Senate's approach: efforts to narrow the definition of "waters" were abandoned; the legislation as ultimately passed, in the words of Senator Baker, "retain[ed] the comprehensive jurisdiction over the Nation's waters exercised in the 1972 Federal Water Pollution Control Act."

The significance of Congress' treatment of the Corps' § 404 jurisdiction in its consideration of the Clean Water Act of 1977 is twofold. First, the scope of the Corps' asserted jurisdiction over wetlands was specifically brought to Congress' attention, and Congress rejected measures designed to curb the Corps' jurisdiction in large part because of its concern that protection of wetlands would be unduly hampered by a narrowed definition of "navigable waters."***

Second, it is notable that even those who would have restricted the reach of the Corps' jurisdiction would have done so not by removing wetlands altogether from the definition of "waters of the United States," but only by restricting the scope of "navigable waters" under § 404 to waters navigable in fact *and their adjacent wetlands*. In amending the definition of "navigable waters" for purposes of § 404 only, the backers of the House bill would have left intact the existing definition of "navigable waters" for purposes of § 301 of the Act, which generally prohibits discharges of pollutants into navigable waters.***

Two features actually included in the legislation that Congress enacted in 1977 also support the view that the Act authorizes the Corps to regulate discharges into wetlands. First, in amending § 404 to allow federally approved state permit programs to supplant regulation by the Corps of certain discharges of fill material, Congress provided that the States would not be permitted to supersede the Corps' jurisdiction to regulate discharges into actually navigable waters and waters subject to the ebb and flow of the tide, "including wetlands adjacent thereto." CWA § 404 (g) (1). Here, then, Congress expressly stated that the term "waters" included adjacent wetlands. Second, the 1977 Act authorized an appropriation of $6 million for completion by the Department of Interior of a "National Wetlands Inventory" to assist the States "in the development and operation of programs under this Act." CWA § 208 (i) (2). The enactment of this provision reflects congressional recognition that wetlands are a concern of the Clean Water Act and supports the conclusion that in defining the waters covered by the Act to include wetlands, the Corps is "implementing congressional policy rather than embarking on a frolic of its own."

C

We are thus persuaded that the language, policies, and history of the Clean Water Act compel a finding that the Corps has acted reasonably in interpreting the Act to require permits for the discharge of fill material into wetlands adjacent to the "waters of the United States." The regulation in which the Corps has embodied this interpretation by its terms includes the wetlands on respondent's property within the class of waters that may not be filled without a permit; and, as we have seen, there is no reason to interpret the regulation more narrowly than its terms would indicate. Accordingly, the judgment of the Court of Appeals is Reversed.

NOTES

1. How secure is this victory for environmental interests?

Given the Court's emphasis on deference to the Corps' construction of the statute so long as "it is reasonable and not in conflict with the expressed intent of Congress," could the Corps amend its regulation to apply only to waters navigable in fact? Could it adopt the position of the 1977 House bill and assert jurisdiction only over wetlands contiguous to waters navigable in fact? Could it return to the definition of "freshwater wetlands" in the 1975 iterim final rules which required "periodic inundation" and prevalence of vegetation that "requires" saturated soil conditions?

Does this decision mean that the district court was wrong in issuing the order in *NRDC v. Callaway, supra* p. 161?

2. Could the Corps adopt a definition of "waters of the United States" for purposes of dredge and fill permitting under Section 404 that was more limited than EPA's definition of the same words for purposes of requiring permits for point source discharges of other kinds of pollutants under Section 402?

3. Is it significant that, unlike virtually every lower court opinion on the jurisdictional issue, the Supreme Court did not say that Congress intended for permitting authority under the Water Act to extend as far as the reach of the federal commerce power? Would you say that it is an open question whether the Corps or EPA *could* control discharges into any water the use or abuse of which might affect interstate commerce (if only in combination with similar discharges)? Does a significant issue remain, in view of footnote 4 to the Court's opinion, whether the Corps has the authority to regulate discharges into wetlands that are not adjacent to bodies of open water?

4. As pointed out by the Court in footnote 9, not only does the Corps have some leeway in determining its own statutory jurisdiction, it has significant discretion in deciding whether to issue, deny, or impose conditions upon permits for activities falling within its jurisdiction. *See* Chapter 14 in this text *infra*.

Also, as illustrated by the Fifth Circuit's opinion in *Avoyelles Sportsmen's League, Inc. v. Marsh*, 715 F.2d 897 (5th Cir. 1983), the Corps' (and ultimately EPA's) determination of what areas do and do not fall within its regulatory definition of wetlands is also entitled to substantial deference. Not only are its *factual* decisions — e.g., on what sorts of vegetation are "typically adapted for life in saturated soil conditions" — to be reviewed only on the administrative record and overturned only if "arbitrary and capricious," its *interpretation* of such terms in the regulation — e.g., only to require an "ability to live" in saturated soil — are to be upheld if "reasonable."

5. For consideration of the likelihood of recovery of compensation by a property owner claiming a "taking" by denial of a dredge and fill permit, see *Deltona Corporation v. United States*, 657 F.2d 1184 (Ct. Cl. 1981), and the Notes following in the text *infra* page 219.

Kelley v. United States

23 ERC 1494 (W.D. Mich. 1985)

OPINION:

RICHARD A. ENSLEN, U.S. District Judge.

In this motion, Defendants contend that Plaintiffs' claim under the Federal Water Pollution Control Act (Clean Water Act or CWA) fails to state a claim upon which relief can be granted.

Defendants have not contested the ability of Plaintiffs to maintain their CERCLA action, except as to the narrow *parens patriae* damages issue.

In a nutshell, this case involves allegations that certain toxic chemicals were released into the ground at the United States Coast Guard Air Station in Traverse City, Michigan, by Coast Guard personnel. Plaintiffs further allege that these chemicals contaminated the groundwater underlying the Air Station and that the plume of contamination is migrating downgradient in a north-easterly direction through East Bay Township and eventually discharging into the East Arm of Grand Traverse Bay. It is undisputed that the Coast Guard neither applied for nor received a permit from either the federal government or the state of this discharge.

Plaintiffs bring this "citizen suit" pursuant to section 505(a) of the Clean Water Act, which provides in pertinent part that:

> Except as provided in subsection (b) of this section [precluding suit except after proper notice], any citizen may commence a civil action on his own behalf —
>
> (1) Against any person (including (i) the United States and (ii) any other governmental instrumentality or agency to the extent permitted by the eleventh amendment to the Constitution) who is alleged to be in violation of (A) an effluent standard or limitation under this chapter . . . .

Section 301(a) of the CWA provides that "[e]xcept as in compliance with this section and [certain other sections of the Act], the discharge of any pollutant by any person shall be unlawful." The term "discharge of a pollutant" is defined in section 502(12) as "any addition of any pollutant to navigable waters from any point source . . . . " For the purposes of the CWA, the term "navigable waters" has been defined very broadly to mean simply "the waters of the United States, including the territorial seas." Some courts have interpreted "navigable waters" as broadly as possible under Congress' commerce power, *United States v. Byrd,* 609 F.2d 1204 (7th Cir. 1979); *Leslie Salt Co. v. Froehlke,* 578 F.2d 742 (9th Cir. 1978), even so far as to exclude from consideration any concept of navigability, in law or in fact, *United States v. GAF Corp.,* 389 F. Supp. 1379 (S.D. Tex. 1975).

Defendants argue that while the term "navigable waters" is construed broadly, Congress did not intend to include groundwater within its definition. Indeed, Defendants maintain that the regulatory and enforcement aspects of the Clean Water Act were not designed to control the discharge of pollutants into the soil and groundwater. Certainly Congress realized the importance of the groundwater pollution issue. It specially directed the Administrator of the Environmental Protection Agency (EPA) to cooperate with the states in establishing a national groundwater surveillance system. CWA section 104(a) (5). It conditioned future grants to any state on the establishment of groundwater quality monitoring procedures. CWA section 106(e) (1). It also directed the EPA to develop and periodically publish the latest scientific criteria for groundwater quality, the effect of its contamination, and information regarding its cleanup. CWA section 304(a)(1), (2). However, Defendants argue that the fact that Congress did not expressly include the term "groundwaters" in most of the regulatory provisions of Title III of the CWA, including section 301(a), indicates a clear intent to leave the regulation of ground-water pollution to the states.

This argument is substantially supported by the legislative history of the 1972 amendments. The senate Committee on Public Works reported:

> Several bills pending before the Committee provided authority to establish Federally approved standards for groundwaters which permeate rock, soil, and other subsurface formations. Because the jurisdiction regarding groundwaters is so complex and varied from State to State, the Committee did not adopt this recommendation.
>
> The Committee recognizes the essential link between ground and surface waters and the artificial nature of any distinction. Thus, the Committee bill requires in section 402 that each State include in its program for approval under section 402 affirmative controls over the injunction or placement in wells of any pollutants that may effect groundwater.

S. Rep. No. 414, 92nd Congress, 1st Sess. 73, reprinted in 1972 U.S. Code Cong. & Ad. News 3739. In response to the Senate's rejection of federal regulatory jurisdiction over groundwater, Representative Aspin introduced an amendment into the House to expressly bring groundwater within the regulatory scope of the Act. After a spirited debate, the Aspin amendment was defeated by a vote of 86-34.

This same legislative history was more thoroughly analyzed in *Exxon Corp. v. Train*, 554 F.2d 1310 (5th Cir. 1977). That court characterized the Senate Report quoted above as "evinc[ing] a clear intent to leave the establishment of standards and controls for groundwater pollution to the states." *Id.* at 1325. Likewise, it concluded that the "House bill, like the Senate bill, did not authorize federal control over any phase of groundwater pollution." *Id.* at 1326.

Plaintiffs seek to distinguish the facts of the principal case from those found in *Exxon*.

The instant complaint alleges that the pollutants released into the ground at the Air Station not only contaminated the groundwater, but are naturally discharging into the Grand Traverse Bay — an undisputed navigable body of water. By comparison, the *Exxon* case dealt with disposal of pollutants into deep wells. The *Exxon* court prefaced its entire discussion with the recognition of the distinction:

> Throughout this opinion, we will use certain terms interchangeably that are not, strictly speaking, equivalent. The main example is our equation of "disposal into deep wells" with "disposal into groundwaters" .... We make this equation because neither party before us argues that the disposal into wells at issue here ... is disposal into anything other than groundwaters. *Specifically, EPA has not argued that the wastes disposed of into wells here do, or might, "migrate" from groundwaters back into surface waters that concededly are within its regulatory jurisdiction .... We mean to express no opinion on what the result would be if that were the state of facts.*

Exxon, 554 F.2d at 1312 n.1 (emphasis added).

Plaintiffs also rely on an unpublished opinion from the Eastern District of Michigan in a case similar to the case at bar. *Kelley v. United States*, No. 70-10199 (E.D. Mich. Oct. 28, 1980). In that opinion, the court ruled that the State Attorney General could maintain an action against the United States under section 505 of the Clean Water Act for an alleged discharge of toxic chemicals into the groundwaters from sites at the Wurtsmith Air Force Base in Alpena, Michigan, where plaintiff claimed the discharge was ultimately affecting surface waters. The court's analysis on this point was brief:

> Defendants cite the case of *Exxon Corp. v. Train*, 554 F.2d 1310 (CA 5, 1977) as their primary authority for the argument that groundwater pollution was not intended to be regulated under

the Federal Water Pollution Control Act, supra. *Plaintiff, however, quite correctly points out that the Court of Appeals for the Fifth Circuit concedes that wastes which migrate from ground-waters back into surface waters are within the EPA's regulatory jurisdiction. Exxon Corp. v. Train, 554 F.2d 1310, 1312, Fn1 (CA 5, 1977).* This Court believes that the type of navigable waters which plaintiff complains of in the instant case is encompassed by the Federal Water Pollution Control Act, supra, notwithstanding defendants' arguments to the contrary.

Kelley v. United States, No. 79-10199, slip op. at 2-3 (E.D. Mich. Oct. 28, 1980) (emphasis added).

I think that the court and the State Attorney General have both misinterpreted footnote one of *Exxon.* The Fifth Circuit did not concede that discharges into the soil will be subject to the regulatory provisions of CWA if the groundwater contaminated thereby eventually migrates into navigable waters. On the contrary, it specifically "express[ed] no opinion on what the result would be [under the CWA] if that were the state of facts." *Exxon,* 554 F.2d at 1312 n.1. Moreover, the remainder of the *Exxon* opinion and the unmistakably clear legislative history both demonstrate that Congress did not intend the Clean Water Act to extend federal regulatory and enforcement authority over groundwater contamination. Rather, such authority was to be left to the states. Therefore, Count I of Plaintiffs' complaint is dismissed.

NOTES

1. This decision is consistent with EPA's present position: that neither federally-set effluent limitations under Section 301 nor federally-issued permits under Section 402 are applicable to discharges into groundwater.

Some support remains, however, for the limited position taken by the Eastern District of Michigan in 1980: that groundwater which communicates with surface water is "navigable water" and, therefore, that point source discharges into it are subject to federal regulation under the Clean Water Act. *See United States v. GAF Corp.,* 389 F. Supp. 1379, 1383 (S.D. Tex. 1975).

The prevailing reading of the legislative history of the 1972 and 1977 Amendments, however, is that Congress intended to leave regulation of discharges into groundwater to the states — at least insofar as the Federal Water Pollution Control Act went.

2. As pointed out in the *Kelley* opinion, Congress did include several provisions in the Water Act to encourage states to protect their groundwaters. Most significantly, Section 402(b)(1)(c) conditions federal approval of a state NPDES plan upon state authority to issue permits which control the disposal of pollutants into wells.

For a time, EPA took the position that the language of Section 402(a)(3), specifying that an EPA-promulgated NPDES plan be subject to the same requirements as a state permit program, meant that EPA could regulate groundwater discharges by any source whose surface water discharges were subject to federal permitting. This position was accepted by the Seventh Circuit in *United States Steel Corp. v. Train,* 556 F.2d 822 (7th Cir. 1977); but, after it was rejected by the Fifth Circuit in *Exxon Corp. v. Train,* 554 F.2d 1310 (5th Cir. 1977), EPA decided to concentrate its groundwater protection strategy on other federal legislation.

3. The Safe Drinking Water Act of 1974 establishes a federal regulatory and permitting system, designed to be "cooperatively" administered by the states, which is supposed to protect against any endangerment of underground sources of drinking water. 42 U.S.C. § 300 f,*et seq.*

Also, as you will see when you study Part II of these materials, the Resource Conservation and Recovery Act (RCRA) of 1976 and its 1984 Amendments provide substantial protection against damage to groundwaters by new land disposals or underground injections of hazardous wastes. Along with RCRA, the Comprehensive Environmental Response, Compensation, and Liability Act (CERCLA) of 1980 provides means for remedying existing hazardous waste disposal sites which cause or threaten contamination of groundwater.

12 POINT SOURCES

Natural Resources Defense Council, Inc. v. Costle

568 F.2d 1369 (D.C. Cir. 1977)

Before: BAZELON, Chief Judge, LEVEN-THAL and MacKINNON, Circuit Judges.

Opinion for the Court filed by Circuit Judge LEVENTHAL.

Concurring Opinion filed by Circuit Judge MacKINNON.

LEVENTHAL, Circuit Judge: In 1972 Congress passed the Federal Water Pollution Control Act Amendments [hereafter referred to as the "FWPCA" or the "Act"]. It was a dramatic response to accelerating environmental degradation of rivers, lakes and streams in this country. The Act's stated goal is to eliminate the discharge of pollutants into the Nation's waters by 1985. This goal is to be achieved through the enforcement of the strict timetables and technology-based effluent limitations established by the Act.

The FWPCA sets up a permit program, the National Pollutant Discharge Elimination System (NPDES), as the primary means of enforcing the Act's effluent limitations. At issue in this case is the authority of the Administrator of the Environmental Protection Agency to make exemptions from this permit component of the FWPCA.

Section 402 of the FWPCA provides that under certain circumstances the EPA Administrator "may . . . issue a permit for the discharge of any pollutant" notwithstanding the general proscription of pollutant discharges found in § 301 of the Act. The discharge of a pollutant is defined in the FWPCA as "any addition of any pollutant to navigable waters from any point source" or "any addition of any pollutant to the

waters of the contiguous zone or the ocean from any point source other than a vessel or floating craft." In 1973 the EPA Administrator issued regulations that exempted certain categories of "point sources" of pollution from the permit requirements of § 402. The Administrator's purported authority to make such exemptions turns on the proper interpretation of § 402.

A "point source" is defined in § 502 (14) as "any discernible, confined and discrete conveyance, including but not limited to any pipe, ditch, channel, tunnel, conduit, well, discrete fissure, container, rolling stock, concentrated animal feeding operation, or vessel or other floating craft, from which pollutants are or may be discharged."

The 1973 regulations exempted discharges from a number of classes of point sources from the permit requirements of § 402, including all silvicultural point sources; all confined animal feeding operations below a certain size; all irrigation return flows from areas of less than 3,000 contiguous acres or 3,000 noncontiguous acres that use the same drainage system; all nonfeedlot, nonirrigation agricultural point sources; and separate storm sewers containing only storm runoff uncontaminated by any industrial or commercial activity. The EPA's rationale for these exemptions is that in order to conserve the Agency's enforcement resources for more significant point sources of pollution, it is necessary to exclude these smaller sources of pollutant discharges from the permit program.

The National Resources Defense Council, Inc. (NRDC) sought a declaratory judgment that the regulations are unlawful under the FWPCA. Specifically, NRDC contended that the Administrator does not have authority to exempt any class of point source from the permit requirements of § 402. It argued that Congress in enacting §§ 301, 402 of the FWPCA intended to prohibit the discharge of pollutants from *all* point sources unless a permit had been issued to the discharger under § 402 or unless the point source was explicitly exempted from the permit requirements by statute. The District Court granted NRDC's motion for summary judgement.*** The EPA has appealed to this court. It is joined on appeal by a number of defendant-intervenors, National Forest Products Association (NFPA), National Milk Producers Federation (NMPF), and the Colorado River Conservation District.

This case thus presents principally a question of statutory interpretation. EPA also argues that even if Congress intended to include the pertinent categories in the permit program, the regulations exempting them should be upheld on a doctrine of administrative infeasibility, *i.e.*, the regulations should be upheld as a deviation from the literal terms of the FWPCA that is necessary to permit the Agency to realize the principal objectives of the Act.

I. LEGISLATIVE HISTORY

*   *   *

The technique for enforcing***effluent limitations is straightforward. Section 301(a) of the FWPCA provides:

> Except as in compliance with this section and sections 302, 306, 307, 318, 402 and 404 of this Act, the discharge of any pollutant by any person shall be unlawful.

Appellants concede that if the regulations are to be valid, it must be because they are authorized by § 402; none of the other sections listed in § 301(a) afford grounds for relieving the exempted point sources from the prohibition of § 301.

> Section 402 provides in relevant part that
>
> the Administrator may, after opportunity for public hearing, issue a permit for the discharge of any pollutant, or com-

bination of pollutants, notwithstanding section 301(a), upon condition that such discharge will meet either all applicable requirements under sections 301, 302, 306, 307, 308, and 403 of this Act, or prior to the taking of the necessary implementing actions relating to all such requirements, such conditions as the Administrator determines are necessary to carry out the provision of this Act.

The NPDES permit program established by § 402 is central to the enforcement of the FWPCA. It translates general effluent limitations into the specific obligations of a discharger.***

The appellants argue that § 402 not only gives the Administrator the discretion to grant or refuse a permit, but also gives him the authority to exempt classes of point sources from the permit requirements entirely.***

Putting aside for the moment the appellants' administrative infeasibility argument, we agree with the District Court that the legislative history makes clear that Congress intended the NPDES permit to be the only means by which a discharger from a point source may escape the total prohibition of § 301(a). This intention is evident in both Committee Reports.***

*   *   *

The EPA argues that since § 402 provides that "the Administrator *may* . . . issue a permit for the discharge of any pollutant" (emphasis added), he is given the discretion to exempt point sources from the permit requirements altogether. This argument, as to what Congress meant by the word "may" in § 402, is insufficient to rebut the plain language of the statute and the committee reports.***The use of the word "may" in § 402 means only that the Administrator has discretion either to issue a permit or to leave the discharger subject to the total proscription of § 301.***

Under the EPA's interpretation the Administrator would have broad discretion to exempt large classes of point sources from any or all requirements of the FWPCA. This is a result that the legislators did not intend.***

There are innumerable references in the

legislative history to the effect that the Act is founded on the "basic premise that a discharge of pollutants without a permit is unlawful and that discharges not in compliance with the limitations and conditions for a permit are unlawful."***

We also note that all the Supreme Court decisions referring to § 402 view the permit as the only means by which a point source polluter can avoid the ban on discharges found in § 301.***

*   *   *

In *E.I. du Pont de Nemours v. Train*, 430 U.S. 112 (1977), the Court held that under FWPCA the EPA can set uniform effluent limitations through industry-wide regulations rather than develop them on an individual basis during the permit issuance process. But the Court, per Justice Stevens, clearly indicated that those limitations were translated into obligations of the discharger through their inclusion in an NPDES permit.

The wording of the statute, legislative history, and precedents are clear: the EPA Administrator does not have authority to exempt categories of point sources from the permit requirements of § 402.***

II. ADMINISTRATIVE INFEASIBILITY

The appellants have stressed in briefs and at oral argument the extraordinary burden on the EPA that will be imposed by the above interpretation of the scope of the NPDES program. The spectre of millions of applications for permits is evoked both as part of appellants' legislative history argument — that Congress could not have intended to impose such burdens on the EPA — and as an invitation to this court to uphold the regulations as deviations from the literal terms of the FWPCA necessary to permit the agency to realize the general objectives of that act.***

A. *Uniform National Effluent Limitations*

EPA argues that the regulatory scheme intended under Titles III and IV of the FWPCA requires, first, that the Administrator establish national effluent limitations and, second, that these limitations be incorporated in the individual permits of dischargers. EPA argues

that the establishment of such limitations is simply not possible with the type of point sources involved in the 1973 regulations, which essentially involve the discharge of runoff— *i.e.*, wastewaters generated by rainfall that drain over terrain into navigable waters, picking up pollutants along the way.

There is an initial question, to what extent point sources are involved in agricultural, silvicultural, and storm sewer runoff. The definition of point source in § 502 (14), including the concept of a "discrete conveyance," suggests that there is room here for some exclusion by interpretation. We discuss this issue subsequently. Meanwhile, we assume that even taking into account what are clearly point sources, there is a problem of infeasibility which the EPA properly opens for discussion.

EPA contends that certain characteristics of runoff pollution make it difficult to promulgate effluent limitations for most of the point sources exempted by the 1973 regulations:

> The major characteristic of the pollution problem which is generated by runoff . . . is that the owner of the discharge point . . . has no control over the quantity of the flow or the nature and amounts of the pollutants picked up by the runoff. The amount of flow obviously is unpredictable because it results from the duration and intensity of the rainfall event, the topography, the type of ground cover and the saturation point of the land due to any previous rainfall. Similar factors affect the types of pollutants which will be picked up by that runoff, including the type of farming practices employed, the rate and type of pesticide and fertilizer application, and the conservation practices employed. . . .

> An effluent limitation must be a precise number in order for it to be an effective regulatory tool; both the discharger and the regulatory agency need to have an identifiable standard upon which to determine whether the facility is in compliance. That was the principal of the passage of the 1972 Amendments.

Federal Appellants' Memorandum on "Impossibility" at 7-8 (footnote omitted). Implicit in EPA's contentions is the premise that there must be a uniform effluent limitation prior to issuing a permit. That is not our understanding of the law.

*   *   *

As noted in *NRDC v. Train,* the primary purpose of the effluent limitations and guidelines was to provide uniformity among the federal and state jurisdictions enforcing the NPDES program and prevent the "Tragedy of the Commons" that might result if jurisdictions can compete for industry and development by providing more liberal limitations than their neighboring states. The effluent limitations were intended to create floors that had to be respected by state permit programs.

But in *NRDC v. Train* it was also recognized that permits could be issued before national effluent limitations were promulgated and that permits issued subsequent to promulgation of uniform effluent limitations could be modified to take account of special characteristics of subcategories of point sources.***

Another passage in *NRDC v. Train* touches on the infeasibility problem. *** In that case this court fully appreciated that technological and administrative constraints might prevent the Administrator from developing guidelines and corresponding uniform numeric effluent limitations for certain point sources anytime in the near future. The Administrator was deemed to have the burden of demonstrating that the failure to develop the guidelines on schedule was due to administrative or technological infeasibility. *** It is a number of steps again to suggest that these problems afford the Administrator the authority to exempt categories of point sources from the NPDES program entirely.

With time, experience, and technological development, more point sources in the categories that EPA has now classed as exempt may be amenable to national effluent limitations achieved through end-of-pipe technology or other means of pollution control. EPA has noted its own success with runoff from mining operations.***

In sum, we conclude that the existence of uniform national effluent limitations is not a necessary precondition for incorporating into the NPDES program pollution from agricultural, silvicultural, and storm water runoff point sources. The technological or administrative infeasibility of such limitations may result in adjustments in the permit programs, as will be seen, but it does not authorize the Administrator to exclude the relevant point source from the NPDES program.

B. *Alternative Permit Conditions under § 402(a)*

EPA contends that even if it is possible to issue permits without national effluent limitations, the special characteristics of point sources of runoff pollution make it infeasible to develop restrictions on a case-by-case basis. EPA's implicit premise is that whether limitations are promulgated on a class or individual source basis, it is still necessary to articulate any limitation in terms of a numerical effluent standard. That is not our understanding.

Section 402 provides that a permit may be issued upon condition "that such discharge will meet either all applicable requirements under sections 301, 302, 306, 307, 308 and 403 of this Act, *or prior to taking of necessary implementing actions relating to all such requirements, such conditions as the Administrator determines are necessary to carry out the provisions of this Act,*" (emphasis added). This provision gives EPA considerable flexibility in framing the permit to achieve a desired reduction in pollutant discharges. The permit may proscribe industry practices that aggravate the problem of point source pollution.

EPA's counsel caricatures the matter by stating that recognition of any such authority would give EPA the power "to instruct each individual farmer on his farming practices." Any limitation on a polluter forces him to modify his conduct and operations. For example, an air polluter may have a choice of installing scrubbers, burning different fuels or reducing output. Indeed, the authority to prescribe limits consistent with the best practicable technology may be tantamount to prescribing that technology. Of course, when alternative techniques are available, Congress intended to give the discharger as much flexibility as possible in choosing his mode of compliance. We only indicate here that when numerical effluent limitations are infeasible, EPA may issue permits with conditions designed to reduce the level of effluent discharges to acceptable levels. This may well mean opting for a gross reduction in pollutant discharge rather than the fine-tuning suggested by numerical limitations. But this ambitious statute is not hospitable to the concept that the appropriate response to a difficult pollution problem is not to try at all.

It may be appropriate in certain circumstances for the EPA to require a permittee simply to monitor and report effluent levels; EPA manifestly has this authority. Such permit conditions might be desirable where the full extent of the pollution problem is not known.

C. *General Permits*

Finally, EPA argues that the number of permits involved in the absence of an exemption authority will simply overwhelm the Agency. Affidavits filed with the District Court indicate, for example, that the number of silviculture point sources may be over 300,000 and that there are approximately 100,000 separate storm sewer point sources. We are and must be sensitive to EPA's concerns of an intolerable permit load. But the District Court and the various parties have suggested devices to mitigate the burden — to accommodate within a practical regulatory scheme Congress's clear mandate that all point sources have permits.***

Section 402 does not explicitly describe the necessary scope of a NPDES permit. The most significant requirement is that the permit be in compliance with limitation sections of the Act described above. As a result NRDC and the District Court have suggested the use of area or general permits. The Act allows such techniques. ***

In response to the District Court's order, EPA promulgated regulations that make use of the general permit device, 42 Fed. Reg. 6846-53 (Feb. 4, 1977). The general permit is addressed to a class of point source dischargers, subject to notice and opportunity for public hearing in the geographical area covered by the permit. Although we do not pass on the validity of the February, 1977, regulations, they serve to dilute an objection of wholesale infeasibility.

Our approach is not fairly subject to the criticism that it elevates form over substance, that the end result will look very much like EPA's categorical exemption. It is the function of the courts to require agencies to comply with legislative intent when that intent is clear, and to leave it to the legislature to make adjustments when the result is counterproductive. At the same time, where intent on an issue is unclear, we are instructed to afford the administering agency the flexibility necessary to achieve the general objectives of the Act.***

There is also a very practical difference between a general permit and an exemption. An exemption tends to become indefinite: the problem drops out of sight, into a pool of inertia, unlikely to be recalled in the absence of crisis or a strong political protagonist. In contrast, the general or area permit approach forces the Agency to focus on the problems of specific regions and requires that the problems of the region be reconsidered at least every five years, the maximum duration of a permit.

D. *Other Interpretational Powers*

Many of the intervenor-appellants appear to argue that the District Court should be reversed because the categories exempted by EPA are nonpoint sources and are not, in fact, point sources. We agree with the District Court "that the power to define point and nonpoint sources is vested in EPA and should be reviewed by the court only after opportunity for full agency review and examination." The only issue precisely confronted by all the parties and properly framed for our consideration is whether the Administrator has authority to exempt point sources from the NPDES program. We also think that we should, for similar reasons, not consider at this time the appropriate definition of "discharge of any pollutant" as used in § 402. The American Iron and Steel Institute as *amicus curiae* has pressed upon us the argument that the term "discharge" as used in § 402 was intended to encompass only "volitional flows" that add pollutants to navigable waters. Most forms of runoff, it is argued, do not involve volitional flows.

We assume that FWPCA, however tight in some respects, leaves some leeway to EPA in the interpretation of that statute, and in that regard affords the Agency some means to consider matters of feasibility. However, for reasons already noted, we do not consider these particular contentions as to interpretation on the merits.

III. CONCLUSION

As the Supreme Court recently stated in a FWPCA case, "[t]he question . . . is not what a court thinks is generally appropriate to the regulatory process, it is what Congress intended . . . ." *E.I. du Pont de Nemours & Co. v. Train,* 430 U.S. 112, 138 (1977). *** Imagination conjoined with determination will likely give EPA a capability for practicable administration. If not, the remedy lies with Congress.

So ordered.

MacKinnon, *Circuit Judge,* concurring: I concur in the very sound and practical construction set forth in the foregoing opinion. Any person concerned with the actual application and enforcement of laws would necessarily be concerned by the application of the relevant legislation to all point sources in agriculture — and particularly to irrigated agriculture. Concern would also lie in the congressional admission that *present* technology is inadequate to enable our citizens to meet the standards and deadlines the Act imposes; in passing the law, Congress was relying on the future "invention [of] new and imaginative developments that will allow us to meet the objectives of our bill." In gambling parlance, Congress in enacting the law was "betting on the come." It is relying on our citizens in the near future to develop the complex technology to meet all the law's standards and objectives on time. The difficulty with that approach is that the hopes of Congress in this respect, like that of any gambler, might not be realized. The agency in this case, however, has shown that it takes a realistic view of both the situation and the task of meeting the difficult requirements and objectives of the Act. I sincerely hope that the ability of the agency to issue section 402 permits—including general area permits — will permit it to meet the present and future compliance problems posed by the Act in a practical way.

NOTES

1. In strictly construing the statutory definition of point source and denying exemptions from the Act's permitting requirements, did the court close one escape valve only to leave open others with as much, if not more, potential for abuse?

After the court precluded the possibility of exemptions for circumstances in which traditional point source regulation is infeasible, it accommodated the administrative infeasibility argument by holding that uniform national numerical standards are not required. Instead it would allow (1) individualized determinations, (2) process controls rather than end-of-the-pipe standards, and (3) general permits which (4) require no more than monitoring and reporting. Is such dilution of the NPDES permitting system more threatening to the fabric of the Water Act than allowing exemptions in exceptional cases?

2. Congress's response in 1977 was limited to providing relief for farmers and ranchers. It amended Section 502(14) to exempt return flows from irrigated agriculture from the definition of point source.

3. EPA responded to the court's invitation to use its "interpretational powers" by promulgating restricted definitions of "concentrated animal feeding operation," "storm water point source," and "silvicultural point source." *See* 40 C.F.R. §§ 122.23, 122.26, and 122.27 (1985).

For those concentrated animal feeding operations within the definition, the BPT and BAT limitations promulgated were significant: no discharge of waste water to navigable waters from any such animal feedlots (except for the duck subcategory). *See* 40 C.F.R. § 412 (1985).

EPA's narrow definition of silvicultural point source, for purposes of permitting under Section 402, only includes those discrete conveyances related to either "rock crushing and gravel washing" or "log sorting and storage" — activities for which effluent limitations are set under other point source categories. *See* 40 C.F.R. §§ 429 and 436 (1985). Do you think that EPA has such broad discretion to limit the definitions of particular types of point sources?

4. EPA has yet to promulgate nationwide effluent limitations for storm sewers. Instead it has left the limitations to be set in the issuance of general permits encompassing geographic or political areas — for example an entire city or county. *See* 40 C.F.R. § 122.28 (1985). Thus far, EPA's approach to regulation of storm sewer discharges has been to authorize general area-wide permits which (a) approve existing discharge levels, (2) require some monitoring, and (3) encourage incorporation of any nonpoint source restrictions in existence.

5. Although an unpermitted point source discharge into waters of the United States is necessary to a violation of the Clean Water Act, state law often is not so limited. *See*, e.g., Section 35-11-301(a) of the Wyoming Statutes, barring "the discharge of any pollution or wastes into the waters of the state" — with "discharge" defined in Section 35-11-103(c)(vii) to be "any addition of any pollution or wastes to any waters of the state." "Waters of the state" is defined in Section 35-11-103(c)(vi) to mean "all surface or ground water within Wyoming." *See People v. Platte Pipe Line Co.*, 649 P.2d 208 (Wyo. 1982).

Sierra Club v. Abston Construction Company

620 F.2d 41 (5th Cir. 1980)

Before GODBOLD, RONEY and FRANK M. JOHNSON Jr. Circuit Judges.

RONEY, J.:

In this suit to enforce portions of the Federal Water Pollution Control Act Amendments of 1972 against coal strip miners, the issue is whether pollution carried in various ways into a creek from defendant coal miners' strip mines is "point source" pollution controlled by the Act.

Sediment basin overflow and the erosion of piles of discarded material resulted in rainwater carrying pollutants into a navigable body of water. Since there was no direct action of the mine operators in pumping or draining water into the waterway, the district court by summary judgment determined there was no violation of the Act because there was no "point source" of the pollution. Deciding the district court interpreted too narrowly the statutory definition of the prohibited "point source" of pollution, and

that there remain genuine issues of material fact, we reverse.

Defendants Abston Construction Co., Mitchell & Neely, Inc., Kellerman Mining Co. and The Drummond Co. [hereinafter miners] operate coal mines near Daniel Creek, a tributary of the Black Warrior River, in Tuscaloosa County, Alabama. They each employ the strip mining technique, whereby rock material above the coal — the overburden — is removed, thereby exposing the coal that is close to the land surface. When the overburden is removed, it is pushed aside, and forms "spoil piles." During the mining operations, and thereafter if the land is not reclaimed by replacing the overburden, the spoil piles are highly erodible. Rainwater runoff or water draining from within the mined pit at times carried the material to adjacent streams, causing siltation and acid deposits. In an effort to halt runoff, the miners here occasionally constructed "sediment basins," which were designed to catch the runoff before it reached the creek. Their efforts were not always successful. Rainfall sometimes caused the basins to overflow, again depositing silt and acid materials into Daniel Creek.

Plaintiff Sierra Club brought a "citizen suit" under the Federal Water Pollution Control Act Amendments of 1972 (the Act), claiming defendants' activities were proscribed "point sources" of pollution. The State of Alabama through its attorney general was allowed to intervene with similar claims.***

The parties do not dispute the ultimate fact that these pollutants appeared in the creek due to excess rainfall. Nor is there any disagreement the activities would be prohibited if the pollutants had been pumped directly into the waterways. The parties differ only on the legal responsibility of the miners for controlling the runoff and the legal effect of their efforts to control the runoff.

Plaintiff may prevail in its citizen suit only if the miners have violated some effluent limitations under the Act. 33 U.S.C.A. § 1365(a)(1)(A). Those limitations, in turn, apply only to "point sources" of pollution, as defined in the Act.

The term "point source" means any discernible, confined and discrete conveyance, including but not limited to any pipe, ditch, channel, tunnel, conduit, well, discrete fissure, container, rolling stock, concentrated animal feeding operation, or vessel or other floating craft, from which pollutants are or may be discharged. 33 U.S.C.A. § 1362(14). Nonpoint sources, on the other hand, are not due to be controlled.***

Thus, the issue is whether defendants' activities amounted to the creation of point sources of pollution. The district court ruled they did not. On the facts before it, the district court found the pollution had not resulted "from any affirmative act of discharge by the defendants." Instead, any water and other materials that were deposited in Daniel Creek were carried by natural forces, mostly erosion caused by rainwater runoff, even though such erosion was "facilitated by the acts of defendants of creating pits and spoil banks in the course of their mining operation."

A preliminary question here is whether the Act may be applied to mining activities at all. The district court, although holding the miners here did not create point sources of pollution, conceded, correctly, we think, that "some strip mine operations may involve the discharge of pollutants in ways which would trigger application of the Act's enforcement provisions."

*   *   *

As to whether the activities here fall under the definition of point sources of pollution, three positions are asserted: plaintiff's, defendants' and a middle ground presented by the Government. We adopt the Government's approach.

Plaintiff would merely require a showing of the original sources of the pollution to find a statutory point source, regardless of how the pollutant found its way from that original source to the waterway. According to this argument, the broad drainage of rainwater carrying oily pollutants from a road paralleling a waterway, or animal pollutants from a grazing field contiguous to the waterway, would violate the Act. Whether or not the law should prohibit such pollution, this Act does not. The focus of this Act is on the "discernible, confined and discrete" conveyance of the pollutant, which would exclude natural rainfall drainage over a broad area.

Defendants, on the other hand, would exclude from the point source definition any discharge of pollutants into the waterway through ditches and gullies created by natural erosion and rainfall, even though the pollutant and the base material upon which the erosion could take place to make gullies was created by the mine operation, and even though the miners' efforts may have permitted the rainfall to flow more easily into a natural ditch leading to the waterway. This interpretation, essentially adopted by the district court, too narrowly restricts the proscription of the Act because it fails to consider fully the effect the miners' activity has on the "natural" drainage.

The United States, which participated in the case as *amicus curiae*, takes a middle ground: surface runoff collected or channeled by the operator constitutes a point source discharge. Simple erosion over the material surface, resulting in the discharge of water and other materials into navigable waters, does not constitute a point source discharge, absent some effort to change the surface, to direct the waterflow or otherwise impede its progress. Examples of point source pollution in the present case, according to the Government, are the collection, and subsequent percolation, of surface waters in the pits themselves. Sediment basins dug by the miners and designed to collect sediment are likewise point sources under the Government's view even though the materials were carried away from the basins by gravity flow of rainwater.

We agree with the Government's argument. Gravity flow, resulting in a discharge into a navigable body of water, may be part of a point source discharge if the miner at least initially collected or channeled the water and other materials. A point source of pollution may also be present where miners design spoil piles from discarded overburden such that, during periods of precipitation, erosion of spoil pile walls results in discharges into a navigable body of water by means of ditches, gullies and similar conveyances, even if the miners have done nothing beyond the mere collection of rock and other materials. The ultimate question is whether pollutants were discharged from "discernible, confined, and discrete conveyance[s]" either by gravitational or nongravitational means. Nothing in the Act relieves miners from liability simply because the operators did not actually construct those conveyances, so long as they are reasonably likely to be the means by which pollutants are ultimately deposited into a navigable body of water. Conveyances of pollution formed either as a result of natural erosion or by material means, and which constitute a component of a mine drainage system, may fit the statutory definition and thereby subject the operators to liability under the Act.

*   *   *

United States v. Earth Sciences, Inc., 599 F.2d 368 (10th Cir. 1979), involved application of the Act to a gold leaching process. There, an unusually rapid melting of snow caused primary and reserve pumps [*sic,* "sumps"], designed to catch excess runoff and gold leachate, to overflow, resulting in the discharge of a pollutant into a creek. The United States brought an enforcement action under the Act,

charging the mine had discharged a pollutant into navigable waters from a point source. After disposing of defendant's argument that mining is strictly a nonpoint source of pollution, the Tenth Circuit considered whether overflows from Earth Science's operations were point sources, and whether there had actually been a discharge under the Act. Earth Sciences argued the reference to "conveyance" in the point source definition. 33 U.S.C.A. § 1362(14), requires a ditch or pipe, "or some instrument intended to be used as a conduit." In rejecting defendant's approach, the court found,

> The undisputed facts demonstrate the combination of sumps, ditches, hoses and pumps is a circulating or drainage system to serve this mining operation. Despite the large capacity (168,000 gallons for the reserve sump) we view this operation as a closed circulating system to serve the gold extraction process with no discharge. When it fails because of flaws in the construction or inadequate size to handle the fluids utilized, with resulting discharge, whether from a fissure in the dirt berm or overflow of a wall, the escape of liquid from the confined system is from a point source. Although the source of the excess liquid is rainfall or snow melt, this is not the kind of general runoff, considered to be from nonpoint sources under the [Act].

599 F.2d at 374.

The court also rejected defendant's contention that the Act covers only the intentional discharge of pollutants into navigable waters. Section 1362(12), the court noted, "defines discharge of pollutants as 'any addition of any pollutant to navigable waters from any point source.' " Id. (court's emphasis). Thus, the court held that even unintentional discharges of pollutants from a mine system designed to catch runoff during periods of excess melting met the statutory definition of a point source.

Under the view of the law adopted here, there remain genuine issues of material fact. Viewed in a light most favorable to Sierra Club, the party opposing the motion for summary judgment, the affidavits and depositions considered by the district court indicate that significant amounts of dirt, sand and other solid particles were transported from the spoil banks by rain-water to Daniel Creek. Earl Bailey, a Sierra Club vice president and a professor at the University of Alabama, testified by affidavit that he observed

> gullies and ditches running down the sides of steep spoil piles created by Abston Construction Company. The sedimentation and pollutants are carried through these discernible, confined and discrete conveyances to Daniel Creek.

> *　　*　　*

Dwight Hicks, who served as defendant Drummond Co.'s manager of reclamation and environmental control, testified that in some areas, drainage basins were constructed to catch sediment flowing down the outer edges of the spoil piles. Hicks noted the basins were constructed along a "drainage course," by placing earthen material on the lower end of a slope. He described construction of the "B-21" dam as follows:

> [T]hat's just the general type dam section that is put into the small drainage course with a standpipe and an emergency spillway.
> The material is either pushed in or hauled in after residual vegetation is removed. It is compacted and a standpipe, the primary means of outflow, is installed, and then an emergency spillway is built around the side of it. Hicks added that in the event of a measurable amount of precipitation, water and small amounts of sediment would drain through the sediment basin outflow.

> *　　*　　*

On some occasions, according to the various affidavits and depositions, severe rainfall caused some of the sediment basins to overflow, spilling out their contents, and again those materials flowed toward the creek. Rainwater trapped in the mine pits themselves also eventually percolated through the banks and flowed toward the creek, carrying with it acid and chemicals from the pit.

Thus, additional findings are necessary to determine the precise nature of spoil basins constructed by defendant Drummond. In light of Hicks's statement that a "standpipe and an emergency spillway" were constructed to guard against spoil basin overflow, we note that a "pipe" from which pollutants are discharged may be a point source of pollution. This design could likewise fit under the Earth Sciences finding that "the escape of liquid from [a] confined system is from a point source, since the affidavits and depositions suggest that water and other materials escaped from the mines and sediment basins, eventually finding their way to Daniel Creek. Furthermore, factual findings are lacking insofar as the sediment basins and other devices may be characterized as encompassing "container[s] . . . from which pollutants are or may be discharged."

　　*　　*　　*

Although the point source definition "excludes unchanneled and uncollected surface waters, surface runoff from rainfall, when collected or channeled by coal miners in connection with mining activities, constitutes point source pollution.

The district court's decision is reversed and the case remanded for further proceedings consistent with this opinion.

REVERSED AND REMANDED.

NOTES

1. Assuming that the facts are as testified to by Professor Bailey and Mr. Hicks, what are the point sources? The mine pits? The spoil piles? The sediment basins? The spillways of the sediment basins? Their outflow pipes? The eroded "gulleys" and "ditches" which convey the runoff from the mine pits, spoil piles, and basin overflows to Daniel Creek? Or, the "whole system"?

2. Doesn't the Act require that a "discernible, discrete conveyance" of the pollutants into navigable water be found? Should courts be narrow or expansive in their construction of the definition of "point source" when a significant, and remediable, water pollution problem exists?

3. In the case of *United States v. Earth Sciences, Inc.*, 599 F.2d 368 (10th Cir. 1979), which is cited in *Abston*, the Tenth Circuit "had no problem finding a point source" in a gold mining operation (at least insofar as it failed to contain pollutants). Its opinion provided the following description of the Earth Sciences operation:

> The events which gave rise to this action occurred at Earth Sciences' gold leaching operation on the Rito Seco Creek in Costilla County, Colorado, and were stipulated by the parties. Gold leaching is a process whereby a toxic substance, here a sodium cyanide-sodium hydroxide water solution, is sprayed over a "heap" of gold ore, separating the gold from the ore. The leachate solution is then collected and the gold extracted for commercial sale. The center of Earth Sciences' operation is a 3 1/2- to 4-acre pile of gold ore on top of an impermeable plastic membrane and 12 inches of sand constructed with a gradual slope, causing the leachate solution to funnel to one end into a small fiberglass-lined pool, called the primary sump. The solution is pumped from the primary sump into a processing trailer where the gold is removed, and then back onto the heap or into the primary sump. A 168,000-gallon reserve sump is available to catch excess leachate or runoff in emergency situations. The entire operation consists of several open excavations lined with plastic membrane, the processing trailer and pumps, all designed to be a closed system without any pollutant discharge.
>
> Warm April temperatures caused faster melting than expected of a blanket of snow covering the heap, filling the primary and reserve sumps to capacity. This caused a one-to five-gallon-per-minute discharge of the sodium cyanide-sodium hydroxide leachate solution into the Rito Seco Creek for about a six-hour period. The solution is stipulated to be a pollutant under the FWPCA. Earth Sciences did not report the discharge to either state or federal environmental authorities.
>
> A few days later the Colorado Division of Wildlife received a report of dead fish on the Rito Seco, causing a state inspector and two other wildlife employees to visit the Earth Sciences site. The inspector interviewed Earth Sciences employees and verified that a discharge had occurred. While the state employees were photographing and taking water samples of the operation, the reserve sump overflowed a second time, discharging approximately ten gallons per minute into the Rito Seco for two hours, until a bulldozer was used to construct a dirt berm around the edge of the reserve sump to stop the flow. Within a week Earth Sciences constructed another reserve sump with an additional capacity of 398,000 gallons.

> *   *   *

> Five days after the EPA order was issued a sampling team of two EPA employees visited the Earth Sciences site. Groundwater seeps of approximately one gallon per minute were observed below the sumps running toward the Rito Seco and partially gathering into pools near the creek. Samples taken from two of these pools were found to contain cyanide.

Id. at 370-71.

As quoted by the Fifth Circuit, apparently favorably, the Tenth Circuit did not quibble about which component was the point source:

> *** We have no problem finding a point source here. The undisputed facts demonstrate the combination of sumps, ditches, hoses and pumps is a circulating or drainage system to serve this mining operation.

The usage of the reserve sump here fits the Webster's Third New International Dictionary (1976) definition of "sump pit" as "a pit at the lowest point in a circulating or drainage system." Despite the large capacity (168,000 gallons for the reserve sump) we view this operation as a closed circulating system to serve the gold extraction process with no discharge. When it fails because of flaws in the construction or inadequate size to handle the fluids utilized, with resulting discharge, whether from a fissure in the dirt berm or overflow of a wall, the escape of liquid from the confined system is from a point source. Although the source of the excess liquid is rainfall or snow melt, this is not the kind of general runoff considered to be from nonpoint sources under the FWPCA.
Id. at 374. Do you agree with such a general view of an entire system as a point source?

4. As mentioned in the *Abston* decision, the Tenth Circuit in *Earth Sciences* also held that violators were strictly liable under the *civil* action provisions of the Act. *Intent* is not required for liability — not intent to discharge or, apparently, even intent that the source of the discharge be a means of conveying effluent; *i.e.*, it may be a break in a retaining wall.

5. Other than mine operators, judging from the reported decisions, mushroom farmers seem to have had the most problems with the overflows from their operations being deemed illegal point source discharges. *See United States v. Frezzo Brothers, Inc.*, 602 F.2d 1123 (3d. Cir. 1979). *Also see United States v. Oxford Royal Mushroom Products, Inc.*, 487 F. Supp. 852 (E.D.Pa. 1980).

National Wildlife Federation v. Gorsuch

693 F.2d 156 (D.C. Cir. 1982)

Before: ROBINSON, Chief Judge; WALD, and BORK, Circuit Judges.

WALD, Circuit Judge: The National Wildlife Federation petitioned the district court for a declaration that the Administrator of the Environmental Protection Agency (EPA) has a nondiscretionary duty to require dam operators to apply for pollutant discharge permits under § 402(a) of the Clean Water Act and for an order directing her to perform that duty. The district court issued the requested declaration and order, from which EPA and the numerous defendant-intervenors (principally electric utilities and water agencies) now appeal. The sole issue is whether certain dam-induced water quality changes constitute the "discharge of a pollutant" as that term is defined in § 502(12) of the Act. ***

I. BACKGROUND

A. *Dam-Induced Water Quality Changes*

Dams cause a variety of interrelated water quality problems, both in reservoirs and in river water downstream from a dam. ***

1. *Low Dissolved Oxygen*

Water released from a reservoir through a dam into downstream water may be low in dissolved oxygen. The river below the dam will remain oxygen-depleted for some distance, although the river will gradually become reaerated through wind mixing as it flows downstream. If the oxygen level is too low, fish cannot survive. Also, a river low in oxygen has limited ability to break down pollutants and other organic matter. Because dissolved oxygen is important both for fish and for breakdown of organic matter, it is an important measure of water quality.

Only large storage dams have low dissolved oxygen problems, and then only during warmer months and only when water is released from the lower part of the reservoir. During warm months, deep reservoirs, like deep natural lakes, stratify into a cold, dense lower layer and a warmer, lighter upper layer. The upper layer, called the "epilimnion," is aerated by wind mixing; oxygen is also produced by photosynthesis. Thus, water quality in the upper layer is good. The lower level, called the "hypolimnion," is too deep to be aerated by wind action and light levels are too low to support photosynthesis. Organic decomposition, which consumes oxygen, leads to a continual net depletion of dissolved oxygen. Depletion continues until "fall turnover," when the two layers break up and the reservoir returns to full aeration.

*   *   *

Several techniques can be used to prevent release of oxygen-depleted water. First, for many dams, water can be released from the epilimnion (which occurs automatically for natural lakes). Older dams were built with reservoir outlets at one level only, usually deep in the dam so that the outlet would remain below the surface of the reservoir even in dry years when the reservoir was low. Many newer dams, however, have outlets at several levels, permitting the dam operator to release high-quality epilimnion water. In single-outlet dams, one can aerate the reservoir (by pumping compressed air down to the hypolimnion) or destratify it (by pumping cold water from the hypolimnion to the surface). Alternatively, one can aerate the hypolimnion water as it is released from the reservoir, either by injecting air or by creating turbulence.

The record does not indicate the number of dams for which discharge of low-oxygen water is a significant problem, nor the cost of the various methods of mechanical aeration. But the problem is serious for at least some dams, and the cure is apparently expensive.

2. *Dissolved Minerals and Nutrients*

If dissolved oxygen is totally depleted from the hypolimnion, a further problem develops. A number of minerals and plant nutrients, insoluble under normal "aerobic" conditions, are soluble in zero-oxygen "anaerobic" water. These compounds — including iron, manganese, and phosphates — therefore tend to be leached from bottom muds into the reservoir. High concentra-

tion of these minerals and nutrients, released into the down-stream river, can harm fish, make the water unpalatable for drinking, and foster undesirable plant growth.

*   *   *

Control of mineral leaching primarily involves destratifying or mechanically aerating the reservoir to prevent the hypolimnion from becoming totally depleted, or else discharging water from the epilimnion. When building a new dam, site preparation (*e.g.,* removing organic soils) can reduce future leaching. Once again, the record reveals neither the number of dams for which mineral leaching is a significant problem nor the cost of cure.

3. *Temperature Changes*

In a thermally stratified reservoir, the lower hypolimnion layer will generally be colder than the upstream river, while the upper epilimnion layer will be warmer. Some species of fish can survive only in warm water; others can survive only in cold water. Thus, cold hypolimnion water, even if fully oxygenated, will harm or kill warm water fish but benefit cold water fish; conversely, warm epilimnion water will harm or kill cold water fish and benefit warm water fish. In some cases, cold water discharges may be desirable — to create a trout fishery, for example. Also, colder water has higher capacity to assimilate wastes, both because decomposition is slower and because oxygen is more soluble in cold water. In short, dams cause *changes* in the temperature of downstream water, and some of the time, but not all of the time, those changes are undesirable.

Changes in the temperature of downstream water can be prevented in dams with multiple outlet levels by release of an appropriate mix of epilimnion and hypolimnion water. For some dams without multiple outlet levels, destratifying the reservoir may be feasible. However, the goal of maintaining downstream water temperature, because it requires a mix of warm and cold water, may conflict with the goal of maintaining downstream oxygen levels, which calls for release of warm epilimnion water.

4. *Sediment*

Generally, large reservoirs act as sediment traps; the water velocity decreases (compared to the upstream river) and sediment settles to the bottom of the reservoir. Thus, water released from the dam will contain less sediment than upstream water. This is generally viewed as an improvement in water quality. However, the river will "tend to restore its equilibrium [sediment] loading by scouring the downstream channel." Also, the reservoir will tend to fill with sediment, which in some cases can require periodic dredging or sluicing. Dredging may temporarily increase sediment load in the reservoir (and hence in the downstream water); sluicing is a deliberate attempt to have the river carry accumulated sediment downstream.

Sediment release can be reduced by careful dredging or by filtering. There is no evidence in the record to suggest that increased sediment is a major problem.

5. Supersaturation

When water plunges at high velocity from the reservoir into the downstream river, it becomes mixed with air. Depending on the velocity and turbulence of the falling water and the depth of the receiving basin, this can cause downstream water to become "supersaturated" — aerated in excess of normal concentration. Supersaturated water does not harm people and is suitable for most uses, but can be fatal to fish; documented fish kills have occurred at a number of dams.

Supersaturation can be prevented or reduced to nonfatal levels by reducing the turbulence of the falling water (water released from a spillway at the top of a dam is more turbulent than water released through a pipe in the dam), increasing reservoir capacity to reduce the need for spillway releases during flood periods, using a shallow receiving basin below the dam, or constructing spillway deflectors. Supersaturation does not appear at present to be a major problem. ***

6. Other Water Quality Changes

Dams also cause numerous other changes in the nation's waters, not directly at issue in this litigation. On the positive side, dams can prevent floods, store drinking and irrigation water, provide a clean source of electric power (thus reducing other sources of pollution), moderate stream flow, and provide recreation opportunities. On the negative side, they can indirectly affect ground water quality and reduce stream flow and hence waste-assimilative capacity. In short, dams affect environmental quality in a large number of ways, both good and bad.

B. Legal Issue Presented

The issue in this case is one of statutory construction — which if any of the water quality changes caused by dams must be regulated under the National Pollutant Discharge Elimination System (NPDES) established by § 402 of the Clean Water Act. Under § 402(a), "the Administrator may, after opportunity for public hearing, issue a permit for the discharge of any pollutant." Unless the Administrator issues an NPDES permit, "the discharge of any pollutant by any person [is] unlawful." Id. § 301(a). Section 502(12) defines the key phrase "discharge of a pollutant" as "any addition of any pollutant to navigable waters from any point source." Thus, for dams to require NPDES permits, five elements must be present: (1) a pollutant must be (2) added (3) to navigable waters (4) from (5) a point source.

The parties agree that a dam can, in some circumstances, be a "point source,"[22] and that both the reservoir and the downstream river are "navigable waters" within the statutory meaning whether or not they are navigable in fact. They dispute whether low dissolved oxygen, cold, and supersaturation are "pollutants" and whether any of the disputed water quality problems constitute the "addition" of a pollutant "from" a point source.

The Wildlife Federation argues that any adverse change in the quality of reservoir water from its natural state involves a "pollutant" and

---

[22]"Point source" is defined in § 502(14) as:

> any discernible, confined and discrete conveyance, including but not limited to any pipe, ditch, channel, tunnel, [or] conduit . . . from which pollutants are or may be discharged.

The pipes or spillways through which water flows from the reservoir through the dam into the downstream river clearly fall within this definition, and EPA has required NPDES permits for the discharge of grease, oil, or trash through the outlet works of a dam.

that release of polluted water through the dam into the downstream river constitutes the "addition" of a pollutant to navigable waters "from" a point source. If this is correct, the Administrator has a nondiscretionary duty to regulate dams under § 402.[25]

EPA argues, on the other hand, that for addition of a pollutant from a point source to occur, the point source must *introduce* the pollutant into navigable water from the outside world; dam-caused pollution, in contrast, merely passes through the dam from one body of navigable water (the reservoir) into another (the downstream river). Also, while conceding that all adverse water quality changes are "pollution" — broadly defined in § 502(19) as "the man-made or man-induced alteration of the chemical, physical, biological, and radiological integrity of water" — EPA argues that low dissolved oxygen, cold, and supersaturation are not included in the narrower statutory term "pollutant," defined in § 502(6), as:

> dredged spoil, solid waste, incinerator residue, sewage, garbage, sewage sludge, munitions, chemical wastes, biological materials, radioactive materials, heat, wrecked or discarded equipment, rock, sand, cellar dirt and industrial, municipal, and agricultural waste discharged into water.

In EPA's view, the Act divides the causes and control of water pollution into two categories, *point sources of pollutants* (regulated through the § 402 permit program) and *nonpoint sources of pollution* (regulated by the states through "areawide waste treatment management plans" under § 208. The latter category is defined by exclusion and includes all water quality problems not subject to § 402.

*   *   *

*** The district court thus ruled in favor of the Wildlife Federation on the meaning of both

---

[25]If the releases constitute the discharge of a pollutant, the Administrator *must* regulate dams and cannot issue a categorical exemption from the permit requirements. Natural Resources Defense Council, Inc. v. Costle, 568 F.2d 1369 (D.C. Cir. 1977).

*   *   *

"addition" and "pollutant." Recognizing that the large number of dams in the country made issuing individual permits impractical, it ordered EPA to establish "effluent limitations or other performance standards for dams on a categorical, as opposed to a case-by-case basis."

*   *   *

II. DEFERENCE TO EPA

Because we agree with the district court that neither the language of the Act nor its legislative history conclusively supports either side's interpretation of § 402, we make a threshold inquiry into how much deference to give to EPA's construction. In our view, the district court erred in failing to give enough deference to EPA's construction of the Act. First, as a general rule, courts must give " 'great deference to the interpretation given the statute by the officers or agency charged with its administration.' " Here, EPA certainly has responsibility for administering the Act. Indeed, since deference is "ultimately 'a function of Congress' intent,' " we find it noteworthy that Congress expressly meant EPA to have not only substantial discretion in administering the Act generally, but also at least some power to define the specific terms "point source" and "pollutant."

Several other factors point to increased deference due to EPA's interpretation. EPA's construction was made contemporaneously with the passage of the Act, and has been consistently adhered to since. Also, construction of the Act is likely to require scientific and technical expertise. ***

*   *   *

III. THE REASONABLENESS OF EPA'S INTERPRETATION

*   *   *

If we conclude that EPA's interpretation is inconsistent with the language of the Clean Water Act, as interpreted in light of the legislative history, or if it "frustrate[s] the policy that Congress sought to implement," no amount of deference can save it. But if the agency's construction neither contradicts the language of the statute nor frustrates congressional policy, our inquiry is a limited one. The agency's construction must be upheld if, in light of the appropriate degree of deference, it is "sufficiently reasonable," even if it is not "the only reasonable one or even the reading the court would have reached" on its own.

Our analysis proceeds in two stages. Section A considers the language and legislative history of the specific substantive provisions of the Act relating to dams; section B then considers the general legislative purposes underlying the Act. ***

A. *Specific Substantive Provisions*

*   *   *

1. *"Pollutant"*

Low dissolved oxygen, cold, and super-saturation do not plainly fall within the statutory list of pollutants in § 502(6) — "dredged spoil, solid waste, incinerator residue, sewage, garbage, sewage sludge, munitions, chemical wastes, biological materials, radioactive materials, heat, wrecked or discarded equipment, rock, sand, cellar dirt and industrial, municipal, agricultural waste discharged into water." These dam-induced changes are water *conditions*, not substances added to water. Section 502(6), however, primarily lists substances; "heat" is the only listed water condition. Moreover, the wording of § 506(6) makes us cautious in adding new terms to the definition. Congress used restrictive phrasing — "[t]he term 'pollutant' *means* dredged spoil, [etc.]" — rather than the looser phrase "includes," used elsewhere in the Act. As a general rule, " '[a] definition which declares what a term "means" . . . excludes any meaning that is not stated.' "

The Wildlife Federation argues that super-saturation and changes in temperature and oxygen level are indisputably "pollution " as that term is defined in § 502(19), and that it would be pointless to recognize dam-induced water changes as pollution without treating these same changes as involving a pollutant. The argument has some superficial appeal. The Supreme Court, however, has ruled that certain radioactive materials are not "pollutants" even though they undoubtedly emit "pollution." *Train v. Colorado Public Interest Research Group, Inc.*, 426 U.S. 1

(1976). Moreover, under usual rules of statutory construction, use of two different terms is presumed to be intentional, especially when the legislation specially defines both terms. Finally, EPA's policy-oriented explanation for the distinction — that Congress purposely limited federal NPDES permit program to certain well-recognized pollutants and left control of other water-altering substances or conditions to the states under § 208 — is quite plausible.

The legislative history, while not entirely consistent with the statutory language, further suggests that the Act does not require EPA to treat dam-induced water conditions as "pollutants." ***

*   *   *

And, while Congress did not intend the term "pollutant" to be all-inclusive, we find, at the same time, strong signals in the legislative history that it also entrusted EPA with at least some discretion over which "pollutants" and sources of pollutants were to be regulated under the NPDES program. ***

Given this focused legislative intent concerning deference to EPA's interpretation of these definitional provisions, we must accept that interpretation unless it is manifestly unreasonable. *** In fact, EPA has given the statute a natural reading, both on its face and in light of the legislative history. ***

2. *"Addition" of a Pollutant "from" a Point Source*

The Act does not define what constitutes the "addition" of a pollutant. The parties agree that water quality problems that occur within a reservoir (*e.g.*, dissolved minerals) are nonpoint pollution, for lack of a point source. The Wildlife Federation argues, however, that the statutorily necessary "addition . . . from a point source" occurs when (1) a dam causes pollutants to enter the reservoir and (2) the polluted water subsequently passes through the dam — the point source — into the formerly unpolluted river below. EPA responds that addition from a point source occurs only if the point source itself physically introduces a pollutant into water from the outside world. In its view, the point or nonpoint character of pollution is established when the pollutant first enters navigable water, and does not change when the polluted water later passes through the dam from one body of navigable water (the reservoir) to another (the downstream river). As for supersaturation, which does not exist in the reservoir, EPA argues that it occurs downstream, *after* the water is released from the dam.

In our view, the language of the statute permits either construction. The legislative history does not provide much help either. Throughout its consideration of the Act, Congress' focus was on traditional industrial and municipal wastes; it never considered how to regulate facilities such as dams which indirectly cause pollutants to enter navigable upstream water and then convey these polluted waters downstream. Congress did consider *downstream* water changes caused by dams such as saltwater intrusion, *see* § 304(f)(2)(E), but had no occasion to consider whether NPDES permits were desirable for dams because downstream changes are not amenable to the technological controls required for point sources.

Although Congress did not expressly address whether EPA should have discretion to define the term "addition," we note that it gave the agency reasonable discretion to define two other necessary components of the § 402 permit program — "point source" and "pollutant." On that basis, we consider it likely that Congress would have given EPA similar discretion to define "addition" had it expected the meaning of the term to be disputed. Therefore, EPA's interpretation must be accepted unless manifestly unreasonable, and we do not find it so. ***

3. The Primacy of § 402 in the Legislative Scheme

The Wildlife Federation also argues that the definitions of "pollutant" and "addition" should be read broadly because the NPDES permit program is Congress' preferred method of water pollution control and would have been applied to all sources of pollution had Congress thought that it was technologically feasible to do so. There is indeed some basis in the legislative history for the position that Congress viewed the NPDES program as its most effective weapon against pollution. ***

Nonetheless, it does not appear that Congress wanted to apply the NPDES system wherever feasible. Had it wanted to do so, it could easily have chosen suitable language, *e.g.*, "all pollution released through a point source." Instead, as we have seen, the NPDES system was limited to "addition" of "pollutants" "from" a point source.

The legislative history of the 1977 amendments further bolsters the view that the division of pollution control efforts between discharge permits under § 402 and areawide waste management plans under § 208 was not just a device for separating out pollution sources amenable to NPDES technological controls. Rather, Congress viewed state pollution control programs under § 208 as in part an "experiment" in the effectiveness of state regulation. ***

*   *   *

4. *Provisions Specifically Referring to Dams*

Several other sections of the statute refer specifically to dams. To the very limited extent that these sections are relevant, they support EPA and hence reinforce our conclusion that EPA's position is reasonable. In particular, EPA relies on § 304(f)(2)(F), which requires it to develop:

> processes, procedures, and methods to control [nonpoint source] pollution resulting from —
>
> . . . .
>
> (F) changes in the movement, flow, or circulation of any navigable waters or ground waters, including changes caused by the construction of dams, levees, channels, causeways, or flow diversion facilities.

In its view, this section demonstrates congressional intent that some water quality changes caused by dams be regulated as nonpoint pollution. But even under the Wildlife Federation's reading, downstream bank erosion due to decreased sediment load or variable water releases, saltwater intrusion due to reduced flow, and pollution of the reservoir itself would be nonpoint source pollution. Thus, Congress' mention of dam-induced changes in § 304 as nonpoint source pollution provides only mild support for EPA's position since some dam-caused water quality changes will be treated as nonpoint pollution in any event.

*   *   *

B. *The Purposes of the Act*

We conclude, then, on the basis of the text and history of the Act, that EPA's construction of relevant substantive provisions is reasonable. We consider next the Wildlife Federation's argument, accepted by the district court, that EPA's construction nonetheless will plainly frustrate the general congressional purposes underlying the Act. We find that it does not.

1. *The Text of the "Purposes" Section*

The district court, in giving "pollutant" and "addition" a broad reading, relied heavily on the "purposes" section of the Act, § 101(a). That section declares (emphasis added):

> The objective of this [Act] is to restore and maintain the chemical, physical, and biological integrity of the Nation's waters. In order to achieve this objective it is hereby declared that, consistent with the provisions of the [Act] —
>
>   (1) it is the national goal that the discharge of pollutants into the navigable waters be eliminated by 1985;
>
>   (2) it is the national goal that wherever attainable, an interim goal of [fishable and swimmable] water be achieved by July 1, 1983;
>
>   (3) it is the national policy that the discharge of toxic pollutants in toxic amounts be prohibited . . . .

Undeniably, Congress' strong statement of its objective must color EPA's and our interpretation of specific provisions of the Act. But, as any student of the legislative process soon learns, it is one thing for Congress to announce a grand goal, and quite another for it to mandate full implementation of that goal. Read as a whole, the

Clean Water Act shows not only Congress' determined effort to clean up our polluted lakes and rivers, but also its practical recognition of the economic, technological, and political limits on total elimination of all pollution from all sources. The Act contains numerous requirements that cost be taken into account in establishing effluent limits, as well as assorted exemptions from those limits. Moreover, the purposes section, in its own right, suggests that Congress recognized that the substantive provisions of the Act fall short of completely achieving the announced goals of the Act. Congress hedged the purposes section by making it apply only as "consistent with the provisions of this [Act]," and explicitly distinguished between the congressional "policy" to eliminate discharge of toxic pollutants and the presumably weaker "goal" of eliminating discharge of all pollutants.

Moreover, even if we accept the purposes section at face value, it is only suggestive, not dispositive of whether EPA must issue NPDES permits for dams. ***

In addition to our general doubts, expressed above, about how heavily to rely on the broad goals of the Act, we find specific indication in the Act that Congress did not want to interfere any more than necessary with state water management, of which dams are an important component. Section 101(g) states:

> It is the policy of Congress that the authority of each State to allocate quantities of water within its jurisdiction shall not be superseded, abrogated, or otherwise impaired by this [Act].

In light of its intent to minimize federal control over state decisions on water *quantity*, Congress might also, if confronted with the issue, have decided to leave control of dams insofar as they affect water *quality* to the states. ***

2. *The Legislative History of the "Purposes" Section*

In short, based on the text of the Act, EPA's interpretation cannot be said to plainly frustrate congressional purposes. Our review of the history of the 1972 Act and the 1977 amendments also leaves us unsure what Congress would have decided to do about dam-caused pollution if it had focused on the issue. Congress might have regulated dams under § 402 (as the Wildlife Federation desires), or under § 208 (as EPA has done), or even under an entirely new section specifically crafted to deal with dams.

*   *   *

The legislative history, then, indicates that Congress' avowed purpose to minimize pollution was not nearly so unequivocal as to make unreasonable EPA's interpretation of the specific provisions of the Act relating to dams. ***

***How broadly we construe the congressional "purpose" will inevitably turn in part on the practical or "policy" consequences of the choice. There is special reason to defer to the agency's policy choices. Contemporaneous construction by the agency should also receive substantial weight because the agency was in a better position in 1973 to decide how broadly to characterize Congress' intent than we are almost a decade later. In this case, EPA's views on dam-induced pollution merit deference as both contemporaneous and infused with its expert evaluation of the seriousness of the problem, the cost of cure, and the effectiveness of state regulation. We think, therefore, that the district court erred in relying on the legislative goals expressed in § 101(a) to invalidate EPA's otherwise reasonable construction of the NPDES permit program as excluding dam-caused pollution.

3. *Policy Considerations*

Finally, as a policy matter (and recognizing our limited role in reviewing agency policy decisions) we are not convinced that EPA's decision to leave dam regulation to the states was so misguided as to frustrate congressional policy. EPA contends that requiring permits for 2,000,000 dams would be an impossible task. Yet, so far as the record shows, most, if not all of the dams that cause water quality problems are large hydroelectric dams. Thus, the number of dams that would require permits is probably no more than the 50,000 "large" dams in the country, and quite possibly only the 3,000 or so dams that are large enough to generate significant amounts of hydroelectric power. That is a manageable number even if it turns out to be impractical to issue categorical permits. Nor are we persuaded by EPA's

argument that because the NPDES program requires discharge of pollutants to be eliminated to the extent technologically feasible, it will preclude beneficial dam-caused water changes, such as cold water discharges to support a trout fishery. It should be feasible for EPA to define "pollutant" to exclude beneficial water quality changes.

On the other hand, dam-caused pollution is unique because its severity depends partly on whether other sources have polluted the upstream river. The NPDES program, however, requires EPA to issue nationally uniform standards, and thus would not allow the agency to take full account of the interrelationship between dam-caused pollution and other pollution sources. Moreover, dams are a major component of state water management, providing irrigation, drinking water, flood protection, etc. In light of these complexities, which the NPDES program was not designed to handle, it may well be that state areawide water quality plans are the better regulatory tool.

Also, the severity of dam-caused pollution is highly site-specific. Common forms of NPDES limits (x% reduction in biochemical oxygen demand (BOD) or y pounds of BOD per ton of industrial output) would entail major costs at one dam, and only minor costs at another. Thus, it would be difficult at best for EPA to determine what level of reduction is obtainable by using the "best available technology *economically achievable*" for each "category or class" of polluter. Clean Water Act § 301(b)(2)(A) (emphasis added). Control that is economically feasible at one site may be infeasible at another. Conversely, major expenditures might be required for dams where, say, dissolved oxygen levels are slightly reduced immediately below the dam, but not enough to harm fish, and the river is fully reaerated within a few miles.

Finally, we cannot say, on the record before us, that federal intervention is needed because the states have abdicated their § 208 responsibility over a truly pressing national problem. The record does not show how vigorous state enforcement has been, but at least some efforts have been made to remedy dam-caused pollution. Supersaturation and sediment releases appear to be minor problems. As discussed earlier, temperature changes are not always harmful, are not easily controllable at single-outlet dams, and can apparently be readily controlled at multiple-outlet dams. Low dissolved oxygen and dissolved minerals and nutrients are the most serious problems, but EPA has the authority, when it reviews state water pollution control plans, to insist if need be on stronger efforts in the future. Also, new dams cannot be built unless they comply with state water quality requirements; thus the problem is largely limited to existing dams.[78]

*   *   *

[78]See § 401(a)(2). 33 U.S.C. § 1341(a)(2).

V. CONCLUSION

In closing, we emphasize the narrowness of our decision. It is not our function to decide whether EPA's interpretation of the term "discharge of a pollutant" is the best one or even whether it is more reasonable than the Wildlife Federation's interpretation. We hold merely that EPA's interpretation is reasonable, not inconsistent with congressional intent, and entitled to great deference; therefore, it must be upheld. The judgment of the district court is *reversed*.

NOTES

1. Do you agree with EPA's application of the five (?) required elements for "discharge of a pollutant" to the various water quality effects caused by dams? Do you agree that the court properly deferred to EPA's construction and application of these terms?

2. If EPA had not conceded the issue, is it debatable whether or not dams (especially their discharge ducts and spillways) are "point sources"?

3. Aren't at least several of the dam-induced water quality changes mentioned by the court within the statutory list of "pollutants" in Section 502 (6)? Is detrimentally hot epilimnion water released from a dam not "heat"? Shouldn't the same be said of detrimentally cold hypolimnion water released? Aren't farm fertilizers dissolved by anaerobic conditions in dams and then discharged "agricultural wastes"? Aren't sediments stirred up by dredging or released when sluicing "biological materials," "sand," or "cellar dirt"?

4. Are such pollutants not "additions" (to higher-quality downstream waters) "from" a point source (the spillway or discharge duct of a dam) when such pollutants were not present in the water prior to its impoundment?

5. Is this judicial deference or abdication to agency policy choices? How much is the court's deference influenced by policy considerations — especially the difficulty of imposing meaningful 301 limitations and the offense to states rights interests in regulation of surface waters?

6. What if an industry had impounded, used, and then released from a spillway cold, mineral-laden water that was low in dissolved oxygen? Would you then expect the court to defer to an EPA refusal to treat this as the discharge of a pollutant subject to NPDES permitting?

7. If EPA changed its mind, could it treat these dam-induced water quality changes as discharges of pollutants and subject them to NPDES permitting?

What would an NPDES permit for a dam look like?

What would the effluent limitations required by Sections 301 and 306 look like?

With the great variety of dams and differing water quality effects, how could uniform national standards be promulgated?

What did the district court envision in ordering EPA to establish "effluent limitations on a categorical, as opposed to a case-by-case basis"?

8. For a very cursory decision by the Eighth Circuit reaching a result similar to that of the D.C. Circuit, see *Missouri v. Department of the Army*, 672 F.2d 1297 (8th Cir. 1982). There the court held that soil erosion and reduction of dissolved oxygen downstream of a hydroelectric dam, both allegedly caused by release of water from the dam, did not constitute the addition of a pollutant from a point source.

9. In *United States v. Tennessee Water Quality Control Board*, 19 ERC 1826 (6th Circuit 1983), the State of Tennessee and recreational users of a stretch of the Ocoee River argued that TVA's diversion of water from the river (by means of a dam) into a flume that led to a hydroelectric power-house four and one-half miles downstream, from which the water was returned to the riverbed, required a state water quality permit. Through curious reasoning, the Sixth Circuit concluded that, since the dam, diversion, and powerplant did not result in the discharge of pollutants from a point source, the state could not subject the project to the requirements of its discharge permit program — leaving open the possibility of state imposition of non-point source controls.

Weinberger v. Romero-Barcelo
456 U.S. 305 (1982)

JUSTICE WHITE delivered the opinion of the Court.

The issue in this case is whether the Federal Water Pollution Control Act (FWPCA or the Act) requires a district court to enjoin immediately all discharges of pollutants that do not comply with the Act's permit requirements or whether the district court retains discretion to order other relief to achieve compliance. The Court of Appeals for the First Circuit held that the Act withdrew the courts' equitable discretion. We reverse.

I

For many years, the Navy has used Vieques Island, a small island off the Puerto Rico coast, for weapons training. Currently all Atlantic Fleet vessels assigned to the Mediterranean and the Indian Ocean are required to complete their training at Vieques because it permits a full range of exercises under conditions similar to combat. During air-to-ground training, however, pilots sometimes miss land-based targets, and ordnance falls into the sea. That is, accidental bombings of the navigable waters and, occasionally, intentional bombings of water targets occur. The District Court found that these discharges have not harmed the quality of the water.

In 1978, respondents, who include the Governor of Puerto Rico and residents of the

island, sued to enjoin the Navy's operations on the island. Their complaint alleged violations of numerous federal environmental statutes and various other acts. After an extensive hearing, the District Court found that under the explicit terms of the Act, the Navy had violated the Act by discharging ordnance into the waters surrounding the island without first obtaining a permit from the Environmental Protection Agency (EPA).

Under the FWPCA, the "discharge of any pollutant" requires a National Pollutant Discharge Elimination System (NPDES) permit. 33 U.S.C.§ 1311(a). The term "discharge of any pollutant" is defined as

". . . any addition of any *pollutant* to the waters of the contiguous zone or the ocean from any *point source* other than a vessel or other floating craft." 33 U.S.C. § 1362(12) (emphasis added).

Pollutant, in turn, means,

". . . dredged spoil, solid wastes, incinerator residue, sewage, garbage, sewage sludge, *munitions*, chemical wastes, biological materials, radioactive materials, heat, wrecked or discarded equipment, rock, sand, cellar dirt and industrial, municipal and agricultural waste discharged into water ...."33 U.S.C. § 1362(6) (emphasis added).

And, under the Act, a "point source" is

"any discernible, confined and discrete *conveyance*, including but not limited to any pipe, ditch, channel, tunnel, conduit, well, discrete fissure, container rolling stock, concentrated animal feeding operation, or *vessel* or *other floating craft from which pollutants are or may be discharged* ...." 33 U.S.C. § 1362(14) (emphasis added).

Under the FWPCA, the EPA may not issue an NPDES without state certification that the permit conforms to state water quality standards. A state has the authority to deny certification of the permit application or attach conditions to the final permit. 33 U.S.C. § 1341.

As the District Court construed the FWPCA, the release of ordnance from aircraft or from ships into navigable waters is a discharge of pollutants, even though the Environmental Protection Agency, which administers the Act, had not promulgated any regulations setting effluent levels or providing for the issuance of a NPDES permit for this category of pollutants. Recognizing that violations of the Act "must be cured," the District Court ordered the Navy to apply for a NPDES permit. It refused, however, to enjoin Navy operations pending consideration of the permit application. It explained that the Navy's "technical violations" were not causing any "appreciable harm" to the environment.[4] "Moreover, because of the importance of the island as a training center, the granting of injunctive relief sought would cause grievous, and

perhaps irreparable harm, not only to Defendant Navy, but to the general welfare of this Nation." The District Court concluded that an injunction was not necessary to ensure suitably prompt compliance by the Navy. To support this conclusion, it emphasized an equity court's traditionally broad discretion in deciding appropriate relief and quoted from the classic description of injunctive relief in *Hecht Co.* v. *Bowles,* 321 U.S. 321, 329-330 (1944): "The historic injunctive process was designed to deter, not to punish."

The Court of Appeals for the First Circuit vacated the District Court's order and remanded with instructions that the court order the Navy to cease the violation until it obtained a permit. 643 F. 2d 835 (1981). Relying on *TVA* v. *Hill,* 437 U.S. 153 (1978), in which this Court held that an imminent violation of the Endangered Species Act required injunctive relief, the Court of Appeals concluded that the District Court erred in undertaking a traditional balancing of the parties' competing interests. "Whether or not the Navy's activities in fact harm the coastal waters, it has an absolute statutory obligation to stop any discharges of pollutant until the permit procedure has been followed and the Administrator of the Environmental Protection Agency, upon review of the evidence, has granted a permit." The court suggested that if the order would interfere significantly with military preparedness, the Navy should request that the President grant it an exemption from the requirements in the interest of national security.

*　　*　　*

II

It goes without saying that an injunction is an equitable remedy. It "is not a remedy which issues as of course," or "to restrain an act the injurious consequences of which are merely trifling." *** The Court has repeatedly held that the basis for injunctive relief in the federal courts has always been irreparable injury and the inadequacy of legal remedies.

Where plaintiff and defendant present competing claims of injury, the traditional function of equity has been to arrive at a "nice adjustment and reconciliation" between the competing claims, *Hecht Co.* v. *Bowles, supra,* at 329. In such cases, the court "balances the conveniences of

---

[4]The District Court wrote,
"In fact, if anything, these waters are as aesthetically acceptable as any to be found anywhere, and Plaintiff's witnesses unanimously testified as to their being the best fishing grounds in Vieques. ... [I]f truth be said, the control of large areas of Vieques [by the Navy] probably constitutes a positive factor in its over all ecology. The very fact that there are in the Navy zones modest numbers of various marine species which are practically non-existent in the civilian sector of Vieques or in the main island of Puerto Rico, is an eloquent example of *res ipsa loquitur.*"

the parties and possible injuries to them according as they may be affected by the granting or withholding of the injunction." *Yakus* v. *United States,* 321 U.S. 414, 440 (1944). "The essence of equity has been the power of the chancellor to do equity and to mold each decree to the necessities of the particular case. Flexibility rather than rigidity has distinguished it." *Hecht Co.* v. *Bowles, supra,* at 329.

In exercising their sound discretion, courts of equity should pay particular regard for the public consequences in employing the extraordinary remedy of injunction. *** The grant of jurisdiction to insure compliance with a statute hardly suggests an absolute duty to do so under any and all circumstances, and a federal judge sitting as chancellor is not mechanically obligated to grant an injunction for every violation of law.

These commonplace considerations applicable to cases in which injunctions are sought in the federal courts reflect a "practice with a background of several hundred years of history," a practice of which Congress is assuredly well aware. Of course, Congress may intervene and guide or control the exercise of the courts' discretion, but we do not lightly assume that Congress has intended to depart from established principles. ***

In *TVA* v. *Hill,* we held that Congress had foreclosed the exercise of the usual discretion possessed by a court of equity. *** The purpose and language of the statute under consideration in *Hill,* not the bare fact of a statutory violation, compelled that conclusion. Section 1536 of the Act requires federal agencies to "insure that actions authorized, funded, or carried out by them do not jeopardize the continued existence of [any] endangered species . . . or result in the destruction of habitat of such species which is determined . . . to be critical." The statute thus contains a flat ban on the destruction of critical habitats.

It was conceded in *Hill* that completion of the dam would eliminate an endangered species by destroying its critical habitat. Refusal to enjoin the action would have ignored the "explicit provisions of the Endangered Species Act." Congress, it appeared to us, had chosen the snail

darter over the dam. The purpose and language of the statute limited the remedies available to the district court; only an injunction could vindicate the objectives of the Act.

That is not the case here. An injunction is not the only means of ensuring compliance. The FWPCA itself, for example, provides for fines and criminal penalties. Respondents suggest that failure to enjoin the Navy will undermine the integrity of the permit process by allowing the statutory violation to continue. The integrity of the nation's waters, however, not the permit process, is the purpose of the FWPCA. As Congress explained, the objective of the FWPCA is to "restore and maintain the chemical, physical and biological integrity of the Nation's waters."

This purpose is to be achieved by compliance with the Act, including compliance with the permit requirements. Here, however, the discharge of ordnance had not polluted the waters, and, although the District Court declined to enjoin the discharges, it neither ignored the statutory violation nor undercut the purpose and function of the permit system. The court ordered the Navy to apply for a permit.[9] It temporarily, not permanently, allowed the Navy to continue its activities without a permit.

***That the scheme as a whole contemplates the exercise of discretion and balancing of equities militates against the conclusion that Congress intended to deny courts their traditional equitable discretion in enforcing the statute.

***Although the ultimate objective of the FWPCA is to eliminate all discharges of pollutants into the navigable waters by 1985, the statute sets forth a scheme of phased compliance. As enacted, it called for the achievement of the "best practicable control technology currently available" by July 1, 1977 and the "best availa-

---

[9]The Navy applied for an NPDES permit in December, 1979. In May, 1981, the EPA issued a draft NPDES permit and a notice of intent to issue that permit. The FWPCA requires a certification of compliance with state water quality standards before the EPA may issue an NPDES permit. 33 U.S.C. § 1341(a). The Environmental Quality Board of the Commonwalth of Puerto Rico denied the Navy a water quality certificate in connection with this application for an NPDES in June, 1981. ***

ble technology economically achievable" by July 1, 1983. ***

The FWPCA directs the Administrator of the EPA to seek an injunction to restrain immediately discharges of pollutants he finds to be presenting "an imminent and substantial endangerment of the health of persons or to the welfare of persons." 33 U. S. C. § 1364(a). This rule of immediate cessation, however, is limited to the indicated class of violations. For other kinds of violations, the FWPCA authorizes the Administrator of the EPA "to commence a civil action for appropriate relief, including a permanent or temporary injunction, for any violation for which he is authorized to issue a compliance order . . . ." 33 U. S. C. 1319(b). The provision makes clear that Congress did not anticipate that all discharges would be immediately enjoined. Consistent with this view, the administrative practice has not been to request immediate cessation orders. "Rather, enforcement actions typically result, by consent or otherwise, in a remedial order setting out a detailed schedule of compliance designed to cure the identified violation of the Act." Brief for United States 17. ***

Both the Court of Appeals and respondents attach particular weight to the provision of the FWPCA permitting the President to exempt Federal facilities from compliance with the permit requirements. 33 U. S. C. § 1323. They suggest that this provision indicates Congressional intent to limit the court's discretion. According to respondents, the exemption provision evidences Congress' determination that only paramount national interests justify failure to comply and that only the President should make this judgment.

We do not construe the provision so broadly. We read the FWPCA as permitting the exercise of a court's equitable discretion, whether the source of pollution is a private party or a federal agency, to order relief that will achieve *compliance* with the Act. The exemption serves a different and complementary purpose, that of permitting *noncompliance* by federal agencies in extraordinary circumstances. ***

Should the Navy receive a permit here, there would be no need to invoke the machinery of the Presidential exemption. If not, this course remains open. ***

Like the language and structure of the Act, the legislative history does not suggest that Congress intended to deny courts their traditional equitable discretion. ***

III

This Court explained in *Hecht Co.* v. *Bowles,* 321 U. S. 321 (1944), that a major departure from the long tradition of equity practice should not be lightly implied. *** We do not read the FWPCA as foreclosing completely the exercise of the court's discretion. Rather than requiring a District Court to issue an injunction for any and all statutory violations, the FWPCA permits the District Court to order that relief it considers necessary to secure prompt compliance with the Act. That relief can include, but is not limited to, an order of immediate cessation.

The exercise of equitable discretion, which must include the ability to deny as well as grant injunctive relief, can fully protect the range of public interests at issue at this stage in the proceedings. The District Court did not face a situation in which a permit would very likely not issue and the requirements and objective of the statute could therefore not be vindicated if discharges were permitted to continue. Should it become clear that no permit will be issued and that compliance with the FWPCA will not be forthcoming, the statutory scheme and purpose would require the court to reconsider the balance it has struck.

Because Congress, in enacting the FWPCA, has not foreclosed the exercise of equitable discretion, the proper standing for appellate review is whether the district court abused its discretion in denying an immediate cessation order while the Navy applied for a permit. We reverse and remand to Court of Appeals for proceedings consistent with this opinion.

JUSTICE STEVENS, dissenting.

The appropriate remedy for the violation of a federal statute depends primarily on the terms of the statute and the character of the violation. Unless Congress specifically commands a particular form of relief, the question of remedy remains subject to a court's equitable discretion. Because the Federal Water Pollution Control Act does not specifically command the federal courts to issue an injunction every time an unpermitted discharge of a pollutant occurs, the Court today is obviously correct in asserting that such injunctions should not issue "automatically" or "mechanically" in every case. It is nevertheless equally clear that by enacting the 1972 amendments to the FWPCA Congress channeled the discretion of the federal judiciary much more narrowly than the Court's rather glib opinion suggests. Indeed, although there may well be situations in which the failure to obtain an NPDES permit would not require immediate cessation of all discharges, I am convinced that Congress has circumscribed the district courts' discretion on the question of remedy so narrowly that a general rule of immediate cessation must be applied in all but a narrow category of cases. The Court of Appeals was quite correct in holding that this case does not present the kind of exceptional situation that justifies a departure from the general rule.

The Court's mischaracterization of the Court of Appeals' holding is the premise for its essay on equitable discretion. This essay is analytically flawed because it overlooks the limitations on equitable discretion that apply in cases in which public interests are implicated and the defendant's violation of the law is ongoing. Of greater importance, the Court's opinion grants an open-ended license to federal judges to carve gaping holes in a reticulated statutory scheme designed by Congress to protect a precious natural resource fom the consequences of ad hoc judgments about specific discharges of pollutants.

*   *   *

IV

The decision in *TVA* v. *Hill* did not depend on any peculiar or unique statutory language. Nor did it rest on any special interest in snail darters. The decision reflected a profound respect for the law and the proper allocation of lawmaking responsibilities in our government. There we refused to sit as a committee of review. Today the Court authorizes free thinking federal judges to do just that. Instead of requiring adherence to carefully integrated statutory procedures that assign to nonjudicial decisionmakers the responsibilities for evaluating potential harm to our water supply as well as potential harm to our national security, the Court unnecessarily and casually substitutes the chancellor's clumsy foot for the rule of law.

I respectfully dissent.

NOTES

1. If the Supreme Court had addressed the issue, could the Navy's bombings of the waters around Vieques be found to be anything other than the "discharge of any pollutant"?

If not, was there any escape from the requirement of an NPDES permit? What do you suppose would be appropriate terms for such a permit? Would each individual point source, each ship and plane discharging the ordnance, have to have a separate permit?

2. Was this not a situation demonstrably suited for a presidential exemption under Section 313?

If this relief was readily available, should it affect the court's attitude toward granting injunctive relief? How?

3. Was *TVA v. Hill* so easily distinguished? Should it have been overruled, not distinguished? Which case is the rule and which the exception — *Hill* or *Romero-Barcelo*?

If express statutory mandates — e.g., no discharge of any pollutant without a permit — are not controlling, how is one to know the real "purpose" of legislation? How helpful to deciding the necessity of injunctive relief is it to say that the purpose of the Clean Water Act is to "restore and maintain the . . . integrity of the Nation's waters."

4. *Could* the district court properly have issued an injunction in this case? Would it *ever* be required to enjoin the Navy bombing? What if the Navy had refused to follow the court's order to apply for a permit? What would be an appropriate sanction for such contempt?

5. As noted by the court, Section 401 (a) requires state certification of compliance with local standards before EPA may issue a permit. What if Puerto Rico adheres to its refusal to issue the Navy a certificate? Could the district court still refuse to enjoin the bombing?

6. Would the same broad equitable discretion exist for a trial judge asked to enjoin an industrial discharger operating (with or without a permit) in gross violation of the applicable effluent limitations? Should it matter whether or not a variance was available? Whether or not the discharger had applied for a variance? Whether or not it had been denied?

13   NONPOINT SOURCES

Natural Resources Defense Council, Inc. v. Costle

564 F.2d 573 (D.C. Cir. 1977)

Before: McGowan, Leventhal and Robb, Circuit Judges.

Opinion for the Court filed by Circuit Judge Robb.

Robb, Circuit Judge: The Natural Resources Defense Council and the Environmental Defense Fund (referred to collectively as NRDC) brought an action in the District Court seeking (1) a declaratory judgment construing section 208 of the Federal Water Pollution Control Act Amendments of 1972, 33 U.S.C. § 1288, and (2) an order directing the Administrator of the Environmental Protection Agency (EPA) to promulgate regulations consistent with the plaintiffs' interpretation of the Act. National Forest Products Association (NFPA), an organization representing firms and local organizations engaged in the forest products industry, was permitted to intervene as a defendant. The District Court granted the plaintiffs' motion for summary judgment and ordered the EPA to promulgate regulations consistent with the court's construction of section 208. *Natural Resources Defense Council v. Train*, 396 F. Supp. 1386 (D.C.D.C. 1975). Both NFPA and EPA filed notices of appeal but thereafter EPA voluntarily dismissed its appeal and has now intervened as an appellee to defend the District Court's decision. The Commonwealth of Virginia and the State of Washington have filed briefs *amicus curiae* in support of the position taken by NFPA. We affirm.

The Federal Water Pollution Control Act Amendments of 1972, 33 U.S.C. § 1251 *et seq.*, establish "a comprehensive program designed 'to restore and maintain the chemical, physical, and biological integrity of the Nation's waters . . . .'" *Natural Resources Defense Council v. Train*, 315, 510 F.2d 692, 695 (1974). A central feature of this attack on the problem of water pollution is section 208. 33 U.S.C. § 1281. ***

Section 208(a) provides that State and local agencies shall develop and implement areawide waste treatment management plans to achieve the Act's 1983 goal of fishable and swimmable waters. Section 208(a)(1) directs the Administrator of EPA by regulation to publish guidelines for the identification of those areas having substantial water control problems. Section 208(a)(2) provides that "The Governor of each State . . . shall identify each area within the State which, as a result of urban-industrial concentrations or other factors, has substantial water quality control problems." The Governor shall then "designate (A) the boundaries of each such area, and (B) a single representative organization, including elected officials from local governments or their designees, capable of developing effective areawide waste treatment management plans for such area." In the case of an area located in two or more states the Governors of the respective states are to consult and cooperate "toward designating" the boundaries of the interstate area and "toward designating" a "representative organization" to develop effective areawide waste treatment management plans. Sec. 208(a)(3). If no designation is made by a Governor or Governors the "chief elected officials of local governments within an area may by agreement designate" an area and "a single representative organization" capable of developing the waste treatment management plan. Sec. 208 (a)(4). Section 208(a)(5) provides: "Existing regional agencies may be designated under paragraphs (2), (3), and (4) of this subsection." Section 208(a)(6), upon which the controversy in this case has focused, provides: "The State shall act as a planning agency for all portions of such State which are not designated under paragraphs (2), (3), or (4) of this subsection."

Section 208(b)(1) provides that not later than one year "after the date of designation of any organization" under section 208(a) "such organization shall have in operation a continuing area-wide waste treatment management planning process." Section 208(b)(2) in turn specifies the required elements of a proper waste treatment plan. Section 208(b)(2) (A)-(E) applies to the establishment of long-term preventive point source regulatory programs and section 208(b) (2) (F)-(K) relates to programs for identifying and controlling non-point source pollution from agriculture, silviculture, mining, construction and other similar activities. The waste treatment management plans are to be certified annually by the Governors and submitted to the Administrator for his approval. Sec. 208(b)(3). The Administrator is directed to "make grants to any agency designated under subsection (a) of this section [208] for payment of the reasonable costs of developing and operating" the waste treatment planning processes "under subsection (b) of this section." Sec. 208(f)(1). These grants shall be 100% of the costs for each of the three fiscal years beginning June 30, 1973, and not more than 75% of such costs in each succeeding fiscal year. Sec. 208(f)(2).

As we have said, section 208(a)(1) of the Act provides that the Administrator of EPA shall by regulation publish guidelines for the identification of those areas having substantial water quality control problems. After some delay EPA promulgated such regulations. At this time EPA took the position that the State when acting as a "planning agency" under section 208(b)(6) was not required to develop a section 208 plan for all areas of the State which had not been "designated." In a subsequent regulation promulgated June 3, 1974, EPA suggested that a State could

fulfill its section 208 planning requirements for undesignated areas by planning under section 303(e) of the Act. Planning under section 303(e) includes some, but not all the elements required by section 208 plans.

It appears that only about 5% of the nation's waterways were in areas "designated" for local planning. Thus, if the EPA's original interpretation of the statute was correct, 95% of the country's area was not subject to section 208 planning. In particular the long-term preventive programs of section 208(b)(2)(F)-(K), for identifying and controlling non-point source pollution from agriculture, silviculture, mining, construction and other similar activities, were not required or were limited to areas in which they could have little or no effect.

Responding to the EPA regulations NRDC notified the Administrator of its intention to file an action for a declaratory judgment that (1) section 208(a)(6) requires the same type of planning in local and State planning areas, and (2) so far as they were inconsistent with that requirement the EPA regulations were invalid. As a result, at a conference with counsel for NRDC on August 29, 1974 EPA's associate general counsel provided counsel for NRDC with an EPA memorandum of law which indicated substantial agreement with NRDC's position. ***

Although EPA had signified this agreement with NRDC, regulations implementing the agreement were not forthcoming. Accordingly, NRDC filed its complaint for a declaratory judgment construing section 208 (a) (6) and for an order directing EPA to promulgate appropriate regulations. After some skirmishing during which EPA averred that it intended to promulgate such regulations but was not required to do so, NRDC filed its motion for summary judgment. At this stage of the case our appellant National Forest Products Association intervened. NFPA contended, and argues before us, that section 208 (a) (6) does not require statewide planning and that any such planning in areas which have not been "designated" for local planning is a matter for State discretion.

The District Court granted NRDC's motion for summary judgment. Emphasizing that section 208 must be read "in the context of the entire Act so that its purpose together with the intent of the whole Act may be effectuated," the court held that section 208 is a "critical provision in a broad, far-reaching Act" which requires comprehensive statewide planning:

> [Section 208] contains unique authority to control water pollution from point sources (e.g., factory or pipe discharge) . . . and from nonpoint sources (e.g., mining or agricultural runoff). Its implementation features distinguish it from Section 303 (e) of the Act, which emphasizes ongoing State planning and limits State efforts to stationary sources of pollution. The Section is also intended to coordinate and integrate other planning, construction, and discharge permit provisions of the Act. Section 208 charts a course not only for the cleaning up of polluted waters but also for the prevention of future pollution by identifying problem sources, regulating construction of certain industrial facilities, and developing processes to control runoff sources of pollution. While Section 208 focuses on "urban-industrial" areas with substantial water quality control difficulties, it also directs attention to other geographical locations with water pollution problems, such as forests, mining areas, farms, and salt water inlets. As a "bottom line" for the Section 208 waste treatment management activities, the Act prescribes a 1983 goal of clean waterways. *Id.* at 1389. [Citations omitted]

The District Court stressed the critical importance of section 208 (a) (6) as "the residual clause in the areawide waste treatment management planning provisions". *Id* at 1390. The court explained that:

> [Section 208(a)(6)] deals with the non-designated or "leftover" portions of the State . . . . The plain implication is that [Section 208(a)(6)] empowers the State to achieve what other [designated] planning organizations . . . . are directed to achieve . . . . It would be illogical for Congress to set forth a detailed scheme for

State, interstate, and local water pollution planning — and then to lump the remainder of State territory into a residuary provision with veiled instructions to the state, to do as it saw fit regarding waste treatment control . . . . There are presently only about 85 designated problem areas in the United States, leaving an estimated 95% of the nation's waterways non-designated . . . . Surely the Congress did not intend Section 208 planning to be the exception rather than the rule . . . . *Id.* at 1390.

The court recognized that the intensity of planning might not be as great in the state planning portions of a State:

> As [NRDC, and Environmental Defense Fund] have stressed on numerous occasions, the subsection (a) (6) regulations will not call for rigorous planning where no pollution problems exist. Rural areas need not implement safeguards for urban pollution problems, and vice versa; planning can be tailored to a region's peculiar problems . . . . A State may certify large portions of its territory as pollution-free and concentrate on preventive measures for these portions as well as on abatement measures for the substantial problem areas. *Id.* at 1391-92.

*   *   *

The court therefore held (1) that section 208 (a) (6) requires that the States implement full section 208 planning in all areas which are not locally designated, (2) that such planning must include the same elements required by section 208(b)(2) for designated areas, (3) that construction grants under Title II and discharge permits under Title IV must be consistent with such State plans, and (4) that under section 208 (f) federal funding must be made equally available to State and local planning agencies.

The court did not attempt to formulate specific regulations implementing its decision but rather directed that EPA do so:

> It is not for this Court . . . to define or promulgate the subsection (a)(6)

regulations. Hopefully, EPA's draft regulations already address the complexities of a State's subsection (a)(6) planning role and delineate the need for State and local cooperation. In any event, a full and prompt rulemaking proceeding will enable interested parties including the States to offer further comments to EPA with reference to the content of the proposed guidelines. *Id.* at 1392.

On July 16 and September 8, 1975 EPA published final regulations implementing the District Court's order. 40 C.F.R., Parts 130 and 131, 40 Fed. Reg. 55.321 (Nov. 28, 1976).

We have referred at length to the District Court's opinion because we agree with its conclusions and substantially agree with its reasoning. We think, as did the District Court, that section 208 sets up a comprehensive scheme for the elimination of water pollution in all areas of a State, both urban-industrial areas and agricultural and forest areas. We think it unreasonable to believe that the Congress intended to exempt from this scheme 95% of the State's areas. We need to consider only briefly the specific arguments to the contrary pressed upon us by NFPA.

NFPA argues first that the "plain language of § 208 [demonstrates] that the § 208(b)(2) planning requirements are only required in those areas, and by those organizations, 'designated' under §§ 208(a)(2)-(4)." In support of this argument NFPA engages in a microscopic scrutiny of the words used in section 208. ***

We are not persuaded by this exercise in semantics. We think the statute must be given a reasonable interpretation, not parsed and dissected with the meticulous technicality applied in testing a common law indictment or deed creating an estate in fee-tail. It is plain to us on the face of section 208 that Congress itself has "designated" the State to act as the entity charged with developing waste treatment management plans under section 208 (b)(2) for non-designated regions.***

*   *   *

Having scrutinized the words of the statute NFPA turns to its legislative history and argues that this history demonstrates that Congress did not intend to require 208 (b) planning for portions of a State not "designated" under sections 208 (a)(2)-(4). We have carefully considered this legislative history and NFPA's somewhat involved argument but are not persuaded. ***

Finally, NFPA argues that as construed by the District Court section 208 violates the Tenth Amendment by compelling the States to expend their own funds and to exercise their own sovereign powers in carrying out a federal regulatory program established by Congress. In response the government says this argument is not properly before us because it was not raised in the District Court and because NFPA has no standing to assert the rights of the States under the Tenth Amendment.

We hold that NFPA is entitled to make its constitutional argument in support of its proposed construction of the statute. It is of course familiar doctrine that a statute should if possible be construed so as to avoid constitutional infirmities, and NFPA is entitled to argue that its construction will eliminate the infirmities it perceives in section 208 as construed by EPA and the District Court. Turning to the merits of the argument, however, we reject it. The District Court's order merely directs EPA to promulgate regulations for the submission of State section 208 plans. As NFPA concedes in its brief (P. 40) the Act contains no provision for enforcement of any obligation that may be imposed upon a State under section 208. In the absence of any provision for sanctions the EPA may of course employ the accepted and traditional means of gaining State compliance by withholding funds under section 208 (f), but that method of stimulation would not violate the Tenth Amendment. *See District of Columbia v. Train*, 521 F.2d 971, 993 (1975).

The judgment of the District Court is *Affirmed*.

NOTES

1. The regulatory attention which has been given to point sources of pollution over the past near decade and a half — with a substantial degree of success — has not focused nearly so sharply on nonpoint sources. Consequently, nearly half the present conventional pollutant load in the nation's waters comes from runoff from urban areas, agriculture, silviculture, mines, and construction sites. Some activities, such as mining and pesticide application, moreover, cause substantial loads of toxic pollutants to enter our waters otherwise than through discrete conveyances. Other kinds of degradation of water, such as saltwater intrusion and adverse changes in the flow or reach of surface and ground waters, also are usually included in the nonpoint source category. All these various causes of water pollution have at least one thing in common: they are not amenable to the usual end-of-the-pipe control strategies. All too often, therefore, they have gone without adequate regulation.

2. Provisions in the Clean Water Act do, of course, address nonpoint source pollution problems, in a fashion. As described by Judge Robb in the preceding decision, Section 208 provides that the designated state and local agencies were to have expeditiously developed and implemented "areawide waste treatment management plans." The required ingredients of such plans, which are specified in Section 208(b)(2), fall into three broad categories: assurance of adequate POTWs; regulation of industrial, commercial, and residential development so as to minimize water quality impacts; and control of nonpoint sources of pollution. This provision identifies four contributors to nonpoint pollution and requires the designated state agencies to establish procedures and methods (expressly including land use requirements) to control them to the extent feasible: (1) agriculture and silviculture, (2) mine-related sources, (3) construction activities, and (4) causes of salt water intrusion. In repeated instances, the Act mandates that such plans, once prepared, be submitted to EPA for its approval.

In addition, Section 303(e) requires that each state have an EPA-approved "continuing planning process" to protect all waters within the state. Required elements of plans resulting from such continuing planning processes include, *inter alia*, effluent limitations for point sources, calculation of total maximum daily loads and the other means necessary to attain designated water quality standards, and incorporation of the areawide waste management plans prepared pursuant to Section 208.

EPA has integrated the overlapping planning obligations under Sections 208(b) and 303(e) (and a couple of other sections), terming the result a "water quality management plan." Typically, the weakest parts in such combined plans are those covering nonpoint source controls.

3. What appear to be several important incidents are attached to approval of 303(e)/208(b) plans.

According to Section 303(e)(2), "The Administrator shall not approve any State permit program [under 402 or 404] for any State which does not have an approved continuing planning process under this section."

According to Section 208(d), after a plan complying with Section 208(b) has been approved for an area, "The Administrator shall not make any grant for construction of a publicly owned treatment works under [Section 201] within such area except . . . for works in conformity with such plan."

Section 208(e) states: "No permit under Section 402 of this title shall be issued for any point source which is in conflict with a plan approved pursuant to subsection (b) of this section."

Section 208(f) provides for federal funding of up to 75% of the cost of developing and implementing a qualifying 208 plan.

4. A variety of means of controlling nonpoint sources of pollution are available to state and local governments.

Pollutants in runoff from urban areas can be controlled by the routing of storm sewers through treatment works, but this may be prohibitively expensive for areas without combined storm and sanitary sewer systems. Suspended solids, however, can be settled out in detention basins. The only other strategies feasible for most communities are those directed toward diminishing the amounts of pollutants which enter the storm sewers. This can be accomplished by street cleaning and by ordinances requiring covering or treatment of raw materials storage piles; prohibiting the discharge of such things as crankcase oil, paint, and large amounts of detergents into storm sewers; imposing limits on applications of pesticides and fertilizers; setting design standards for parking lots, shopping centers, etc., that will minimize runoff; and requiring retention of silt from construction sites.

Agricultural runoff carrying pollutants is controlled primarily through soil conservation programs and regulation of irrigation practices administered at state and district levels. Such programs may be effective at controlling siltation and salinity, but few have included regulation of pesticide and fertilizer application. The emphasis in most states is upon prevention of soil erosion. Pesticide regulation usually does not extend beyond that conducted pursuant to the Federal Insecticide, Fungicide, and Rodenticide Act (FIFRA). 7 U.S.C. § 135 *et seq.* Under Section 208(j) of the Clean Water Act, added by the 1977 Amendments, the U.S. Department of Agriculture was authorized to provide substantial financial assistance to farmers and ranchers who would enter into contracts agreeing to use specified "best management practices" (BMPs) to control nonpoint source pollution from their lands — a promising program frustrated from its inception by lack of federal funds.

BMPs for forestry practices also have been identified by EPA, but few states have enacted any authority to implement such measures. What restrictions on runoff from silvicultural operations exist are usually no more than the Forest Service imposes as conditions in its timber leasing.

Runoff from construction sites can be controlled by retention barriers, sedimentation ponds, regulation of slope and contour during and after construction, reseeding and revegetation of cleared land, and planning of drainage systems. Some states do have legislation requiring that such measures be taken if projects exceed a certain size, but most states do not. The severe runoff problems that can accompany highway construction are addressed in requirements set by state highway departments and in design standards imposed as a condition of federal funding.

Nonpoint source discharges from mines have received little state attention except when covered by federal legislation. Surface runoff and damage to groundwater from operating and abandoned coal mines is adequately addressed by the Surface Mining Control and Reclamation Act of 1977. 30 U.S.C §§ 1201-1328. SMCRA, however, applies only to *coal* mining. At other kinds of mines, federal standards to control nonpoint pollution exist only when the mining is conducted on federal lands or when it is concurrent with *point* source pollution. Under Section 304(e) of the Clean Water Act, added by Congress in 1977, EPA was authorized to set BMPs to control runoff, leakage, spillage, and drainage of toxic or hazardous pollutants from any site which also contains a point source. Such nonpoint controls may be supplemental to effluent limitations for *any* point source category, not just mining operations. EPA has been slow, however, to utilize this new authority.

5. Despite the availability of the means of controlling nonpoint sources of pollution, serious efforts to formulate effective 208 plans have been made by few states. And even those plans which look impressive on paper are often not enforceable or enforced. For the widely-held view that EPA's lack of emphasis on nonpoint source controls is at least partially to blame, see Lazarus, *Non-Point Source Pollution,* 2 HARV. ENVTL. L. REV. 176 (1977).

6. The primary reason that Section 208 is not taken seriously by most states is because they don't *have* to. Section 208 ostensibly requires states to tell some very powerful constituencies — farmers, miners, and construction contractors — how to run their operations. Without some substantial encouragement by federal carrots or sticks, state governments are naturally going to shy away from such tasks. Consider what federal leverage exists.

Can EPA promulgate a 208 plan for a state that does not submit an adequate one — or any at all? Does anything in Sections 208 or 303(e) suggest that authority lies with anyone but state, local, or regional agencies?

What happens if a state submits a plan but does not implement it? *See* Section 208(b)(4)(D). Could EPA enforce it?

What federal funding may be withheld from states that do not submit or implement 208 plans? *See* Section 208(d) and (f).

Could EPA withhold NPDES permitting authority from a state which does not submit an adequate 208 plan? *See* Section 303(e)(2) and (e)(3)(B).

Could EPA veto a 402 permit in conflict with an approved 208 plan? *See* Section 208(e). What if the 208 plan had no application to point source permitting? What if no 208 plan was in effect?

Could a state be forced by court order to submit or implement a 208 plan? Does the language of the statute make such state action mandatory? Would the Constitution allow such compulsion of state governmental functions?

14   DREDGE AND FILL

Preface to Final Rules Implementing Section 404

Title 33 — Navigation and Navigable Waters
Chapter 11 — Corps of Engineers,
Department of The Army
Regulatory Programs of the
Corps of Engineers*

*   *   *

HISTORICAL BACKGROUND

The Department of the Army, acting through the Corps of Engineers, is responsible for administering various Federal laws that regulate certain types of activities in specific waters in the United States and the oceans. The authorities for these regulatory programs are based primarily on various sections of the River and Harbor Act of 1899 (33 U.S.C. 401 et seq.), Section 404 of the Federal Water Pollution Control Act Amendments of 1972 (33 U.S.C. 1344) and Section 103 of the Marine Protection, Research and Sanctuaries Act of 1972 (33 U.S.C. 1413). Each of these laws will be discussed in further detail below.

THE RIVER AND HARBOR ACT OF 1899

Until recently, the regulatory programs of the Corps of Engineers were administered only pursuant to various sections in the River and Harbor Act of 1899. These include: Section 9 (33 U.S.C. 401); Section 10 (33 U.S.C. 403); Section 11 (33 U.S.C. 404); and Section 13 (33 U.S.C. 407).

---

*This material is from the "supplementary information" provided by the Corps of Engineers as a preface to final rules for its programs implementing § 404 of the Water Act and related statutes, 42 Fed. Reg. 37122-64 (July 19, 1977).

Section 9 requires a permit from the Corps of Engineers to construct any dam or dike in a navigable water of the United States. The consent of Congress is also required if the navigable water is interstate, and the consent of the appropriate state legislature is required if the water is intrastate. Bridges and causeways constructed in navigable waters of the United States also require permits under Section 9, but the authority to issue these permits was transferred to the U.S. Coast Guard in 1966 when the Department of Transportation was created.

Section 10 identifies other types of structures or work in or affecting navigable waters of the United States that are prohibited unless permitted by the Corps of Engineers. However, unlike Section 9, the consent of Congress or a State legislature is not required. Section 10 requires permits from the Corps for structures in navigable waters such as piers, breakwaters, bulkheads, revetments, power transmission lines, and aids to navigation. It also requires permits for various types of work performed in navigable waters, including dredging and stream channelization, excavation and filling. In addition, any work that is performed outside the limits of a navigable water which affects its navigable capacity may also require a Section 10 permit.

The 1899 Act was enacted to protect navigation and the navigable capacity of the nation's waters. Section 11 focuses on this basic concern by allowing the Secretary of the Army to establish harbor lines landward of which piers, wharves, bulkheads, and other structures or work could be built or performed without a Corps permit. However, as will be noted below, these harborlines now serve only as guides to defining the offshore limits of these activities from the standpoint of their impact on navigation. They can no longer be relied upon as a substitute for the requirement to obtain a permit under the 1899 Act.

Violation of the provisions and requirements of Section 9, 10 or 11 of the 1899 Act can result in criminal prosecution. Section 12 specifies criminal fines that range between $500 and $2,500 per day of violation and/or imprisonment, either or both of which may be imposed upon conviction. In addition, Section 12 also provides for injunctive relief that may be sought by the United States to respond to violations of these Sections, including the restoration of the area to its original condition. See *U.S. v. Moretti,* 478 F.2d 418 (5th Cir. 1975).

Until 1968, the Corps administered the 1899 Act regulatory program only to protect navigation and the navigable capacity of the nation's waters. The permit requirements of the Act were limited in their application to waters that were presently used as highways for the transportation of interstate or foreign commerce.

On December 18, 1968, the Department of the Army revised its policy with respect to the review of permit applications under Sections 9 and 10 of the 1899 Act. It published in the FEDERAL REGISTER a list of additional factors besides navigation that would be considered in the review of these applications. These included: fish and wildlife; conservation; pollution; aesthetics; ecology; and the general public interest. (33 CFR 209.120.)

The 1968 change in policy identified this new type of review as a "public interest review." It was adopted in response to a growing national concern for environmental values as they related to our nation's water resources and in response to related Federal legislation, such as the Fish and Wildlife Coordination Act (16 U.S.C. 661 et seq.), that required the consideration of some of these concerns in Federal decision-making. Enactment of the National Environmental Policy Act on January 1, 1970 (42 U.S.C. 4331 et seq.) gave further support to this change in policy.

The "public interest review" received its first judicial test in the case of *Zabel v. Tabb,* 430 F. 2d 199 (5th Cir. 1970), *cert. den.* 401 U.S. 910 (1972) in which the Court upheld the denial by the Corps of a landfill permit for fish and wildlife reasons (and not reasons related to navigation). In reaching this decision, the Court reaffirmed the Department of the Army's position that it was "acting under a Congressional mandate to collaborate and consider all of these factors" when it reached that decision.

In further response to the adoption of this public interest review, the Department of the Army revised its harborline regulation (33 CFR 209.150) on May 27, 1970. This revision made it clear that permits were required for any work commenced landward of an established harborline after May 27, 1970, and that these permit applications would receive a full public interest review. Of course, navigation concerns in this public interest review will be guided, in large part, by the presence of established harborlines.

During 1972, the Corps of Engineers reviewed all judicial decisions in which the term "navigable waters of the United States" had been interpreted in order to identify all waters to which Sections 9 and 10 of the 1899 Act could be applied. This analysis was made in response to the Federal government's growing concern over the protection of the nation's water resources and the need to protect those resources through the full mandate of available Federal laws.

On September 9, 1972, the Corps of Engineers published an administrative definition of the term "navigable waters of the United States" in the FEDERAL REGISTER (subsequently codified as 33 CFR 209.260). This definition was intended for use in the Corps' administration of Sections 9 and 10 of the 1899 Act ***.

*   *   *

THE REFUSE ACT PERMIT PROGRAM

On April 7, 1971, the Corps of Engineers implemented the first nationwide program to regulate the discharge of pollutants into the nation's waters. Authority for this permit program was based on Section 13 of the River and Harbor Act of 1899 (33 U.S.C. 407), commonly referred to as "The Refuse Act," which prohibits the discharge of "refuse matter" into navigable waters of the United States or their tributaries, or onto the banks of such waters if the "refuse matter" is likely to be washed into a navigable water. Regulations to implement this permit program were published in 33 CFR 209.131. On December 24, 1971, the permit program was enjoined by the District Court for the District of Columbia in the case of *Kalur v. Resor*, 335 F. Supp. 1 (D.D.C.1971).

The Refuse Act permit program remained suspended until October 18, 1972, when Congress enacted the FWPCA. Section 402 of the FWPCA established the National Pollutant Discharge Elimination System program, which subsumed the Refuse Act permit program. Section 402 (a)(5) provides that no permits may be issued under Section 13 of the 1899 Act for discharges into waters of the United States after 18 October 1972. However, the Refuse Act prohibitions can only be lifted by the issuance of an NPDES permit, and the Refuse Act remains a viable Federal enforcement mechanism for the discharge of pollutants into these waters without such a permit.

SECTION 404 OF THE FWPCA

On October 18, 1972, Congress enacted the Federal Water Pollution Control Act Amendments of 1972 with the announced purpose of restoring and maintaining the chemical, physical, and biological integrity of the Nation's waters. ***

Section 301 of the FWPCA prohibits the discharge of pollutants from discernible conveyances (defined as "point sources") into "navigable waters," (defined in the FWPCA as "the waters of the United States, including the territorial seas"), unless the discharge is in compliance with Section 402 or 404 of the Act. ***

Section 404 of the FWPCA establishes a permit program, administered by the Secretary of the Army, acting through the Chief of Engineers, to regulate the discharge, into the waters of the United States, of dredged material and of those pollutants that comprise fill material. Applications for Section 404 permits are evaluated by using guidelines developed by the Administrator of EPA, in conjunction with the Secretary of the Army (see 40 CFR 230). The Chief of Engineers can make a decision to issue a permit that is inconsistent with those guidelines if the interests of navigation require. Section 404 (c) gives the Administrator, EPA, further authority, subject to certain procedures, to restrict or prohibit the discharge of any dredged or fill material that may cause an unacceptable adverse effect on municipal water supplies, shellfish beds and fishery areas (including spawning and breeding areas), wildlife, or recreational areas.

Violation of the prohibition specified in Section 301 of the FWPCA against discharging pollutants into the waters of the United States without a required permit under Section 402 or 404, or permit conditions, or of other requirements of the FWPCA, can result in civil fines of not more than $10,000 per day of violation, criminal fines of up to $50,000 per day of violation, imprisonment, and/or injunctive relief, including restoration of the area to its original condition. The exact provisions for Federal enforcement of the FWPCA are established in Section 309. (33 U.S.C. 1319).

*   *   *

Deltona Corporation v. United States

657 F. 2d 1184 (Ct. Cl. 1981)

Before FRIEDMAN, Chief Judge, SKELTON, Senior Judge, and KUNZIG, Judge.

KUNZIG, Judge, delivered the opinion of the court:

In this case, plaintiff contends that it has suffered an uncompensated taking as the consequence of federal regulation affecting its development of a planned subdivision along the

Gulf coast of Florida. The statutes in question — § 10 of the Rivers and Harbors Appropriation Act of 1899 and § 404 of the Federal Water Pollution Control Act Amendments of 1972 — and implementing regulations thereunder, prohibit, *inter alia*, dredging and filling in navigable waters without the authorization of the Department of the Army. The latter, stressing environmental factors, has thus far steadfastly refused to grant plaintiff the permits it needs to finish its project. We hold that while plaintiff may indeed have sustained an economic loss, the loss is not such as to constitute a Fifth Amendment taking under the circumstances herein.

I. BACKGROUND

A. Applicable Statutes and Regulations: A Pattern of Stiffening Requirements.

1. *Section 10 of the Rivers and Harbors Appropriation Act of 1899* (Rivers and Harbors Act), provides in part:

> That the creation of any obstruction not affirmatively authorized by Congress, to the navigable capacity of any of the navigable waters of the United States is hereby prohibited. . . .

The section goes on to outlaw various structures in any navigable water of the United States except those initiated by plans recommended by the Chief of Engineers and authorized by the Secretary of the Army. Section 10 then states that it shall not be lawful to excavate or fill, or in any manner to alter or modify the . . . capacity of . . . the channel of any navigable water of the United States, unless the work has been recommended by the Chief of Engineers and authorized by the Secretary of War [now the Army] prior to beginning the same.

*   *   *

The Secretary of the Army has delegated to the Corps of Engineers the authority to issue or deny Section 10 permits. ***

The Supreme Court has described Section 10 as a type of "general proscription" or "ban," the intent being "to benefit the public at large by empowering the federal government to exercise its authority over interstate commerce with respect to obstructions" in the navi-

gable waters of the United States. *California v. Sierra Club*, 451 U.S. 287 (1981).

2. *Section 404 of the Federal Water Pollution Control Act Amendments of 1972*, (FWPCA), generally prohibits the "discharge of dredged or fill material into . . . navigable waters" absent a permit from the Army Corps of Engineers. *See also* FWPCA § 301.[4] The term "navigable waters" is defined by FWPCA as "the waters of the United States, including the territorial seas," 33 U.S.C. § 1362(7)(1976). It is now well settled that Congress, by adopting this 1972 definition, "asserted federal jurisdiction over the nation's waters to the maximum extent permissible under the Commerce Clause of the Constitution,"***and intended a departure from the traditional tests used to delimit Corps jurisdiction under the Rivers and Harbors Act, *viz,* tidal waters extending to the mean high water mark and/or waters susceptible to use to transport interstate or foreign commerce.***

*   *   *

3. *The implementing regulations* adopted by the Corps of Engineers pursuant to its statutory authority have grown increasingly complex and rigorous since the late 1960's. This, for us, is the key legal event in the case at bar.

Until 1968, the Corps administered the Rivers and Harbors Act solely in the interest of navigation and the navigable capacity of the nation's waters. However, on December 18, 1968, in response to a growing national concern for environmental values and related federal legislation, the Corps revised its regulations to implement a new type of review termed "public interest review." Besides navigation, the Corps would consider the following additional factors in reviewing permit applications: fish and wildlife, conservation, pollution, aesthetics, ecology, and the general public interest.

---

[4]Section 404(a) provides: "The Secretary of the Army, acting through the Chief of Engineers, may issue permits, after notice and opportunity for public hearings for the discharge of dredged or fill material into the navigable waters at specified disposal sites." The companion provision, Section 301(a), reads: "Except as in compliance with this section and section . . . 404 of this Act, the discharge of any pollutant by any person shall be unlawful."

On April 4, 1974, the Corps published further revised regulations so as to:

a) incorporate new permit programs under Section 404 of the FWPCA;

b) incorporate the requirements of new federal legislation by adding to the factors to be weighed in the public interest review, including: economics; historic values; flood damage prevention; land-use classification; recreation; water supply and water quality;

c) adopt further criteria to be considered in the evaluation of each permit application, including the desirability of using appropriate alternatives; the extent and permanence of the beneficial and/or detrimental effects of the proposed activity; and the cumulative effect of the activity when considered in relation to other activities in the same general area;

d) institute a full-fledged wetlands policy to protect wetlands subject to the Corps' jurisdiction from unnecessary destruction.

The inauguration of the wetlands policy should especially be noted, as it plays a leading role in the forthcoming scenario.

The last general revision of Corps regulations occurred on July 19, 1977. The purpose was merely to simplify and reorganize the existing body of rules to make them more understandable.

B. Facts.

In 1964, plaintiff, Deltona, purchased for $7,500,000 a 10,000 acre parcel on the Florida Gulf coast with the intention of developing a water-oriented residential community, Marco Island. The property, then completely undeveloped, lay astride the mean high water mark and contained large areas of dense mangrove vegetation, including wetlands. Deltona's master plan called for more than 12,000 single family tracts, numerous multifamily sites, school and park areas, shopping districts, marinas, beaches and regular utilities. Structurally, the project revolved about the "finger-fill" or "landfinger"

concept and would necessitate considerable dredging and filling as well as the permanent destruction of much of the natural mangrove vegetation.

Deltona divided Marco Island into five construction or permit areas to be built consecutively. These five areas, in order of scheduled completion, were Marco River, Roberts Bay, Collier Bay, Barfield Bay and Big Key. Each separate stage would take three to four years to complete. While partitioned for these limited purposes, in operation, the Marco Island community would be a thoroughly integrated, unified whole.

Because Deltona's proposed dredge and fill activities were to take place in "navigable waters of the United States" as that term is used in the Rivers and Harbors Act, it was required to obtain the proper permit from the Army Corps of Engineers before any of the work could legally get underway in 1964. Also, because its proposed dredge and fill activities were to take place in "navigable waters" as used in the FWPCA, Deltona was required after 1972 to obtain a permit from the Army Corps under that statutory scheme as well. Deltona's problems which culminated in the instant law suit stem from its inability to obtain all the permits which it needs to complete its project.

When in 1964 Deltona applied for a dredge and fill permit for the Marco River area, the Corps' policy, as we have seen, was merely to consider the likely adverse impact which issuance would have upon navigation. In this case, the Corps routinely granted the necessary permit on October 27, 1964.

The second construction area was Roberts Bay. Deltona obtained its dredge and fill permit on December 18, 1969, this time pursuant to the so-called "public interest review" which had been adopted by the Corps a year earlier. The permit, however, was issued subject to the following express conditions: first, Deltona's "understand[ing] that all permit applications are independent of each other and that the granting of this permit does not necessarily mean that future applications for a permit or permits in the general area of the proposed work by Marco Island Development Corporation or others will be similarly granted; second, its "agree[ment] . . . not [to] advertise or offer for sale as suitable building lots parcels of land which (1) are in whole or in part seaward of the mean high water line and which (2) could not be made suitable for the erection of residences or other structures in the absence of a Department of the Army fill permit that has not yet been issued."

Deltona applied for Corps of Engineers dredge and fill permits for the Collier Bay, Barfield Bay, and Big Key construction areas on April 9, 1973. By this time, the permit requirement imposed by § 404 of the FWPCA had been added to that already imposed by § 10 of the Rivers and Harbors Act. In a written decision dated April 15, 1976, the Chief of Engineers denied Deltona's application to dredge and fill in Barfield Bay and Big Key, while granting its application for Collier Bay.

The permit denials were premised upon "overriding national factors of the public interest." The decision indicated that "Corps regulation[s] . . . identify certain types of wetlands considered to perform functions important to the public interest."

> These include wetlands that serve important natural biological functions (including food chain production, general habitat, and nesting, spawning, rearing and resting sites for aquatic or land species); wetlands set aside as sanctuaries or refuges; wetlands which are significant in shielding other areas from wave action, erosion, or storm damage (including barrier beaches); and wetlands that serve as valuable storage areas for storm and flood waters.

The decision continued: "A review of the permit file clearly indicates that the mangrove wetlands involved in these permit applications fulfill each of these functions in a most significant way." Consequently, under governing regulations, denial of the permits was mandated unless it could be shown that "the benefits of the proposed alteration . . . outweigh[ed] the damage to the wetlands resource, and that the proposed alteration [was] necessary to realize those benefits." The Chief of Engineers concluded that Deltona had failed to make the requisite factual showing as to both elements.

By contrast, "[t]he permit file reveal[ed] that a significant amount of destruction ha[d] already occurred to the mangrove wetlands associated with the Collier Bay application" and that a "considerable amount of dredging and filling" had taken place, resulting in the creation of a large number of lots and approximately forty homes.[10] The Chief of Engineers wrote: "It is my position, therefore, that this area has been already so dedicated to development that it would no longer be in the public interest to preclude completion of that development."

Deltona quickly filed suit in federal district court challenging the legality of the permit denials under the Administrative Procedure Act, 5 U.S.C. §§ 701-706 (1976). On January 14, 1981, the court ruled that the Corps of Engineers had acted reasonably and lawfully in denying Deltona the permits to dredge and fill in Barfield Bay and Big Key. *Deltona v. Alexander*, No. 76-473 [15 ERC 1508] (M.D.Fla., Jan. 14, 1981). The *validity* of the permit denials is therefore not before this court. Deltona does not take issue with this basic point.

Deltona notes with much vigor that prior to the adverse decision by the Corps of Engineers, it had obtained all the necessary county and state permits to go forward with the development of Barfield Bay and Big Key and had entered into contracts of sale covering approximately 90% of the lots in those two areas.[11] As a practical matter, however, it cannot consummate its plans

---

[10]The construction had occurred around 1971 at a time when there was some confusion concerning Corps jurisdiction over the particular tract involved. The tract was also closely associated with the more fully developed areas in Marco River and Roberts Bay. Overall, Collier Bay contained only a very small amount of mangrove vegetation.

[11]Under Deltona's plan, individual lots at the Marco Island community were to be purchased from Deltona for cash or on an installment basis, with purchasers making a down payment and subsequent installment payments over various periods of time, depending on the type of lot, location, and payment plan selected by the individual purchaser. In some cases, periodic payments on contracts would extend over a period of time as long as 8½ years from the date of sale.

without the federal permits. The question before this court is whether plaintiff has suffered an uncompensated taking as the consequence of federal regulation. Under the specific facts and circumstances of this case, and the tests enunciated by the courts, we conclude that plaintiff has not.

II. ANALYSIS

A. Basic Constitutional Principles.

The Just Compensation Clause of the Fifth Amendment provides: "[N]or shall private property be taken for public use, without just compensation."***

*   *   *

It is well established as a matter of law that government regulation can effect a Fifth Amendment taking. *See, e.g., Penn Central Transp. Co. v. New York City,* 438 U.S. 104, 123 (1978) (no taking found on the specific facts of that case).***

While "Government hardly could go on if to some extent values incident to property could not be diminished without paying for every such change in the general law," *Pennsylvania Coal Co. v Mahon,* 260 U.S. 393, 413 (1922), the principle generally applied is that "if regulation goes too far it will be recognized as a taking." *Id.* at 415 ***.

B. The Crucial Factor Herein and the Parties' Positions.

The crucial factor in the case is that since the late 1960's the regulatory jurisdiction of the Army Corps of Engineers has substantially expanded pursuant to § 404 of the FWPCA and—under the spur of steadily evolving legislation — the Corps has greatly added to the substantive criteria governing the issuance of dredge and fill permits within its jurisdiction. Recall that when Deltona initially purchased the Marco Island property in 1964, the regulatory jurisdiction of the Corps was limited to "navigable waters of the United States" and the lone substantive criterion for the issuance of Corps dredge and fill permits was the likely adverse impact upon navigation. Pursuant to this relatively undemanding standard, Deltona routinely succeeded in 1964 in obtaining the first permit for which it applied. By 1976, when the Barfield Bay and Big Key applications were denied, the situation had been radically transformed. The Corps' jurisdiction now extended to all "navigable waters" and the substantive criteria for granting permits had been significantly stiffened. Deltona's particular stumbling block, as we have seen, was its inability to satisfy the Corps' recently inaugurated wetlands protection policy. The impact is self-evident. As the result of an unforeseen change in the law, Deltona is no longer able to capitalize upon a reasonable investment-backed expectation which it had every justification to rely upon until the law began to change.

*   *   *

C. Tests for Determining Whether Regulation Effects a Taking.

*   *   *

While "[t]he economic impact of the regulation on the claimant and, particularly, the extent to which the regulation has interfered with distinct investment-backed expectations are, of course, relevant considerations," *Penn Central Transp. Co., supra,* the decisions of the Supreme Court "uniformly reject the proposition that diminution in property value, standing alone, can establish a 'taking.'" *Id.* at 131, *citing, Euclid v. Ambler Realty Co.,* 272 U.S. 365 (1926)(75% diminution in value caused by zoning law); *Hadachek v. Sebastian,* 239 U.S. 394(1915)(87.5% diminution in value). Similarly, the Court has branded as fallacious the "contention that a 'taking' must be found to have occurred whenever the land-use restriction may be characterized as imposing a 'servitude' on the claimant's parcel." *Penn Central Transp. Co., supra,* at 130 n.27. Instead, "the 'taking' issue in these contexts is resolved by focusing on the uses the regulations permit." *Id.* at 131. In one of its most recent pronouncements, the Court crystallized its thinking as follows: "The application of a general zoning law to particular property effects a taking if the ordinance does not substantially advance legitimate state interests . . . or denies a[n] owner economically viable use of his land . . . ." *Agins v. City of Tiburon,* 447 U.S. 255, 260 (1980); *accord, Hodel v. Virginia Surface Mining and Reclamation Ass'n,* 452 U.S. 264, (1981). *** The *Agins* Court also commented that "the question necessarily requires a weighing of private and public interests." *Id.* at 261.

In applying the foregoing considerations, it is important to bear in mind the Supreme Court's admonition:

"Taking" jurisprudence does not divide a single parcel into discrete segments and attempt to determine whether rights in a particular segment have been entirely abrogated. In deciding whether a particular governmental action has effected a taking, this Court focuses rather both on the character of the action and on the nature and extent of the interference with rights in the parcel *as a whole* . . . .

Penn Central Transp. Co., supra, at 130-131 (emphasis supplied).

D. Application of These Tests to the
   Case at Bar.

*   *   *

Although we have accepted that the expansion of the Corps' regulatory jurisdiction and the stiffening of its requirements for granting permits have substantially frustrated Deltona's reasonable investment-backed expectation with respect to Barfield Bay and Big Key, this development neither "extinguish[es] a fundamental attribute of ownership," *id.*, nor prevents Deltona from deriving many other economically viable uses from its parcel — however delineated. Indeed, the residual economic value of the land is enormous, both proportionately and absolutely. A few statistics will suffice. In the aggregate, Barfield Bay and Big Key contain only 20% of the total acreage of Deltona's original purchase in 1964 and 33% of the developable lots. All the necessary federal permits for the development of the remainder of Marco Island — Marco River, Roberts Bay, and Collier Bay — have been granted. If we focus solely upon the three construction areas which became subject to the new federal restrictions promulgated during the early 1970's — Collier Bay, Barfield Bay, and Big Key — the salient fact emerges that while Deltona has been blocked from going forward at Barfield Bay and Big Key, it has obtained

all the necessary clearances for Collier Bay, a tract approximately 25% of the three areas together. Most striking, even within Barfield Bay and Big Key, there are located 111 acres of uplands which can be developed without obtaining a Corps permit and whose total market value is approximately $2.5 million. Deltona only paid $1.24 million for all of Barfield Bay and Big Key in 1964.

Therefore, in the terms of *Agins, supra,* the statutes and regulations at issue in this case substantially advance legitimate and important governmental interests and do not deprive Deltona of the economically viable use of its land. Instead, Deltona's remaining land uses are plentiful and its residual economic position very great. Reduced to its essentials, this case merely presents an instance of some diminution in value. The Supreme Court, however, has squarely held that mere diminution, standing alone, is insufficient to establish a taking. *See Penn Central Transp. Co., supra,* at 131. Thus, "it cannot be said that the impact of general land-use regulations has denied [plaintiff] the 'justice and fairness' guaranteed by the Fifth . . . Amendment . . . ." *Agins, supra,* at 263.

Moreover, when Deltona acquired the property in 1964, it knew that the development it contemplated could take place only if it obtained the necessary permits from the Corps of Engineers. Although at that time Deltona had every reason to believe that those permits would be forthcoming when it subsequently sought them, it also must have been aware that the standards and conditions governing the issuance of permits could change. ***

In *Penn Central Transp. Co., supra,* the Supreme Court rejected as "quite simply untenable" the contention that property owners "may establish a 'taking' simply by showing that they have been denied the ability to exploit a property interest that they heretofore had believed was available for development . . . ." *Supra,* at 130. That is precisely this case. Deltona has been denied the ability to exploit its property by constructing a project that it theretofore had believed "was available for development."

While plaintiff may very well be correct in

its alternative assertion that it has been denied the highest and best economic use for its property, it is obvious from the Supreme Court tests we have cited that such an occurrence does *not* form a sufficient predicate for a taking.***

*　　*　　*

We are not insensitive to the fact that the permit denials have placed Deltona in a highly difficult situation, legally and financially. The Fifth Amendment, however, does not provide a solution. In addition, Deltona certainly bears a great deal of responsibility for its current plight by having rushed into many land sale contracts before having obtained all the necessary federal permits which would enable it to meet its obligations. Note that Deltona had been specifically warned against this when it obtained its Roberts Bay permit in 1969.

In sum, we have rejected plaintiff's argument that the denial of highest and best use can constitute a taking. We have found that subsequent to Deltona's purchase of the land in question, a significant change occurred in the statutes and regulations affecting its land-use, and that this development did have a significant impact upon the values incident to Deltona's Marco Island property. However, in view of the many remaining economically viable uses for plaintiff's property, and the substantial public benefits which the new statutes and regulations serve to bring about, we have concluded that no taking occurred.

*　　*　　*

NOTES

1. Deltona's experience illustrates the impact of Section 404 of the 1972 Amendments, and the Corps' progressively more stringent interpretation of its responsibilities thereunder, upon the prospects of an applicant seeking to obtain a permit to dredge and fill in wetlands.

2. What if Deltona had made no application for a permit for any of the five areas until after the 1972 Amendments and all permission to engage in any dredging and filling in any wetlands on the entire parcel had been denied? Would it have been arbitrary and capricious for the Corps to base its denial exclusively on a policy of preserving wetlands areas demonstrated to be critical to the maintenance of a viable estuarine ecology? Would such a total restriction have allowed recovery for a "taking"?

3. If today someone bought a partially submerged reef covered with mangroves for $500,000, the entire value of which was based on its potential for resort development, would a taking occur if the investment were completely lost in the denial of a 404 permit?

4.What impact, if any, will the Supreme Court's 1985 decision in *United States v. Riverside Bayview Homes, Inc., supra* page 170, have on recovery of compensation by those denied dredge and fill permits?

5.For the only case thus far discovered by the author in which a landowner denied a dredge and fill permit by the Corps was held to have suffered a "taking" entitling it to just compensation, see *Florida Rock Industries, Inc. v. United States*, 22 ERC 1943 (Ct. Cl. 1985).

The details of the Corps' policies and procedures for issuance of dredge and fill permits under Section 404 of the Clean Water Act, as well as under the Rivers and Harbors Act and other related statutes, can be found at 33 C.F.R. §§ 320.1 - 384.13 (1985).

Most basically, Section 404 establishes a separate permit system for the discharge of dredged or fill material. Such dredged or fill material subject to Section 404 is excepted from the general permit system under Section 402. Permits are issued by the Army Corps of Engineers pursuant to EPA guidelines which protect environmental values. If the EPA guidelines would prohibit a disposal site, the Corps may nevertheless approve the site because of "the economic impact of the site on navigation and anchorage." Section 404(b). EPA, however, has the final authority: it may deny or restrict a site for disposal if, after public hearing, it concludes that the discharge of dredged or fill materials "will have an unacceptable adverse effect on municipal water supplies, shellfish beds and fishery areas (including spawning and breeding areas), wildlife, or recreational areas." Section 404(c).

The wide-ranging factors and policies considered by the Corps of Engineers in exercising its discretion to issue, deny, or condition a dredge and fill permit is set out in 33 C.F.R. § 320.4 (1985). Also, keep in mind that most proposals for dredge and fill permits by the Corps are subject to the substantive and procedural requirements of the National Environmental Policy Act. *See* the Corps' "Policies and Procedures for Implementing NEPA," 33 C.F.R. § 230 (1985); *Sierra Club v. Sigler*, 695 F.2d 957 (5th Cir. 1983).

Prior to the 1977 Amendments, permit-issuing authority under the FWPCA for dredge and fill activities could not be delegated to the states, as could permitting authority for discharges of other pollutants under Section 402. The 1977 Amendments, however, allow permitting authority to be delegated to the states for discharges of dredged or fill material into waters other than those meeting the traditional test of navigability and their adjacent wetlands. Such delegation follows standards similar to those required for approval of state NPDES permit plans under Section 402. EPA retains supervisory authority over the state permitting programs and can veto individual permits or withdraw permitting authority from the state if it finds that the state program is not being administered according to statutory requirements. Section 404(t), however, separately guarantees the states the independent right to impose their own requirements and thereby concurrently control dredging and filling within their jurisdictions (to the extent such state requirements do not adversely affect navigation).

The 1977 Amendments gave the Corps authority to issue five-year "general" permits on a state, regional, or national basis for any category of activities involving discharges of dredged or fill material if it determines that the activities "will have only minimal cumulative adverse effect on the environment." Section 404(e). For activities within such a general permit no individual permit is required. Regulations promulgated in 1977 established five nationwide general permits for minor dredging and filling activities (such as utility lines and minor road work) and two nationwide general permits for any type of discharge into (1) the headwaters (with streamflow of less than 5 c.f.s.) of non-tidal rivers and streams and their adjacent wetlands and (2) lakes less than ten acres in size.

Regulations promulgated in 1982 increased the number of general permits for specific activities to twenty-five and established an expansive general permit for all discharges into any non-tidal waters that are not part of a surface water system tributary to interstate waters or navigable waters of the United States (eliminating the acreage limitation of the 1977 regulations). 33 CFR 330.4, 330.5. The Corps also asserted the authority to issue other general permits whenever it "would result in avoiding unnecessary duplication of regulatory control exercised by another federal, state, or local agency provided it has been determined that the environmental consequences of the action are individually and cumulatively minimal." 33 CFR 323.2 (n) (2). Under this assertion of authority, the Corps created several general permit programs that substantially turned over regulation of most dredge and fill activities to the states. A suit filed by the National Wildlife Federation challenging the legality of these general permit programs resulted in a settlement whereby the Corps would resume regulatory control in significant respects: *e.g.*, proposals that would affect ten acres or more of wetlands would require individual permits; those that would affect more than one acre would require notice to the Corps, which might then impose conditions on the project. Also, the Corps agreed to abide by the broad jurisdictional definition of "wetlands" recognized by the Fifth Circuit in *Avoyelles Sportmen's League, Inc. v. Marsh*, 715 F.2d 897 (5th Cir. 1983).

A comprehensive survey of cases involving federal dredge and fill permitting in wetlands areas can be found in Want, *Federal Wetlands Law: the Cases and the Problems*, 8 HARV. ENVTL. L. REV. 1 (1984).

Also, the 1977 Amendments added a new provision whereby certain activities, primarily those related to agriculture and forestry, would be exempted from the 404 permit program. Application of this new subsection (f) was a major issue in the case which follows.

Avoyelles Sportsmen's League, Inc.
v.
Alexander
473 F. Supp. 525 (W.D. La. 1979)

SCOTT, N.S., Chief D. J.

Plaintiffs brought this declaratory and injunctive action alleging that landclearing operations being carried on by the private defendants have and will: alter and modify the course, condition and capacity of the navigable waters of the United States in violation of § 10 of the Rivers and Harbors Act of 1899. 33 U.S.C.A. § 403; result in the discharge of dredged and fill material into the waters of the United States in violation of § 404 of the Federal Water Pollution Control Act (hereinafter FWPCA). 33 U.S.C.A. § 1344; result in the discharge of pollutants into the waters of the United States in violation of § 402 of the FWPCA, 33 U.S.C.A. § 1342; and violate Louisiana State law under Louisiana Civil Code arts. 667 and 857. The plaintiffs requested that we compel the federal defendants to regulate the landclearing activities and enjoin the landclearing activities until the extent of the federal defendants' jurisdiction has been determined and permits applied for under 33 U.S.C.A. §§ 403, 1342 and 1344.

The land subject to this proceeding and being cleared is an approximately 20,000 acre tract (hereinafter referred to as the Lake Long Tract) situated in Avoyelles Parish, Louisiana between the Grassy Lake State Management Area and the Spring Bayou State Management Area. It lies within the Bayou Natchitoches basin which, along with the Ouachita, Black and Tensas river basins, makes up the Red River backwater area. The Bayou Natchitoches basin itself is an area comprised of approximately 140,000 acres. Much of this basin has been cleared of forest but before the private defendants' land clearing operations commenced, approximately 80,000 acres of this area still was forested. Consequently, prior to the commencement of the private defendants' land clearing operations, the Lake Long tract represented one-quarter of the remaining forested acreage in the Bayou Natchitoches basin.

The Bayou Natchitoches basin serves as a major overflow or backwater area for the Red River. Backwater flooding occurs in the Bayou Natchitoches basin when the Red River rises to a point where the waters cannot flow downstream efficiently and instead flow west into Bayou Natchitoches, then into Bayou Jeansonne, over the Lake Long tract and further westward into the Spring Bayou State Management area. Generally, during the recession of backwater floods, the flood waters on the Lake Long tract drain in an easterly direction back into the Red River.

More than half of the tract, i.e., everything at or below 45.8 feet MSL, is subject to the average annual flood.[4] Virtually all of the tract, i.e., everything at or below 49.6 feet MSL, is subject to the average biannual flood.

The clearing of the Lake Long Tract, began in June of 1978. Sometime prior to that loggers had harvested much of the commerically valuable hardwoods with chainsaws. Thereafter, the private defendants took various steps to remove all the remaining trees and vegetation from the tract so that it could be put to agricultural use and specifically into soybean production.

Initially, bulldozers outfitted with shearing blades cut the timber and vegetation at or just above ground level. The shearing blades were V-shaped, had a serrated edge and flat bottom and were approximately 18-20 feet in length. The blades were adjusted to be free floating so that they would ride along the top surface of the ground. Occasionally, however, the blades would gouge the surface of the ground. Although the blades were adjusted to ride on the ground surface, they did scrape the leaf litter and humus that overlaid the soil as they moved from tree to tree.

After the shearing was completed in a section, bulldozers outfitted with rake blades pushed the felled trees into windrows. The upper portion of the raking blade was solid whereas the lower portion had tines that permitted soil to pass through the openings. The raking blades were also outfitted so that they generally operated on top of the soil. However, in the process of windrowing the trees and debris, soil and leaf litter was also scraped into the windrows. Various photos introduced into evidence showing the burned windrows revealed that soil was piled up during the windrowing process. It is not clear whether the blades themselves or the broom-like action of the trees and brush that they were pushing actually scraped the soil and the overlying leaf litter. In any event the photographic evidence clearly demonstrated that soil and leaf litter

was piled up during the windrowing process—this movement filled in low areas and along with the discing which followed, had a levelling effect on the surface of the land.

The trees and other vegetation that had been windrowed were then burned. The remaining ashes were later disced into and across the tract. Some of the felled trees and other debris would not burn. This material was buried in four or five pits, each approximately 50 feet long and 6 feet deep that had been dug with backhoes by the private defendants.

Tractors pulling chunk rakes would go over the areas that had been sheared and windrowed and rake together any remaining debris. Basically, the chunk rakes were sets of tines that were outfitted on cultivators that had had their blades removed. The chunk rakes gathered the small debris into piles where it was presumably burned. These ashes were also disced into the soil.

After the shearing, windrowing and chunk raking the land was disced to prepare it for soybean cultivation. A disc is a bowl-shaped blade that cuts into the ground and fluffs the soil up. The discs used on this tract were 24 inches in diameter and would cut into the ground approximately 9 inches. During discing some soil would ride in front of the disc and would be redeposited in other areas of the tract, resulting in substantial displacement and redepositing of the soil itself.

Defendants also dug a drainage ditch that was approximately three-quarters of a mile long. The earth excavated from the ditch was piled alongside the ditch and was to be spread over the adjacent area. Construction of at least four or five miles of additional ditches were contemplated for soybean cultivation.

On November 7, 1978 we granted a temporary restraining order whereby the private defendants were prohibited from engaging in any further landclearing activity. More specifically, they were prohibited from conducting ditch excavation, altering the surface of the land, logging, except by chainsaw, destroying vegetation, plowing, discing, or discharging any biologic material or pollutants onto the

---

[4]Basically the average annual flood means certain elevations on the tract can be expected to flood every year based on a statistical average.

land. They were permitted to clean up debris already on the ground.

On January 17, 1979 it was ordered that the federal defendants prepare a final wetland determination within sixty days. The private defendants were permitted to engage in normal cultivation, plowing and seeding without obtaining a permit on the land already cleared, approximately 10,000 acres. The private defendants were ordered to and agreed under protest, to apply for permits under § 404 for any ditching, levee construction and drainage work construction on the land already cleared. As to the uncleared land, the prohibitions of the temporary restraining order remained unchanged.

On March 26, 1979 the federal defendants filed their final wetland determination which designated certain portions of the tract, including substantial portions of the cleared lands, to be wetlands. Thereafter the private defendants filed objections to this determination.

The wetland determination also contained a statement concerning what activities of the private defendants were subject to the permit requirements of § 404.

"A section 404 permit is not required for the shearing of trees where no earth (other than de minimis)is moved in the process and the trees are promptly removed through burning or other means. However, under the facts of this case as they are known to the government, a section 404 permit will be required for construction of drainage ditches in the wetland area delineated by the government in Exhibit I. While it is the government's understanding that the non-Federal defendants do not plan to build any dikes or levees in the waters of the United States, permits will be required if their plans change. Plowing, discing, and raking of the sort observed on the tract so far will not require a permit."

Both the plaintiffs and the private defendants objected to the Government's statement on the activities issue. Thereafter, it was decided to bifurcate the jurisdictional issue, i.e., what areas

of the tract constitute wetlands, from the activities issue outlined in the statement attached to the government's determination. In accordance with this bifurcation it was agreed that the activities issue would be tried first. For the purposes of the trial on this issue it was stipulated, without prejudice to any party's rights to contest the validity of the final wetland determination, that the final wetland determination filed on March 26, 1979 was correct and that the wetland area was subject to the strictures of the FWPCA. Consequently, the only issue now before us is whether the type of activities allowed in the government's statement, such as the shearing of trees to convert forested wetlands to other purposes, require permits under the FWPCA and § 10 of the Rivers and Harbors Act of 1899. We hold that permits are required under § 404 of the FWPCA.

The declared objective of the FWPCA "is to restore and maintain the chemical, physical, and biological integrity of the nation's water." § 101(a) of the Act. Basically, two different types of pollution, subject to different programs of regulation, are envisioned by the Act, those that emanate from point sources and those that derive from non-point sources. Point sources of pollution except those exempted under § 404(f)(1) are regulated by permit programs under §§ 402 and 404 of the FWPCA.[5] Other sources of pol-

---

[5]The phrase "point source pollution" as utilized hereafter shall refer to point source pollution not exempt under the provisions of § 401(f)(1).

We are well aware of the dispute as to whether the activities mentioned in § 404(f)(1) are excluded from the Act because Congress felt that these activities do not involve the discharge of dredged or fill material or whether those activities involve dredged or fill material but are exempt. The Government contends the former, that they do not involve dredged or fill material and that other activities of normal farming and silviculture that do involve the discharge of dredged or fill material would be subject to the permit program unless exempted by § 404(f)(1)(B) through (E). On the other hand the *amici curiae* (National Forest Products Association, American Paper Institute, and Louisiana Forestry Association) contend that § 404(f)(1)(A) exempts all normal agricultural and silvicultural activities, even those involving the discharge of dredged or fill material. Although we believe that the position of the section, the specific language of § 404(f)(1) and the physical character of the activity described therein clearly indicate that § 404(f)(1)(A)

lution are regulated under the § 208 best management practice program and do not require a permit.[6]

Section 301(a) of the FWPCA is the keystone of the Act's attack on point sources of pollution. That section makes it unlawful to "discharge any pollutant" into the waters of the United States unless a permit is granted under §§ 402 or 404. Although the literal terms of § 301(a) do not make it clear that it is directed only at point sources of pollution, the definition of "discharge of a pollutant" in § 502(12) of the FWPCA makes this fact evident.

> "The term 'discharge of a pollutant' and the term 'discharge of pollutants' each means (A) any addition of any pollutant to navigable waters from any point source, (B) any addition of any pollutant to the waters of the contiguous zone or the ocean from any point source other than a vessel or other floating craft."

§ 502(14) of the FWPCA defines a point source as any "discernible, confined, and discrete conveyance."

The permit program that is of primary concern in this litigation, § 404, regulates the discharge of dredged or fill material and is administered by the Corps of Engineers. The term "dredged material" and "fill material" are not defined in the Act, however, they are defined in the Corps regulations implementing the § 404 program:

> "The term 'dredged material' means material that is excavated or dredged from water of the United States." 33 C.F.R. § 323.2(k).

> "The term 'discharge of dredged material' means any addition of dredged material into the waters of the United States.****The term does not include plowing, cultivating, seeding and harvesting for the production of food, fiber, and forest products."* 33 C.F.R. § 323.2(1). (Emphasis supplied).

> "The term 'fill material' means any material used for the primary purpose of replacing an aquatic area with dry land by changing the bottom elevation of a water body.***" 33 C.F.R. § 323.2(m).

> "The term 'discharge of fill material' means the addition of fill material into waters of the United States. The term generally includes, without limitation, the following activities: placement of fill that is necessary to the construction of any structure in a water of the United States; the building of any structure or impoundment requiring rock, sand, dirt or other material for its construction; site development fills for recreational, industrial, commercial, residential, and other uses; causeways or road fills; dams and dikes; artificial islands; property protection and/or reclamation devices such as rip-rap, groins, seawalls, breakwaters, and revetments; beach nourishment; levees; fill for structures such as sewerage treatment facilities; intake and outfall pipes associated with power plants and subaqueous utility lines; and artificial reefs. *The term does not include plowing, cultivating, seeding and harvesting for the production of food, fiber, and forest products."* 33 C.F.R. § 323.2(n).

However, as indicated above, a permit is not required for all discharges of dredged or fill material. § 404(f)(1) exempts certain activities from the permit program. The exemptions contained in § 404(f)(1)(A) and (C) are pertinent herein. They provide:

> "(f)(1) except as provided in paragraph (2) of this subsection, the discharge of dredge or fill material—

---

activities involve the discharge of dredged and fill material, we need not resolve this dispute since we have determined that the clearing activities do not constitute normal farming or silviculture and is also barred as an exemption under § 404(f)(2).

[6]In 1977 the Clean Water Act amendments to the FWPCA amended §208 such that some dredge and fill activities that have little or no adverse impact on the waters of the United States can be regulated under a state best management practice program under § 208(b)(4)(B). There has been no contention that Louisiana has such a program or that the defendants' activities are properly regulated under § 208(b)(4)(B).

(A) from normal farming, silviculture, and ranching activities such as plowing, seeding, cultivating, minor drainage, harvesting for the production of food, fiber, and forest products, or upland soil and water conservation practices;

*   *   *

(C) for the purpose of construction or maintenance of farm or stock ponds of irrigation ditches, or the maintenance of drainage ditches;

*   *   *

is not prohibited by or otherwise subject to regulation under this section or section 301(a) or 402 of this Act (except for effluent standards or prohibitions under § 307)."

Yet, the § 404(f)(1) exemptions are not absolute since they are subject to the limitations of § 404(f)(2) which provide

"Any discharge of dredged or fill material into the navigable waters incidental to any activity having as its purpose bringing an area of the navigable waters into a use to which it was not previously subject, where the flow or circulation of navigable waters may be impaired or the reach of such waters may be reduced, shall be required to have a permit under this section."

Since "navigable waters" includes wetlands, 33 C.F.R. 323.2(a), it is clear that the following issues must be resolved in determining whether any or all of the private defendants' landclearing activities require a permit under § 404: (1) are there any point sources of pollution? (2) if so, is there a discharge of dredged or fill material? (3) if so, does the activity constitute normal farming or silviculture activities which are exempted from the permit program under § 404(f)(1)(A) and (4) if so, will the activities result in a change in the use of the land so that the flow or circulation of the waters may be impaired or that reach of the waters may be reduced thereby making the exemption unavailable under § 404(f)(2).

(1) Are there any point sources of pollution? § 502(14) of the FWPCA defines a point source as:

"any discernible, contained and discrete conveyance, including but not limited to any ... ditch, channel ... discrete fissure, container, rolling stock ... from which pollutants are or may be discharged .... "

We determine that defendants' land-clearing equipment (bulldozers fitted with V-blades, bulldozers fitted with raking blades, and the tractor-pulled rakes), ditch excavation equipment (the backhoe used to excavate the three-quarter mile drainage ditch as well as any equipment used to excavate the proposed drainage ditches) and discing equipment, (unless used in connection with "normal farming"), are point sources. The general definition of point source and the illustrative examples connote that a point source is an isolable, identifiable activity that conveys a pollutant, dredged or fill material. The operation of defendants' equipment was certainly an identifiable and isolable activity. It also conveyed dredged or fill material since it collected, gathered and transported the sheared trees and vegetation, leaf litter and soil across the wetland which, for reasons set out below, we determine to be dredged material. It is clear beyond cavil that any machinery used in ditch excavation is a point source since such machinery excavates the wetland soil and then discharges this soil back into the wetland.

This determination is buttressed by the cases of *U.S. v. Fleming Plantations*, 12 E.R.C. 1705 (E.D. La. 1978), and *U.S. v. Holland*, 373 F. Supp. 665 (M.D.Fla. 1974). In the former case it was determined that marsh buggies and draglines were point sources. In the latter case it was determined that dump trucks, draglines and bulldozers were point sources.

(2) Is there a discharge of dredged or fill material? As just indicated above, we have determined that the sheared trees and vegetation and scraped soil and leaf litter constitute dredged or fill material. We will deal first with the sheared trees and vegetation. To reiterate, 33 C.F.R.

§ 323.2(k) defines dredged material as "material that is excavated or dredged from waters of the United States." This essentially means that excavated material is the removal of some part of the waters of the United States. When dealing with a traditional water body such as a lake or a river, this would involve digging up the bottom or floor of the water body. However, herein we are not dealing .with such traditional water bodies. Rather the area in dispute has been determined to be a wetland. The term "wetlands" is defined as:

> "those areas that are inundated or saturated by surface or ground water at a frequency and duration sufficient to support, and that under normal circumstances do support, *a prevalence of vegetation typically adapted for life in saturated soil conditions.* Wetlands generally include swamps, marshes, bogs and similar areas." 33 C.F.R. 323.2(c). (Emphasis supplied.)

The above quoted definition makes it clear that wetlands include the vegetation that grows thereon. Such lands in the absence of vegetation can supply hardly any of the purposes of the Act. Consequently, in determining what constitutes dredged material in a wetland area, the inquiry does not end at the surface of the earth or water. Rather, any such inquiry must also consider vegetation, the very thing that defines a wetland. Accordingly, we determine that clearing the land of trees and vegetation, which are parts of the waters of the United States under 33 C.F.R. § 323.2(a) and (c) constitutes the discharge of dredged material.

Our determination that the soil and detritus was scraped up and conveyed across the tract is buttressed by the fact that many of the small sloughs were filled and the larger ones were partially filled in the landclearing process. The process had a levelling effect which also qualified the material moved as fill material.

We feel that our determination follows the spirit as well as the letter of the law. A basic policy of the FWPCA is the protection of our nation's wetlands and the important functions they serve. The legislative history of the Clean Water Act amendments of 1977 reflects an abiding congressional concern with the functional importance of wetlands.

The Corps regulations implementing the § 404 program set out some basic policies for evaluating permit applications. Particularly pertinent herein is § 320.4(b)(1) which begins by declaring that:

> "Wetlands are vital areas that constitute a productive and valuable public resource, the unnecessary alteration or destruction of which should be discouraged as contrary to the public interest."

The section then goes on to identify wetlands that are considered important to the public because of the functions they perform. 320.4(b)(2):

> "(i) Wetlands which serve important natural biological functions, including food chain production, general habitat, and nesting, spawning, rearing and resting sites for aquatic or land species;
>
> "(ii) Wetlands set aside for study of the aquatic environment or as sanctuaries or refuges;
>
> "(iii)Wetlands the destruction or alteration of which would affect detrimentally natural drainage characteristics, sedimentation patterns, salinity distribution, flushing characteristics, current patterns, or other environmental characteristics;
>
> "(iv) Wetlands which are significant in shielding other areas from wave action, erosion, or storm damage. Such wetlands are often associated with barrier beaches, islands, reefs and bars;
>
> "(v) Wetlands which serve as valuable storage areas for storm and flood waters;
>
> "(vi) Wetlands which are prime natural recharge areas. Prime recharge areas are locations where surface and ground water are directly inter-connected; and
>
> "(vii) Wetlands [which] through natural water filtration processes serve to purify water."

Section 320.4(b)(3) goes on to provide that when the Corps conducts the public interest review for permit applications for wetland areas it should take into account the cumulative effect of many minor changes or alterations.

"Although a particular alteration of wetlands may constitute a minor change, the cumulative effect of numerous such piecemeal changes often results in a major impairment of the wetland resources. Thus, the particular wetlands site for which an application is made will be evaluated with the recognition that it is part of a complete and interrelated wetland area."

The evidence demonstrated that the Lake Long wetland area performed the functions mentioned in 33 C.F.R. § 320.4(b)(2)(i), (iii), (v) and (vii). Aside from the flood storage capacity function recognized in 33 C.F.R. § 320.4(b)(2)(v) which will not be affected by the removal of the wetland vegetation, the evidence disclosed that the other wetland functions performed by the Lake Long Tract will be seriously impaired, if not destroyed, by permanent removal of the wetland's vegetation since the vegetation on the land, not the land itself, makes these functions possible.

Functions identified in 33 C.F.R. § 320.4(e)(2)(i): Forested wetland provides habitat for many animals such as deer, otter, beaver and nutria. Of course, cleared agricultural land does not provide food and shelter for these animals.

The permanent removal of the trees and vegetation will also result in a loss of detritus—an important link in the aquatic food chain. Detritus, a particulate organic material formed when bacteria, insects and other small organisms feed on the fallen leaves that have accumulated on the forest floor (referred to as leaf litter), is an important source of food energy for the fish and shellfish of the Natchitoches Basin and Red River. Fish and shellfish that are carried into the backwater area feed heavily on detritus. The receding flood waters carry out detrital material into the Red River where it is used as food.

Clearing of the wetland's vegetation will also seriously impair fish spawning. Fish that inhabit the Red River and its basins spawn in the backwater areas. Many of these fish are broadcast spawners—they spew their eggs out into the water which attach to vegetation by means of an adhesive material that covers them. The eggs won't have any vegetation on which to attach after clearing and as a result the eggs will fall to the bottom where they will be covered with silt resulting in suffocation of the embryo. Fish nursery grounds will also be adversely affected by the clearing. Many fish larvae use the backwater area as a nursery where they feed on detritus and seek out vegetated areas for protection from predators. This will no longer be possible if the wetlands are cleared.

Functions identified in 33 C.F.R. § 320.4(b)(2)(iii): Sedimentation patterns will be adversely affected by clearing since there would be a drastic increase in the amount of sedimentation produced by the wetland. Forested wetland produces only three-quarters of a ton of sediment per acre yearly whereas agricultural land produces substantially more than five tons of sediment per acre yearly.

In addition, there will be an increase in the rate of erosion if the land is cleared. The forest overstory tends to break the momentum of precipitation and thereby decrease the impact of the precipitation on the soil lying below. The leaf litter and humus which covers the forest floor also protects the underlying soil from the impact of precipitation. If cleared, the soil would be subject to the full impact of the rain and will erode at a quicker rate than it would if it remained forested. Of course, this increased erosion helps explain why sedimentation will be greatly increased after clearing.

The wetland's natural drainage characteristics will also be affected by clearing since precipitation runs off agricultural land much quicker than it does from forested land. On forested land, leaf litter and humus lying on the forest floor absorbs much of the precipitation and thereby slows down the rate of drainage. Additionally, tree roots slow down the rate of drainage since they trap and hold precipitation. Needless to say, the rate of drainage will be further increased by any ditching activities.

Function identified in 33 C.F.R. § 320.4(b)(2)(vii): As precipitation slowly drains off a forested area it percolates through the leaf litter and humus which tends to purify it. If there is no leaf litter and humus to act as a filtration system, needless to say, this purification process will be seriously impaired if not destroyed.

The FWPCA would be emasculated insofar as wetlands are concerned were we to conclude that the permanent removal of the wetland's vegetation in the process of converting it to agricultural land was not subject to the § 404 permit program. As the above discussion makes evident, wetlands are important to the public interest because of the various functions they perform. If you destroy a wetland's ability to perform these functions, you have in effect destroyed the wetland insofar as the public interest is concerned. Many of the functions that wetlands perform are dependent on the presence of vegetation. Obviously, if a wetland area is cleared of its vegetation it would no longer functionally exist in many respects and the public interest will be seriously affected. Common sense dictates that an activity that results in the effective destruction of a wetland resource should be subject to regulation under an Act that has as its purpose the restoration and maintenance of the "chemical, physical and biological integrity" of our nation's wetlands.

(3) Does the activity of the private defendants constitute normal farming or silviculture so as to be exempt from the § 404 permit program by § 404(f)(1)(A)? We note at the outset that the legislative history to the Clean Water Act indicates that the exemptions to the § 404 permit program should be narrowly construed.

The literal terms of § 404(f)(1)(A) indicate that only activities that are part of an *ongoing* agricultural or silvicultural operation were intended to be exempted from the permit program and not activities, such as the private defendants' landclearing operations, which convert forested bottomland into farmland. 404(f)(1)(A) speaks in terms of "normal" farming and silviculture. The word "normal" connotes an established and continuing activity. Moreover, the examples of normal farming and silviculture activity set out in 404(f)(1)(A) are also activities that would only occur on a continuing basis as part of an ongoing farming or forestry operation. There is not the slightest hint in the terminology of § 404(f)(1)(A) that the defendants' land

conversion activities are comprehended under its terms. Bulldozers equipped with V-blades or with raking blades are not farming equipment. Clearing timber is not an agricultural pursuit. No farming operation was or could have been contemplated until after the acreage was cleared.

Although clear-cutting may be part of a normal silviculture operation under other circumstances, it is clear that the private defendants' clear-cutting was not part of a normal silviculture operation herein since no regeneration of the timber is contemplated.

(4) Finally we are buttressed in our conclusion that the defendant's land conversion activities are not exempt under 404(f)(1)(A) by the fact that 404(f)(2) specifically takes away the exemption for activities that involve converting the use of the land. Even assuming arguendo that the clearing activities were normal farming or silviculture, the evidence demonstrated that these activities would fall within the technical terms of the 404(f)(2) limitation. Under that provision activities that would be exempted under 404(f)(1)(A) are denied exempt status if they are incidental to an activity which will convert a wetlands area to another use where the reach of the water may be reduced or the flow or circulation of the water may be impaired.

Private defendants' clearing of the land so that it could be used for soybean production was definitely a change in use. Since wetlands do not functionally exist apart from the vegetation that defines it, the clearing of all of the wetlands' vegetation will, in essence, destroy the wetland and, consequently, reduce the reach of the waters of the United States. Furthermore, the circulation and flow of the water will be impaired since the evidence demonstrated that the land would drain at a faster rate after clearing. Additionally, during the clearing process small sloughs were filled and larger ones partially filled thereby levelling the land which will affect natural drainage patterns resulting in an alteration and impairment of the circulation and flow of the water. Of course, any ditching would surely impair the circulation and flow of the water since the ditches would accelerate drainage.

We find the government's statement is untenable. In essence the government contends that if you use landclearing equipment which moves earth (other than de minimis) to clear a wetland, a permit is required under § 404. But if you clear the wetland "where no earth (other than de minimis) is moved" you can clear and destroy every acre of wetlands in the United States with impunity and without applying for a permit. It seems to us that the government has ignored the purposes of the Act and has applied engineering and construction methodology and theory to an environmental problem, totally frustrating the purposes of the Clean Water Act.

> "There is no question that the systematic destruction of the nation's wetlands is causing serious, permanent ecological damage. The wetlands and bays, estuaries and deltas are the nation's most biologically active areas. They represent a principal source of food supply. They are the spawning grounds for much of the fish and shellfish which populate the oceans, and they are passages for numerous upland game fish. They also provide nesting areas for a myriad of species of birds and wildlife."

Remarks of Sen. Muskie during Senate debate on § 404. Leg. History 869. If the destruction and conversion of wetlands to another purpose is accomplished, does it really matter whether it is accomplished "where no earth (other than de minimis) is moved" or otherwise?

More specifically, does it make sense, as the Government's statement implies, that the excavation of a ditch 6 feet deep and 100 feet long requires a § 404 permit (is destructive of wetlands) but that the clearing of 20,000 acres of forest wetlands by methods involving only de minimis movement of earth does not (is not destructive of such wetlands)? The factual situation in this very proceeding demonstrates the error implicit in the Government's statement.

Since we have determined that defendants' land clearing activities are subject to the § 404 permit program, we find it unnecessary to decide whether there was any violation of § 10 of the Rivers and Harbors Act of 1899 and § 402 of the FWPCA. *U.S. v. Fleming Plantations,* 12 E.R.C. 1705 (E.D. La. 1978).

Up to this point in the opinion we have been concerned with the uncleared wetlands on the Lake Long Tract, as the Government determination of March 26, 1979, has defined "wetlands." We now are concerned with the cleared wetlands on that tract. If the private defendants' clearing activities were not exempt under the provisions of § 404(f)(1)(A) as we have now determined then perhaps the private defendants should be ordered to restore the forested wetlands, *U.S. v. Fleming Plantations, supra.* But in our final injunction and order dated May 4, 1979, the private defendants were permitted to engage in normal farming operations on all wetlands that were cleared prior to the issuance of the temporary restraining order. This decision was based on the following equitable considerations: Defendants' land clearing operations began in the summer of 1978. They had cleared several thousand acres when the Corps issued a cease and desist order so that it could determine what areas of the tract were wetlands and thus subject to its jurisdiction under the § 404 program. The private defendants stopped their land clearing activities in compliance with the cease and desist order. Subsequently the Corps surveyed the tract and made a determination of what areas it considered to be wetlands. On November 7, 1978, this court granted a temporary restraining order that prohibited all land clearing and ditching activities on the tract. The defendants have not engaged in any land clearing activities or ditching activities since the TRO was granted. Unfortunately, the final wetland determination filed on March 26, 1979 by the federal defendants differed from the determination that had been made at the time of the cease and desist order by the Corps. As a result, the private defendants cleared some area of the tract that had initially been determined not to be wetlands and which were subsequently determined to be wetlands in the March 26, 1979 wetland determination. There has been no evidence of any bad faith on the part of the defendants who at all times have acted in full compliance with the directives of the Corps and this court. Under such circumstances, we feel that the private defendants should be permitted to conduct normal farming operations on the land already cleared with the exception

that no ditching will be conducted without § 404
permits on any of the wetland area including
those areas that had already been cleared.

NOTES

1. Assuming, as the court does, that "wetlands" under the Corps' jurisdiction are involved, do you agree with this decision? Consider it step by step.

Should the shearing of trees and the raking and discing that was carried out here be deemed the "discharge of dredged or fill material" under Section 404?

If so, should it be exempt under subsection (f)(1)(A) as a discharge from "normal farming or silviculture activities"?

Even if the (f)(1) exemption presumptively applies, should the exemption be denied under the (f)(2) limitation for activities which will convert a wetland to another use where the reach of the water may be reduced or the flow or circulation impaired? Construed literally, wouldn't this limitation swallow most exemptions under (f)(1)?

Would this holding require a coastal rice farmer to obtain a 404 permit before every planting and harvest? Would it require him to do so before he cleared a new field for planting?

Would such wetland landclearing activities as occurred in *Avoyelles* be an appropriate subject for a "general permit" under Section 404 (e)(1)?

2. In the similar case of *United States v. Huebner*, 752 F.2d 1235 (7th Cir. 1985), the court held that the clearing, scraping, plowing, and furrowing incident to expansion of cranberry beds into a wetland involved the discharge of dredge and fill material without a permit. Also, as did the Fifth Circuit in *Avoyelles*, the Seventh Circuit held that Congress intended that Section 404(f)(1) exempt from the permit process only "narrowly defined activities . . . that cause little or no adverse effects . . . [and which do not] convert more extensive areas of water into dry land or impede circulation or reduce the reach and size of the water body." 752 F.2d at 1241, quoting from legislative history.

3. In *United States v. M.C.C. of Florida, Inc.*, 23 ERC 1318 (5th Cir. 1985), the defendant construction company was charged with having violated the Rivers and Harbors Act and the Clean Water Act when the propellers of its tugs devastated the bottom vegetation within a wildlife refuge. The Fifth Circuit held that, when the tug propellers cut into the bottom, uprooting and destroying the sea grass and depositing bottom sediment on adjacent sea grass beds, it constituted the unpermitted dredging of a channel and "excavation," "alteration," and "modification" of navigable water in violation of Section 10 of the Rivers and Harbors Act. Also, the court held that the "redeposit" of the sediment and vegetation that was cut and uprooted by the propellers upon the adjacent sea grass beds was the "discharge of a pollutant" without the permit required by Section 404 of the Water Act.

4. The private defendants in the *Avoyelles* case were at least fortunate in one significant respect: they were not required to restore the cleared wetlands to their original forested state.

As burdensome, expensive, and difficult to carry out as such a restoration order may be, similar orders have been issued against other developers who have dredged and/or filled wetlands without obtaining permits from the Corps of Engineers. *See*, for example, *United States v. Joseph G. Moretti, Inc.*, 478 F.2d 418 (5th Cir. 1973) and its subsequent history at 387 F. Supp. 1404 (S.D. Fla. 1974), 526 F.2d 1306 (5th Cir. 1976) 423 F.Supp. 1197 (S.O. Fla. 1976), 592 F.2d 1189 (5th Cir. 1979). Poor Mr. Moretti was not only ordered to fill all the canals which he had dug for his new mobile home park on a Florida key, he was ordered to perform the extremely difficult task of replanting and restoring destroyed mangroves.

Most restoration orders such as the one imposed on Mr. Moretti have been issued under the authority of Section 10 of the Rivers and Harbors Act, which expressly empowers a federal district court to order the removal of "structures" erected in violation of the Act.

However, in more recent cases the general injunctive relief provision in the Clean Water Act has been used by courts to order restoration of wetlands without application of the Rivers and Harbors Act. *See*, for example, *Parkview Corp. v. Corps of Engineers*, 490 F.Supp. 1278 (E.D.Wis. 1980); *United States v. Fleming Plantations*, 12 ERC 1705 (E.D.La. 1978).

In *United States v. Sexton Cove Estates, Inc.*, 526 F.2d 1293 (5th Cir. 1976), the Fifth Circuit expressed general criteria, which have been followed in other circuits, for judicial evaluation of the propriety of a restoration order. The restoration plan must be carefully designed to confer maximum environmental benefits, at the same time that it is "tempered with a touch of equity." In essence, the same basic principle applies as when any other equitable relief is sought: "The degree and kind of wrong and the practicality of the remedy must be considered in the formulation of that remedy." 526 F.2d at 1293. Such considerations caused the Seventh Circuit in *U.S. v. Huebner* to overturn the trial court's restoration order, saying that it was "a draconian exercise of judicial discretion to order undone a ten-acre expansion of cranberry beds which it took the Huebners several years to develop and which beds are not inherently incompatible with the surrounding wetlands." 752 F.2d at 1246. In *U.S. v. M.C.C.*, the Fifth Circuit held that the trial court correctly rejected restoration of the sea grass beds damaged by the tug propellers as too speculative and too costly; but it did, in principle, approve of requiring the defendant to pay for restoration of *other* areas in South Florida in "mitigation" of the harm it caused to the nonrestorable area. 23 ERC at 1323.

5. On the second issue in the bifurcated *Avoyelles* case — the correctness of EPA's determination that approximately eighty percent of the Lake Long Tract was "wetland" subject to regulation under the Clean Water Act — the district court subsequently decided that over ninety percent of the tract was wetland. *See Avoyelles Sportmen's League, Inc. v. Alexander*, 511 F. Supp. 278 (W.D. La. 1981).

When both parts of the case were appealed, the Fifth Circuit affirmed the district court's ruling that the landclearing activities constituted the "discharge of dredged or fill material" and that the (f)(1) exemption did not apply. The Court of Appeals, however, found EPA's determination of how much of the tract was "wetland" subject to 404 permitting not to have been arbitrary and capricious — rejecting both the district court's more expansive application of the classification and the landowners' arguments for a more narrow one. *See Avoyelles Sportmen's League, Inc. v. Marsh*, 715 F.2d 897 (5th Cir. 1983).

Monongahela Power Company v. Alexander

507 F.Supp. 385 (D.D.C. 1980)

Smith, J.

MEMORANDUM

Plaintiffs, three power companies, bring this action against the United States Army Corps of Engineers (the Corps) and various individuals acting in their official capacities. They seek injunctive and declaratory relief regarding the Corps' denial of their application for a permit for the Davis Pumped Storage Hydroelectric Project (the Project), a complex of dams designed to produce power. Prior to the Corps' denial, a license to construct and operate the Project had been issued by the Federal Power Commission

(FPC), the predecessor of the Federal Energy Regulatory Commission (FERC).[1]***

Plaintiffs' threshold contention, that the Corps is without jurisdiction to either grant or deny a permit, is based on the premise that Congress has vested all authority over hydroelectric projects in the FPC and its successors, to the exclusion of any other federal agency. This comprehensive authority is dated back to the Federal Water Power Act of 1920 (codified at 16 U.S.C. §§ 792 *et seq.*(1976)(the Water Power Act). Defendants respond that the Corps has concurrent jurisdiction pursuant to Section 404 of the Federal Water Pollution Control Act Amendments of 1972. That section requires a permit issued by the Corps for any discharge of dredged or fill material into navigable waters, a process which construction of the Project would admittedly involve. Resolution of this apparent statutory conflict entails an inquiry into the origins and purposes of both Acts.

Prior to the enactment of the Water Power Act, federal control over water power was characterized by duplicative and overlapping regulatory jurisdiction. Authority to license water power projects was shared among three agencies: the Department of Interior, the Department of Agriculture, and the Secretary of War. The Water Power Act was intended to coordinate the exercise of federal jurisdiction; and to that end the Act created the FPC with authority over federal water power projects.

At the time of its passage, the Water Power Act was administratively interpreted as concentrating all licensing authority in the FPC and providing "a complete and detailed scheme for the development . . . of all the water power resources of the public domain." 32 Op. Att'y Gen. 525, 528 (1921).***

During the existence of the FPC, the courts interpreted this authority in the same manner. Prominent among the decisions is *First Iowa Hydroelectric Cooperative v. FPC*, 328 U.S. 152 (1946), in which the Court examined the purposes and powers of the Water Power Act and found that

It was the outgrowth of a widely supported effort of the conservationists to secure enactment of a complete scheme of national regulation which would promote the comprehensive development of the water resources of the Nation, in so far as it was within the reach of the federal power to do so, instead of the piecemeal, restrictive, negative approach of the River and Harbor Acts and other federal laws previously enacted. *Id.* at 180.
***

Congress itself has also construed the authority of the FPC as exclusive. When the authority was transferred to FERC pursuant to the Department of Energy Organization Act of 1977 (codified at 42 U.S.C. § 7172(a)(1) (Supp. III 1979)(the Energy Organization Act)). Congress stated in the Conference Report that:

Section 402(a) describes the exclusive jurisdiction of the Commission over certain functions transferred from the FPC. This exclusive jurisdiction consists of functions transferred from the FPC which will be within the sole responsibility of the Commission to consider and to take final agency action on without further review by the Secretary or any other executive branch official.

Specifically included in this "exclusive jurisdiction" is power to issue licenses for hydroelectric projects.

While defendants and intervenors dispute the label "exclusive," and while the language used to describe the FPC's authority does vary, the reach of its jurisdiction prior to 1972 was clear. Congress had created an agency and centralized in it *all* federal authority for licensing federal water power projects. This exclusive licensing authority preempted any conflicting state regulation and precluded any concurrent federal jurisdiction. This historic statutory policy was apparently reaffirmed at the time of the passage of the Energy Organization Act. Were it not for the existence of the FWPCAA, there would be no difficulty in holding that the FPC's power here was exclusive.

---

[1]Unless the context demands otherwise, the energy licensing authority will be referred to as the FPC, rather than the FERC.

However, the FWPCAA does exist and does disrupt the otherwise clear statutory mandate of the FPC. Section 404 of the FWPCAA gives the Corps power to grant or deny permits for discharges of "dredged or fill material" into navigable waters. There is no exception for FPC-licensed hydroelectric projects. Since the Project concededly requires such a discharge, the Corps asserts that it, as well as the FPC, has the duty and the authority to license the project. Defendants contend that had Congress intended to preserve the FPC's exclusive licensing procedure, it could easily have done so and that the absence of an exemption in the 1972 FWPCAA is indicative of Congressional intent to give the Corps the power disputed here. They argue that this construction is further strengthened by the Clean Water Act of 1977, in which Congress passed a number of specific exemptions to the Corps' licensing authority but again failed to exempt hydroelectric projects.***

This omission in 1977 is all the more striking in that Congress was on notice that the FWPCAA had been construed as applicable to water power projects. *See Scenic Hudson Preservation Conference v. Callaway.* 370 F. Supp. 162(S.D.N.Y. 1973), *aff'd per curiam* 499 F.2d 127 (2d Cir. 1974) (discussed more fully *infra*). The seemingly inevitable conclusion is that Congress, by not exempting FPC-licensed projects, intended them to be subject to the Corps' licensing jurisdiction.

That, indeed, was the holding in the only case which has confronted the apparent conflict between the FPC's exclusive jurisdiction and the Corps' general authority:

Con Ed would infer an exception from the [FWPCAA] for hydroelectric plants on the theory that Congress could not have intended to interfere with jurisdiction of the FPC in view of the long settled policy, discussed above, of allowing that agency unique control over the production of hydroelectric power. The argument is persuasive at first blush, but even more plausible is plaintiffs' contention that Congress would not design an Act which on its face is all-

inclusive, but for specifically enumerated exceptions, and yet intend to establish an unmentioned exception of the scale suggested here. Without any indication that Con Ed's reading of the Congressional will is accurate, the carving out of so major an exception would be improper. If this was Congress' intention and the omission is mere oversight, the remedy rests in Congress' hands . . . .

Scenic Hudson Preservation Conference v. Callaway, 370 F. Supp. 162, 170 (S.D.N.Y. 1973). This finding was affirmed in a per curiam opinion describing the District Court's opinion as "well-considered." 499 F.2d at 128. While such a precise holding would normally govern any disposition here, two intervening events have diminished its authority.

First, Congress has now given an indication that the FPC's hydroelectric jurisdiction should be construed as exclusive, notwithstanding the FWPCAA. *See* H.R. Rep. No. 539, *supra.* Although the statement clearly describes the FPC jurisdiction as exclusive, and was made after both the FWPCAA and the decision in *Scenic Hudson*, it is difficult to determine the weight it should be accorded. Had the Energy Organization Act actually created the FPC power at issue here, the Conference Report language would be controlling. The FPC's power would be exclusive, whatever duplicative licensing power the Corps might have possessed would have been repealed,[2] and the decision in *Scenic Hudson* overruled. If, on the other hand, the statement were merely a legislative comment upon a previously enacted statute, it would still be entitled to "some consideration as a secondarily authoritative expression of expert opinion."***

While allowing the statement even this minimal consideration would cast doubt upon the

---

[2]Defendants and Intervenors have questioned whether the Energy Organization Act should be construed as repealing by implication the concurrent jurisdiction of the Corps. Because of the Court's disposition of the issue of the Corps' jurisdiction, that question need not be dealt with.

continuing validity of *Scenic Hudson*, the better course is to interpret its authority as somewhere between the two extremes. The Energy Organization Act did not simply transfer to FERC certain powers of the FPC; it created additional ones and consolidated others. It was a sweeping transformation of the entire field of energy regulation. As such, the statement is as much an indication of the jurisdiction Congress intended to allocate to FERC in 1977 as it is an expression of its understanding of prior legislation. Although it did not, perhaps, conclusively overrule *Scenic Hudson*, nor repeal whatever concurrent jurisdiction the Corps may have had under the FWPCAA, the statement is sufficiently authoritative to undermine the precedential value of the contrary conclusion in *Scenic Hudson*.

The second intervening event was *Train v. Colorado Public Interest Research Group*, 426 U.S.A. (1976), where the Supreme Court ruled that there do exist inferable exceptions to the facially inclusive licensing authority vested by the FWPCAA in the Corps. The FWPCAA was found inapplicable to the discharge of nuclear pollutants, the regulation of which the Atomic Energy Commission (AEC) considered within its sole jurisdiction. The Court noted that the regulatory authority of the AEC was "comprehensive," and preemptive of any state regulation. It further noted that it would expect a "clear indication of legislative intent" to change such a "pervasive regulatory scheme." Examining the relevant legislative history, it then found that Congress had specifically intended to preserve the preexisting regulatory plan. If there were similar legislative history in the FWPCAA preserving the jurisdiction of the FPC, *Train* would obviously be controlling. However, no such history can be found and that crucial distinction allows each side to claim *Train* as its own. Defendants contend that the case allows this Court to look only to the legislative history of the FWPCAA to find an exemption for hydroelectric projects. Since no such exemption can be found, none could have been intended, just as *Scenic Hudson* concluded. Plaintiffs insist, conversely, that *Train* overrules *Scenic Hudson* by

implication, and this appears the better argument.

The key lies in the three-step approach implicit in the Court's analysis in *Train*. First, there must be a comprehensive or pervasive regulatory plan which is threatened with change by subsequent statute. If such a situation exists, the Court will next search for Congressional intent to preserve the preexisting regulatory framework, a search which was successful in *Train*. Not finding any intent to preserve, a third step would be necessary before the Court would recognize any change in an established regulatory plan: it would look for and normally expect to find a specific Congressional intent to make such a change. *Id.* ***

However, even the third step implicit in the *Train* analysis does not dispose of the dispute here. Although the regulatory scheme administered by the FPC is as comprehensive and pervasive as the nuclear regulation at issue in *Train*, the legislative history of the FWPCAA reveals neither an intent to preserve the FPC jurisdiction, nor an intent to change it. Thus to resolve the statutory conflict other principles of statutory construction must be examined.

The first principle applicable is the "cardinal rule" that repeals by implication are not favored.*** That is undoubtedly the situation here. If the Corps' concurrent and duplicative jurisdiction over FPC-licensed projects is found valid, the statutory policy of centralized, coordinated licensing procedures for such projects, dating back to 1920, will be repealed. There is also no doubt that the repeal would be by implication since there is no evidence that Congress specifically and consciously intended to effect such a repeal. Under such circumstances the second applicable precept is that a court can find an implied repeal only if the two statutes are "irreconcilable."***

In essence, then, the Court's duty here is to compare the two statutes in purpose and operation, to attempt to give effect to both, and to repeal the exclusive authority of the FPC only if it is clearly repugnant to the purpose and operation of the FWPCAA.

An analysis of the sets of factors used by the

two agencies in reaching determinations under the respective statutes reveals no substantial or overriding differences. The operation of the FWPCAA requires that before the Corps issues a permit under Section 404, all relevant factors must be carefully weighed and the benefits balanced against the detriments. These factors include "conservation, *economics*, esthetics, general environmental concerns, historic values, fish and wildlife values, flood damage prevention, land use, navigation, recreation, water supply, water quality, *energy needs*, safety, food production, and, in general, the needs and welfare of the people." 33 CFR § 320.4(a)(1979)(emphasis added). A permit will only be granted if it is in the "public interest." *See also* W. Rodgers, *Environmental Law* § 4.7, at 407 (1977). The Corps must also consider whether the benefits of the project outweigh the damage to wetlands. 33 CFR § 320.4(b)(4)(1979).

The operation of the FPC under its exclusive statutory authority has been described by the Supreme Court:

The questions whether the proponents of a project "will be able to use" the power supplied is relevant to the issue of the public interest. So too is the regional need for the additional power. But the inquiry should not stop there. A license under the Act empowers the licensee to construct, for its own use and benefit, hydroelectric projects utilizing the flow of navigable waters and thus, in effect, to appropriate water resources from the public domain. The grant of authority to the Commission to alienate federal water resources does not, of course, turn simply on whether the project will be beneficial to the licensee. Nor is the test solely whether the region will be able to use the additional power. The test is whether the project will be in the public interest. And that determination can be made only after an exploration of all issues relevant to the "public interest," including future power demand and supply, alternate sources of power, the

public interest in preserving reaches of wild rivers and wilderness areas, the preservation of anadromous fish for commercial and recreational purposes, and the protection of wildlife.

The need to destroy the river as a waterway, the desirability of its demise, the choices available to satisfy future demands for energy—these are all relevant to a decision.

Udall v. FPC, 387 U.S. 428, 450 (1967). Moreover, the FPC has adopted as part of its decision-making process the guidelines and goals of the National Environmental Protection Act. That procedure echoes the balancing process used by the Corps in Section 404 permit applications. Specifically included among the factors which must be reported to and evaluated by the FPC are "areas of critical environmental concern, e.g., wetlands" 18 C.F.R. App. A. § 2.2.3, at 137 (1979). Finally, the FPC also uses its own regulations on conservation of natural resources, which were issued pursuant to the Federal Power Act, 16 U.S.C. §§ 791a-828 (1976), a successor to the Water Power Act. It is thus apparent that each agency evaluates approximately the same elements in arriving at the ultimate goal of the public interest. Consequently, the operations of each agency under the relevant statutes are neither irreconcilable nor repugnant to each other.

Even allowing that the operations may be similar, defendants nevertheless assert that the purposes and goals of each agency under the respective statutes are so different as to be inconsistent. They contend, citing *Scenic Hudson,* that although the FPC may review the same environmental factors as the Corps, it is not required to do so. This is not entirely accurate. The Supreme Court and other courts have consistently held that such factors are relevant to an FPC decision and *must* be considered.***

Defendants' objections are thus reduced to the proposition that while both agencies may be required to consider approximately the same factors, the Corps is required to weigh more heavily the environmental issues, especially those concerning preservation of wetlands.

This difference in perspective is attributed to the disparity between the purposes of the statutes: the Water Power Act's prime orientation is power development while the FWPCAA's is preservation of water resources. Although this difference is not insignificant, the similarities in purpose and operation are more persuasive. The Court's duty here is to repeal the FPC's exclusive authority only if it is positively repugnant to or irreconcilable with the FWPCAA. Given the FPC's substantial environmental responsibilities, it cannot fairly be said that the difference in emphasis and perspective of the FWPCAA rises to a level sufficient to support an implied repeal. Accordingly, an exemption for FPC-licensed projects from the licensing requirements of the FWPCAA must be inferred. The Court finds that the Corps was therefore without jurisdiction to either grant or deny the permit at issue here.

An appropriate order follows.

NOTES

1. Although this court may be correct that only the Second Circuit had previously addressed the issue directly, most probably that was because all parties assumed that the Corps was on solid ground in requiring 404 permits for dredging and filling incident to hydroelectric projects. Obviously, that position was not invulnerable to attack.

2. If the dam is to be built on a "navigable water of the United States," doesn't Section 9 of the Rivers and Harbors Act of 1899 very expressly confer jurisdiction in the Corps? Section 9 reads as follows:

> It shall not be lawful to construct or commence the construction of any bridge, dam, dike, or causeway over or in any port, roadstead, haven, harbor, canal, navigable river, or other navigable water of the United States until the consent of Congress to the building of such structures shall have been obtained and until the plans for the same shall have been submitted to and approved by the Chief of Engineers and by the Secretary of the Army: Provided, That such structures may be built under authority of the legislature of a State across rivers and other waterways the navigable portions of which lie wholly within the limits of a single State, provided the location and plans thereof are submitted to and approved by the Chief of Engineers and by the Secretary of the Army before construction is commenced: And provided further, That when plans for any bridge or other structure have been approved by the Chief of Engineers and by the Secretary of the Army, it shall not be lawful to deviate from such plans either before or after completion of the structure unless the modification of said plans has previously been submitted to and received the approval of the Chief of Engineers and of the Secretary of the Army.

3. Even if the district court opinion in *Monongahela* is allowed to stand, its significance is lessened by a controversial new subsection (r) added to Section 404 by the 1977 Amendments which exempts all federal projects specifically authorized by Congress from both the federal and state permit programs, if an environmental impact statement analyzing the effects of dredge and fill activity associated with the project is submitted to Congress prior to authorization of the project or appropriation of funds, and before the actual discharge of dredged or fill material.

As explained in the Corps' "historical background" at the beginning of this section, before enactment of the Federal Water Pollution Control Act Amendments of 1972, Sections 10 and 13 of the Rivers and Harbors Act of 1899 provided some measure of protection for the nation's waters, shores, and wetlands.

Section 10 prohibits creation of "obstructions" not authorized by Congress to navigable waters of the United States and makes it unlawful "to excavate or fill, or in any manner to alter or modify the course, condition, or capacity *** of the channel of any navigable water of the United States" without authorization of the Corps of Engineers.

Section 13 (commonly known as the "Refuse Act") prohibits the deposit of refuse in, or on the bank of, navigable waters of the United States, or any tributary from which the refuse will wash into such waters, without a Corps of Engineers permit.

Under the authority of Section 13, in 1971 the Corps established a program requiring all industries discharging into navigable waters of the United States to apply for permits. In processing permit applications, decisions on questions of navigation and anchorage were to be made by the Corps; decisions on questions of water quality impacts were to be made by EPA. Due to a federal court injunction, however, only a handful of these permits were issued before passage of the FWPCA Amendments of 1972. The 1972 Amendments did not repeal the Refuse Act, but they did deprive it of virtually all importance relative to water pollution. Section 402 provides that permits under the FWPCA shall be deemed permits under the Refuse Act and that no more permits under the Refuse Act are to be issued.

Section 10 retains more vitality. In *Zabel v. Tabb*, 430 F.2d 199 (5th Cir. 1970), cert. denied, 401 U.S. 910 (1971), the Fifth Circuit approved the Corps' authority to deny or condition permits to dredge or fill in navigable waters of the United States on ecological grounds unrelated to navigation. To the extent dredge and fill activities covered by Section 10 constitute the "*discharge* of dredged or fill material" under Section 404 of the FWPCA, Section 10 will impose no additional requirements on a permit applicant. However, if it is possible to dredge without *discharging* into navigable waters, Section 10 may continue to impose permit requirements on activity not covered by Section 404.

Minnehaha Creek Watershed District v. Hoffman
597 F.2d 617 (8th Cir. 1979)

Before HEANEY and McMILLIAN, Circuit Judges, and TALBOT SMITH, Senior District Judge.

HEANEY, Circuit Judge.

The United States Army Corps of Engineers and various officials of the Corps appeal from the judgment of the District Court which permanently enjoined the Corps from asserting regulatory jurisdiction over the waters of Lake Minnetonka in Hennepin County, Minnesota, under § 10 of the Rivers and Harbors Act of 1899. *** The District Court also permanently enjoined the Corps from asserting regulatory jurisdiction over the placement of riprap and construction of dams in Lake Minnetonka under the Federal Water Pollution Control Act. We affirm in part and reverse in part.

*   *   *

Lake Minnetonka is a natural lake, navigable in fact, lying entirely within Hennepin County, Minnesota. The total surface area of the lake is approximately 22.5 square miles. The lake's depth averages forty feet, although there are isolated spots with depths up to one hundred feet. No permanent tributaries empty into Lake Minnetonka. The lake's single outlet is Minnehaha Creek, which flows eastward from Gray's Bay for approximately 20-22 miles, until it empties into the Mississippi River.

Prior to settlement of the area surrounding the lake in the mid-19th century, Indians navigated the lake by canoe. In 1852, a dam and sawmill were constructed on Minnehaha Creek at Minnetonka Mills, a short distance from where Lake Minnetonka flows into Minnehaha Creek. After the construction of this dam, the lake's water level increased sufficiently to allow the navigation of steam-powered boats and the flotation of logs on the lake. Steamers were used for the carriage of passengers and mail across the lake until 1926. Grain and lumber were shipped or floated on the lake to distribution points, where they were then shipped by rail. Beginning in 1890 and continuing thereafter, Lake Minnetonka was a thriving resort area, with North American and foreign tourists using the lake as a means of transportation from one shore point to another.

Present use of Lake Minnetonka is primarily recreational, by both local residents and travelers from other states. Centers of urban population around the lake include the towns of Mound, Excelsior and Wayzata. Rail service to shoreline communities is provided by the Burlington Northern and the Chicago and Northwestern Railroads.

The flow of Minnehaha Creek is intermittent; during a large part of the summer and fall, the flow is inadequate to permit the passage of any form of navigation. There is no history of navigation on the creek of either a private or a commercial nature. Navigation on that portion of the creek between Lake Minnetonka and Minnetonka Mills was rendered impossible by the construction of the dam at the source of the creek at Gray's Bay in 1897.

On May 16, 1916, the Army Corps of Engineers advised the Minneapolis Street Railway Company that construction of a bridge across an arm of Lake Minnetonka would require the Corps' approval. The Corps did not exercise active jurisdiction over the lake again until February 14, 1975, when it issued a "Determination of Navigability" which concluded that Lake Minnetonka and that portion of Minnehaha Creek above Minnetonka Mills are "navigable waters of the United States," and are, thus, subject to Corps' jurisdiction under the Rivers and

Harbors Act. The Corps has since asserted its regulatory authority over the lake under both the Rivers and Harbors Act and under § 404 of the F.W.P.C.A.

The appellees brought this action, seeking a declaratory judgment that Lake Minnetonka and Minnehaha Creek above Minnetonka Mills are not "navigable waters of the United States" within the meaning of the Rivers and Harbors Act. The appellees requested the entry of an order directing the Corps to withdraw the "Determination of Navigability" of February 14, 1975, and permanently enjoining the Corps from exercising regulatory jurisdiction over Lake Minnetonka or Minnehaha Creek under the Rivers and Harbors Act. The appellees also sought a declaratory judgment that 33 C.F.R. § 323.2(n), promulgated by the Corps, is invalid insofar as it attempts to extend the Corps' permitting program under § 404 of the F.W.P.C.A. over the placement of riprap and the construction of dams in navigable waters. They sought a permanent injunction against the Corps' assertion of regulatory jurisdiction pursuant to this regulation over the placement of riprap and the construction of dams in Lake Minnetonka and Minnehaha Creek.

Upon cross-motions for summary judgment, the District Court held for the appellees on both counts and granted all the relief requested. Applying the test set forth in *The Daniel Ball v. United States*, 77 U.S. (10 Wall.) 557 (1871), the court held that although both Lake Minnetonka and Minnehaha Creek above Minnetonka Mills are navigable waters, since their capability of use for navigation is undisputed, they are not "navigable waters of the United States" as that phrase is used in the Rivers and Harbors Act because they are located entirely within one state and have no interstate waterway connection with other navigable waters. The court held that the Corps lacked jurisdiction over the placement of riprap and the construction of dams in the lake and in the creek since, in its view, such activities do not constitute the "discharge of [a] pollutant" under § 301 of the F.W.P.C.A.***

A. Jurisdiction of the Corps of Engineers Under the Rivers and Harbors Act of 1899

In *The Daniel Ball v. United States, supra,*

the United States Supreme Court set forth what was to become the foundational test for determining federal regulatory power over the coastal or inland waters of the United States. Waters subject to federal regulatory jurisdiction, or "navigable waters of the United States," were defined by the Court as follows:

> Those rivers must be regarded as public navigable rivers in law which are navigable in fact. And they are navigable in fact when they are used, or are susceptible of being used, in their ordinary condition, as highways for commerce, over which trade and travel are or may be conducted in the customary modes of trade and travel on water. And they constitute navigable waters of the United States within the meaning of the Acts of Congress, in contradistinction from the navigable waters of the States, when they form in their ordinary condition by themselves, or by uniting with other waters, a continued highway over which commerce is or may be carried on with other States or foreign countries in the customary modes in which such commerce is conducted by water.

Id. at 563.

Although *The Daniel Ball* was a case brought in admiralty, the Court did not base its decision on federal maritime or admiralty jurisdiction but rather on federal power over coastal and inland waterways under the Commerce Clause. The Court stated that since the river in question flowed into Lake Michigan, an interstate waterway, a public navigable waterway is formed which is "brought under the direct control of Congress in the exercise of its commercial power." The Court cited its prior statement in *Gilman v. Philadelphia*, 70 U.S. (3 Wall.) 713 (1866), that "'[t]he [federal] power to regulate commerce comprehends the control***of all the navigable waters of the United States which are accessible from a state other than those in which they lie. For this purpose they are the public property of the nation, and subject to all the requisite legislation by Congress'". *The Daniel Ball v. United States, supra* at 564, quoting *Gilman*

v. Philadelphia, supra at 724-725. Although it has since been established that federal admiralty and maritime jurisdiction and federal power under the Commerce Clause are not necessarily coextensive, the test for federal jurisdiction over navigable waters which was set out in *The Daniel Ball* has been consistently applied by the Supreme Court in cases involving federal power under the Commerce Clause.***

The extent of federal regulatory power under § 10 of the Act, under which the Corps claims jurisdiction in the instant case, is limited to "navigable *** waters of the United States." Since this is the precise phrase which was defined by the Supreme Court in *The Daniel Ball* and which was used in that case and others to describe the reach of the federal commerce power over navigable waters prior to the enactment of the first Rivers and Harbors Act in 1890, we must assume that Congress intended the phrase to have the meaning which it had acquired in contemporary judicial interpretation. *** Indeed, virtually all courts which have interpreted the various provisions of the Rivers and Harbors Act of 1899 have begun with the basic definition of "navigable waters of the United States" set forth in *The Daniel Ball.*

Applying *The Daniel Ball* test to the waters at issue here, we agree with the District Court that Lake Minnetonka, and that portion of Minnehaha Creek above Minnetonka Mills, are not "navigable waters of the United States" as required for federal regulatory jurisdiction under § 10 of the Rivers and Harbors Act of 1899. *The Daniel Ball* test is bipartite: first, the body of water must be navigable in fact;[6] and second, it must itself, or together with other waters, form a highway over which commerce may be carried on with other states. All parties agree that both Lake Minnetonka, and that portion of Minnehaha Creek above Minnetonka Mills are navigable in fact. These waters do not,

---

[6]"Navigability in fact" has been broadened by later decisions of the Supreme Court to include bodies of water which were navigable in their natural state although they may not presently be so, or which, although traditionally considered to be non-navigable, might be made navigable with reasonable improvements.

however, form themselves, or in conjunction with other navigable waters, a continued highway over which interstate commerce can be conducted. Lake Minnetonka is located entirely within the State of Minnesota, with Minnehaha Creek as its sole connecting waterway. Although the portion of Minnehaha Creek above Minnetonka Mills is navigable, the remainder of the creek is not. Lake Minnetonka and the upper, navigable portion of Minnehaha Creek are not, therefore, part of a navigable interstate waterway, and federal regulatory jurisdiction under the Rivers and Harbors Act over these waters does not exist.

The Corps of Engineers contends, however, that federal regulatory jurisdiction under the Rivers and Harbors Act does not require that a body of water be part of an interstate waterway system, as long as it is a segment of a commercial highway, which may consist of water, rail or road connections. The Corps contends that since Lake Minnetonka and the upper portion of Minnehaha Creek have interstate road and rail connections, this is enough to make them "navigable waters of the United States" for the purposes of regulatory jurisdiction under the Act.

We disagree. Although the first prong of *The Daniel Ball* test has been broadened in later Supreme Court decisions, the second prong of this test, requiring a navigable interstate linkage by water, has remained unchanged.***

In *Hardy Salt Company v. Southern Pacific Trans. Co., supra,* a case almost factually identical to the one at bar, the Tenth Circuit rejected the argument that the Great Salt Lake in Utah was a navigable water of the United States for the purpose of jurisdiction under the Rivers and Harbors Act because it was a conduit for the transportation of goods which were shipped interstate by rail.*** Other courts which have recently considered this question have similarly concluded that entirely intrastate bodies of water, with no navigable interstate waterway linkage, are not subject to federal regulatory jurisdiction under the Rivers and Harbors Act.***

We do not, by our holding, imply that Congress could not extend federal regulatory jurisdiction under its commerce power to include such bodies of water.***

B. Jurisdiction of the Corps of Engineers Over the Construction of Dams and Placement of Riprap in Navigable Waters Under Section 404 of the Federal Water Pollution Control Act.

The District Court found, and all parties agree, that Lake Minnetonka and Minnehaha Creek above Minnetonka Mills are "navigable waters" as that term is used in the Federal Water Pollution Control Act, and, thus, the Corps of Engineers has jurisdiction under § 404 of the Act, 33 U.S.C. § 1344, to regulate the discharge of dredge or fill material into these waters. The parties disagree, however, as to whether the construction of dams and the placement of riprap constitute the discharge of dredge or fill material as envisioned by that section.

The District Court held that such activities do not come within the purview of § 404 because they do not constitute the discharge of a pollutant under § 301(a) of the Act. The court held that although § 502(6), 33 U.S.C. § 1362(6), includes "rock, sand, [and] cellar dirt" in the definition of "pollutant," the Act did not intend to extend federal jurisdiction to all matters which incidentally require rock or sand for construction. It held that since there was no evidence that the construction of dams or riprap significantly alter water quality, "there is no federal interest under the [Act] in the activity." The court declared 33 C.F.R. § 323.2(n), promulgated by the Corps, invalid insofar as it purports to regulate the construction of dams and riprap, and permanently enjoined the Corps from asserting regulatory jurisdiction over these activities in Lake Minnetonka and in that portion of Minnehaha Creek above Minnetonka Mills.*Id.*

We believe that the District Court interpreted the scope of the Act too narrowly. The Federal Water Pollution Control Act Amendments of 1972 were enacted after a Congressional finding that "the [prior] national effort to abate and control water pollution has been inadequate in every vital aspect ***". The purpose of the Amendments was broad and remedial, with their stated objective being "the restor[ation] and main[tenance] [of] the chemical, physical, and biological integrity of the Nation's waters." Section 101(a).

*   *   *

In keeping with far-reaching objectives of the Act, "pollutant" is very broadly defined. Section 502(6) 33 U.S.C. § 1362(6), defines this term as follows:

> The term "pollutant" means dredged spoil, solid waste, incinerator residue, sewage, garbage, sewage sludge, munitions, chemical wastes, biological materials, radioactive materials, heat, wrecked or discarded equipment, rock, sand, cellar dirt and industrial, municipal, and agricultural waste discharged into water. This term does not mean(A) "sewage from vessels"*** or (B) water, gas, or other material which is injected into a well to facilitate production of oil or gas***.

"Pollution" is also defined by the Act to mean "the man-made or man-induced alteration of the chemical, physical, biological, and radiological integrity of water." Section 502(19).

We believe that the construction of dams and riprap in navigable waters was clearly intended by Congress to come within the purview of §§ 301 and 404 of the Act. By including rock, sand and cellar dirt in the list of polluting substances, Congress recognized that the addition of these substances could affect the physical, as well as the chemical and biological, integrity of a waterbody. Since the construction of dams or riprap admittedly involves the placement of rock, sand or cellar dirt into the body of water, such activities would appear to come within the plain meaning of the Act.

Our interpretation of the Act as subjecting the construction of dams and riprap in navigable waters to the Corps' permitting program under § 404 is reinforced by the regulations promulgated by the Corps. The Corps has defined "fill material" under § 404 as follows:

> The term ["fill material"] generally includes without limitation, the following activities: Placement of fill that is necessary to the construction of any structure in a water of the United States; the building of any structure of impoundment requiring rock, sand, dirt or other material for its construction; site-development fills for recreational, industrial, commercial, residential, and other uses; causeways or road fills; dams and dikes; artificial island; property protection and/or reclamation devices such as riprap, groins, seawalls, breakwaters, and revetments, beach nourishment; levees; fill for structures such as sewage treatment facilities;***.
> 33 C.F.R. § 323.2 (n)(1977).
> ***

*   *   *

We find no justification in the Act for the District Court's conclusion that a significant alteration in water quality must be demonstrated before the addition of a particular substance to navigable waters can be classified as the discharge of a pollutant. Congress has, by the inclusion of certain substances in the definition of "pollutant" found in § 502(6), 33 U.S.C. § 1362(6), determined that the discharge of these substances in navigable waters is subject to the Act's control requirements.***

*   *   *

The District Court further held, and the appellees urge, that the construction of dams and the placement of riprap in Lake Minnetonka and in Minnehaha Creek should not be subject to the Corps' § 404 permitting program because that program is duplicative of state and local regulatory efforts. As commendable as such state and local efforts might be, they cannot supplant the duty of the Corps to enforce the provisions of the Act. It is important to note, however, that under § 67(b) of the Clean Water Act of 1977, a state may administer its own permit program for the regulation of the discharge of dredged or fill materials into navigable waters, other than traditionally navigable waters and adjacent wetlands, after approval of the state plan by the Administrator of the Environmental Protection Agency. Upon E.P.A. approval of a state plan, the federal program for the regulation of the discharge of dredged or fill materials into these waters will be suspended. *See* 33 U.S.C. § 1344(g)(1). If the State of Minnesota wishes to administer its own permit program for the discharge of dredged or fill material into these waters, it may make application for this authority in accordance with the statutory procedure. Until it does and until its program is approved, the Corps must fulfill its statutory obligation.

C. Summary.

In summary, we affirm the order of the District Court insofar as it declares that Lake Minnetonka and that portion of Minnehaha Creek above Minnetonka Mills are not navigable waters of the United States within the meaning of the Rivers and Harbors Act of 1899, insofar as it directs the Secretary of the Army to withdraw the "Determination of Navigability" of February 14, 1975, and insofar as it permanently enjoins the Corps of Engineers from asserting regulatory jurisdiction under the Rivers and Harbors Act of 1899 over these waters. We reverse the order of the District Court insofar as it declares 33 C.F.R. § 323.2(n), promulgated by the Corps under § 404 of the Federal Water Pollution Control Act, to be invalid, and insofar as it permanently enjoins the Corps from asserting regulatory jurisdiction over the construction of dams and the placement of riprap in Lake Minnetonka and that portion of Minnehaha Creek above Minnetonka Mills under § 404 of that Act.

Affirmed in part and reversed in part. Each party will bear its own costs.

NOTES

1. Consistent with this decision (and, indeed, with blackletter law), the D.C. Circuit in *National Wildlife Federation v. Alexander*, 613 F.2d 1054 (D.C. Cir. 1979), held that the North Dakota State Water Commission was not required by Section 10 of the Rivers and Harbors Act to obtain a permit from the Corps to construct a drainage channel that would empty into Devils Lake, a natural lake wholly within the state's borders which lacked any interstate connection by water.

Therefore, even though construction of the drainage channel would be an "excavation," and a "modification" or "alteration," Section 10 could not be applied.

Could, however, Section 404 of the Clean Water Act be applied to the cutting of the channel into Devils Lake?

2. Note that now private suits to block activities undertaken in violation of Section 10 of the Rivers and Harbors Act cannot be maintained in light of the Supreme Court's holding in *California v. Sierra Club*, 451 U.S. 287 (1981), that Section 10 created no implied private right of action on behalf of persons injured by its violation.

15   COMMON LAW REMEDIES

Milwaukee v. Illinois

451 U.S. 304 (1981)

JUSTICE REHNQUIST delivered the opinion of the Court.

When this litigation was first before us we recognized the existence of a federal "common law" which could give rise to a claim for abatement of a nuisance caused by interstate water pollution. *Illinois v. Milwaukee*, 406 U.S. 91 (1972). Subsequent to our decision, Congress enacted the Federal Water Pollution Control Act Amendments of 1972. We granted certiorari to consider the effect of this legislation on the previously recognized cause of action.

I

Petitioners, the City of Milwaukee, the Sewerage Commission of the City of Milwaukee, and the Metropolitan Sewerage Commission of the County of Milwaukee, are municipal corporations organized under the laws of Wisconsin. Together they construct, operate, and maintain sewer facilities serving Milwaukee County, an area of some 420 square miles with a population of over one million people. The facilities consist of a series of sewer systems and two sewage treatment plants located on the shores of Lake Michigan 25 and 39 miles from the Illinois border, respectively. The sewer systems are of both the "separated" and "combined" variety. A separated sewer system carries only sewage for treatment; a combined sewer system gathers both sewage and storm water runoff and transports them in the same conduits for treatment. On occasion, particularly after a spell of wet weather, overflows occur in the system which result in the discharge of sewage directly into Lake Michigan or tributaries leading into Lake

Michigan. The overflows occur at discrete discharge points throughout the system.

Respondent Illinois complains that these discharges, as well as the inadequate treatment of sewage at the two treatment plants, constitute a threat to the health of its citizens. Pathogens, disease-causing viruses and bacteria, are allegedly discharged into the lake with the overflows and inadequately treated sewage and then transported by lake currents to Illinois waters. Illinois also alleges that nutrients in the sewage accelerate the eutrophication, or aging, of the lake. Respondent Michigan intervened on this issue only.

Illinois' claim was first brought to this Court when Illinois sought leave to file a complaint under our original jurisdiction. *Illinois v. Milwaukee*, 406 U.S. 91 (1972). We declined to exercise original jurisdiction because the dispute was not between two States and Illinois had available an action in federal district court. The Court reasoned that federal law applied to the dispute, one between a sovereign State and political subdivisions of another State concerning pollution of interstate waters, but that the various laws which Congress had enacted "touching interstate waters" were "not necessarily the only federal remedies available." *Id.*, at 101, 103. Illinois could appeal to federal common law to abate a public nuisance in interstate or navigable waters. The Court recognized, however, that:

"It may happen that new federal laws and new federal regulations may in time pre-empt the field of federal common law of nuisance. But until that time comes to pass, federal courts will be empowered to appraise the equities of the suits alleging creation of a public nuisance by water pollution." *Id.*, at 107.

On May 19, 1972, Illinois filed a complaint in the United States District Court for the Northern District of Illinois seeking abatement, under federal common law, of the public nuisance petitioners were allegedly creating by their discharges.

Five months later Congress, recognizing that "the Federal water pollution control program ... has been inadequate in every vital aspect," *** passed the Federal Water Pollution Control Act Amendments of 1972. *** Petitioners operated their sewer systems and discharged effluent under permits issued by the Wisconsin Department of Natural Resources (DNR), which had duly qualified under § 402(b) of the Act as a permit granting agency under the superintendence of the EPA. Petitioners did not fully comply with the requirements of the permits and, as contemplated by the Act, § 402(b)(7), the state agency brought enforcement action in state court. On May 25, 1977, the state court entered a judgment requiring discharges from the treatment plants to meet the effluent limitations set forth in the permits and establishing a detailed timetable for the completion of planning and additional construction to control sewage overflows.

Trial on Illinois' claim commenced on January 11, 1977. On July 29 the District Court rendered a decision finding that respondents had proved the existence of a nuisance under federal common law, both in the discharge of inadequately treated sewage from petitioners' plants and in the discharge of untreated sewage from sewer overflows. The court ordered petitioners to eliminate all overflows and to achieve specified effluent limitations on treated sewage. A judgment order entered on November 15 specified a construction timetable for the completion of detention facilities to eliminate overflows. Separated sewer overflows are to be completely eliminated by 1986; combined sewer overflows by 1989. The detention facilities to be con-

structed must be large enough to permit full treatment of water from any storm up to the largest storm on record for the Milwaukee area. Both the aspects of the decision concerning overflows and concerning effluent limitations, with the exception of the effluent limitation for phosphorus, went considerably beyond the terms of petitioners' previously issued permits and the enforcement order of the state court.

On appeal, the Court of Appeals for the Seventh Circuit affirmed in part and reversed in part.***The court reversed the District Court insofar as the effluent limitations it imposed on treated sewage were more stringent than those in the permits and applicable EPA regulations. The order to eliminate all overflows, however, and the construction schedule designed to achieve this goal, were upheld.

II

Federal courts, unlike state courts, are not general common law courts and do not possess a general power to develop and apply their own rules of decision. The enactment of a federal rule in an area of national concern, and the decision whether to displace state law in doing so, is generally made not by the federal judiciary, purposefully insulated from democratic pressures, but by the people through their elected representatives in Congress. *Erie* recognized as much in ruling that a federal court could not generally apply a federal rule of decision, despite the existence of jurisdiction, in the absence of an applicable Act of Congress.

When Congress has not spoken to a particular issue, however, and when there exists a "significant conflict between some federal policy or interest and the use of state law," the Court has found it necessary, in a "few and restricted" instances, to develop federal common law. See, *e.g., Clearfield Trust Co. v. United States,* 318 U. S. 363, 367 (1943).***We have always recognized that federal common law is "subject to the paramount authority of Congress."***Federal common law is a "necessary expedient," and when Congress addresses a question previously governed by a decision rested on federal common law the need for such an unusual exercise of lawmaking by federal courts disappears.***

*   *   *

Contrary to the suggestions of respondents, the appropriate analysis in determining if federal statutory law governs a question previously the subject of federal common law is not the same as that employed in deciding if federal law pre-empts state law. In considering the latter question "we start with the assumption that the historic police powers of the States were not to be superseded by the Federal Act unless that was the clear and manifest purpose of Congress." While we have not hesitated to find pre-emption of state law, whether express or implied, when Congress has so indicated, or when enforcement of state regulations would impair "federal superintendence of the field," our analysis has included "due regard for the presuppositions of our embracing federal system, including the principle of diffusion of power not as a matter of doctrinaire localism but as a promoter of democracy." Such concerns are not implicated in the same fashion when the question is whether federal statutory or federal common law governs, and accordingly the same sort of evidence of a clear and manifest purpose is not required. Indeed, as noted, in cases such as the present "we start with the assumption" that it is for Congress, not federal courts, to articulate the appropriate standards to be applied as a matter of federal law.

III

We conclude that, at least so far as concerns the claims of respondents, Congress has not left the formulation of appropriate federal standards to the courts through application of often vague and indeterminate nuisance concepts and maxims of equity jurisprudence, but rather has occupied the field through the establishment of a comprehensive regulatory program supervised by an expert administrative agency. The 1972 amendments to the Federal Water Pollution Control Act were not merely another law "touching interstate waters" of the sort surveyed in *Illinois v. Milwaukee* and found inadequate to supplant federal common law. Rather, the amendments were viewed by Congress as a "total restructuring" and "complete rewriting" of the existing water pollution legislation considered in that case.***Congress' intent in enacting the amend-

ments was clearly to establish an all-encompassing program of water pollution regulation.***No Congressman's remarks on the legislation were complete without reference to the "comprehensive" nature of the amendments.***The establishment of such a self-consciously comprehensive program by Congress, which certainly did not exist when *Illinois v. Milwaukee* was decided, strongly suggests that there is no room for courts to attempt to improve on that program with federal common law.

Turning to the particular claims involved in this case, the action of Congress in supplanting the federal common law is perhaps clearest when the question of effluent limitations for discharges from the two treatment plants is considered. The duly issued permits under which the city commission discharges treated sewage from the Jones Island and South Shore treatment plants incorporate, as required by the Act, the specific effluent limitations established by EPA regulations pursuant to § 301 of the Act. There is thus no question that the problem of effluent limitations has been thoroughly addressed through the administrative scheme established by Congress, as contemplated by Congress. This being so there is no basis for a federal court to impose more stringent limitations than those imposed under the regulatory regime by reference to federal common law, as the District Court did in this case.***Federal courts lack authority to impose more stringent effluent limitations under federal common law than those imposed by the agency charged by Congress with administering this comprehensive scheme.

The overflows do not present a different case. They are point source discharges and, under the Act, are prohibited unless subject to a duly issued permit. As with the discharge of treated sewage, the overflows, through the permit procedure of the Act, are referred to expert administrative agencies for control. All three of the permits issued to petitioners explicitly address the problem of overflows.***As issued***, these permits require the city commission "to initiate a program leading to the elimination or control of all discharge overflow and/or bypass points in the ***Collector System . . . to assure attainment of all applicable Water Quality Standards."***

The enforcement action brought by the DNR in state court resulted in a judgment requiring "[e]limination of any bypassing or overflowing which occurs within the sewerage systems under dry weather by not later than July 1, 1982." Wet weather overflows from separated sewers were to be subject to a coordinated effort by the commissions resulting in correction of the problem by July 1, 1986, pursuant to a plan submitted to the DNR. As to the combined sewer overflows, the commissions were required to accomplish an abatement project, with design work completed by July 1, 1981, and construction by July 1, 1993. Annual progress reports were required to be submitted to the DNR.

It is quite clear from the foregoing that the state agency duly authorized by the EPA to issue discharge permits under the Act has addressed the problem of overflows from petitioners' sewer system. The agency imposed the conditions it considered best suited to further the goals of the Act, and provided for detailed progress reports so that it could continually monitor the situation. Enforcement action considered appropriate by the state agency was brought, as contemplated by the Act, again specifically addressed to the overflow problem. There is no "interstice" here to be filled by federal common law: overflows are covered by the Act and have been addressed by the regulatory regime established by the Act. Although a federal court may disagree with the regulatory approach taken by the agency with responsibility for issuing permits under the Act, such disagreement alone is no basis for the creation of federal common law.

Respondents strenuously argue that federal common law continues to be available, stressing that neither in the permits nor the enforcement order are there any effluent limitations on overflows. This argument, we think, is something of a red herring. The difference in treatment between overflows and treated effluent by the agencies is due to differences in the *nature* of the problems, *not* the extent to which the problems have been addressed. The relevant question with overflow discharges is not, as with discharges of treated sewage, what concentration

of various pollutants will be permitted. Rather the question is what degree of control will be required in preventing overflows and ensuring that the sewage undergoes treatment. This question is answered by construction plans designed to accommodate a certain amount of sewage that would otherwise be discharged on overflow occasions. The EPA has not promulgated regulations mandating specific control guidelines because of a recognition that the problem is "site specific."***Decision is made on a case-by-case basis, through the permit procedure, as was done here. Demanding specific regulations of general applicability before concluding that Congress has addressed the problem to the exclusion of federal common law asks the wrong question. The question is whether the field has been occupied, not whether it has been occupied in a particular manner.[18]

The invocation of federal common law by the District Court and the Court of Appeals in the face of congressional legislation supplanting it is peculiarly inappropriate in areas as complex as water pollution control.***Not only are the technical problems difficult—doubtless the reason Congress vested authority to administer the Act in administrative agencies possessing the necessary expertise—but the general area is particularly unsuited to the approach inevitable under a regime of federal common law. Congress criticized past approaches to water pollution control as being "sporadic" and "ad hoc," apt characterizations of any judicial approach applying federal common law.

It is also significant that Congress addressed in the 1972 amendments one of the major concerns underlying the recognition of federal common law in *Illinois v. Milwaukee*. We were concerned in that case that Illinois did not have any forum in which to protect its inter-

---

[18]The point is perhaps made most clear if one asks what inadequacy in the treatment by Congress the courts below rectified through creation of federal common law. In imposing stricter effluent limitations the District Court was not "filling a gap" in the regulatory scheme, it was simply providing a different regulatory scheme. The same is true with overflows. The District Court simply ordered planning and construction designed to achieve more stringent control of overflows than the planning and construction undertaken pursuant to the permits. ***

ests unless federal common law were created. In the 1972 amendments Congress provided ample opportunity for a State affected by decisions of a neighboring State's permit granting agency to seek redress. Under § 402(b)(3), a state permit granting agency must ensure that any State whose waters may be affected by the issuance of a permit receives notice of the permit application and the opportunity to participate in a public hearing. Wisconsin law accordingly guarantees such notice and hearing. Respondents received notice of each of the permits involved here, and public hearings were held, but they did not participate in them in any way. Section 402(b)(5) provides that state permit granting agencies must ensure that affected States have an opportunity to submit written recommendations concerning the permit applications to the issuing State and the EPA, and both the affected State and the EPA must receive notice and a statement of reasons if any part of the recommendations of the affected State are not accepted. Again respondents did not avail themselves of this statutory opportunity. Under § 402(d)(2)(A), the EPA may veto any permit issued by a State when waters of another State may be affected. Respondents did not request such action. Under § 402(d)(4) of the Act, added in 1977, the EPA itself may issue permits if a stalemate between an issuing and objecting State develops. The basic grievance of respondents is that the permits issued to petitioners pursuant to the Act do not impose stringent enough controls on petitioners' discharges. The statutory scheme established by Congress provides a forum for the pursuit of such claims before expert agencies by means of the permit granting process. It would be quite inconsistent with this scheme if federal courts were in effect to "write their own ticket" under the guise of federal common law after permits have already been issued and permittees have been planning and operating in reliance on them.

Respondents argue that congressional intent to preserve the federal common law remedy recognized in *Illinois v. Milwaukee* is evident in §§ 510 and 505(e) of the statute. Section 510 provides that nothing in the Act shall preclude States from adopting and enforcing limitations on the discharge of pollutants more stringent than those adopted under the Act. It is one thing, however, to say that States may adopt more stringent limitations through state administrative processes, or even that States may establish such limitations through state nuisance law, and apply them to in-state dischargers. It is quite another to say that the State may call upon *federal* courts to employ *federal* common law to establish more stringent standards applicable to out-of-state dischargers.***Section 510 clearly contemplates state authority to establish more stringent pollution limitations; nothing in it, however, suggests that this was to be done by federal court actions premised on federal common law.

Subsection 505(e) provides:

> "Nothing in this *section* shall restrict any right which any person (or class of persons) may have under any statute or common law to seek enforcement of any effluent standard or limitation or to seek any other relief (including relief against the Administrator or a state agency)" (emphasis supplied).

Respondents argue that this evinces an intent to preserve the federal common law of nuisance. We, however, are inclined to view the quoted provision as meaning what it says: that nothing in § 505, the citizen suit provision, should be read as limiting any other remedies which might exist.

Subsection 505(e) is virtually identical to subsections in the citizen suit provisions of several environmental statutes. The subsection is common language accompanying citizen suit provisions and we think that it means only that the provision of such suit does not revoke other remedies. It most assuredly cannot be read to mean that the Act as a whole does not supplant formerly available federal common law actions but only that the particular section authorizing citizen suits does not do so. No one, however, maintains that the citizen suit provision preempts federal common law.

We are thus not persuaded that § 505(e) aids respondents in this case, even indulging the unlikely assumption that the reference to "common law" in § 505(e) includes the limited *federal* common law as opposed to the more routine state common law.

*   *   *

We therefore conclude that no federal common law remedy was available to respondents in this case. The judgment of the Court of Appeals is therefore vacated, and the case remanded for proceedings consistent with this opinion.

JUSTICE BLACKMUN, with whom JUSTICE MARSHALL and JUSTICE STEVENS join, dissenting.

*   *   *

I

The Court's analysis of federal common law displacement rests, I am convinced, on a faulty assumption. In contrasting congressional displacement of the common law with federal pre-emption of state law, the Court assumes that as soon as Congress "addresses a question previously governed" by federal common law, "the need for such an unusual exercise of lawmaking by federal courts disappears." This "automatic displacement" approach is inadequate in two respects. It fails to reflect the unique role federal common law plays in resolving disputes between one State and the citizens or government of another. In addition, it ignores this Court's frequent recognition that federal common law may complement congressional action in the fulfillment of federal policies.

It is well-settled that a body of federal common law has survived the decision in *Erie R. Co. v. Tompkins*, 304 U.S. 64 (1938).***Chief among the federal interests served by this common law are the resolution of interstate disputes and the implementation of national statutory or regulatory policies.

Both before and after *Erie*, the Court has fashioned federal law where the interstate nature of a controversy renders inappropriate the law of either State. See, *e.g., Nebraska v. Wyoming*, 325 U.S. 589 (1945)***(apportioning waters of interstate stream).***

*   *   *

This Court also has applied federal common law where federally created substantive rights and obligations are at stake. Thus, the Court has been called upon to pronounce common law that will fill the interstices of a pervasively federal framework, or avoid subjecting relevant federal interests to the inconsistencies in the laws of several States. If the federal interest is sufficiently strong, federal common law may be drawn upon in settling disputes even though the statute or Constitution alone provides no precise answer to the question posed.

*   *   *

Thus, quite contrary to the statements and intimations of the Court today, *Illinois v. Milwaukee* did not create the federal common law of nuisance. Well before this Court and Congress acted in 1972, there was ample recognition of and foundation for a federal common law of nuisance applicable to Illinois' situation. Congress cannot be presumed to have been unaware of the relevant common-law history, any more than it can be deemed to have been oblivious to the decision in *Illinois v. Milwaukee*, announced six months prior to the passage of the Federal Water Pollution Control Act Amendments of 1972 (Act or Amendments). The central question is whether, given its presumed awareness, Congress, in passing these Amendments, intended to prevent recourse to the federal common law of nuisance.

The answer to this question, it seems to me, requires a more thorough exploration of congressional intent than is offered by the Court. Congress had "spoken to" the particular problem of interstate water pollution as far back as 1888, and in 1948 did so in a broad and systematic fashion with the enactment of the Water Pollution Control Act. In *Illinois v. Milwaukee*, the Court properly regarded such expressions of congressional interest as not an obstacle but an incentive to application of the federal common law. The fact that Congress in 1972 once again addressed the complicated and difficult problem of purifying our Nation's waters should not be taken as presumptive evidence, let alone conclusive proof, that Congress meant to foreclose pre-existing approaches to controlling interstate water pollution. Where the possible extinction of federal common law is at issue, a reviewing court is obligated to look not only to the magnitude of the legislative action but also with some care to the evidence of specific congressional intent.

II

In my view, the language and structure of the Clean Water Act leave no doubt that Congress intended to preserve the federal common law of nuisance. Section 505 (e) of the Act reads:

"Nothing in this section shall restrict any right which *any person* (or class of persons) may have under *any statute or common law* to seek enforcement of any effluent standard or limitation *or to seek any other relief* (including relief against the Administrator or a State agency)." (emphasis added).

The Act specifically defines "person" to include States, and thus embraces respondents Illinois and Michigan. § 502 (5). It preserves their right to bring an action against the governmental entities who are charged with enforcing the statute. Most important, as succinctly stated by the Court of Appeals in this case: "There is nothing in the phrase 'any statute or common law' that suggests that this provision is limited to state common law." 599 F. 2d 151, 163 (CA7 1979). To the best of my knowledge, every federal court that has considered the issue has concluded that, in enacting § 505(e), Congress meant to preserve federal as well as state common law.

*   *   *

[U]nder the statutory scheme, any permit issued by the EPA or a qualifying state agency does not insulate a discharger from liability under other federal or state law. To the contrary, the permit granted pursuant to § 402(k) confers assurances with respect to certain specified sections of the Act, but the requirements under other provisions as well as separate legal obligations remain unaffected.

The Court offers three responses to this view of congressional intent.*** The Court thus reads § 505(e) as though Congress has said that " 'this section' does not take away any pre-existing

remedies, but the remainder of the statute does." This is an extremely strained reading of the statutory language, and one that is at odds with the manifest intent of Congress to permit more stringent remedies under both federal and state law.***

The Court also relies on certain language contained in the legislative history of the 1972 amendments. *Ante*, at 11-12. Based on the remarks of several of the Act's proponents that this was the most comprehensive water pollution bill prepared to date, the Court finds a strong congressional suggestion that there is no room for improvement through the federal common law. But there is nothing talismanic about such generalized references. The fact that legislators may characterize their efforts as more "comprehensive" than prior legislation hardly prevents them from authorizing the continued existence of supplemental legal and equitable solutions to the broad and serious problem addressed. Moreover, the Court ignores express statements of legislative intent that contradict its position.***

This deliberate preservation of all remedies previously available at common law makes no distinction between the common law of individual States and federal common law. Indeed, the legislative debates indicate that Congress was specifically aware of the presence of federal common law, and intended that it would survive passage of the 1972 amendments.***

Finally, the Court attaches significance to the fact that the 1972 amendments provided a more rigorous administrative mechanism for addressing interstate controversies.***

***[C]ontrary to what the Court implies, Congress never intended that failure to participate in the § 402 administrative process would serve as a jurisdictional bar. Nothing in the language of § 402 suggests that a neighboring State's participation in the permit-granting process is anything other than voluntary and optional. Indeed, the Conference Committee considering the 1977 amendments to the Act was presented with a proposal that *would* have made such participation a jurisdictional prerequisite. This proposal was not adopted by the

Conference Committee and among its opponents was the Department of Justice.***

The Justice Department's position on the survival of federal common law is consistent with the stance taken by the EPA both in this litigation and throughout the period since the 1972 Amendments were enacted. The EPA in fact has relied upon the federal common law of nuisance in addition to the remedies available under the statute in seeking to protect water quality. As the agency charged with enforcing and implementing the Act, EPA's interpretation of the scope and limits of that statute is entitled to considerable deference. Where, as here, the agency has publicly and consistently acted upon its interpretation, congressional silence is not without significance, particularly since this area has been a subject of frequent and intense legislative attention.***

III

Assuming that Congress did preserve a federal common law of nuisance, and that respondents properly stated federal common law claims for relief, there remains the question whether the particular common law applied here was reasonable.***

The Act sets forth certain effluent limitations. As did the Court of Appeals, a court applying federal common law in a given instance may well decline to impose effluent limitations more stringent than those required by Congress because the complainant has failed to show that stricter standards will abate the nuisance or appreciably diminish the threat of injury. But it is a far different proposition to pronounce as does the Court today, that federal courts *"lack authority* to impose more stringent effluent limitations under federal common law than those imposed" under the statutory scheme.***

The problem of controlling overflows is particularly amenable to application of this common law authority. As the courts below found, see 599 F.2d, at 167-168, the sewer systems operated by petitioners include some 239 bypass or overflow points from which raw sewage is discharged directly into Lake Michigan or into rivers that flow into the lake. In a single month in 1976, discharge from 11 of the 239 discrete overflow points amounted to some 646 million gallons of untreated sewage.***

No provision of the Act explicitly addresses the discharge of raw sewage into public waters from overflow points. While the Administrator has issued regulations that define secondary treatment in terms of certain minimum levels of effluent quality, he also has acknowledged that combined sewer overflows raise special concerns that must be resolved on a case-by-case basis. This record demonstrates that both Congress and the Administrator recognized the inadequacy of the statutory scheme. It surely does not show that these responsible parties intended no role for the federal common law.

*   *   *

IV

There is one final disturbing aspect to the Court's decision. By eliminating the federal common law of nuisance in this area, the Court in effect is encouraging recourse to state law wherever the federal statutory scheme is perceived to offer inadequate protection against pollution from outside the State, either in its enforcement standards or in the remedies afforded. This recourse is now inevitable under a statutory scheme that accords a significant role to State as well as federal law. But in the present context it is also unfortunate, since it undermines the Court's prior conclusion that it is federal rather than state law that should govern the regulation of *inter*state water pollution. Instead of promoting a more uniform federal approach to the problem of alleviating interstate pollution, I fear that today's decision will lead States to turn to their own courts for statutory or common law assistance in filling the interstices of the federal statute. Rather than encourage such a prospect, I would adhere to the principles clearly enunciated in *Illinois v. Milwaukee,* and affirm the judgment of the Court of Appeals.

NOTES

1. What effect should be given to the savings clause of Section 505(e)? Should federal common law be distinguished from state common law?

Indulging in the "unlikely assumption" that the reference to "common law" in the savings clause *does* include actions under the federal common law, does the remainder of the Act indicate that such actions are displaced? Do any sections specifically apply? Sections 309 and 402(b)(7) address enforcement of the Act. Do they constitute displacement?

2. Should a court be able to impose more stringent effluent standards than those imposed in the Section 402 permit issued by the responsible agency? Is this what the lower courts had done here? Shouldn't the Clean Water Act be read to at least protect a complying permittee against such a result?

3. Should a state's participation in hearings on permits in a neighboring state have any effect on its ability to seek relief from harm caused by pollution discharged in that state? How can one state protect itself against discharges under a permit issued by another state? The Court cites Section 402(b)(3), (b)(5), (d)(2)(A), and (d)(4) as provisions in the Clean Water Act in which "Congress provided ample opportunity for a state affected by decisions of a neighboring state's permit granting agency to seek redress." Do these provisions insure that the affected state's standards will be incorporated into the permit, or merely that it will have a forum for making its views known?

Could any other sections in the Act be utilized to control discharges from another state? Consider Section 301 (b)(1)(C) as implemented by Sections 402 (a)(1) and (b)(1)(A). Should these sections be read to require that a permit issued by one state incorporate any more stringent effluent standards established by another affected state? How about reading them to at least require protection of other states' *water quality* standards?

4. Consider the last paragraph in the dissent. Can one state invoke its *own* common law of nuisance to control pollution originating in an adjoining state? Should it expect protection under the nuisance law of the source state? Don't such questions raise the very problems which the *federal* common law of nuisance was designed to solve?

5. On remand of the case from the Supreme Court, the Seventh Circuit held that application of the statutory and common law of Illinois was likewise preempted by the Clean Water Act. *Illinois v. Milwaukee,* 731 F.2d 403 (7th Cir. 1984). The savings clauses in Sections 505(e) and 510 were read only to preserve rights to relief under statutes and common law of the state within which the discharge occurred. (In neither this case nor the companion case of *Scott v. City of Hammond* did the state or individual plaintiffs claim a violation of the law of the state of discharge.) To allow the law of the state in which any injury occurred to apply would, in the Seventh Circuit's mind, undermine the uniformity and state cooperation envisioned by the Clean Water Act for interstate waters.

The contrary conclusion was reached by the federal district court in Vermont in *Ouellette v. International Paper Co.,* 602 F. Supp. 264 (D. Vt.), *aff'd,* 23 ERC 1703 (2d Cir. 1985). There the court held that various Vermont residents owning property on Lake Champlain might invoke the Vermont common law of nuisance in an action for damages and injunctive relief against a paper mill for its discharges across the lake in New York. The Second Circuit affirmed in a three-paragraph per curiam opinion, and the U.S. Supreme Court granted certiorari on March 24, 1986 *(International Paper Co. v. Ouellette,* No. 85-1233).

6. Congress has not provided for federal regulation of nonpoint discharges, or insured that the states will do so. Does the Clean Water Act nevertheless preclude the use of the federal common law of nuisance to enjoin a harmful nonpoint discharge?

7. During the time between *Illinois v. Milwaukee,* in 1972, and the principal case, lower federal courts were divided as to whether:

a) The federal common law of nuisance could be invoked only by a state. Compare *Parsell v. Shell Oil Co.,* 421 F. Supp. 1275 (D. Conn. 1976), with *Byram River v. Village of Port Chester,* 394 F. Supp. 618 (D. N. Y. 1975).

b) The doctrine applied only to interstate waters. Compare *Illinois v. Outboard Marine Corp.,* 619 F.2d 623 (7th Cir. 1980), with *Committee for Consideration of Jones Falls Sewage System v. Train,* 539 F.2d 1006 (4th Cir. 1976).

c) The doctrine could be used only to obtain injunctive relief. Compare *Parsell v. Shell Oil Co., supra,* with *National Sea Clammers Ass'n. v. City of New York,* 616 F.2d 1223 (3d Cir. 1980).

The principal case would largely seem to render those questions moot. In *Milwaukee,* though, a court arguably was substituting its judgment for that of the authorized expert agency with respect to effluent limitations. Suppose that a state or individual sued a discharger under the federal common law of nuisance, seeking damages for harm caused by discharges in violation of Section 402 permits. Suppose further that an injunction would be of no value since the harm had already occurred. Wouldn't a court merely be fulfilling its traditional role in awarding damages? The Clean Water Act does not provide for private damages, nor would such damages seem to conflict with the purposes of the Act. Insofar as it provides damages for violations of Section 402 permits, the federal common law of nuisance should not be displaced by the Act, should it?

Middlesex County Sewerage Authority
v.
National Sea Clammers Association
453 U. S. 1 (1981)

JUSTICE POWELL delivered the opinion of the Court.

In this case, involving alleged damage to fishing grounds caused by discharges and ocean dumping of sewage and other waste, we are faced with questions concerning the availability of a damages remedy, based either on federal common law or on the provisions of two Acts—the Federal Water Pollution Control Act (FWPCA), as amended, 33 U.S.C. § 1251 *et seq.,* and the Marine Protection, Research, and Sanctuaries Act of 1972 (MPRSA), 33 U.S.C. § 1401 *et seq.*

I

Respondents are an organization whose members harvest fish and shellfish off the coast of New York and New Jersey, and one individual member of that organization. In 1977, they brought suit in the United States District Court for the District of New Jersey against petitioners — various governmental entities and officials from New York, New Jersey and the Federal Government. Their complaint alleged that sewage, sewage "sludge," and other waste materials were being discharged into New York Harbor and the Hudson River by some of the respondents. In addition it complained of the dumping of such materials directly into the ocean from maritime vessels. The complaint alleged that, as a result of these activities, the Atlantic Ocean was becoming polluted, and it made special reference to a massive growth of algae said to

---

[4] The complaint alleged that this growth of algae was caused by the discharges of sewage and "covered an area of the Atlantic Ocean ranging from approximately the southwest portion of Long Island, New York, to a point approximately due east of Cape May, New Jersey, and extending from a few miles offshore to more than 20 miles out to sea." Complaint ¶ 35, App. 25a. Respondents' Brief in this Court states that when "this massive algal bloom died, its residuals settled on the ocean floor, creating a condition of anoxia, or oxygen deficiency, in and about the water near the ocean's floor. This condition resulted in the death and destruction of an enormous amount of marine life, particularly with respect to the shellfish and other ocean-

have appeared offshore in 1976.[4] It then stated that this pollution was causing the "collapse of the fishing, clamming and lobster industries which operate in the waters of the Atlantic Ocean."

Invoking a wide variety of legal theories, respondents sought injunctive and declaratory relief, $250 million in compensatory damages, and $250 million in punitive damages. The District Court granted summary judgment to petitioners on all counts of the complaint.

In holdings relevant here, the District Court rejected respondents' nuisance claim under federal common law, see *Illinois v. Milwaukee*, 406 U.S. 91 (1972), on the ground that such a cause of action is not available to private parties. With respect to the claims based on alleged violations of the FWPCA, the court noted that respondents had failed to comply with the 60-day notice requirement of the "citizen suit" provision in § 505 of the Act. This provision allows suits under the Act by private citizens, but authorizes only prospective relief, and the citizen plaintiffs first must give notice to the EPA, the State, and any alleged violator. Because respondents did not give the requisite notice, the court refused to allow them to proceed with a claim under the Act independent of the citizen-suit provision and based on the general jurisdictional grant in 28 U.S.C. § 1331. The court applied the same analysis to respondents' claims under the MPRSA, which contains similar citizen-suit and notice provisions. Finally, the court rejected a possible claim of maritime tort, both because respondents had failed to plead such claim explicitly and because they had failed to comply with the procedural requirements of the federal and state tort claims acts.

The United States Court of Appeals for the Third Circuit reversed as to the claims based on the FWPCA, the MPRSA, the federal common law of nuisance, and maritime tort. 616 F. 2d 1222 (1980).***

***Although the court was not explicit on this question, it apparently concluded that suits for *damages*, as well as for injunctive relief, could

be brought under the FWPCA and the MPRSA.

With respect to the federal common law nuisance claims, the Court of Appeals rejected the District Court's conclusion that private parties may not bring such claims. It also held, applying common law principles, that respondents "alleged sufficient individual damage to permit them to recover damages for this essentially public nuisance." It thus went considerably beyond *Illinois v. Milwaukee, supra,* which involved purely prospective relief sought by state plaintiff.[15]

Petitions for a writ of certiorari raising a variety of arguments were filed in this Court***. We granted these petitions, limiting review to three questions: (i) whether FWPCA and MPRSA imply a private right of action independent of their citizen-suit provisions, (ii) whether all federal common law nuisance actions concerning ocean pollution now are pre-empted by the legislative scheme contained in the FWPCA and the MPRSA, and (iii) if not, whether a private citizen has standing to sue for damages under the federal common law of nuisance. We hold that there is no implied right of action under these statutes and that the federal common law of nuisance has been fully pre-empted in the area of ocean pollution."[17]

II

The Federal Water Pollution Control Act*.***

The Marine Protection, Research, and Sanctuaries Act of 1972, sought to create comprehensive federal regulation of the dumping of materials into ocean waters near the United States coastline. Section 101 of the Act requires a permit for any dumping into ocean waters, when the material is transported from the

---

[15]The court also held that respondents had offered allegations sufficient to make out a claim of maritime tort, cognizable under admiralty jurisdiction. It did not decide whether the Federal Tort Claims Act, with its various procedural requirements, applies to any of respondents' federal-law claims against federal defendants, although it did hold that the Act precluded a "money damage recovery against federal agencies based on state law."

[17]We therefore need not discuss the question whether the federal common law of nuisance could ever be the basis of a suit for damages by a private party.

---

bottom dwellers and other marine life unable to escape the blighted area." Brief for Respondents 4.

United States or on an American vessel or air-craft.[19] In addition, it requires a permit for the dumping of material transported from outside the United States into the territorial seas or in the zone extending 12 miles from the coastline, "to the extent that it may affect the territorial sea or the territory of the United States."

The exact nature of the respondents' claims under these two Acts is not clear, but the claims appear to fall into two categories. The main contention is that the EPA and the Army Corps of Engineers have permitted the New Jersey and New York defendants to discharge and dump pollutants in amounts that are not permitted by the Acts. In addition, they seem to allege that the New York and New Jersey defendants have violated the terms of their permits. The question before us is whether respondents may raise either of these claims in a private suit for injunctive and monetary relief, where such a suit is not expressly authorized by either of these Acts.

A

It is unnecessary to discuss at length the principles set out in recent decisions concerning the recurring question whether Congress intended to create a private right of action under a federal statute without saying so explicitly. The key to the inquiry is the intent of the legislature. We look first, of course, to the statutory language, particularly to the provisions made therein for enforcement and relief. Then we review the legislative history and other traditional aids of statutory interpretation to determine congressional intent.

These Acts contain unusually elaborate enforcement provisions, conferring authority to sue for this purpose both on government officials and private citizens. ***

These enforcement mechanisms, most of which have their counterpart under the MPRSA, are supplemented by the express citizen-suit provisions in § 505(a) of the FWPCA and § 105(g) of the MPRSA. These citizen-suit provisions authorize private persons to sue for injunctions

to enforce these statutes. Plaintiffs invoking these provisions first must comply with specified procedures — which respondents here ignored — including in most cases 60 days' prior notice to potential defendants.

In view of these elaborate enforcement provisions it cannot be assumed that Congress intended to authorize by implication additional judicial remedies for private citizens suing under MPRSA and FWPCA. As we stated in *Transamerica Mortgage Advisers, supra,* "it is an elemental canon of statutory construction that where a statute expressly provides a particular remedy or remedies, a court must be chary of reading others into it." 444 U.S. at 19. In the absence of strong indicia of a contrary congressional intent, we are compelled to conclude that Congress provided precisely the remedies it considered appropriate.

As noted above, the Court of Appeals avoided this inference. Discussing the FWPCA, it held that the existence of a citizen-suit provision in § 505(a) does not rule out implied forms of private enforcement of the Act. It arrived at this conclusion by asserting that Congress intended in § 505(a) to create a limited cause of action for "private attorneys general" — "non-injured member[s] of the public" suing to promote the general welfare rather than to redress an injury to their own welfare. ***

There are at least three problems with this reasoning. First, the language of the savings clause on which the Court of Appeals relied is quite ambiguous concerning the intent of Congress to "preserve" remedies under the FWPCA itself. It merely states that nothing in the citizen-suit provision "shall restrict any right which any person . . . may have under any statute or common law to seek enforcement of any effluent standard or limitation or to seek any other relief." It is doubtful that the phrase "any statute" includes the very statute in which this statement was contained.

Moreover, the reasoning on which the Court of Appeals relied is flawed for another reason. It draws a distinction between "non-injured" plaintiffs who may bring citizen suits to enforce provisions of these Acts, and the "injured" plaintiffs in this case who claim a right to sue under the Acts, not by virtue of the citizen-suit provisions, but rather under the language of the savings clauses. In fact, it is clear that the citizen-suit provisions apply only to persons who can claim some sort of injury and there is, therefore, no reason to infer the existence of a separate right of action for "injured" plaintiffs. "Citizen" is defined in the citizen-suit section of the FWPCA as "a person or persons having an interest which is or may be adversely affected." § 505(g). It is clear from the Senate Conference Report that this phrase was intended by Congress to allow suits by all persons possessing standing under this Court's decision in *Sierra Club v. Morton,* 405 U.S. 727 (1972). ***

*   *   *

The Court of Appeals also applied its reasoning to the MPRSA. But here again we are persuaded that Congress evidenced no intent to authorize by implication private remedies under these Acts apart from the expressly authorized citizens suits. ***

***Thus, the structure of the Acts and their legislative history both lead us to conclude that Congress intended that private remedies in addition to those expressly provided should not be implied. Where, as here, Congress has made clear that implied private actions are not contemplated, the courts are not authorized to ignore this legislative judgment.

B

Although the parties have not suggested it, there remains a possible alternative source of *express* congressional authorization of private suits under these Acts. Last Term, in *Maine v. Thiboutot,* 448 U.S. 1 (1980), the Court construed 42 U.S.C. § 1983 as authorizing suits to redress violations by state officials of rights created by federal statutes. Accordingly, it could be argued that respondents may sue the municipalities and sewerage boards among the petitioners under the FWPCA and MPRSA by virtue of a right of action created by § 1983.

***The claim brought here arguably falls within the scope of *Maine v. Thiboutot* because it involves a suit by a private party claiming that a federal statute has been violated under color of state law, causing an injury. The Court,

however, has recognized two exceptions to the application of § 1983 to statutory violations. In *Pennhurst State School and Hospital v. Halderman,* 451 U.S. 1 (1981), we remanded certain claims for a determination (i) whether Congress had foreclosed private enforcement of that statute in the enactment itself, and (ii) whether the statute at issue there was the kind that created enforceable "rights" under § 1983. *Id.,* at 451 U.S. 1. In the present case, because we find that Congress foreclosed a § 1983 remedy under these Acts, we need not reach the second question whether these Acts created "rights, privileges, or immunities" within the meaning of § 1983.

When the remedial devices provided in a particular act are sufficiently comprehensive, they may suffice to demonstrate congressional intent to preclude the remedy of suits under § 1983. *** As discussed above, the FWPCA and MPRSA do provide quite comprehensive enforcement mechanisms. It is hard to believe that Congress intended to preserve the § 1983 right of action when it created so many specific statutory remedies including the two citizen-suit provisions.***

III

The remaining two issues on which we granted certiorari relate to respondents' federal claims based on the federal common law of nuisance.***In this case, we need not decide whether a cause of action may be brought under federal common law by a private plaintiff, seeking damages. The Court has now held that the federal common law of nuisance in the area of water pollution is entirely pre-empted by the more comprehensive scope of the FWPCA, which was completely revised soon after the decision in *Illinois v. Milwaukee.* See *Milwaukee v. Illinois,* 451 U.S. 304 (1981).

This decision disposes entirely of respondents' federal common law claims, since there is no reason to suppose that the pre-emptive effect of the FWPCA is any less when pollution of coastal waters is at issue. To the extent that this case involves ocean waters not covered by the FWPCA, and regulated under the MPRSA, we see no cause for different treatment of the pre-emption question. The regulatory scheme of the MPRSA is no less comprehensive, with respect to ocean dumping, than are analogous provisions of the FWPCA.[32]

We therefore must dismiss the federal common law claims because their underlying legal basis is now pre-empted by statute. As discussed above, we also dismiss the claims under the MPRSA and the FWPCA because respondents lack a right of action under those statutes. We vacate the judgment below with respect to these two claims, and remand for further proceedings.

JUSTICE STEVENS, with whom JUSTICE BLACKMUN joins, concurring in the judgment in part and dissenting in part.

*　　　*　　　*

Although I agree with the Court's disposition of the implied private right of action question in these cases, I write separately to emphasize that the Court's current approach to the judicial task of fashioning appropriate remedies for violations of federal statutes is out of step with the Court's own history and tradition. More importantly, I believe that the Court's appraisal of the intent expressed by Congress in the Federal Water Pollution Control Act Amendments of 1972 (Clean Water Act) and the Marine Protection, Research, and Sanctuaries Act of 1972 (MPRSA) with respect to the availability of private remedies under other federal statutes or the federal common law is palpably wrong.

In the present context of these cases, we of course know nothing about the ultimate merits of the claims asserted by respondents. As the cases come to us, however, we must make certain assumptions in analyzing the questions presented. First, we must assume that the complaint speaks the truth when it alleges that the petitioners have dumped large quantities of sewage and toxic waste in the Atlantic Ocean and its tributaries and that these dumping operations have violated the substantive provisions of the Clean Water Act and the MPRSA. Second, we

must also assume that these illegal operations have caused an injury to respondents' commercial interests.*** Finally, we must assume that, apart from these two statutes, the dumping operations of petitioners would constitute a common law nuisance for which respondents would have a federal remedy. The net effect of the Court's analysis of the legislative intent is therefore a conclusion that Congress, by enacting the Clean Water Act and the MPRSA, deliberately deprived respondents of effective federal remedies that would otherwise have been available to them. In my judgment, the language of both statutes, as well as their legislative history, belies this improbable conclusion.

I

The Court's holding that Congress decided in the Clean Water Act and the MPRSA to withdraw the express remedy provided by 42 U.S.C. § 1983 seems to rest on nothing more than the fact that these statutes provide other express remedies and do not mention § 1983. Because the enforcement mechanisms provided in the statutes are "quite comprehensive," the Court finds it "hard to believe that Congress intended to preserve the § 1983 right of action . . . ." *Ante*, at 18. There are at least two flaws in this reasoning. First, the question is not whether Congress "intended to preserve the § 1983 right of action," but rather whether Congress intended to withdraw that right of action. Second, I find it not at all hard to believe that Congress intended to preserve, or, more precisely, did not intend to withdraw, the § 1983 remedy because Congress made this intention explicit in the language of both statutes and in the relevant legislative history.

*　　　*　　　*

Despite their comprehensive enforcement mechanisms, both statutes expressly preserve all legal remedies otherwise available. The statutes state in so many words that the authorization of an express remedy in the statute itself shall not give rise to an inference that Congress intended to foreclose other remedies. Thus, § 505(e) of the Clean Water Act states:

"Nothing in this section shall restrict any right which any person (or

---

[32]Indeed, as noted *supra*, at n. 14 [deleted herein], the ocean dumping of sewage sludge must end altogether by December 31, 1981. To the extent that Congress allowed some continued dumping of sludge prior to that date, this represents a considered judgment that it made sense to allow entities like petitioners to adjust to the coming change.

class of persons) may have under any statute or common law to seek enforcement of any effluent standard or limitation or to seek any other relief (including relief against the Administrator or a State agency)." 33 U.S.C. § 1365(e).

And, §105(g)(5) of the MPRSA states:

"The injunctive relief provided by this subsection shall not restrict any right which any person (or class of persons) may have under any statute or common law to seek enforcement of any standard or limitation or to seek any other relief (including relief against the Administrator, the Secretary, or a State agency)." 33 U.S.C. § 1415(g)(5).
***

*   *   *

***Thus, the Court holds that the statutory phrase "any statute" does not refer to the Clean

Water Act or the MPRSA; the Court apparently also holds that it does not refer to § 1983, even though that statute clearly qualifies as "any *other* statute" or "any *other* law," within the meaning of the legislative history.

*   *   *

II

*   *   *

Today, the Court pursues the pre-emption rationale of *Milwaukee v. Illinois* to its inexorable conclusion and holds that even noncompliance with the requirements of the Clean Water Act and the MPRSA is a defense to a federal common law nuisance claim. Because JUSTICE BLACKMUN has already exposed in detail the flaws in the Court's treatment of this issue, see *Milwaukee v. Illinois, supra*, at 335, *et seq.* (dissenting opinion), I merely note that the reasoning in his dissenting opinion in *Milwaukee* applies with special force in this case.

*   *   *

NOTES

1. Did *Milwaukee* actually hold that the federal common law of nuisance had been entirely pre-empted by the Water Act?

2. Should the Court have distinguished this case from *Milwaukee*?

The standard for finding pre-emption of federal common law which the Court used in *Milwaukee* was whether Congress had spoken directly to a question. While Congress has spoken to the question of water pollution control, it has not addressed compensation for harm caused by water pollution: nowhere does the Act provide for private damages. Isn't this exactly the type of statutory interstice that federal common law is intended to fill? See *United States v. Little Lake Misere Land Co.*, 412 U.S. 580, 593 (1973), where the Court said: "the inevitable incompleteness presented by all legislation means that interstitial federal law making is a basic responsibility of the federal courts." In that case, the Court also cited the following language with approval:

At the very least, effective Constitutionalism requires recognition of power in the federal courts to declare, as a matter of common law or "judicial legislation," rules which may be necessary to fill in interstitially or otherwise effectuate the statutory patterns enacted in the large by Congress. In other words, it must mean recognition of federal judicial competence to declare the governing law in an area comprising issues substantially related to an established program of government operation. Mishkin, 105 U. Pa. L. Rev., at 800. 412 U.S. 580, 593.

At least in a situation similar to *Sea Clammers*, where damages were sought and permits were violated, wouldn't a court be fulfilling its proper role in awarding damages?

3. The denial of an implied private right of action is consistent with the Supreme Court's recent policy of restricting the availability of such actions. See *California v. Sierra Club*, 451 U.S. 287 (1981), decided the same day as *Milwaukee*. In that case the plaintiffs claimed that they had an implied private right of action to enjoin violations of Section 10 of the Rivers and Harbors Act. The Supreme Court found no Congressional intent to allow a private remedy for violations of the Act and refused to imply the existence of such a remedy.

4. If an action is based in part on a violation of the Water Act, but is not necessarily aimed at enforcement of the Act, is any policy served by requiring compliance with the citizen-suit provision? Are any private actions other than a Section 505 suit available? How can a plaintiff recover damages for harm caused by discharges in violation of a Section 402 permit?

5. As noted on page 257 *supra*, on remand of the Supreme Court's decision in *Milwaukee v. Illinois* the Seventh Circuit held that the Clean Water Act preempted both state and private claims for relief from harm caused by out-of-state sewage discharges insofar as they were based upon the statutory or common law of the state in which the injury occured. It left open the possibility of applying the law of the state in which the discharges originated to impose more stringent standards than required by the federal law. 731 F.2d at 413, 414.

Should the savings clauses in Sections 505(e) and 510 be given such a restricted construction? Is such a holding necessary in order to preserve "uniformity" and "state cooperation" in "reconciliation of competing uses of an interstate body of water?" See 731 F.2d at 410, 414. Would it matter if only *damages*, rather than injunctive relief, were sought under the law of the state in which the injury occurred?

The reasoning of the Seventh Circuit was rejected in *Ouellette v. International Paper Co.*, 602 F. Supp. 264 (D. Vt.), *aff'd*, 23 ERC 1703 (2d Cir. 1985), *cert. granted*, (March 24, 1986, No. 85-1233). The Vermont federal district court also emphasized that the case before it was a claim for *damages*, brought by lakeshore property owners in Vermont invoking the Vermont common law of nuisance against a paper mill across the lake in New York:

> Plaintiffs have not attempted to impose legislatively defined standards or limitations on defendant. Plaintiffs seek compensatory damages, the purpose of which, of course, is to compensate parties for injuries or for interference with the use and enjoyment of their property. Such damages may have an indirect regulatory effect, yet the discharger remains free to operate so long as it pays for the injury it causes. *** The application of state law in this situation is no more intrusive on the sovereignty of foreign states than the application of one state's product liability law to a manufacturer located in another state.

6. Would any obstacle exist to the application of the law of the *state of discharge* in order to recover *damages*, particularly when the harm is accompanied by a violation of state and/or federal permitting requirements? This, of course, assumes that such a state remedy exists and that it applies to harm caused to interests outside the state.

Even if the statutory or common law of the state in which the pollution originates offers some possibility of relief, would a *state* court within that state be an ideal forum to press such a claim by "foreign" interests? How could subject matter jurisdiction exist in federal court?

If suit is brought in state or federal court in the plaintiff's home state, additional problems of obtaining *in personam* jurisdiction might arise. Even under a state long-arm statute, there would be a question of whether a discharger had sufficient minimum contacts within the state where the harm occurred. Would a county or city sewerage authority be likely to have the requisite contacts in the affected state? If the state long-arm statute considers a tort to be sufficient contact, where did the tort occur? Where the pollution was discharged or where it caused the harm?

7. An interesting state law parallel to the *Sea Clammers* and *Milwaukee* decisions arose in

Stoddard v. Western Carolina Regional Sewer Authority, 23 ERC 2105 (4th Cir. 1986). There riparian landowners downstream from a grossly malfunctioning and inadequate POTW claimed that the Sewer Authority had taken their property without just compensation in violation of the South Carolina constitution when it discharged effluent that caused massive algal blooms, fish kills, and severe odors which interfered with the use of their property. The Sewer Authority argued that the South Carolina regulatory scheme enacted pursuant to the Clean Water Act pre-empted the "common law" just compensation remedy (even though the discharges were in viola-tion of the state-issued NPDES permit). The Fourth Circuit rejected this argument, holding that the "savings clause" of the South Carolina Pollution Control Act expressly preserved remedies other than those provided by the statute. (It also held that the Clean Water Act did not preempt recovery under state law.)

8. The plaintiffs in *Sea Clammers* also asserted a claim based on federal *maritime tort*. The Circuit Court held that this constituted a valid claim, 616 F.2d 1222, 1236 (1980), but the Supreme Court did not review this issue.

Maritime tort is a part of the body of admiralty law which came to the United States from England along with the concepts of common law and equity. The Constitution has been construed to have incorporated this admiralty law as it then existed as the law of the United States, subject to the power of Congress to alter. Federal courts have exclusive jurisdiction over maritime torts. To invoke that jurisdiction, a plaintiff must show that the tort occurred in a maritime locality (most courts hold that "navigable" waters are sufficient), and that there exists a significant relationship between the tort and a traditional maritime activity (injury to the fishing industry generally meets this requirement). After establishing jurisdiction, a plaintiff must then prove that a tort occurred which caused injury to the plaintiff.

Does the Water Act preempt the field of maritime tort with respect to injuries caused by water pollution?

When the federal government has attempted to utilize maritime tort law to supplement its claims under Section 311 of the Act for the costs of cleaning up oil spills, the courts have held that Congress intended Section 311 to provide the government's exclusive remedy against the owner or operator of discharging vessel. *See In re Oswego Barge Corporation*, 664 F.2d 327 (2d Cir. 1981), included in text *infra* p. 284, and decisions from other circuits noted *infra* p. 291. On the other hand, and illustrating that these preemption holdings turn on the niceties of the particular statutory structures, in *United States v. M/V Big Sam*, 681 F.2d 432 (5th Cir. 1982), included in text *infra* p. 293, the Fifth Circuit held that the Federal government was not precluded from bringing a maritime tort action to recover its oil cleanup costs from a negligent third party which caused the discharge from another vessel.

Although Section 311(o) seems to expressly preserve private damage claims under existing law for harm caused by a discharge of oil or a hazardous substance, the First Circuit has held that the Clean Water Act *as a whole* preempted a maritime tort claim based on nuisance principles which was brought by commercial fishermen against dischargers of toxic pollutants that had dam-aged their fishing grounds. *Conner v. Aerovox, Inc.*, 730 F.2d 835 (1st Cir. 1984).

The statutory language, however, has been interpreted to permit *state* statutory provisions for assessing cleanup costs and damages against dischargers of oil into state territorial waters to be invoked by either the state or its private citizens. *See Askew v. American Waterways Operators, Inc.*, 411 U.S. 325 (1973); *Steuart Transportation Co. v. Allied Towing Corp.*, 596 F.2d 609 (4th Cir. 1979), and Notes in this text *infra* pp. 291-92.

9. Although the result should depend on the particular statutory scheme, ever since the Supreme Court's decisions in *Milwaukee* and *Sea Clammers* the lower courts have not been recep-tive to assertion of federal common law of nuisance claims in any context in which federal environmental legislation has been enacted. *See United States v. Price*, 523 F. Supp. 1055 (D.N.J. 1981), included in text *infra* p. 315, holding that RCRA and CERCLA preempted the federal government's use of federal common law of nuisance to remedy hazards posed by chemical dumping at a landfill. *Also see City of Philadelphia v. Stepan Chemical Co.*, 544 F. Supp. 1155 (E.D. Pa. 1982), for a similar holding when a municipality attempted to invoke the federal common law of nuisance to recover costs of cleaning up hazardous wastes.

State common law nuisance claims have proven more durable. *See New York v. Shore Realty Corp.*, 759 F.2d 1032 (2d Cir. 1985), included in text *infra* p. 361, in which the state was allowed an injunction to compel cleanup of a hazardous waste disposal site, alternatively based on CERCLA and state nuisance law (but without discussion of the possibility of preemption). On the other hand, in *New England Legal Foundation v. Costle*, 632 F.2d 936 (2d Cir. 1981), the Second Circuit held that the Clean Air Act preempted state common law nuisance actions, at least to the extent a permit or variance authorized the conduct.

16   SPILLS OF OIL AND HAZARDOUS SUBSTANCES

Two years before Congress passed the 1972 Amendments to the Water Pollution Control Act, giving us NPDES permitting and uniform effluent limitations on point sources of pollution, it had enacted complex legislation concerning liability for spills of oil and hazardous substances in the Water Quality Improvement Act of 1970. This legislation was reenacted, in somewhat modified form, as Section 311 of the 1972 Amendments; and it has remained in the Clean Water Act as a regulatory and liability scheme covering spills of oil and hazardous substances that is largely separate and apart from the rest of the Act.

Read through this comprehensive section, and then consider the following short-hand summary.

Spills and discharges of oil and hazardous substances into the nation's waters are regulated by Section 311 of the Act, an intricate provision that addresses three elements of the problem: spill prevention, spill cleanup, and liability for spills and cleanup costs. Enforcement authority is extended over all waters of the United States out to the 200-mile limit of the fisheries management zone.

While this section states a zero discharge policy, it in fact proscribes only the discharge of harmful quantities of oil and hazardous substances. EPA has interpreted "harmful quantities" of oil to be those which violate applicable water quality standards or which cause a film, sheen, or discoloration of the surface or deposition of a sludge upon bottoms and shorelines. Hazardous substances are defined by Section 311(b)(2)(A) as those which "present an imminent and substantial danger to the public health or welfare, ... fish, wildlife, shellfish, shorelines and beaches."

Defining "harmful quantities" of hazardous substances other than oil has been a source of controversy. EPA published regulations in March of 1978 designating 271 chemicals as hazardous and establishing a five-part classification system which adopted a one-pound measure as the "harmful quantity" for the most toxic category. Multiples of one pound were stated as harmful quantities for less toxic categories, as an alternative to more complex standards that would account for the volume and character of receiving waters. This program was set aside by a reviewing court in August of 1978 because it did not consider receiving water characteristics. EPA and the successful industry challengers subsequently agreed upon a compromise which would salvage its extensive list and one-pound-multiples approach. This proposal was enacted by amendment of Section 311 in October, 1978.

The 1978 Amendments changed "harmful quantities" to "quantities which may be harmful," dropped the requirement that receiving waters be considered in determining risks of harm, and very substantially reduced the maximum civil penalties for illegal discharges which EPA could seek in court.

1. Spill Prevention

Discharges in harmful quantities are prohibited; dischargers who violate the prohibition are subject to administrative civil penalties of up to $5,000 per offense. Alternatively, violators may be subject to civil actions brought in court by EPA for civil penalties of up to $50,000, or up to

$250,000 for willful negligence or misconduct. The primary purpose of these penalty provisions is to deter and punish violators; other provisions provide for recovery of clean-up costs by the government. Persons in charge of discharging sources are required to immediately notify appropriate agencies or be subject to criminal prosecution for failure to do so. Information gained from such notification cannot be used in any criminal case related to the discharge violation.

2. Spill Cleanup

The President is directed to establish a National Contingency Plan for removal of oil and hazardous substances, including prepositioning of equipment and supplies for cleanup of spills. EPA and the Coast Guard are authorized to coordinate planning with state agencies to insure earliest possible notice of discharges. The government is given authority to destroy or remove any vessel which threatens a pollution hazard, and to seek injunctions against sources which threaten harmful discharges. When discharges occur, federal and state agencies have lead responsibilities for cleanup and removal of oil and hazardous substances.

3. Liability for Cleanup Costs

Owners and operators of vessels and onshore and offshore facilities are liable to the U.S. government for the actual costs of cleaning up and removing spills. The maximum exposure for onshore and offshore facilities is $50 million, which may be reduced by the President for any class of facilities, but not below $8 million. Maximum liability for vessels is the greater of $125 per gross ton or $125,000 for inland barges, and $150 per gross ton or $250,000 for other vessels. If discharges are caused by willful misconduct, the full amount of cleanup costs can be recovered even in excess of the maximum limits stated.

Owners and operators of discharging vessels and facilities can escape cleanup liability for discharges caused solely by acts of God or war, negligence on the part of the government, or acts or omissions of third parties. Persons who cause a vessel or facility of another to discharge harmful quantities are similarly liable to the government for cleanup costs. Owners in some cases may be held liable for acts of third parties, but are subrogated to the rights of the government against them in such cases. Owners may recover their own costs of cleanup from the government when discharges are caused solely by causes other then their own acts.

Costs of cleanup may include the following elements:

(a) actual costs of removal of oil and hazardous substances;
(b) costs of mitigating damage to the public health or welfare caused by discharges;
(c) costs of coordination of all public and private efforts to remove or eliminate threatened discharge hazards;
(d) costs incurred by state and federal agencies in restoration or replacement of natural resources damaged by discharges.

Owners of vessels over three hundred gross tons, including barges, are required to establish evidence of financial responsibility in accordance with the maximum limits stated above.

States remain free to impose liability for damages sustained by them or private interests, under state law, including damages in excess of cleanup costs recoverable under Section 311 in a few cases.

Now that you have had this basic overview, you are ready to explore some of the issues which have arisen under Section 311 in a few cases.

United States v. Chevron Oil Company
583 F.2d 1357 (5th Cir. 1978)

Before RONEY, TJOFLAT and HILL, Circuit Judges.

RONEY, Circuit Judge:

This appears to be the first appellate case concerning harm to the environment within the context of the penalty provisions of the Federal Water Pollution Control Act Amendments of 1972. In this case the issue is clearly presented as to whether or not the definition of harm to the environment promulgated by the Executive Branch pursuant to the statute must yield in a particular situation when the evidence shows that no harm in fact resulted to the environment from the spill in question.

In this action brought by the United States against defendant Chevron Oil Company to enforce a civil penalty for discharging oil into the navigable waters, the district court granted summary judgment for the Government. We reverse and remand for entry of summary judgment for Chevron. The statutory scheme in question prohibits discharges of "harmful quantities" of oil, and the administrative regulations state that any spill that causes a "sheen" on the water is harmful. While we hold that the regulation establishing the "sheen test" is generally valid, it is invalid as applied to the facts of this case in which the uncontradicted evidence at the administrative hearing showed that although this spill produced a sheen, it did not have a harmful effect.

Statutory Scheme: 33 U.S.C.A. § 1321(b) and the "Sheen Test"

* * *

Section 1321(b)(3) prohibits the discharge of oil *"in harmful quantities as determined by the President under"* § 1321(b)(4). Section 1321(b)(4) instructs the President to issue regulations indicating "those *quantities* of oil . . . the discharge of which, at such times, locations, circumstances, and conditions, will be harmful . . . ."

Enforcement of these provisions is provided for by § 1321(b)(6). When a discharge of oil in violation of § 1321(b)(3) occurs, the Coast Guard may assess the owner, operator, or person in charge of the vessel or facility a civil penalty of up to $5,000, provided that notice and an opportunity for a hearing is provided. 33 U.S.C.A. § 1321(b)(6). Finally to aid in the detection of oil spills, § 1321(b)(5) requires any "person in charge" of a vessel or facility to immediately report any discharge in violation of § 1321(b)(3) to the appropriate agency. The section also provides criminal penalties for a failure to so notify.

From this summary of the statutory scheme, it is apparent that the entire regulatory structure of the Act hinges on the term "harmful quantities as determined by the President." The President exercised the authority given him by Congress and determined that "at all times and locations and under all circumstances and conditions," discharges of oil which cause "a film or sheen upon or discoloration of the surface of the water" are determined to be harmful. 40 C.F.R. § 110.3 (1977).[5] Chevron challenges the validity of this regulation known as the "sheen test" as applied to the facts of this case in which the uncontradicted evidence showed that Chevron's oil spill caused a sheen but was not "harmful."

---

[5]The regulation provides in full:
§ 110.3 *Discharge into navigable waters harmful.*

For purposes of section 311(b) of the Federal Act [33 U.S.C.A.§ 1321(b)], *discharges of such quantities of oil* into or upon the navigable waters of the United States or adjoining shorelines *determined to be harmful to the public health* or welfare of the United States, *at all times and locations and under all circumstances and conditions,* except as provided in § 110.6 of this part, *include discharges which:*

(a) Violate applicable water quality standards, or

(b) *Cause a film or sheen upon or discoloration of the surface of the water* or adjoining shorelines or cause a sludge or emulsion to be deposited beneath the surface of the water or upon adjoining shorelines.
(Emphasis added.) The exception in § 110.6 of the Regulations is not applicable to this case. It provides that "discharges of oil from a properly functioning vessel engine are not deemed to be harmful."

Chevron's Oil Spill

The facts concerning this spill were developed at an administrative hearing before the Coast Guard, a transcript of which is in the record, and are not in dispute.

Chevron is the owner-operator of an oil and gas producing structure located in Lake Salvadore in St. Charles Parish, Louisiana. This structure stands in about eleven feet of water and is approximately two miles from the nearest shore. A vent or flare pipe is found some 150 feet away. On November 7, 1972, a malfunction resulted in the discharge through the vent pipe of approximately one-half to one barrel of crude oil. Since a barrel of crude oil contains 42 gallons, 21 to 42 gallons of oil were spilled. A Chevron employee corrected the malfunction and recovered about one-half barrel of the discharged oil which had remained within the casing surrounding the vent pipe. He also noticed a "slight sheen" on the water which he estimated was about 20 feet in width and 50 feet in length. Chevron notified the Coast Guard of the spill as required by § 1321(b)(5).

The Coast Guard proposed that Chevron be fined $1,000 for the oil spill pursuant to § 1321(b)(6). The statutorily guaranteed hearing was held at Chevron's request. At that hearing, the above facts were elicited from Chevron personnel, and Chevron called Dr. John Mackin as an expert witness. He was accepted by the Coast Guard "as an expert biologist in the field of marine life and marine organisms and as an expert in the effect of oil in such marine life and organisms." He testified that under the circumstances of the spill as testified to at the hearing, it was his opinion that this spill did not have a harmful effect on the environment of Lake Salvadore, despite the presence of a "sheen" upon the water. Dr. Mackin also testified that the toxicity of oil is a function of its concentration, and a sheen does not show quantity or concentration. He felt that the sheen test of 40 C.F.R. § 110.3 was inappropriate for determining the harmful effects of an oil spill.

The Government did not produce any evidence at the hearing.

After the hearing, the Coast Guard confirmed the $1,000 penalty assessment, and Chevron exhausted its administrative remedies. The Government then brought this suit in district court to collect the penalty. 28 U.S.C.A. § 1355. Both sides moved for summary judgment on the basis of the undisputed facts set out above.

In addition, over Chevron's objections, the Government submitted to the district court an affidavit of Kenneth Biglane, the Director of the Division of Oil and Special Materials Control for the Environmental Protection Agency. The affidavit dealt not with the specific facts of the present spill but with the reasons for the sheen test's adoption. Mr. Biglane stated that "smaller spills [of 10 barrels or less] have a seriously degrading effect on the environment." He averred that the "environmental damage caused by discharges of oil in quantities sufficient to produce a sheen on the surface of the water has been widely recognized," and he mentioned several scientific studies and reports which supported that statement. Therefore, it was his opinion "that an oil spill sufficient to produce a film or sheen on the surface of the water is large enough to cause harm to the environment." Based on this premise and the "enforcement workability of the sheen test," he concluded that the test "is well suited to define a discharge which damages the environment . . . ."

The district court found that the differences of opinion between Chevron's expert, Dr. Mackin, and those who promulgated the sheen test regulation "would appear to be inevitable and unavoidable in any determination as subjective as the definition of harmful quantities of oil" and that these differences did not make the regulation unreasonable or arbitrary. The judge therefore granted summary judgment for the Government, relying primarily on the Ninth Circuit case of *United States v. Boyd*, 491 F.2d 1163 (9th Cir. 1973).

United States v. Boyd and Its Progeny

Boyd involved a criminal prosecution for failure to report a spill of "approximately thirty gallons" in which the validity of the sheen test was challenged as applied to the § 1321(b)(5) duty to report harmful discharges. Boyd challenged the sheen test on the ground that it "defines as 'harmful' a broader class of oil discharges than Congress intended . . . ." *Id.* at 1166.

The Ninth Circuit upheld the sheen test on the facts of the case before it. It relied on the legislative history and the same Biglane affidavit which was submitted to the district court in the case *sub judice*. One factor which the court found persuasive in the reporting context was the "workability" and "simplicity" of application of the sheen test:

> [O]ne salutary aspect of the sheen test is the simplicity of its application. The statute and Regulation read together amount to a clear command to a ship captain: "If you can see the spill, report it!"

Id. at 1169. The court also relied on Biglane's conclusion that a discharge large enough to cause a sheen is large enough to cause harm to the environment, noting that this statement was supported by the scientific studies cited in the affidavit and was not refuted by Boyd. The court upheld the sheen test, concluding that "[n]othing has been shown, on the facts in this case, to indicate that the Department's Regulations determining harmfulness go beyond the statutory mandate." *Id.* at 1170.

Several district courts have upheld the sheen test's validity as a definition of harmfulness in suits brought by the Goverment to collect § 1321 (b) (6) civil penalties. Those cases rely on *Boyd* and its reasoning without discussion of any possible distinctions between § 1321 (b) (5) reporting cases and § 1321 (b) (6) penalty cases. In addition, like *Boyd,* there was no proof in any of these cases that the sheen test might cover *de minimis* oil spills.

These cases merely followed *Boyd* without adding anything to it. The present case requires us to analyze *Boyd* and to determine whether its reasoning is still controlling where there is evidence that the spill was not harmful even though it caused a "sheen" on the water.

Validity of the Sheen Test as a Basis for Imposing a Civil Penalty for Chevron's Spill

Congress could have prohibited *all* oil spills in the navigable waters of the United States. Indeed, the Senate version of the Water Quality Improvement Act of 1970 prohibited *all* dis-

charges. The House version of the bill prohibited only "substantial" discharges. The conference committee substituted the present prohibition on "harmful quantities as determined by the President."[9] It is clear from this that certain *de minimis* discharges are not prohibited by § 1321 (b). Congress delegated to the President the authority to enact regulations to separate these nonprohibited *de minimis* quantities from prohibited "harmful" quantities.

Of course, instead of allowing the President to define "harmful quantities," Congress could have enacted the "sheen test" as part of § 1321 (b). Had Congress done so, Chevron concedes that the sheen test would have been valid even as applied to the facts of this case. For the reasons given in the Biglane affidavit and in the *Boyd* opinion, there is a reasonable basis for the sheen test even if the test is somewhat broader than necessary to achieve the congressional objective of prohibiting only harmful oil spills.

As a *regulation*, however, the sheen test cannot be any broader than congressionally authorized. *Boyd* and its progeny upheld the sheen test because there was no evidence in those cases that the test exceeded the statutory mandate. The court in *Boyd* refused to hypothesize such a situation in the absence of proof in the record:***

In the case *sub judice,* the "hypothetical" situation mentioned in *Boyd* has become a reality. According to the uncontradicted evidence of Chevron's expert, Dr. Mackin, Chevron's spill was not harmful despite the fact that it caused a sheen. Thus it would appear that the sheen test as applied to the facts of this case exceeds the scope of the congressionally delegated authority.

We need not, however, strike down the regulation. As the court in *Boyd* found, the sheen test is very workable, and there is a proven scientific connection between a sheen and harmful quantities of oil. The sheen test provides a useful

---

[9] A general declaration of congressional policy against discharging any oil was also inserted into the Act:

> The Congress hereby declares that it is the policy of the United States that there should be no discharges of oil or hazardous substances into or upon the navigable waters of the United States. . . .

33 U.S.C.A. § 1321(b)(1). *See also id.* § 1251.

general criterion, but one which will occasionally cover nonprohibited *de minimis* spills. Any quantification adopted in an area such as this is liable to hit nonharmful spills in certain circumstances.

The solution to the problem can be found in the hearing provided by § 1321 (b) (6). A defendant must be allowed to offer proof at that hearing that its spill was not harmful despite the presence of a sheen. By "not harmful" we mean only that the quantity of oil spilled was *de minimis, not* that a harmful quantity was spilled but fortunately did not *actually* cause any harm. Because the sheen test provides a generally valid and useful standard, it creates a rebuttable presumption that any spill which causes a sheen is "harmful" and therefore prohibited by § 1321 (b)(3). Evidence of a sheen thus provides a sufficient basis for the Government to assess the § 1321 (b) (6) civil penalty *unless* a defendant proves that its spill was not harmful under the circumstances. If a defendant introduces such

evidence, as Chevron did here through Dr. Mackin, the Government must rebut with evidence that defendant's spill was of a harmful quantity under the circumstances.[12] Since the Government in the case *sub judice* did not come forward with any evidence at the administrative hearing, the penalty cannot be enforced.

Accordingly, the district court's grant of summary judgment is reversed, and the case is remanded for entry of summary judgment for defendant Chevron.

---

[12]We need not now decide whether the sheen test also creates only a rebuttable presumption in the context of § 1321(b)(5)'s duty to report harmful spills. While the statutory language is the same, the purpose of the reporting requirement is to enable an expeditious cleanup of the spill rather than to penalize for it, and that might allow the sheen test to serve as an irrebuttable presumption in that context. Since Chevron reported the spill and also concedes the validity of the reporting requirement even on the facts of this case, the sheen test as applied to §1321(b)(5)'s reporting requirement is not before us.

NOTES

1. Amendments to the Act in October, 1978, changed the language of both the prohibition in Section 311 (b) (3) and the determination required of the President in Section 311 (b)(4) to read "quantities . . . which [or "as"] *may* be harmful." (Emphasis added.)

Should this change in language cause the Fifth Circuit to change its holdings?

EPA has not amended its controlling regulation, 40 C.F.R. Section 110.3 (1982), in light of this opinion; but notice that the Fifth Circuit expressly stated that the regulation was not being struck down anyway.

2. Do you think that the Fifth Circuit was correct as a matter of law? As a matter of policy? If you were representing the government in other circuits, would you concede that *Chevron* controls? If you were representing the discharger in an administrative penalty case, would you cite *Chevron* and attempt to introduce evidence that the spill was not harmful? (The author has found no reported subsequent decisions on point.)

Notice that under Section 311 (b)(6)(A) the "gravity of the violation" is to be considered by the Coast Guard in determining the amount of the penalty. If a penalty of less than $2,000 was proposed by the Coast Guard, would it be economical to request an evidentiary hearing? Would it be economical to present scientific evidence in an attempt to rebut the "presumption" of harmfulness?

3. If we assume that *Chevron* remains good law for administrative assessment of civil penalties for oil spills, should it be applied to the reporting requirement of Section 311 (b)(5)? Are different considerations involved?

Notice that Section 311 provides that failure to report a spill of a quantity of oil (or a hazardous substance) which "may be harmful" can result in a fine of up to $10,000 and/or imprisonment for up to one year. Is it consistent with the Fifth Amendment to thus compel reporting of information which is used against the responsible party in an administrative proceeding to assess a civil penalty of $5,000 under Section 311 (b)(6)(A)? What if it is used by EPA as the basis for a civil action in court under Section 311 (b)(6)(B) to collect a $50,000 penalty? *See United States v. Ward*, 448 U.S. 242 (1980).

4. Notice that all relevant provisions in Section 311 — whether for reporting, imposition of civil penalties, or recovery of cleanup costs — apply to discharges of "hazardous substances" as well as oil in quantities which may be harmful. Indeed, it was the difficulty which the government had in designating harmful quantities of hazardous substances other than oil which led to the insertion of the word "may" into subsections (b)(3) and (b)(4) of Section 311.

As of this writing, 301 substances have been designated as hazardous by the Administrator of EPA pursuant to Section 311 (b)(2)(A). *See* 40 C.F.R. § 116.4, Tables A & B (1982). The quantity of each of these 301 hazardous substances which "may be harmful" (and which, therefore, is "reportable") has been specified as 1 pound, 10 pounds, 100 pounds, 1,000 pounds, or 5,000 pounds — depending upon the toxicity and extent of the hazard associated with each substance. In general, any person in charge of a vessel or facility which discharges into the water a quantity equal to or exceeding the quantity specified for a designated substance (within any 24-hour period) is subject to the reporting, penalty, and cleanup requirements of the Act. *See* 40 C.F.R. §§ 117.21, 117.22, and 117.23 (1982). Since the Act was amended in 1978 primarily to authorize this regulatory scheme, it has thus far remained unchallenged.

5. Notice that the various provisions of Section 311 apply to discharges (1) into or upon "the navigable waters of the United States" or adjoining shorelines; (2) into or upon the contiguous zone; (3) in connection with deepwater port or outer continental shelf activities; and (4) those which may affect natural resources belonging to or under the exclusive authority of the United States. This last category specifically includes protection of all marine fisheries resources on the continental shelf and all fish within 200 miles of shore. *See* the Magnuson Fishery Conservation and Management Act, 16 U.S.C. § 1801, *et seq.*

The only peculiarity is in the use in Section 311 of the term "navigable waters of the United States," rather than the term "navigable waters" which, as discussed in *United States v. Holland, supra,* has been interpreted to include much more than traditional maritime jurisdiction within the sweep of Sections 402 and 404. EPA and the Coast Guard, however, have consistently applied Section 311 to discharges into all "waters of the United States," the definition of "navigable waters" in Section 502 (7). *See* 40 C.F.R. §§ 110.2, 112.3 (k), and 116.3. Thus far, the courts have accepted this application without attaching any significance to the different terminology. *See, e.g., United States v. Texas Pipe Line Co.*, 611 F.2d 345 (10th Cir. 1979), in which a company whose pipeline was struck by a bulldozer was held liable for a $2,500 administrative penalty under Section 311 when oil escaped into an unnamed tributary of a small creek, even though there was no evidence that the creek was flowing at the time.

6. Notice that a civil penalty or liability for failure to report can only be imposed on a vessel discharging oil or a hazardous substance beyond 12 miles if the vessel is "otherwise subject to the jurisdiction of the United States." Sections 311 (b)(5) and (6). Consider how this phrase is defined in Section 311 (a)(17). Does this leave a significant gap in enforcement against the many foreign flag vessels? Does the same gap exist in recovery of cleanup costs under Sections 311 (f) and (g)?

7. When is a discharger of oil or a hazardous substance liable under Section 311, and when is he liable under Sections 301 and 309? The term "discharge," as defined in Section 311 (a) (2) of the 1972 Amendments was broad enough to include a great many point source discharges. In 1978, the definition was amended to exclude the three circumstances now expressly mentioned.

Does this remove all possibility of overlap and dual liability? What if an industrial point source of oil pollution which is required to have an NPDES permit discharges without ever applying for one? Is it liable under Section 309 or Section 311 or both?

United States
v.
Coastal States Crude Gathering Company

643 F.2d 1125 (5th Cir. 1981)

Before INGRAHAM, POLITZ and WILLIAMS, Circuit Judges.

POLITZ, Circuit Judge:

Coastal States Crude Gathering Company (Coastal) appeals a summary judgment in favor of the United States enforcing a "civil" penalty in the amount of $5,000 against Coastal pursuant to 33 U.S.C. § 1321 (b)(6). We amend the judgment to provide for a penalty of $1,000 and, as amended, affirm.

Finding no genuine issue of material fact, the district court summarized the facts as follows:

> Both parties agree that there is no genuine issue as to any material fact in this case. On or about June 7, 1977, approximately 5,200 barrels of gasoline were discharged into Nueces Bay, near Corpus Christi, Texas, from a product pipeline known as the Houston 12-inch pipeline owned and operated by the Defendant. The gasoline escaped from the pipeline through a small "hairline" fracture at a point well outside the navigational channel in Nueces Bay. At the point of the fracture in the pipeline, Nueces Bay was at least four feet deep, and the pipeline was buried at a depth of at least three feet below the bottom of the Bay. The pipeline in question had been installed by the Defendant in accordance with all applicable governmental regulations and standard industry practice.

It seems that the discharge resulted solely from the acts of an unknown third party. Inspection of the pipeline, conducted immediately after the discharge was discovered, revealed that the leak was caused when the pipe was struck by a vessel owned by an unknown third party traveling well outside the navigation channel in Nueces Bay. The vessel struck the pipeline with enough force to penetrate the two inches of concrete in which the pipeline had been encased and to dent and gouge the body of the pipe.

In brief and in oral argument counsel for Coastal forcefully contends that the imposition of a monetary penalty on Coastal for a discharge resulting solely from the acts of an unknown third person violates the Fifth Amendment proscription against the taking of property without due process of law. The district court rejected this contention, upheld the constitutionality of the statute, granted summary judgment to the United States and ordered Coastal to pay a civil penalty of $5,000. ***

***Section 1321 (b)(3) prohibits the "discharge of oil or hazardous substances (i) into or upon the navigable waters of the United States . . . in such quantities as may be harmful." Congress prescribed various remedies and penalties, including the civil penalty established by § 1321 (b)(6). Under this section, after notice and an opportunity for a hearing the Secretary of the department in which the Coast Guard is operating shall assess a civil penalty of up to $5,000 for each violation of § 1321(b)(3) by any owner, operator, or person in charge of an onshore facility, offshore facility or vessel from which oil or a hazardous substance has been discharged. In determining the amount of the civil penalty the section directs the Secretary to consider three factors: "the appropriateness of such penalty to the size of the business of the owner or operator charged, the effect on the owner or operator's ability to continue in business, and the gravity of the violation."

Section 1321 (b)(6) provides no defense to the assessment of the civil penalty; indeed, it establishes an absolute liability standard which obviates the need for a finding of fault. By way of contrast, one of the other remedies contained in the Act, liability for clean-up costs, does provide certain defenses. Under § 1321(f) the owner or operator of a facility or vessel from which there has been a discharge may defend against a claim that it is liable for clean-up costs by showing that the discharge was caused solely by an act of God, an act of war, negligence on the part of the United States Government, or an act or omission of a third party.

The district court properly held that this statutory scheme, as applied to impose a civil penalty upon the owner of a discharging facility regardless of fault, is not violative of the Fifth Amendment due process clause. To evaluate properly the legislation we must look to the whole of the statutory scheme. The proceeds resulting from the imposition of civil penalties, as noted by our colleagues in the Seventh Circuit:

> are to be deposited in a revolving fund which is to be used to finance a National Contingency Plan for the containment, dispersal, and removal of spills; the clean-up maritime disaster discharges; the reimbursement of clean-up costs incurred by owners or operators who are able to establish one of the four defenses; and the administration of the act.

United States v. *Marathon Pipe Line Co.,* 589 F.2d 1305, 1309 (7th Cir. 1978).

In order to satisfy due process requirements, the legislative means must bear "a reasonable relation to a proper legislative purpose" and be

"neither arbitrary nor discriminatory." *Nebbia* v. *New York,* 291 U.S. 502, 537 (1934). The statutory provision under challenge here satisfies these criteria. We concur with the Seventh Circuit's conclusion expressed in *Marathon Pipe,* 589 F.2d at 1309:

> The purpose of the FWPCA and of section 1321 is to achieve the result of clean water as well as to deter conduct causing spills. The civil penalty serves the Act's goal of pollution-free water by providing a means of funding the administration and enforcement of the Act.

The intendment of the statute is clear: Congress places a major part of the financial burden for achieving and maintaining clean water upon those who would profit by the use of our navigable waters and adjacent areas, and who pollute same. We find this shifting of the burden from the public to the offending users — albeit good faith, non-negligent users — to be a valid exercise of congressional powers. The imposition of a civil monetary penalty, on a strict liability basis, is reasonably related to the purposes of the statutory scheme and is not unconstitutional.

The Secretary assessed a fine of $1,000 after obviously weighing and considering the three statutory criteria. We are persuaded that the third factor, the gravity of the violation, was given substantial consideration as indeed it should have been. Coastal built and maintained its pipeline in accordance with all prevailing governmental rules and regulations and industry practices; it bore no fault in the rupture and discharge and immediately corrected the leak and pursued available measures to clean up the affected area. The Secretary was quite apparently impressed by this and set the penalty at twenty percent of the maximum allowed. We consider this assessment fair and just. In the complaint filed by the government, the penalty prayed for was the maximum available under § 1321 (b)(6). We think the prayer and judgment for $5,000 was the result of inadvertence. Regardless, under the circumstances reflected in this record we believe the civil penalty of $5,000 is inappropriate and find appropriate the

$1,000 as originally assessed by the Secretary. The judgment will be modified to assess a penalty of $1,000.

*   *   *

NOTES

1. Such imposition of "strictest" liability for (b)(6) civil penalties upon dischargers regardless of fault has been applied by the other federal circuits in which the issue has arisen.

In *United States v. Marathon Pipe Line Co.,* 589 F.2d 1305 (7th Cir. 1978), for example, the Coast Guard's assessment of a $2,000 civil penalty against a pipeline company was upheld on the following facts:

> On November 20, 1975 Marathon was notified by local police that a pipeline owned by it had ruptured and was discharging crude oil into the Kaskaskia River in southern Illinois. The company immediately took steps to contain the spill and reported the occurrence to the United States Environmental Protection Agency. In all, 19,992 gallons of crude oil were discharged from the pipeline and 10,920 gallons were recovered or burned, so that approximately 9,072 gallons escaped downriver. Subsequent investigation by the company revealed that a bulldozer had struck the four-inch buried pipe back in June or July of 1975 while hired to dig an irrigation ditch for the owners of the land. The bulldozer operator had reported the damage to the landowners, but as the latter thought that the pipeline was no longer in use, neither ever reported the damage to Marathon. The location of the pipeline was a matter of public record, the easement having been duly recorded with the local recorder's office, and the pipeline was marked in accordance with all federal regulations. It is undisputed that the eventual split in the line resulted from the bulldozer damage and that Marathon was in no way at fault in not learning of either the digging or the damage at any time prior to the spill.

589 F.2d at 1306. *See also United States v. Tex-Tow, Inc.,* 589 F.2d 1310 (7th Cir. 1978), decided the same day as *Marathon,* in which the operator of a barge was held liable for a $350 civil penalty because of gasoline discharged into the Mississippi River when the barge settled, as it was being filled at the dock, upon an underwater steel piling of which the barge operator could have had no reasonable way of knowing.

2. Substantive due process challenges to absolute liability under subsection (b)(6) were also rejected in *Marathon* and in *Tex-Tow,* using the same analysis followed by the Fifth Circuit in *Coastal States.* Two of the three judges who participated in the two Seventh Circuit decisions, however, expressed their dissatisfaction with the law in concurring opinions.

> Wood, Circuit Judge, concurring. As I believe Judge Castle has correctly analyzed the applicable law I join in his opinion, but as a matter of principle do so with some reluctance.
> The company which will have to pay this fine can no doubt do so without any economic pain. I recognize, however, no justification for the basic unfairness it involves. The company is concededly not guilty of the slightest fault. It in no way caused the accident, except it was in business. Just being in the business of supplying critical energy or other needs for our society scarcely justifies this type of penalty being imposed by someone in a government agency. I fail to see how it will deter or remedy anything. The company did not con-

ceal the accident, but actively engaged in efforts to contain the spill. This fine and others as unjustified will only be passed along to the consuming public. Little good can be accomplished in these particular circumstances by this unusual process which is generally considered to be contrary to the accepted principles of law and equity.

Bauer, Circuit Judge, concurring. *** While I also agree that the responsibilities of this court go no further than such a legal analysis — without contested facts — I am also joining in Judge Wood's concurring remarks. It seems to me that the Coast Guard, having been given such a fantastic amount of leeway by the Congressional action involved, should pay closer attention to the purposes for which the legislation was passed — environmental protection. To punish a business engaged in enterprises essential to our national well being for an unfortunate accident when the business is faultless, seems to be a self-defeating exercise of power. "Strict liability" concepts normally refer to compensation, not punishment without fault.

Marathon, 589 F.2d at 1310. (Same reservations expressed in concurrences in *Tex-Tow.*)

Is the standard of review under substantive due process so deferential as to leave judges who feel so strongly opposed to such strict liability no room to declare the provision unconstitutional? Do you agree with them as a matter of policy? Should Congress respond?

3. In *Marathon,* no member of the Seventh Circuit panel was willing even to find an abuse of discretion in the Coast Guard's assessment of a $2,000 civil penalty on the pipeline. The court recognized that the statute directed the Coast Guard to consider, in setting a penalty, the "gravity of the violation;" but it accepted the Coast Guard's interpretation of this factor to include the size of the spill as well as the degree of culpability. In *Marathon* the spill was of nearly 20,000 gallons of oil. The discharge in *Coastal States* was of 218,400 gallons (5,200 barrels) of gasoline. Did the Fifth Circuit properly reduce the penalty in *Marathon* from $5,000 to $1,000?

United States v. LeBeouf

621 F.2d 787 (5th Cir. 1980)

Before THORNBERRY, ANDERSON and THOMAS A. CLARK, Circuit Judges.

THORNBERRY, J.

In this appeal from judgment against the Government in its suit to recover clean-up costs under 33 U.S.C. § 1321 (1976) for an oil spill from appellee's tanker barge, we must interpret the clause in section 1321 (f)(1) that establishes a third-party defense for the owners of the discharging vessel. Because we conclude that the tugboat hired by the appellees in this case does not constitute a "third party" under section 1321 (f)(1), we reverse the judgment and remand the case to the court below.

I. Facts.

The parties stipulated the facts as follows. LeBeouf is in the business of transporting petroleum products in tanker barges. In 1974 LeBeouf contracted with Bayou Marine Corporation to obtain a tug and crew that would tow the non-self propelled tanker barge LBT # 4 on an itinerary specified by LeBeouf. Bayou secured the M/V Harding R, a tug owned by Barracuda Marine Corporation. The tug crew loaded and unloaded LeBeouf's cargo at the places and times designated in LeBeouf's itinerary. LeBeouf engaged in no other supervision over the crew. In March 1974 the tug crew unloaded oil from the LBT # 4 at Westwego, Louisiana. A tug crewman who was working as a tankerman without a license, in violation of 33 C.F.R. § 155.710(a)(2) (1979), accidentally opened the wrong valve and discharged sixty barrels of crude oil onto the Mississippi River.

Neither LeBeouf, Bayou, nor Barracuda cleaned up the oil spill. Finally the Coast Guard contracted to clean up the spill at a total cost of $38,689. The Government sued to recover this cleanup cost under the Federal Water Pollution Control Act, 33 U.S.C. § 1321, in March 1977. The district court dismissed the Government's suit against LeBeouf because it concluded that the oil spill was caused by a "third party" under section 1321 (f)(1).

II. Third-Party Defense under Section 1321 (f)(1).

Under section 1321(f)(1) the owner or operator of the discharging vessel is liable to the Government for the costs of cleaning up an oil spill

> [e]xcept where an owner or operator can prove that a discharge was caused solely by (A) an act of God, (B) an act of war, (C) negligence on the part of the United States Government, or (D) an act of omission of a third party without regard to whether any such act or omission was or was not negligent, or any combination of the foregoing clauses . . .

In cases involving inland oil spills, section 1321(g) requires the Government to sue the owner or operator of the discharging vessel for clean-up costs before it can sue a "third party" who may have caused the spill. The statute does not define what constitutes such a "third party."

LeBeouf contends that the term "third party" in section 1321(f)(1) should be interpreted broadly to include all parties — such as the tugboat in this case — over whom the owner-operator has no direct control or supervision.***

A broad interpretation of the term "third party" was rejected by the First Circuit in *Burgess v. M/V Tamano*, 564 F.2d 964,981-82 (1st Cir. 1977), in which the court expressly discussed what constitutes a "third party" under section 1321(f)(1). In *Burgess* the court held that a super-

tanker's temporary local pilot did not constitute a "third party" under section 1321(f)(1). As a result, the owners of the supertanker were held liable for an oil spill that occurred because the local pilot negligently ran the supertanker into a submerged ledge in a Maine harbor. The court concluded that the legislative purpose in drafting section 1321 as a strict liability statute would be undermined unless the third-party defense was narrowly interpreted. Even though the local pilot might be regarded as an independent contractor, he could not constitute a "third party" because the pilot acted for the ship and was subject to its ultimate control. In dicta the court reasoned that a shipyard that installed a defective valve would likewise not constitute a "third party" for the purpose of protecting the shipowner from liability for an oil spill caused by the defect in the valve. If a vandal opened the valve and caused the spill, however, the court said that the third-party defense would apply.

Following the reasoning of the First Circuit in *Burgess*, we conclude that the third-party defense in section 1321(f)(1) must be narrowly interpreted. The statute's comprehensive scheme for preventing and cleaning up oil spills would be undermined if barge owners like LeBeouf could escape strict liability merely by hiring out their operations to tugs and independent contractors. A narrow interpretation of the third-party defense would make it consistent with the other section 1321(f)(1) defenses, which include only narrow exceptions such as acts of God, acts of war, and instances in which the Government's own negligence is the sole cause of the spill. The only significant legislative history relating to the third-party defense also suggests that a narrow interpretation is proper; a committee report indicates that the drafters' primary purpose for including the third-party defense was to cover situations in which a third-party ship collided with an unrelated, oil-carrying vessel and caused a spill.

Under the analysis used in *Burgess*, the tug in this case does not constitute a "third party" that would protect LeBeouf from liability for clean-up costs under section 1321. LeBeouf hired the tug to act in its place. Although the tug operated as an independent contractor, LeBeouf held ultimate control over it by hiring it in the first place, specifying its itinerary, and retaining it throughout the job. Our narrow interpretation of the third-party defense promotes the goals of the statute and of traditional tort policy because it will encourage barge owners like LeBeouf to select tugs carefully and to insure against potential losses. LeBeouf can also require a tug to indemnify it for losses caused by the tug's conduct alone.

Because the tug does not constitute a "third party" for the purpose of protecting LeBeouf from liability under section 1321, we reverse the judgment and remand the case to the court below.

REVERSED AND REMANDED.

NOTES

1. Given the massive dollar amount of liability which can be imposed on a discharger for cleanup costs under Section 311(f) of the Act, it seems only reasonable that some defenses would apply.

If the government can prove that a discharge "was the result of willful negligence or willful misconduct within the privity and knowledge" of the owner or operator, it is liable for the full amount of the costs of removal. Absent such proof of culpability, Section 311 imposes monetary limits on liability; but the financial exposure is still high. Onshore and offshore facilities may be held liable for up to $50,000,000. The upper limit for vessels is $150 per gross ton of the vessel ($125 per ton for inland oil barges). With the average oil tanker approaching 50,000 tons, this means that the average maximum liability for an oil spill from a tanker is currently nearly $7,500,000. On the other hand, if a significant amount of the oil transported in one of these tankers is lost and is deposited on shores or in wetlands, the amount of damage usually far exceeds these limits.

Prior to the passage of Section 311, the Limitation of Liability Act, 46 U.S.C. § 183, originally enacted by Congress in 1851, allowed a shipowner to limit its liability to the value of the vessel (after the event giving rise to the damage) and "her freight then pending." For example, after the Torrey Canyon broke up on a reef off the coast of Cornwall in 1967, the tanker's owners invoked the Limitation Act to limit recovery to $50, the value of the one remaining lifeboat. A claimant could lift the limitation only by proving that the injury was caused within the owner's "privity or knowledge." The language used in Section 311 (f)(1), "notwithstanding any other provision of law," has been read to embody congressional intent that the Limitation Act not apply to recovery of cleanup costs under Section 311. *See In re Hokkaido Fisheries Co.*, 506 F. Supp. 631 (D. Alas. 1981). *Also see* Gillmore and Black, THE LAW OF ADMIRALTY at 828 (2d ed. 1975). (The same phrase is employed in subsection (g), covering nondischarging vessels which are responsible for a spill, and which have the same dollar per gross ton liability limits under the statute for non-willful acts.)

The addition of paragraph (f)(4) in 1977, allowing the costs of "restoration or replacement of natural resources" to be included in recoverable cleanup costs, increased the likelihood of reaching the statutory limits in the event of a substantial spill.

2. The Fifth Circuit's refusal to apply the third party defense in the *LeBeouf* case may be understandable. But in what circumstances should a discharge be found to have been "caused solely by . . . an act or omission of a third party"? What about the situation in the *Coastal States* case? What about when a bulldozer ruptures a crude oil pipeline, as in *United States v. Marathon Pipe Line Co.*, described in note 1 following *Coastal States, supra*? Should it matter if the pipeline company had not taken reasonable precautions to prevent such mishaps from occurring?

3. The court in *LeBeouf* mentions a circumstance in which a vandal opens a valve on an oil barge as an example of the sort of case in which the third party defense would apply. In vandalism cases which have arisen under the parallel provisions of Section 311(i), however, the discharger who has been victimized by vandals has not always been allowed to recover his cleanup costs from the government. In *Minneapolis Park and Recreation Board v. United States*, 18 ERC 1015 (Ct. Cl. 1982) for example, the Park Board was denied recovery of its costs incurred in cleaning up oil discharged when vandals opened a valve and switched on the pump to an oil storage tank in the park. The court found that the Park Board for 19 years had not known how much oil was left in the unused tank, had not erected any barrier on the bridge which provided access to the building in which the pump and valves were housed, had failed to remove the fuses for the unused pump, had not shut off the electricity to the building even though it was not being used at the time, and had failed to adequately patrol the area or take other precautionary action after previous incidents of vandalism. This the Court of Claims held not to constitute reasonable care on the part of the Park Board which would allow the spill to be attributed solely to the acts of third parties. Its own acts and omissions were found to have contributed to the discharge. *Also see Travelers Indemnity Co. v. United States*, 17 ERC 1677 (Ct. Cl. 1982), in which the court denied recovery to the insurer of privately-owned oil storage tanks, holding that it failed to show that a locked gate and chain link fence around the tanks was an adequate precaution against vandalism, when it was admitted that the switch to the pump was left on during closing hours. The most recent of what has become a long line of decisions denying recovery to dischargers who are the victims of vandals is *Atlantic Richfield v. United States*, 19 ERC 1999 (Ct. Cl. 1982).

Compare, on the other hand, the Court of Claims' award of nearly $100,000 in costs of cleaning up a vandalism-caused oil spill in *Union Petroleum Co. v. United States*, 651 F.2d 734 (Ct. Cl. 1981). There the court found that unknown vandals who opened the valves on two railroad tank cars at Union Petroleum's oil terminal and distribution facility during a labor strike were the sole cause of the discharge. The oil company was held to have exercised reasonable precautions in fencing and lighting the area, in providing an oil separator and a spill containment system, and, despite no such previous acts of vandalism, in taking increased security measures during the strike.

4. In light of these decisions in the Court of Claims, is it safe to say that proof of reasonable care on the part of a discharger will give rise to the third party defense under Sections 311(f), (g) and (i) when another party's intentional or negligent conduct is involved? Consider the following case.

Reliance Insurance Company v. United States
677 F.2d 844 (Ct. Cl. 1982)

BENNETT, Judge, delivered the opinion of the court:

This case involves an action by plaintiff to recover from defendant the costs incurred in the cleanup and removal of oil spilled into one of the navigable waterways of the United States. *** The specific question presented is whether the oil spill "was caused solely by * * * an act or omission of a third party" within the meaning of section 1321(i)(1)(D). The case is now before the court on cross-motions for summary judgment.

For the reasons set forth hereafter, we deny plaintiff's claim and grant defendant's motion for summary judgment.

I

Plaintiff, Reliance Insurance Company, is the insurance carrier for the Smith-Rice Company (hereinafter Smith-Rice), a California enterprise engaged in the business of maritime barge and derrick operations. Smith-Rice owns real property located at 2199 Clement Avenue, Alameda, California, which borders the Alameda

Estuary, a navigable waterway of the United States running between Alameda and Oakland, California.

In 1976, Smith-Rice decided to dredge a portion of its Clement Avenue property and remove 75 existing wood pilings and other timber debris in order to extend its waterfront sheetpile bulkhead 200 feet and to add a graded rip-rap slope, thereby creating a permanent shoreline wall. This project was intended to create additional mooring space for Smith-Rice's derrick barges and other floating equipment, replace deteriorating wood pilings and generally reclaim ground which had been gradually lost through action of the tidal canal. Prior to commencing the dredging, Smith-Rice secured approval from the proper local, state and federal authorities.

Since the dredged material was to be disposed of in the San Francisco Bay at a site near Alcatraz Island, Smith-Rice retained the soil engineering firm of Lawney-Kaldveer Associates to conduct test borings and to take core samples from various elevations and depths within the area to be dredged. This was done to determine whether or not the soil showed evidence of or contained pollutant materials. Results from these tests failed to reveal the existence of any subsurface pollutants. However, on or about March 11, 1977, while engaged in its dredging operations, Smith-Rice uncovered an underground deposit of an oily pollutant which discharged into the Alameda Estuary. Smith-Rice immediately notified the United States Coast Guard, which undertook to clean up the spill at a cost of $36,815.28. This expense was paid by plaintiff, as insurer for Smith-Rice. On April 16, 1979, plaintiff filed a petition in this court to recover from the United States the amount of this payment.

II

*   *   *

As presently constituted, the Federal Water Pollution Control Act flatly prohibits the discharge of harmful quantities of oil or hazardous substances into the navigable waters of the United States. 33 U.S.C. § 1321(b)(3). The statute holds owners or operators of discharging vessels and facilities strictly liable for actual cleanup costs, subject to certain limited defenses. 33 U.S.C. § 1321(f)(1)-(3). Upon proof of one of these defenses, an owner or operator is entitled to recover its reasonable cleanup costs from the United States. 33 U.S.C. § 1321(i)(1).

III

The conditions for imposition of absolute liability having otherwise been met, plaintiff seeks recovery under section 1321(i)(1)(D) by contending that the deposit of subsurface oil it discovered was the result of the acts or omissions of third parties including former but unrelated owners of the Clement Avenue property.

Section 1321(i)(1)(D) requires, as a precondition to reimbursement, that the discharge be *"caused solely by * * * an act or omission of a third party."* (Emphasis added.) We are called upon to decide the precise meaning of this statutory language. ***

Plaintiff contends that an act or omission of an owner or operator is not a cause of a spill if committed without fault. According to plaintiff, an owner or operator can recover under section 1321(i)(1)(D) when it can be shown (1) that the act or omission of a third party was a cause of the spill and (2) that even though the spill would not have occurred "but for" some act or omission of the claimant, the act or omission was neither willful nor negligent. In other words, in plaintiff's view, the question of whether or not the spill was "caused solely by" the act or omission of a third party turns on whether Smith-Rice acted with reasonable care. Supporting this interpretation of the law, plaintiff alleges that Smith-Rice took reasonable precautions before dredging by testing for subsurface pollutants and that its lack of knowledge as to the existence of the oil deposit absolves it from culpability, thereby rendering the third party solely responsible for the spill.

In response, defendant construes section 1321(i)(1)(D) to require that a claimant first establish that a third party was the "immediate cause" of the spill and then show that it did not contribute to the spill through some negligent act or omission. Defendant submits that the act or omission of a third party was not solely responsible for the oil spill since the dredging by Smith-Rice was the immediate cause of the discharge.***

IV

We find neither of the foregoing positions of the parties to be wholly consistent with the statute. As previously stated, section 1321 imposes absolute liability on an owner or operator for an oil spill, limited only where the spill is "caused solely by" one or more of four enumerated exceptions. It is implicit in this limitation that the conduct of the owner or operator cannot be a contributing cause of the spill. Thus, correlative to any inquiry into whether a spill was caused solely by a third party is an evaluation of the owner's or operator's own conduct. Where the act or omission of an owner or operator is a necessary antecedent to the spill, it is a contributing cause which bars recovery. *Union Petroleum Corp.* v. *United States* 651 F.2d 734, (1981).

Plaintiff would have us mitigate this result, however, in instances where an owner or operator could establish that his conduct was not negligent. This we cannot sanction, for there is no standard of limited liability incorporated within the exception of section 1321(i)(1)(D). ***

When this court has had prior occasion to consider the scope of the third-party exception, it has been only required to determine whether some omission on the part of the owner or operator facilitated the spill; that is, whether the owner's or operator's failure to act amounted to conduct which contributed to the spill to such an extent that it could not be said that the independent act or omission of a third party was the sole cause. While the affirmative actions of an owner or operator are easily identified and, therefore, are readily susceptible to evaluation, an omission to act is only understood within the framework of a legal duty to act. Absent a legal duty to act, a pre-existing, passive condition cannot be fairly held an omission for causative purposes.

A legal duty to act may be restated as an obligation, to which the law will give recognition and effect, to conform to a particular standard of conduct. With respect to section 1321 this standard of conduct must reflect Congress' strong concern for the protection of the nation's water resources and is, accordingly, very high. Yet, to give practical effect to the statutory exceptions, this standard of conduct must necessarily be less than absolute. Consequently, in recognition of this congressionally ordained standard of conduct, the court has had need to articulate, at various times, the requisite degree of care needed to satisfy an owner's or operator's legal duty. It is only within this context that the concept of due care has found expression in our prior decisions. Plaintiff is decidedly mistaken in its effort to extend this concept beyond its obvious, but limited, utility in defining the legal duty to which an owner or operator is bound to conform.

In the present case, since we are confronted with an affirmative act, rather than an omission to act, on the part of Smith-Rice, we need not repeat such an analysis. Under these circumstances, we proceed directly to a determination of whether this act was a contributing cause of the discharge into the Alameda Estuary, such as to preclude the act or omission of any third party from being the sole cause thereof.

Defendant endeavors to persuade us that we should read "caused solely by" to mean the immediate cause of the spill. While such an interpretation may be plausible under the particular facts of this case, its obvious emphasis on considerations of timing suggests a purely mechanical administration that could, in certain situations, lead to anomalous and unjust results. We are, therefore, unable to embrace this argument.

Instead, it appears to us that the proper construction to be given to the phrase "caused solely by" can be drawn from the purpose and intent of the statute itself. The legislative history of section 1321 demonstrates Congress' desire for a comprehensive solution to the nation's oil spill problem. After lengthy and extensive discussion, Congress determined that a system of absolute liability with specified limits best protected the public interest. Such a system, it was felt, properly placed the cost for an oil spill on the responsible party, and not on the general public. After deciding on the nature of the liability, Congress then considered the circumstances under which an owner or operator should be exempt from the imposition of such liability. Only in those instances which Congress believed to be completely beyond the control of the owner or operator would they be excused from liability. Any conduct, however slight, on the part of an owner or operator contributing to a spill would negate relief, even though such conduct might have operated in concert with greater third-party conduct to produce the spill. In other words, only where the owner's or operator's conduct was so indirect and insubstantial as to displace him as a causative element of the discharge would he be relieved of responsibility and, correspondingly, financial liability.

V

Viewed in this light, we cannot say that the activities of Smith-Rice were so indirect and insubstantial as to not be a cause of the subject oil spill. While the existence of the deposit of oil may have resulted from the act or omission of a third party, it is undeniable that it was Smith-Rice's dredging which allowed that oil to discharge into the Alameda Estuary. To us, this dredging was a significant element in the causal chain leading to the ultimate spill, since without this direct intervention it is reasonable to assume that the deposit of oil eventually dislodged would have remained undisturbed.

Therefore, it is concluded that the acts of Smith-Rice were a contributing cause to the oil spill and that, consequently, the spill was not caused solely by the act or omission of any third party as required by the statute. Plaintiff has failed to establish its right to recovery under section 1321(i).

*   *   *

NOTES

1. Under this reasoning, can you think of any circumstances in which the owner or operator of a discharging facility would be entitled to the third party defense if "but for" his actions the discharge would not have occurred?

What if the only action by the owner of a pipeline company was in laying the pipeline which someone else ruptured while dredging? Should this situation be distinguished, as the government argued, by holding that laying the pipeline was not the "immediate cause"? On the other hand, what if the only action by the owner was in opening a valve which broke off due to defective construction by a third-party manufacturer? What if the valve had been sabotaged by a disgruntled former employee to break when opened?

2. If, despite all due care on the part of the owners and operators of an oil barge and its tug, the barge was slashed open when it struck debris deposited in the channel by the contractor constructing an adjoining breakwater, would either the tug or the barge owner be held liable for cleanup costs?

What if the debris had washed into the channel during a violent hurricane? Should the "act of God" provision then apply? What if the debris had been deposited in the channel during an annual spring runoff which commonly washed such obstructions into the waterway? *See Sabine Towing and Transportation Co. v. United States*, 666 F.2d 561 (Ct. Cl. 1981), in which a shipowner's claim for cleanup costs under Section 311 (i) was denied because the court did not consider debris deposited in the Hudson River during the "freshet" spring runoff to have been an "act of God," but rather to have been a foreseeable natural condition giving rise to costs of operation which should be borne by vessel owners.

In Re Oswego Barge Corporation
664 F.2d 327 (2d Cir. 1981)

Before VAN GRAAFEILAND and NEWMAN, Circuit Judges, and DUMBAULD, District Judge.

NEWMAN, Circuit Judge:

In the aftermath of a massive oil spill in the St. Lawrence Seaway, the United States filed claims for cleanup costs against the owner of the discharging vessel. Some of the claims were based on § 311 of the Federal Water Pollution Control Act (FWPCA), 33 U.S.C. § 1321 (1976); others were based on traditional maritime law, the federal common law of public nuisance, and § 13 of the Rivers and Harbors Act of 1899, 33 U.S.C. § 407 (1976) (§ 13 is known as the Refuse Act). The District Court for the Northern District of New York (Howard G. Munson, Chief Judge) dismissed the FWPCA claims without prejudice, and those claims have been refiled in a separate action that is still pending. This appeal is from a judgment dismissing all of the remaining claims on the ground that they are preempted by the provisions of the FWPCA.***

The oil spill occurred on June 23, 1976, when the Barge "Nepco 140," while being towed by the Tug "Eileen C," grounded in fog in American territorial waters, causing a discharge of oil into the St. Lawrence Seaway. The appellee Oswego Barge Company ("Oswego") owned the barge and had chartered the tug. As a result of the spill, the United States alleges it spent $8,062,981 to clean its territorial waters and reimbursed Canada, pursuant to an executive agreement, for the $768,265 Canada spent to clean Canadian waters.

On June 30, 1976, Oswego filed in the Northern District of New York a petition for exoneration from or limitation of liability pursuant to the Limitation of Liability Act of 1851, 46 U.S.C. § 183 (1976) ("Limitation Act"). The District Court ordered all claimants to submit their claims by December 31, 1976. On December 15, 1976, the United States submitted a claim seeking recovery of up to $9,000,000 from Oswego. Invoices were tendered by the Government to Oswego in the total amount of $8,831,246, including $768,265 paid by the United States to

Canada. On November 13, 1978, the District Court ruled on Oswego's motion to dismiss the claim presented by the United States. First, the District Court dismissed, without prejudice, the Government's claim to the extent that it was based on § 311 of the FWPCA, because recovery under that statute would not be subject to the Limitation Act Fund. The Government refiled its claim based on the FWPCA in a separate action, *United States v. Tug Eileen C,* No. 79 CV 117 (N.D.N.Y., filed Feb. 23, 1979), which is still pending. Second, to the extent that the Government's claim for cleanup costs rested on the Refuse Act, the common law of nuisance, or maritime tort law, the District Court ruled that the Government's right to proceed was precluded by the exclusive provisions of the FWPCA. ***

*   *   *

On appeal the Government contends that by enacting the FWPCA Congress did not intend to limit the availability of other remedies that would be consistent with the general purpose of the FWPCA to prevent the discharge of oil into United States waters. The Government asserts that the FWPCA was enacted only to insure a minimum recovery of oil pollution cleanup expenses and was not intended to preclude supplementary remedies that would also help prevent oil spills.***

1. The Claim for Cleanup of United States Waters

To determine whether the Government is limited to FWPCA remedies in its claim against Oswego for costs of cleaning up pollution of United States waters requires some understanding of the background against which Congress enacted § 311. Before 1970, the Government's statutory remedy for recovery of its cleanup costs was the Oil Pollution Act of 1924. Recovery was available only upon proof of gross negligence or willfulness on the part of the discharging vessel. Non-statutory remedies required proof of the elements of a public nuisance [5] or a maritime tort,[6] and any non-statutory recovery would be limited by the Limitation Act to the value of the vessel after the accident unless the act causing the spill was within the privity or knowledge of the vessel owner.

Recognizing the inadequacy of these remedies, Congress included a detailed scheme for recovery by the United States of oil spill cleanup costs in § 102 of the Water Quality Improvement Act of 1970 ***. Two years later, in the course of a comprehensive restructuring of water pollution laws, Congress reenacted the oil spill cleanup provisions of § 102 in slightly modified form as § 311 of the FWPCA, 33 U.S.C. § 1321 (1976) (hereafter cited as § 1321). Under § 1321 (f)(1) the Government, with exceptions not relevant to this appeal, can recover its cleanup costs under a theory of strict liability from the vessel owner or operator, up to specified dollar limits. The Government can recover its total cleanup costs if it can prove "willful negligence or willful misconduct within the privity and knowledge of the owner." The Act also requires vessels to establish evidence of financial responsibility up to the limits for recovery based on strict liability. The Oil Pollution Act of 1924 was expressly repealed, but no mention was made of either the preservation or repeal of additional remedies for cleanup costs under theories of public nuisance, maritime tort, or the Refuse Act.

Non-Statutory Theories of Recovery

In order to determine whether the FWPCA preempts theories of recovery based on public nuisance or maritime tort, we must first bring into focus the nature of the claims the Government is asserting. Many passages in the Government's statement of its claim in the District Court and in its brief in this Court suggest that the Government is attempting to pitch liability upon two different bodies of law: federal com-

mon law and maritime law. To the extent that maritime law is judge-made, it can be viewed as simply one branch of federal common law. But we understand the Government to use the phrase "federal common law" in contrast to maritime law, i.e., referring to judge-made law pronounced on the law side of the district courts (or in the exercise of equity jurisdiction). *See, e.g., Illinois v. Milwaukee,* 406 U.S. 91 (1972); *Clearfield Trust Co. v. United States,* 318 U.S. 363 (1943). In particular, the Government contends that its claim for recovery of cleanup costs may be based upon that aspect of federal common law revived or discovered in *Illinois v. Milwaukee, supra:* public nuisance resulting from interstate pollution of navigable water. With respect to maritime law, the Government is less precise in describing the pertinent aspects of this body of law on which it grounds liability for cleanup costs; the Government simply says Oswego is liable for a "maritime tort."

As we analyze the Government's nonstatutory theories, they both must rest upon maritime law. The essential facts supporting the legal theories are that a vessel discharged oil into navigable waters of the United States and the United States incurred costs in cleaning up the oil from those waters. The facts satisfy the elements of admiralty jurisdiction — a maritime locality and a significant relationship to a traditional maritime activity. Whatever federal liabilities arise from these facts, only maritime law, both judge-made and statutory, creates them. In referring to both maritime law and federal common law as the sources of liability, the Government is apparently searching for bodies of law that will support theories of negligence and public nuisance. But maritime law, unless preempted by the FWPCA, can comprehend both theories. Negligent conduct causing loss to others constitutes a traditional maritime tort. *Pope & Talbot, Inc. v. Hawn,* 346 U.S. 406, 413 & n.6 (1953). Whether non-negligent conduct amounting to a public nuisance creates liability within maritime law is more debatable, but this type of "maritime nuisance tort" has been recognized. We therefore conclude that both of the Government's nonstatutory theories of recovery are based upon liabilities arising from judge-made maritime law.

---

[5] If the theory was the common law of public nuisance, the Government would have had to show "an unreasonable interference with a right common to the general public."

[6] The maritime tort could involve a claim of negligence or, borrowing from common law, a claim of public nuisance.

Refuse Act Theory of Recovery

The Government presents its theory of recovery based on the Refuse Act as if it were a statutory cause of action, but this theory also rests ultimately upon judge-made maritime law, though differing from the non-statutory nuisance and negligence theories in that they involved maritime law *liabilities*, whereas the Refuse Act theory involves a judicially created maritime *remedy*.

The Refuse Act, which is § 13 of the Rivers and Harbors Act of 1899, makes it unlawful to discharge any refuse matter into navigable water of the United States, and "refuse matter" has been construed to include oil accidentally discharged. *United States v. Standard Oil Co.*, 384 U.S. 224 (1966). While the Rivers and Harbors Act does not provide explicit remedies enabling the United States to recover costs incurred in removing anything placed in navigable water in violation of the various prohibitions of the Act, the authority of federal courts to fashion cost recovery remedies for the United States has been recognized. *Wyandotte Transportation Co. v. United States*, 389 U.S. 191 (1967) (costs of removing vessel negligently sunk in violation of § 15). In this case, the remedy sought by the Government to recover cleanup costs for an oil spill in violation of § 13 is a judge-made remedy, and, since the source of the spill is a vessel operating on navigable waters, the judge-made remedy to enforce § 13 must be grounded in non-statutory maritime law.

Criteria for Gauging Statutory Preemption of Judge-Made Law

In order to determine whether the liabilities and remedies grounded in judge-made maritime law have been preempted by the FWPCA, we next consider the criteria for assessing when federal statutes displace judicial law-making authority. In particular we examine whether the Supreme Court's approach to statutory preemption of judge-made law applies to maritime law as rigorously as it now appears to apply to non-maritime federal common law.

With respect to non-maritime federal common law, the Court has recently articulated a strict test for determining the preemptive effect of a federal statute. *City of Milwaukee v. Illinois*, 101 S.Ct. 1784 (1981). Instead of inquiring whether "Congress ha[s] affirmatively proscribed the use of federal common law," we are to conclude that federal common law has been preempted as to every question to which the legislative scheme "spoke directly," and every problem that Congress has "addressed." While federalism concerns create a presumption *against* preemption of state law, including state common law, separation of powers concerns create a presumption *in favor of* preemption of federal common law whenever it can be said that Congress has legislated on the subject.

Applying this test, the Court concluded in *City of Milwaukee* that the FWPCA preempted the federal common law of public nuisance in the area of interstate water pollution, at least to the extent of displacing the authority of a district court to impose more stringent effluent limitations upon sewer systems than those promulgated pursuant to § 301 of the Act. In *Middlesex County Sewerage Authority v. National Sea Clammers Ass'n*, 101 S.Ct. 2615 (1981), the Court more broadly characterized *City of Milwaukee* as a determination that "the federal common law of nuisance in the area of water pollution" has been "entirely pre-empted" by the FWPCA. *Id.* at 2627.

The Supreme Court has recognized however, that the federal judiciary has a more expansive role to play in the development of maritime law that in the development of non-maritime federal common law.***

In recognizing a substantial law-creating function for federal courts in maritime law, the Supreme Court appears to have applied the presumption of statutory preemption somewhat less forcefully to judge-made maritime law than to non-maritime federal common law. In several cases the Court has approved the creation of new rights pursuant to judge-made maritime law despite the presence of arguably preempting federal statutes. Thus, in *Moragne v. States Marine Lines, Inc.*, 398 U.S. 375 (1970), the Court created a maritime wrongful death action for deaths occurring within state territorial waters, notwithstanding that the maritime wrongful death action created by Congress was limited to deaths occurring on the high seas. Death on the High Seas Act (DOHSA), 46 U.S.C. §§ 761-768 (1976).***

Even more pertinent to the issues on this appeal are cases in which the Court has ruled that preexisting judge-made maritime law remains in force notwithstanding the enactment of statutes that arguably preempt the judge-made law.***

Though judge-made maritime law has thus been less easily displaced by statutory preemption than non-maritime federal common law, preemption of maritime law has occurred both as to prior judge-made law and the authority to fashion new law. *** These cases suggest that a presumption of legislative preemption applies to judge-made maritime law, though less forcefully than it applies to non-maritime federal common law.

We also think it reasonable to conclude that the force of the presumption of preemption is somewhat reduced when the judge-made law arguably preempted by a new statute is a remedy fashioned by admiralty or common law courts in aid of a preexisting statute. The presumption thus will have less force in this case when we proceed to consider whether the FWPCA preempts the judge-made maritime remedy entitling the Government to collect cleanup costs for violations of the Refuse Act. The presumption still retains more force than it would have if the issue were whether the FWPCA impliedly repeals any of the substantive provisions of the Refuse Act, for repeals of statutes by implication are disfavored. On the other hand, the presumption of preemption does not apply as forcefully as it would apply, after *City of Milwaukee,* to bodies of federal common law, such as public nuisance arising from interstate water pollution, that are related to generalized federal interests, rather than to specific federal statutes. Judicially created remedies in aid of statutes like the Refuse Act fall somewhere between the federal common law of nuisance and the specific commands of the Refuse Act in their resistance to implied preemption by the FWPCA.

Ultimately determining whether non-statutory maritime law, as to both liabilities and remedies, survives enactment of a statute requires a careful analysis of several factors that the Supreme Court has considered relevant in assessing whether the presumption of preemption has been overcome. Any terms of the statute explicitly preserving or preempting judge-made law are of course controlling, as is clear evidence of Congressional intent to achieve such results. In the absence of clearly expressed legislative intent, legislative history may provide useful guidance. The "scope of the legislation" must be assessed. *City of Milwaukee v. Illinois, supra.* A judgment must be made whether applying judge-made law would entail "filling a gap left by Congress' silence" or "rewriting rules that Congress has affirmatively and specifically enacted." *Mobil Oil Corp. v. Higginbotham, supra,* 436 U.S. at 625. The detail and comprehensiveness of a statute will frequently aid this determination. Finally, Congress is less likely to have intended preemption of "long-established and familiar principles" of "the common law or the general maritime law." *Isbrandtsen Co. v. Johnson,* 343 U.S. 779, 783 (1952), *quoted in Edmonds v. Compagnie Generale Transatlantique, supra,* 433 U.S. at 263. In sum, we recognize, as *City of Milwaukee* instructs, that the doctrine of separation of powers creates a presumption that legislation preempts the role of federal judges in developing and applying federal common law, but we also recognize that it is not a simple task to determine the force and proper application of this presumption. With these principles in mind, we turn to the impact of the FWPCA upon the Government's non-FWPCA theories of recovery.

FWPCA Preemption

Without any doubt the FWPCA legislates on the subject of recovery by the United States of its costs of cleaning up oil spilled into American waters. Section 1321(f) establishes a comprehensive remedial scheme providing for both strict liability up to specified limits and recovery of full costs upon proof of willful negligence or willful misconduct within the privity and knowledge of the owner. We must therefore start with a presumption that non-FWPCA maritime liabilities and remedies for oil spill cleanup costs of the United States have been preempted.

This presumption is not rebutted by the language of FWPCA. The remedies created by § 1321(f)(1) are established "notwithstanding any other provisions of law." While various meanings can be drawn from this phrase, we think it means that the remedies established by the FWPCA are not to be modified by any preexisting law. The main objective apparently was to assure that the limits on recoveries established by § 1321(f) are not to be varied by the different limits established by the Limitation Act. The "notwithstanding" phrase is not a preservation of preexisting bases of recovery.

Nor do any of the savings clauses of the FWPCA aid the Government's position. Section 511(a) of the Act, 33 U.S.C. § 1371(a), preserves the "authority or functions" of United States officers and agencies "not inconsistent" with the Act. It would torture the meaning of these words to interpret them as preserving "authority" of the United States to use non-FWPCA remedies to collect cleanup costs from discharging vessels. Elsewhere in the Act, when Congress sought to preserve a preexisting liability and remedy — the liability of vessel owners for damages to property from oil spills, 33 U.S.C. § 1321(o)(1) (1976), precise language was used, disclaiming any effect upon vessel owners' "obligations" under any provision of law. Moreover, § 1321(o) itself demonstrates that Congress used the term "authority" to mean something other than pursuing a legal remedy. Subsection (3) of § 1321(o) preserves certain aspects of federal "authority" (not pertinent to cleanup costs), thereby indicating, by comparison with subsection (1)'s reference to vessel owners' "obligations" that "authority" does not refer to the right to collect upon an owner's liability. In any event, whatever "authority" is preserved by § 1371(a) must be consistent with the Act, thereby raising the issue, to be considered *infra*, whether non-FWPCA remedies would be consistent with the remedies of § 1321(f). *See Steuart Transportation Co. v. Allied Towing Corp.*, 596 F.2d 609, 616 (4th Cir. 1979).

The liability that is preserved by § 1321(o)(1) concerns only damage to property and does not include recovery of oil removal costs, *Steuart Transportation Co. v. Allied Towing Corp., supra*, 596 F.2d at 616; *United States v. Dixie*

Carriers, Inc., 627 F.2d at 741-42, at least in circumstances like this case where the Government incurred cleanup costs in the exercise of its responsibilities for navigable waters and not in connection with restoring damaged Government property.

Arguably of more significance is § 1321(h)(2), which preserves the Government's rights against "any third party whose actions may in any way have caused or contributed to" an oil spill. This clause does not directly aid the Government's claim because cleanup costs are sought in this case from the discharging vessel's owner, and not from a third party. Nevertheless the existence of subsection (h) lends some support to the Government's position. It would be anomalous, the Government contends, for Congress to preserve non-FWPCA remedies against third parties (including vessels) if it had intended to abolish such remedies against discharging vessels and their owners. But even if the Government is correct that subsection (h) preserves all non-FWPCA remedies against all third parties, it would be even more anomalous for Congress to have drafted express language to preserve such remedies against third parties while leaving the preservation of such remedies against ship owners to be inferred by courts. *** None of the savings clauses of the Act preserves the non-statutory remedies the Government is asserting in this case.

The Government invites us to interpret the Act as not preempting non-statutory remedies by relying on isolated statements drawn from the legislative history of the FWPCA. *** However, *City of Milwaukee* instructs us to be cautious in making even educated guesses about Congressional intent when the consequence would be to maintain a common law remedy on a subject dealt with in legislation. Suffice it to say that we do not find evidence of Congressional intent that rebuts the presumption of legislative preemption.

An analysis of each of the Government's three non-FWPCA theories of recovery indicates that the other factors that we have identified as relevant to an assessment of whether the presumption of preemption has been overcome are likewise of no help to the Government's position. These other factors include the scope of the preempting legislation, its detail and compre- hensiveness, whether the judge-made law is fill- ing a gap in legislation or effectively rewriting the statute, and how well established the judge- made law was at the time of the statute's passage.

With respect to the Government's maritime nuisance tort theory, the Supreme Court has ruled in *City of Milwaukee* and *National Sea Clammers* that the comprehensive provisions of the FWPCA regarding effluent discharges preempt the public nuisance ingredient of this approach, at least in the context of non-maritime federal common law. We see no reason why the "often vague and indeterminate nuisance con- cepts," *City of Milwaukee, supra,* 101 S.Ct. at 1792, to whatever extent imported into maritime law, should survive the comprehensive and detailed provisions of the FWPCA regarding Government recovery of oil spill cleanup costs. The contours of a federal common law of public nuisance are unsettled, and the recognition of such concepts within maritime law is of recent vintage. *See Burgess v. M/V Tamano,* 370 F.Supp. 247 (D.Me. 1973).

To whatever extent judge-made remedies for violation of the Refuse Act include recovery for cleanup costs based on strict liability,[23] such remedies would be plainly inconsistent with the FWPCA, because the strict liability remedy of the FWPCA is subject to dollar limitations, while recovery of damages under the Rivers and Har- bors Act of 1899, when permitted at all, is not subject to the limits of the Limitation Act. Allow- ing the Government a judge-made damage remedy without limits in strict liability under the Refuse Act would amount to "rewriting rules that Congress has affirmatively and specifically enacted." *Mobil Oil Corp., supra.*

Whether the presumption of preemption of non-FWPCA liabilities and remedies based on negligence has been overcome requires further analysis. If the FWPCA means what it says in permitting recovery of full cleanup costs upon

proof of "willful negligence or willful miscon- duct" within the knowledge and privity of the owner, such a remedy would be inconsistent with a maritime negligence remedy, since the latter would avoid the limits of the Limitation Act sim- ply upon proof of ordinary negligence within the privity or knowledge of the owner.*** On the other hand, if, as the Government contends, the reference in § 1321(f) to "willful negligence or willful misconduct" is only an inartistic way of expressing ordinary negligence, then Congress has, for no apparent reason, created an FWPCA negligence remedy for full costs to stand along side a similar maritime tort remedy.

Whatever degree of negligence applies to a claim for full costs under § 1321(f), a holding against preemption would result in a four-tiered scheme of liabilities: strict liability under the FWPCA up to FWPCA limits, common law lia- bility for negligence not within the knowledge or privity of the owner up to Limitation Act limits, common law liability for negligence within the knowledge or privity of the owner without limits (because the Limitation Act would not apply), and FWPCA liability for "willful negligence or willful misconduct" within the privity and knowledge of the owner (because the FWPCA limits would not apply). The FWPCA would be the basis for recovery on the two ends of the spectrum of recoveries, but judge-made law would be the basis for the two means of recovery in the middle. A statute would have to specify such an unwieldy scheme with express provisions before a court could assume that it may continue to administer the common law components of such an arrangement.[27] Without

---

[23]The District Court assumed that the vessel owner would be strictly liable to the United States for viola- tions of the Refuse Act. The Fifth Circuit has also assumed that recovery under the Refuse Act would be on a strict liability basis. *United States v. Dixie Car- riers, Inc., supra,* 627 F.2d at 744.

*   *   *

[27]The anomalies that would result if common law remedies were not preempted are accentuated by the fact that the Limitation Act would impose upon claims for negligence not within the privity or knowledge of the owner limits that could be either higher or lower than the limits of the FWPCA upon the statutory cause of action for strict liability. The variation in limits arises because the Limitation Act sets limits based on the value of the vessel after the spill, whereas the FWPCA sets dollar limits based on tonnage. If the ves- sel is still valuable after the spill, the Limitation Act may provide limits far higher than those of the FWPCA; on the other hand, if the vessel is rendered of little or no value by the occurrence that caused the spill, the Limitation Act limits would be far below those of the FWPCA.

such an express provision, judge-made remedies falling within the scope of the remedies provided by the statute are preempted, at least in the context of a statute as comprehensive as § 1321.

For all these reasons, we agree with those courts that have ruled, even prior to *City of Milwaukee*, that § 1321(f) has preempted the Government's non-FWPCA remedies against a discharging vessel for cleanup costs. *See, e.g., United States v. Dixie Carriers, Inc., supra; Steuart Transportation Co. v. Allied Towing Corp., supra; United States v. Tug J.P. McAllister,* Civ. No. 76-462 (D.P.R. Apr. 3, 1980). *See also Tug Ocean Prince, Inc. v. United States, supra,* 584 F.2d at 1162.

2. The Claim for Cleanup of Canadian Waters

The Canadian portion of the United States' claim concerns only the costs of cleaning up oil from Canadian waters. The United States seeks to recover the money it reimbursed Canada for cleanup costs that Canada incurred. We disagree with the District Court that this portion of the Government's claim has been preempted by the FWPCA and reverse the Court's denial of the Government's motion to amend its complaint to amplify the reimbursement claim.

The FWPCA explicitly limits its coverage to Government recovery of costs for the cleanup of American territorial waters. 33 U.S.C. § 1321(b)(1) (1976) declares that "it is the policy of the United States that there should be no discharges of oil or hazardous substances into or upon the navigable waters of the United States, adjoining shorelines, or into or upon the waters of the contiguous zone," § 1321(b)(3) prohibits "[t]he discharge of oil . . . into or upon the navigable waters of the United States, adjoining shorelines, or into or upon the waters of the contigu-

ous zone," and § 1321(c)(1) authorizes the President to act to remove oil discharges "into or upon the navigable waters of the United States, adjoining shorelines, or into or upon the waters of the contiguous zone." The broader purpose of the FWPCA in its entirety is "to restore and maintain the chemical, physical, and biological integrity of the Nation's waters." The legislative history further supports the conclusion that the FWPCA concerns only the cleanup of pollution in American waters.***

While a statute might have a preemptive effect upon some matters outside its coverage, the preemption analysis we have discussed leaves no possibility that the FWPCA has any effect on claims for cleaning the territorial waters of foreign countries. *** Obviously the FWPCA does not purport to affect Canada's rights to sue a vessel discharging into American waters oil that pollutes Canadian waters. And we find nothing in the statute to suggest that Congress intended to alter any rights the United States may have to collect money reimbursed to Canada for Canada's costs, whether the claim of the United States for reimbursement is derived from treaty obligations, subrogation, or otherwise. In rejecting the contention that the reimbursement claim is preempted by the FWPCA, we express no views on whether the United States is entitled to reimbursement, nor whether public nuisance or more traditional maritime tort law or treaty rights provide a basis for Oswego's liability.

*   *   *

Accordingly, the judgment is affirmed in part, reversed in part, and remanded to permit the Government to amend its complaint to amplify its claim for money reimbursed to Canada.

NOTES

1. Do you agree with the Second Circuit that Section 311 precludes recovery of cleanup costs by the federal government from dischargers under theories of federal common law, maritime tort law, or as an implied remedy for violation of the Refuse Act? Every court which has considered these questions thus far is in agreement with this decision. *See, e.g., Steuart Transportation Co. v. Allied Towing Corp.*, 596 F.2d 609 (4th Cir. 1979); *United States v. Dixie Carriers, Inc.*, 627 F.2d 736 (5th Cir. 1980) — both decided against the government, even prior to the Supreme Court's 1981 decisions in *City of Milwaukee* and *Sea Clammers*.

2. Do you agree with the court's construction of Section 311(o)(1) not to apply to the federal government's recovery of oil removal costs, at least when they were not incurred in restoring damaged *government* property? Obviously, such a distinction between "damage to property" and "oil removal costs" leaves open the possibility of the government's using maritime tort law to recover, for example, for oil damage to Padre Island National Seashore.

3. Can common law theories of recovery be used by the federal government for recovery of damage to wildlife? Sections 311(f)(1) and (2) may, of course, be utilized by the federal or state governments to recover the costs of restoring or replacing natural resources (presumedly, including wildlife). But what if, to escape the Act's liability limits, the federal government also sues for damages to "its" wildlife under common law? *See In re Steuart Transportation Co.*, 495 F. Supp. 38 (E.D. Va. 1980), on remand from the Fourth Circuit, in which the district court upheld the rights of both the federal government and the Commonwealth of Virginia to seek recovery under both the "public trust doctrine" and the doctrine of *parens patriae* for the destruction of some 30,000 migratory birds, whether or not either had any real "ownership" of the birds.

4. Does the Clean Water Act preempt state statutes or common law which would allow the *state* to recover its cleanup costs and/or damages for destruction of natural resources within the state? Consider the express language of sections 311(o)(1) and (2).

In *Askew v. American Waterways Operators, Inc.*, 411 U.S. 325 (1973), this issue early on came before the Supreme Court in an attack by shipowners on the Florida Oil Spill Prevention and Control Act, which provided *inter alia*, for liability to the state for "all costs of cleanup of other damage incurred by the state and for damages resulting from injury to others." After reviewing Section 311 of the federal act, with particular emphasis on the plain meaning of subsection (o), the Court had no difficulty in sustaining the Florida statute:

> While the Federal Act is concerned only with actual cleanup costs incurred by the Federal Government, the State of Florida is concerned with its own cleanup costs. Hence there need be no collision between the Federal Act and the Florida Act ***. ***
>
> Moreover, since Congress dealt only with "cleanup" costs, it left the States free to impose "liability" in damages for losses suffered both by the States and by private interests. ***

411 U.S. 335-36.

Left open by the Court, however, was whether recovery under the Florida statute was limited to the amount specified in the federal Water Act or subject to the federal Limitation on Liability Act. When the former issue was raised in *Steuart Transportation Co. v. Allied Towing Corp., supra*, in an effort by the barge owner to limit recovery by the Commonwealth of Virginia of its cleanup costs under state statute, the Fourth Circuit found in Section 311(o)(2) a "clear manifestation of Congress' intention to let states recover their cleanup costs without regard to the limitation imposed on the federal government" by the Water Act. Since *Steuart* had been denied relief under the Limitation Act, the court did not consider whether the Water Act removed the liability limits of the Limitation Act for recovery under state law. Phrasing this latter issue in that manner, as did the Supreme Court in *Askew*, may assume a negative answer.

Given the Fourth Circuit's holding in *Steuart Transportation*, when Virginia applied its statute to another barge owner in *In re Complaint of Allied Towing*, 478 F. Supp. 398 (E.D. Va. 1979), the owner was forced to accept the application of Virginia's statute to recovery of cleanup costs. It argued, however, that it could not be held liable under the state statute for damages to Virginia's natural resources and property, since these costs were recoverable either by the federal government on the state's behalf under Section 311(f)(4) or by the state on its own behalf under Section 311(f)(5). These express statutory remedies, added by the 1977 Amendments, were argued to preempt recovery under state law for damage to natural resources. In light of the specific terms of subsection (o), the court refused to accept this argument; it held that the state was now provided the choice of either utilizing the federal strict liability remedy or using its own statutory means of recovery. The federal legislation was read merely to provide the states with an alternative remedy for destruction of their natural resources.

See also Commonwealth of Puerto Rico v. SS Zoe Colocotroni, 628 F.2d 653 (1st Cir. 1980), in which the court allowed the local Environmental Quality Board to recover the reasonable cost of restoring natural resources — e.g., mangroves and marine animals — destroyed by an oil spill, as authorized by Puerto Rican legislation. (But the court found it improper and excessive to measure damages according to the cost of planting containerized mangrove plants and purchasing replacements for the marine animals destroyed.)

Should a state also be allowed to invoke maritime tort law in order to recover for damages caused by an oil spill? See State of California v. S.S. Bournemouth, 307 F. Supp. 922 (C.D. Calif. 1969).

   5. Nothing in Section 311 provides a private right of action for damages for violation of the Act, and none can be judicially created in light of Middlesex County Sewage Authority v. National Sea Clammers Ass'n (1981), supra.

Despite Sea Clammers, doesn't Section 311(o) clearly preserve independent private rights to recovery under (1) state statutory and common law remedies and (2) federal maritime tort law of negligence and unseaworthiness? Recall that neither of these theories of recovery were addressed by the Supreme Court in Sea Clammers, and that, in any event, the express provision of Section 311(o) was inapplicable there since the claim did not involve a discharge of oil or hazardous substances.

Indeed, in Askew v. American Waterways Operators, Inc. (1973), supra, the Supreme Court had already held that in enacting Section 311 Congress had left the states free to impose liability in damages for losses suffered by private interests as well as the states themselves. Given the express language in subsection (o), may not such liability be based on state common law as well as state statutes?

Several states have enacted legislation establishing private remedies for damages caused by spills of oil and hazardous substances. See, e.g., FLA. STAT. ANN. § 376.011 et seq.; OR. REV. STAT. § 468.780 et seq.

Despite the seemingly unambiguous language in Section 311(o), the First Circuit recently held that the Clean Water Act as a whole preempted a federal maritime tort claim for damages based on nuisance principles which was brought by commercial fishermen against dischargers of toxic pollutants who had damaged their fishing grounds. Conner v. Aerovox, Inc., 730 F.2d 835 (1st Cir. 1984). The court left open the question whether an action in maritime tort under a negligence theory would be allowed, but its wholesale incorporation of the Supreme Court's reasoning in Sea Clammers would seem to leave little room for private recovery of damages based on any federal maritime tort theory.

The First Circuit's decision in Conner v. Aerovox was contrary to the apparent assumptions, at least, of other federal courts which had previously allowed private actions based in maritime tort for damages caused by oil and chemical spills. These earlier decisions were instead concerned with the issues of who could recover and for what sorts of damages—largely questions of "proximate cause"—under both state and federal tort law.

For example, in Burgess v. M/V Tamano, 370 F. Supp. 247 (D. Me. 1973), the court held that, although fishermen and clammers had no individual property rights in the aquatic life harmed by an oil spill, they could sue (under state and maritime tort law) for the tortious invasion of a public right, having suffered damages greater in degree than the general public. Claims of beach businessmen for damages from loss of customers due to the oil-fouled beaches and coastal waters, however, were dismissed by the court in *M/V Tamano*, based on the reasoning that these were indirect losses occasioned by damages to public property in which they had no interest other than that which was derivative from the interest of the public at large. See the similar holding allowing commercial fishermen to invoke federal maritime law and state tort law to recover for damages to their livelihoods caused by an oil spill in *Union Oil Co. v. Oppen*, 501 F.2d 558 (9th Cir. 1974). Compare *Louisiana v. M/V Testbank*, 752 F.2d 1019 (5th Cir. 1985), in which the court denied recovery to shipping interests, seafood enterprises, and recreational fishermen for loss of economic opportunities caused by a temporary closing of the Mississippi River after a spill of toxic chemicals, because their economic losses were not accompanied by any physical damage to their proprietary interests.

These decisions allowed commercial fishermen to recover for damages to their businesses even though the fishing grounds fouled and/or closed because of the spills belonged to the state and federal governments. Do such holdings comport with a literal reading of Section 311 (o)(1)?

Keep in mind that damage to fishing grounds outside state territorial waters (generally 3 miles) is probably beyond the jurisdiction of state law, while federal maritime law will reach maritime-type injuries occurring in any navigable waters of the United States.

United States v. M/V Big Sam

681 F.2d 432 (5th Cir. 1982)

Before WISDOM, RANDALL, and TATE, Circuit Judges.

TATE, Circuit Judge:

The United States appeals from the dismissal of its suit against the Motor Vessel BIG SAM and its owner to recover oil spill cleanup costs.
***

*   *   *

Factual Context of the Issues

The case originated out of a collision in the Mississippi River between the M/V BIG SAM and the T/B BUTANE, April 25, 1975, which resulted in hull damages to and oil spill from the BUTANE. The BIG SAM is a twin screw towboat, 155 gross tons, which at the time of the collision was owned by Zito Towing, Inc. and bareboat chartered by Tri-Capt., Inc. Due to negligent navigation and an inexperienced pilot, the BIG SAM collided with the tank barge BUTANE, owned and operated by Delta Barge Line. The collision caused 280,000 gallons of oil to be discharged from the BUTANE. Delta Barge Line immediately began cleanup opera-

tions. After spending over $50,000 in cleaning up and protecting water intakes, Delta turned the operation over to the U.S. Coast Guard, which spent almost $300,000 more to finish cleaning up the spill.

The United States brought this suit against the BIG SAM (in rem). Zito (its owner), and Tri-Capt (the vessel's bareboat charterer),[1] alleging causes of action based upon (a) § 1321(g) of the Act, (b) the Refuse Act, 33 U.S.C. § 407, and (c) general negligence (maritime tort law), to recover its cleanup costs. The findings in litigation between the private parties were stipulated,[2] under which the sole cause of the collision was

---

[1]The United States initially also sued the BUTANE (the discharging vessel) and Delta, its owner and operator. The government does not complain of the dismissal of these parties from the suit, as exculpated from liability because the negligence of the BIG SAM was the sole cause of the collision. *See* § 1321(f).

[2]*See Naptha Barge Co. v. Continental Navigation Co.*, 1978 A.M.C. 501, No. 75-1281 (E.D. La. 1977). In this suit, Delta (the owner of the discharging vessel

the negligence of the BIG SAM, the non-discharging third-party vessel. The district court held that liability was determined exclusively by § 1321(g); that under that section no in rem remedy against the vessel was recognized; and that under § 1321(g) Tri-Capt, the bareboat charterer (by now insolvent), was solely at fault and that it alone was thus liable in the amount of $15,500, the limit of liability under the circumstances as provided by § 1321(g).

The government contends that the district court erred in not affording an in rem remedy against the solely negligent vessel, and in its holding that § 1321(g) of the Act provided the exclusive remedy against a third-party non-discharging vessel solely at fault. Before reaching these contentions, we will set forth briefly an overview of sections of the Act relevant to the issues before us.

The Statutory Scheme

*   *   *

The Act imposes liability for cleanup costs on "dischargers," and cleanup costs incurred by the government are recoverable under § 1321(f) (1),(2),(3) from the discharging vessel or facility. If, however (as here), the sole cause of the accident is the act or omission of a third party, the government is permitted to recover its cleanup costs from such sole-cause third-party. § 1321(g). The Act also expressly provides that the liabilities thereby provided "shall *in no way* affect any rights" that a discharging vessel or facility, *or the United States*, may have against any third party whose acts "may *in any way* have caused or contributed to the discharge." § 1321(h) (emphasis supplied).

BUTANE) recovered from Tri-Capt (the bareboat charterer of the BIG SAM) damages, civil penalties paid to the Coast Guard under § 1321(b), costs expended to protect water intake, and the *initial and aborted cleanup costs incurred by Delta*. The right to recover the latter is expressly recognized by § 1321(h), which provides:

> The liabilities established by this section shall in no way affect any rights which (1) the owner or operator of a vessel or of an onshore facility or an offshore facility may have against any third party whose acts may in any way have caused or contributed to such discharge, or . . . .

*   *   *

A primary issue of this appeal is the interrelationship between subsections (f),(g), and (h), with regard to the liability of a sole-cause non-discharging vessel. ***

Subsection (f) imposes a strict liability standard under which the United States may recover from a discharger its cleanup costs up to stated limits without a showing of fault. The discharger may, however, escape this strict liability if he shows that the discharge was caused solely by an act of God, an act of war, negligence on the part of the United States — or an act or omission of a third party. On the other hand, if the United States proves that the discharge "was the result of willful negligence or willful misconduct within the privity and knowledge of the owner," the owner is liable to the United States for the full amount of the cleanup costs.

Subsection (g) comes into play when the discharger proves that the discharge "was caused solely by an act or omission" of a third party *"without regard to whether such act or omission was or was not negligent."* If the discharger can so prove, then the third party is liable for cleanup costs up to stated limits (a strict liability, without fault) — in the case of a vessel, as of 1975 the statutory liability of the "owner or operator . . . shall not exceed $100 per gross ton of such vessel or $14,000,000, whichever is the lesser." However, if the United States can prove that the discharge was "the result of willful negligence or willful misconduct within the privity and knowledge of such third party," then the United States may recover from the third party for the full amount of its cleanup costs. Subsection (g) (see note 6) does not expressly recognize an in rem remedy for cleanup costs as a maritime lien, as does subsection (f)(1)(see note 5) with respect to the discharging vessel.

Subsection (h) relates only to third parties whose act "in any way" caused or contributed to the discharge. It provides that the liabilities established by the Act "shall in no way affect any rights" against such third party that either the discharging vessel-facility or the United States may have.

Subsection (g), third-party liability.

The principal issue raised with regard to third-party liability is whether subsection (g) provides the exclusive remedy for the government's recovery of oil-spill cleanup costs. Before reaching that issue, however, we will first decide two subsidiary issues of statutory interpretation with regard to that subsection's imposition of strict (no fault) liability upon a third-party vessel whose act or omission was the sole cause of a discharge: (1) whether the Act contemplated that *either* the owner of the non-discharging vessel *or* the operator (the bareboat charterer) shall be so liable, or whether instead the statutory terms contemplate joint and several liability; and (2) whether subsection (g)'s silence as to an in rem remedy against a non-discharging third-party vessel, precludes an admiralty court from affording one to the government? No decision cited to us has touched upon these issues other than the opinion of the district court in the present case.

(1) *Liability of "owner or operator":* Subsection (g), which emerged from the 1970 Congressional conference committee without explanation, speaks in terms of the liability of the "owner *or* operator" of the non-discharging third-party vessel. ***

*   *   *

As statutorily defined, the term "owner or operator" refers both to the owner and to the bareboat charterer, and thus in our opinion subsection (g) affords the government a remedy against either or both. Having in mind the intent of the Act to provide an effective remedy through strict liability for recovering cleanup costs from oil spills on navigable waters, it would seem that this construction is more consistent with the legislative purpose than one that would permit an offending vessel or its owners to insulate themselves from liability through a bareboat charter to, as here, an impecunious and uninsured charterer. ***

*   *   *

We therefore find that the liability of the owner and the operator under subsection (g) is not alternative but is instead joint and several.

*   *   *

(2) *In rem remedy against the non-discharging vessel:* In disallowing an in rem remedy, the district court persuasively noted: *(a)* while an in rem remedy is expressly recognized

against the *discharging* vessel by subsection (f), subsection (g) is silent as to the availability of such a remedy against (as here) the non-discharging third-party vessel: *(b)* that, due to the exclusive remedy provided by the Act (a holding we disapprove below), no independent maritime tort has been created that would give rise to a maritime lien.

As to (a), we should first note that the inclusion of in rem language in subsection (f) is indicated by the conference report as clarifying the existence of the remedy, not as creating it. *** We are unable to find any Congressional intent in subsection (g) that no in rem remedy should be allowed as against a third-party non-discharging vessel that caused or contributed to the discharge.

As to (b), the decision of the issue under the present facts is clear. The sole fault of the accident causing the oil spill was the *negligence* of the BIG SAM. Under the Act, the United States may be responsible for removing the substance from the navigable waters unless it is determined that the removal will be done properly by the discharger. As stated in this context, "[n]egligent conduct causing loss to others constitutes a traditional maritime tort." *Matter of Oswego Barge Corp.,* 664 F.2d 327, 334 (2d Cir. 1981).***

Thus, even if subsection (g) of the Act provides an exclusive remedy (which below we hold it does *not*), the damages caused to the United States (its cleanup costs) — even if (as we below reject) subject to the liability limits of the Act — result from a maritime tort, at least when caused by the negligence of a non-discharging vessel on the navigable waters.

A maritime lien, necessary as a prerequisite for the in rem action, may arise out of a tort claim against a vessel. Suit may be brought against the vessel in rem in the proceeding to enforce the lien. Tort liens may arise against a vessel even when it is under the control of persons neither the owner nor the owner's agents, including that of a bareboat charterer.

Thus, the statutory no-fault remedy of limited liability provided by subsection (g) is here grounded also upon the sole negligence of the non-discharging third-party vessel. We see no reason why, at least as to a negligent third-party non-discharging vessel, the United States may not exercise an in rem remedy under the general maritime law to recover oil-pollution cleanup costs incurred as a result of conduct that constitutes a maritime tort, even though subsection (g) might limit the recovery whether or not the sole-cause act or omission was tortious under the present facts. We need not here decide whether the United States likewise has an in rem remedy when the sole-cause act or omission did not constitute negligence.

Subsection (g): Exclusive Remedy for Government's Recovery of Oil-Spill Cleanup Costs against Negligent *Third-Party Non-Discharging Vessel?*

Subsection (f) relates to oil-spill liability of discharging vessels or facilities, and subsection (g) relates to such liability for third parties whose act or omission is the sole cause of the discharge. In virtually identical terms these subsections provide for (a) a strict (no fault) liability up to stated limits (excusable only by the intervening sole cause of a limited specified nature) and (b) full liability for all such costs if the discharge was the result of willful negligence or willful misconduct within the privity and knowledge of the discharger or third party. By reference to the legislative history, the government persuasively argues that the specification of these two new remedies was not intended to exclude other remedies available for the recovery of damages (costs of cleanup) caused by oil-spill, such as for those through simple negligence (a maritime tort) of a vessel without the owner's privity or knowledge, where the owner's liability is limited to the value of the vessel and its freight, see 46 U.S.C. § 183(a).

With regard to subsection (f), relating to the liability of a discharging vessel, this argument has been rejected by this and other courts.***

*   *   *

However, at this point we must note that a facet of the reasoning was that the Act itself did not show any intent to permit other remedies against the *discharger* than those stated by subsection (f).***

In holding that the Act provides an exclusive remedy as against the *discharger, Oswego Barge*

contained a thoughtful and well-reasoned discussion of the criteria for gauging whether the Act had preempted (as against the *discharger)* other causes of action there asserted, which included both the maritime tort (simple negligence) and the Refuse Act actions, both here presently asserted by the United States against the present *third party* non-discharging vessel. We see no need to reiterate the detailed reasoning of that opinion, but we here note and adopt the salient features of that decision's excellent analysis of the applicable criteria as to whether the Act [referred to as the "FWPCA" in that opinion] had preempted other statutory or judge-made maritime law remedies.

*   *   *

Subsection (h)(2): Express Preservation of Judge-Made Maritime Tort Remedy to Recover Damages Caused by Oil Spill?

As noted in *Oswego Barge,* "[a]ny terms of the statute explicitly preserving or preempting judge-made law are of course controlling." 664 F.2d at 339. Although no such preservation is evidenced by the statutory language with regard to the liability of *dischargers* to the United States, subsection (h)(2) unequivocally states that "[t]he liabilities established by this section [1321] shall in no way affect any rights which . . . the United States Government may have against any *third party* whose actions may in any way have caused or contributed to the discharge of oil or hazardous substance."*** Thus, as against third parties causing or contributing to an oil spill, the United States may assert other causes of action than those established by subsection (g), or at least any others that are not inconsistent with the remedies thereby provided.

If the BIG SAM's negligence was a concurring instead of sole cause of the accident, no statutory provision of the Act applies to prevent the government's recovery of the non-discharging vessel's apportioned share of the oil-spill cleanup-cost damage occasioned by its contributing negligence. *United States v. City of Redwood City,* 640 F. 2d 963, 969-70 (9th Cir. 1981). We can see no functional reason, nor does the legislative history afford any suggestion of such a purpose, that the government's remedy against the negligent third party vessel should be less because that negligence was the sole instead of merely a contributing cause of the accident.

The government here asserts two causes of action beyond those provided by subsection (g): (1) a maritime tort action, based upon the negligence of the BIG SAM, and (2) an alleged implied action for violation of the Refuse Act. We now turn to these two causes of actions alleged:

(1) *Maritime Tort:* As we previously noted, under traditional maritime principles, negligent conduct on the navigable waters that causes loss to another constitutes a maritime tort. *See, e.g., Oswego Barge, supra,* 664 F.2d at 334, 343-44, "Oil pollution in navigable waters has been deemed a tort for which the United States is entitled damages." *United States v. City of Redwood City,* 640 F.2d 963, 969-70 (9th Cir. 1981). Even prior to the enactment of the 1970 predecessor of the present Act, at least one federal district court had recognized a cause of action in maritime tort in favor of a state government for damages caused by an oil discharge into the state territorial waters. *State of California, etc. v. S.S. Bournemouth,* 307 F. Supp. 922, 926-28 (C.C.Cal. 1969).***

Before us, the government only raises the issue of whether, by virtue of subsection (h)(2)'s express preservation, it is permitted to assert its cause of action in maritime tort against the BIG SAM and its owner, to recover damages to the government (the oil-spill cleanup costs) caused solely by the BIG SAM's negligence, under circumstances where the conduct occurred without the privity or knowledge of the owner—so that the owner is entitled to the limitation of personal liability provided by 46 U.S.C. § 183(a) of no more than the value of the vessel and its freight. We have little hesitation in declaring that such a remedy is not inconsistent with the remedy provided by subsection (g).***

We expressly do not reach two issues, unnecessary for us to decide under present facts: (1) whether a maritime tort not subject to the limitation of liability because of the owner's knowledge or privity would be inconsistent with the remedy provided by the Act for willful conduct or willful negligence; and (2) whether the maritime tort remedy provides a recovery that is cumulative to or concurrent with the remedy provided by subsection (g).[16]

(2) *The Refuse Act:* Section 13 of the Rivers and Harbors Act, 33 U.S.C. § 407 (commonly referred to as the "Refuse Act") prohibits the discharge of "refuse matter" (which has judicially been interpreted to include oil) from any vessel into the navigable waters of the United States. The United States argues that a civil remedy action is implied by that statute, and it seeks recovery on that basis also.

With regard to the remedy against the discharger, the courts have consistently held that any Refuse Act remedy for cleanup damages is inconsistent with the remedy against the discharger provided by the subsection (f) and is therefore preempted by that latter statute. *Oswego Barge, supra,* 664 F.2d at 343; *Dixie Carriers, supra,* 627 F.2d at 740. The essential reasoning is that any such strict liability remedy held to be implied by the Refuse Act, would provide recovery of damages without limitation, while subsection (f) in providing strict (no fault) liability provides for specified limits.

For identical reasons, we affirm the district court's conclusion that subsection (g), providing for strict liability in limited amount against a faultless third-party causing the accident, is inconsistent with the no-limitation strict liability remedy to be implied from the Refuse Act.

Conclusion

Accordingly, we AFFIRM the district court's dismissal of the United States claim insofar as based upon the Refuse Act; but we REVERSE the dismissal of the government's maritime tort claim and the district court's disallowance of an in rem remedy for the subsection (g) cleanup-cost damages resulting from the BIG SAM's negligence. The case is remanded for further proceedings not inconsistent with this opinion.

---

[16]If cumulative, the government might recover both the subsection (g) limits and the limitation-of-liability limits, where its actual cost exceeded the highest of the two. If concurrent, the United States would recover only the higher of the two limits. Here, however, the record indicates that the value of the vessel is substantially greater than the $300,000 cleanup-cost damages sustained by the government.

NOTES

1. Doesn't it seem anomalous that Congress would have preserved the government's common law causes of action against non-discharging third parties in Section 311(h), but would have preempted any such common law claims against dischargers under the construction given Section 311(f) by the courts?

Is this peculiar discrepancy in exposure to liability dictated by the statutory language and structure?

2. Does this holding create, as to third parties, the "four-tiered scheme of liabilities" characterized as "unwieldy" and unlikely to have been contemplated by Congress by the Second Circuit in *Oswego Barge*, at footnote 27, *supra* p. 289?

Notice that the Fifth Circuit expressly did not reach the issue as to whether a maritime tort action *not* subject to the limitation of liability, because of the owner's knowledge or privity, would be inconsistent with the Act's provision for unlimited liability only for "willful negligence or willful misconduct." Is such overlap of the two causes of action so peculiar as to cause *Big Sam* to be limited to negligence without the owner's privity? If this were done, would it create an even more anomalous scheme?

3. Illustrating perhaps as much as anything else that the Act does not provide a logical comprehensive recovery scheme, Section 311(g) only creates liability for a third party who is the *sole* cause of a discharge. It does not provide for any statutory recovery against third parties who are *contributing*, but not sole causes of a spill.

In *United States v. Bear Marine Services*, 509 F. Supp. 710 (E.D. La. 1980), the court held that the Water Act had not affected the government's right to proceed under maritime tort law against the owner of a marine terminal whose mooring dolphin allegedly punctured an oil barge. After deciding *Big Sam*, the Fifth Circuit vacated the order granting leave for interlocutory appeal, stating that "the reasoning of *Big Sam* leaves little doubt that such a tort action is also maintainable against a non-sole-cause, non-discharging third party." *United States v. Bear Marine Services*, 696 F.2d 1117 (5th Cir. 1983).

With no recovery available against a non-sole-cause third party vessel under Section 311, it would make no sense to find any preemption of a maritime tort claim, even if recovery was without limitation because of privity or knowledge of the vessel owner. Reconsidering the issue left open in *Big Sam*, should the Act be read to allow unlimited liability for those who *contribute* to a spill, but to impose limits on maritime tort recovery for those who are the *sole* cause?

Keep in mind that liability under maritime tort law is not restricted to *vessels*, and that the same is true for recovery under Sections 311(f) and (g) of the Act, while the Limitation of Liability Act affords protection only to vessels. Obviously, liability issues in the case of maritime oil spills are going to be complex, regardless of how the court handles preemption questions.

4. Do you agree with the court's different view of the Refuse Act claim in *Big Sam*? Is it readily distinguishable? Does the court's reasoning imply that it would not allow maritime tort recovery if the Limitation Act did not limit recovery? Does it imply that it would not allow non-statutory recovery under strict liability—*e.g.*, under an "unseaworthiness" claim?

II
LAND DISPOSAL OF HAZARDOUS WASTES

1 THE RESOURCE CONSERVATION AND RECOVERY ACT

State Hazardous Waste Programs Under the Federal Resource Conservation and Recovery Act

David Schnapf, 12 ENVTL. L. 679 (1982)

* * *

HISTORY AND STRUCTURE OF THE RCRA HAZARDOUS WASTE PROGRAM

* * *

In 1965, Congress enacted the Solid Waste Disposal Act (SWDA), plunging the federal government into the field of waste management for the first time. Congress recognized that serious problems could result from improper waste disposal practices, yet the role established for the federal government was quite modest. The SWDA provides monetary grants to states for planning, training, research, demonstration projects, and similar activities. The law does not define the concept of "hazardous" waste, although Congress recognized that improper waste disposal practices "create serious hazards to the public health, including pollution of air and water resources, accident hazards . . . [and] create public nuisances."

Five years later, Congress enacted the Resource Recovery Act of 1970. This law followed the pattern set by the SWDA for federal involvement, although greater emphasis was placed on resource recovery and on means of reducing waste generation.

Section 212 of the Resource Recovery Act required EPA to prepare a "comprehensive report and plan for the creation of a system of national disposal sites for the storage and dis-posal of hazardous wastes," to be submitted to Congress by October, 1972. Hazardous waste was not defined but was said to include "radioactive, toxic chemical, biological, and other wastes which may endanger public health or welfare."

In June of 1973, EPA submitted its report to Congress, revealing that the agency had largely ignored its charge to develop a plan for a national disposal site system. Instead, the report focused on the need for a federal regulatory program, noting that "land-based hazardous waste treatment, storage, and disposal activities are essentially unregulated by Federal and State laws." The report included proposed legislation which would establish such a regulatory program.

Following the pattern established by the Clean Air Act and the Clean Water Act, EPA's legislative proposal held states responsible for program implementation; minimum standards would be set and enforced by EPA. The report rejected a totally federal system because of "the difficulty in proving conclusively that the hazards . . . justify total Federal involvement, the prohibitive costs and administrative burdens . . . [and a desire not to preclude state involvement] in what is essentially a state problem." Likewise, EPA rejected a "state only" control program because of "its total dependence on the States for the adoption and enforcement of [a control program], the nonavailability of Federal back-up enforcement authority, [and] the potential for extreme nonuniformity between the individual States adopting control programs." ***

*   *   *

There were virtually no operating state hazardous waste programs when the EPA legislation was proposed. ***

EPA's proposed legislation was introduced in both the House and the Senate in early 1973, but was not enacted by the ninety-third Congress. In 1975 the Ford administration withdrew its support for federal hazardous waste legislation, citing budgetary constraints.

Finally, with very little fanfare and almost no debate, Congress enacted RCRA, directing EPA to establish a comprehensive regulatory program governing the management of hazardous waste.[34] RCRA was signed into law by President Ford on October 21, 1976. Although details differ, the major components of RCRA resemble the legislation EPA had proposed three years earlier.

The federal role under the SWDA was primarily the provision of grants and technical assistance to the states. By contrast, subtitle C of RCRA establishes the framework for a regulatory program and gives EPA primary responsibility for ensuring that hazardous wastes are properly managed. RCRA's "cradle-to-grave" approach to hazardous waste management regulates the generation, transportation, and ultimate disposal of hazardous waste. A manifest system is mandated to track all movements of hazardous waste. In addition, RCRA creates a permit program with technical standards covering all hazardous waste treatment, storage, and disposal facilities. EPA is directed to determine which wastes are hazardous for the purposes of subtitle C control. Finally, although EPA was given primary responsibility, Congress intended that EPA would turn over to the states most of the responsibility for program implementation.

EPA has at least five distinct roles under RCRA. First, and perhaps foremost, the agency is responsible for setting minimum standards and other regulatory program requirements. Second, the agency is responsible for the operation of a federal program in states that choose not to develop their own programs. Third, the agency must regulate and police state programs. It is required to establish regulations governing state programs, to review and authorize state programs meeting the EPA requirements, and to oversee state programs and withdraw "authorization" when a state program ceases to meet the EPA requirements. Fourth, the agency engages in a range of activities which assist states in their efforts. These activities include the provision of grants, technical assistance, and counsel to aid in solving both generic and specific hazardous waste problems. It is this role which most closely resembles the cooperative spirit of a partnership. Fifth, RCRA casts EPA in the role of an enforcer, giving the agency enforcement power even in states that have authorized programs.

*   *   *

---

[34]Resource Conservation and Recovery Act, Pub. L. No. 94-580, 90 Stat. 2796 (codified as amended at 42 U.S.C. §§ 6901-6987 (1976 & Supp. III 1979).

Hazardous Waste Management Under RCRA: An Overview of the Statute and the EPA's Current Program

Theodore L. Garrett, 13 NAT. RESOURCES L. NWSLTR. 1 (1981)*

The Resource Conservation and Recovery Act of 1976 (RCRA) provides a comprehensive Federal program for the regulation of solid wastes. This statute greatly expands the role of the Federal government in the field of solid waste disposal, with particular emphasis on the regulation of hazardous waste. ***

The major regulatory program of RCRA is contained in Subtitle C and covers the management of solid wastes which are defined as hazardous. Section 1004(5) of the Act defines a hazardous waste as a solid waste which, because of its quantity, concentration or physical, chemical or infectious characteristics may "(A) cause, or significantly contribute to an increase in mortality or an increase in serious irreversible, or incapacitating reversible illness; or (B) pose a substantial present or potential hazard to human health or the environment when improperly treated, stored, transported, or disposed of, or otherwise managed." 42 U.S.C. § 6903(5).

Identification and Listing of
Hazardous Waste

After defining hazardous wastes in this broad fashion, Congress required the EPA to publish criteria for identifying the characteristics of hazardous wastes and for listing hazardous wastes.***

On May 19, 1980, EPA published its initial regulations under Section 3001 of RCRA, 40 C.F.R. Part 261. (45 Fed. Reg. 33,119) These regulations identify four characteristics to be used by persons handling solid wastes to determine if that waste is a hazardous waste, namely (1) ignitability, those substances posing a fire hazard during routine management; (2) corrosivity, the ability to corrode standard containers or to dissolve other wastes; (3) reactivity, the tendency to explode under normal management conditions, to act violently when mixed with water, or to generate toxic gases; and (4) toxicity as determined by a specific extraction procedure resulting in the presence of certain toxic materials at levels greater than those specified.

In addition, EPA's Part 261 regulations contain a list of specific hazardous wastes, including various process wastes and chemical products which, if discarded, must be managed as hazardous waste. Included in the list are some readily identifiable wastes that possess any of the above four hazardous wastes characteristics as well as wastes meeting the criteria for acute hazard or toxicity.***

*   *   *

Finally, EPA has excluded certain wastes as not subject to the hazardous waste controls. These include domestic sewage, industrial waste water discharges, wastes (other than sludges or listed wastes) that are reused or recycled, utility wastes, and certain other wastes.

Notification of Hazardous Waste Activity

Section 3010 of RCRA sets forth a notification procedure that applies to all persons who generate or transport hazardous wastes or who own or operate a facility for the treatment, storage or disposal of hazardous wastes. 42 U.S.C. § 6930. Such persons must notify EPA of their status as generators, transporters, owners, or operators within 90 days after EPA promulgates regulations that identify or list hazardous wastes. This notification is a prerequisite for transporting, treating, storing, or disposing of hazardous wastes.***

*   *   *

EPA's notification form requires each facility to state the location and describe the hazardous waste activity and the wastes handled. Any hazardous wastes handled during the preceding three-month period must be reported. A new generator or transporter must apply to EPA for an identification number before any hazardous waste can be transported.***

Standards Applicable to Generators of
Hazardous Wastes

Section 3002 of RCRA requires EPA to publish regulations applicable to generators of hazardous wastes. 42 U.S.C. § 6922. These regulations are to establish requirements regarding recordkeeping, labeling, the use of a manifest system, and submission of reports.***

Under these regulations, a generator of solid waste must determine if his waste is hazardous, or excluded according to the definitions, criteria, and lists set forth in Part 261. If the waste is neither excluded nor specifically listed, the generator must then determine whether the waste meets the "hazardous" criteria. The generator must accomplish the latter by testing the waste according to specific methods or by applying his knowledge of the hazard characteristic of the waste in light of the materials or processes used.

*   *   *

A generator of solid waste must prepare a manifest for all shipments of hazardous wastes that are sent to offsite treatment, storage, or disposal facilities. The manifest serves as a tracking device, to provide relevant information to persons handling the wastes, and to provide proper records.

***In particular, the manifest must contain the name and address of the generator, the names of all transporters, the name and address of the permitted facility designated to receive the wastes, EPA identification numbers of all those who handle the wastes, the Department of Transportation description of the wastes, the quantity of waste and number of containers, and the generator's signature certifying that the waste has been properly labeled, marked and packaged in accordance with EPA and DOT regulations. There are current efforts under way to develop a uniform national manifest.

With respect to the operation of the system, the generator must sign one copy of the manifest, and must present the initial transporter with sufficient copies to allow each subsequent handler of the waste to retain a copy, together with an extra copy to be returned to the generator by the designated disposal facility.***

One point which should be emphasized is that generators must ship their wastes off that site promptly to avoid being classified as a storage facility. A generator who accumulates wastes on his property for more than 90 days is considered to be "storing" waste, and is required to obtain a facility permit under Section 3005 of RCRA. A generator may accumulate hazardous wastes on-site for 90 days or less without a RCRA permit.

Standards Applicable to Transporters of Hazardous Wastes

Section 3003 of RCRA authorizes EPA to promulgate standards for hazardous waste transporters. 42 U.S.C. § 6923.***

The EPA regulations for transporters were developed jointly by EPA and the Department of Transportation.***

The EPA regulations require that a transporter of hazardous wastes have an EPA identification number and comply with the manifest system for tracking hazardous wastes by refusing to accept hazardous wastes that are not accompanied by a manifest. In addition, the transporter must return a manifest to the generator, and deliver the manifest to subsequent transporters or the operators of the designated facility. The transporter must deliver the waste to the designated facility or the next designated transporter.*** Finally, a transporter is required to take immediate action on discharges or spills, including the reporting of a discharge and clean up of any hazardous waste discharged during transportation.

*   *   *

Standards for Hazardous Waste Treatment, Storage and Disposal Facilities

Section 3004 of RCRA authorizes EPA to publish performance standards applicable to owners and operators of facilities for the treatment, storage, or disposal of hazardous wastes. 42 U.S.C. § 6924. In particular, the statute authorizes EPA to establish requirements with respect to records maintenance; reporting, monitoring, and inspection and compliance with the manifest system; operating methods, techniques and practices for the treatment, storage or disposal of wastes; the location, design and construction of hazardous wastes facilities; contingency plans; maintenance, training and financial responsibility; and compliance with permit requirements for treatment, storage, or disposal.

*   *   *

The initial regulations under Part 264 are the first phase of the standards which will be used to issue permits for hazardous waste treatment, storage, and disposal facilities. Included are the requirements with respect to preparedness for and prevention of hazards, contingency planning in emergency procedures, the manifest system, and recordkeeping and reporting (Subparts C, D and E). Also included are general requirements with respect to identification numbers, required notices, waste analysis, security at facilities, inspection of facilities, and personnel training. (Subpart B).***

Part 265 of the regulations published on May 19, 1980, establishes the requirements applicable during the interim status period. These regulations apply during the period after an owner or operator has applied for a permit, but prior to final action on the application. 40 C.F.R. § 265.1. The regulations deal with preparation for and prevention of hazards, contingency planning and emergency procedures, the manifest system, recordkeeping and reporting, ground water monitoring, facility closure and post-closure care, financial requirements, the use and management of containers. (Subparts C-I). The regulations also contain requirements for the design and operation of tanks, treatment facilities, landfills, incinerators, and other facilities. (Subparts J-R). Additional requirements include those with respect to identification numbers, notices, waste analysis, security at facilities and personnel training. (Subpart B).

*   *   *

Permits for Treatment, Storage or Disposal Facilities

Section 3005 of RCRA requires that any person who owns or operates a facility for the treatment, storage, or disposal of hazardous waste must receive a permit from EPA or a state authorized to conduct its own hazardous waste program. 42 U.S.C. § 6925.

*   *   *

An existing facility achieves interim status and is considered to have a permit if notification is filed with EPA and Part A of the permit application is submitted within the time allowed. The interim status continues until EPA acts upon Part B of the permit. During this time, the facility must comply with the interim status standards promulgated under section 3004 of RCRA.

State Programs

Section 3006 of RCRA allows states to apply to EPA for authorization to administer the solid waste program.***

Under the EPA regulations, state programs that are substantially equivalent to the federal program may receive interim authori-

zation. To qualify for interim authorization, a state must submit a program which is substantially the same as the federal program with respect to the universe of waste control, the substance of the standards, the procedures with which it is administered, and must cover all types of hazardous waste facilities in the state.***

Enforcement and Inspection

*   *   *

Enforcement of Subtitle C of RCRA is governed by section 3008, 42 U.S.C. § 6928. EPA under this provision may either issue a compliance order or commence a civil action in a district court. Compliance orders are required to state the nature of the violation, specify the time for compliance, and assess a civil penalty. Failure to take corrective action within the time specified subjects the violator to a civil penalty of $25,000 for each day of violation and to suspension or revocation of the permit. In addition, section 3008(9) provides for the assessment of a $25,000 civil penalty for each day of a violation of any requirement of Subtitle C.

Section 3008(d) of RCRA establishes criminal liability where any person knowingly transports hazardous wastes to an unpermitted facility; knowingly treats, stores, or disposes of hazardous wastes without a permit; or knowingly makes a false statement in a permit application, manifest, report or other document. Upon first conviction, the above violations are subject to a fine of not more than $25,000 and imprisonment not to exceed one year for each year of violation, or both. Subsequent convictions are punishable by fines of up to $50,000 or by imprisonment for not more than two years or both. A recently passed amendment to section 3008(e) of RCRA provides enhanced felony penalties for certain life-threatening conduct.

Conclusion

The above is but a brief summary of some of the principal features of the statutory provisions and regulations announced to date by EPA. It is too soon to assess the success of this program. A number of the major statutory provisions have not yet been implemented by the Agency. Other provisions of the statute, and in particular the provisions relating to the control of hazardous wastes, are the subject of regulations only recently issued by EPA and which are now undergoing careful scrutiny by the public. Litigation is presently pending as to EPA's regula-

tions, and it is reasonable to anticipate that there will be congressional oversight and further administrative proceedings. These programs are complex, and will have great significance for all companies that generate, transport, store, treat, and dispose of solid wastes.

EPA's New Land Disposal Standards

Susan Bromm, 12 ENVTL. L. REP 15027 (1982)

On July 26, 1982, the Environmental Protection Agency (EPA) promulgated the long awaited hazardous waste land disposal standards.[1] Publication of these regulations, which apply to hazardous waste landfills, surface impounds, waste piles, and land treatment facilities, completes the core hazardous waste management regulatory program under Subtitle C of the Resource Conservation and Recovery Act (RCRA). Further regulatory activity is planned, however, to "fine tune" existing regulations. The new regulations, which form the basis for granting permits to new and existing hazardous waste land disposal facilities, rely on a two-pronged approach for protection of human health and the environment. They establish a performance-oriented groundwater protection standard, implemented through groundwater monitoring and, if contamination is detected, corrective action. In addition, they prescribe performance-based design and operating standards aimed at preventing the release of waste and waste constituents during the facility's operating life and post-closure care period.

*   *   *

As a result, final state authorization can begin, allowing states to administer their own permitting programs, once they were determined to be "equivalent" to and "consistent" with the federal program.

---

[1] 47 Fed. Reg. 32274-373 (July 26, 1982).

Regulatory Framework

Under the two-pronged approach of the new regulations, facilities are subject to both the groundwater protection requirements and a set of design and operating requirements, specific to the type of facility (i.e., landfill, waste pile, surface impoundment, or land treatment). In defining which waste management components are subject to the groundwater protection requirements, EPA uses the term "regulated unit." A unit is a contiguous area of land on or in which waste is placed. Examples of units include a single surface impoundment or a single waste pile. A "regulated unit" is any unit that receives hazardous waste after January 26, 1983 (the effective date of the regulations). All regulated units are subject to the groundwater protection provisions unless they have been constructed with a double liner system incorporating a leak detection system between the liners.*** Also exempt from the groundwater protection requirements are facilities located in areas with deep, tight soils (*e.g.*, clay) that will prevent the migration of leachate to groundwater for at least 30 years after closure.

All permitted facilities are subject to the design and operating requirements; however, "existing portions" of existing facilities are not required to install liners or leachate collection and removal systems. By definition, existing portions are land areas on which wastes have been placed prior to permit issuance. Thus, lateral expansions of existing facilities after permit issuance are required to meet the liner requirements.***

Existing facilities are, however, subject to all other design and operating standards. These standards are roughly equivalent to the interim status standards under which existing facilities are now regulated, although in some cases they are expressed in terms of a more specific performance standard. Included in these generally applicable design and operating standards are run-on and run-off control, wind dispersal control, restrictions on the disposal of ignitable and reactive wastes, restrictions on the disposal of incompatible wastes, restrictions on the disposal of liquids in landfills, and final cover (cap) requirements for disposal facilities.

*   *   *

Groundwater Protection Standard

The heart of the groundwater protection requirements is the assumption that significant leachate plumes reaching groundwater can and will be detected and removed through corrective action (e.g., counter pumping). This requirement represents a significant step forward from the interim status standards, which mandate groundwater monitoring to detect contamination but do not establish a groundwater protection standard or prescribe a "cure" when contamination occurs. Although there is limited experience with corrective action to remove contamination from groundwater, this is likely to be a very expensive undertaking and should provide an economic incentive for owners and operators to employ designs and operating practices that minimize the chance that corrective action will be necessary.

The groundwater protection program is comprised of three phases—detection monitoring, compliance monitoring, and the corrective action program. New facilities and existing facilities at which no groundwater contamination has been detected during the interim status period will initially begin in the detection monitoring phase.*** This monitoring must continue throughout the facility's operating

life and the post-closure care period (normally 30 years after closure).***

If detection monitoring indicates that leachate has reached groundwater, the second phase of the program, compliance monitoring, is triggered. Once leachate is detected, the owner or operator must analyze groundwater for specific hazardous constituents that are known to be in the waste at the facility and determine their concentrations.*** EPA will then (after a public hearing) modify the permit to include a groundwater protection standard. This standard identifies the hazardous constituents for which monitoring must be conducted and the allowable concentration limits for these constituents.***

Compliance monitoring begins when leachate is detected and must continue for a number of years equal to the entire operating life of the facility.*** If the concentration limits established in the permit are not exceeded during this period, compliance monitoring ceases. However, should the specified concentration limits be exceeded at any time during the compliance monitoring phase, a corrective action program must be instituted.

If compliance monitoring indicates an excessive concentration of hazardous constituents, the owner or operator must immediately notify EPA and within six months submit an application for a permit modification for a corrective action program. This application must explain what actions the owner/operator proposes in order to return groundwater quality to within the acceptable concentration limits established in the compliance monitoring phase. The application must also include a groundwater monitoring scheme to verify the results of corrective action. Corrective action must continue until groundwater quality at the waste management boundary is again within the limits established in the groundwater protection standard for the unit.

*   *   *

Corrective action requirements are described in terms of the performance to be achieved, namely returning the concentration of hazardous constituents in the groundwater to within established concentration limits by removing the hazardous constituents or treating them in place. The regulations do not specify what type of corrective action must be undertaken, leaving this open for a case-by-case determination. The preamble suggests that containment of contaminated groundwater via slurry walls is not adequate alone; however, the use of slurry walls with counter pumping may constitute an acceptable corrective action program.

*   *   *

Design and Operating Standards

While the groundwater protection measures are *curative* in nature, the design and operating requirements are aimed at *preventing* groundwater contamination. As mentioned previously, new landfills, surface impoundments, and waste piles are required to have liner systems; existing portions of these facilities are not. Liner systems must be designed to prevent any migration of wastes out of the facility into adjacent subsurface soil or groundwater or surface water during the facility's operating life and closure period.

At storage facilities, migration of waste into the liner is acceptable, because storage facilities, by definition, will remove all wastes and contaminated liners at closure. This standard permits the use of single clay liners at waste piles and storage surface impoundments. Disposal facility liners, on the other hand, must be designed to prevent migration of wastes into the liner as well as the subsurface soil. In effect, this rules out the use of clay liners at disposal facilities. EPA states in the preamble that, to its knowledge, only synthetic liners will meet this standard.

Both new and existing surface impoundments and landfills must place a final cap on the facility at closure to minimize the infiltration of precipitation and run-on. This in turn is intended to minimize the generation of leachate after closure.

New landfills and waste piles are required to have leachate collection and removal systems to remove leachate generated during the operation of the facility and, in the case of landfills, during the post-closure care period.***

The new regulations include restrictions on the disposal of liquids in landfills that parallel the corresponding provisions in the interim status standards. Containers holding liquids may not be placed in landfills unless all free-standing liquid is absorbed, solidified, or otherwise eliminated. Bulk liquids may only be disposed of in landfills with liners and leachate collection and removal systems which meet the performance standard specified for new facilities.

*   *   *

Implementation

All hazardous waste management facilities in existence on November 19, 1980 were required to file a notification and Part A of a permit application with EPA. The actual permitting process begins when the Agency calls in Part B of a facility's permit application. Part B applications for land disposal facilities will be called in as soon as the standards become effective on January 26, 1983.

In accordance with previously promulgated regulations, owners and operators have at least six months from the date of request to submit their Part B application. After a draft permit has been developed, public notice is given and a comment period is provided. A public hearing on the draft permit will be held if there is a "significant degree of public interest." After the close of the public comment period and the public hearing, significant public comments are addressed and a final permit decision is made. Permits become effective 30 days after the service of notice of the decision.

In a separate Federal Register notice,[40] also published on July 26, 1982, EPA announced that states could immediately begin applying for the final phase of state authorization. Once a state receives final authorization, it takes over the principal role of issuing permits and enforcing permit conditions.

*   *   *

With the promulgation of this crucial "final piece" of hazardous waste management stan-

---

[40] 47 Fed. Reg. 32378 (July 26, 1982).

dards, the RCRA program is on the verge of moving foward into full-scale implementation. When these regulations become effective on January 26, 1983, there will indeed be a "cradle-to-grave" management system for hazardous waste.

The Hazardous and Solid Waste Amendments of 1984: A Dramatic Overhaul of the Way America Manages Its Hazardous Wastes

William L. Rosbe and Robert L. Gulley, 14 ENVTL L. REP. 10458 (1984)

The Resource Conservation and Recovery Act (RCRA), required the Environmental Protection Agency (EPA) to establish a regulatory program for "cradle to grave" management of hazardous wastes. EPA did not promulgate the first set of those regulations until 1980. The full package of rules, essentially completed in mid-1982, is extremely complex and difficult for EPA and the regulated community to implement. In 1983, Congress began consideration of bills to reauthorize the RCRA program. During hearings on the bills, many members of Congress expressed frustration with what they perceived as EPA's inability or unwillingness to promulgate all of the regulations required to implement the RCRA program and with the "loopholes" in the regulations that EPA did promulgate. These concerns culminated in the Hazardous and Solid Waste Amendments of 1984 (Amendments),[3] which President Reagan signed into law on November 8, 1984.

The Amendments do much more than reauthorize RCRA. Instead, they will cause "a dramatic overhaul of the way America manages its hazardous wastes." First, Congress has brought up to 15 million metric tons of hazardous wastes and over 130,000 new generators within the ambit of RCRA's hazardous waste

management regulations by narrowing EPA's small quantity generator exemption. Second, Congress effectively has directed EPA to phase out land disposal of hazardous wastes by prohibiting land disposal of most hazardous wastes unless extraordinarily stringent conditions are satisfied. Third, Congress has added two major regulatory programs to RCRA—one for managing leaking underground storage tanks and a second for regulating the burning of fuels that contain used oil or hazardous wastes. Fourth, Congress has broadened EPA's authority to require cleanup of environmental problems caused by hazardous waste facilities. It has done so by expanding EPA's ability to require corrective actions at interim status facilities and at permitted facilities with inactive units and by broadening RCRA's imminent hazard provision to allow EPA to require corrective actions at abandoned hazardous waste sites. Finally, Congress has expanded the public's role in forcing cleanup of hazardous waste pollution by allowing citizen suits to enforce RCRA's imminent hazard provision when EPA fails to do so adequately.***

The Small Quantity Generator Exemption

RCRA directs EPA to promulgate regulations establishing standards for generators of hazardous wastes "as may be necessary to protect human health and the environment."[5] When first deciding how to implement RCRA, EPA realized that it lacked sufficient administrative resources to regulate all hazardous waste gen-

---

[3]Pub. L. No. 98-616, 96 Stat. 3221 (forthcoming). The only version of the amendments available at press time is in the Conference Report, H.R. REP. No. 1133, 98th Cong., 2d Sess. (1984). Citations to the 1984 Act [hereinafter cited as Amendments] and to the analysis in the Report [hereinafter cited as Conference Report] both refer to this document.***

*   *   *

[5]RCRA § 3002.

erators. EPA chose to make the standards applicable only to generators of 1000 or more kilograms per month ("kg/mo") of hazardous wastes, but committed itself to phasing in small quantity generators down to 100 kg/mo within two to five years.

Apparently impatient with EPA's failure to keep its commitment, Congress now has directed EPA to promulgate standards by March 31, 1986, for generators of between 100 and 1000 kg/mo of hazardous wastes.[9] The Amendments expressly allow EPA to make these standards different from those currently imposed on generators of greater than 1000 kg/mo of hazardous wastes, but require that the standards be "sufficient to protect human health and the environment." The new standards, at a minimum, must require that all hazardous wastes generated by these small quantity generators be treated, stored, and disposed of at a hazardous waste facility with either interim status or a permit under RCRA, except that these generators may, prior to disposal, store up to 1000 kg of hazardous wastes on site for no longer than 180 days.

*   *   *

Congress included a so-called "hammer" if EPA does not promulgate the new standards by March 31, 1986. If EPA misses the deadline, the wastes generated by these small quantity generators would not escape regulation, but rather would be subject to what are, in effect, congressional regulations. Unless EPA promulgates the new standards by March 31, 1986, small quantity generators must (1) manifest their hazardous wastes for off-site disposal; (2) treat, store, or dispose of their hazardous wastes at interim status or permitted facilities; (3) file manifest exception reports as required of generators producing greater than 1000 kg/mo of hazardous wastes; and (4) retain copies of all manifests for up to three years. These statutory requirements would remain in effect until EPA promulgates the required standards.

---

[9]Amendments, *supra* note 3, sec. 221(a), RCRA § 3001(d)(1).

The new small quantity generator provisions will subject over 130,000 new generators to regulation — more than double the 60,000 that notified EPA in 1980 that they were generators. Most of these generators will be small businesses, such as dry cleaning establishments and gasoline stations. This category of generators will need to spend up to $100 million each year to comply with the new regulations. Another effect of these provisions will be that an additional 15 million metric tons of hazardous wastes will be sent to hazardous waste treatment, storage, and disposal facilities each year. To date, in most areas of the country, where local ordinances do not bar it, hazardous wastes generated by small quantity generators typically have been sent to municipal landfills that are not required to meet strict waste management standards and, in fact, are now known to create many environmental problems.***

Congress was aware of these effects and problems, but decided that the broader coverage was necessary to protect human health and the environment. It is not clear, however, that Congress considered fully the impact of the small quantity generator requirements in relation to other major changes mandated by the Amendments. For example, by March 31, 1986, all hazardous wastes generated by small quantity generators will have to be disposed of in permitted or interim status facilities. By the same time, however, other provisions in the Amendments will effectively prohibit some, if not all, forms of land disposal for many hazardous wastes and impose stringent, minimum technological requirements for all other hazardous waste facilities. The almost inevitable result will be a greatly reduced number of hazardous waste facilities available to receive the wastes generated by the small quantity generators. Where will these newly regulated wastes be disposed of? Congress apparently envisioned that small quantity generators would resort to incineration and other new technologies to handle their wastes. Yet incineration is only effective for destroying organic compounds and there is limited incineration capacity available. And the Amendments do nothing to expedite the permitting of hazardous waste incinerators and little to facilitate the development of new technologies. The new requirements for safer disposal combined with the decreasing number of hazardous waste facilities at which disposal will be legal will drive up the disposal costs for small businesses and increase their resistance to compliance. Unless EPA is equipped to undertake massive enforcement efforts against these newly regulated generators, the small generator provision, at best, may do little to relieve the risks posed by the 15 million metric tons of wastes produced each year by the small quantity generators.

Land Disposal Provisions

Land disposal of liquids and highly mobile or persistent hazardous wastes can present significant long-term risks to ground and surface water because, eventually, the wastes or their constituents will leak or leach from the disposal unit. Nonetheless, since land disposal is less expensive than the primary alternatives of incineration or physical-chemical treatment, it is by far the most commonly employed method for disposing of hazardous wastes. To avoid the risks from land disposal of hazardous wastes and to encourage the development of new treatment and disposal technologies, Congress enacted land disposal provisions that effectively phase out land disposal as a method of hazardous waste management.

Congress' policy regarding land disposal of hazardous wastes is simple and straightforward: (1) "reliance on land disposal should be minimized or eliminated"; and (2) "land disposal, particularly landfill and surface impoundment, should be the least favored method for managing hazardous waste."[25] Three major provisions in the Amendments implement this policy. The first prohibits, or severely restricts, land disposal of hazardous and non-hazardous liquids. The second effectively phases out land disposal of many hazardous wastes by all or most types of facilities. The third imposes stringent, minimum technological requirements on all existing and new landfills and surface impoundments.

To ensure that EPA would not fail to give full and immediate effect to these provisions, Congress set out with great specificity what EPA must do and by what dates. Moreover, to ensure that EPA would not fail to meet the deadlines, Congress included statutory prohibitions (more "hammers") that will go into effect automatically if EPA misses the deadlines.

Land Disposal of Liquids

Congress was particularly concerned with land disposal of liquids. Because liquids can readily leak from a land disposal unit or move within the wastes in a unit, Congress enacted measures to prohibit or minimize the land disposal of liquids. ***After May 8, 1985, the Amendments prohibit disposal of bulk and non-containerized liquid hazardous wastes in any landfill.[27]***By February 8, 1986, EPA must promulgate regulations to minimize the disposal of containerized liquid hazardous wastes in landfills and to minimize the presence of free liquids in containerized hazardous wastes in landfills.***

Land Disposal of Specified Hazardous Wastes

The Amendments prohibit all methods of land disposal (except deep well injection) of the so-called "California list" hazardous wastes[31] (effective in 32 months) and of the dioxin-containing listed hazardous wastes and listed spent solvents (effective in 24 months), "unless [EPA] determines that the prohibition of one or more methods of land disposal of such waste is not required in order to protect human health and the environment for as long as the waste remains hazardous...."***A method of land disposal is not "protective of human health and the environment" for these wastes unless an

---

[25]*Id.*, sec. 101(a)(7), RCRA § 1002(b)(7).

[27]*Id.*, sec. 201(a), RCRA § 3004(c)(1). In the interim, existing regulatory limitations on liquids in landfills remain in effect. *Id.*

[31] The "California list" of hazardous wastes includes liquid hazardous wastes and sludges containing specified concentrations of cyanide, heavy metals or arsenic, highly acidic liquids, liquids containing 50 or more parts per million of PCBs and halogenated organic compounds in total concentrations of 1000 mg/kg or greater. *Id.*, sec. 201(a), RCRA § 3004(d)(2).

interested person demonstrates "to a reasonable degree of certainty" that there will be "no migration of hazardous constituents" from the disposal unit for "as long as the wastes remain hazardous."[36] These tests are nearly impossible to satisfy. Thus, the Amendments will effectively prohibit the land disposal of these wastes.

Disposal in Deep Injection Wells

Congress required EPA to review the disposal of the California-list wastes, specified dioxin-containing wastes, and listed spent solvents in deep injection wells within 45 months and to promulgate regulations prohibiting such disposal if it "may be reasonably determined" that such disposal method may not be "protective of human health and the environment." If, however, EPA fails to make that determination for any of these wastes by the deadline, the disposal of that waste into any deep injection well will be prohibited.[38]

Other Listed Hazardous Wastes

EPA must submit to Congress a schedule for reviewing all other listed hazardous wastes in order to determine whether one or more methods of land disposal of those wastes should be prohibited.[39] Not later than specified dates several years after enactment, EPA must promulgate, for each waste, regulations prohibiting all methods of land disposal, except those that EPA determines will be "protective of human health and the environment." Congress again included "hammers."***If EPA "fails to promulgate regulations, or make a determination" regarding any listed waste within 66 months, land disposal of such waste is prohibited.

The Amendments authorized two types of variances from these land disposal prohibitions.***

*　　　*　　　*

Minimum Technological Requirements

In the Amendments, Congress established minimum technological requirements for existing and new landfills and surface impoundments in order to ensure that the landfill or surface impoundment is designed to minimize the risk of hazardous wastes or their constituents migrating from the unit and to ensure that any such migration will be detected if it does occur. Any permit issued after November 8, 1984 for a new or replacement landfill or surface impoundment or a lateral expansion of an existing facility must require, at a minimum, two or more liners, a leachate collection system above (in the case of a landfill) and between the liners, and groundwater monitoring.[51]***

Most interim status surface impoundments must comply with the new minimum technological requirements within four years.[55]***

Effects of Land Disposal Restrictions

By these Amendments, Congress effectively has required EPA to phase out most, if not all, methods of land disposal of hazardous wastes. To the extent that any method of land disposal might still be allowed, Congress has shifted the burden to EPA to take action before the statutory prohibitions take effect and to industry to urge that EPA act in time. It is doubtful that EPA is capable of meeting the statutory deadlines, even with prodding from industry, unless it can develop simple new procedures for evaluating land disposal methods' protection of health and the environment. Even if EPA develops such procedures, the burden placed on a company to demonstrate "to a reasonable degree of certainty" that there will be "*no* migration of hazardous constituents" from the unit "for as long as the waste remains hazardous" may be virtually insurmountable. Thus, industry may, instead, elect to invest in incineration and physical-chemical treatment as methods of managing the California list wastes, dioxin-containing wastes, and listed spent solvents rather than attempt to obtain an exception for a method of land disposal for these

---

[36]*Id.*, sec. 201(a), RCRA §§ 3004(d)(1),(e)(1).
[38]*Id.*, sec. 201(a), RCRA § 3004(f)(3).
[39]*Id.*, sec. 201(a), RCRA § 3004(g)(1).***

[51]*Id.*, sec. 202(a), RCRA § 3004(o)(1).***
[55]*Id.*, sec. 215, RCRA § 3005(j)(1).***

wastes. With regard to the other listed wastes, industry may decide to focus its efforts on urging EPA to promulgate reasonable treatment standards that would avoid the regulatory prohibitions rather than trying to overcome the burden necessary to obtain an exception. If this happens, Congress will have effectively achieved its goal of forcing the increased use of non-land disposal hazardous waste management methods and the development of new hazardous waste management technology. Whether the waste disposal industry can respond, within the time allowed, to this new technology-forcing imperative with enough effective treatment and incineration capacity to handle the growing hazardous waste load remains to be seen.

*   *   *

Major New Regulatory Programs

The Amendments create two major new regulatory programs. One governs leaking underground storage tanks.[63] The other applies to burning fuels containing used oil or hazardous wastes.[64]

*   *   *

Corrective Actions

The Amendments expand EPA's ability to take corrective actions to prevent or remedy surface or groundwater contamination from leaking active and inactive land disposal units. EPA's current regulations do not allow EPA to require permitted facilities to correct releases from inactive units or to require corrective actions at interim status facilities. The Amendments close both of these loopholes.

*   *   *

The Amendments also expand EPA's authority to address problems at inactive sites which are not subject to the permitting process. RCRA § 7003 currently grants EPA authority to immediately restrain any person "contributing to" disposal of any solid or hazardous waste that "may present an imminent and substantial

endangerment." Several courts interpreted § 7003 not to authorize EPA to bring an imminent hazard suit against parties who previously contributed wastes to an abandoned site that presents an imminent hazard.[93] Under this interpretation, EPA would lack the authority under § 7003 to address problems at abandoned hazardous waste sites and would have to resort to the Comprehensive Environmental Response, Compensation, and Liability Act (CERCLA) to correct these problems. The Amendments expressly extend the scope of § 7003 to allow EPA to bring a suit against "any person," including any "past or present" generator, transporter, or owner or operator of a hazardous waste facility "who has contributed or who is contributing" to an activity that "may present an imminent and substantial endangerment to health or the environment."[94]

*   *   *

By expanding the parties whom EPA can sue under § 7003 to past and present generators, transporters, and owners/operators, Congress now authorizes EPA to use RCRA to address both active and inactive hazardous waste sites that present an imminent and substantial endangerment and makes EPA's authority under CERCLA § 106 and RCRA § 7003 virtually identical. The overall effect of the corrective action provisions and the change in the imminent hazard provision in the Amendments is to make EPA's RCRA authority overlap extensively with its authority under CERCLA to address releases from hazardous waste facilities.

Citizen Suits

The expansion in the parties who can be sued under RCRA's imminent hazard provision is particularly significant in light of the fact that the Amendments authorize citizen suits to

___

[63]Amendments, *supra* note 3, sec. 601(a), RCRA §§ 9001-9010.***
[64]*Id.*, sec. 204, RCRA §§ 3004(p)-(s), 3010.

[93]E.g., United States v. Northeastern Pharmaceutical & Chemical Co., 579 F. Supp. 823, 14 ELR 20212 (W.D. Mo. 1984); United States v. Wade, 546 F. Supp. 785, 12 ELR 21051 (E.D. Pa. 1982); and United States v. Waste Industries, 556 F. Supp. 1301, 13 ELR 20286 (E.D.N.C. 1982).
[94]Amendments, *supra* note 3, sec. 402(a), RCRA § 7003(a).***

enforce the imminent hazard provision when EPA is not adequately addressing the problem. RCRA authorizes a citizen suit in a federal district court (a) against any person alleged to have violated any permit standard, regulation, condition, requirement, or order under RCRA, or (2) against EPA for allegedly failing to perform a non-discretionary duty.[98] District courts have interpreted this provision not to grant a private right of action to enforce RCRA's imminent hazard provision.[99] In response to these decisions, Congress amended the citizen suit provision to allow suits to enforce the imminent hazard provision.[100] * * *

*   *   *

Conclusion

It may be unrealistic to expect EPA to complete all the tasks required by the 1984 RCRA Amendments. To fulfill the statutory requirements, EPA must complete over 30 rulemakings and meet over 50 deadlines—most of them within the next two years. The Amendments treble the number of generators that EPA will

---

[98]RCRA §§ 7002(a)(1), (2).
[99]City of Gallatin v. Cherokee, 563 F. Supp. 94, 13 ELR 20395 (E.D. Tex. 1983); Luckie v. Gorsuch, 13 ELR 20400 (D. Ariz. Feb. 25, 1983); *but see* Jones v. Inmont Corp., 14 ELR 20485 (S.D. Ohio Apr. 26, 1984).
[100]Amendments, *supra* note 3, sec. 401(a), RCRA § 7002(a)(1)(B).

have to regulate. They create two major new programs covering hundreds of thousands of private entities and require EPA to process promptly permits for over 1500 hazardous waste facilites. And Congress has placed the onus of making the new RCRA program succeed totally on EPA.

The success or failure of the new RCRA program may be preordained by the nature of the Amendments. Even a casual review reveals that they do not resemble traditional environmental statutes. In nearly all previous environmental legislation, Congress has established broad environmental goals and delegated to the agency the authority to make the technical and scientific decisions necessary to implement those goals. In contrast, the Amendments have the specificity and detail of regulations and confer only limited discretion on EPA for implementing those regulations. Congress clearly has invaded the bailiwick of the administrative agency by engaging in highly technical and scientific decision-making. Thus, the success or failure of the amended RCRA program depends in large part on the real world effect of Congress' decisions. If EPA's attempt to implement the new hazardous waste management program fails, any assessment of the blame for the failure should give equal consideration to the wisdom of Congress' new approach to environmental legislation as to EPA's "incompetence and lack of will."

From the complex provisions of RCRA and its implementing regulations discussed in the preceding articles, what is encompassed in the expression "cradle-to-grave" management of hazardous wastes should be evident. Certainly Congress's major concern was the prevention of future "Love Canals" through regulation of all persons who wanted to continue generation, transportation, and disposal of hazardous wastes. If the high expectations of the 1984 Amendments are even approximately realized, the United States will have substantially reduced the dangers from newly generated hazardous wastes within this country. But what about the present dangers from disposal sites existing before RCRA's stringent regulations took effect?

The first six subchapters of RCRA, which establish the regulatory scheme, contain virtually nothing addressed to the dangers of inactive or abandoned toxic waste dumps. One section in the 1976 Act, however, which could have been easily overlooked in subchapter VII, containing the "Miscellaneous Provisions," was soon recognized for its potential application to the task of remedying the serious problems caused by hazardous wastes disposed of prior to the imposition of any meaningful controls.

§ 7003. Imminent hazard

(a) Authority of Administrator.—Notwithstanding any other provision of this chapter, upon receipt of evidence that the handling, storage, treatment, transportation or disposal of any solid waste or hazardous waste may present an imminent and substantial endangerment to health or the environment, the Administrator may bring suit on behalf of the United States in the appropriate district court to immediately restrain any person contributing to such handling, storage, treatment, transportation or disposal to stop such handling, storage, treatment, transportation, or disposal or to take such other action as may be necessary. The Administrator shall provide notice to the affected State of any such suit. The Administrator may also, after notice to the affected State, take other action under this section including, but not limited to, issuing such orders as may be necessary to protect public health and the environment.

The following case should give you a feel for why this little section soon became the most controversial and heavily-litigated section in the whole of RCRA.

United States v. Price ("Price I")

523 F. Supp. 1055 (D.N.J. 1981)

BROTMAN, District Judge:

For fundamental and deeply rooted psychological reasons, as well as more mundane utilitarian considerations, it is characteristic of man to bury that which he fears and wishes to rid himself of. In the past, this engrained pattern of behavior has generally proven harmless and, indeed, has often led man to restore to the earth the substances he had removed from it. In today's industrialized society, however, the routine practice of burying highly toxic chemical wastes has resulted in serious threats to the environment and to public health. The dangers are especially acute when buried chemical wastes threaten to contaminate the underground aquifers, upon which half of the nation relies for its supply of drinking water.

The United States brought the instant action for injunctive relief to remedy the hazards posed by chemical dumping that occurred at Price's Landfill in Pleasantville, New Jersey during 1971 and 1972. The action was brought pursuant to section 1431 of the Safe Drinking Water Act ("SDWA"), 42 U.S.C. § 300i, section 7003 of the Resource Conservation and Recovery Act ("RCRA"), 42 U.S.C. § 6973, and the federal common law of nuisance. Defendants are the present owners of the now dormant landfill and the persons who owned and managed the landfill in the

early 1970's when it was in operation. Currently being considered by the court are the government's motion for a preliminary injunction and defendants' motions for summary judgment and to compel the joinder of additional defendants. In accord with Rule 65, Fed.R.Civ.P., the court now renders the following findings of fact and conclusions of law.

*   *   *

[In lieu of the extremely detailed eighty-seven enumerated findings of fact by the trial court, the author of the text substitutes the following summary of the facts by the Third Circuit when the case went up on appeal. 688 F.2d 204, 208-09.]

Price's Landfill is a twenty-two acre lot situated on the border of the City of Pleasantville and the Township of Egg Harbor in New Jersey. It was owned by Charles and Virginia Price from 1960 until 1979 when they sold it to the present owners, A.G.A. Partnership.

In 1970, on his initial application for a license to conduct a sanitary landfill operation, Charles Price listed the materials he intended to accept for disposal at Price's Landfill. He specifically excluded "Chemicals (Liquid or Solid)." In his proposed landfill design, submitted on September 29, 1971, he made no provision for the disposal of chemical wastes despite the fact that earlier that year he had begun accepting chemical wastes for disposal at the landfill.

When Charles Price applied to renew his permit in February 1972, for the first time he sought permission to accept and dispose of chemical wastes. His permit was renewed, however, only on the condition that no soluble liquid industrial wastes, petrochemicals, waste oils, sewage sludge or septic tank wastes be disposed at the site. Nevertheless, Price's Landfill continued to accept chemical and industrial wastes for disposal in direct contravention of the conditions of the license.

During 1971 and 1972, Price's Landfill accepted for disposal approximately 9 million gallons of assorted industrial and chemical wastes. These wastes were disposed of with minimal precautions. Frequently, they would be poured into the refuse from an open spigot on a tank truck; at other times, drums of chemicals would simply be buried under the refuse. The dumping of chemical wastes at Price's Landfill ended in November of 1972, and, in 1976, the operation of the site as a commercial landfill ceased.

Upon purchasing the property in 1979, A.G.A. Partnership acknowledged in writing that the site had been used as a landfill. Although two of the three members of the A.G.A. Partnership, including the member who negotiated the purchase, were licensed real estate brokers, no one inquired whether hazardous wastes had been deposited there. Neither did anyone from or on behalf of A.G.A. inspect the property or take steps to determine if the landfill had been properly closed.

As a result of the chemical dumping which occurred during 1971 and 1972, water samples drawn from the area in and around Price's Landfill during the years 1979-81 were found to contain numerous contaminants in quantities likely to create grave hazards to human health. Among the contaminants were: arsenic, a highly toxic metal and an established human carcinogen; lead, a toxic metal and a suspected human carcinogen and teratogen; benzene, a highly toxic petroleum derivative and a potent carcinogen and teratogen; vinyl chloride, a toxic halogenated hydrocarbon and a suspected carcinogen and

mutagen; and 1,2 dichloroethane, a toxic chlorinated hydrocarbon, and a suspected carcinogen and teratogen.

Geohydrological evidence presented to the district court revealed that contaminants leaching down through the groundwater and away from Price's Landfill are forming a plume or region of contamination emanating into the Cohansey Aquifer, a saturated geologic deposit supplying water to approximately 35 private wells, and to 10 of the Atlantic City Municipal Utility Authority's 12 operating public wells. Many of the private wells are already contaminated beyond use, and 4 of the municipal wells are in imminent danger of serious contamination. Atlantic City has no readily accessible alternative source of water should these wells become contaminated.

These facts led the district court to conclude that Atlantic City's public water supply is in imminent and substantial danger of serious contamination by substances leaching from Price's Landfill. The court found that an extensive geohydrological study of the area around the landfill was "essential in devising a strategy to contain and mitigate the pollution and to protect Atlantic City's water supply," and that it was "imperative that such a study be done immediately." In ruling on various motions for summary judgment, the district court expressed its belief that the defendants could ultimately be held liable for the cost of abating this toxic hazard.

[Despite these findings, the District Court denied the government's motion for a preliminary injunction (1) to compel the defendants to fund a study to determine the extent of the problem posed by the leachate from Price's Landfill and (2) to require them to provide an alternative water supply to those private well owners whose wells were contaminated. Its most emphasized basis for refusing the requested relief was its reasoning that to require such payments and expenditures of money would have been the equivalent of awarding money damages, something beyond the equitable power of the court on a motion for preliminary injunction. On appeal, although the Third Circuit found it not beyond the discretion of the trial court to wait until after trial to determine whether to grant the requested relief, it held that, as a matter of law, the court's remedial powers, both under traditional equitable doctrines and under RCRA, empowered it to order such payments and expenditures of money.]

*   *   *

II. *The Summary Judgment Motions*

    The standard for summary judgment is, of course, a stringent one. Summary judgment may only be granted "when the pleadings, depositions, answers to interrogatories, and admissions on file, together with the affidavits, if any, show that there is no genuine issue as to any material fact and that the moving party is entitled to a judgment as a matter of law." Fed.R.Civ.P. 56(c).

    Defendants raise a number of arguments in support of their summary judgment motions. First, they argue that the Government has no cause of action, given the instant facts, under the federal common law of nuisance. Second, they argue that, because they are not presently dumping chemicals at the landfill, they are not liable under either the RCRA or the SDWA. Third, they contend that those statutes should not be applied retroactively to impose liability for acts they performed several years before the statutes became effective. Finally, each of the defendants argues, albeit for somewhat different reasons, that he is not a proper defendant in the action brought under those statutes. We shall consider these arguments in the context of the claims for relief to which they relate.

A. *The Federal Common Law of Nuisance Claim*

    Initially, defendants contend that the Government has no cause of action against them under the federal common law of nuisance. We agree.

    The type of claim raised here is simply outside the bounds of the federal courts' law making authority. It is well established that the federal courts do not have the authority to make law that is inherent in state common law courts. *City of Milwaukee v. Illinois and Michigan.* 451 U.S. 304, (1981). The scope of the federal courts'

law making authority is much more limited than the area in which Congress may legitimately legislate: indeed, the former is limited to situations "where there is an overriding federal interest in the need for a uniform rule of decision or where the controversy touches basic interests of federalism." *Illinois v. City of Milwaukee,* 406 U.S. 91, 105 n.6 (1972). It is uncontested that the pollution at issue here, unlike that at issue in *Illinois,* is intrastate in all relevant respects. Coping with such intrastate pollution neither requires a uniform federal rule of decision nor implicates important federalism concerns. *See* 42 U.S.C. §§ 6901 (a)(4) ; 6941; *but see United States v. Solvents Recovery Serv. of New Eng.,* 496 F. Supp. 1127, 1135-38 (D.Conn. 1980). In brief, this is not a proper area for the development of federal common law.

    In addition, even if this were an appropriate area for federal common law, any such common law has been preempted by the enactment of the RCRA and, more recently, the Comprehensive Environmental Response, Compensation, and Liability Act of 1980 (CERCLA), 42 U.S.C. § 9601 *et seq.* In determining whether a federal statute has preempted federal common law, we start with the understanding that "it is for Congress, not federal courts, to articulate the appropriate standards to be applied as a matter of federal law." *City of Milwaukee, supra.* 101 S.Ct. at 1792. The comprehensive nature of the schemes established by the RCRA and the CERCLA require us to conclude that, if federal common law ever governed this type of activity, it has since been preempted by those statutes. *See Middlesex Cty. Sewerage Auth. v. National Sea Clammers Ass'n.* 453 U.S. 1 (1981). Therefore, defendants' summary judgment motions will be granted insofar as the Government's federal common law claims are concerned.

B. *The RCRA Claim*

    The Government brings this action under the imminent hazard section of the RCRA, which provides as follows:

> Notwithstanding any other provision of this chapter, upon receipt of evidence that the handling, storage, treatment, transportation or disposal of any solid

waste or hazardous waste may present an imminent and substantial endangerment to health or the environment, the Administrator may bring suit on behalf of the United States in the appropriate district court to immediately restrain any person contributing to such handling, storage, treatment, transportation or disposal to stop such handling, storage, treatment, transportation, or disposal or to take such other action as may be necessary. The Administrator shall provide notice to the affected State of any such suit. The Administrator may also, after notice to the affected State, take other action under this section including, but not limited to, issuing such orders as may be necessary to protect public health and the environment.

42 U.S.C. § 6973(a).[3] Section 7003 is but one of several imminent hazard provisions that Congress has included in environmental statutes. These provisions are broadly drafted to give appropriate Government officials the right to seek judicial relief or take other appropriate action to avert imminent and substantial threats to the environment or public health.

Defendants raise three related but distinct arguments with respect to the Government's section 7003 claim. First, they argue that the statute is purely prospective and does not apply to disposal sites, such as Price's Landfill, that are no longer in active operation. Second, they contend that the statute, which became effective in 1976, should not be applied retroactively to impose liability for acts they performed in 1971 and 1972. Third, defendants argue that they are not persons "contributing to" the handling or disposal of hazardous wastes and, therefore, that they are not liable under the statute. In support of their arguments, defendants note the uncontested facts that chemical dumping at the land-

fill ceased in November of 1972 and that all dumping ceased in 1976. The A.G.A. defendants note the additional facts that they were never actively involved in the dumping that occurred at the landfill and that they never knew of the chemical wastes that had been dumped there until 1979. Nonetheless, for the reasons indicated below, we conclude that defendants are not entitled to summary judgment with respect to the Government's RCRA claim.

Defendants' first argument is that section 7003 is purely prospective, designed to prevent future dumping in certain circumstances but not to remedy the effects of past waste disposal practices. There is some merit to this argument, but we do not see it as a sufficient basis for granting summary judgment. Two basic principles of statutory construction guide our analysis of section 7003: first, that we should look first and foremost to the plain language of the statute, which "controls when sufficiently clear in its context," and second, that we should pay close attention to the manner and context in which that language is being used. A straightforward reading of section 7003, which is quoted above, reveals that it is not a general clean up provision and that its thrust is basically prospective. The statute is, we note, written in the present tense, and Congress employed words, such as "stop" and "restrain," that clearly denote a prospective orientation. Hence, we agree with defendants that section 7003 was essentially intended to allow the Administrator to prevent future harm, not cure past ills. *But cf. Solvents Recovery Serv. of New Eng., supra.* 496 F. Supp. at 1139-41. That does not lead, however, to the conclusion that summary judgment is warranted.

The Government correctly observes that RCRA's definition of "disposal," one of the activities within the ambit of section 7003, is quite broad. Section 2 of RCRA defines disposal as "the discharge, deposit, injection, dumping, spilling, leaking, or placing of any solid waste or hazardous waste into or on any land or water so that such solid waste or hazardous waste or any constituent thereof may enter the environment or be emitted into the air or discharged into any waters, including ground waters." 42 U.S.C. § 6903(3). Not only is this definition quite broad

---

[3]Defendants argue that the RCRA should only apply to cases of interstate pollution. That argument is utterly without merit. Section 7003 neither states nor implies that it is applicable only when hazardous wastes have crossed state lines. ***

but, significantly, it includes within its purview leaking, which ordinarily occurs not through affirmative action but as a result of inaction or negligent past actions. In addition, the statute broadly authorizes the Administrator to bring suit to enjoin "such other action as may be necessary."[4] The Government therefore argues that it is entitled to relief under section 7003, notwithstanding the fact that the active disposal of wastes at the landfill ceased over five years ago.

We conclude that the statute does not authorize a general clean up of dormant waste disposal sites, but that the Government may rely upon it to prevent further harm to the environment. By its plain language, the statute authorizes relief restraining further disposal, *i.e., leaking*, of hazardous wastes from the landfill into the groundwaters. *See United States v. Vertrac Chem. Corp.*, 489 F. Supp. 870,885 (E.D. Ark. 1980); *Midwest Solvent Recovery, Inc., supra.* 484 F. Supp. at 144-45. That disposal need not result from affirmative action by the defendants but may be the result of passive inaction. In brief, section 7003 does not mandate the clean up of the ten years of leachate contamination that has emanated from the landfill. It does, however, authorize Goverment suits to restrain the continued leaking of wastes in a manner that may present an imminent hazard to the environment or to health. Thus, although the relief available to the Government under section 7003 will be somewhat limited, defendants are not entitled to summary judgment with respect to that claim.

Defendants' second argument is closely related. They observe that section 7003 was not adopted and did not become effective until 1976, and they argue that the statute was not meant to apply retroactively to acts that preceded that date. Hence, because the dumping of toxic wastes at Price's Landfill ceased in 1972, defendants argue that the statute cannot be used to impose liability on them.

We find this argument unpersuasive for reasons that are, to a significant extent, implicit in earlier discussion. The gravamen of a section 7003 action, as we have construed it, is not defendants' dumping practices, which admittedly ceased with respect to toxic wastes in 1972, but the present imminent hazard posed by the continuing disposal (*i.e.*, leaking) of contaminants into the groundwater. Thus, the statute neither punishes past wrongdoing nor imposes liability for injuries inflicted by past acts. Rather, as defendants themselves argue, its orientation is essentially prospective. When construed in this manner, the statute simply is not retroactive. It merely relates to current and future conditions.

Admittedly, from a practical perspective, defendants may be compelled under our reading of the statute to remedy the continuing effects of acts they performed prior to the statute's adoption. But we do not conceive of this as contrary to the purposes of the RCRA, one of the objectives of which was to require the "conversion of existing open dumps to facilities which do not pose a danger to the environment or to health." 42 U.S.C. § 6902(3). Indeed, Congress has subsequently confirmed that it intended section 7003 to apply to "events which took place at some time in the past but which continue to present a threat to the public health or the environment." Nor can it seriously be questioned that Congress has the authority to require the clean up of waste disposal sites that are currently presenting a hazard to the environment or to health. Because the gravamen of a section 7003 action is the current existence of a hazardous condition, not the past commission of any acts, we see no retroactivity problem with the statute.

Defendants' third argument is that they are not persons within the ambit of liability defined by the statute. They note that section 7003 authorizes relief from "any person contributing to" the disposal of hazardous wastes, and they argue that they are not contributing to any such disposal. The peculiar difficulty presented by this case is that the property was sold in 1979 by the persons who had previously operated the landfill to several persons who had no previous con-

---

[4] Although this phrase can be read as authorizing the Administrator to take "such other action as may be necessary," such a reading tenders the final sentence of section 7003 meaningless. We therefore interpret the "such other action" clause as referring to the type of judicial relief that the Agency may pursue. This reading accords with the broad grant of remedial authority that one would expect to find in an imminent hazard provision.

nection with the landfill or the waste disposal operation. Therefore, in analyzing this third argument, we must take into account the somewhat distinct positions of the Price defendants and the A.G.A. defendants.

The Price defendants operated the landfill from 1969 through 1976 and eventually sold the property in 1979. They argue that they are not now contributing to the disposal of wastes and that they are therefore not liable under the act. Their reading of the statute, however, is too confined. We have earlier noted the extremely broad statutory definition of disposal to encompass the passive leaking of contaminants from the landfill. It is evident that the current leaking of contaminants from the landfill is being contributed to in large measure by the failure of the Price defendants to store properly the chemical wastes. Certainly, that proper storage should have been done in 1971 and 1972, when the wastes were originally deposited in the landfill. But it cannot be denied that their continued failure to rectify the hazardous condition they created has been and is contributing to the leaking that is now occurring.

Thus, the critical question with respect to the Price defendants is whether their statutory duty to prevent the disposal of contaminants from the landfill ended when they sold the property in 1979. We conclude that their sale of the property did not relieve them of their accountability under the statute. We reach this conclusion, in large part, because the actions and inaction of the Price defendants are the primary cause of the hazardous situation that now exists. Although the current owners of the property may well also have a duty to prevent the continued disposal of contaminants from the landfill, it would be inequitable to require them to bear the entire burden of a situation that was largely caused by others. More importantly, society's interests in deterring the improper disposal of hazardous wastes and in alleviating serious hazards as quickly as possible mandate that those responsible for the disposal of such wastes not be able to shirk their statutory responsibilities by simply selling the property on which the wastes are stored.

Our conclusion that the Prices are proper defendants, notwithstanding their sale of the property, is supported, albeit indirectly, by the limited legislative history that is available.*** They are proper defendants notwithstanding their sale of the property, and their summary judgment motion will be denied insofar as the section 7003 claim is concerned.

In some respects, a more troubling question is presented with regard to the liability of the A.G.A. defendants. They bought the property several years after all dumping had ceased and therefore argue that they never have and are not now "contributing to" the disposal of any hazardous wastes. This argument, however, is predicated on the same erroneous premise as that underlying the Price defendants' contentions—the idea that "disposal" requires some active behavior. That is simply not so. As owners of the property, the A.G.A. defendants are, we conclude contributing to the disposal (*i.e.*, leaking) of wastes merely by virtue of their studied indifference to the hazardous condition that now exists. The idea that ownership imposes responsibility for hazardous conditions on one's land is certainly not novel. *See Vertrac Chem. Corp., supra.* 489 F. Supp. at 877. Admittedly, the A.G.A. defendants did not create that hazardous condition. Nonetheless, they were aware, at the time they purchased the property, that it had been used as a landfill. As sophisticated investors, they had a duty to investigate the actual conditions that existed on the property or take it as it was. They deliberately chose the latter course. Moreover, they became aware in the summer of 1979 that toxic chemicals had been dumped at the landfill, but they have done nothing to abate the hazardous condition that exists. Under these circumstances, the A.G.A. defendants may be held responsible to stop the continued leaking of contaminants from the site.

*   *   *

***Accordingly, the summary judgment motion of the A.G.A. defendants will be denied insofar as the Government's RCRA claim is concerned.

C. *The SDWA Claim*

The Government also seeks relief pursuant to the imminent hazard provision of the SDWA, section 1431***. ***An extended discussion of the requirements of this statute is unnecessary at this time. What is immediately apparent, however, is that in several respects the section is more broadly drawn than the comparable provision of the RCRA. The legislative history of section 1431 confirms that its broad reach was purposeful: "Section 1431 reflects the Committee's determination to confer completely adequate authority to deal promptly and effectively with emergency situations which jeopardize the health of persons."

Defendants raise identical objections to the section 1431 claim as they did to the Government's section 7003 claim. Largely for the reasons discussed above, we will deny defendants' summary judgment motions with respect to the section 1431 claim. In addition, we note that section 1431 does not have the language that led us to conclude that section 7003 was intended only to prevent the future disposal of contaminants into the environment. Although section 1431 is prospective in the sense that its concern is alleviating present imminent hazards, the legislative history of the statute reveals that Congress intended to authorize broad forms of affirmative relief, including the treatment or reduction of hazardous situations and the provision of alternate water supplies, where appropriate. Although we need not and do not decide at this time what forms of relief are appropriate under this statute, it may well be that the relief available under section 1431 is broader than that available under section 7003 of the RCRA.

The gravamen of a section 1431 action is the present existence of an imminent hazard. Defendants' retroactivity argument is as unsound here as it was in the context of the RCRA claim. In addition, we note that the legislative history of section 1431 indicates that the Administrator may seek appropriate relief from State and local officials, area or point source polluters, or *"any other person whose action or inaction* requires prompt regulation to protect public health." *Id.* (emphasis added). It is even clearer under section 1431 than under section 7003 that both the Price defendants and the A.G.A. defendants are liable for appropriate relief.

*   *   *

IV: *Conclusion*

The miraculous achievements of modern technology have led to many advances in our standard of living and our way of life. Among the by-products of modern technology, however, are materials that pose a grave threat to the environment and, indeed, to our continued existence. For many years we have done our best to ignore this fact. It is, after all, simply human to avoid problems, rather than deal with them, whenever we can. The instant situation is the direct result of such an atavistic approach to the problems posed by modern technology. The lesson to be learned from this situation and others like it is a simple one: if we brush our problems under the carpet or bury them under the earth, they are not solved; we only postpone dealing with them. We hope that this case and similar ones will teach all concerned that short-term solutions to the problem of hazardous waste disposal are no longer a viable approach, nor do they remedy the problems posed by past thoughtlessness.

NOTES

1. Do you agree with the court's rulings on all three arguments which the defendants made against application of § 7003 to them?

Did the language of § 7003 easily lend itself to construction in a manner that would provide a remedy for the effects of past waste disposal? If Congress had intended this application could it not have made its intent more clearly evident?

Is there any constitutional impediment to application of a statute "retroactively" to impose a civil remedy for present hazards caused by action taken prior to passage of the legislation?

How are either the past operators of the landfill or the real estate developers who now own it presently "contributing to" the leaking or other disposal? Is it equitable to hold the present owners responsible for the waste disposal practices of previous owners? What if the present owners had no inkling when they purchased the property that it had ever been used for waste disposal? Could they be treated differently if, in fact, this provision imposes strict liability?

2. As a practical matter, do you see any distinction between application of Section 7003 to compel the cleanup of an inactive waste disposal site (which the district court apparently would not accept) and its application "to restrain the continued leaking of wastes" that present a hazard?

On appeal, the judges of the Third Circuit wrote so as to correct any impression that the trial court might have had that its remedial powers under Section 7003 were limited:

> The unequivocal statutory language and this legislative history make it clear that Congress, by enacting section 7003, intended to confer upon the courts the authority to grant affirmative equitable relief to the extent necessary to eliminate any risks posed by toxic wastes. Under section 7003, a court could not order the cleanup of a waste disposal site which posed no threat to health or the environment. There is no doubt, however, that it authorizes the cleanup of a site, even a dormant one, if that action is necessary to abate a present threat to the public health or environment. It is also clear that if a threat to human health can be averted only by providing individuals with an alternate water supply, that remedy, in an appropriate case, may be granted under the authority of section 7003.

United States v. Price, 688 F.2d 204, 213-14 (3d Cir. 1982).

3. Do you agree with the court in *Price* that the government had no cause of action under federal common law of nuisance? If so, for what reason: because of preemption or because no interstate effects were shown? As recognized, *United States v. Solvents Recovery Service,* 496 F. Supp. 1127 (D. Conn. 1980), held that interstate effects were unnecessary for recovery under federal common law of nuisance for groundwater pollution.

4. Several other federal district courts construed Section 7003 to provide a remedy for present hazards caused by past waste disposal. *See United States v. Reilly Tar & Chemical Corp.,* 546 F. Supp. 1100 (D. Minn. 1982); *United States v. Hardage,* 18 ERC 1687 (W.D. Okla. 1982); *United States v. Diamond Shamrock Corp.,* 17 ERC 1329 (N.D. Ohio 1981); *United States v. Solvents Recovery Service,* 496 F. Supp. 1127 (D. Conn. 1980); *United States v. Vertac Chemical Corp.,* 489 F. Supp. 870 (E.D. Ark. 1980).

Obviously, however, room for disagreement existed. *See United States v. Waste Industries, Inc.,* 556 F.Supp. 1301 (E.D.N.C. 1982), in which the court held that Section 7003 did not apply to either the past operators or present owners of an abandoned landfill. *Also see United States v. Northeastern Pharmaceutical and Chemical Co.,* 579 F.Supp. 823 (W.D. Mo. 1984), and *United States v. Wade,* 546 F.Supp. 785 (E.D. Pa. 1982), in which the courts refused to apply Section 7003 to parties who previously generated hazardous wastes deposited in subsequently abandoned sites.

5. In 1984, Congress amended Section 7003(a) to provide as follows:

> **(a) Authority of Administrator.**—Notwithstanding any other provision of this chapter, upon receipt of evidence that the past or present handling, storage, treatment, transportation or disposal of any solid waste or hazardous waste may present an imminent and substantial endangerment to health or the environment, the Administrator may bring suit on behalf of the United States in the appropriate district court against any person (including any past or present generator, past or present transporter, or past or present owner or operator of a treatment, storage, or disposal facility) who has contributed or who is contributing to such handling, storage, treatment, transportation or disposal to restrain such

person from such handling, storage, treatment, transportation, or disposal, to order such person to take such other action as may be necessary, or both. A transporter shall not be deemed to have contributed or to be contributing to such handling, storage, treatment, or disposal taking place after such solid waste or hazardous waste has left the possession or control of such transporter if the transportation of such waste was under a sole contractual arrangement arising from a published tariff and acceptance for carriage by common carrier by rail and such transporter has exercised due care in the past or present handling, storage, treatment, transportation and disposal of such waste. The Administrator shall provide notice to the affected State of any such suit. The Administrator may also, after notice to the affected State, take other action under this section including, but not limited to, issuing such orders as may be necessary to protect public health and the environment.

Would the new Section 7003 apply to the Prices—that is, the past operators of the landfill presently presenting an imminent hazard? Would it apply to the A.G.A. Partnership—that is, the present owners of the abandoned site? Notice that, even under the amended version, defendants must have "contributed to" or be "contributing to" the disposal, etc. Does this leave room for purchasers (with or without knowledge of conditions) to escape liability?

6. Section 7003 only authorizes action by the federal government. Prior to the 1984 amendments, no private right of action existed to implement this imminent hazard provision. In 1984, however, Congress amended the citizen suit provision in Section 7002 to authorize any person to bring a civil action to remedy an imminent hazard of the same description as found in Section 7003. *See* Section 7002(a)(1)(B) and (b)(2).

2 THE COMPREHENSIVE ENVIRONMENTAL RESPONSE, COMPENSATION, AND LIABILITY ACT ("SUPERFUND")

Superfund at Square One: Promising Statutory Framework Requires Forceful EPA Implementation

11 ENVTL. L. REP. 10101 (1981)

Over the last several years public attention has focused increasingly on the risks associated with hazardous wastes and other toxic substances. Incidents of environmental contamination at locales such as Love Canal, New York, Toone, Tennessee, and Gray, Maine have fueled the controversy and have led to claims that releases of toxic substances and hazardous wastes constitute a serious threat to public health and the environment. Indeed, as reports of such incidents have mounted, so have the estimated costs of addressing the problem. The Council on Environmental Quality (CEQ), for example, has suggested that cleanup costs alone for abandoned hazardous waste sites could run well into the billions of dollars. Moreover, the cleanup costs resulting from the improper disposal of hazardous substances represent only one facet of the larger and more general problem of environmental pollution and damages to private citizens caused by toxic chemicals.

* * *

During the last few sessions of Congress, a growing number of legislative proposals have been advanced to address the problem of pollution-related injuries. This situation peaked during the 96th Congress, which considered more than 20 bills involving liability and compensation for toxic substances pollution and other forms of environmental contamination. After a series of fits and starts, the 96th Congress enacted the "Superfund" in the closing hours of the legislative session.[11]

CERCLA

The new law is formally called the Comprehensive Environmental Response, Compensation, and Liability Act (CERCLA) and applies to hazardous waste sites and other sources of hazardous substances pollution.***

The concept of a "release" of a hazardous substance is critical to the operation and implementation of many provisions of CERCLA.[13] Essentially, CERCLA authorizes

---

[11]Pub. L. 96-510, 42 U.S.C. § 9601 et seq., ELR STAT. & REG. 41941.

[13]"Release" is broadly defined in the Act at § 101(22), as ". . . any spilling, leaking, pumping, pouring, emitting, emptying, discharging, injecting, escaping, leaching, dumping, or disposing into the environment . . . ." 42 U.S.C. § 9601(22), ELR STAT. & REG. 41943. However, the definition of "release" specifically excludes those exposures resulting from specified discharges of nuclear materials, workplace emissions, most engine exhausts, and "normal" fertilizer applications. Id.

governmental responses to actual and threatened releases of a wide range of harmful substances. Parties causing releases of such substances may then be held liable without regard
to fault for certain damages resulting from the
release, which primarily include government-
incurred costs for cleanup, removal, and resource
restoration. To ensure that such injuries are
redressed, the law establishes a $1.6 billion
Hazardous Substances Response Fund, financed
jointly by industry and the federal government
over five years. When polluters are unknown, or
are unable or unwilling to provide recompense,
a claim for specified damages may be filed
against the fund. Payment of claims by the fund
then subrogates the fund to the rights of the claimant. Thus, fund representatives can attempt to
recover claim payments from the party responsible for the hazardous substance release. Within
this broad statutory framework, the new law
establishes various procedures and principles
governing notification, response authority, liability, and the filing of claims.

Notification

Section 102 of CERCLA requires the
government to designate hazardous substances
and establish reportable quantities for such substances. Until such quantities are developed specifically by EPA, releases of more than one pound
of a hazardous substance must be reported
except those for which reportable quantities have
been established under § 311(b)(4) of the Federal
Water Pollution Control Act.

Section 103 of the Act requires that in the
event of a reportable release from a vessel or
facility, "any person in charge of" that vessel
or facility must "immediately notify the
National Response Center established under
the Clean Water Act of such release," and must
do so, "as soon as he has knowledge of any
release . . . ."***

Response Authority

Section 104 of the Act provides the federal
and state governments with a fairly sweeping
mandate to mitigate and respond to pollution
and requires the President to broaden the scope
of the National Contingency Plan for oil and
hazardous materials spills under the Clean Water

Act. Unless the President or his delegates determine that the party responsible for an actual or
threatened pollution release will take appropriate remedial action, the President may arrange
for pollution removal and remedial operations
whenever:

- any hazardous substance is released or
there is a substantial threat of such a
release into the environment, or
- there is a release or substantial threat
of release into the environment of any
pollutant or contaminant which may
present an imminent and substantial
danger to the public health or welfare
. . . . [20]

---

[20]CERCLA § 104(a)(1). A hazardous substance is
defined as:

. . . (A) any substance designated pursuant to
section 311(b)(2)(A) of the Federal Water Pollution Control Act, (B) any element, compound, mixture, solution, or substance
designated pursuant to section 102 of this
Act, (C) any hazardous waste having the
characteristics identified under or listed pursuant to section 3001 of the Solid Waste Disposal Act (but not including any waste the
regulation of which under the Solid Waste
Disposal Act has been suspended by Act of
Congress), (D) any toxic pollutant listed under
section 307(a) of the Federal Water Pollution
Control Act, (E) any hazardous air pollutant
listed under section 112 of the Clean Air Act,
and (F) any imminently hazardous chemical
substance or mixture with respect to which
the Administrator has taken action pursuant
to section 7 of the Toxic Substances Control
Act. The term does not include petroleum,
including crude oil or any fraction thereof
which is not otherwise specifically listed or
designated as a hazardous substance under
subparagraphs (A) through (F) of this paragraph, and the term does not include natural
gas, natural gas liquids, liquefied natural gas,
or synthetic gas usable for fuel (or mixtures
of natural gas and such synthetic gas);

Id. § 101(14). A pollutant or contaminant includes:

. . . any element, substance, compound, or
mixture, including disease-causing agents,
which after release into the environment and
upon exposure, ingestion, inhalation, or
assimilation into any organism, either directly
from the environment or indirectly by ingestion through food chains, will or may reasonably be anticipated to cause death, disease,
behavioral abnormalities, cancer, genetic

However, except in certain emergencies and in cases where the states are cooperating in alleviating the pollution, the President's principal response actions are limited to a period of six months or to the expenditure of $1 million in response costs, whichever occurs first.[21]

Liability

The liability scheme under § 107 of CERCLA for governmental pollution response costs, other necessary costs of response to pollution under the National Contingency Plan, and damages to natural resources reflects a complex legislative evolution.***

Furthermore, while the term "strict liability" is not used in the Act, CERCLA indirectly provides for strict liability by its failure to contain general defenses based on the exercise of due care.[27] In other words, responsible parties cannot escape liability for their actions by alleging that they exercised due care. In this sense then, responsible parties remain strictly liable for the consequences of releases that they caused. However, CERCLA provides for defenses based on acts of war or acts of God. In addition, the Act authorizes a defendant to avoid liability if he or she shows that the pollution was caused by an independent third party (one not related by contract or employment) and that the defendant has exercised due care with respect to that party and that polluting substance. However, since this defense does not apply to employees of the defendant or to most other third parties directly or indirectly related by contract with the defendant, as may often be the case between generators, transporters, and disposers, this provision should not restrict those state courts that otherwise might impose joint and several liability on such parties under state law.

Section 107(c) provides limits on liability. However, these do not apply where the polluter fails to cooperate in cleanup efforts, where knowing violation of certain regulations is the primary cause of pollution, or where willful negligence or misconduct has occurred. In such instances, unlimited liability may be imposed for specified types of damages, including damages for natural resource injuries. Such damages are paid generally to the United States and to the state in which the resources are located, owned, or managed. Under § 107(f), however, liability for such damages may not be imposed if they occurred wholly prior to CERCLA's enactment.

Interestingly, while CERCLA purportedly precludes awards of compensation for private injuries, the Act explicitly allows recovery for "any other necessary costs of response incurred by *any other person* consistent with the National Contingency Plan." On its face, this language would seem to permit a private cause of action for damages under CERCLA if a person acts in a manner "consistent" with the National Contingency Plan (NCP). Thus, for example, the existing NCP developed under the Clean Water Act authorizes a wide range of actions to prevent pollution from threatening "the public health or welfare"***.

If similarly broad authority is incorporated in the NCP as revised under CERCLA, private parties harmed or threatened by pollution may be able to engage in a wide variety of pollution mitigation and response activities and may recover their costs under CERCLA.

While this may unexpectedly expand the scope of CERCLA's liability provisions, the Act also contains certain potentially significant qualifications to and exemptions from liability. It does not cover damages from releases of pollutants pursuant to federal permits, or from the application of a registered pesticide; nor does it cover damages resulting from activities which

---

mutation, physiological malfunctions (including malfunctions in reproduction) or physical deformations, in such organisms or their offspring.

Id. § 104(a)(2).

[21]CERCLA § 104(b) & (c). The Act distinguishes between pollution "removal" and "remedial action." Removal refers generally to cleanup and short-term relief. *Id.* § 101(23). Remedial actions are those that are "consistent with permanent remedy taken instead of or in addition to removal." *Id.* § 101(24). "Response" is broadly defined under the Act to include both removal and remedial action. *Id.* § 101(25).

[27]CERCLA § 107. This approach is similar to that taken under § 311(f) of the Clean Water Act, which essentially imposes strict liability on parties deemed to have caused pollution.

were previously determined in an environmental impact statement to involve an "irreversible and irretrievable" commitment of natural resources.***

Fund Uses and Claims

Approximately $1.38 billion of the $1.6 billion fund is derived from a tax on oil, specified organic chemicals, and certain heavy metals. The remainder comes from governmental expenditures. The fund may be used for the following purposes: (1) payment of governmental response costs incurred under the Act's response authority provisions; (2) payment of other necessary response costs under the National Contingency Plan established under § 311 of the Clean Water Act (to be revised under CERCLA); (3) payment of claims asserted and compensable but unsatisfied under § 311 of the Clean Water Act; and (4) payment for certain other purposes, including monitoring resource losses, restoring, replacing, rehabilitating, or acquiring the substantial equivalent of damaged resources, conducting epidemiological studies, and purchasing cleanup equipment.[41]

Claims may include necessary response costs incurred under the National Contingency Plan and damages arising out of injury to natural resources. Under § 112, claims may be asserted against the fund after being presented to the party responsible for the facility or vessel from which a hazardous substance has been released or to any other known, potentially liable person. Claims for resource damages may be asserted only for those resources belonging to, managed by, or protected by state or federal governments. Funds are not available, however, for resource injuries occurring wholly before the enactment of CERCLA or for claims resulting from multiple-source, long-term exposures to ambient concentrations of air pollutants.

If a claim has not been satisfied by a known, potentially liable party within 60 days, the claimant has the option of initiating an action in court against that party or presenting the claim to the fund. If the claim is presented to the fund, the President must attempt to promote and arrange a settlement between the claimant and the alleged polluter. Where a settlement is not reached within 45 days, the President may either make an award or decline to make an award. If the President makes an award and the claimant is dissatisfied with the amount, he may appeal the President's determination to the federal courts. If the President declines to make an award, appeals to arbitrators and the courts may follow.

Once a claim is paid, the fund or the party paying the claim is subrogated to the rights of the claimant. This entitles such parties to seek recovery of claim payments in another proceeding. Thus, the Act is intended to redress injuries, and where possible, to encourage the eventual assignment of liability for statutorily compensable damages. These principles are potentially valuable in both deterring pollution and preventing excessive depletion of fund resources.

Other Provisions

In addition to the provisions discussed above, CERCLA has several other interesting features. It confers upon the federal government broad authority to abate imminent and substantial dangers to the public health and welfare.

*   *   *

Preemption may become an important issue under CERCLA. Under § 114, no one may be required to pay into any state or other fund for compensating claimants who could recover under CERCLA. This preemption language will be especially significant to states such as New Jersey and Florida, both of which have pollution spill funds.

Implementation

EPA's efforts to implement CERCLA naturally will be critical to the prevention and mitigation of environmental contamination from the release of hazardous substances and pollutants. Because of limitations on fund monies and resources, EPA must establish priorities for addressing such releases.***

---

[41]CERCLA § 111(a)(1)-(4), (b), (c). Claims may be filed up to three years after discovery of the loss or the date of the Act's enactment, whichever is later. *Id.* § 112(d).

Approximately 9,200 waste sites have been identified for assessment by EPA under CER-CLA, with an additional 200-400 being added to this list every month. Approximately 2,000 sites have been evaluated thus far; of these, approximately 350 have been determined to require enforcement or remedial action. EPA is expected to focus its energies on encouraging privately financed cleanup efforts, thus conserving fund resources for situations where this is not possible.

*   *   *

Conclusion

Superfund started out as an ambitious attempt to use liability as a complement to regulatory intervention in reducing the risks from toxic substances. By facilitating the process by which polluters are held liable for the damages they cause, it was hoped, such injuries would be redressed and an added measure of pol-lution deterrence would be achieved. As enacted, the current Comprehensive Environmental Response, Compensation and Liability Act does not wholly abandon these principles, but it incor-porates them in a law of more limited scope and impact. For one thing, oil spills are generally not covered. In addition, by restricting the primary coverage of the law to governmental cleanup, resource restoration, and pollution response costs, Congress has indicated its reluctance to modify legal principles traditionally relegated to state control. Thus, private citizens injured by toxic substances generally must continue to litigate such claims in state court according to the common law and other legal rules applied in that particular jurisdiction.[65]

---

[65]Whether barriers to recovery under state law allow for adequate compensation for such injuries has been the subject of considerable debate.

NOTES

In CERCLA, Congress expressly provided several means of remedying the dangers caused by inactive hazardous waste disposal sites: (1) a civil action or an administrative order by the federal government under the imminent endangerment abatement authority of Section 106; (2) cleanup by the federal government or by a state, and recovery of their response costs from responsible parties under Section 107(a)(4)(A) and (C); (3) recovery of response costs by "any other person" from responsible parties under Section 107(a)(4)(B); (4) cleanup and claims against the "Superfund" for such response costs incurred by private or governmental entities in carrying out the national contingency plan.

Congressional creation of these available remedies in CERCLA, however, did not cause the federal government to forego use of Section 7003 of RCRA to abate the dangers presented by inactive hazardous waste dumps. Instead, its strategy was to invoke Section 7003 along with all available authority under CERCLA in its lawsuits against all persons whom it deemed in any sense responsible. This dual strategy obviously has been sanctioned by the changes to Section 7003 made by the 1984 RCRA amendments.

United States
v.
Reilly Tar and Chemical Corporation
546 F. Supp. 1100 (D. Minn. 1982)

MAGNUSON, District Judge

The United States, the State of Minnesota (the State), the City of St. Louis Park and the City of Hopkins bring these actions against the Reilly Tar & Chemical Corporation (Reilly Tar) under section 7003 of the Resource Conservation and Recovery Act of 1976 (RCRA), 42 U.S.C. § 6973 (1976 & Supp. IV 1980), and section 107 of the Comprehensive Environmental Response, Compensation, and Liability Act of 1980 (CERCLA), 42 U.S.C.§ 9607 (Supp. IV 1980), for alleged contamination of the ground and groundwater in and around the City of St. Louis Park, Minnesota. The United States also asserts a claim against Reilly Tar based upon section 106(a) of CERCLA. 42 U.S.C. 9606(a) (Supp. IV 1980). The State of Minnesota and the cities of St. Louis Park and Hopkins also assert a series of state law claims arising out of the waste disposal practices underlying their federal claims. Reilly Tar has moved for dismissal of the claims for lack of jurisdiction and for failure to state a claim upon which relief can be granted under *Fed. R.Civ.P.* 12(b)(1) and (6). The motions to dismiss are denied.

Factual Allegations

The factual allegations as contained in the complaints are as follows.

In 1917, Reilly Tar, an Indiana corporation, began to operate a plant in St. Louis Park, Minnesota where it refined coal tar into creosote oil and other products, and treated wood products with creosote oil and other preservatives. For fifty-five years, until the plant ceased operations in 1972, Reilly Tar generated chemical wastes which were handled, stored, treated and disposed of at the Reilly Tar site.

In June 1973, the City of St. Louis Park purchased the Reilly Tar site and transferred its ownership to the Housing and Redevelopment Authority of St. Louis Park, a municipal corporation incorporated under the laws of Minnesota.

From May 1978 through January 1980, defendants Oak Park Village Associates, Rustic Oaks Condominium, Inc. and Philip's Investment Co. purchased part of the Reilly Tar site from the Housing and Redevelopment Authority. TCF Service corporation is the successor in interest to Rustic Oaks Condominium, Inc. The United States and State of Minnesota named these entities as defendants only to insure that the remedial measures they seek can be fully implemented.

In 1970, the State of Minnesota and the City of St. Louis Park sued Reilly Tar in state court for violating state law concerning air and surface water pollution at the Reilly Tar site. The state amended its complaint in 1978 to allege groundwater pollution. That suit is pending.

Plaintiffs further allege that Reilly Tar spilled, leaked and discharged chemical wastes generated at the Reilly Tar site directly into the ground there, and that the wastes are in the ground at and surrounding the site. These chemicals have leached and migrated into the groundwater beneath and surrounding the site and will continue to do so.

The groundwater beneath the Reilly Tar site is part of a system of several aquifers which supplies water to St. Louis Park and other parts of the Minneapolis-St. Paul metropolitan area. Many industrial and drinking water wells have been drilled into the aquifers. Inadequate groutings and casings in some of the wells permit further migration of the chemicals between the aquifers. One well at the Reilly Tar site is 909 feet deep, and is plugged with coal tar at a depth of approximately 590 feet.

St. Louis Park and Hopkins, as well as other municipalities, obtain drinking water for their residents from the system of aquifers extending beneath the Reilly Tar site. During 1978 and 1979, St. Louis Park closed five drinking water wells because the water was contaminated with chemicals from the Reilly Tar plant. In 1981, Hopkins closed a drinking water well for the same reason. Chemicals from the Reilly Tar operation have contaminated the groundwater in one aquifer at least two miles north of the site, and in another at least one and one-half miles east and southeast of the site. Unless preventive measures are taken, leaching and migration of groundwater will continue to move the chemicals from the Reilly Tar site through the aquifers and into the drinking water for the Minneapolis-St. Paul metropolitan area.

Chemical wastes resulting from the refining of coal tar into creosote oil and other products, and the treatment of wood products with creosote oil and other materials, usually fall within three distinct groups: neutral oils, tar acids, and tar bases. Neutral oils include polynuclear aromatic hydrocarbons (PAH) compounds such as fluoranthene, acenaphthene, benzopyrene, benzathracene, pyrene, and chrysene. Tar acids consist of phenolic compounds such as phenol and cresols. Tar bases consist of basic nitrogen compounds such as acridines and naphthylamines.

Some creosote oil causes cancer in animals and has been associated with occupational cases of cancer in humans. The body absorbs creosote oil through the skin, and on ingestion through the intestinal tract. Acute exposure may produce vomiting, vertigo, respiratory difficulties, headaches, and convulsions. Exposure to high concentrations may also cause hypertension.

Many PAH compounds found in wastes resulting from the refining of creosote oil are animal carcinogens and are suspected human carcinogens. In addition, interaction among the various PAH compounds may enhance their carcinogenic and other toxic effects. Some PAH compounds are cocarcinogens, substances which enhance the carcinogenic activity of cancer causing substances.

Phenolic compounds found in the tar acids resulting from the refining of creosote oil are toxic. Ingestion may cause vomiting, paralysis, convulsions, coma and death. Prolonged exposure to phenolic compounds may impair kidney, liver, and lung functions. Phenol is a tumor promoter, which when exposed to certain car-

cinogens, increases their carcinogenic activity.

Plaintiffs also allege that the substances Reilly Tar disposed of are classified as hazardous substances by regulations promulgated under the Solid Waste Disposal Act Amendments of 1980.

The State, Hopkins, and St. Louis Park each allege that they have incurred substantial expenses because of Reilly Tar's conduct; that their costs and actions were consistent with the national contingency plan; that they have presented their claims to Reilly Tar under 42 U.S.C. § 9612(a)(Supp. IV 1980); and that Reilly Tar has denied liability and taken no action to satisfy their claims.

The United States alleges that since the passage of CERCLA, it has incurred and will continue to incur response costs in responding to the hazard created by the release and threatened release of hazardous substances from the site. It also alleges that Reilly Tar is liable to it for such costs.

Section 7003 of the Resource Conservation and Recovery Act (RCRA)

All plaintiffs have brought claims against Reilly Tar under section 7003 of the Resource Conservation and Recovery Act of 1976, 42 U.S.C. § 6973.

*   *   *

Reilly Tar seeks dismissal of the section 7003 claims primarily on three grounds. First, it contends that section 7003 is jurisdictional only and provides no substantive standards for determining liability. Liability under the statute, it argues, must be based on the federal common law of nuisance,[1] which applies only to pollution having interstate effects. No interstate effects having been alleged in this case, Reilly Tar contends the section 7003 claim must be dismissed.

Not all courts have accepted the argument that section 7003 is jurisdictional only, *United States v. Diamond Shamrock Corp.* [17 ERC 1329] (N. D. Ohio May 29, 1981), and of those that have accepted the argument, some refuse

---

[1]No plaintiff in this case purports to be bringing any claim based on federal common law nuisance. ***

to limit section 7003 to groundwater pollution having interstate effects. *United States v. Solvents Recovery Service of New England,* 496 F. Supp. 1127 (D. Conn. 1980). Congress did not intend to restrict section 7003 to the rare instance where groundwater pollution caused by hazardous waste disposal crosses state lines. Conditioning a section 7003 claim on an allegation of interstate effect would be inconsistent with the character of the pollution which is the target of the statute and incompatible with the nature and extent of the federal concern embodied in RCRA.***

Second, Reilly Tar asserts that section 7003 is limited to injunctive actions to restrain ongoing activities, and because it ceased operations in 1972 there is nothing to enjoin. It also contends the statute was not meant to apply to prior owners of inactive sites.

Although Reilly Tar no longer engages in ongoing activities at the site, this is no basis for dismissing the action. Other courts have held that a complaint based upon section 7003 need not contain an allegation of ongoing acts of disposal.***

*   *   *

Because of the Price holding, at this stage of the proceedings the court is not prepared to hold that section 7003 cannot be applied to prior owners of inactive sites.

Third, Reilly Tar argues that the facts alleged "do not amount to the sort of disastrous emergency situation required for invocation of a provision meant to deal with 'imminent and substantial endangerments.'" It contends that section 7003 may be invoked only in true emergency situations and not as a substitute procedure for chronic and recurring problems that may be dealt with under other statutes.

*   *   *

The facts alleged in the complaints are sufficient to establish an imminent and substantial endangerment to health or the environment. Plaintiffs allege that many of the chemicals found in wastes disposed of by Reilly Tar are carcinogens and toxic. For over fifty-five years these wastes were spilled, leaked and discharged directly into the ground at the site, and from

there entered and continue to enter the groundwater which is used as a water supply for the City of St. Louis Park and the surrounding area. The City of St. Louis Park has already closed five wells and the City of Hopkins has closed one. Unless preventative measures are taken, the contaminants will continue to move through the leaching and migration of groundwater into the drinking water for the Minneapolis-St. Paul metropolitan area.

*   *   *

Reilly Tar is correct in stating that section 7003 should not be used as a substitute procedure for chronic and recurring pollution problems that may be dealt with under other statutes.***

Although the alleged groundwater contamination in this case may be a recurring or chronic problem, it may also be, or develop into, one that presents an imminent and substantial endangerment to health or the environment. The legislative history Reilly Tar relies on indicates only that section 7003 should not be used as a substitute for other procedures. While section 7003 should not become a *substitute* for other reasonably available and adequate response authorities, it certainly may be used to *supplement* the response actions taken by the government agencies under other environmental statutes. Even though response actions under other statutes may also be appropriate in this case, this does not mean that plaintiffs cannot resort to section 7003 as well.

*   *   *

Finally, Reilly Tar contends that the relief sought in the complaints is beyond that contemplated by section 7003, and requests that the prayers for relief be limited accordingly. The scope of the relief to which plaintiffs may be entitled under the statute is a matter more appropriately left to further proceedings.

Comprehensive Environmental Response, Compensation and Liability Act (CERCLA) Claims.

On December 11, 1980, after extensive hearings and some last minute amendments, Congress enacted the Comprehensive Environmental Response, Compensation, and Liability Act (CERCLA) of 1980 to provide for liability, compensation, cleanup, and emergency response to hazardous substances released into the environment.

CERCLA authorizes state and federal governments to institute actions for the containment, cleanup, and removal of hazardous wastes. 42 U.S.C. § 9604. The Act establishes a Hazardous Substances Response Fund, financed jointly by industry and the federal government. 42 U.S.C. § 9631. The fund is available to compensate state and federal governments for containment, cleanup, and removal of hazardous wastes if the responsible parties cannot be identified or are unable to undertake such activities themselves. 42 U.S.C. 9611, 9612. Section 107 of the Act imposes liability on responsible parties for government response costs and damages to natural resources, subject to specified dollar limits and certain enumerated defenses. 42 U.S.C. § 9607. The statute contains a provision, broader than section 7003 of RCRA, which authorizes judicial action when an imminent and substantial endangerment to the public health, welfare or the environment is caused by an actual or threatened release of a hazardous substance. 42 U.S.C. § 9606. Finally, it requires that the President prepare a revised "national contingency plan" to reflect and carry out the responsibilities and powers created by the Act. 42 U.S.C. § 9605.

*   *   *

A review of the statute and the Committee Reports reveals at least two congressional concerns that survived the final amendments to the Act. First, Congress intended that the federal government be immediately given the tools necessary for a prompt and effective response to problems of national magnitude resulting from hazardous waste disposal. Second, Congress intended that those responsible for problems caused by the disposal of chemical poisons bear the costs and responsibility for remedying the harmful conditions they created. To give effect to these congressional concerns, CERCLA should be given a broad and liberal construction. The statute should not be narrowly

interpreted to frustrate the government's ability to respond promptly and effectively, or to limit the liability of those responsible for cleanup costs beyond the limits expressly provided.

Section 106(a) CERCLA Claims

The United States asserts a second claim for relief based on section 106(a) of CERCLA. 42 U.S.C. § 9606(a). Section 106(a) is a broadly written imminent hazards provision.*** Section 106(a) provides:

> (a) In addition to any other action taken by a State or local government, when the President determines that there may be an imminent and substantial endangerment to the public health or welfare or the environment because of an actual or threatened release of a hazardous substance from a facility, he may require the Attorney General of the United States to secure such relief as may be necessary to abate such danger or threat, and the district court of the United States in the district in which the threat occurs shall have jurisdiction to grant such relief as the public interest and the equities of the case may require. The President may also, after notice to the affected State, take other action under this section including, but not limited to, issuing such orders as may be necessary to protect public health and welfare and the environment.

*   *   *

Reilly Tar*** seeks dismissal of the section 106(a) claim on substantially the same grounds it raised for dismissal of the section 7003 RCRA claims: (1) the statute is jurisdictional only, therefore, liability must be based upon the federal common law of nuisance which applies only where an interstate effect is alleged; (2) the statute does not apply to prior owners of inactive sites; and (3) the complaint fails to allege sufficient facts to establish an imminent and substantial endangerment to the public health, welfare or the environment. Those arguments are without merit.

First, section 106(a) neither expressly nor impliedly states that it applies only where hazardous wastes cross state lines, nor should that requirement be read into it. 42 U.S.C. § 9606(a). The language of section 106(a), like that of section 7003 of RCRA, suggests a contrary conclusion.***

Although the equitable principles of federal common law nuisance actions may apply to determine what remedies are appropriate, Congress did not intend section 106(a) to incorporate the element of interstate effect required in federal common law nuisance actions.

Second, nothing in the language of section 106(a) indicates that it cannot in appropriate circumstances be invoked against the prior owner of a disposal site. Section 106(a) is broader in scope than section 7003 of RCRA, and whatever concerns the court has regarding the applicability of section 7003 to *prior owners* of inactive sites do not apply to section 106(a). Section 106(a) of CERCLA contains no limitations on the classes of persons within its reach. Nor does it contain language indicating that it applies only to present owners of waste disposal sites.

In addition, as noted above, section 106(a) empowers the federal courts to grant "such relief as the public interest and the equities of the case may require." *Id.* This broad grant of equitable power to the federal courts is not limited in its application to those who are the present owners of disposal sites. The equities of this case, as they appear in the complaints, do not suggest that Reilly Tar should escape the statute's reach.

Third, there is no merit to Reilly Tar's argument that this case does not present the sort of emergency situation that section 106(a) was meant to cover. The earlier discussion on what constitutes an "imminent and substantial endangerment" under section 7003 is generally applicable here as well. Taking the facts alleged in the complaint as true, it cannot be said with positive assurance that there exists no imminent and substantial endangerment to the public health, welfare or the environment.

*   *   *

Accordingly, Reilly Tar's motion to dismiss the section 106 claim is denied.

Section 107 CERCLA Claims.

All plaintiffs seek recovery from Reilly Tar for response costs incurred as a result of the contamination under section 107(a) of CERCLA. 42 U.S.C. § 9607(a). The State of Minnesota has also asserted a claim for natural resource damages under section 107(a)(4)(C). The section provides in part:

(a) Notwithstanding any other provision or rule of law, and subject only to the defenses set forth in subsection (b) of this section—

*   *   *

(2) any person who at the time of disposal of any hazardous substance owned or operated any facility at which such hazardous substances were disposed of,

*   *   *

(4) ... From which there is a release, or a threatened release which causes the incurrence of response costs, of a hazardous substance, shall be liable for —

(A) all costs of removal or remedial action incurred by the United States Government or a State not inconsistent with the national contingency plan;

(B) any other necessary costs of response incurred by any other person consistent with the national contingency plan; and

(C) damages for injury to, destruction of, or loss of natural resources, including the reasonable costs of assessing such injury, destruction, or loss resulting from such a release.
Id.

Reilly Tar seeks dismissal without prejudice of all claims for response costs brought under section 107(a), contending that these claims are premature because the national contingency plan revisions called for by section 105 have not been finally adopted. *See* 42 U.S.C. § 9605. There is no merit to that argument. Congress did not intend final adoption of the revisions to the national contingency plan to be prerequisite for bringing suit to recover response costs under section 107(a).

*   *   *

Section 101 of the Act defines the "national contingency plan" as "the national contingency plan published under section 1321(c) of Title 33 [Section 311(c) of the Federal Water Pollution Control Act] or revised pursuant to section 9605 of this Act." 42 U.S.C. § 9601(3). Section 105 of the Act requires the President, within 180 days after the enactment of CERCLA, to revise and republish the national contingency plan for the removal of oil and hazardous substances, to reflect and effectuate the responsibilities and powers created by CERCLA. 42 U.S.C. § 9605. This revision is to include a section known as the "national hazardous substance response plan" which shall establish procedures and standards for responding to releases of hazardous substances and pollutants. *Id.* Among other things, the plan is to specify procedures, techniques, materials, equipment and methods to be used in identifying, removing, or remedying releases of hazardous substances comparable to those required under the plan developed under section 311 of the FWPCA. 42 U.S.C. § 9605(1)-(9). Finally, section 105 provides: "Following publication of the revised national contingency plan, the response to and actions to minimize damage from hazardous substances releases, shall, to the greatest extent possible, be in accordance with the provisions of the plan." 42 U.S.C. § 9650.

* * *

Reilly Tar argues that since the Plan has not yet been finally adopted, the section 107 claims must be dismissed as premature. It reasons one cannot determine whether the costs incurred are consistent or inconsistent with a Plan that does not yet exist.

The Reports of both the Senate and House Committees indicate that Congress did not intend revision of the Plan be a prerequisite to liability under the Act.***

* * *

To impose the interpretation urged by Reilly Tar would penalize those agencies that took prompt action and act as a disincentive to prompt action until the Plan is finally adopted. Congress, recognizing the significance of the problem and the importance of immediate responses in many cases, did not intend that final adoption of the revised plan be a prerequisite to begin an action against a private party to recover response costs under section 107(a).

Reilly Tar also seeks to limit liability under section 107(a) to those costs for which response fund expenditures may be made under section 111, 42 U.S.C. 9611, and contends ultimately that the existence of the cooperative agreement between the state and federal government called for by section 104(c)(3), 42 U.S.C. 9604(c)(3), is a condition to liability under section 107. The complexities of defendant's argument require that it be set out in some detail.

Section 112 of the Act sets forth the procedures for filing and determining claims against the Fund. 42 U.S.C. § 9612. Section 112(a) requires a party seeking recovery from either the Fund or a private party to first present the claim to the responsible party. If the claim is not satisfied within sixty days, the claimant may elect to commence an action against either the Fund or the responsible party.***

***Reilly Tar argues that *all* claims, whether against the Fund or a private party, must be assertable against the Fund under section 111. 42 U.S.C. § 9611. It then turns to section 111(a), which provides in part:

(a) The President shall use the money in the Fund for the following purposes:

(1) payment of governmental response costs incurred pursuant to section 9604 of this title, including costs incurred pursuant to the Intervention on the High Seas Act. . . .

Reilly Tar then argues that section 111 provides for reimbursement of government response costs, "but only, 'government response costs incurred pursuant to section [104].'" It then turns to section 104, arguing that certain requirements of that section have not been met. Specifically, it claims that the cooperative agreement called for by section 104(c)(3) has not been entered into. Section 104(c)(3) prohibits the President from taking "remedial"[5] actions under

---

[5]There are two types of response actions under CERCLA: removal actions and remedial actions. The Act provides extensive definitions for each type of response action. 42 U.S.C. § 9601(23) and (24). Gener-

section 104 unless a cooperative agreement between the President and the affected state containing certain conditions has been entered into. 42 U.S.C. § 9604(c)(3).***

Reilly Tar's complex analysis of the Act is incorrect. Most importantly, Reilly Tar errs in attempting to link liability under section 107 to the authorized uses of the Fund provided in section 111. Liability under section 107(a) is independent of the authorized uses of the Fund under section 111 and of the cooperative agreement called for by section 104(c)(3).

In determining what conditions must be met before a party can be held liable for response costs under section 107(a), the obvious place to begin is with the language of section 107(a) itself. The first clause of that section provides:

> *Notwithstanding any other provision or rule of law* and subject *only* to the defenses set forth in subsection (b) of this section. . . .

42 U.S.C. § 9607(a) (emphasis added).

From this language it is apparent that Congress did not intend that courts engage in the complex inquiry and statutory tracing of the various sections Reilly Tar relied on. Section 107(a) was meant to stand by itself; liability under it can be determined without the numerous inquiries suggested by the defendant. The plain language of the statute says so. Liability for the specified response costs under section 107(a) is absolute, subject only to the defenses listed in section 107(b), which are acts of God, acts of war, and certain acts or omissions of third parties. 42 U.S.C. § 9607(b).

There is no claim before the court seeking recovery from the Fund. The authorized uses of the Fund provided by section 111 are therefore not relevant to this action. Nor is there any suit before this court seeking to compel the President to enter into a cooperative agreement with Minnesota under section 104(c)(3). *See* 42 U.S.C. § 9604(c)(3). Whether there should be a cooper-

---

ally, removal actions are short term cleanup actions while remedial actions contemplate a long term approach consistent with a permanent remedy.

ative agreement between the President and Minnesota as provided by section 104(c)(3) is not material in determining Reilly Tar's potential liability under section 107(a).

Natural Resource Damages Claim.

The State of Minnesota has also asserted a claim for natural resources damages under section 107(a)(4)(C). 42 U.S.C. § 9607(a)(4)(C). Reilly Tar seeks dismissal of the natural resources damage claim on two grounds. First, it argues that the claim is premature because certain regulations and administrative procedures called for by the Act with respect to the assessment of natural resources damages have not yet been established. Specifically, Reilly Tar refers to section 301(c) of the Act, 42 U.S.C. § 9651(c), and sections 111(h) and (i), 42 U.S.C. § 9611(h) & (i).

Section 301(c) requires the President to promulgate regulations for the assessment of natural resources damages resulting from the release of hazardous substances.***

Section 111(h) provides that for purposes of the Act, federal officials designated by the President under the national contingency plan are to assess natural resources damages. 42 U.S.C. § 9611(h). Their assessment is given the evidentiary status of a rebuttable presumption on behalf of any claimant in any judicial or adjudicatory proceeding under the Act.***

Dismissal is not appropriate even though the regulations required by section 301(c) have not been promulgated and the assessment mechanism provided by section 111(h) does not yet exist. Legislative history and other provisions of the statute support this conclusion.

The legislative history indicates that the provisions regarding promulgation of regulations and assessment by federal officials were intended to provide a standardized method for determining natural resource damages that would be efficient in both time and cost.***

Congress was aware of the difficulties plaintiffs faced in establishing damages to natural resources and sought to facilitate, not block, such claims through the regulation and assessment procedures of section 301(c) and 111(h).

Furthermore, to interpret the Act as Reilly Tar suggests would, in effect, suspend the operation of section 107(a)(4)(C) until the regulations and assessment procedures are enacted. Congress did not intend to render the section imposing natural resources damages a nullity until then.***

The court is not unmindful of the practicalities of this litigation. Environmental litigation often lasts several years and it is certainly possible that the court will not be called upon to determine the ultimate merits of the State's natural resource damage claim until long after the regulations and assessment procedures are in place. A dismissal now would not serve a realistic purpose.

Reilly Tar's final argument is that under section 107(f) the court should dismiss the State's claim to the extent that it seeks recovery for damages that occurred before the enactment of CERCLA. Section 107(f) provides in part:

> There shall be no recovery under the authority of subparagraph (C) of subsection (a) of this section where such

damages and the release of a hazardous substance from which such damages resulted have occurred wholly before December 11, 1980.

42 U.S.C. § 9607(f).

Under section 107(f) Reilly Tar may escape liability for natural resource damages only where both the damages and the release occurred *wholly* before December 11, 1980. *Id.* Section 107(f) precludes liability under section 107(a)(4)(C) only where (1) all releases ended before December 11, 1980, and (2) no damages were suffered on or after December 11, 1980 as a result of the release. The complaint alleges continuing releases and damages from the release. The extent to which Reilly Tar will be entitled to escape liability under section 107(f) is a fact question to be resolved in future proceedings.

Accordingly, IT IS ORDERED that Reilly Tar's motions to dismiss are denied.

NOTES

1. Was the court correct to view these allegations as stating a claim of "imminent and substantial endangerment" under Section 7003 of RCRA? Notice that the language expressing this substantive standard is virtually the same in Section 7003 of RCRA and Section 106 of CERCLA. Would any circumstances exist, therefore, in which Section 7003 would add anything to the government's suit against an owner or operator under Section 106?

2. In view of the 1984 amendments to RCRA, which imminent hazard provision now has the broader application — that in RCRA or that in CERCLA? Might not the express terms in Section 7003 bring a court to hold a party liable when it would hesitate to apply the very general language of Section 106? On the other hand, to the extent any "gaps" remain in liability under Section 7003, could Section 106 be used to fill them?

3. Under the original CERCLA legislation, no private right to invoke Section 106 was provided. *See Velsicol Chemical Corp. v. Reilly Tar and Chemical Corp.,* 21 ERC 2118 (E.D. Tenn. 1984); *Cadillac Fairview/California, Inc. v. Dow Chemical Co.,* 21 ERC 1108 (C.D. Calif. 1984). As of this writing, however, CERCLA reauthorization bills pending in Congress include provisions analogous to that in the 1984 RCRA amendments, which would allow citizens to sue in federal court to abate any endangerment covered by Section 106.

4. Notice that in *Reilly Tar* the cities and the state, as well as the federal government, made claims against the defendants based on Section 107. Was there any problem with any of these plaintiffs as proper parties to recover response costs? Judicial decisions have consistently held that Section 107 (a)(4)(B) creates a private right of action for response costs. *See, e.g., Walls v. Waste Resource Corp.,* 761 F.2d 311 (6th Cir. 1985); *Pinole Point Properties, Inc. v. Bethlehem Steel Corp.,* 596 F. Supp. 283 (N.D. Cal. 1984); *Jones v. Inmont Corp.,* 584 F.Supp. 1425 (S.D. Ohio 1984); *City of Philadelphia v. Stepan Chemical Co.,* 544 F.Supp. 1135 (E.D. Pa. 1982).

5. One often-litigated issue is whether CERCLA may be used for recovery of cleanup costs incurred prior to its effective date of December 11, 1980. For affirmative answers, *see United States v. Ward,* 23 ERC 1391 (E.D. N.C. 1985); *Town of Boonton v. Drew Chemical Corp.,* 23 ERC 1289 (D.N.J. 1985); *United States v. Shell Oil Co.,* 605 F.Supp. 1064 (D. Colo. 1985). For negative answers, *see United States v. Wade,* 21 ERC 1348 (E.D. Pa. 1984); *United States v. Northeastern Pharmaceutical and Chemical Co.,* 579 F.Supp. 823 (W.D. Mo. 1984).

Is it not beyond cavil, however, that costs may be recovered for *post*-enactment cleanup responses to releases and acts of disposal that took place before the effective date of CERCLA? For a curious decision seemingly based upon a negative conclusion, *see Nunn v. Chemical Waste Management, Inc.,* 22 ERC 1763 (D. Kan. 1985).

6. Section 107(a)(4)(A) of CERCLA requires that response costs recoverable by the federal government or states be "not inconsistent with the national contingency plan;" and Section 107(a)(4)(B) requires response costs incurred by any other person to be "consistent with the national contingency plan." Was the court correct to allow claims under these provisions to be made before the national contingency plan had been revised to cover land disposal of hazardous wastes? [The revision to the plan has now been made. See 47 Fed. Reg. 31180 (1982).]

Under Section 111(a)(1), governmental response costs may be paid out of the superfund if "incurred pursuant to Section 104" (which authorizes federal and cooperating state action "consistent with the national contingency plan"). Under Section 111(a)(2), response costs incurred by any other person can be paid out of the fund if they were incurred "as a result of carrying out the national contingency plan" and "approved under said plan." EPA has interpreted this requirement in Section 111(a)(2) quite restrictively to require certification by its Washington office prior to the taking of any private response action for which costs are recoverable from the fund. *See* 40 C.F.R. § 300.25 (d). Indeed, EPA has imposed so many requirements for private recovery of response costs from the fund that one author asserts that it has virtually precluded private parties from obtaining such reimbursement. *See Thomas, Municipal and Private Party Claims Under Superfund,* 13 ELR 10272 (1983). This may mean that, as a practical matter, a municipality or private party may be more likely to recover its costs under Section 107 than from the fund.

7. Before the government can undertake any "remedial" action (as distinguished from "removal"), the state in which the release has occurred must have entered into a contract or cooperative agreement with the President in which it has agreed, *inter alia,* to pay 10 percent of the total cost of the remedial action. *See* Section 104(c)(3). Does this provision block long-term federal remedies in "uncooperating" states which are unwilling to contribute to financing the cost of cleanup?

The court holds that an action against a responsible party under Section 107 need not await a "cooperative agreement." But if the federal government is barred by Section 104(c)(3) from taking remedial action in the absence of such an agreement with the state, doesn't this in effect block recovery under Section 107 of what could be a significant item of response costs?

For other cases holding that response costs may be recovered in the absence of a cooperative agreement by a civil action under Section 107, *see Ohio v. Georgeoff,* 19 ERC 1113, (N.D. Ohio 1983); *New York v. General Electric Co.,* 592 F. Supp. 291 (N.D.N.Y. 1984). For a decision to the contrary, *see Wickland Oil Terminals v. Asarco, Inc.,* 590 F. Supp. 72 (N.D. Cal. 1984).

Unlike other federal environmental legislation, CERCLA does not mandate state implementation plans. It does, however, encourage states to enact hazardous waste legislation in order to enable the federal government to provide remedial action at waste sites in the state and in order to be eligible for reimbursement from the superfund. For a good article on state hazardous waste laws and their relationship to CERCLA, *see* Comment, *State Hazardous Waste Superfunds and CERCLA: Conflict or Complement,* 13 ELR 10348 (1983).

8. Section 107(a)(4)(C) creates a cause of action for damages for injury or destruction of natural resources, apart from costs of removal or remedial action, but without saying who are the proper parties to make such a claim. Section 107(f), however, seems to limit such recovery to the federal government and to any state owning or managing the resources—by implication precluding private recovery under Section 107 for such damages.

Now read sections 111(h) and 301 (c). Do you agree with the court's holding that the State of Minnesota could recover for natural resource damages prior to promulgation of federal regulations for the assessment of such damages?

Do you agree with the court's construction of the last sentence in Section 107(f) to preclude recovery for natural resource damages only where both the damages and the release occurred wholly before December 11, 1980? Given the statutory language, isn't it hard to disagree? Under such construction, are many substantial claims for natural resource damages apt to be barred by this sentence?

Much more significant to potential governmental plaintiffs is Section 112(d). After you have read it, check the definition of "damages" in Section 101(6). This means that claims by the United States or state governments for natural resource damages which were discovered before December 11, 1980, had to be filed by December 11, 1983. Does this apply to claims against the superfund as well as civil actions? Does it apply to recovery of response costs as well as natural resource damages? Whatever the ultimate construction by the courts, prudence caused a raft of claims, both in court and against the fund, to be filed in the week preceding December 11, 1983.

For two articles on recovery of natural resource damages under CERCLA, *see* Breen, *CERCLA's Natural Resource Damage Provisions: What Do We Know So Far?* 14 ELR 10304 (1984); Breen, *Natural Resource Recovery by Federal Agencies — A Roadmap to Avoid Losing Causes of Action,* 13 ELR 10324 (1983).

9. Although a private litigant may invoke Section 7003 of RCRA to obtain abatement of an imminent hazard to his person and property, and he may utilize Section 107 of CERCLA to recover response costs incurred, nothing in RCRA or CERCLA (as of this writing) provides a cause of action for *damages* to his person or property. To recover for personal injury from "toxic torts," one must turn to state tort law, statutory or common. For a good comment on recent efforts to utilize state common law to recover damages for physical and emotional harm from exposure to chemicals escaping from hazardous waste dumps, *see* Reed, *Hazardous Waste and the Common Law: Will New Jersey Clear the Way for Victims to Recover?* 15 ELR 10321 (1985).

10. The cases read thus far have concerned governmental claims against past and present owners and operators of hazardous waste disposal sites. The resources of these defendants may be far too little to begin to pay the sorts of claims being made for response costs and damages. In order to find pockets deep enough to satisfy judgments in cases such as these, the government has turned to the generators of the wastes (and, ultimately, their insurers). The varying success which it has achieved in these efforts under RCRA and CERCLA is illustrated by the following cases.

United States v. Wade ("Wade I")

546 F. Supp. 785 (E.D. Pa. 1982)

NEWCOMER, J:

Before me is defendant Gould, Inc.'s motion to dismiss the amended complaint of plaintiff Unites States of America ["the government"] in this civil action brought under section 7003 of the Resource Conservation and Recovery Act ["RCRA"] and section 106 of the Comprehensive Environmental Response, Compensation, and Liability Act of 1980 ["CERCLA"]. The government seeks to use these statutory injunctive relief provisions to impose liability upon defendant Gould and five other chemical companies for their past generation of hazardous chemical wastes which were subsequently disposed of upon a property located at 1 Flower Street, Chester, Pennsylvania ["the Wade site"]. The government seeks to recover from Gould and other off-site generators for expenses incurred, or to be incurred, in planning and carrying out a clean-up of the Wade site.***

*   *   *

FACTS

The Wade site has been used for disposal of hazardous chemical wastes for a period of time unspecified in the complaint. Generators of hazardous waste products, like Gould, contracted with the ABM Disposal Service (also a defendant in this suit but not involved in this motion) to have the substances drained into tank cars and drums. ABM then brought them to the Wade site and either stored the tanks or drums there, or emptied them directly onto the soil, through which they are currently draining into the Delaware River. On February 2, 1978, a fire broke out on the site which caused further damage to the several thousand drums and tank cars, which are now in a corroding, leaky and charred condition. After the fire, the Environmental Protection Agency (hereinafter "EPA"), in conjunction with the Pennsylvania Department of Environmental Resources, conducted tests on the site which demonstrated, the complaint alleges, that some fifty hazardous chemical substances are currently present in the soil. Some, like benzene, are toxic in themselves, and some, like decane, are

potential fire hazards. Several small fires have in fact spontaneously ignited on the site since 1978. Water sampling conducted by the same agencies since 1978 indicates that some of the dangerous chemicals are currently migrating through the soil into the Delaware River.

The complaint alleges that Gould, among others, generated these substances and caused them to be brought to the site; that the substances are hazardous wastes under the definition in section 1004(5)(27) of RCRA, and that the current leaking of the chemicals into the soil and the water constitutes "disposal" which creates an "imminent ... endangerment" to public health or the environment, so as to bring the site under the terms of the emergency injunctive relief provisions, section 7003 of RCRA and section 106(a) of CERCLA. The complaint does not allege that Gould is currently dumping waste on the site, that it was negligent in its past disposal, or that it has any current connection with the site.

The government filed suit against Gould when it amended its complaint for the second time on November 10, 1981, to include certain off-site generators of the hazardous wastes now on the Wade site. It sought an injunction forbidding any further dumping on the site and ordering Gould, among others, to "abate" the hazard by reimbursing the goverment for costs incurred or to be incurred in planning and implementing a clean-up of the Wade site. Gould responded by filing the motion which is now before the Court to dismiss the complaint against it. Gould argues that section 7003 and section 106 do not impose liability on non-negligent past generators of hazardous waste who have no present connection with the dump site.

DISCUSSION

Upon a motion to dismiss brought under F.R.Civ.P. 12(b)(5), the facts alleged in the complaint must be taken as true. I accept, therefore, that as a result of past disposal of hazardous chemical wastes, dangerous chemicals are present in the soil on the Wade site and are currently being discharged into the atmosphere and into the Delaware River. I also accept as true that these discharges constitute an imminent and substantial endangerment to the public health and the environment (Amended Complaint, ¶¶ 35, 45) and that Gould and the others were generators of hazardous chemical wastes which were transported to the Wade site (¶ 46).

The question before me, therefore, is whether, as a matter of law, the statutory provisions relied on by the government confer substantive liability on non-negligent off-site generators of hazardous waste for past disposal of such waste which now creates an imminent hazard.

*   *   *

1. *Section 7003 of RCRA.*

***The section authorizes the Administrator of the EPA "upon receipt of evidence that the handling, storage, treatment, transportation or disposal of any solid waste or hazardous waste may present an imminent and substantial endangerment to health or the environment," to bring suit "to immediately restrain any person contributing to such storage, treatment, transportation or disposal . . . . " 42 U.S.C. § 6973(a).

*   *   *

While I am inclined to the view that current leaking of previously dumped waste does not constitute "disposal" enjoinable under the clear language of section 7003, I need not resolve this issue in light of my conclusion that section 7003 may not, in any case, be used to confer liability on non-negligent past off-site generators of hazardous waste. As the government concedes, no court has yet construed section 7003 to be applicable to past off-site generators. I believe this is because there is nothing in the statutory language or the legislative history that would authorize such a considerable extension of liability.

The government argues that since section 7003 grants the EPA authority to restrain "any person contributing" to the disposal of hazardous waste, it must therefore encompass "generators" since "[g]enerators are the first and perhaps the most important actors in the chain of events leading to the ultimate disposal of the waste." There are, however, numerous other actors in this chain of events. Were I to accept the government's logic, I might be constrained to impose liability, through section 7003, upon the original manufacturers or miners of the chemicals which Gould uses in its manufacturing processes. Because there is no logical limit, given the breadth of the statutory language, to the number and type of persons who might be construed to be "contributing to" the disposal of hazardous waste, a court must look for clear legislative guidance before reading section 7003 to confer substantive liability upon so vast a class of potential defendants as off-site generators. There is no statutory definition of "a person contributing to" hazardous waste disposal. In the absence of Congressional guidance, it is not reasonable to define the term so broadly.

***Yet, the fragmentary legislative history does not support the government's contention that Congress intended section 7003 to impose strict liability upon generators of hazardous waste. The original House and Senate reports on RCRA yield no sign of such an intent.

*   *   *

The inapplicability of section 7003 to the present case is also demonstrated by the type of relief for which the government prays. Since the complaint does not allege that any of the generators is currently disposing of waste on the Wade site or that there is any threat that they will resume their past practice of doing so, I cannot sensibly grant the government's prayer that they be permanently restrained from doing so. The government's essential request, therefore, is contained in paragraphs three and four of the prayer for relief, in which the Court is asked to "enjoin" the defendant among others, to pay the cost of drawing up and implementing a plan to clean up the Wade site. I am also asked to require the defendant to reimburse the government for expenses already incurred toward this end. Since Gould is no longer dumping on the site and is not the owner of the property, it cannot comply with any such injunction except by paying money. The government's prayer for relief, though phrased in injunctive terms, is transparently a prayer for money damages.***

*   *   *

2. Section 106(a) of CERCLA.

The government's second statutory claim, under section 106 of CERCLA, or "Superfund," must also fail. Because CERCLA is so new and has not as yet been construed by any court, the government urges that I analogize section 106, the emergency injunctive relief section of CERCLA, to section 7003. Given my analysis of section 7003, *supra*, such an analogy would not avail the government.

CERCLA was specifically designed to plug gaps in the government's then existing anti-pollution program. In particular, it was designed to deal squarely with the problem of abandoned or "orphan" hazardous waste dumps, a problem which RCRA had not adequately addressed.[19] The method chosen by Congress was the creation of a revolving "Superfund," which was to be funded by a tax on generators of hazardous waste products. The heart of the statute is contained in section 104, "Response Authorities," which gives the EPA the authority to undertake emergency clean-up measures when it determines that an abandoned site presents, or may present "an imminent and substantial danger to public health." 42 U.S.C. § 9604. Congress intended section 104 to work in tandem with section 107, the liability section. By the terms of section 107, the government is authorized to sue designated classes of persons to reimburse the Superfund for emergency clean-up, removal and containment actions which it undertook under section 104. Section 107 clearly includes generators of hazardous waste among those potentially liable to be sued for clean-up costs incurred under section 104. Moreover, the provision which applies to generators is written in the past tense and clearly applies to past generators and transporters.[21] Had the government, therefore, under-

taken to clean up the site under section 104, and then proceeded against Gould under section 107, the statutory authority to support such actions would have been clear.

The government has, however, ignored sections 104 and 107 and chosen instead to proceed under section 106(a) of CERCLA, which confers upon the EPA the authority to seek emergency injunctive relief when presented with evidence of an "imminent and substantial endangerment to the public health."[22] 42 U.S.C. § 9606. The government argues that because Congress intended past off-site generators to be liable under the statutory scheme established by sections 104 and 107, it must also have intended that they be liable under the emergency injunctive relief authority of section 106. In the absence of any evidence that Congress intended section 106 to be used in this way, and in face of the clear and carefully detailed legislative provision of another route to the same result, I cannot agree with the government's contention.

The language of section 106 gives no hint of an intent to confer liability on past generators. Like section 7003 of RCRA, and significantly, unlike section 107, it is written in the present tense. It authorizes the government to seek immediate injunctive relief because of "an actual or threatened release of a hazardous substance from a facility . . . ." It authorizes the EPA to supplement any action undertaken by a local government to meet this imminent hazard, and "to

---

[19]The enactment of "Superfund" was preceded by lengthy Congressional hearings into the infamous abandoned chemical waste dump at Love Canal, near Niagara Falls, New York. *Hazardous Waste Hearings*, note 8, *supra*.

[21]Section 107 confers liability upon "any person who by contract, agreement, or otherwise arranged for dis-

posal or treatment, or arranged with a transporter for transport for disposal or treatment, of hazardous substances owned or possessed by such person . . . ." 42 U.S.C. § 9607(a)(3). ***

[22]The government does not, in its memorandum, straightforwardly state the reason it has chosen to proceed via section 106 of CERCLA. A reason may be that the Superfund, as enacted, is inadequate to address the enormous public health problem posed in our country by abandoned or inactive hazardous waste sites. When describing the scope of the problem before the Joint Committee which considered CERCLA, EPA Assistant Administrator Thomas C. Jorling stated that approximately 1-2000 of the 30-50,000 waste disposal sites in the U.S. pose potential threats to public health or the local environment. He estimated that 25-44 billion dollars would be needed to clean up these potentially dangerous sites. *Hazardous Waste Hearings*, note 6, *supra*, at 37, 38.

*   *   *

secure such relief as may be necessary to abate such danger or threat . . . . " 42 U.S.C. § 9606(a). A straightforward reading of this language requires that I conclude that Congress intended section 106(a) to be used in emergency situations where hazardous waste was currently being discharged or threatened to be discharged "from a facility"[23] and where such discharge could be stopped by an injunction. Such a reading of section 106 as applicable to current emergencies where responsible parties may be ordered to comply with an injunction renders the section a complement to sections 104 and 107 which are so clearly addressed to the present health problems caused by abandoned sites.

The government argues, however, that a "harmonious" reading of the statute requires a conclusion that section 106 provides an alternative route through which the EPA may, at its option, address the problem of abandoned sites. The "harmonious" reading for which the government contends will be better achieved, this Court believes, by acknowledging that Congress intended each provision to serve a specific purpose in this extensively debated legislative program. Where Congress after extensive debate, has clearly designated its choice of a method for obtaining money damages from past off-site generators whose waste products have contributed to the critical problem posed by abandoned chemical dumps, it is the role of EPA and this Court to carry out the unambiguous legislative intent.***

An appropriate order will be entered.

*   *   *

ORDER

AND NOW, this 7th day of September, 1982, it is hereby Ordered that defendant Gould's motion to dismiss the amended complaint is GRANTED. The amended complaint is hereby DISMISSED as against Apollo Metals, Inc., Congoleum Corporation, Gould, Inc., H.K. Porter Company, Inc., Sandvik Steel, Inc. and Superior Tube Company.

AND IT IS SO ORDERED.

---

[23]Section 101(a) of CERCLA, 42 U.S.C. § 9601(9), defines "facility" quite broadly to include both "building, structure, installation" as well as "any site or area where a hazardous substance has been deposited, stored, disposed of, or placed . . . ." The Wade site is unquestionably a facility under the statutory definition, and I must reject defendant's argument which seeks to limit the phrase's applicability.

NOTES

1. Obviously, this decision was a big blow to the government's strategy to use the "imminent hazard" provisions in RCRA and CERCLA against past generators in order to obtain cleanup of inactive and abandoned dumps without bearing at least the initial expense itself. With only the $1.6 billion Superfund to draw on, it is easy to see why the government was so unhappy with this holding.

2. Was the claim under Section 7003 properly dismissed? Can this decision be reconciled with *Reilly Tar's* application of Section 7003 to a (negligent?) past on-site generator who was also owner and operator of the facility? Would a principled basis exist for different treatment? Would any language in the original Section 7003 support such a distinction?

3. Was the claim under Section 106(a) of CERCLA properly dismissed? How could the court first say that CERCLA "was designed to deal squarely with the problem of abandoned or 'orphan' hazardous waste dumps," but then go on and refuse to allow Section 106 to be applied? Would it have allowed application of Section 106 to a past operator? To a present generator? Was it saying that only Section 107 might appropriately be used against those responsible for abandoned sites? If so, as you will see in the next case, courts may require the government to undertake the expense of cleanup before Section 107 can be used, an obvious barrier with available funds so limited.

4. In *United States v. Hardage*, 18 ERC 1687 (W.D.Okla. 1982), without any real legal analysis or distinctions, the court imposed liability under Section 7003 of RCRA and Sections 106 and 107 of CERCLA for all costs of cleanup upon the owners (past and present) of a hazardous waste dump which had been inactive since November, 1980.

In *United States v. Northeastern Pharmaceutical and Chemical Co.*, 579 F. Supp. 823 (W.D. Mo. 1984), the Court refused to hold Section 7003 applicable to non-negligent past off-site generators, at the same time that it held Section 106 applicable to them.

5. What would be the proper holding following the 1984 amendments to Section 7003 of RCRA? Does any doubt remain as to its application to off-site generators who contributed in the past to the disposal of hazardous waste that is presently causing an imminent and substantial danger?

What is the proper standard of liability under Section 7003? Under Section 106 of CERCLA? Should past off-site generators be liable only if negligent in arranging for disposal at the site? Or should they be held strictly liable? If so, should they have any affirmative defenses? Consider the analysis in the next case.

United States v. Price ("Price III")

577 F. Supp. 1103 (D.N.J. 1983)

BROTMAN, District Judge.

This is a complex environmental action instituted by the United States of America pursuant to § 1431 of the Safe Water Drinking Act (SWDA), 42 U.S.C. § 300i; § 7003 of the Resource Conservation and Recovery Act (RCRA), 42 U.S.C. § 6973, and Comprehensive Environmental Response, Compensation, and Liability Act (CERCLA), 42 U.S.C. § 9601, *et seq* (Supp. IV 1980). The case comes before this court on a motion by generator-defendant Hoffman-LaRoche Corporation for summary judgment.

*   *   *

On September 21, 1981, two days prior to this court's decision on the preliminary injunction issue, plaintiff filed a second amended complaint adding thirty-five defendants. The new defendants included individuals and corporations who allegedly generated and/or dumped the hazardous waste at Price's Landfill. The amended complaint also added two additional claims brought under CERCLA. Due to the timing of the amendment, this court did not have

an opportunity to consider the effect of CERCLA as a statutory basis for this case.***

*   *   *

***In an effort to expedite the action, the court suggested that just one generator defendant, Hoffman-LaRoche (Roche), move for summary judgment. If this action proved successful, others could take appropriate action.

*   *   *

Factual Background

The facts pertinent hereto are thoroughly outlined in this court's previous decision in this case. *See United States v. Price*, 523 Supp. 1055, 1057-66. The only new relevant facts relate to the development of the government's case against Roche. In its summary, the government notes that Roche had a place of business in Nutley, New Jersey. Laboratory chemicals were generated at the Nutley plant and subsequently packed into drums. Roche paid a transporter, Scientific Chemical Processing Company (SCP) to pick up the drums and dispose of them. The president of SCP, Carl Ling, testified at a deposition that he went to the Nutley plant numerous times, packed the drums and deposited them at various landfills. The empty drums were supplied by Roche and the chemicals included acids, bases, and organic liquids. Ling also remembered that he took some lab packs to Price's Landfill, however, he could not link directly the Roche lab packs with those waste materials dumped at the landfill.

The government also produced three loading tickets, discovered in Price's business records, which indicate that waste chemicals originating at Roche's plant ended up at Price's Landfill. The one ticket mentioned in the summary is dated June 9, 1972. Since the summary was compiled, the government has produced two more loading tickets from approximately the same time period. Furthermore, the government maintains that they possess other facts which suggest that more than three loads of Roche's waste were deposited at the landfill during the period in question.

*   *   *

Section 107

The initial question that must be addressed in this motion, is whether CERCLA, by its own terms, precludes the government from seeking monetary or equitable relief from potentially responsible parties prior to expending any of the superfund allocated for that purpose. ***

It appears with respect to § 107, that the government must first begin the cost of the clean-up and incur some expenses before it can initiate an action. 42 U.S.C. § 107(a)(1); *see Brown v. Georgeoff,* 562 F. Supp. 1300 (N.D. Ohio 1983).***

***Because of its failure to establish an action under § 107, any claims brought solely under that section are hereby dismissed without prejudice.

Section 106

The government also asserts claims under § 106(a) which read as follows (heading used for § 106 is "abatement actions"):

"In addition to any other action taken by a State or local government, when the President determines that there may be an imminent and substantial endangerment to the public health or welfare or the environment because of an actual or threatened release of a hazardous substance from a facility, he may require the Attorney General of the United States to secure such relief as may be necessary to abate such danger or threat, and the district court of the United States in the district in which the threat occurs shall have jurisdiction to grant such relief as the public interest and the equities of the case may require. The President may also, after notice to the affected State, take other action under this section including, but not limited to, issuing such orders as may be necessary to protect public health and welfare and the environment."

The defendants maintain that § 106(a) was not drafted with this type of action in mind. *** Moreover, defendants point to a recent decision in a case involving similar facts, in which the court held that § 106(a) was not applicable to non-negligent, off-site generators that were no longer actively dumping waste in the landfill. *United States v. Wade,* 546 F. Supp. 784 (E.D.Pa. 1982). ***

Wade is the only case decided to date in which the government attempted to hold non-negligent, off-site generators liable under § 106(a). *But see United States v. Outboard Marine Corp.,* 556 F. Supp. 54 (N.D.Ill. 1982): *United States v. Reilly Tar & Chemical Corp.,* 546 F.Supp. 1100 (D. Minn. 1982). (In both *Outboard Marine* and *Reilly Tar* the defendant was the owner of the landfill. It must be noted, however, that in both cases the court found that § 106(a) applied to *past* actions.)***

After carefully analyzing the statutory language and the purposes of CERCLA, this court must respectfully disagree with both the reasoning used and the result arrived at in *Wade.* The comparison between § 106(a) and § 7003 is inevitable. In fact, as the court in *Reilly Tar* recognized, the imminent hazard provisions of § 106(a) are even broader than those articulated in § 7003. Moreover, the court in *Wade* construed

§ 106(a) in the same narrow manner that it construed § 7003. The decision in *Wade*, however, was prior to the Third Circuit decision in this case, *United States v. Price*, 688 F.2d 204 (3rd Cir. 1982), in which the court held that § 7003 could be applied to a dormant site if it poses a current threat to the environment or to public health.***

Defendant also argues that Congress was reluctant to involve the courts in the clean up process and therefore provided a superfund along with the necessary statutory mechanism for implementation. While this may have been one purpose behind the superfund, it does not necessarily preclude the government from also seeking emergency relief from potentially responsible parties under § 106(a). The primary purpose of CERCLA was to "[accelerate the] elimination of unsafe hazardous waste sites." In view of the overriding need, it is doubtful that Congress would draft § 106 intending it to apply only prospectively. It is far more likely that Congress envisioned possible problems with the government funding numerous cleanups and drafted § 106(a) as a viable alternative or concurrent means of achieving the same goal.[8] If, in fact, Congress did not intend the EPA to pursue remedial action with respect to past sites, other than just by use of the superfund, it would have been forced to allot more money to the fund itself. In other words, if the EPA is forced to use the superfund, and finance the entire clean up operation prior to even initiating an action for those costs against responsible parties, the $1.6 billion allocated to the fund would be depleted almost immediately. *See* Eckhardt, *The Unfinished Business of Hazardous Waste Control*, 33 Baylor L. Rev. 263 (1981). Moreover, according to the defendant's interpretation, once the superfund is depleted, the government will have no further recourse against potentially lia-

ble parties, since there will be no costs incurred. This result makes no sense both practically and in light of the objectives with which Congress promulgated the legislation.

For the above reasons and in view of the broad and ambiguous language used in § 106(a), this court hereby holds that CERCLA was intended and should apply to past off-site generators if the circumstances indicate an "imminent and substantial endangerment." Since there is no dispute that Price's landfill requires immediate action, it is not improper for the government to sue the defendants for relief under § 106(a).

Liability Under § 106(a).

The second issue raised by defendant concerns that standard of liability applicable pursuant to § 106(a). The defense argues that even if § 106(a) does apply to the instant case, the proper standard of care should be negligence, not strict liability. Such reasoning assumes that either § 107, which defines liability does not apply to § 106(a), or that § 107 does not set forth a standard of strict liability. We disagree with both arguments and for the following reasons conclude that the defendant generators in the instant case should be held strictly liable for their alleged acts.

In analyzing the standard to be applied under § 106, we must first determine whether the section as drafted contains an independent definition of liability. Of the two courts that have heard actions under § 106(a), one applied the § 107 standards of liability. *United States v. Outboard Marine, supra,* and the other held that § 106 was substantive and contained its own standards. *United States v. Reilly Tar, supra.* The court in *Reilly Tar* quoted the phrase "the public interest and the equities of the case" and concluded that such language implied that Congress intended a standard similar to that used in federal common law nuisance actions.

The *Reilly Tar* interpretation is difficult to fathom given the result of *Milwaukee v. Illinois,* 451 U.S. 304 (1981) where the Supreme Court held that federal common law of nuisance had been preempted in the area of water pollution due to the recent outbreak of complex legislation.***

---

[8]While CERCLA seems to encourage swift government action, it allots only $1.6 billion dollars to the superfund. Even the lowest estimates regarding clean up costs exceed that figure by almost 5 billion dollars, Eckhardt, *supra,* 33 Baylor L. Rev. 263 (1981), and the EPA estimates that such costs will actually run from 13.1 billion as high as 22.1 billion dollars just to take care of the 1200-2000 most dangerous inactive sites.

This court fully concurs with the result reached in *Outboard Marine****. ***

After deducing that the § 107 definition of liability applies in the instant action, we must next determine the proper standard as articulated in that section.*** We note that although the term "strict" was deleted at the last minute, it still appears that Congress intended to impose a strict liability standard subject only to the affirmative defenses listed in § 107(b). *See* Note, *Generator Liability Under Superfund for Cleanup of Abandoned Hazardous Waste Dumpsites*, 130 U.Pa.L. Rev. 1229, 1252-58 (1983). This conclusion is reinforced by virtue of the fact that Congress left the "due care" defense in the statute, a defense which would be rendered meaningless in the absence of strict liability. 42 U.S.C. § 9607(b)(3). Moreover, the strict liability standard fits most closely with the legislative aims of CERCLA which include goals such as cost-spreading and assurance that responsible parties bear their cost of the cleanup. The fulfillment of these Congressional goals is more likely to be effectuated if the defendants who allegedly contributed to the environmental mess are now held to a very stringent standard of liability. Though strict liability may impose harsh results on certain defendants, it is the most equitable solution in view of the alternative—forcing those who bear no responsibility for causing the damage, the taxpayers, to shoulder the full cost of the cleanup.

Finally, we turn to the "due care" affirmative defense set forth in § 107(b)(3) which reads as follows:

"an act or omission of a third party other than an employee or agent of the defendant, or than one whose act or omission occurs in connection with a contractual relationship, existing directly or indirectly with the defendant . . . if the defendant establishes by a preponderance of the evidence that (a) he exercised due care with respect to the hazardous substance concerned, taking into consideration the characteristics of such

hazardous substance, in light of all relevant facts and circumstances and (b) he took precautions against foreseeable acts or omissions of any such third party and the consequences that could foreseeably result from such acts or omissions;"

42 U.S.C. § 107(b)(3).[12] Roche contends that the government has not alleged a lack of due care in its complaint and therefore this court must assume that the requirements of § 107(b)(3) have been satisfied. The above-cited section, however, constitutes an affirmative defense. As a result, the burden of proof is on the party raising the defense, in this instance, Roche. In fact, the language of the subsection specifically states that the defendant must establish "by a preponderance of the evidence" that due care was exercised. 42 U.S.C. § 107(b)(3). Obviously, at this point in the litigation, Roche is not able to prove that it exercised due care, in part because the company has not been presented with the full range of evidence implicating it in the dumping scheme (if such evidence does, in fact, exist). Since Roche has the burden of proving the "due care defense," and has not yet satisfied that burden, its motion for summary judgment must be denied.

In light of the reasons set forth in this opinion this court concludes that Roche can be held liable under § 106(a) of CERCLA, as a potential past, nonnegligent, offsite generator of hazardous waste deposited at Price's Landfill.

*   *   *

---

[12]The relevant legislative history cited by defendant reads, in part, as follows:

"The mere act of generation or transportation of hazardous waste or the mere existence of a generator's or transporter's waste in a site with respect to which clean up costs are incurred would not, in and of itself, result in liability under § 3071 (predecessor version of section 107)."

H.R. Rep. No. 96-1016, *supra* at 34, reprinted in 1980 U.S. Code Cong. & Ad. News 6119, 6139.

NOTES

1. In the court's dismissal without prejudice of the government's claim under Section 107, what did it mean by requiring the government to "first begin the cost of cleanup and incur some expenses"? Does this suggest that this court would award the government its prospective costs of full response if it had merely made a beginning on the job of cleaning up and remedying a hazardous waste problem? Or does it simply mean that the government may *bring* an action under Section 107 before it has completed a cleanup job, but that it can obtain a final judgment only for those costs actually incurred?

Several federal district courts have held that a plaintiff may obtain declaratory relief under Section 107 that a defendant will be liable for future response costs not yet incurred. *See Pinole Point Properties, Inc. v. Bethlehem Steel Corp.,* 596 F.Supp. 283, 291-92 (N.D. Cal. 1984), and other decisions cited therein.

2. Do you agree with this decision, rather than that in *Wade,* as to the applicability of Section 106 to non-negligent past off-site generators? Is practical necessity, given the inadequate size of the "superfund," an adequate justification for this holding? If, as has been proposed in Superfund reauthorization bills, the fund is expanded to over $10 billion, should courts continue to construe Section 106 in this manner?

3. Was this court correct to apply strict liability to a claim under Section 106? Where did this idea come from? Was the court justified in incorporating into Section 106 the liability scheme from Section 107, seemingly in its entirety, including the affirmative defenses from subsection (b)? The same conclusion — that Section 106 incorporated Section 107's standard for liability, and that it was *strict* — was reached in *United States v. Northeastern Pharmaceutical and Chemical Co., Inc.,* 579 F. Supp. 823 (W.D. Mo. 1984).

4. Except for the parenthetical exclusion for carriage under tariffs and by rail, do you see any difference in the affirmative defenses set out in Section 107(b) and those contained in Section 311(f) of the Water Act? Does not the elaboration on the third-party defense in Section 107(b) reflect the judicial constructions of the third-party defense when asserted in oil-spill cases?

5. If a generator exercised all due care in packaging its waste, choosing its transporter, and insuring that the transporter delivered the waste to a permitted disposal site, could it nevertheless be held liable under Section 107 for a spill of the waste by the transporter? Notice the exclusion from the third-party defense in Section 107(b) for acts which occur in connection with a "contractual relationship." What about holding such a "duly careful" generator liable for acts of the operator of the disposal facility? What is an "indirect" contractual relationship?

Could a generator be held liable under Section 107 for the cleanup of a facility containing its hazardous wastes if it proved that it did not know where its wastes would end up when they were turned over to the transporter? Would the "release" be caused *solely* by the disposal facility — with whom it had no contractual relationship? Or would it also be caused by the transporter? Would the generator be deemed to have exercised due care if it claimed that it delivered the hazardous wastes to the transporter without any idea where they would be disposed of?

Apart from any availability of the third-party defense — would the generator be found to have "arranged for disposal . . . at any facility . . . from which there is a release" if the generator did not know where the wastes were bound? Reconsider this question after reading the next two cases.

United States v. Wade ("Wade II")

577 F. Supp. 1326 (E.D. Pa. 1983)

NEWCOMER, District Judge.

*   *   *

This is a civil action brought by the United States against several parties allegedly responsible for the creation of a hazardous waste dump in Chester, Pennsylvania. The government seeks injunctive relief against Melvin R. Wade, the owner of the dump site, ABM Disposal Service, the company which transported the hazardous substances to the site, and Ellis Barnhouse and Franklin P. Tyson, the owners of ABM during the time period at issue ("non-generator defendants"). The government also seeks reimbursement of the costs incurred and to be incurred in cleaning up the site from the non-generator defendants as well as from Apollo Metals, Inc., Congoleum Corporation, Gould, Inc. and Sandvik, Inc. ("generator defendants").

The claims for injunctive relief are brought pursuant to § 7003 of the Resource Conservation and Recovery Act of 1976 ("RCRA") and § 106 of CERCLA. The claims for monetary relief are based on § 107(a) of CERCLA as well as a common law theory of restitution. Presently before the Court are the government's motions for partial summary judgment on the issue of joint and several liability under § 107(a) against each of the defendants. In addition, each of the generator defendants has moved for summary judgment.

*   *   *

The generator defendants' motions for summary judgment on the CERCLA claims generally advance two arguments. First, they argue that the government has not and cannot establish the requisite causal relationship between their wastes and the costs incurred by the government in cleaning up the site. Second, assuming the government can establish liability under the Act, the generator defendants argue that it has recovered all costs to which it could possibly be entitled.***

*   *   *

A. THE CAUSATION ARGUMENT

*   *   *

Even assuming the government proves that a given defendant's waste was in fact disposed of at the Wade site, the generator defendants argue it must also prove that a particular defendant's actual waste is presently at the site and has been the subject of a removal or remedial measure before that defendant can be held liable. In the alternative, the generator defendants argue that at a minimum the government must link its costs incurred to waste of the sort created by a generator before that generator may be held liable.***

The liability provision of CERCLA provides in relevant part as follows:

> Notwithstanding any other provision or rule of law, and subject only to the defenses set forth in subsection (b) of this section— . . .
>
> (3) Any person who by contract, agreement, or otherwise arranged for disposal or treatment or arranged with a transporter for transport for disposal or treatment of hazardous substances owned or possessed by such person, by any other party or entity, at any facility owned or operated by another party or entity and containing *such* hazardous substances... (4) ... from which there is a release, or a threatened release which causes the incurrence of response costs, of *a* hazardous substance, shall be liable for—
>
> (A) All costs of removal or remedial action incurred by the United States Government or a state not inconsistent with the national contingency plan.

42 U.S.C. § 9607(a) (emphasis added).***

Part of the generator defendants' argument revolves around the use of the word "such" in referring to the "hazardous substances" contained at the dump site or "facility." It could be read to require that the facility contain a particular defendant's waste. On the other hand it could be read merely to require that hazardous substances like those found in a defendant's waste must be present at the site. The legislative history provides no enlightenment on this point. I believe that the less stringent requirement was the one intended by Congress.

The government's experts have admitted that scientific technique has not advanced to a point that the identity of the generator of a specific quantity of waste can be stated with certainty. All that can be said is that a site contains the same kind of hazardous substances as are found in a generator's waste. Thus, to require a plaintiff under CERCLA to "fingerprint" wastes is to eviscerate the statute. Given two possible constructions of a statute, one which renders it useless should be rejected. Generators are adequately protected by requiring a plaintiff to prove that a defendant's waste was disposed of at a site and that the substances that make the defendant's waste hazardous are also present at the site.[3]

*   *   *

I turn now to the generator defendants' contention that the government must link its costs incurred to wastes of the sort created by them.

A reading of the literal language of the statute suggests that the generator defendants read too much into this portion of its causation requirement. Stripping away the excess language, the statute appears to impose liability on a generator who has (1) disposed of its hazardous substances (2) at a facility which now contains hazardous substances of the sort dis-

posed of by the generator (3) if there is a release of that or some other type of hazardous substance (4) which causes the incurrence of response costs. Thus, the release which results in the incurrence of response costs and liability need only be of "a" hazardous substance and not necessarily one contained in the defendant's waste. The only required nexus between the defendant and the site is that the defendant have dumped his waste there and that the hazardous substances found in the defendant's waste are also found at the site. I base my disagreement with defendants' reading in part on the Act's use of "such" to modify "hazardous substance" in paragraph three and the switch to "a" in paragraph four.

Additional support for my reading may also be found in the legislative history of the Act.***

Deletion of the causation language contained in the House-passed bill and the Senate draft is not dispositive of the causation issue. Nevertheless, the substitution of the present language for the prior causation requirement evidences a legislative intent which is in accordance with my reading of the Act.

*   *   *

B. COSTS RECOVERABLE UNDER THE ACT

*   *   *

No useful purpose will be served by conducting a lengthy trial on the merits if it is clear at the outset that the federal government is not entitled to any compensation from these defendants; however, I do not believe this is the case. First, the government is clearly not barred by § 104 from spending additional money at the site which would be recoverable from these defendants if liability is otherwise established. In addition, the amount the federal government, as opposed to the Commonwealth of Pennsylvania, has received from the settling defendants is unclear. Finally, the intent of the parties as to the appropriation of the settlement fund has not been established. Because I do not believe the issue is clear I will deny the generator defendants' motion for summary judgment insofar as it is based on the conten-

[3] I also reject the arguments that the government must establish that the generator selected the site at which the wastes were dumped and that transfer of ownership of the waste to ABM at the time of pick-up for disposal absolves the generator of liability. Neither argument finds any support in the language of the statute.

tion that the government has no recoverable damages.

C. JOINT AND SEVERAL LIABILITY

The government seeks partial summary judgment holding each defendant jointly and severally liable under section 107(a) of CER-CLA. Assuming certain statutory prerequisites are established, I believe the Act permits, but does not require, the imposition of joint and several liability. For reasons discussed below, I do not believe the facts are adequately developed for a determination of whether joint and several liability should be imposed in this case. My conclusions on this issue have recently been confirmed in *United States v. Chem-Dyne Corp.*, 572 F.Supp. 802 (S.D.Ohio 1983).

The generator defendants' argument that CERCLA does not permit the imposition of joint and several liability is based on the deletion from the Act of an explicit reference to joint and several liability and on Senator Helms' explanation of the deletion:

Retention of joint and several liability in S. 1480 received intense and well-deserved criticism from a number of sources, since it could impose financial responsibility for massive costs and damages awards on persons who contributed only minimally (if at all) to a release or injury. Joint and several liability for costs and damages was especially pernicious in S.1480 not only because of the exceedingly broad categories of persons subject to liability and the wide array of damages available, but also because it was coupled with an industry-based fund. Those contributing to the fund will be frequently paying for conditions that they had no responsibility in creating or even contributing to. To adopt a joint and several liability scheme on top of this would have been grossly unfair. The drafters of the Stafford-Randolph substitute have recognized this unfairness and the lack of wisdom in eliminating any meaningful link between culpable conduct and financial responsibility. Consequently,

all references to joint and several liability in the Bill have been deleted.

126 Cong.Rec. at S15004 (Nov. 24, 1980)

A reading of the entire legislative history, however, reveals that deletion of the reference to joint and several liability was intended to avoid mandatory application of that standard to a situation where it would produce inequitable results. For example Senator Randolph, who introduced the amendment deleting reference to joint and several liability, commented "we have deleted any references to joint and several liability, relying on common law principles to determine when parties should be severally liable." 126 Cong.Rec. at S14964 (Nov. 24, 1980). Similar comments were made by Representative Waxman. *Id.* at H11799 (Dec. 3, 1980).***

Thus, I believe that in deleting the reference to joint and several liability Congress intended that courts apply common law principles in determining the scope of liability under CERCLA. Having reached this conclusion I must now determine whether state or federal common law controls. As noted above, the legislative history is not conclusive on this point, and the legislators' understanding of the common law was not uniform.

Federal courts may create federal common law when "necessary to protect uniquely federal interests." *Texas Industries v. Radcliff Materials*, 451 U.S. 630, 640 (1981). The problems presented by improper disposal of hazardous wastes have become problems of national magnitude. One factor giving rise to the enactment of CERCLA was the failure of states to address adequately the growing problem of hazardous waste dumps. At the time of CER-CLA's passage, the EPA estimated that as many as 30,000 to 50,000 inactive and uncontrolled hazardous waste sites existed in the United States, about 20 to 30 percent of which contained wastes created by offsite generators. The EPA estimated that clean-up of the 1200 to 2000 most dangerous sites would cost $13.1 billion to $22.1 billion.

State common law varies on the imposition of joint and several, as opposed to apportioned, liability on joint polluters. Thus, resort to state law on this issue would result in needless uncertainty and lack of uniformity. A liability standard which varies from state to state would undermine the policy of the statute by encouraging illegal dumping in states with lenient liability laws. Because of the strong federal interest in the abatement of toxic waste sites and the need for a uniform liability standard I conclude that Congress intended the development of a federal common law on the issue of the scope of liability under § 107 of CERCLA and that this is an area in which the development of such law is proper.

I agree with the *Chem-Dyne* decision that joint and several liability should be imposed in cases brought under § 107 of CERCLA unless the defendants establish that a reasonable basis exists for apportioning the harm amongst them. This rule would be in accord with the position adopted by the Restatement (Second) of Torts:

> (1) Damages for harm are to be apportioned among two or more causes where
>> (a) there are distinct harms, or
>> (b) there is a reasonable basis for determining the contribution of each cause of a single harm.

Restatement (Second) of Torts § 433A

> (2) Where the tortious conduct of two or more actors has combined to bring about harm to the plaintiff, and one or more of the actors seeks to limit his liability on the ground that the harm is capable of apportionment among them, the burden of proof as to the apportionment is upon each such actor.

Restatement (Second) of Torts § 433B.

Such a rule does not unfairly hamper the ability of the government to recover its costs incurred in cleaning up hazardous waste dump sites.[13] Likewise it helps to ameliorate the

harshness of the liability provisions of the statute. Finally, it appears to embody the general congressional intent of placing liability for toxic waste clean-up as nearly as possible on those responsible for creating the hazard.

D. DEFINITION OF "HAZARDOUS SUBSTANCE"

One final issue contested by all the generator defendants centers on the statutory definition of "hazardous substance." The statute defines that term as "any substance" designated pursuant to the provisions of specified federal environmental protection laws. In establishing the generator defendants' liability the government relies on a list of "hazardous substances" promulgated pursuant to § 311(b)(2)(A) of the Federal Water Pollution Control Act (FWPCA) and the list of "toxic pollutants" promulgated pursuant to § 307 of the FWPCA. These lists are contained in 40 C.F.R. § 116.4 and § 401.15, respectively. The government maintains that the presence of any of the listed substances or pollutants in a generator's waste makes that waste a "hazardous substance" for purposes of CERCLA liability without regard to concentration or quantity.

Not all discharges of "hazardous substances" or "toxic pollutants" lead to FWPCA liability. Instead, liability is imposed if a discharge contains a "reportable quantity" of a hazardous substance, §311(b)(4), or is in excess of the "effluent standards" for a toxic pollutant. § 307(d). Reportable quantites for hazardous substances are listed at 40 C.F.R. § 117.3 and effluent standards for certain toxic pollutants are published at 40 C.F.R. § 129.4 *et seq.*

The generator defendants contend the government's motion for summary judgment must be denied because the government has failed to establish that their wastes contain a reportable quantity of hazardous substances under § 311 or toxic pollutants in excess of the stated effluent guidelines under § 307. Indeed, the government denies the necessity of so doing. The government contends that under CERCLA no reportable quantity or effluent standard need be determined for hazardous substances incorporated by reference to §§ 307 and 311 of

---

[13]   Of course certain issues, which I need not decide, could have a bearing on this. For example, left undecided is the problem of who bears the burden of insolvent or unavailable defendants.

FWPCA. Only substances designated as hazardous pursuant to § 102 of CERCLA have reportable quantity requirements for CERCLA purposes.

*   *   *

*** Having already concluded that triable issues exist I need not decide this issue at this time; however, in the interest of expediting trial once it begins I will rule on this issue now. What the government must prove to establish that a defendant's wastes are hazardous is that the waste contains an unspecified quantity of substances designated as hazardous or toxic under the statutes specified in CERCLA's definition of "hazardous substance."

Certainly the definition of hazardous substances contained in § 101 of CERCLA supports the government's position. The definition refers only to the provisions of FWPCA authorizing the designation of hazardous substances and toxic pollutants and not to those authorizing promulgation of reportable quantities or effluent standards. Likewise § 107 makes no reference to reportable quantities or effluent standards as do its FWPCA counterparts. On the other hand, as the generator defendants point out, this interpretation could lead to the absurd result that a penny is a hazardous substance, the disposal of which could lead to CERCLA liability, by virtue of the inclusion of copper on the list of toxic pollutants promulgated pursuant to § 307 of FWPCA.

Nevertheless, merely incorporating FWPCA effluent standards and reportable quantities into CERCLA requirements is not without its problems. First, I am not persuaded that incorporation of standards created with respect to water pollution into a statute directed at the disposal of hazardous wastes on land makes any sense. If it does not it lessens the probability that such incorporation was intended by Congress.

Second, I am unclear why Congress would incorporate these standards from FWPCA into CERCLA when § 102 of CERCLA establishes reportable quantities for purposes of the statute's reporting requirements. That section provides as follows:

(b) Unless and until superseded by regulations establishing a reportable quantity under subsection (a) of this section for any hazardous substance as defined in section 9601(14) of this title, (1) a quantity of one pound, or (2) for those hazardous substances for which reportable quantities have been established pursuant to section 1321(b)(4) of Title 33, such reportable quantity, shall be deemed that quantity, the release of which requires notification pursuant to section 9603(a) or (b) of this title.

42 U.S.C. § 9602(b). This provision may have been aimed at the fact that EPA has promulgated effluent standards for only a few toxic pollutants designated pursuant to § 307(a) of FWPCA and apparently has no plans to promulgate additional standards in the immediate future.

Third, given the standard established by § 102 for designating additional substances as hazardous, Congress may well have intended to vest a great deal of discretion in the Executive branch in its prosecutorial decisions. A substance may be designated as hazardous if, upon release into the environment, it "may present substantial danger to the public health or welfare or the environment." 42 U.S.C. § 9602(a).

Similarly, the interim standard for reportable quantities under CERCLA—one pound for all substances except those designated pursuant to § 311(b)(2)(A) of FWPCA—suggests that Congress intended a result almost as drastic as the one the generator defendants posit. If Congress intended CERCLA liability only for those whose discharges contained reportable quantities of hazardous substances, and if the reportable quantities are determined by reference to § 102, a defendant could be held liable for the disposal, not of one penny, as the defendants fear, but of a pound of pennies.

Finally, I believe the defendants' fears of draconian liability are overstated. Given my ruling on joint and several as opposed to apportioned liability, a defendant whose sole contribution to a hazardous waste dump site was a copper penny would not be responsible for the entire cost of cleaning up the site.

*   *   *

NOTES

1. Do the court's holdings on these three issues mean that if the government can prove only that a few drums of benzene generated by Dow Chemical Co. were disposed of in a large hazardous waste dump containing hundreds of thousands of gallons of toxic chemicals, only one of which is benzene, and that some of the hazardous wastes are leaking into the environment, on this evidence Dow Chemical could be stuck with the entire tab for cleanup costs? Dow's problem would be exacerbated if no solid evidence exists linking the waste with any other party with funds and/or insurance that could make any significant contribution to the costs — not necessarily a hypothetical situation in a context in which impecunious owners, operators, and transporters and fragmentary records have been the norm.

Under these circumstances, would a reasonable basis exist for determining Dow's contribution to the harm? How would Dow establish a reasonable basis for apportionment?

2. Does the *Wade II* decision contain the potential for carrying the "deep pocket" approach to recovery to unprecedented extremes? Is it justifiable? Will it be if Congress increases the size of the Superfund to $10 billion?

3. Several other courts have similarly held that CERCLA allows imposition of joint and several liability on defendants. *See United States v. Chem-Dyne Corp.*, 572 F.Supp. 802 (S.D. Ohio 1983); *United States v. Northeastern Pharmaceutical and Chemical Co.*, 579 F.Supp. 823 (W.D. Mo. 1984); *United States v. South Carolina Recycling and Disposal, Inc.*, 20 ERC 1753 (D.S.C. 1984); *United States v. A & F Materials Co.*, 578 F.Supp. 1249 (S.D. Ill. 1984).

4. For a view decidedly opposed to holding one generator responsible for the cleanup of wastes produced by others, *see* Rogers, *Three Years of Superfund*, 13 ELR 10361 (1983). For other articles on imposition of liability on generators for hazards posed by past disposal of their wastes, *see* Rogers, *The Generators' Dilemma in Superfund Cases*, 12 ELR 15049 (1982); Reed, *Conservation Chemical: Generator Liability for Imminent Hazards on the Docket*, 13 ELR 10208 (1983).

5. The first judicial order actually apportioning response costs among generators was issued on March 3, 1986, in *United States v. Ottati & Goss, Inc.*, No. C80-225 (D.N.H. 1986). In the order, Judge Loughlin ruled that, under CERCLA, the federal government's response costs for removing drums of hazardous waste from a disposal site were to be apportioned among the defendant generators according to the number and precentage of drums each generator sent at the site. The Judge held that the number of drums discarded there by each generator constituted "a reasonable basis for determining the contribution of each cause of the harm" according to the standard expressed in the Restatement (Second) of Torts § 433A.

6. EPA estimates that the average expenditure per Superfund site is $12 million. When a company faces cleanup obligations that are grossly disproportionate to its size, it may have little choice but to seek shelter in bankruptcy.

In *Ohio v. Kovacs*, 105 S. Ct. 705 (1985), the Supreme Court held that the obligation of the operator of a hazardous waste disposal site to comply with a state court injunction requiring it to clean up the site was dischargeable in bankruptcy. Where it was clear that the only type of performance in which the State was interested, or which was feasible, was the payment of money to defray cleanup costs, the injunction had become a "debt" or "liability on a claim" subject to discharge under the Bankruptcy Code. The Court's unanimous decision, however, was expressly limited to the circumstances of the case. At the conclusion of Justice White's opinion, he went so far as to specify numerous issues *not* decided by the Court — including whether anyone left in possession of the site must nevertheless comply with state environmental laws (which might require cleanup). 105 S. Ct. at 711-12. Although the *Kovacs* case itself involved the discharge of a liability on a claim arising under *state* environmental law, the Court's analysis seems clearly to apply as well to claims brought under *federal* environmental statues, particularly Section 107 of CERCLA. More difficult issues are raised by cleanup orders under Section 106 of CERCLA and Section 7003 of RCRA. For a comprehensive treatment of the impact of bankruptcy upon hazardous waste cleanup liabilities, and vice-versa, see Drabkin, Moorman, and Kirsch, *Bankruptcy and the Cleanup of Hazardous Waste: Caveat Creditor*, 15 ELR 10168 (1985).

The Supreme Court was not in such accord in deciding the next hazardous waste/bankruptcy cases to come before it, *Midlantic National Bank v. New Jersey Department of Environmental Protection* and *O'Neill v. City of New York* 106 S. Ct. 755 (1986). The decision of the 5/4 majority in these two consolidated cases, however, was straightforward: a trustee in bankruptcy may not abandon contaminated real or personal property in contravention of state laws that are reasonably designed to protect the public health or safety from identified environmental hazards. (Again, the Court's reasoning would seem to apply as well to federal environmental statutes and regulations.) As pointed out by Justice Rehnquist's dissent, the majority opinion may mean that the public interest in forcing a hazardous waste cleanup is placed ahead of the claims of other creditors. Would this be a desirable result?

New York v. General Electric Company
592 F.Supp. 291 (N.D. N.Y. 1984)

Before Roger J. Miner, D.J.

*   *   *

Defendant GE operates several manufacturing plants in the State of New York, including plants at Hudson Falls and Fort Edward, New York. According to plaintiff's complaint, in the early 1960's GE disposed of between four and five hundred fifty-five gallon drums of used transformer oil from those two plants through sales to the South Glens Falls Dragway, Inc., Allie Swears, and Carl Becker. The oil, which contained hazardous substances including polychlorinated biphenyls ("PCBs") and dibenzofurans, was used at the South Glens Falls Dragstrip ("dragstrip") for purposes of dust control.[4] In 1982 and 1983, chemical analyses of soil samples taken by plaintiff from the dragstrip and its environs revealed PCB contamination as high as 2900 parts a million and dibenzofuran contamination as high as 12 parts

---

[4] Apparently, South Glens Falls Dragway, Inc., was disolved some time around 1970 and the dragstrip has not been used for organized racing for a number of years. The dragstrip is regularly used, however, by the public for picnics, walks, and dirt-bike riding.

a billion. Analysis of air samples taken in June of 1983 indicated PCB contamintion in the ambient air as well. This contamination apparently results in release of PCBs into the ambient air by volatilization as well as migration of the contaminants through the soil and towards the groundwater.***

On November 30, 1983, pursuant to section 112(a) of CERCLA, the state presented its claim to defendant for damages to the natural resources and "for the costs of removal, remediation and response with respect to the identification, definition, monitoring, control and abatement of the contamination at and around the South Glens Falls Dragstrip." Amended complaint, ¶20. GE has failed to satisfy the claim for these items***.

This relatively simple factual background lays the predicate for three causes of action set forth in plaintiff's amended complaint. The first cause of action alleges that GE is strictly liable under section 107(a)(3) of CERCLA "for all damages sustained and to be sustained by the land, wildlife, biota, groundwater, ambient air and other such natural resources of the State and for all costs and expenses incurred or to be incurred by the State of New York for the removal, remediation and response to all contamination at and in the environs of the South Glens Falls Dragstrip ...."Amended complaint, ¶23. The second and third causes of action concern alleged violations of state statutory and common law. GE has not moved against these claims on the merits but rather has only taken the position that the dismissal of New York's federal CERCLA claims would require dismissal of the state claims under the jurisprudential considerations of pendent jurisdiction.

*   *   *

A. *Applicability of section 107*

GE argues that there is no basis for liability under Section 107 of CERCLA, the relevant subsection of which provides for liability of persons

> who by contract, agreement, or otherwise arranged for disposal or treatment, or arranged with a transporter for transport for disposal or treatment, of hazardous substances owned or possessed by such person, by any other party or entity, at any facility owned or operated by another party or entity and containing such hazardous substances
> . . . .

42 U.S.C. §9607(a)(3). GE's argument is twofold: First, it argues that because a dragstrip is not a hazardous waste facility there can be found no liability under section 107(a)(3). Second, it contends that liability may not be premised upon section 107(a)(3) because it did not "contract or otherwise arrange for 'disposal or treatment' " of the transformer oil within the meaning of the statute. This Court rejects both of defendant's contentions.

*** Section 101(9) of CERCLA defines "facility" in exceptionally broad terms, to include:

> (A) any building, structure, installation, equipment, pipe or pipeline (including any pipe into a sewer or publicly owned treatment works), well, pit, pond, lagoon, impoundment, ditch, landfill, storage container, motor vehicle, roll-

ing stock, or aircraft, or (B) any site or area where a hazardous substance has been deposited, stored, disposed of or placed, or otherwise come to be located
. . . .

42 U.S.C. §9601(9). ***

Arguing that "[t]he legislative history leaves no question as to the reach of Section 107(a)(3)," GE suggests that mere sales of chemicals to an entity other than a hazardous dump site simply are not within the statute's contemplation. Because the dragstrip here at issue was not "a facility owned and operated by another party . . . *containing such hazardous substances,*" GE views its actions as not within the statutory proscription. The thrust of its argument is that a covered facility may only be one already containing hazardous substances. This construction, GE argues, is consistent with the legislative history of CERCLA which evinced a congressional concern regarding the problems attendant upon "dump sites," for example, sites such as the "Valley of the Drums" in Kentucky. Since the complaint has not alleged that the dragstrip was ever used for other than its principal purpose, i.e., automobile racing, or that hazardous wastes had previously been disposed of there, GE urges the Court to find no liability. Although not lacking entirely in intuitive appeal, the Court finds GE's hypertechnical construction to be unsupported by the legislative history and contradicted by simple common sense.

First, the broad language employed in section 101(9) dispels any notion that CERCLA was designed to cover only traditional dump sites. That section expressly covers buildings, pipelines, motor vehicles, rolling stock, aircraft and *any area* where hazardous substances come to be located. Moreover, the legislative history makes clear Congress' intent to address the problem of hazardous wastes rather than merely a particular category of disposal sites. Indeed, it appears that Congress sought to deal with every conceivable area where hazardous substances come to be located, including not only the Valley of the Drums, but, for example, dirt roads in Texas contaminated with nitrobenzene and cyanide as a result of oiling, radium waste sites scattered throughout Colorado found to be "under restaurants, in empty lots where children play. [and] near factories . . . ," tanks filled with toxic chemicals abandoned near the Nanticoke River in Maryland, PCBs dumped into the Hudson River, and spills of hazardous substances on the George Washington Bridge.

*   *   *

GE also argues it is not a responsible party under section 107(a)(3) since it did not "arrange[] for disposal or treatment" of hazardous substances within the meaning of the statute. "Disposal" is defined under section 101(29) of CERCLA by reference to section 1004 of the Solid Waste Disposal Act, 42 U.S.C. §6903, which defines disposal as

> the discharge, deposit, injection, dumping, spilling, leaking, or placing of any solid waste or hazardous waste into or on any land or water so that such solid waste or hazardous waste or any constituent thereof may enter the environment or be emitted into the air or discharged into any waters, including ground waters.

42 U.S.C. §6903(3). Specifically, GE contends that the complaint alleges only that it sold or otherwise supplied used transformer oil to the South Glens Falls Dragway, Inc., and not that it entered into an agreement or arrangement to have the oil deposited or otherwise placed on the dragstrip. At most, GE suggests, the complaint alleges only that it "entered into an agreement to supply oil to the drag strip in the ordinary course of commerce to be used as the drag strip owners saw fit," and concludes that "Congress never intended to make a supplier liable for the subsequent action of a purchaser in the ordinary course of a business other than waste disposal." Because the conduct giving rise to any response costs here was the application of the oil to the dragstrip by its owners, GE urges that it cannot therefore be held liable.

GE's contention must be rejected for a number of reasons. First, because this is a motion to dismiss, the allegations in plaintiff's complaint must be construed most favorably in plaintiff's behalf. Section 107(a)(3) imposes liability for response costs upon "any person who by contract, agreement, or otherwise arranged for disposal or treatment of hazardous substances. . . ." Here, plaintiffs have alleged that GE disposed of hazardous substances by arranging with the South Glens Falls Dragway to remove the substances from GE's plants with knowledge or imputed knowledge that the substances would be deposited on the land surrounding the dragstrip. The Court is not prepared to hold that the complaint does not allege an arrangement for the disposal of wastes.

***At least as a pleading matter, it appears clear that GE arranged or contracted with other parties to dispose of its waste; accordingly, it is not entitled to avoid liability. Finally, it is equally clear that a waste generator's liability under CERCLA is not to be so facilely circumvented by its characterization of its arrangements as "sales." *See United States v. A & F Materials, Co.*, 20 ERC 1957 (S.D. Ill. 1984).

B. *Failure to incur response costs*

Defendant next argues that plaintiff's complaint must be dismissed because plaintiff has not yet expended funds for the clean-up of the hazardous waste site. *See* 42 U.S.C. §9607 (a)(4)(A) (providing for recovery of "costs of removal or remedial action *incurred*" (emphasis added)).*** Moreover, GE suggests that costs of investigation are not response costs under 42 U.S.C. §§9601(23)-(25). Finally, GE claims that costs "to be incurred" are not recoverable as costs under a plain reading of section 107.

With respect to this aspect of the motion to dismiss, several points are in order. First, plaintiff's complaint specifically sets forth a claim for damages to the state's natural resources in addition to its claim for response costs, 42 U.S.C. §9607(a)(C), and there is no requirement that money must be expended by the state before it can seek to recover for damages to natural resources. Second, it is clear that plaintiff has properly alleged recoverable response costs under section 107(a)(A) and (C). Specifically, ¶ 21 of the amended complaint alleges that the state "has incurred and will continue to incur expenses and costs. . . ." As a pleading matter, that allegation must be construed in the light most favorable to plaintiff and, contrary to GE's suggestion, plaintiff need not particularize the costs thus far incurred.

Finally, those initial response costs undertaken thus far by plaintiff are clearly authorized as costs of response under section 101(23). Removal action is defined under that section to include "such actions as may be necessary to monitor, assess, and evaluate the release or threat of release of hazardous substances. . . ."[12]***

In a supplemental memorandum submitted prior to oral argument, GE has brought to the Court's attention the decision of the District Court of California in *Cadillac Fairview/California, Inc. v. Dow Chemical Co.* [21 ERC 1108] (C.D. Cal. Mar. 5, 1984), assertedly supportive of the proposition that investigative costs are not recoverable. Citing with approval the decision in *D'Imperio v. United States*, 575 F.Supp. 248 (D.N.J. 1983), the *Cadillac Fairview* court held that clean-up costs incurred in fencing off a site and conducting chemical analyses, were not recoverable. That decision is distinguishable, however, in at least two respects. First, the action before the court entailed interpretation of section 107(a)(B) rather than section 107(a)(A) and (C). That section is applicable to parties other than federal or state governments and establishes significantly different cost recovery criteria. Second, it is clear that the *Cadillac Fairview* court did not look at all to the strictures of section 101(23) and (25) which expressly provide that costs associated with monitoring, assessing, and evaluating the release or threat of release of hazardous substances are recoverable under section 107(a)(A).

Finally, GE contends that future response costs are not recoverable under CERCLA. The Court declines to reach this particular issue at this juncture since, even if future costs are not recoverable, the foregoing discussion establishes that plaintiff has otherwise stated a claim for costs incurred.[14]

C. *Failure to comply with notice provisions*

Based on section 112(a) of CERCLA, 42 U.S.C. §9612(a), GE claims that plaintiff's complaint must be dismissed for failure to comply with that section's sixty-day notice requirement. According to GE, section 112(a) provides that a claim "shall be presented in the first instance to the owner, operator, or guarantor . . . of . . . [a] facility from which a hazardous substance has been released . . . , and to any other person known to the claimant who may be liable . . ." under section 107. 42 U.S.C. §9612(a). Only if such a claim is not satisfied within sixty days of its presentation may suit be brought. While GE received a letter from plaintiff on November 30, 1983 advising it of the substance of the assertion of liability, it claims that such notice was defective in two respects. First, the letter did not request a sum certain, *see supra* note 15, and second, suit was filed just eight days later. Accordingly, GE argues that the present action must be dismissed.

GE acknowledges that this is a case of first impression, noting that no other court has yet confronted the question of whether failure to comply with the sixty-day notice requirement amounts to a jurisdictional defect. It argues, however, that courts interpreting notice provisions in similar environmental protection statutes have found such requirements to be in fact jurisdictional.***

First, and perhaps most importantly, defendant's reliance on the sixty-day notice requirement is misplaced. The first sentence of section 112(a) expressly provides that "[a]ll

---

[12] There is no dispute that plaintiff has in fact undertaken field and laboratory work in order to monitor, assess, and evaluate the release and threat of release of hazardous substances and has incurred expenses as a consequence of these efforts.

[14] The parties have presented the Court with three cases on the issue of future costs. *United States v. Price*, 13 Env. L. Rep. 20843 (D.N.J. 1983), urged by GE, apparently holds that future costs are not recoverable. *United States v. Northeastern Phamaceutical & Chemical Co.*, 20 ERC 1401 (W.D. Mo. 1984), and *United States v. Wade*, 20 ERC 1277 (E.D. Pa. 1983), noted by plaintiff, on the other hand, held that costs "to be incurred" are recoverable. None of the decisions is generous in analysis, although the *Wade* court reasons that permitting future recovery "better effectuates the purposes of the Act . . . ." 20 ERC at 1283. Since there is no need to pass on this question now, the Court defers judgment on this aspect of the complaint pending further briefing by the parties.

claims which may be asserted against the Fund [the Superfund] pursuant to section 9611 of this title shall be presented in the first instance to the owner . . . ." 42 U.S.C. §9612(a). It is clear, therefore, that the notice provision applies only to actions in which a claim is sought to be made against the Fund; it does not apply when a CERCLA case is merely brought against a responsible party such as GE. Notification in Fund cases is a necessary prerequisite aimed at conserving the assets of the Superfund by encouraging responsible parties to pay clean-up costs before a plaintiff is forced to look to Fund money. Because New York's suit here involves claims for certain costs which may not be asserted against the Fund, but only against GE, the provisions of section 112(a) are not applicable.

Second, the Court is persuaded that in any event, the sixty-day requirement is not jurisdictional. The cases cited by GE, which arose in the context of suits involving other environ-mental statutes, embodied interpretations of significantly different statutory mechanisms. Unlike the Clean Water Act and the Clean Air Act, which impose notice requirements that are compatible with those statutes' preference for initial administrative rather than private action, the purpose of CERCLA seems only to require notice in order to facilitate negotiated settlements. The fact that sixty days elapsed prior to the instant motions comports with the pragmatic approach to the notice requirement, since the parties were afforded adequate time in which to avoid any court intervention.

*   *   *

On balance, there can be no question that New York has stated a claim for cost recovery and natural resources damages cognizable under CERCLA. Accordingly, GE's motion to dismiss the complaint must be denied.

It is so Ordered.

NOTES

1. Did the court have to stretch the language of the statute to bring GE within it?

Is there any doubt that the dragstrip was a "facility" under these circumstances? In *United States v. Ward*, 23 ERC 1391 (E.D. N.C. 1985), the court had no difficulty holding that the shoulders of rural roads onto which PCB oil was sprayed from a moving truck constituted a "facility" within the broad definition of Section 101(9) of CERCLA.

Compare Fishel v. Westinghouse Electric Corp., 23 ERC 1329 (M.D. Pa. 1985), in which the court held that the accidental discharge of hazardous wastes at a Westinghouse plant did not subject it to the permit requirements and regulations applicable to a "disposal facility" under RCRA; on the other hand, Westinghouse's *intentional* discharges at the plant did make it liable for violation of the permit requirements of RCRA. (The definitions in the two acts are not the same, however, nor do they serve the same purpose.)

2. Did the question of whether GE "arranged for disposal" at the dragstrip present a more difficult issue? What if GE had no knowledge, "imputed" or otherwise, that the PCB oil would be deposited on the land at the dragstrip? What if the evidence showed that GE had simply waived goodbye to the PCBs at the plant gate, not knowing, nor wanting to know, where they were bound? Would a literal reading of Section 107(a)(3) allow liability to be imposed on GE? Would the "spirit" of the legislation?

In the *Ward* case, cited in the note above, the court made short shrift of the defendants' contention that they did not "arrange for disposal" of the PCB oil on the roadsides because they merely arranged for an associate to "get rid of" the oil without being aware of *where* he planned to discharge it. "To give the statute the interpretation argued by the *Ward* defendants would allow generators of hazardous wastes to escape liability under CERCLA by closing their eyes to the method in which their hazardous wastes were disposed of. This would encourage exactly the type of blatant disregard for the consequences of hazardous waste disposal that occurred here." 23 ERC at 1398.

In *United States v. A & F Materials Co.*, 582 F.Supp. 842 (S.D. Ill. 1984), McDonnell Douglas Corporation generated a spent caustic solution in the manufacture of jet aircraft. Pursuant to McDonnell Douglas's invitation to bid, the caustic solution was sold for $.072 per gallon to an oil recycling business for use in neutralizing the acidic oil it produced. Despite the sale of the caustic solution (deemed hazardous waste) in a "marketplace" transaction, the court found that McDonnell Douglas "arranged for disposal" of its waste at the oil recycling company. The fact that the disposal was through a sale was irrelevant. To the court, "the relevant inquiry is *who decided* to place the waste into the hands of a particular facility." 582 F.Supp. at 845. For McDonnell Douglas, the arrangement served the purpose of disposal.

In *A & F Materials*, the court distinguished *United States v. Westinghouse Electric Co.*, 14 ELR 20483 (S.D. Mo. 1983). There Monsanto manufactured PCBs which it sold to Westinghouse for use as an insulator in electrical equipment. The fact that Westinghouse subsequently dumped equipment containing some of these PCBs in a landfill was not enough to make Monsanto liable in a third-party complaint filed by Westinghouse. Monsanto was held not to have "arranged for disposal," but to have made a bona fide sale of a commercial product. A critical distinction to the *A & F Materials* court was that Monsanto did not arrange to have the PCB-laden appliances placed in the landfill; Westinghouse did. To Monsanto, the sale of the PCBs were for Westinghouse's use in manufacturing.

In *Missouri v. Independent Petrochemical Corp.*, 22 ERC 1167 (E.D. Mo. 1985), the defendant arranged to have dioxin disposed of at one facility from which it was subsequently removed (apparently without the defendant's involvement) and deposited at a second facility. When the state sought to impose liability on the defendant for costs of cleaning up the second site, the defendant maintained that the state had failed to state a claim because it had not alleged that defendant had arranged for disposal at the site from which there was a release. Rather than deciding the issue of whether or not a defendant under Section 107 had to have arranged for disposal at the particular facility at which the release resulted in the incurrence of response costs, the court used more facile reasoning and held that a "release" from the first site occurred when the dioxin was transported to and disposed of at the second site. Thus the state was entitled to recover its costs of cleaning up the site that was the "depository of the first release." 22 ERC at 1168.

Can you distill from these cases any single guiding principle as to when a generator will or will not be deemed to have "arranged for disposal" at a facility? For a very good analysis of the issue, see Comment, *"Arranging For Disposal" Under CERCLA: When is a Generator Liable?* 15 ELR 10160 (1985).

3. On the question of whether a plaintiff bringing an action under Section 107 has to provide sixty days notice to defendants, the technical reading of the statute in the *General Electric* case seems to be correct: the notice provision in Section 112 seems to apply on its face only to claims *against the Fund.* This result, however, is so contrary to holdings concerning the notice requirements in the citizen-suit provisions of other federal environmental legislation (although their wording is significantly different) that cautious attorneys bringing actions under Section 107 should still provide sixty days notice to potentially liable parties prior to filing suit. The view of the overwhelming majority of courts is that the notice requirements in the citizen-suit provisions of the Clean Air Act, the Clean Water Act, the Surface Mining Act, RCRA, etc., are jurisdictional; and it is unforgiveable to be poured out of court on such grounds midway through a lawsuit. *See Walls v. Waste Resource Corp.*, 761 F.2d 311 (6th Cir. 1985), in which the court upheld dismissal of claims asserting violations of RCRA and the Clean Water Act for plaintiffs' failure to give the required sixty days notice, while it left open the question whether the notice provision in Section 112(a) of CERCLA applied to private cost recovery actions under Section 107.

New York v. Shore Realty Corp.

759 F.2d 1032 (2d Cir. 1985)

Before FEINBERG, Chief Judge, OAKES and
NEWMAN, Circuit Judges.

OAKES, Circuit Judge:

This case involves several novel questions
about the scope of the Comprehensive Environmental Response, Compensation, and Liability
Act of 1980 ("CERCLA") and the interplay
between that statute and New York public nuisance law.***

On February 29, 1984, the State of New
York brought suit against Shore Realty Corp.
("Shore") and Donald LeoGrande, its officer
and stockholder, to clean up a hazardous waste
disposal site at One Shore Road, Glenwood
Landing, New York, which Shore had acquired
for land development purposes. At the time of
the acquisition, LeoGrande knew that hazardous waste was stored on the site and that
cleanup would be expensive, though neither
Shore nor LeoGrande had participated in the
generation or transportation of the nearly
700,000 gallons of hazardous waste now on the
premises.*** On October 15, 1984, the district
court granted the State's motion for partial
summary judgment. Apparently relying at
least in part on CERCLA, it directed by permanent injunction that Shore and LeoGrande
remove the hazardous waste stored on the
property, subject to monitoring by the State,
and held them liable for the State's "response
costs." In the alternative the court based the
injunction on a finding that the Shore Road site
was a public nuisance. Following a remand by
this court on December 14, 1984, the district
court on January 11, 1985, stated with more
particularity the undisputed material facts
underlying its decision finding defendants liable for the State's response costs and clarifying
its earlier decision by basing the injunction
solely on state public nuisance law. The court
also modified its earlier decision by suggesting
that CERCLA does not authorize injunctive
relief in this case.

*　　*　　*

FACTS

*　　*　　*

LeoGrande incorporated Shore solely for
the purpose of purchasing the Shore Road
property. All corporate decisions and actions
were made, directed, and controlled by him. By
contract dated July 14, 1983, Shore agreed to
purchase the 3.2 acre site, a small peninsula
surrounded on three sides by the waters of
Hempstead Harbor and Mott Cove, for condominium development. Five large tanks in a field
in the center of the site hold most of some
700,000 gallons of hazardous chemicals located
there, though there are six smaller tanks both
above and below ground containing hazardous
waste, as well as some empty tanks, on the
property. The tanks are connected by pipe to a
tank truck loading rack and dockage facilities
for loading by barge. Four roll-on/roll-off containers and one tank truck trailer hold additional waste. And before June 15, 1984, one of
the two dilapidated masonry warehouses on
the site contained over 400 drums of chemicals
and contaminated solids, many of which were
corroded and leaking.[3]

It is beyond dispute that the tanks and
drums contain "hazardous substances" within
the meaning of CERCLA. 42 U.S.C. § 9601(14).
The substances involved—including benzene,
dichlorobenzenes, ethyl benzene, tetrachlo-
roethylene, trichloroethylene, 1,1,1-trichlo-
roethene, chlordane, polychlorinated biphenyls
(commonly known as PCBs), and bis (2-ethy-
lhexyl) phthalate—are toxic, in some cases carcinogenic, and dangerous by way of contact,
inhalation, or ingestion. These substances are

---

[3] When these drums concededly were "bursting and
leaking," Shore employees asked the State to enter
the site, inspect it, and take steps to mitigate the
"life-threatening crisis situation." Pursuant to stipu-
lation and order entered on June 15, 1984, Shore
began removing the drums. Some may still remain at
the site.

present at the site in various combinations, some of which may cause the toxic effect to be synergistic.

The purchase agreement provided that it could be voided by Shore without penalty if after conducting an environmental study Shore had decided not to proceed. LeoGrande was fully aware that the tenants, Applied Environmental Services, Inc., and Hazardous Waste Disposal, Inc., were then operating — illegally, it may be noted—a hazardous waste storage facility on the site. Shore's environmental consultant, WTM Management Corporation ("WTM"), prepared a detailed report in July, 1983, incorporated in the record and relied on by the district court for its findings. The report concluded that over the past several decades "the facility ha[d] received little if any preventive maintenance, the tanks (above ground and below ground), pipeline, loading rack, fire extinguishing system, and warehouse have deteriorated." WTM found that there had been several spills of hazardous waste at the site, including at least one large spill in 1978. Though there had been some attempts at cleanup, the WTM testing revealed that hazardous substances, such as benzene, were still leaching into the groundwater and the waters of the bay immediately adjacent to the bulkhead abutting Hempstead Harbor. After a site visit on July 18, 1983, WTM reported firsthand on the sorry state of the facility, observing, among other things, "seepage from the bulkhead," "corrosion" on all the tanks, signs of possible leakage from some of the tanks, deterioration of the pipeline and loading rack, and fifty to one hundred fifty-five gallon drums containing contaminated earth in one of the warehouses. The report concluded that if the current tenants "close up the operation and leave the material at the site," the owners would be left with a "potential time bomb." WTM estimated that the cost of environmental cleanup and monitoring would range from $650,000 to over $1 million before development could begin. After receiving this report Shore sought a waiver from the State Department of Environmental Conservation ("DEC") of liability as landowners for the disposal of the haz-

ardous waste stored at the site. Although the DEC denied the waiver, Shore took title on October 13, 1983, and obtained certain rights over against the tenants, whom it subsequently evicted on January 5, 1984.

Nevertheless, between October 13, 1983, and January 5, 1984, nearly 90,000 gallons of hazardous chemicals were added to the tanks. And during a state inspection on January 3, 1984, it became evident that the deteriorating and leaking drums of chemicals referred to above had also been brought onto the site. Needless to say, the tenants did not clean up the site before they left. Thus, conditions when Shore employees first entered the site were as bad as or worse than those described in the WTM report. As LeoGrande admitted by affidavit, "the various storage tanks, pipelines and connections between these storage facilities were in a bad state of repair." While Shore claims to have made some improvements, such as sealing all the pipes and valves and continuing the cleanup of the damage from earlier spills, Shore did nothing about the hundreds of thousands of gallons of hazardous waste standing in deteriorating tanks. In addition, although a growing number of drums were leaking hazardous substances, Shore essentially ignored the problem until June, 1984. *See supra* note 3.

On September 19, 1984, a DEC inspector observed one of the large tanks, which held over 300,000 gallons of hazardous materials, with rusting floor plates and tank walls, a pinhole leak, and a four-foot line of corrosion along one of the weld lines. On three other tanks, flakes of corroded metal "up to the size and thickness of a dime" were visible at the floorplate level.*** In addition, defendants do not contest that Shore employees lack the knowledge to maintain safely the quantity of hazardous chemicals on the site. And, because LeoGrande has no intention of operating a hazardous waste storage facility, Shore has not and will not apply for a permit to do so. Nor do defendants contest that the State incurred certain costs in assessing the conditions at the site and supervising the removal of the drums of hazardous waste.

CERCLA

*   *   *

CERCLA authorizes the federal government to respond in several ways. EPA can use Superfund resources to clean up hazardous waste sites and spills. 42 U.S.C. § 9611. The National Contingency Plan ("NCP"), prepared by EPA pursuant to CERCLA, *id.* § 9605, governs cleanup efforts by "establish[ing] procedures and standards for responding to releases of hazardous substances." At the same time, EPA can sue for reimbursement of cleanup costs from any responsible parties it can locate, *id.* § 9607, allowing the federal government to respond immediately while later trying to shift financial responsibility to others.*** In addition, CERCLA authorizes EPA to seek an injunction in federal district court to force a responsible party to clean up any site or spill that presents an imminent and substantial danger to public health or welfare or the environment. 42 U.S.C. § 9606(a).***

Congress clearly did not intend, however, to leave clean up under CERCLA solely in the hands of the federal government. A state or political subdivision may enter into a contract or cooperative agreement with EPA, whereby both may take action on a cost-sharing basis. 42 U.S.C. § 9604(c), (d). And states, like EPA, can sue responsible parties for remedial and removal costs if such efforts are "not inconsistent with" the NCP. *Id.* § 9607(a)(4)(A). While CERCLA expressly does not preempt state law, *id.* § 9614(a), it precludes "recovering compensation for the same removal costs or damages or claims" under both CERCLA and state or other federal laws, *id.* § 9614(b), and prohibits states from requiring contributions to any fund "the purpose of which is to pay compensation for claims . . . which may be compensated under" CERCLA, *id.* § 9614(c). Moreover, "any . . . person" who is acting consistently with the requirements of the NCP may recover "necessary costs of response." Finally, responsible parties are liable for "damages for injury to, destruction of, or loss of natural resources, including the reasonable costs of assessing such injury, destruction, or loss

resulting from such a release." 42 U.S.C. § 9607(a)(4)(C).

Congress intended that responsible parties be held strictly liable, even though an explicit provision for strict liability was not included in the compromise. Section 9601(32) provides that "liability" under CERCLA "shall be construed to be the standard of liability" under section 311 of the Clean Water Act, 33 U.S.C. § 1321, which courts have held to be strict liability***. *** Strict liability under CERCLA, however, is not absolute; there are defenses for causation solely by an act of God, an act of war, or acts or omissions of a third party other than an employee or agent of the defendant or one whose act or omission occurs in connection with a contractual relationship with the defendant. 42 U.S.C. § 9607(b).

DISCUSSION

A. *Liability for Response Costs Under CERCLA*

We hold that the district court properly awarded the State response costs under section 9607(a)(4)(A). The State's costs in assessing the conditions of the site and supervising the removal of the drums of hazardous waste squarely fall within CERCLA's definition of response costs, even though the State is not undertaking to do the removal.***

1. *Covered Persons.* CERCLA holds liable four classes of persons:

(1) the owner and operator of a vessel (otherwise subject to the jurisdiction of the United States) or a facility,[15]

(2) any person who at the time of disposal of any hazardous substance owned or operated any facility at which such hazardous substances were disposed of,

(3) any person who by contract, agreement, or otherwise arranged for disposal or treatment, or arranged with a transporter for transposrt for disposal or treatment, of hazardous sub-

---

[15] CERCLA defines the term "facility" broadly to include any property at which hazardous substances have come to be located. *See* 42 U.S.C. §9601(9).

stances owned or possessed by such person, by any other party or entity, at any facility owned or operated by another party or entity and containing such hazardous substances, and

(4) any person who accepts or accepted any hazardous substances for transport to disposal or treatment facilities or sites selected by such person.

42 U.S.C. § 9607(a). As noted above, section 9607 makes these persons liable, if "there is a release, or a threatened release which causes the incurrence of response costs, of a hazardous substance" from the facility, for, among other things, "all costs of removal or remedial action incurred by the United States Government or a State not inconsistent with the national contingency plan."

Shore argues that it is not covered by section 9607(a)(1) because it neither owned the site at the time of disposal nor caused the presence or the release of the hazardous waste at the facility.*** Shore claims that Congress intended that the scope of section 9607(a)(1) be no greater than that of section 9607(a)(2) and that both should be limited by the "at the time of disposal" language. By extension, Shore argues that both provisions should be interpreted as requiring a showing of causation. We agree with the State, however, that section 9607(a)(1) unequivocally imposes strict liability on the current owner of a facility from which there is a release or threat of release, without regard to causation.

Shore's claims of ambiguity are illusory; section 9607(a)'s structure is clear. Congress intended to cover different classes of persons differently. Section 9607(a)(1) applies to all current owners and operators, while section 9607(a)(2) primarily covers prior owners and operators. Moreover, section 9607(a)(2)'s scope is more limited than that of section 9607(a)(1). Prior owners and operators are liable only if they owned or operated the facility "at the time of disposal of any hazardous substance"; this limitation does not apply to current owners, like Shore.***

Shore's causation argument is also at odds with the structure of the statute. Interpreting section 9607(a)(1) as including a causation requirement makes superfluous the affirmative defenses provided in section 9607(b), each of which carves out from liability an exception based on causation.***

Our interpretation draws further support from the legislative history. Congress specifically rejected including a causation requirement in section 9607(a).***

Furthermore, as the State points out, accepting Shore's arguments would open a huge loophole in CERCLA's coverage. It is quite clear that if the current owner of a site could avoid liability merely by having purchased the site after chemical dumping had ceased, waste sites certainly would be sold, following the cessation of dumping, to new owners who could avoid the liability otherwise required by CERCLA. Congress had well in mind that persons who dump or store hazardous waste sometimes cannot be located or may be deceased or judgmentproof.***

*   *   *

2. *Release or Threat of Release.* We reject Shore's repeated claims that it has put in dispute whether there has been a release or threat of release at the Shore Road site. The State has established that it was responding to "a release, or a threatened release" when it incurred its response costs. We hold that the leaking tanks and pipelines, the continuing leaching and seepage from the earlier spills, and the leaking drums all constitute "releases." Moreover, the corroding and deteriorating tanks, Shore's lack of expertise in handling hazardous waste, and even the failure to license the facility, amount to a threat of release.

In addition, Shore's suggestion that CERCLA does not impose liability for threatened releases is simply frivolous. Section 9607 (a)(4)(A) imposes liability for "all costs of removal or remedial action." The definitions of "removal" and "remedial" explicitly refer to actions "taken in the event of the threat of release of hazardous substances."

3. *The NPL and Consistency with the NCP.* Shore also argues that, because the Shore Road site is not on the NPL [National Properties

List], the State's action is inconsistent with the NCP [National Contingency Plan], and thus Shore cannot be found liable under section 9607(a). This argument is not frivolous. Section 9607(a)(4)(A) states that polluters are liable for response costs "not inconsistent with the national contingency plan." And section 9605, which directs EPA to outline the NCP, includes a provision that requires EPA to publish the NPL. Nevertheless, we hold that inclusion on the NPL is not a requirement for the State to recover its response costs.

The State claims that, while NPL listing may be a requirement for the use of Superfund money, it is not a requisite to liability under section 9607. The State relies on the reasoning of several district courts that have held that liability under section 9607 is independent of the scope of section 9611, which governs the expenditure of Superfund monies, and by extension, section 9604, which governs federal cleanup efforts. *See, e.g., id.; United States v. Northeastern Pharmaceutical & Chemical Co.,* 579 F.Supp. 823, 850-51 (W.D.Mo. 1984) *("NEPACCO"); United States v. Wade,* 577 F.Supp. 1326, 1334-36 (E.D.Pa. 1983). These courts have reasoned that CERCLA authorizes a bifurcated approach to the problem of hazardous waste cleanup, by distinguishing between the scope of direct federal action with Superfund resources and the liability of polluters under section 9607. While implicitly accepting that Superfund monies can be spent only on sites included on the NPL, they conclude that this limitation does not apply to section 9607. And it is true that the relevant limitation on Superfund spending is that it be "consistent with" the NCP, 42 U.S.C. §9604(a), while under section 9607(a)(4)(A), liability is limited to response costs "not inconsistent with" the NCP.***

***Instead of distinguishing between the scope of section 9607 and the scope of section 9604, we hold that NPL listing is not a general requirement under the NCP. We see the NPL as a limitation on remedial, or long-term, actions—as opposed to removal, or short-term, actions—particularly federally funded remedial actions. The provisions requiring the estab-

lishment of NPL criteria and listing appear to limit their own application to remedial actions.***

CERCLA's legislative history also supports our conclusion. Congress did not intend listing on the NPL to be a requisite to all response actions.***

Moreover, limiting the scope of NPL listing as a requirement for response action is consistent with the purpose of CERCLA. The NPL is a relatively short list when compared with the huge number of hazardous waste facilities Congress sought to clean up. And it makes sense for the federal government to limit only those long-term—remedial—efforts that are federally funded. We hold that Congress intended that, while federally funded remedial efforts be focused solely on those sites on the NPL, states have more flexibility when acting on their own.

Finally, we reject Shore's argument that the State's response costs are not recoverable because the State has failed to comply with the NCP by not obtaining EPA authorization, nor making a firm commitment to provide further funding for remedial implementation nor submitting an estimate of costs.*** Shore apparently is arguing that EPA has ruled that the State cannot act on its own and seek liability under CERCLA. We disagree. Congress envisioned states' using their own resources for cleanup and recovering those costs from polluters under section 9607(a)(4)(A). We read section 9607(a)(4)(A)'s requirement of consistency with the NCP to mean that states cannot recover costs inconsistent with the response methods outlined in the NCP.*** Thus, the NCP's requirements concerning collaboration in a joint federal-state cleanup effort are inapplicable where the State is acting on its own.*** Indeed, the kind of action taken here is precisely that envisioned by the regulations.

4. *Affirmative defense.* Shore also claims that it can assert an affirmative defense under CERCLA, which provides a limited exception to liability for a release or threat of release caused solely by

> an act or omission of a third party other than an employee or agent of the defendant, or than one whose act or

omission occurs in connection with a contractual relationship, existing directly or indirectly, with the defendant (except where the sole contractual arrangement arises from a published tariff and acceptance for carriage by a common carrier by rail), if the defendant establishes by a preponderance of the evidence that (a) he exercised due care with respect to the hazardous substance concerned, taking into consideration the characteristics of such hazardous substance, in light of all relevant facts and circumstances, and (b) he took precautions against foreseeable acts or omissions of any such third party and the consequences that could foreseeably result from such acts or omissions.

42 U.S.C. §9607(b)(3). We disagree. Shore argues that it had nothing to do with the transportation of the hazardous substances and that it has exercised due care since taking control of the site. Who the "third part(ies)" Shore claims were responsible is difficult to fathom. It is doubtful that a prior owner could be such, especially the prior owner here, since the acts or omissions referred to in the statute are doubtless those occurring during the ownership or operation of the defendant. Similarly, many of the acts and omissions of the prior tenants/operators fall outside the scope of section 9607(b)(3), because they occurred before Shore owned the property. In addition, we find that Shore cannot rely on the affirmative defense even with respect to the tenants' conduct during the period after Shore closed on the property and when Shore evicted the tenants. Shore was aware of the nature of the tenants' activities before the closing and could readily have foreseen that they would continue to dump hazardous waste at the site. In light of this knowledge, we cannot say that the releases and threats of release resulting of these activities were "caused solely" by the tenants or that Shore "took precautions against" these "foreseeable acts or omissions."

B. *Injunctive Relief Under CERCLA*

Having held Shore liable under CERCLA for the State's response costs, we nevertheless are required to hold that injunctive relief under CERCLA is not available to the State. Essentially, the State urges us to interpret the right of action under section 9607 broadly, claiming that "limiting district court relief [under section 9607] to reimbursement could have a drastic effect upon the implementation of Congress's desire that waste sites be cleaned." Conceding that section 9607 does not explicitly provide for injunctive relief, the State suggests that the court has the inherent power to grant such equitable relief, citing *Hecht Co. v. Bowles*, 321 U.S. 321, 329 (1944).

The statutory scheme, however, shows that Congress did not intend to authorize such relief. Section 9606 expressly authorizes EPA to seek injunctive relief to abate "an actual or threatened release of a hazardous substance from a facility." Implying the authority to seek injunctions under section 9607 would make the express injunctive authority granted in section 9607 surplusage. In addition, the scope of injunctive relief under section 9607 would conflict with the express scope of section 9606. The standard for seeking abatement under section 9606 is more narrow than the standard of liability under section 9607. Section 9606 authorizes injunctive relief only where EPA "determines that there may be an imminent and substantial endangerment to the public health or welfare or the environment." Section 9607 contains no such limitation.***

If there were any doubt about the statutory language, the legislative history would compel us to reject the State's argument. Congress specifically declined to provide states with a right to injunctive relief.***

C. *Common Law of Public Nuisance*

In challenging the decision below, Shore fails to distinguish between a public nuisance and a private nuisance. The former "is an offense against the State and is subject to abatement or prosecution on application of the proper governmental agency" and "consists of conduct or omissions which offend, interfere with or cause damage to the public in the exercise of rights common to all . . . in a manner such as to . . . endanger or injure the property, health, safety or comfort of a considerable number of persons." The latter, however, "threatens one person or a relatively few. . ., an essential feature being an interference with the use or enjoyment of land . . . . It is actionable by the individual person or persons whose rights have been disturbed."***

Under New York law, Shore, as a landowner, is subject to liability for either a public or private nuisance on its property upon learning of the nuisance and having a reasonable opportunity to abate it. As noted in the *Restatement (Second) of Torts* §839 comment d (1979) [hereinafter cited as *Restatement*]:

> [L]iability [of a possessor of land] is not based upon responsibility for the creation of the harmful condition, but upon the fact that he has exclusive control over the land and the things done upon it and should have the responsibility of taking reasonable measures to remedy conditions on it that are a source of harm to others. Thus a vendee . . . of land upon which a harmful physical condition exists may be liable under the rule here stated for failing to abate it after he takes possession, even though it was created by his vendor, lessor or other person and even though he had no part in its creation.

It is immaterial therefore that other parties placed the chemicals on this site; Shore purchased it with knowledge of its condition—indeed of the approximate cost of cleaning it up—and with an opportunity to clean up the site. LeoGrande knew that the hazardous waste was present without the consent of the State or its DEC, but failed to take reasonable steps to abate the condition. Moreover, Shore is liable for maintenance of a *public* nuisance irrespective of negligence or fault. Nor is there any requirement that the State prove actual, as opposed to threatened, harm from the nuisance in order to obtain abatement. Finally, the State has standing to bring suit to abate such a nuisance "in its role as guardian of the environment."

We also reject Shore's argument that its maintenance of the Shore Road site does not constitute a public nuisance. We have no doubt that the release or threat of release of hazardous waste into the environment unreasonably infringes upon a public right and thus is a public nuisance as a matter of New York law*** ***

The district court could have also found that Shore is maintaining a public nuisance under two alternative theories. Shore's continuing violations of N.Y. Envtl. Conserv. Law §27-0913(1) (not having a permit to store or dispose of hazardous waste), and of *id.* § 27-0914(1) (possessing hazardous waste without authorization), if not of *id.* §27-0914(2) (disposing of hazardous waste without authorization), constitute a nuisance per se. And while we recognize that determining whether an activity is abnormally dangerous depends on the circumstances, a review of the undisputed facts*** convinces us that a New York court would find as a matter of law that Shore's maintenance of the site—for example, allowing corroding tanks to hold hundreds of thousands of gallons of hazardous waste—constitutes abnormally dangerous activity and thus constitutes a public nuisance.

*   *   *

Judgment affirmed.

NOTES

1. Do you find anything remarkable in this decision, one of the very few thus far to have made it through a circuit court?

Was it not predictable, given the language of Section 107(a)(1) and district court precedent, that the liability of the present owner of the site would be upheld, even though it played no part in the placement of the waste on the site?

A more difficult issue was presented in *Cadillac Fairview/California, Inc. v. Dow Chemical Co.*, 21 ERC 1108 (C.D. Cal. 1984). There the court granted a motion to dismiss a claim brought under Section 107 against a development company who was not alleged to have been an owner at any time when the waste disposals complained of were made, but was alleged merely to have owned the site *after* the disposals and prior to the plaintiff's present ownership. Such intervening ownership was held not to be within the coverage of either Section 107(a)(1) or (2).

2. Some difference of judicial opinion remains as to whether a site must be on the national priorities list (the "NPL") in order for Section 107(a) to be applicable. *Compare* the two different holdings by federal district courts in California in 1984 in the context of suits by private parties under Section 107(a)(4)(B): *Cadillac Fairview/California, Inc. v. Dow Chemical Co.*, 21 ERC 1108 (C.D. Cal. 1984), in which NPL listing was held to be a prerequisite; *Pinole Point Properties, Inc. v. Bethlehem Steel Corp.*, 596 F. Supp. 283 (N.D. Cal. 1984), in which NPL listing was held not to be required. *Pinole Point* and *Shore Realty* seem to have the better view: NPL listing is a prerequisite for expenditures of money from the Superfund under Sections 111 and 112, but not for claims against responsible parties under Section 107.

3. In the same vein, most federal district court decisions support the Second Circuit's holding that EPA authorization of the states' cleanup activities, using their own resources rather than Superfund money, is unnecessary. *See Fishel v. Westinghouse Electric Corp.*, 23 ERC 1329 (M.D. Pa. 1985); *Homart Development Co. v. Bethlehem Steel Corp.*, 22 ERC 1357 (N.D. Cal. 1984); *Pinole Point Properties, Inc. v. Bethlehem Steel Corp.*, 596 F. Supp. 283 (N.D. Cal. 1984). *But compare Wickland Oil Terminals v. Asarco, Inc.*, 590 F. Supp. 72 (N.D. Cal. 1984); *Bulk Distribution Centers, Inc. v. Monsanto Co.*, 21 ERC 1080 (S.D. Fla. 1984). (All of these decisions, pro and con recovery without EPA authorization, involved private claims under Section 107(a)(4)(B).)

Does a stronger case for prior EPA approval exist for costs associated with "remedial actions," as distinct from "removal actions"? *See Artesian Water Co. v. New Castle County*, 22 ERC 1345 (D. Del. 1985).

4. Do you agree with the Second Circuit that the "third party" affirmative defense expressed in Section 107(b) was not available to Shore — even with respect to the tenants' conduct after Shore acquired the property? What if Shore had not been aware that its tenants were bringing hazardous wastes onto the property?

5. Do you agree that injunctive relief was not available to the State under Section 107? Remember that only the federal government may seek injunctive relief under the "imminent hazard" provision in Section 106, as it is presently worded. Could a state now use the amended citizen-suit provision in Section 7002(a)(1)(B) of RCRA to accomplish the same purpose? A bill recently passed by the House of Representatives for the reauthorization of CERCLA contains a provision allowing citizens to sue in federal court to abate imminent dangers.

6. Obviously, no state or private party claimant should overlook claims for damages or injunctive relief arising under state statutory or common law. Section 114 (a) of CERCLA expressly preserves such state causes of action, limited only by the prohibition in Section 114(b) against obtaining *double* compensation for damages or removal costs by invoking both state and federal law.

Exxon Corp. v. Hunt
— U.S. — (March 10, 1986)

JUSTICE MARSHALL delivered the opinion of the Court.

The question for our determination is whether §114(c) of the Comprehensive Environmental Response, Compensation, and Liability Act of 1980 pre-empts the New Jersey Spill Compensation and Control Act, N. J. Stat. Ann. §§58:10-23.11 to 58:10-23.11z (West 1982 and Supp. 1985) (Spill Act). We conclude that the Spill Act is pre-empted in part.

I

In 1977 the New Jersey Legislature enacted the Spill Act to respond to the problem of hazardous substance release. Finding that oil spills threatened the health and beauty of the State's natural resources, and that leaks of hazardous chemicals from disposal sites presented a great risk to the public, the legislature intended the Spill Act to protect the citizens and environment of New Jersey through prevention and cleanup of spills and other releases. Those efforts are financed by an excise tax levied upon major petroleum and chemical facilities within the State. The money collected goes into a permanent fund known as the "Spill Fund." The Spill Fund may spend money to clean up releases of hazardous substances, to compensate third parties for certain economic losses sustained as a result of such releases, and to pay administrative and research costs.

In 1980 Congress enacted CERCLA in response to similar concerns. CERCLA imposes an excise tax on petroleum and other specified chemicals. The Act establishes a trust fund, commonly known as "Superfund," 87.5% of which is financed through the excise tax, and the remainder through general revenues. Superfund money may be used to clean up releases of hazardous substances and for certain other purposes. Unlike the Spill Act, CERCLA does not include oil spills within its definition of hazardous substance releases, nor is Superfund money available to compensate private parties for economic harms that result from discharges of hazardous substances. Rather, it seeks to facilitate government cleanup of hazardous waste discharges and pre-

vention of future releases. There are two primary purposes for which the Superfund money may be spent—to finance "governmental response," and to pay "claims." See §111(a) of CERCLA, 42 U. S. C. §9611(a). Governmental response consists of "removal," or short-term cleanup, §9601(23), and "remedial action," or measures to achieve a "permanent remedy" to a particular hazardous waste problem, §9601(24). Claims are demands for reimbursement made upon the Superfund, and also come in two types. One type of claim is a demand by "any other person" for costs incurred pursuant to the federal plan for cleanup of hazardous substances, known as the "national contingency plan." §9611(a)(2). Thus, Superfund may reimburse private parties only to the extent that their cleanup activities are expressly authorized by the Federal Government. The second type of claim is a demand by the Federal or a State government for compensation for damages to natural resources belonging to that government. §9611(a)(3). Superfund money may not be used to pay for injury to persons or property caused by hazardous wastes, except for payment to the Federal and State Governments for their natural resource losses.

This litigation concerns §114(c) of CERCLA, 42 U. S. C. §9614(c), which provides:

"Except as provided in this chapter, no person may be required to contribute to any fund, the purpose of which is to pay compensation for claims for any costs of response or damages or claims which may be compensated under this subchapter. Nothing in this section shall preclude any State from using general revenues for such a fund, or from imposing a tax or fee upon any person or upon any substance in order to finance the purchase or prepositioning of hazardous substance response equipment or other preparations for the response to a release of hazardous substances which affects such State."

Clearly, this provision is meant to forbid the States from imposing taxes to finance certain types of funds. The issue in this case is whether the New Jersey Spill Fund is, in whole or in part, the type of fund that §114(c) pre-empts.

Appellants are corporations that have paid the Spill Act tax since its inception. After unsuccessful attempts to litigate the issue in the federal courts, appellants brought suit in the New Jersey Tax Court against New Jersey and certain of its officials (collectively New Jersey), seeking a declaratory judgment and a refund of taxes paid pursuant to the Spill Act. Appellants claimed that the New Jersey tax was invalid in its entirety under §114(c) and the Supremacy Clause. The Tax Court entered summary judgment for New Jersey***.***

The New Jersey Appellate Division affirmed, as did the New Jersey Supreme Court, 97 N. J. 526, 481 A. 2d 271 (1984). The latter court, like the Tax Court, concluded that "the Spill Fund tax . . . is not preempted by section 114(c) of Superfund insofar as Spill Fund is used to compensate hazardous-waste cleanup costs and related claims that are either not covered or not actually paid under Superfund." *Id.*, at 544, 481 A. 2d, at 281.***

II

This is an express pre-emption case; appellants claim that the plain language of §114(c) forbids state taxation of the type the Spill Act imposes. ***

Section 114(c), unfortunately, is not a model of legislative draftsmanship. The critical language, "no person may be required to contribute to any fund, the purpose of which is to pay compensation for claims for any costs of response or damages or claims which may be compensated under this subchapter," is at best inartful and at worst redundant.***

III

Our task, then, must proceed in three parts. First, we must determine what class of expenses is encompassed within the phrase "costs of response or damages or claims." Then, because at least some of those expenses are covered by §114(c) only to the extent that they "may be compensated" by Superfund, we must determine the meaning of that phrase as well. Finally, if we find an overlap between

§114(c)'s prohibitions and the Spill Act's provisions, we must hold the latter pre-empted.

A

Both parties agree as to the first question. Each concludes that the words "costs of response or damages or claims" are to be read as a unit, and the entire phrase is modified by the phrase "which may be compensated under this subchapter." However, the Solicitor General, appearing on behalf of the United States as *amicus curiae*, adopts a contrary position. He contends that §114(c) should be read to prohibit funds whose purpose is to pay "compensation for [a] claims for any costs of response or damages[,] or [b] claims which may be compensated under this subchapter." Under the Solicitor General's view, therefore, any expense that fits CERCLA's definitions of a "claim" for "costs of response" or "damages" may not be paid by a state fund supported by special taxes, whether or not that expenditure "may" be paid by Superfund.[7] Because "costs of response" covers essentially the entire spectrum of cleanup expenses, see 42 U. S. C. §9604, the Solicitor General's reading of the pre-emptive scope of §114(c) might seem very broad at first reading.

The wide sweep of the Solicitor General's position, however, is tempered considerably by his interpretation of the term "claim." CERCLA defines a "claim" as "a demand in writing for a sum certain." §9601(4). Under the Solicitor General's view, only a private party's demand upon a state fund or Superfund for reimbursement for that party's own cleanup expenses constitutes a "claim." Any State or Federal Government use of a special fund is merely a governmental expenditure, and not the payment of a "claim." Because each of the two clauses created by the Solicitor General's parsing of §114(c) begins with the word

---

[7]An example of a "cost of response" that would not be eligible for Superfund compensation would be the cost of a private party's cleanup efforts if that party did not receive prior authorization from the Federal Government or its agent, see 42 U. S. C. §9611(a)(2). Under the Solicitor General's reading of §114(c), a state fund could not reimburse those costs even though it is clear that they would not be eligible for Superfund money.

"claims," he argues, that section does not prohibit *any* state fund expenditures for a state government's own cleanup efforts. It prohibits only expenditures to reimburse private parties. Were we to accept the Solicitor General's reading of §114(c), therefore, New Jersey could freely tax appellants to pay for its own cleanup costs, even if Superfund might otherwise pay those costs. New Jersey could not, however, tax appellants to pay for third-party cleanup costs, whether or not Superfund might bear those costs. Similarly, New Jersey could not use the Spill Fund to pay for any party's "damages," defined by CERCLA to mean loss of natural resources, even though Superfund covers only "damages" suffered by governments.

* * *

One problem with the Solicitor General's view is that the distinction between a government's own cleanup costs, on the one hand, and "claims," on the other, has not been so consistent throughout CERCLA's history as the Solicitor General suggests.***

* * *

A second reason for rejecting the Solicitor General's argument proceeds from the wording of §114(b). That section provides: "Any person who receives compensation for removal costs or damages or claims pursuant to this chapter shall be precluded from recovering compensation" for the same expenses under any other state or federal law. We consider the similarity between §114(b)'s phrase "removal costs or damages or claims" and §114(c)'s phrase "costs of response or damages or claims" to suggest that Congress intended for the three terms to be read as a unit. When read in conjunction with §111(a), which provides that Superfund money may be spent on payment of governmental response costs, natural resource damages, and third party cleanup claims, it seems likely that Congress intended the phrase "removal costs or damages or claims" to provide a shorthand for the authorized uses of Superfund. This strongly undercuts the Solicitor General's approach, because it suggests that Congress envisioned state funds paying "claims" for *all* of the authorized

uses of Superfund, including state cleanup costs.

***On the balance, then, we conclude that the use of the term "compensation for claims" in §114(c) represents an instance of inartful drafting rather than the intentional drawing of a subtle distinction.

B

Having adopted the parties' view of the interpretation of "costs of response or damages or claims," we must now determine the proper interpretation of the phrase "which may be compensated under this subchapter." The New Jersey Supreme Court read that language very narrowly, concluding that it covered only expenses that are actually paid by Superfund. Appellants, adopting a broader interpretation of "may be compensated," contend that §114(c) pre-empts any fund that is intended, in whole or in part, to pay for the same types of expenses that may be paid by Superfund.

* * *

We find these arguments [of Appellants] persuasive. Congress has already banned double compensation in §114(b), and there is accordingly no reason to read "may be compensated" to mean "is compensated." The contrary view adopted by the New Jersey Supreme Court renders the first sentence of §114(c) surplusage. The language of §114(c) permitting the States to use general revenues for such a fund would also be meaningless under such a narrow reading.

C

Nevertheless, New Jersey contends that the decision below, with one minor modification, is correct. New Jersey concedes that §114(c) is not restricted to cases in which Superfund actually disburses money. New Jersey argues, however, that §114(c) applies only when Superfund pays a claim or *would have* paid the claim had it not already been paid by the state fund.***

New Jersey emphasizes the limited scope of CERCLA. The federal statute does not cover several broad areas—for example, payment for nongovernmental property losses and costs arising from oil spills—that are important aspects of hazardous substances control, and are covered by New Jersey's Spill Act. Moreover, Congress was well aware that the funding level of Superfund was and is insufficient to clean up more than a few of the most dangerous hazardous waste disposal sites. These facts, New Jersey claims, suggest that Congress recognized that Superfund would not solve all of the Nation's hazardous waste problems, and that the States would have to continue their own efforts. It follows that Congress did not intend to pre-empt state taxation to pay for cleanup efforts that the Federal Government was unable to undertake because of unavailability of funds, even though such efforts were of the type that are eligible for Superfund money.

That Congress has not chosen the most comprehensive or efficient method of attacking the problem of hazardous substances discharges, however, is not reason to depart from the language of the statute. Moreover, while we agree with New Jersey that the overall purpose of a statute is a useful referent when trying to decipher ambiguous statutory language, remedying the Nation's toxic waste problems as effectively as possible was not the sole policy choice reflected in CERCLA. Previous attempts to enact a comprehensive hazardous substance response bill were defeated in part because of opposition by the affected industries. It seems clear that the decision to enact a pre-emption provision resulted in part from Congress' concern about the potentially adverse effects of overtaxation on the competitiveness of the American petrochemical industry. That consideration, whether wise or not, cautions against our concluding that Congress would not have wanted to hinder state attempts to clean up hazardous substances in any way.

New Jersey contends, however, that its reading of §114(c) does no violence to the statutory language. It argues that we must look not only to the provisions of CERCLA, but also to the amount of money available in Superfund, before deciding whether a particular expense "may be compensated" by Superfund. New Jersey argues that the availability of Superfund money is sufficiently low, as a practical matter, that only projects that have been actually approved, or are almost certain to be approved, can be termed "eligible" for Superfund financing, and then only to the extent of the approved funding.

We cannot agree. To say that the only expenses that "may be compensated" are those that *are* compensated twists both language and logic further that we are willing to go. Had that been Congress' intent, it surely would have said so in plainer terms than those of §114(c).

Comparisons with the prior bills reinforces our reading of the statute.***

We also fail to find sufficient support for New Jersey's position in the sparse legislative history of the Stafford-Randolph substitute bill that became CERCLA.***

IV

Having decided that "may be compensated" should be given its ordinary meaning, we must define the category of expenses that may be compensated by Superfund. Fortunately, CERCLA itself furnishes an appropriate test. Section 105(8)(B) of CERCLA, 42 U. S. C. §9605(8)(B), requires the President to revise the National Contingency Plan (NCP) to reflect CERCLA's provisions. As part of that revision, the President must create and revise annually a list of sites most in need of federal efforts, now known as the National Priorities List. The NCP currently specifies that removal, or immediate cleanup, will be financed by Superfund only in emergency situations, see 40 CFR §300.65 (1985). Remedial action will be financed only for sites on the National Priorities List, *id.*, §300.68(a). Finally, the Environmental Protection Agency, pursuant to the NCP, has proposed criteria for the use of Superfund money for natural resource claims. See 50 Fed. Reg. 9593 (1985). The NCP, therefore, provides criteria that determine what expenses, at which sites, will be eligible for Superfund money. We therefore conclude that the NCP provides the appropriate measure of whether a given expenditure constitutes "costs of response or damages or claims which may be compensated" by Superfund.

CERCLA also provides that a State must agree to pay at least 10% of the cost of any remedial action for a hazardous waste site within the State. 42 U. S. C. §9604(c)(3)(C). This state share is, by definition, not eligible for Superfund money. We therefore conclude that the 10% state share is not a cost that "may be compensated" by Superfund.

To the extent that appellants argue that §114(c) covers any cleanup or remedial expenses, whether or not eligible for Superfund compensation, we must reject their position. While we have acknowledged Congress' desire to spare the involved industries from excessive taxation, we must assume that Congress meant the words "which may be compensated under this subchapter" to have some meaning. The only plausible explanation for the use of that phrase is that Congress intended to prohibit state funds that covered Superfund-eligible expenses.***

Our remaining task is to determine whether the "purpose" of the Spill Fund is to pay costs that we have found to fall within the scope of pre-emption. As we have explained above, the Spill Fund may be used for six purposes: (1) to finance governmental cleanup of hazardous waste sites; (2) to reimburse third parties for cleanup costs; (3) to compensate third parties for damage resulting from hazardous substance discharges; (4) to pay personnel and equipment costs; (5) to administer the fund itself; and (6) to conduct research. Of these, the latter four are clearly beyond the scope of CERCLA, and are therefore not covered by §114(c). The first two are within the scope of CERCLA, except to the extent that they are intended to provide the 10% state share of remedial costs. Those parts of the statute that permit Spill Fund expenditures beyond this state share for remedial costs for sites on the National Priority List, or for removal costs that are eligible for Superfund compensation under the terms of the NCP, are pre-empted by §114(c).

New Jersey argues, finally, that after the enactment of CERCLA, or at least after the publication of the National Priorities List, all Spill Fund expenditures for purposes (1) and (2) above have been for non-Superfund eligible sites, and therefore are for nonpre-empted purposes. To the extent that the Spill Act permits taxation to support pre-empted expenditures, however, it cannot stand. State legislation is invalid "to the extent that it actually conflicts with federal law," *Pacific Gas & Electric Co.* v. *Energy Resources Commission,* 461 U.S. 190, 204 (1983), and such a conflict has been demonstrated in this case. We leave to the New Jersey Supreme Court the state-law question whether, or to what extent, the non-pre-empted provisions of the statute are severable from the pre-empted provisions. See *Exxon Corp.* v. *Eagerton,* 462 U.S. 176, 196–197 (1983). We decline the dissent's invitation to hold that the Spill Act is valid in its entirety because a substantial portion of its purposes are permissible. Such a holding would be an open invitation to the States to flout federal law by including valid provisions within clearly invalid statutes.

V

To the extent that the New Jersey Supreme Court held that the Spill Act could constitutionally impose a tax to support expenditures for purposes that we have identified above as non-pre-empted, that court's judgment is affirmed. To the extent it held that Spill Act could constitutionally impose a tax to support expenditures for purposes that we have identified as pre-empted, its judgment is reversed and the case is remanded for further proceedings not inconsistent with this opinion.

NOTES

1. Justice Stevens, dissenting (alone), accused the Court of "resolving a lawsuit that has not been filed"—deciding what *expenditures* could properly be made from the New Jersey Spill

Fund—without providing any hint of what impact its conclusion of "partial preemption" would have on appellants' suit for a tax refund. Was this a valid criticism?

2. If the New Jersey Supreme Court on remand holds that the non-preempted provisions of the statute are severable from the preempted provisions, is any tax refund due the appellants?

3. For Justice Stevens, the fact that the tax monies in New Jersey's Spill Fund might be spent on entirely valid, non-preempted purposes should have been sufficient to sustain the tax—leaving to another day a decision on the preemption of state spending of fund monies on activities compensable under Superfund. He would have held contributions to state funds preempted "only if their sole purpose—or perhaps their only non-trivial purpose—was to compensate for claims covered by Superfund." Since this plainly was not the case for the New Jersey fund, he would have upheld the validity of the state's levying contributions to it. Would Justice Stevens' approach have left Section 114(c) with any significant effect?

4. If the New Jersey Supreme Court holds the preempted provisions in the Spill Act severable, for what purposes may the Spill Fund monies be used (other than the four statutory purposes recognized by the Court, payment of costs and damages arising from oil spills, and providing the 10% state share of remedial costs)?

May the state funds be used to reimburse private parties for their cleanup costs incurred without prior authorization from EPA? *See* footnote 7. May they be used by the state to finance "remedial action" at a site not on the NPL? May they be used to cover state or private response costs which are inconsistent with the NCP? If your answers are affirmative to these questions, do you find anything strange about such a statutory scheme?

5. The problem for New Jersey, of course, is that under this decision it is prohibited from using its Spill Fund to pay for cleanup costs or natural resources damages when recovery from the federal Superfund is *purely theoretically* available—even though the level of the Superfund is such that the likelihood of actual compensation may be virtually nil. Do you think that Congress intended such a result? Would it seem more reasonable if Congress increased the size of the Superfund?

6. Hopefully, by the time you read this, Congress will have passed CERCLA reauthorization legislation containing some significant amendments. Present indications are that the amended legislation will set mandatory cleanup schedules for EPA, include a broad citizen-suit provision, and substantially increase the size of the Superfund. One major issue separating the two houses of Congress is the method of financing the fund. The House bill would finance the bulk of a $10.3 billion five-year fund by increasing the present tax on basic chemicals and oil. The Senate bill would raise most of the revenue for a $7.5 billion fund through a general excise tax on manufacturers. Which financing method seems fairer to you?

Another conflict in the different versions of HR 2005 passed by the House and Senate concerns the creation of an oil spill liability fund. The House bill would establish a separate fund to compensate persons harmed by oil spills from ships or offshore production facilities which would be financed by a special tax on oil. The Senate bill has no similar provision, and dispute exists over the extent to which the state oil spill liability funds should be preempted.

Even though the original Superfund program expired at the end of September, 1985, six months later House and Senate conferees still have not been able to resolve all their differences. In March, 1986, both houses responded to EPA's pleas to avoid a total shutdown of the hazardous waste cleanup program and passed a stopgap funding measure signed by the President on April 1 which provided $150 million to keep it operating through May. The hope was that this interim funding would buy the program enough time for the conference committee to iron out the House/Senate differences. As of this writing (April, 1986), however, prospects for passage of a long-term reauthorization bill this session are dimming; and congressmen are beginning to talk of short-term reauthorization of the existing Superfund legislation at an increased level of funding.

The author will not engage in further speculation on the eventual legislative outcome. He only indulges in the vain hope that Congress will solve all the hazardous waste cleanup problems in a manner that will make nothing in this book obsolete before you read it.